D1171050

# IN THIS FARAWAY LAND

by

ORVAL EUGENE FAUBUS

DISCARD

RIVER
ROAD
PRESS

Copyright © 1971
by Orval Eugene Faubus. All Rights Reserved.

This book, or parts thereof,
may not be reproduced in any
form without permission of
the author.

*Printed in the United States of America*

River Road Press
Conway, Arkansas

The author, Orval Eugene Faubus, Combs, Ark,, age 34, then a first lieutenant, Regimental Headquarters, 320th Infantry Regiment, 35th Division, Third Army. The picture was taken at a studio in Nancy, France on or about Oct. 18, 1944.

CENTRAL ARKANSAS LIBRARY SYSTEM
LITTLE ROCK PUBLIC LIBRARY
700 LOUISIANA STREET
LITTLE ROCK, ARKANSAS 72201

iii

## DEDICATION

With admiration for their deeds, and in humility for their sacrifice, this book is dedicated to my fallen comrades of World War II.

*They shall grow not old, as we that are left grow old,*
*Age shall not worry them, nor the years condemn.*
*At the going down of the sun and in the morning*
*We will remember them.*

—From the poem, "To The Fallen," by
Laurence Binyon

*There let them rest, wrapped in her verdant arms,*
*Their task well done. Now, from the smoke-veiled sky,*
*They watch our khaki legions pass to certain victory,*
*Because of them who showed us how to die.*

—From the poem, "To Our First Dead" by
General George S. Patton, Jr.

# ACKNOWLEDGEMENTS

Sources used for reference in the writing of this book, other than the original journal, my 201 file, and other documents from my war service, were:

1. History of the 35th Division published just after the war, together with a roster which purported to contain the names of all enlisted men who served with the division from the time it sailed from the States until it returned. (The names of many men who served with the unit are not contained in the roster, and it was otherwise so mixed up that it was of little use.)

2. The brief 320th Infantry history published in Europe just after the War.

3. A brief booklet about activities of the 35th, entitled "ATTACK."

4. The files of the *Madison County Record, Stars and Stripes*, the *Santa Fe Express* and its successor, *The 35th Divisionaire* and newspaper clippings.

5. A list of officers of the 320th Infantry, including the cause and date of their final termination from the unit, apparently prepared by Capt. Dwight D. Bonham, and mailed to me some years ago by Lt. Col. William F. Northam.

6. Statistics on casualties of the various divisions were taken from the "Order of Battle" reports in the Archives in Washington and were obtained for me by Congressman John Paul Hammerschmidt.

7. Information obtained personally or by correspondence from various individuals, both enlisted men and officers, who served in the 320th.

All those who served in the 320th Regiment and the 35th Division, will clearly understand the difficulty of being completely accurate in listing names, addresses, dates and other facts without access to official records. With access to such records, even then complete accuracy would be impossible. In the confusion and turmoil of battle, with death ever present and many records made from uncertain reports and recollections of the living, absolute authenticity is not always possible. Many facts were lost forever with those who died and others scattered with the captured or the wounded. The men of combat know this well. Each was busy in his own little corner of the great conflict, and often close friends in the same company or battalion did not see each other for days. Therefore I know that my comrades of the war, who by their deeds of bravery and endurance wrote a glorious record which I hope this book somehow portrays, will understand the reasons for any inaccuracies or omissions that are found.

—O. E. F.

# TABLE OF CONTENTS

# INTRODUCTION

This writing entitled, "In This Faraway Land," may be accurately termed a war diary. It may well be the only one of its kind of World War II. In the first place, as a security measure, combat soldiers were discouraged or forbidden to keep diaries, and secondly, few men indeed would take the time or have the inclination to record the events or to set down their thoughts while actually in combat and most of the time under fire.

While doing the writing in the day by day struggle which finally ran to some 300 days, I called it a journal. As opportunity made possible I transferred the finished portions to the safe keeping of a friend, Lt. Frank X. Sperl, Flushing, N. Y., at Division Rear Headquarters which was always miles behind the battle lines. Until the transfer could be made to the safer area the more recently finished parts were kept at the 320th Infantry Headquarters. No part was ever carried with me while on the many trips about the battle lines or combat zones as a liaison officer or on other duties.

There were standing instructions with my friend, that in case I was lost in combat, the writings in his possession were to be mailed to my father, J. S. Faubus, Combs, Arkansas.

After the war ended, all parts were collected and put together to make up the complete document.

The writing was done in longhand with pencil and, in the later portions on a few occasions, with pen, with one exception. The entry of Feb. 24, 1945 was made on the regimental typewriter with which I was semi-skilled. Various kinds of paper were used including the pencil pads of regimental headquarters on which the daily journals of messages and activities were kept, captured German paper, and stationery and notebooks picked up along the way in the various countries in which we fought. The entries were made in many locations under many and varied circumstances.

I got to see more of the many sides of war than most of the participants, first because of my varied duties, and second, simply by surviving the entire period of conflict. Because of my background as a countryman, hunter and woodsman, my ability to read maps, identify terrain features, maintain my bearings in daylight or darkness, give logical orders or instructions, and transmit messages of clarity, I became a sort of general "trouble shooter" for the regiment when it was on the move or in battle. During the brief periods when the regiment was not on the move or in raging combat, I was assigned administrative, legal and literary tasks. These included all phases of courts martial duties, - investigating officer, member of summary courts, special courts and general courts martial, as well as the roles of defense council, Trial Judge Advocate (prosecutor), and witness. Literary tasks included an effort to report, or to secure some publicity on the role and the accomplishments of the regiment in the war, as well as the gathering of data and the compilation of the "after battle" report on the regiment each month. After making the second monthly report, I recall having the thought "I wonder who will make the next one of these." I was fortunate enough to be permitted to make, or help to make, all the 320th's after action reports, except perhaps the last one, at which time I was hospitalized.

It is well to remember, as the reader will often detect, that the writing was done, ofttimes under great stress, and at almost all times under conditions most unfavorable for clarity in writing. No effort was made to re-word or re-phrase any part of the writing while it was being done. There was no time. Very often there were great intervals between the beginning and the ending of a paragraph, or even a sentence. These lapses of time of various lengths were caused by many interruptions as air raids, artillery barrages, trips about the battlefield, and other matters which required my attention to duty. The proper performance of my assigned tasks to the unit in battle, always came first. The writing was strictly secondary, and was done at odd moments in the spare time when I was not otherwise occupied.

None of the writing was ever seen again after the words were set down, until I read the journal after "la guerre fini"

—the war was ended. Consequently, the critical reader can find many places where much improvement can be made in the wording and phrasing, because no change whatsoever has been made to the entries in the original diary. It is reproduced just as it was written during the stress and strain of combat with the 320th Infantry Regiment of the 35th Division.

To help the reader better understand that which was described or related, some words, phrases, paragraphs and sections have been added. These additions have been made from memory or records, to fill in some of the more pertinent incidents and experiences, as well as names and addresses, which went unrecorded at the time of the original writing. Such additions are clearly indicated in order that the original entries remain unchanged.

Preceding the combat diary itself, other writings, in the form of letters to my home town newspaper, done just prior to and during my military training period, have also been reproduced. Aside from the fact that they will have some interest to many readers, the reproductions throw still further light on my background and indicate many of the beliefs and viewpoints held by me at that time. Whether these wartime viewpoints and beliefs were well founded or foolishly held, the reader may judge for himself, as no effort has been made to change or give a new slant to the writings. Most of them are already a matter of record in the columns of The Madison County Record, Huntsville, Arkansas. Other than a few deletions of the more inconsequential passages for the sake of brevity, these precombat letters have been faithfully reproduced.

However, no deletions or changes have been made in the "Journal" or "War Diary" which began within a stone farm house with shrapnel scarred walls through which gaping holes had been made by artillery shells, in the edge of a verdant Norman orchard on the shell-lit summer night of July 11, 1944. The Journal relates fragments, as only it could, of the experiences of the men of battle, beginning with the "tight little corners of hell,"—the hedgerows of Normandy, and then on many other battlefields in other countries that were to follow, experiences of which a great soldier, "Highroad Chawlie," and I began later to speak as happening to us "in this faraway land."

## BACKGROUND OF THE WRITER

With the thought that some knowledge of the background of the person who recorded a small part of the events he witnessed and the thoughts he had while seeing them, might help the reader to better understand and appreciate this documentary of war, the following information is given.

I was born Jan. 7, 1910, on a hillside farm in the Ozark Mountains some two miles north of the village of Combs, Madison County, Arkansas. My parents were John Samuel Faubus and Addie Joslen Faubus, neither of whom had more than a fourth grade education. The little formal learning they acquired was obtained in the inadequate schools of that area of which they were both natives. My mother, one of four children, two boys and two girls, was left fatherless at an early age when her father disappeared into Indian Territory (now Oklahoma). My father, the eldest of six children, three boys and three girls, likewise lost a parent when his father died of pneumonia. When his mother remarried there were added to his family four step-brothers and two step-sisters, and later two half-brothers and a half-sister. Although my father had little or no formal education he read extensively and was known to his neighbors as a "well posted" man.

When my parents married they moved into a rented three-room log farm house and began housekeeping with furniture, utensils and supplies that would now be considered inadequate for an overnight camp.

I was born in the rented log house where my mother was "waited on" by the neighbors and a country doctor who arrived on horseback through a deep snow.

Later that year my father homesteaded a 160-acre hillside farm located across the narrow valley from my birthplace. My parents moved with me into a crude one-room frame house on the homestead when I was less than a year old. To the one-room house was soon added another room, slightly larger than the first, which served as combination living room and bed room, and the original structure became the kitchen. As the family grew in numbers and size a third unit was added, constructed of rough saw mill lumber the same as the earlier structures. We then had a 3-room house —living room, bedroom and kitchen. The erection of a stone chimney using red clay mud as mortar added a large fireplace to the living room. A wood burning cookstove of the smallest, cheapest type was used for cooking in the kitchen and to supply what little warmth could be found on cold winter days. At meal time on the coldest days our redeye gravy would freeze before we could sop it up with the biscuits.

Here in this rough house, situated on a narrow bench of the mountain, bordered by truck patches and small fields, all surrounded by the encompassing hardwood forests, were born my four sisters and two brothers. As in my birth, mother was "waited on" by the country doctor who rode horseback from his home in Combs the two miles to our place, carrying in his saddle bags whatever medicines and instruments were used. He was assisted by neighbor women who were summoned whenever "the time had come."

The eldest children finally came to realize what was happening, and could tell when a new birth was at hand. We were gathered up and sent away to a neighbor's house. No explanations were ever offered and we asked no questions. (In times of crisis or important events we children did exactly as our elders indicated without inquiry or protest, and without hesitation). After several hours we were brought back home and quietly told we had a new baby brother or sister.

It was in this modest dwelling my grandmother died. When I was age 10 beloved Gran'maw Joslen was visiting us in bleak December. After a particularly cheerful breakfast in the cold kitchen she finished before my parents and came into the living room where I was already seated on the floor before the blazing fireplace. She seated herself in a chair and picked up the baby and sat it on her lap. Suddenly her hands dropped to her side, she drew two breaths like a sleeper snoring and then was still. At that moment my father came through the kitchen door and saw her. He grabbed the baby before it could fall and with one word, "Addie"—the tone was sufficient—and a gesture summoned my mother. She rushed to her side but nothing could be done. Grandma was gone.

Her elder son, Will Joslen, was notified via the neighborhood owned telephone system. I saw him round the bend in the road in front of the house, his horse at a wild gallop past the bare trees of winter, tear madly down the short lane and slide to a halt sending the chips of the woodyard flying at the yard gate. I had the thought that there had been not enough time to saddle a horse, yet he had ridden a distance of two miles. The usually smiling face of my uncle was grey and grim as he entered the house.

Word of the death went out across the mountain community, and the neighbors gathered at the home. They took charge of everything, except possibly the purchase of burial clothes for the deceased, and lace and cloth to line the coffin which were bought at one of the village stores by my parents. Neighbor women prepared the body for burial while others cooked food and took care of the house and the children.

Neighbor men made the wooden coffin and the larger wooden box in which it would rest. Others dug the grave. The following day the body in the coffin and box was hauled on a wagon drawn by the work team to the cemetery across the valley.

Here had gathered, along with the relatives, scores of neighbors to pay their last respects. Among them were the singers and a minister to conduct a grave side service. The service ended and the last sad farewells said, the men lowered the coffin into the box, nailed on the top, threw in the red clay soil until the hole was filled, shaped a mound of earth over all and set a field stone at the head of the grave and a smaller one at the foot. Then the people dispersed to their homes.

The neighbors had given their help in time of need, just as they would receive such help in the same or similar circumstances. There was no charge for any service performed. The only financial cost of the death and burial was the price of the materials purchased at the village store which did not approach fifty dollars.

There were no funeral homes in the region then nor any burial insurance plans. Such inovations did not begin to appear in the mountain area until a decade or more later. At that time ministers or singers would take no pay for preaching or singing and would have been shocked, along with everyone else, at the very thought of being paid. It was the same for any other work or service performed for a neighbor (or a stranger for that matter) in time of need.

As the years went by additional acreage was added to the original 160-acre Ozark Mountain homestead until its size was about 300 acres. Years of arduous toil converted a small part of the benches and slopes into rock strewn farm land. The timber by equally backbreaking toil was harvested from the rougher and more inaccessible areas which remained woodland.

Here on this rough mountain farm I was helping to tend the crops and farm animals before I started to grade school, and was helping my father saw timber in the woods at the age of seven. For the market we cut and split timber for the making of ax handles, plow handles and other farm equipment, staves for bourbon barrels and spokes for wagon and artillery wheels. We cut and hauled logs which were sawed into rough lumber by the small sawmills of the region. Thousands of fence posts were made and sold for use in the plains states in the North and West. The main market was provided by the railroads which used crossties. The ties were shaped from logs eight feet in length, using the old fashioned broadax (now obsolete) and the double-bit chopping ax. Those who engaged in this labor as a means of livelihood were the hardest working men who could be found and usually the poorest. They were known as "tie hackers." Not only were they on the lowest rung of the economic ladder but at or near the bottom of the social scale as well.

My father made many things for the home, the farm and for use in the woods, the main reason being that we had no money with which to buy such items. These included parts for wagons and farm equipment, single (swingle) trees, mauls and hoe and ax handles, and for the home, shelves, cupboards, benches, chairs, door latches, etc.

Using the old fashioned mallet and froe I helped him to rive (split) palings (pickets) for yard and garden fences, and boards (shingles) to roof the buildings.

We never had enough money to purchase all the needed wire for fencing. To enclose the small fields, we split hundreds of rails much as Abraham Lincoln had done a hundred years earlier. For many years the crooked rail fence was considered to be a sort of trademark of the Ozarks.

The Ozark Mountain farmers "lived at home,"—that is they produced most of what they used. The crops included corn and wheat for the livestock and poultry, and the grain was also ground into meal and flour at the local mills for the family bread. The produce of truck patches and garden included radishes, lettuce, onions, parsnips, carrots, turnips, peas, beans, okra, cabbage, potatoes of both kinds, pumpkins, squash, cantaloupes, muskmelons, watermelons, strawberries and rhubarb.

A herd of cows furnished milk, butter and meat; sheep and goats supplied meat for the table and wool for the market; flocks of chickens, ducks, geese and guineas furnished eggs and meat, and the feathers were used to make beds. Fields of cane were made into sorghum molasses. From hives of bees or wild bee trees found in the forest was taken honey. Hogs supplied meat and lard (shortening now). Orchards supplied fruits as peaches, apples, cherries, pears and plums, and some farmers had grape vineyards.

In addition to that which was raised, the mountaineers of the region found other sources of food in the forests and fields. Wild plants provided "greens" or salads, poke sallet (salad) being the most common. There were wild plums, grapes and muscadines, wild blackberries, dewberries and huckleberries, and sometimes even wild strawberries. There was wild game, often a welcome change in the table fare, as rabbit, squirrel and raccoon, and many a housewife could prepare a tasty dish of 'possum. In season wild duck and geese could sometimes be bagged for table use and the feathers used for making pillows. (Wild turkey and deer, once plentiful in the Ozarks, had disappeared at the time I was growing up.)

There were fish in the streams for both pastime and food.

The pelts of furbearing animals were sold during the winter season for cash income. As a youth I earned some of my meager spending money by winter trapping and hunting as did other Ozark Mountain boys.

On every farm were house cats to keep down the mice and rats. Every farm family had dogs for one or more purposes—watchdogs to warn of the approach of strangers, and to ward off the wild animals from the poultry and livestock as well as the crops; tree dogs for hunting wild game for food or cash income; fox hounds and occasionally a bird dog for sport. The baying of fox hounds in the chase during the night is a sound almost every mountaineer will always remember.

Teams of horses and mules were the beasts of burden— the source of power for farm and woodland labor and for transportation. We seldom owned work horses as my father preferred mules. They were smaller and less powerful, but were tougher, more tractable, less costly to feed and were less likely to panic in a tight spot as when tangled in wire or with a wagon turnover in the woods.

An Ozark mountaineer's work animals labored almost as steadily as the owner. They were used to do almost everything. They pulled the plows, harrows, mowing machines, hay rakes and sleds in the fields. They pulled the wagons in both field and forest, and along the rough, winding roads to mill and market. Sometimes their work was not ended with the setting sun. After being fed the animals were hitched to the wagon to haul the whole family, sometimes with neighbors added, to church or some social gathering at night. They were often ridden about the farm or to the neighboring village, and sometimes on round trips of 50 miles or more to the county seat. One of my early boyhood chores was to ride a mule with a "turn of corn" to the village grist mill where the corn was ground into corn meal for the family bread.

To the mountain farmer work animals were essential. He could no more "make a living" without horses, mules or oxen to work than could a cowboy without horses to ride.

For cash income other than the sale of timber, there was usually a market for the increase or the excess of almost all the farm family produced. A thrifty, industrious mountaineer could get by with very few purchases of food or of timber products, and limited purchases of clothing and many household items. Most of the time, cloth was purchased and the garments and other cloth items were home made. Shoes were mended and remended on a home cobbler set to make them last as long as possible. This was fortunate indeed, because I remember my father once kept a record of all cash income for a year which amounted to $360.00 for a family of nine.

For the great mass of Ozark Mountain dwellers cash was almost as "scarce as a hen's teeth." The person who held a county office on a salary of $1,500 to $3,600 per year, or a government job as postmaster or rural mail carrier at $2,000 to $3,000 annually, was considered a privileged character. Likewise those men who had regular employment as section hands on the railroad at $3.00 per day for a 10-hour day, six days a week were considered fortunate. A position as cross tie inspector for the timber companies at $50 per month was considered lucrative.

Then on October 29, 1929, known as 'Black Tuesday,' occurred the historic stock market crash which ushered in the Great Depression. Times became even harder. "Prosperity is just around the corner" became the slogan for the business world. But for the hardworking mountaineers that mythical corner had never been turned by so-called prosperity even before the "Black Tuesday" crash of 1929.

Under such economic conditions the great concerns of my family and of all families were serious illness or injury. It is strange to relate that I do not recall ever hearing anyone give voice to these great concerns. They were "taken for granted" and to mention them was unnecessary. During my early boyhood we had heard of such things as hospitals, the nearest one beyond the mountains where the sun set, in the direction from whence the train "came in" on its morning run. But they were not for us. They were too far away and too expensive. Our only hope in time of such dire emergencies came from the country doctors, the "general practitioners" of their day, and from the neighbors.

There was great faith in the skill, the ability and especially the good intentions of these mountain physicians. They did the best they could under very difficult and very primitive conditions for the practice of medicine. In most instances, as was the case with my family, they were not called until the condition of the patient was serious. As long as it was deemed possible home remedies were used for treatment to avoid the expense of "a doctor bill." And to the everlasting credit of the country doctors of the region during my youth, I never heard of one of them refusing a call "no matter how rough the road, or dark the night or stormy the weather," nor how impoverished the family.

The neighbors helped in every way possible. They would "go get the doctor." I remember one wrinkle-faced mountaineer traveling 20 miles on a dark and rainy night over swollen streams and slippery mountains on foot by the dim and wavering light of a kerosene lantern. Just at dawn he arrived at the farm house of the sick person with the doctor in tow. He knelt on the floor a short distance from the bed as the doctor worked. I shall never forget the look of satisfaction on his face when a favorable diagnosis was given. A fleeting smile momentarily lit up his rugged countenance as he arose and, without a word, passed silently through the doorway to go home and rest.

The neighbors came to "set up with the sick" and to "give the medicine." They brought food, helped to cook and "keep house," "do the chores" and gave encouragement and comfort to the members of the family.

Then when illness or injury was over, through death or recovery, if expenses on the family were heavy, an old fashioned box supper or pie supper was held in the community school building. The proceeds were turned over to the family to be used in paying the bills.

In later years as automobiles became more prevalent and roads became passable, the people of the region began to use the hospital 30 miles to the west. Then expenses mounted more rapidly, and many were the hospital and doctor bills paid with the proceeds of neighborhood pie suppers.

The neighbors helped in other ways. In conjunction with their own activities they would take a "turn of corn" to the mill or deliver medicine, groceries and the mail. There were log-rollings where the timber and brush were cut, piled and burned to clear the ground for cultivation. There were "house-raisings" after a dwelling had been destroyed by fire. In a "house-raising" some men brought lumber, others cut logs, others made boards, while the more skillful began to raise the house. When the day had ended a house was virtually completed. The walls had been raised and roofed. The family could move in. The walls sheltered from the wind and there was a "roof over the head." Crude though the structure might be it was an average dwelling for the region, and in it the family continued the pursuit of a livelihood and did the "finishing work" on the house during the "spare time."

Sometimes these "workings" were held to plant or harvest crops when the breadwinner of the family was ill. Many of the rural schools and churches of the mountain region were erected by the same methods.

In many such affairs everyone participated, men and women, young and old. They arrived with work teams pulling wagons on which rode the members of the family along with tools, food, cooking utensils and whatever supplies were needed. While the men and boys worked on the main project, the women and girls prepared a bountiful meal. There was much visiting and good fellowship. If the affair was to help a neighbor, it was arranged at a time when the crisis, whether of fire, illness or other misfortune, had passed. So a good time was had by all. When the day had ended the separations were made in subdued good spirits. The words of parting were, "Now let us know when ye need anything," "We'll be back," "You all come." I never heard anyone say "goodbye." The wagons jolted homeward along the rough roads. Those on foot took the narrow mountain trails. At the end of such a day there glowed within the breasts of these mountain dwellers the deepseated satisfaction and contentment which comes to those who do good. They had taken of their time and labor, often sorely needed for their own interests, to help with a worthwhile community project or give aid to a neighbor in need. Although many of them wouldn't have understood the phrase they had engaged in the "philanthropy of the poor."

To have heard my father talk in those days one would have thought that debts and taxes were the greatest concerns. There was always a debt, created usually by some emergency, about which he worried constantly until it was paid. The real estate and personal property taxes came due in the spring at the worst possible time. The taxes had to be paid in cash at the season when seed and tools had to be purchased for the planting of crops. It was also the time when the family was most often sorely pressed for food for the family and feed for the livestock, because the winter's supplies had been exhausted and nothing yet had been grown for use. As he worried about the debts and taxes my father coupled his expressions of worry with "cussin" the hard times, high prices, the economic system, the unconcerned rich and the disinterested government. To my father obligations, including debts and taxes, must be met.

In those days many transactions were made just by "giving your word." Seldom were instruments drawn up to legalize a sale, trade or purchase, except in the transfer of ownership of land. It was often said, "If a poor man's word is no good, he is no good at all." Since 99 per cent of the mountaineers of that time were poor, great emphasis was placed on the binding force of oral agreements or pledges. A high compliment to a person was contained in the well known expression, "His word is as good as his bond."

My father wanted this to be truly said of him and he wanted to "bring up" his children to observe the same principles. We recognized the teaching as good but his oft repeated concern over financial obligations caused the family many upset moments.

Transportation being by foot, horseback or horsedrawn vehicle, the only modern links with the outside world in the whole country were the railroad and telegraph lines which ran from Fayetteville along the upper White River Valley through the small settlements, including Combs, to Pettigrew. A combination train of freight, mail, express and passenger cars made a round trip from Fayetteville each week day. No night runs were made and there was no night time telegraph or mail service. The highlight of the day in the railroad settlements was when the train came in on the morning run.

In my early manhood in the 1930's a few modern gravel state highways were constructed in the region and automobiles began to appear. Soon county judges were grading the county roads with new machines to prepare them for automobile travel. Bridges across the streams were late in coming. Consequently high water cut off travel periodically on most roads. I well remember that on my last leave at home in the spring of 1944 before going overseas, I had to wade White River to get from my father's house on Greasy Creek to Combs, where I could get bus service for the return to my station at Camp Butner, N. C. Even with my brother's help in wading the swollen stream we were almost washed away and got most of my clothing wet. (This was in strange contrast to the modern highways we found in Germany when we finally got there).

The crude plank and log houses and few stone dwellings were lighted by the old fashioned coal oil (kerosene) lamps, and lanterns were used for nighttime travel or hunting. (The coal oil monopoly of the Rockefeller empire at that time was the basis of that family fortune). There wasn't an electric line in the whole county except a small system at Huntsville which was installed about 1925. The mountain dwellers of the region never saw an electric light except on the rare occasions when they journeyed to the county seat towns of Huntsville or Fayetteville, until the coming of the REA lines in the Roosevelt era.

The principal social life of the region consisted of visits of relatives or neighbors, attendance at church and school programs. There was an occasional music party in a neighborhood home attended by those who lived nearby. Often square dances (now called folk dances) were held in private homes attended by both young and old, except some church people who frowned on this form of entertainment. Round dancing, or ball room dancing, could be found occasionally in a few homes in the settlements but was unknown to most of the mountain residents.

Besides school activities the school house was likewise used as a church and community center. Here the various church denominations held their services when a preacher was available. For the most part the residents of the area attended all of the services without favoring one over another. The main events of community life were school programs, spelling bees, occasional debates, political speakings, Christmas Tree programs, pie suppers and box suppers.

An old-fashioned pie supper or box supper oft proved to be a highlight of the community events. At such an affair each pie or box was auctioned to the highest bidder and it was customary for a man or boy to bid on the box or pie brought by his favorite lady. A favorite maneuver at the auction was to conspire to "run up" the bids on the box or pie being sought by any young swain who was going steady with his fair lady. A counter move was to switch names on the pies, or to secretly get a friend to bid while the object of the conspiracy stopped soon as if the price had already exceeded what he could afford.

Ofttimes the most interesting event of the occasion was the race for the pretty girl's cake. Votes were a penny or a nickel each. A girl never offered herself as a candidate but could be nominated by others. Although it was considered an honor to be nominated, occasionally there were unwilling contestants because someone was nearly always thoughtful enough to nominate those who would create a spirited race. Sometimes the boys and young men from one group or community would spend all they had, and all they could borrow at the time, in an effort to see that their candidate was chosen. Consequently the race for the pretty girl's cake was an important part of the program as a heated contest often brought in more money than the total sales of all the pies.

These old-fashioned box suppers and pie suppers were always good time, good fellowship affairs in our community. The proceeds from the suppers were going to some worthwhile community project or to help some neighbor in need. Many such suppers were held in the Ozark Mountain Region during WWII to raise funds for the war work of the Red Cross.

(In a box supper, a decorated box contained a number of items of the best food that could be prepared. I have many gleeful boyhood recollections of how, as he promoted the sale, a skillful auctioneer made much of the weight of the box, and the various delightful aromas coming from within. And, I recall, there was always enough food to feed the hungry urchins who were not yet old enough, or did not have the money to participate in the bidding. In a pie supper, pies only were brought for sale. Gradually the pie supper became more prevalent until the box supper disappeared from the scene).

My grade school education was acquired in the one-room school of Greenwood (Greasy Creek) and the two-room facility at Combs,—all grades from first to eighth, all subjects and all students. I walked to and from school just like all the other pupils.

Terms usually ranged from three to six months. I attended one term of seven months which was six months paid for with public funds and one month "subscription" school in which the parents paid tuition at so much per student per month.

Upon finishing the eighth grade I walked to the county seat, a distance of 25 miles, and took the two-day teachers' examination. I made a passing grade and was issued a license to teach. At the age of 18 I began teaching at Pinnacle, the second largest one-room district in the county. During my first year in the district there were 74 students enrolled and 80 the second term, all grades, all subjects. Students' ages ranged from 5 to those who were older than the teacher. If an instructor and administrator does a good job in such a situation he must improvise and make double and triple use of much of the time. This I did, and was quite successful as a teacher from the very beginning. The experience in many respects fitted me for service in the United States Armed Forces during the great war.

It is well known that the initiative of the American soldier, his ability to improvise, to make double use of time, and to make on-the-spot decisions in the field, made the American Army superior to any other when training, numbers and equipment were comparable.

To further my education I enrolled in one of the three high schools in the county each year after teaching a term in a smaller rural school. I had little or no money because my salary while teaching was $40 to $70 per month. I often had to borrow funds to complete a school year. My attendance in high school ranged from three to five months each year. I graduated in six years (Huntsville State Vocational School, class of 1934).

My teaching career extended from 1928 to 1938 with the exception of one year during which I worked as a lumberjack in the state of Washington. In the intervals when not in school as teacher or student, I attended Citizens Military Training Camp at Fort Leavenworth, Kansas and Camp Robinson at Little Rock, Arkansas; worked in the forests of Washington; was an itinerant fruit picker from Arkansas to Michigan; lived as a hobo over portions of the country traveling as a hitchhiker or "sidedoor pullman,"—empty box cars on freight trains; did some sawmill work, farm labor, and timber work in the Ozarks.

My only other formal educational training was six hours credit from the University of Arkansas which I earned by attending night courses of the Extension Service at Huntsville while serving as a county official.

In 1935 I applied for admission to Commonwealth College, a so-called labor school located in Polk County near Mena, Arkansas. I was to pay a nominal sum in cash, $15 as I recall, and work on the farm owned by the school for the tuition for a three-month semester. After arriving at the school I learned that students could not receive credits toward a college education, and that the institution had become very much Communist oriented. I left without paying any tuition and without completing any courses of study. (This episode in my life was well publicized after the war during my first campaign for Governor of Arkansas in 1954 and by subsequent newspaper stories and magazine articles).

I was married in 1931 to Miss Alta Haskins of Ball Creek, a neighboring community of Greasy Creek; graduated from high school in 1934; ran for a seat in the legislature in the Democratic Primary of 1936 and lost by four votes; ran for circuit clerk and recorder in 1938 and was elected. After finishing my last term of school, again at Pinnacle, I assumed office Jan. 1, 1939. My son, Farrell Eugene Faubus, was born April 5, 1939. I was re-elected in 1940 for a second term beginning Jan. 1, 1941. In mid 1940 we moved on a farm in the Ball Creek community near Japton where we took care of some livestock to pay the rent, made garden, raised chickens and milked cows. I drove the school bus, 90 miles round trip, leaving home at 6:00 a.m. and returning at 6:00 p.m. While the students were in school I worked in the office from 8 to 4. With the earnings from two jobs and the income from the farm I was making and saving more money than at any time in my life. (The total income would be considered small now).

It was during this time the Japs struck Pearl Harbor, Dec. 7, 1941. I was in class 3-A, having a family and also holding a county elective office. I volunteered and had my status changed to 1-A and was inducted May 17, 1942. A student took over the bus driving job and my wife took over the duties of the office to finish my term. I had received the uncontested Democratic nomination for County Judge, the most important county office, which I gave up to become a private in the U. S. Army.

MADISON COUNTY RECORD
January 29, 1942

OUR DUTY IS AT THE FRONT WITH COMRADES
by ORVAL E. FAUBUS

Hitler has said, "Two worlds are in conflict, and one of them must break asunder." Everyone who is the least bit informed on world affairs knows that this statement is true, even though it was made by the Nazi leader.

This war is not like many of those of which we have studied in the human history of the past. In the past, nations fought until one side gained the victory, or until both sides became tired of the conflict and negotiated a peace. The one which got the worst of the conflict was, as a rule, forced to give up some territory, its fleet, or to pay an indemnity. Then the vanquished was allowed to continue as a sovereign nation unmolested by the victor in the administration of its internal affairs. And many times the defeated nation continued to enjoy all the rights and privileges in the world of trade and foreign affairs that were allowed to the victorious country.

It cannot be so and will not be so after this war if the Axis powers win. We know Adolph Hitler aims at nothing less than complete domination of the world. He is merely using the Japs and Italians to help him accomplish that aim, and they will be given a place in his "new order" which he chooses them to have. The conquered nations and their peoples will be allowed no more rights and privileges than are the inmates of our prison institutions, if as much.

In Hitler's "New Order," the Germanized, or pure Aryan races will take their place as the superior and dominating class of the world. We, with the other conquered peoples, will take our place, as the Poles, Czechs, Greeks and others have already, as the servant class. We will work under German or Jap overseers whenever and wherever we are needed, perhaps without pay as in the Nazi labor camps already established in conquered Europe. We may be allowed to serve in the German army if needed but only as the lowest grade of soldiers. We will not be allowed to go where we choose or to select the kind of work we will do. It will be the master race's policy to determine that. We may or may not be allowed to marry the mate of our own choosing. We may not be allowed to marry at all depending upon the whim of the Aryan rulers.

We do know that Germans have been forbidden to marry Jews, and that in the Nazi countries marriages of 40 years duration have been broken up because one of the parties was a 32nd part Jew or a 16th part Pole. We know, too, that German youth has been conscripted for labor service without pay and without regard to sex. And we further know that hundreds and hundreds of German girls have gone from the Nazi supervised labor camps to homes for unwed mothers, there to give birth to the children of the black-shirted, pure Aryan supervisors.

Aside from their racial practices, we know that all labor organizations have been outlawed; that property is taken from the rightful owners without due process of law; that political activity and free elections do not exist under the Nazis anymore; that Christianity has been branded a false and weak religion and a form of Pagan worship selected to replace it; that church and fraternal organizations have been abolished; and that freedom of expression and freedom of worship are now denied to all peoples under the Nazi rule. All these evils and many more we know to exist in Germany and her allied countries, and we can fully expect them to be forced upon us if we lose this war.

Yet in the face of all these dire evils which threaten to engulf us, it is surprising to note that a number of people cannot even now, at this late hour, see clearly where their duty lies. Or if they do see and understand, are negligent in the performance of that duty, by attempting to evade the draft. Perhaps it could not be truthfully said that any of those who are trying to escape service in the Army, favor any of the evils put forward by Hitler. Yet, if all of us were unwilling to fight to stop them, they would be put upon us almost at once.

If it were a question of safety at home if we stayed and danger at the front only if we went, that would be a different situation. But that is not the case. If we all stay at home, Hitler and his yellow Aryan pals will be here soon, and the danger will be greater for those of us who should go, also for all our relatives and friends. Surely if those who are now reluctant to go to the Army were reluctant to take Hitler's orders they would soon find themselves in great difficulty. So it is not a question of peace or war; the war has already been thrust upon us. It is not a question of danger or safety; the danger already exists. And it will grow greater and nearer our homes if we do not meet it as we should.

Certainly it is true that many of those boys of Madison County who have asked for 2-A classification are needed at home and would be useful on the farm. That is no reason or excuse for deferment. It can be truthfully said that 95 percent of the boys of Madison County are needed at home and would be useful on the farm. Most of the single boys are already in the service and those that remain are no more entitled to deferment than they.

The few professed conscientious objectors may be sincere. However they say by their attitude, "I don't care who is suffering or who is enslaved. I don't want to do anything to help the sufferers or to prevent slavery. Give me a few quotations from the Bible and let me alone." Don't they know that if Hitler wins, that the Bible will be taken from their hands and tossed into a bonfire? And they certainly then will not be let alone. It certainly seems that they are blind indeed if they cannot see that it is their Christian duty to help their government and their neighbors to defend their right to worship God as they choose.

There are some parents who it seems are not encouraging their sons as they should toward their plain duty. Certainly we know that it is a great sorrow to a mother, especially, to see her son go to war. The mothers will probably suffer more than we who go to the front. But we should be able to see and the mothers should see that, as already pointed out, the suffering will be greater if we stay. If the invaders are not stopped over there, the bombers will come, and little boys and girls, and the old will suffer and be killed as well as those of military age.

In Spain where Hitler and Mussolini won their first great foreign victory, 14,000 children under 15 years of age were slain by the bombers with the black crosses. We here did not see them of course but it was gruesome enough to look at the pictures of little folks laid out in long rows on the sidewalks after the attacks.

The same kind of bombing happened in greater or lesser degree in Poland, Norway, Holland, France, Belgium, Yugoslavia and Greece and is yet happening in England, Philippines, Dutch East Indies, Malaya, Hawaii and other places.

We DON'T WANT THAT TO HAPPEN HERE. The only way to prevent it is to stop the aggressors before they get here. Then every boy or man who is called to go to the front should go without hesitation and stop giving his draft board all kinds of trouble by asking for deferment for this reason and that reason. His parents should be brave and understanding about it and not otherwise.

Of course it will work hardships on many, but others are suffering from the same causes. The sacrifices should be as nearly equalized as possible but it will be impossible to make them exactly the same. Remember this. It will be worse if we don't stop them over there. And we would be blind indeed if we expected to win a great struggle for freedom without any sacrifices at all.

Tonight with MacArthur's forces on Bataan Peninsula and Corregidor Island are Sidney Marcum of Combs and Charles Rankin and Henry Rankin of St. Paul, taking all that the Japanese enemy can hand them and holding out, still holding out even though their ultimate fate can hardly be anything but death or surrender. And in all likelihood Lorin Brandenburg of Kingston is either dead on Wake Island or a prisoner of war in Japan. We must not let them down. To do the work at home, there are the married men with families, those physically unfit for the army, the old men, the women and the young boys and girls. The duty of those of us who are called is at the front with our comrades.

## MADISON COUNTY RECORD
February 12, 1942

### FROM ORVAL E. FAUBUS

The article which appeared in the Record recently under my name has received overwhelming approval both by personal comment and by cards and letters. I quote below from two of the written comments, the first from W. B. Dixon of St. Paul. "Just finished reading your fine article in the Record. Makes me prouder that I am a friend of a man who feels as you do. You forgot Kenneth Gabbard who is in the Navy in the Philippines." I knew Kenneth was in the Navy but did not know he was in the Philippines. My best wishes to him and his comrades.

The second is from Mrs. M. M. Guilbeau of the Work and Play School by the Roadside of Delaney and says, "We liked your article in the Record very much. It was simple enough to be understood by anyone and with enough punch to knock all of the 'do-nothings' into line."

And now I might add to those who may disagree with what I wrote, that you are not in disagreement with one man's opinion, but with what the great majority of Madison Countians and Americans think. I might ask, do you believe in Democracy of the United States in which you live, which has protected you and your loved ones, furnished your schools, your courts of justice, and secured to you the right to your religion and all the other privileges and rights which you enjoy? If so, then be governed by the majority's will and do, without protest, the bidding of your government the which there is none better on the face of the earth.

There are no neutral or middle grounds on which to stand in this conflict. You are either fighting against Hitler or you are helping him. Some may not be conscious of the fact that they are helping Hitler and his satellites, but if they are not actively helping in the fight against him, this in itself is a great help to him. If there were enough people who did not help, as for example conscientious objectors, Hitler would have nothing to do but move in and take control. The forces of the Devil represented by Hitler, Mussolini, the Mikado and their minions, bringing slavery, oppression and suffering, are opposed by the forces of Freedom and Christianity. There are no neutral grounds. On which side will you fight? To most of us our duty is clear.

And this duty devolves not alone on those called for military service, but on all those left at home as well. If you are a teacher, a student, a farmer, a worker, or a public official, proceeding along the same old track you followed in peace time, without assuming any extra duties, you are not doing your full duty to your country. If you are a banker, a manufacturer, or cannery operator, and you are not attempting to render greater service at a reasonable charge, you are falling short.

The duty on those at home is as great as on those at the front. We must give and work until it hurts and then give and work some more. If we will do this unstintingly, the boys at the front will have greater service in arms and supplies and can quicker win the victory, and more of them can come back to the homes which they have so bravely left to so nobly do their duty.

Some time before its publication I showed the previous article to a soldier boy in uniform, a former pupil and very dear friend of mine. He wrung my hand and urged me to have it published and said that it truly expressed the feeling of all the boys in the service. He was leaving then to join his company. And although his heart was heavy and he knew his mother's heart was breaking, he went away with his comrades to war as jauntily as he once went off with his team mates to a ball game. He said, "The job must be done. I'm no better than any other boy." He went bravely because he was a man that knew his duty.

I'm afraid I can't go as bravely as he did when my call comes, but I shall go as bravely as I can.

Next week through the courtesy of the Record I shall present a list of names of all the Madison County boys who are now doing their duty in the armed services of Uncle Sam. We shall call it "The Honor Roll of Madison County." If any of you who read this have a son in the armed services who enlisted, will you please send me his name, your names and home community. I have the names of all those who went into the Army through the Local Draft Board so you do not need to send them. If any of you know of a boy in the service whose parents are not here, send me his name. We do not want to miss anyone. However if we do, his name will be included later as we add to the "Honor Roll" of the fighting forces.

And just a word as to how you might help a little the boys in the service. I know from past experience that one of the greatest pleasures to the soldiers is the mail from home. And next to the letters from relatives and sweethearts in the amount of pleasure they can give, is a copy of the home town paper. So subscribe for the Record for your boy or mail him your old copy.

Sincerely, Orval E. Faubus

## MADISON COUNTY RECORD
### February 26, 1942

### OUR SOLDIER BOYS

As announced elsewhere in the Record this week, Orval E. Faubus is preparing for publication a list of names of all men from Madison County in the military service of the United States; and he having stated that he hopes to have the list ready for next week, and in order to avoid duplication we are again carrying over items we have collected for Our Soldier Boys column and will use same in connection with Mr. Faubus' list.

And we are also holding for next week, reports of pie suppers and other Red Cross benefits.

The Editor

## ROLL OF HONOR BEING COMPILED;
## TO BE PUBLISHED NEXT WEEK

Thanks to those of you who are helping me to compile the "Roll of Honor" of the boys and men in the Armed Forces now defending, or preparing to defend us against the ever more threatening "scientific barbarism" of the Japs and the Nazis. I have a list now which I think will run well over 200 but I have been unable to get it ready for publication this week. I will try to have it ready by next week.

Some of the information I have received has been given to the Record for use in its "Our Soldier Boys" column. One thing I have learned which touched me very deeply was that Mrs. Effie Routh of Hindsville has three sons now serving Uncle Sam in the Army, Raymond C. Turner, stationed at Fort Mears, Alaska; Ralph Turner of Camp Bowie, Texas; and Rueben Turner of Fort Sill, Oklahoma. Compared to the service of this woman and her sons, how little seems the service that many of us have rendered.

Others who have as many as two sons in the service are Mr. and Mrs. Nathan Hill of Japton, Mr. and Mrs. E. C. Combs of Combs, Mr. and Mrs. Lon Hudson of Marble, Mr. and Mrs. Abner Mills of Huntsville, Mr. and Mrs. Bert Snow of Huntsville, Mrs. Ora Bolinger of Purdy and Mr. and Mrs. W. W. Pool formerly of Thompson. All their names will appear next week.

It is the least we can do to let these boys and their parents know that we appreciate what they are doing, not alone for us but for all mankind. That was a fine letter from Cletus Ogden which appeared last week.

Sincerely, Orval E. Faubus

## MADISON COUNTY RECORD

## MADISON COUNTY'S CONTRIBUTION TO
## OUR NATION'S GALLANT DEFENDERS

Much interest among Record readers has been increased from week to week since the first announcement by Orval E. Faubus that he was preparing for publication a list of soldiers and sailors from Madison county who are serving in the greatest of all fights for Life, Liberty and Happiness. The desire for that information, however intensely felt, is graciously gratified below, not alone for the careful and complete compilation of the list made by him but also for Mr. Faubus' beautiful introduction of the names. His words will be thrilling to the heart of every American who may read them.

Alfred Hawn, editor

MADISON COUNTY RECORD
March 12th, 1942

Monday, March 9, 1942—

Yesterday I spent a quiet Sunday. I was not feeling very well so spent most of the day inside, going out only to do the ordinary farm chores. As I am away from home for six days of the week from before dawn to late evening, my little boy (not yet three) and I are always glad to spend a day together when opportunity affords. He watched from the window while I milked the cow and his mother fed the chickens. We let him out to help me carry in the wood and he worked in his small way as industriously as a hired hand.

Back inside he helped us case the eggs which had been saved to sell, and then I had to help him with cutouts from his 'ol' tatlog." We played "tetch" with his "wubber" ball and upon his demand, "Daddy, us have a dame," I was forced to lose a number of games of checkers.

After a while one of our neighbors stopped by for a short time on his way to church. We briefly commented on the latest war news and then fell into argument on religion. We called it a discussion, it being all in good humor, as George [George Neal who lived nearby] insists it isn't an argument until tempers begin to flare. We finally broke off with an understanding to thresh the whole matter out at his house later in the day.

And while these things were occurring inside, on the outside the chickens cackled, the cows grazed in the meadow on the slope, a wood hen flew from hill to hill, and nowhere in the expanse of the horizon which encompassed my little home was there any evidence on land or in air of an intruder to break the peace and quiet. A feeling of absolute security pervaded the whole atmosphere and no fear of some immediate danger clouded our minds.

In view of the death and destruction, starvation and disease which is rampant throughout the earth at this time, why is it possible for me and other Americans to still live amid such scenes of peace and plenty as I experienced with my family Sunday? One reason is the fact that we are lucky as to location, being situated as we are at the farthest point from the aggressors' strongholds. But chiefly it is because that others, not so fortunate as to location, have chosen to defend their liberty and their right to peaceful security by force of arms, and by so doing have kept the bloody intruders from our doors.

And now America, jarred at last from its false sense of security by the bombs on Pearl Harbor, is doing its part in the great struggle. Among those taking their place in the great Army of Freedom are the genial, friendly boys from the beautiful hills of Madison County. After some time and labor I have now compiled a more or less complete list of these boys who are now serving in the Armed Forces of the United States. No doubt there will be errors and I will be glad to know of any that you discover.

In making up the list I have discovered that our county has native sons serving in all branches of the armed service, Army, Navy, Air Force, Coast Guard and Marines. As indicated by enlisted men and volunteers, two sectors of Madison County have a high rating in patriotism; the Forum-Marble section and the White River region beginning at St. Paul and running westward through Crosses and including Asher, Thompson and Thorney.

In the list those names preceded by an "E" are enlisted men and those by "V" are volunteers. An enlisted man is one who voluntarily entered the service on his own accord. A volunteer is one who came forward and asked to be taken into the service through the draft board without being called. All others in the list were regularly inducted through the draft service. All of them are doing their duty, one the same as the other.

I want to say that I feel personally thankful to each and all of these 218 men for the service they are rendering to me, my family and the country. Whether or not my family continues in the peaceful security which it now enjoys depends upon the success of these boys and their comrades-in-arms. Each time we worship, each time we eat, each time we lie down to peaceful slumber, we should thank God for these boys. We should thank Him, too, for the daring British seamen, the do-or-die Russians and all their and our allies, and not fail to ask His blessing on all of them.

Orval E. Faubus

The List Follows:

**Huntsville**

Lieut. Van Albertson,
(Reserve Officer called
to active duty)
E—Oliver Frank Farr, Navy
E—Orvil Mills, Navy
E—Wilson Mills, Coast Guard
E—Elmer Wharton, Navy
E—Robert (Bob) Lovecy,
Navy
Lt. Charles Soule, Army
Air Corps
E—Ed Reed, Army
E—Paul Havens, Army
E—Virgil Cromwell, Army
V—Cecil Tom Harper, Army
Fay Walden Laird, Army
Floyd Raymond Laird,
Army
V—Doyle Brown, Army
Millard Wilson Drake,
Army
Nathan Lee Gaskill,
Army
V—Marion Murphy, Army
V—Charles Calvin Gabbard,
Army
V—Eugene Fowler, Navy
Roy Oliver Woods, Army
Maurice Bryan Rice,
Army
V—Roy Edward Ullom, Army

E—Paul Haynes, Army
Lawrence Arthur Jones,
Army
Clay Henry Phillips,
Army
Louie Andrew Phillips,
Army
Everett W. Eubanks,
Army
Edward Phillips, Army
Harley Allison Phillips,
Army
Noel Claud Armes, Army
Thirl Wilson Sisco, Army
William Ray Eubanks,
Army
V—John Dewey Davis, Army
Howard Smith Warren,
Army
Peter Smith Jones, Army
Guilford Paul Eubanks,
Army
Donald Feak Stroud,
Army
E—Lee Peterson, Navy
E—Claude Daniels, Navy
E—Arthur Kenneth Hughes,
Navy
V—Cecil Richardson, Army
Harry Elias Dullivan,
Army
Carl Lemuel Officer,
Army
Lyle Vines, Army

E—Don Clifford Berkley,
Army
E—Ernest Wayne Binam,
Army
E—John T. Elmore, Navy
E—Harold John Nelson,
Navy
E—John Falconer Roberts,
Army
E—Harold Chancellor, Army
E—Allen B. Gage, Army

**Hindsville**

E—Ellery Litterell, Army
E—Raymond C. Turner,
Army
E—Ralph Turner, Army
E—Reuben Turner, Army
E—Ray Long, Army
Calvin Evans, Army
Fred Eli Fulkerson,
Army
Amel Ray Lewis, Army
J. D. Fritts, Army
Edward Lawrence Ing-
mire, Army
John Reuben Litterell,
Army
James Roy Litterell,
Army
E—Hugh Kenneth Edmon-
son, Army
E—Jimmie Ray Smith, Army

**Marble**

E—L. N. Hudson, Army Air
Corps
V—James Woodrow Cain,
Army
V—Claude Parker, Army
V—Clay Parker, Army
V—Fay Gordon Haley, Army

V—Clarence Everett Walls,
Army
V—Norman Ernest Taylor,
Army
E—Ezekiel McKissic, Army
V—James Andrew Ham-
mond, Army
E—Bill Cline, Army
Jimmie Dell Owens,
Army
Ralph Maynard Porter,
Army
John Kenneth Walls,
Army

**Kingston**

Lieut. J. B. Fields,
Lieut. H. C. Fields, Jr.
(These two volunteer-
ed for duty from Offic-
ers Reserve Corps).
Jack Fields, Army
E—Leo E. Perry, Army
Earl Styles, Army
William G. Smelley,
Army
V—Carl William Sparks,
Army
Albert Lawrence John-
son, Army
E—Norman Afton Garton,
Army
V—James Walter Thomas,
Army
E—Earl Little, Army

**Japton**

E—J. D. Hill, Navy
Ervin Guy Hill, Army
V—Kenneth Hollis McCarv-
er, Army
E—Tel Scott, Army
Olen Leary Ball, Army

— 28 —

Kenneth Charles Williams, Army
Paul Raymond McConnell, Army
Arvil Ray Shipp, Army
John Leo Yelvington, Army
Wilson Benjamin Duncan, Army
Arvil Columbus Lewis, Army

## St. Paul
E—Charles Rankin, Army
E—Henry Rankin, Army, (these two boys with MacArthur in the Philippines).
E—Charles Kilgore, Marines
E—Kenneth Gabbard, Navy
V—Calvin Jesse Petree, Army
V—Myron Chaney Langley, Army
V—Ray White, Navy
E—Aaron Justus Sanders, Army
V—Lloyd Cecil Ogden, Army
E—Hugh Clay Rowlett, Army
William David Rowlett, Army

## Crosses
E—Jerome Ritchie, Army
Arlis Ritchie, Army
E—Tyrell Clay Anderson, Navy
E—Haskell Lloyd Gabbard, Army
V—Paul Stufflebeam, Army
E—John Fred Gabbard, Army

E—Clyde Edward Warford, Army
John Easley, Army
E—Woodrow Anderson, Army

## Formerly of Thompson
E—Jack Don Pool, Navy
E—Walter (Biby) Pool Jr., Army
E—Reuben Lloyd Robbins, Army
E—Wallace William Watts, Army

## Delaney
E—Ralph Buck, Army
V—Atchison Morris Foster, Army

## Patrick
Henry Nelson Tackett, Army
E—Ernest Alvin Combs, Army
Mark Boyd, Army

## Combs
E—Sidney Marcum, Army (with MacArthur in the Philippines).
E—Harry Brougher, Navy
E—Bob Hughey, Army
E—Gorman (Joe) Riddle, Army
E—Bert Combs, Army
E—Blaine Combs, Navy
James Jackson Patrick, Army
Carl Edward Benson, Army

## Dutton
E—Charles Bernard Wist, Navy
Woodrow Combs, Army

**Red Star**
Carl Samuels, Army
E—Voris Orval Calloway,
Army

**Pettigrew**
E—John W. Gibson, Navy
Troy Dailey, Army
E—Harvey Monroe Hunt,
Navy
E—Howard Hugh Hunt,
Navy
Loy Charles Smith, Army
Aubra Shrode, Army
E—Dorsey C. Watson, Army
Millard Melvin Franklin,
Army
E—Fred Allison Smith,
Navy
Claud Leo Seals, Army
James Gerard Gray,
Army
Sanford Sylvester Gray,
Army
E—William H. Donahou,
Army
E—Lewis C. Dunkle, Army

**Boston**
Artsel Hunter, Army
Clifford Brutton Mag-
gard, Army
Herschel H. Johnson,
Army
Melvin Clarence Mag-
gard, Army
E—David Charles Duncan,
Navy

**Aurora**
Loris Eaton Whelchel,
Army
Robert Henry Lee Cor-
nett, Army

Leman Clarence Officer,
Army
E—Arthur Edward Fetter,
Army
E—Max McElhaney, Army

**Witter**
E—William Cletus Ogden,
Army Air Corps
Oren Brandenburg,
Army
Keith Elbert Anderson,
Army
E—Seth Jones, Navy

**Clifty**
V—Henry Orbin Ingle, Army
E—Leonard Bruce Presley,
Army
Oscar Calvin Wilhite,
Army
Rollie Wesley Beaver,
Army
Sol Evans, Army
Charles Alexander Isley,
Army
E—Thomas Nathan Clemens,
Army

**Alabam**
E—Wyatt Gladstone Har-
mon, Army
E—Delman Smith, Navy
V—George Nulph, Army
V—Harvel Thomas Hatfield,
Army
E—Howard Hatfield, Army

**Purdy**
E—Arthur Snow, Army
E—Joe Snow, Army
Albert Quincy Bolinger,
Army
E—Tom Bolinger, Army

**Wharton**
V—John Kermit Beasley, Army
E—Everett D. Jones, Army
Garland Joseph Parson, Army
Olen Leonard Stansell, Army

**Rock House**
Jack Radford Wilson, Army

**Whitener**
E—Herman M. Boatright, Army
E—Albert Eugene Johnson, Army
E—Eugene Phillip Pitts, Army
E—Shelton Gaddis, Army
Trenton Jones, Army
Coy Jones, Army

**Wesley**
Lt. Irvin Wilson, Army Reserve
V—Tommy Washington McCoy, Army
E—Paul Watson, Army
Tilman Franklin Bennett, Army
Carl Leon Duncan, Army
E—Marston John Ross, Army
E—Vol Wilson Sharp, Army
Clyde Walker Ledbetter, Army

**Drakes Creek**
V—Curtis Reid Scott, Army
V—Everett J. Cornelison, Army
V—Everett Earnest Powell, Army

Milburn Samuels, Army
Hubert Carl McDougal, Army
Noel Hobart Sisemore, Army

**Cannon Creek**
V—Milton Kendrick Cooper, Army
Jesse Henry Patrick, Army

**Asher**
V—Julian Woodrow Ledford, Army
V—James Franklin McConnell, Army
E—Lee Patterson, Army

**Thorney**
E—George Davenport, Army
E—James L. Kirksey, Army
Ernest Clayton Allison, Army
Oscar Guy Dunaway, Army
E—James Dyke, Army
Luther L. McElhaney, Army
E—Dan Hoskins Jr., Navy
E—Blake Vanlandingham, Army
(This man, a brother of C. L. Vanlandingham of Thorney, has 17 years service. He was stationed in the Philippines at the outbreak of war and if not killed or captured is with MacArthur or the guerilla fighters in the islands).

## ADDITIONS TO "ROLL OF HONOR"

According to information received, the following should have been included in the original list.

**Huntsville**
E—Jack Keck, Navy
E—E. G. Blankenship, Navy Air Corps
E—Elmer Boatright, Army
**Red Star**
E—Clive Calloway, Navy
**Wesley**
E—Donald Thompson, Army

**Forum-Alabam**
E—John Nulph, Army
E—Woodrow Harmon, Army
**Clifty**
E—Dale E. Hardy, Army
Erwin C. Hardy, Army
**Japton**
E—Grandenberry Scott, Army
Isaac Witt, Army

The following named have recently entered the U. S. service:

**Japton**
V—Melvin Thos. Mitchell, Army
V—Everett James Samples, Army
Denver Samples
**Asher**
Jesse Floyd McConnell, Army
Dan Boone Drain, Army
Eugene Fulkerson, Army
**Cannon Creek**
Emory Virgil Tincher, Army
**St. Paul**
William Howard Hooper, Army
**Combs**
Bert Woods, Army
**Wharton**
Wm. Ellis Keck, Army

**Weathers**
Clyde B. Burk, Army
**Hindsville**
Kenneth Wilson Lane, Army
**Witter**
John Calvin Morgan, Army
**Red Star**
Everett Samuels, Army
**Huntsville**
Raymond Gerald Hallam, Army
**Drakes Creek**
Leo Sizemore, Army
**Clifty**
William Fred Allen, Army

This makes a total of 250 men listed as Madison Countians now serving in the Armed Forces.

Orval E. Faubus

## MADISON COUNTY RECORD
### March 26, 1942

### ADDITIONS TO "ROLL OF HONOR"

Thanks to Mrs. Orin Penny, W. B. Dixon, W. I. Cook, Mrs. M. H. Shumate, Lillie Taylor and all of you who have been helpful in the compiling and correcting of the list.

And remember that enlisted men designated as **E** are also volunteers as all enlistments whether in Army, Navy or any other branch of the service must be voluntary.

Here are some more young men overlooked in the original list:

**St. Paul**
E—Howard Marcum, Army
E—Roy Hill, Army

**Cannon Creek**
E—Hubert Robbins, Army
Tom L. Robbins, Army
**Witter**
Bearl Keck, Army

These listed below recently entered the service.

**St. Paul**
Wm. Melvin Gregory, Army
Abe Gregory, Army
Harvey Lawrence Langley, Army

**Boston**
Olaf Dale Hunter, Army

**Red Star**
Ben Hammond, Army

**Witter**
Elmer Charles Deaton, Army

**Thorney**
Vird Ray Hill, Army
Chester Melton O'Neal, Army

**Wesley**
Gordon Ezry Faulkner, Army

**Kingston**
Arnold Nolen Yingst, Army

**Whitener**
Virgil Elmer Aaron McCoy, Army

**Huntsville**
Hugh Horace Barnes, Army
Fred Louis Hallam, Army

This brings the total of those listed up to now to 268. These men are doing their duty to their country and are therefore protecting us and the privileges we enjoy. Let us not be slackers on the home front. Turn in your old auto tags, deposit your old tooth paste and shaving cream tubes at the drug store, gather your old scrap iron for the time Uncle Sam will need it, grow more crops than you will need, produce more and more milk and eggs, don't hoard sugar as there is enough for everyone if we use it sensibly, pay your taxes and remember that you are getting off light compared with people in other countries. This is a job for all of us.

Orval E. Faubus

## MADISON COUNTY RECORD
### April 16, 1942

## MORE ADDITIONS TO "ROLL OF HONOR"

The following names were overlooked when making the original list:

**Clifty**
Lawrence Elmo Samuels, Army

**St. Paul**
Rex Albert Bivens, Army

**Patrick**
E—Elbert "Dud" Combs, Army

**Witter**
E—Marvin G. Hawley, Army

These boys recently entered the armed services:

**Dutton**
E—Carroll Smith, Navy
Russell Weatherby, Army

**Hindsville**
E—Frank Earl Fullerton, Navy

**Aurora**
Alvis Lewis, Army
Chesley Charles Dennis, Army

**Combs**
Henry Marvin Thornsberry, Army

Gerald D. Eversole, Army
Claud Daniel Perkins, Army

**Boston**
Dorther Elmer Maggard, Army

**Loy**
Hugh Francis Parson, Army

**St. Paul**
John Durgan Robinson, Army

— 34 —

| Wesley | Huntsville |
|--------|------------|
| Quentin Carol Counts, Army | Dorsie Willie Butts, Army |
| **Drakes Creek** | George Murphy, Army |
| James Paul Sisemore, Army | Paskel Hamilton, Army |
| | Clarence Hopper, Army |

This brings the total of men listed as Madison Countians in the Armed Forces of the United States to 289.

I want to thank all of you who have been of help to me in compiling the original list, in making corrections, and keeping the list up to date.

I would be glad to give the whereabouts of each man and his present rank in the service, but that as you know is impossible. The soldiers and marines are being stationed in different parts of the earth and many of the sailor lads will be over much of it before the war is ended. But wherever they are they are doing their duty to us and to mankind, and we may well be proud of them. Our hopes our best wishes and our prayers are for their safety and their success. They and we can take comfort in the scripture "He who would lose his life for my sake will save his." They are working and fighting, not alone for themselves but for us and other people of the world who want to be free. Therefore their efforts are for "the least of these, My brethren," "For inasmuch as ye did it unto the least of these, My brethren, ye did it unto Me."

Orval E. Faubus

## Madison County Record
April 23, 1942

### BOTTLE-NECK IN ARKANSAS

Last fall I received a telegram from a friend and former pupil of mine. It was sent from Seattle, Wash., and read: "Have job in Boeing Aircraft plant, $1.00 per hour. Must have birth certificate before I can go to work. Send it immediately at my expense care of State Hotel. (Signed) Jake Mation." Enclosed was a check for the fees.

I immediately rushed a request to Little Rock. I waited and Jake waited until we both gave up in disgust. I had quite forgotten the matter until some six or seven weeks later I received from the Bureau a communication which said in substance, "We have searched the files and find no birth record. Please fill out the enclosed blank, etc."

Six weeks, mind you, to search the files of one year for one county. At that rate it would have taken, as it often does, from three to five months to have obtained a finished certificate.

The last I heard of Jake he had gone back in the mountains of Washington to a mining job where he was not required to have a birth certificate.

I have heard nothing further from the Bureau regarding the fifty cents I sent for the certificate, and of course all Jake's expense in hotel bills, telegrams, etc., was wasted, for so far as I know he has not yet obtained a certificate.

At another time last fall a friend of mine asked me to obtain birth certificates for his four girls as they were required to have them before being allowed to work in the cannery. I mailed a request with the proper information.

After the usual delay there came a reply saying that two of them were on file and two were not. I had the parties fill out the blanks which were enclosed and returned them accompanied by the correspondence to aid them in checking the matter. That was letter No. Two. After a long wait I sent Letter No. Three inquiring about the matter. The reply contained the same information as the first and two more blanks to be filled out. I sent Letter No. Four explaining that blanks had already been properly filled out and returned to them for those births not on file. Their answer acknowledged the receipt of the blanks, stated that they had been filed and that two were already on file, but their fees for birth certificates were fifty cents each, so would I please send them two dollars.

I checked at the bank and found that my check for two dollars, which I sent in the first letter, had long ago been paid. And so Letter No. Five explaining this contained also a few more or less blistering remarks about inefficiency and a request for immediate service as I was getting tired of overburdening the postal service in my efforts to obtain the certificates. A few days later I received the certificates but the canning season was long since over.

My experience with the Bureau has not been confined alone to the field of correspondence. Sometime ago when I was to make a trip to Little Rock, a lady asked me to see if

I could secure a birth certificate for her son, as after three letters and two telegrams she seemed unable to get any favorable action. I went to the Bureau while there and made known my wants, and gave the proper information. The birth record was not on file but a blank properly filled out had been sent to them for filing. The office force took turns searching for the blank, and when one of them would give up another would try the task awhile.

While waiting I asked the young girl at the door for some blanks to take back with me, so that I would not have to write for them when I received a request from some person whose birth was not on record. She flippantly informed me that they did not trust anyone.

Others were there as I trying to get waited upon. One youth trembling with suppressed anger, told of how he had written four letters from his place of employment in Michigan and had never received a single reply, of how he had finally been "laid off" his job because he had not obtained his birth certificate, of how he had been forced to drive the 1,100 miles from his home to Little Rock to obtain the same. Others there told similar stories, one of them having come from Texas. After three hours wait I finally left without getting the certificate. However some good came of my efforts. While the young lady door-keeper was looking the other way, I slipped a goodly portion of the blanks into my pocket and brought them back to my office, and as long as they lasted they saved many Madison County applicants even longer delays in getting their birth certificates.

I do not think there is need to moralize on what I have written above. The object lesson is plain for anyone to see. These administrative "bottle-necks" are just as damaging to the war effort as strikes, walk-outs, floods or enemy submarines. Because of this particular "bottle-neck" a needed aircraft worker is kept from a job; a man drives 2200 miles for a fifty cent certificate in spite of the need to conserve tires and gasoline to say nothing of the man-hours of labor lost; a youth is kept waiting and waiting to get into the Air Corps in the face of the fearful fact that our very existence depends upon their immediate training.

I think that the Governor of Arkansas, Homer M. Adkins, is a fine, sincere man, and in many ways has made the state a good official. In view of this I am inclined to think that he does not know of this "bottle-neck" in his administration. However, the head of the Bureau of Vital Statistics is his appointee and he is, in a measure, responsible for its actions. It is certain that should he have opposition the Bureau's record would not be an asset in overcoming it, and in any event it will not be a feather in his administrative cap.

Since the Bureau's lack of proper service is in many ways hampering the war effort, it is high time action was taken by someone to remedy the situation. And, war or no war, such slothful inefficiency should not be tolerated anywhere and especially not in the field of government.

As I write this final paragraph I see outside the boys going off to war. Among them I see five former pupils and school mates and many more friends. I ask you, I ask everyone, can we longer tolerate such "bottle-necks" as we know exist in many places, and thus by so doing let our boys down? The answer must be, we cannot and we will not.

Sincerely, Orval E. Faubus

# CHAPTER I

## SERVICE AS ENLISTED MAN

### MADISON COUNTY RECORD
### May 14, 1942

## CIRCUIT CLERK FAUBUS CALLED INTO THE ARMY

The following announcement is patriotically self explanatory: — The Editor.

To the People of Madison County:

Sunday morning, May 17, I, with a number of other young men, leave for Little Rock to be inducted into the Army of the United States, there to do our duty in defending the freedom and security of all of us.

I have been instructed by the Attorney General's office at Little Rock that I can hold my office and at the same time serve in the Armed Forces. Therefore, I am appointing my wife, Mrs. Alta M. Faubus, as my legal deputy, and she, with Miss Pauline Hillard, also a legally appointed deputy clerk, will serve you in my office while I am away.

I can assure you that the service which my wife and Miss Hillard will give you will be honest and faithful. Also they will attempt to be helpful to you in many ways that I have tried to be, although not a part of the official duties of the office.

My appreciation for the friendliness and many acts of kindness of the people of Madison County, I assure you is more deeply felt than I can express. I am very sorry to leave what has been to me a pleasant task. But duty calls and I'm sure that most of you will understand.

Three things in life every individual must inevitably face: duty, death and the judgment. We may avoid doing our duty when we face it, but we cannot avoid the last two. Those of us who face our duties as we should, can face death bravely and need have no fear of the judgment. It will not be so with the coward or the slacker, whether from military duty in times such as these or from any other duty which he may face. Duties can be, and are, at times avoided but never death and the judgment.

The pain or the sorrow of my leaving will perhaps be no greater nor less than that of the others who will go, or of those who have gone before, or of those who will follow. The going will be rough and unpleasant for many of us, but the way cannot always be smooth and sunny. Duties are often unpleasant and hard.

May I thank you again for my pleasant associations with you. I'm sure that you will be as kind to my wife and little son as you have been to me. All of you can and should be kind and considerate to the families of those in the service. I assure you that we who serve in the Armed Forces will greatly appreciate any consideration shown our families, and we will just as greatly resent any unkindness toward them.

Sometime soon the Record will carry a statement by me relative to "The War and my Candidacy for County Judge." For the present let me say, not "good-bye" but "so long," for most of us expect to be back.

Sincerely, Orval E. Faubus
Democratic Candidate for County Judge


MADISON COUNTY RECORD
May 21, 1942


23 MORE MEN FROM MADISON CO.
May 18, 1942

We left Huntsville Sunday, May 17, and I write this at the end of our first day in Camp Robinson. A busy day it has been with examinations both physical and mental, induction and issuance of uniforms. Some of the boys are somewhat blue, but many are actually happy and all are outwardly light-hearted.

All of our bunch of twenty-three have been accepted except two, Winfred Warford of Crosses and Ira Madewell of Kingston.

The young Perkins boy of Combs was the life of the party, with Fritts of Huntsville a close second. We hope that we can be stationed somewhere together, but we don't know where we'll go or when.

Pvt. George Boyd, formerly of the F. S. A. of Huntsville, just called me over the announcement system. I went and brought him down to the tent for a visit.

The boys with me said to request their folks or some one (any of you) to send a copy of the Madison County Record to each of them whenever they got permanently stationed. Following is the latest addition to the Madison County Honor Roll. Will someone please carry on this work after this one, as it will not be possible for me to do so.

**Huntsville**
Clyde Richard Bailey, Army
Tony Trinkle, Army
Nolen F. Lanningham, Army
Clay McElhaney, Army
Clyde Othar Hopper, Army
Darrel R. G. Fritts, Army

**Drakes Creek**
Lether William Ledbetter, Army

**Marble**
Arthur Hugh Tice, Army

**Clifty**
V—Millard F. Clark, Army
Homer Lloyd Worley, Army
Charles Leander McCoy, Army
Willard Bohannan, Army

**St. Paul**
James Marvin Haskins, Army

**Delaney**
E—Richard Edward Buck, Navy
Loy Everett Vanbrunt, Army

**Japton**
Arlis Chester Sisemore, Army
George William Corbett, Army

**Loy**
Oren Jesse Austin, Army

**Kingston**
Warren Andrew Yingst, Army

**Crosses**
E—Waldo Aleshire, Navy

**Whitener**
Fred Dodson, Army

Combs
E—Howard Stephens, Army
   Charles Cleo Perkins,
     Army

Shirley Thornsberry,
   Army
V—Orval Eugene Faubus,
   Army

If I remember correctly the last previous list brought the total of Madison countains in the armed forces to 289. These 23 additional men make now a total of 312.

We who serve here hope that you at home will do your duty. It is likely that each of you can do a little more. We who are in the camps or at the front cannot. We are giving our all.

Sincerely, Pvt. Orval E. Faubus

## MADISON COUNTY RECORD
May 28, 1942

### ORVAL FAUBUS IS REALLY IN ARMY NOW

Camp Robinson,
May 24, 1942

Dear Home Folks:

As this is written I am still at Camp Robinson with no orders for shipment. Of the original 21 of us inducted I think all have been shipped but me. None of the "selectees" are informed as to when or where they are going even when they are shipped, but I have since found out where a part of them are gone.

Trinkle, Laningham, McElhaney, Yingst, Sisemore, Tice, Vanbrunt and Thornsberry were sent to Camp Grant, Illinois; Corbitt, McCoy, Haskins and Hopper went to Camp Wolters, Texas; Ledbetter and Perkins to Camp Claiborne, La.; and Clark was sent to Jefferson Barracks, Mo. All were in fine spirits when I saw them last.

I have seen no one as yet who considers it a pleasure to be in the Army, but all are determined to do their best to become good soldiers and get the unpleasant job over with as soon as possible. It is my opinion that the Army would remain intact if all the men were told tomorrow that they were free to go home, and wait for Hitler to come here if he should, or stay and make sure that he doesn't. There is a much higher degree of patriotism manifest here than at home.

The part of the Army I've seen certainly is pro-Russian, and really heartfelt in their praise of the Russian efforts to stop Hitler. They feel that when we are able to match their accomplishments that the war will soon be over.

Most soldiers are sincerely disgusted with the "isolationists" as a whole, and also with the so-called "non-interventionist" groups in Congress. In their opinion Roosevelt would have had the nation much better prepared if Congress had backed up his efforts toward preparedness before Pearl Harbor. However, they don't like the President's easy going attitude toward slackness and inefficiency in members of the government. They feel that all members of the government who are not able to "deliver the goods" or fail to do so, should be weeded out. Also they are out-spoken in their bitterness toward Jesse Jones and the dollar-a-year men who they think have let them and the country down by their failure to do things which they could have done to better prepare the nation for war.

Many married men are being inducted now. One county's quota was made up entirely of married men with a single exception. Another's quota was more than three-fourths married men, and almost all of the county groups had correspondingly large numbers of married men. Also many of those who are single have dependents. From my observations during the past week it seems that the Madison County Local Board has been very lenient in the induction of men with dependents as compared with other counties.

For example, a selectee by the name of Frazier, an old CMTC acquaintance of mine from Mississippi county, was inducted this week. He has a blind father of whom he is the only support, and in addition he had to dispose of about 150 acres of planted crops, mostly spinach, because of his induction.

To such men, many of whom are now in the service and many more being inducted every day, the bill now before Congress to increase the soldier's pay will be a great help. They were beginning to be a little disgusted with the delay in passing the bill but it seems now that it will be enacted right away.

Certainly no one needs a pay increase more than the men in the ranks of the Armed Forces. They are rendering as great a service if not greater than anyone or any other group toward the preservation of our country. By the time they pay for insurance, toilet articles, hair cuts, lost property, bus fare while on furlough, and incidental expenses for recreation, what can they have left from $21.00 or $30.00? Those with dependents still won't have much spare cash even with the pay increase.

Many individuals who were or are prosperous in civilian life are being inducted now. I saw a railroad fireman Thursday who left a job which paid $350.00 per month. From our own county was Perkins who was earning $8.00 per day, Stephens who was making $16.00 per day, and Eversole who left a position of $250.00 per month.

I saw Willis Sisemore of Washington county this week. He is a native of Madison and wanted to be listed on the "Honor Roll" from our county.

To the list should be added also the name of Earl Shinn Jr. of St. Paul who enlisted this week. I saw him with his uniform on a few minutes ago.

All of you who have relatives in the service, don't forget to write to them. The mail from the home folks is the greatest pleasure in a soldier's life. And don't forget to send the home town paper.

Put forth more effort to win the war, encourage the men of the service and frown upon any slackers whom you encounter.

Sincerely, Pvt. Orval E. Faubus

[My first Army pay was at the rate of $21.00 per month. But the end of my second or third month of service Congress had increased the salary to $50.00 per month for privates in the Army].

MADISON COUNTY RECORD
June 11, 1942

FROM ORVAL FAUBUS

Record readers are sure to enjoy the following letter from Orval E. Faubus, the first he has written since he was transferred from Camp Robinson about three weeks ago.

—The Editor

Dear Home Folks:

We have really settled down to work here at Camp Wolters. I was so sore and tired yesterday and day before that I could hardly get in or out of my bunk. The feeling was due in part to my third typhoid shot, but the hiking with light pack and hand grenade practice we had on Friday would make anyone sore who was not in shape.

The executive officer of my company is a Mexican, De La Cruz by name, [Lt. Gilbert L. De La Cruz] a very handsome fellow, well liked by all the men, and I think very efficient. He has the (to us) funny Mexican accent in his speech, like Caesar Romero in the movies. Our top sergeant, Jay J. Stahyr, is a husky blond who dwarfs me by comparison in size. He is efficiency personified and as direct as a gun-shot in his instructions. He appears to be a gentleman in every respect.

My platoon sergeant [Sgt. Allen J. Hebert, Houma, La., we said Hee-bert but it was pronounced A-bair] is a diminutive fellow from southern Louisiana, who says "woik" and "woise" for "work" and "worse". He looks to weigh a little over 100 pounds but he can handle a rifle and give orders like a husky twice his size. He is very efficient and painstaking in his instructions. By chance I happened to hear him giving orders to the other non-coms who assist him. He said, "Now, dammit! if you're out there giving instructions and they ask you a question you can't answer, say 'I don't know.' Ask me and I'll tell you if I know. If I don't know I'll say so, and we'll find out for the men. It is no disgrace to say 'I don't know,' but it is a disgrace to try to bluff your way through."

And I say in all sincerity that that is the attitude and spirit which will build an efficient and willing army of high morale and keep it that way. I'm sorry that all commissioned and non-commissioned officers do not have the correct attitude but for the most part I believe they do.

The recruits of the company, numbering about 240, are chiefly from Minnesota, North Dakota and Iowa, with some from Nebraska, Ohio, Illinois and Indiana. It certainly does not sound like home to hear them talking but they are a nice bunch of men. They say "Krist" and "by gol" and "'dis," "dese," "dose," and "dere" for this, these, those and there. On the whole I think they are more courteous and better educated than the men of the ranks from the South, which is a result of better educational facilities in the North. They are, perhaps, easier to organize into a smoothly working organization than the men of the hill sections, who are more independent and I think show more initiative.

I'm sure more funny things happened among the Arkansas troops at Camp Robinson than happen here. There was the tall Arkansawyer on grass cutting detail, who walked up to the Colonel and said, "Y'know, I didn't know it was hay makin' time for y'all down in this part of the country." The Colonel (they're up next to generals, of course) just grinned and walked away.

Also there was the recruit who was a member of a sod-hauling detail. A Jap (an American soldier of Japanese descent) was driving the truck hauling the sod away, and while he was gone the sod detail rested. After a quick return trip the recruit walked up to the Jap driver and said, "See here, private, if you don't hurry so fast I won't have to work so hard, and I'll be a little easier on your grandpa when I get over there."

And there was the new recruit who was made a member of the guard. After being instructed how to halt and identify intruders and what to say to them, he was set to walking post at night armed with a rifle. The officer of the guard went out to check the sentries to see if they were performing their duties properly. He approached the recruit who promptly halted him and demanded to know who was there. The officer replied and there followed a silence which continued until finally the officer questioned, "Well, can't you think of what to say next?" "No," came the reply, "but you're a dead son-of-a-b---h if you move before I do."

There are twelve of us Arkansans in this company who were sent here from Camp Robinson. All are volunteers for the same service as I except one who is a volunteer for the parachute troops. All are pretty well informed and likewise interested in politics, and one, like myself, was a public official. He was serving his second term as Mayor of Plummerville when he volunteered.

The camp here appears to be located in a slight depression surrounded by low hills which are covered with a low growth of trees. While hiking through the woods during the past week I discovered that they are filled with many beautiful wild flowers. The yellow ones with purple hearts (black-eyed susans we called them at home) were everywhere, with here and there, standing above them were tall plumed flowers of a brilliant red hue, and scattered over the ground were many more kinds of blue, red and purple. I thought of my little boy and what pleasure they would be to him. He would walk among them and with many exclamations of delight would gather a great bouquet. The low ones would be knee high on his short legs, the yellow ones would be waist high and shoulder high and the bright red colors would wave above his little round head. Truly, I thought, a correct setting for peace.

But here were no peaceful homes or little children at play. Uniformed men armed with deathful weapons tramped among the trees, their heavy shoes crushing the tender petals of the flowers as they took the training which would give them the skill and hardness with which to wage successful war. In their ears were not the peaceful sounds of farm, or city or the songs of birds, but instead the calls of commanders, the chatter of machine guns as the gunners practiced, and ever and anon the deep-throated roar of warplanes overhead.

Not the things in which we take pleasure nor the things we would have if the world were as it should be, but they are the things we choose to have now, which we are glad to see at this time, and which we must have in order to survive. For the men who are training here to become successful soldiers will be no menace to any peaceful country. They will not go out bent upon murder and rape of innocent people nor the loot and destruction of their property. They will go out to stop the murder machines and the terrorist slave rule of Hitler and the Japs.

In times such as these men of peace must go to war, in order to restore for themselves that peace which they love, and maintain it for their posterity.

It is my intention, my wish and my will to become a trained soldier in order to protect the little boy of whom I thought as I tramped through the flowers. And not only him but all others who need protection.

Pvt. Orval E. Faubus
Co. "B" 55th Bn.,
Camp Wolters, Texas

[Camp Wolters was an Infantry Replacement Training Center—abbreviated IRTC.

The twelve Arkansawyers in my group shipped from Camp Robinson were:

Thomas L. Temple, III, Little Rock
Thomas M. Tipton, Blytheville
Ben M. Wilbanks, Plummerville
James E. Fleming, West Memphis
William B. Morrison, Vandale
Stephen W. Bowker, Jonesboro
Joseph A. Spades, Walnut Ridge
Ronald B. Sumlin, Little Rock
Edward R. Reynolds, Manila
L. C. Spillers, unknown (a volunteer for the paratroops)
Richard V. Green, Pine Bluff
Orval E. Faubus, Huntsville]

## MADISON COUNTY RECORD
July 2, 1942

### FROM ORVAL E. FAUBUS

Sunday, June 21, 1942

Dear Home Folks:

Today is very hot; the temperature is probably considerably above 100 degrees. We sit in barracks and sweat, and any soldier who tries to sleep soon awakens saturated with perspiration.

Sunday is the soldier's day of rest, except for those few who get extra duty or are engaged in the type of work which must go on, as guards, cooks, buglers, etc. A large percentage of them go to church. For most the balance of the day is spent in catching up on sleep and rest, letter writing, reading and going to a movie in the evening. Those who have relatives living near, or visitors, may have the weekend off from camp and need not return until reveille on Monday morning.

With the exception of Sunday, the life of a trainee is a busy one. He spends six full days of work, regular hours of training from 6 a. m. to 4:30 p. m. and after that the cleaning of weapons, cleaning of barracks, arranging of clothing, rolling of packs, etc., may keep him busy until 8 p. m. or later.

Four Arkansawyers at Camp Wolters, Tex., as basic trainees in the summer of 1942. Left to right, Thomas L. L. Temple, Little Rock; Edward R. Reynolds, Manila; Faubus, and Ben M. Wilbanks, Plumerville.

Left to right—Charles L. McCoy, Clifty; Marvin Haskins, St. Paul; Orval E. Faubus, Huntsville; Jim Rowlett, St. Paul; all of Arkansas, and all "flatfoot" rookies in basic training at Camp Wolters, Texas during the summer of 1942.

He wanted to "join up" like his Dad, insisted on the uniform and learned to salute. Farrell Eugene Faubus, at age three or four, son of Lt. Faubus.

Pfc Hugh Fritts of Thorney, Ark., killed in action in France in Alsace-Lorraine in September, 1944, while serving as an infantryman with Company I, 137th Infantry Regiment, 35th Division. The photograph was taken at his home in February 1944.

Left to right, Arthur B. Bestul, Dennison, Minn.; Faubus and Stephen W. Bowker, Jonesboro, Ark. (now of North Little Rock); basic trainees at Camp Wolters, Texas during the summer of 1942.

Some GI Joes of Company F, 320th Infantry, at Camp San Luis Obispo, Calif., on the day the unit left for Camp Rucker, Ala. Sgt. Sweeney of Co. F has the barber tools and is preparing to save a buddy the cost of a GI haircut. (photo from Lt. Gene Trask, Winterset, Iowa)

Lt. Eugene F. Trask, Winterset (or Washington) Iowa, and Lt. Arthur J. Manzi, Worcester, Mass., officers in Co F 320th Inf., at Camp San Luis Obispo, Calif. (photo from Trask)

Lts. Sidney Silverman of Detroit, Mich., and Orval E. Faubus of Huntsville, Ark., officers of Co F and later of Regtl. Hqs., 320th Infantry, during the training days before going overseas.

Pictured above are members of the Intelligence and Reconnisance Platoon (I&R Plat) of Hq Co, the 320th Inf. Regt., at Camp Rucker, Ala., 1943, before the Division left for winter maneuvers in Tennessee. All these men entered combat with the unit.

1st Row, left to right: Pvt. Joseph Crisafulli, Newark, N. J.; S/Sgt. William "Muscles" Smith, Chicago, Ill.; 1st Lt. Sidney Silverman, Detroit, Mich.; Pvt. Reginald W. Lockhart, Long Beach, Calif.

2nd Row: Pvt. Cecil Combs, Kentucky; Pvt. Raymond E. "Smitty" Smith, Jr., Cleveland, Ohio; Pvt. Arnold Peterson, Minneapolis, Minn.; Pvt. John E. Douglas, Ottawa, Kans.

3rd Row: Pvt. Ben F. Burnham, Durango, Colo.; Pvt. Robert Whittington, Thurston, Ohio; Pvt. "Honest" John Holloway, address unknown; Pvt. Evans, Dayton, Ohio, (full name unknown);

4th Row: Cpl. Ralph "Nub" Brown, Ogallala, Neb.; Pvt. William "Wild Bill" Bailey, Dodge City, Kans.; Pvt. Sherryl Bunn, Germantown, Ohio; Pvt. Robert R. "Red" Rhodes, Elkins, W. Va.

5th Row: Sgt. Joseph Harris, Chattanooga, Tenn.; Cpl. Kauko Aho, New York, N. Y.; Sgt. "Big Buddy" Ferran, Mt. Shasta, Calif.; (listed on regtl. roster as Raymond P. Ferron, Palo Alto, Calif.); Sgt. Fred Smead, Yakima, Wash.; Pvt. William A. "Bill" Dickson, Barnesville, Ohio; Pvt. Donald F. Riedel, Cleveland, Ohio. Not shown in picture: Pvt. Jack "Blackie" Blackmore, Liberal, Kans.; and Pvt. Carl R. Taçke, Wauwatosa, Wisc. (photo from Bill Dickson).

The bugle call for reveille begins our working day. We fall out of barracks and line up in the grey dawn. The electric lights still shining in the fading darkness remind me of white flowers. We are facing eastward across the plains, and almost always, as I gaze out toward where the sun will rise, I think of familiar scenes and loved ones out in that direction which I have left behind. However, one cannot let his mind wander for long. The stern voice of the platoon sergeant, calling the roll and for reports, abruptly brings one back to reality. A soldier whether in training or combat must learn to be always alert. I am at times not as alert as I should be and I must admit that I sometimes get into hot water because I am here in a Texas training camp and my mind in Arkansas.

Each morning, too, I think of my little boy during the policing (cleaning up) of the platoon area. The match stems I pick up remind me of how he liked to gather up handfuls of them to drive into the ground. The last day we spent together in Huntsville he gathered as many as he could hold in his small hand, and was saving them until he could secure a hammer. I persuaded him to leave them in the school bus by telling him that we would return for them sometime. They were the last things I remember seeing when I stepped out of the bus the last time; a little bunch of burnt match stems scattered over the floor by the driver's seat, symbol of a little boy's faith in what Daddy tells him. I don't know when we'll be able to go back and get them.

The news from home has been bad for me this week. The last I heard from my wife she was still in the hospital at Fayetteville, and death had come to some of my old friends. The boy who slept beside me, Dieterich, [Walter L. Dieterich, St. Ansgar, Iowa] received a telegram that his father had died and went home on emergency furlough.

It is sometimes very tough on the boys in the service and those at home as well. But we are still well off and have many things to be thankful for, when we consider our welfare as compared to the condition of the conquered countries and the battle fronts. I know my folks are among friends, and that law and order and those in authority are still on the side of the weak and the just.

Consider for a moment two recent events, the wiping out of the Czech town of Lidice and the siege of Sevastopol, and you will see how much worse our condition could be (and will be if we lose the war). The Czech town, population 1200, was completely wiped out, all the men were shot, the women sent to concentration camps, and the children to "educational" centers, and the town was destroyed utterly, and its name stricken from German records. To bring this home to yourself, imagine the same thing applied to the home town of Huntsville. See in your mind the men all marched off to death, the editor, the undertaker, the postmaster, the mail carriers, the merchants, the barbers, the county officers, the service station men, the teachers, farmers, all of them, taking their last agonizing looks at their families as they are herded away to be shot. Then the women are separated from their children and herded away to the barbed-wire encircled camps to be slaves to the Nazi masters, who may rape or kill them at their will.

The little children, helplessly and mercilessly taken from their homes and parents, if they are considered the right type, will be taught the Nazi idealogy. If not they will be liquidated, which means that in some way they will be done away with. Then last of all the town and the homes which the people knew are burned and destroyed.

In the Russian Black Sea port of Sevastopol, besieged by the Germans and Rumanians, the women and all the children large enough are armed as the men and taking part in the defense of the city. It was related how one girl sniper, 18 years of age, was cut off among enemy troops and shot her way back to her own lines, killing 15 of the enemy. The town is constantly bombed from the air and shelled by the German heavy artillery. The bombs and the shells fall on houses as well as forts, on women and children as well as soldiers. Great mounds of earth thrown up by the bursting shells bury whole homes or gun crews. Yet they hold out day after day and their motto is "not one step backward" and no surrender.

I'm sure the people of Madison County and of America do not want to undergo such things as the people of the conquered regions and the battle fronts are enduring. And yet we have people who will not sacrifice a little of their pleasure in order to buy Defense Bonds, who will not contribute to the Red Cross or the USO. We still have conscientious objectors and those who wish to evade the draft. There are still those who are thinking more of making money than of winning the war. Perhaps there are not many of that type, but if there is only one, that is too many.

I tell you people at home that it is time for EVERYONE to realize that we are in a total war, a global war, a war for the world, in which EVERYTHING is at stake. We can all put our undivided efforts together and maintain what we have, or we can dilly-dally along and reap hell and destruction, misery and suffering as long as we survive, which may not be for long.

We yet have much to be thankful for, but anything for which we are thankful is a blessing we should be willing to try to keep. Remember the rain falls on the just and on the unjust, and likewise the bombs and shells. The innocent and helpless have not been spared anymore than the fighting men.

The war is drawing ever closer. I think every day now of the boys in Alaska, and wish them success and good luck in throwing back the little yellow devils who are moving in. Word has just been flashed over the radio that the Japs are shelling Vancouver Island near Seattle, Wash. Tobruk has fallen and the British admit that it is a major disaster. It seems that Sevastopol cannot long stand against the forces being hurled against it by the Germans. The grand strategy of the Axis now evolving is to drive to the oil fields of the Near East through British held territory rather than through the Russian lines.

As a result of my last letter in the Record I have made contact here with Geo. W. Corbitt of Wesley, Charles L. McCoy of Clifty and Marvin Haskins of St. Paul. Clyde O. Hopper of Huntsville is here but I have not yet seen him. Also because of the Record I received letters from my aunt in Colorado, [Mrs. J. S. Johnson of Denver] my grandmother in Oklahoma, [Mrs. J. W. Nelson of Tahlequah] my friend, Rev. Norman Drake of Fayetteville, and others in Madison County. Thanks a lot to those who wrote. The letters were appreciated very much.

I wish to urge all of you who have sons or relatives in the service to write to them as often as possible. I have mentioned this before, but I want to impress it upon you strongly. Many of you may wonder why a soldier is so anxious to receive mail.

I'll try to explain briefly why he desires mail from home. With that one exception, a man of the Armed Services is almost completely isolated from the life he once knew, including the friendly ties of home and loved ones. In addition he suffers the loss of civilian freedom and initiative which he has been accustomed to exercise so freely. The mail call, with its news of home and loved ones, is the most pleasant break in the monotonous day of work and drill.

The most envied man in the company is the fellow who never misses his name at mail call, especially those who have sweethearts, and perhaps the bluest is the soldier who returns to his barracks empty handed. You at home! Don't wait for him to write. He may not have time. Sometimes he hardly has five minutes leisure during the day. If father, mother, brother and sister will take turns about, the writing need not be a burden to you.

And be certain you don't forget the home town paper. It is sometimes better than a whole bunch of letters. If your soldier boy is permanently located subscribe for him. If not, send him your copy each week, or buy an extra copy and mail to him. It is a mighty small thing to do for your soldier boy, who is doing so much for you. Best wishes.

Pvt. Orval E. Faubus
Co. B, 55th Bn.,
Camp Wolters, Texas

## MADISON COUNTY RECORD
### July 16, 1942

### FROM ORVAL FAUBUS

Camp Wolters, Texas
July 5, 1942

Dear Home Folks,

The hours have seemed long to me today. I attended church this morning and have spent the remainder of the day attempting to catch up on my correspondence. Lights are already out in barracks now but I have availed myself of the opportunity to do some writing on the company typewriter in the orderly room.

Today marks the end of the fifth week of our training cycle with eight more to go. I am a part of what is known as the "Heavy Weapons Company." The principal weapons of the company are the 81 mm mortar and the heavy .30 caliber machine gun. We also train with the rifle, bayonet and pistol. We have already finished with the rifle, bayonet and mortar training and are now engaged in learning to use the machine gun. We have just about finished with it, and my platoon won the company competition in setting up the gun ready for firing.

Perhaps the most interesting work was that with the mortar. As all military men know it is what is known as a high trajectory weapon. You could set one of them in one of those deep hollows there in the Ozarks and drop a shell right over the mountain onto a house on the other side. The aim is adjusted from instructions given by an observer at some point on top of the hill. Our gun crew did a good job in the firing of the mortars.

Camp Wolters' first blackout since our arrival here caught me with my face half-shaven. The intermittent moaning of the sirens, the cries of "lights out" and "cigarettes out" from noncoms, and the scurrying of the men all gave it an air of reality. Later planes could be heard approaching and we saw them overhead. We were glad that the eyes of a true-hearted American boy were looking down on us rather than those of a sinister Jap or a cruel Nazi.

Our company put on a show for the battalion last week. It is surprising how much talent you can discover in a bunch of men like this. We had a choir which sounded like professionals, there were two singers who had formerly been radio entertainers, another was a former music teacher and could play more than two dozen musical instruments, another was an excellent tap dancer, another a pianist, and so on. Temple of Arkansas announced that Congress had passed an act providing that from now on officers were to be elected rather than appointed, and made a speech in the interest of his candidacy for Lieut. Colonel that brought the house down. Willbanks, the former Mayor of Plummerville, Arkansas, acted as master of ceremonies.

I like the bunch of men with whom I am soldiering better and better. They represent various nationalities and religions. Being from the North for the most part, the roster of their names makes a difficult list for a sergeant to read. There are common names like Smith, Jones, Murphy and White. But how would you like rolling your tongue over a list containing the following, Baarstad, Bjorgum, Blascyk, Bogulslawski, Borgheiinck, Brezinski, Fleischfresser, Gonzagowski, Haatvedt, Kavaya, Lillegard, Liebhaber, Motschenbacker, Najmajstr, Reshtar, Sharpshair, Skaar, and Torgrimson. These are just some samples picked at random from the company roster.

The wit and humor of the men provide the greatest relief from the monotony of the daily drill. There are always some more or less comical men in a group of this size. But sometimes the greatest laughs are caused by statements made in serious vein. On one occasion the instructor had explained to the class that overhead fire was fire directed over the heads of friendly troops. Later on he asked, "What is meant by overhead fire?" "Sir," answered a recruit, "it is firing over the friendly enemy."

A recruit from Minnesota with a pronounced Northern brogue came leisurely into the barracks to find to his surprise that something had to be done in a hurry. "Gees," he exclaimed, "Why don't dey tell a guy dese t'ings." He is a fine fellow but I am constantly amused by the way he talks. On the other hand many of the men from other sections are just as amused at my speech as I am at theirs.

One day the tall, shy Dupont, little Feagins and the scholarly Bestul (the music teacher) were cleaning rifles. They had worked long and hard if not efficiently on one of the new Garands, and four times had thought it finished and sent it to the supply room, and just as many times the eagle-eyed supply sergeant had rejected it on inspection. After the fourth trip Bestul remarked, "I say fellows, this is running into work. Something must be done. Anyone have any suggestions?"

"No I haven't," replied Feagins, "but I agree that something must be done. I don't think I can hold out more than one more trip to see that sergeant."

Dupont who stutters on occasion was looking out the window at the setting sun, and made answer. "Wh-wh-wh-why, w-we might wait until the sun goes down, and he can't see so well, and then take it up." [James W. Dupont, St. Croix, Ind., Edward Feagins, Bloomfield, Iowa, Arthur B. Bestul, Dennison, Minn.]

The fun, pleasure and friendship are mixed with hardship, grief and enmity. As I have been writing this, a soldier in another company had become somewhat intoxicated and slashed his wrists in what was thought to be a suicide attempt and has been taken to the hospital.

Well, it is time for bed check (12:15) and I must stop.

Pvt. Orval E. Faubus,
Co. B, 55th Bn.,
Camp Wolters, Texas

MADISON COUNTY RECORD
July 30, 1942

FAUBUS WITHDRAWS CANDIDACY FOR JUDGE

Orval E. Faubus has withdrawn his candidacy for the Democratic nomination for county judge of Madison County. The reason for his action is his enlistment in Army service, as is stated in a notice published in this issue of the Record by the chairman and secretary of the Democratic County Central Committee, in connection with which notice is a call for a mass meeting of Democrats from all over the county to be held at Huntsville, Monday, August 3, in joint session with the central committee.

Probable candidates for the nomination made vacant by Mr. Faubus' withdrawal and friends of such candidates are urged to be present.

The County Central Committee declares the race for the nomination for county judge is wide open to anyone and all who are eligible to enter same.

MADISON COUNTY RECORD
September 10, 1942

FROM ORVAL E. FAUBUS

Camp Wolters, Texas
August 31, 1942

Dear Home Folks:

At last I find time and opportunity for a few lines to you again. You will recall that I told you once before that Sunday was the soldiers' day of rest, and that they usually spent the day by attending church and writing letters, with perhaps, a movie in the evening. Well, during the last few weeks I have spent five Sundays "on duty," two doing table waiting, one on guard, one on K. P. and one filling sand bags with which to buttress machine guns on the firing line. Also during the past few weeks we have had a number of night hikes and night problems, one of which was the oft-mentioned jaunt to Baker Hollow. We went out one night, stayed for one night problem, and returned to camp on the third. We started on the return at 9:00 P. M. and reached camp at 5:30 A. M., covering a distance of almost 20 miles with full field equipment.

The field equipment, which includes rifle, bayonet, cartridge belt, canteen filled with water, gas mask, rain coat, mess equipment, and the main body of the pack, which includes a number of articles is estimated to weigh 65 or 70 pounds. So you can imagine that we were a tired, footsore and weary bunch of soldiers at the end of the journey.

However, I think the hardest day which I have experienced was the one I spent on K. P. after a ten mile hike the night before. We were finished with the hike, which was with full field equipment, at 1:00 A. M. We arose at 5:00 A. M. so sore we could hardly move, and began doing the kitchen work. The balance of the company had another hike that night and we had to do the work four times instead of three, and did not get to go off duty until 1:30 A. M. the next morning, a stretch of over 20 hours of real work with less than two hours rest during the period. And you don't have to take my word about it being real work; ask any soldier who has ever performed the unpleasant task, and just about all of them have.

To some of you who may not understand the job, the K. P. stands for "kitchen police," and an average day's duties adds up something like this — washing and rinsing 900 plates, 750 cups, 250 cereal bowls, 300 bowls, 75 pitchers, 75 butter dishes, 750 forks, 750 knives, 750 teaspoons, 200 table spoons, the dozens of great cooking pots and pans (the hardest of all), the clearing away, the washing and resetting of 75 tables, the sweeping and mopping thrice daily of the long mess hall, and one scrubbing of the same, peeling 30 gallons of spuds, cleaning four sacks of corn, two bushels of carrots or an equal amount of some other kind of food. There are also a dozen other jobs which go along with these duties, as washing sinks, cleaning the grease trap (the most distasteful), cleaning garbage cans, washing the huge stove, washing the windows, etc., and all this done by six disgusted soldiers.

So when your soldier boy writes home and says "I'm K. P. now," don't think he's been promoted. There is a joke which goes the rounds among each bunch of trainees. There was the new recruit who after a few weeks service, wrote home to his mother and said, "I'm a kitchen policeman now," and she replied, "Well, Son, don't be too hard on the boys. Remember you were once a rookie yourself."

One evening last week I was standing in front of the Service Club, thinking of attending a show in order to remove a little gloom from my spirits. I stepped upon a post in order to see over the waiting line which was rather long, and in stepping down I lost my balance and caught the shoulder of another soldier standing near. On looking into his face, as I apoligized, I was overjoyed to recognize the friendly, familiar features of an old friend of South Madison County, Jim Rowlett. I'll not attempt here to express the feelings one has when there occurs the chance encounter with a friendly face in a far-away land. However, he had soon told me of Clyde Davis of St. Paul who is in the same company with him, and I had told him of Corbitt of Drakes Creek, McCoy of Clifty, Haskins of St. Paul and Hopper of Huntsville, all here in Camp Wolters.

Most of us got together the next Sunday and took some pictures and talked and thought of the "Hills of Home," the St. Paul reunion, the annual "decorations" we used to attend; the watermelon field on a dewy morning; the friendly fields of ripening corn and squirrel huntin' time comin' on; of how in the evening we could eat a nice home cooked meal of all the good things so abundant in the Ozarks, and then sit out on the porch or in the yard while the coolness of the evening settled down about us, while the shadow of the mountain lengthened across the valley and enveloped the hill beyond, and from out the darkest shadow in a deep hollow a hoot owl called and down the slope a whippoorwill began in measured cadence his melancholy chant; later the little frogs began their lonesome songs, and the soft darkness, which had stolen upon us from without the encroaching shadows, was made vibrant by the music of the katydids.

— 57 —

We finally got so homesick that we had to change the subject, for we well realize that many long and weary miles and many dangerous situations lie between us and the time when we will be free to come back and enjoy the things of which we thought and talked.

I wish to acknowledge letters from the following which I have not answered, and thank them for their kindness and thoughtfulness: my aunt, Mrs. A. G. Mast of El Paso, Texas; my aunt, Mrs. Minnie Johnson of Fairplay, Colorado, who says she won't miss my answering so much if she can read my letters in the Record; my grandmother, Mrs. J. W. Nelson of Tahlequah, Oklahoma, who also read my letters in the Record and wrote to ask me not to forget to pray; Rev. Norman Drake of Fayetteville; Mrs. Davis of California who writes that she does not know me but that her father knew me well; Mr. Owens and Mr. Hopper of the Welfare Department of Ozark, Arkansas; my sister, June, and Arch Brandenburg and daughter, Ottilee, of Pateros, Washington; Pvt. Homer Worley who wrote that he was shipping from Fort Knox, Kentucky; Sgt. J. Woodrow Ledford of Camp Crowder, Missouri; Pvt. C. E. Shinn Jr. of Chanute Field, Illinois; Pvt. Shirley Thornsberry who was shipping from Camp Grant, Illinois; my nieces, Betty Jo and Billie June Pool of Fayetteville; and my friends in Madison County, Clay McBroom, Olen Garrett, Grover Harris, Ewell Couch, J. J. Crumpacker and Mr. and Mrs. L. A. Nelson. Thanks also to you who have written and to whom I have found time to reply.

To those of you who say you look for my letters first, I'll say I'm glad you find them interesting. To you who said you had subscribed for the Record in order to read my letters, I'm sure you'll get more than your money's worth in reading the Madison County Record whether any of my letters appear in its columns or not.

I certainly enjoy the letters from the other boys in the service which appear in the Record from time to time. Since the Japs bombed Dutch Harbor I have thought often of Morris Foster and "Cotton" Murphy and the other boys stationed there. The old man who sells papers here in camp calls the Japs "yaller-bellies." Since our forces have been winning in the Pacific he comes through the barracks almost every morning yelling "Mac-Arthur's boys and the Australians have killed 500 more of the yallerbellies."

Thanks to Pvt. John K. Wall for his nice comment on my letters. He is located not very far from where I am stationed.

I wish to extend my heartfelt sympathy to the relatives of Carroll Smith, killed in action. The glory and honor due to him is all the greater because his defense of his country and the sacrifice of his life was entirely voluntary on his part.

Sincerely,

Pvt. Orval E. Faubus
Co. B, 55th Bn.,
Camp Wolters, Texas

[Carroll Smith was the first Madison Countain to give his life in WWII. The American Legion post at Huntsville, Hayes-Smith post no. 137, in which I hold a life membership, is named for him and the first Madison Countain to give his life in WWI.]

MADISON COUNTY RECORD
September 24, 1942

ORVAL E. FAUBUS BACK IN CAMP

September 13, 1942

Dear Home Folks:

Well, I'm back at camp in Texas after a short stay in the Ozarks of Arkansas, which was like an all too brief sojourn in Paradise. In answer to the many questions about home and the Ozarks the most fitting phrase I could think of was "just a bit of heaven."

It really is a wonderful country, and even before I thought of coming to the Army I had learned to enjoy and be thankful for every day of life there. It was a pleasure just to see the sun rise, and a wonderful thing to view its many golden settings. (Especially do I recall the touching beauty of the sunsets I have seen from Alonzo Ledford's farm on Pinnacle Mountain). It was good to see the rain fall, the flowers bloom, the leaves put forth, or the crystal clear brooks to flow, and gladsome almost beyond expression to come home in the cool of a summer evening and see my little boy race across the green lawn, his small, tender, short legs working rythmically, his face shining with pure delight to greet his daddy. Good, too, to attend the church services on Sunday and mingle with the friendly neighbors; and to be seated in the little white-washed building and find descending upon me with the singing and the prayer that "peace which passeth all understanding." And all the other pleasures and joys of that country which if enumerated could not be listed in one issue of the Record.

Upon my return here I found the confusion, the hustle and bustle of settling and straightening out a newly inducted bunch of trainees. They, like the members of the preceding cycle, are entirely new to army life, and are asking many questions and making many wise cracks. I remember the rough talking member of my group who, after arrival here, wrote to his draft board and said, "Dear Draft Board, I'm 'Deep in the Heart of Texas,' wish you were here with me." I recalled the many times I had heard the students on my school bus sing the song, and hadn't suspected that I would soon be there literally. But the word "Heart" in the song title soon gave way to "heat" or "hell" [here] which somewhat changed the meaning much to the displeasure of the natives of the Union's largest state.

The members of my old company have almost all been shipped, and are scattered to the four corners of the U. S. and some already on their way to other parts of the earth. The acquaintances each of us has made, the friendships gained, the faces each had come to know and like and by whose side marched for a time, have gone away and few, if any at all, will ever be seen again during this life's journey.

The Madison Countians, Hopper, Corbitt, Haskins and McCoy have already gone, and Rowlett and Davis are going if not already gone. (God speed them and God bless them. I enjoyed their company while we were together.) By the time you read this it is likely that I will also be on my way. You who have written or intend to write to me wait for my next address, and I hope you all write.

The brief acquaintances and friendships of life, and especially Army life, cause me to recall in ever more recurring frequency, the poem I like so much.

"Ships that pass in the night, and speak each other in
     passing,
Only a signal blown, and a distant voice in the darkness;
So on the ocean of life, we pass and speak one another,
Only a look and a voice, then darkness again, and a si-
     lence".

The war must be won. We must go on. The glorious bravery of the Russians who are dying for us, as well as for their
own people, make us ashamed that we have not done more. Although the partings may often be bitterly sad and painful,
we must hurry on and stand by their side, else we do not deserve the blessings and freedom we enjoy.

Pvt. Orval E. Faubus
Co. B, 55th Bn.,
Camp Wolters, Texas

MADISON COUNTY RECORD
October 8, 1942

FROM ORVAL E. FAUBUS

Camp Wolters, Texas
September 27, 1942

Dear Home Folks:

This is a beautiful fall day here in Texas. Last night
was cool and I had to spread my overcoat on my bunk to
keep from freezing because the heating system had not yet
begun to function. This morning the air was very snappy,
but the warm sun in a clear sky and the absence of any breeze
(unusual in Texas) have brought a warm autumnal day.
Many boys sit about the barracks in the warm sun; others
engage in soft ball games or throw a football back and forth;
many more sit in barracks or in the recreation hall writing
to the folks at home.

There isn't much foliage in camp so it looks much the
same. The Palo Pinto Hills (thanks to J. D. Easley, editor
of the Clarion, or I would have not known their name) are
still green but around the edges of the woods can be seen
the beginnings of autumn colors. Of course the beauty of
these hills is as nothing compared to that of the Ozarks. I

know they have not yet put on their full autumn dress of incomparable color and beauty, but on such a day as this in the hills of Madison County, Arkansas, there can be heard in the early morning the sound of squirrels busily working on the bountiful fall harvests of acorns, nuts and chinquapins, mingled with the call of wandering blue jays and the cawing of raiding crows. The grass-hoppers (hopper-drasses my little boy calls them; he got the word turned around when we first told him the name of the little creatures and it sounded so funny we never attempted to correct him) will be singing their last songs as they stretch their legs in the sunny grass and here and there can be seen stray butterflies, laggards of the southward flight, paying their farewell calls to the autumn flowers.

On such a Sabbath day as this in the Ozarks, the little children will be playing gleefully in the warmth of the roadways and the fields. The older boys will be 'a-huntin'' in the woods or maybe taking a final dip in the old swimmin' hole. Here and there will be parties of young and old of all ages on delightful excursions into the fragrant woods known as "chinquapin hunting." With the help of that delightful chinquapin game of "hull gull" the lads and lassies will be getting acquainted and perchance making a "date" for some social event of the coming night. Groups of women will be seen leisurely talking before the church or beside the farmhouse. The men will be congregated beside the barn or the roadside, where the more energetic will possibly be engaged in a game of horseshoes, while the remainder sit or loll on the browning grass or the warm sand, and talk of war and politics, and compare the present season's abundant harvest with that of former years. (Bet there is such a group right now, if the day there is pretty, beside the old Sycamore tree at the forks of the road on Greasy Creek,—Time: Sunday afternoon, September 27, 1942).

It is a delightful country and a friendly lovable people which we Madison County boys left when we went away to the war. Because it is such a country inhabited by such a people is the reason we are in the Army camps, on the sea and on the battlefields. Because if Hitler and the Japs should win the war the people could no longer live their lives as they now do. Their easy going friendly attitude would cease to be, and they would live in fear and slavery as now live the people of the conquered countries. Under Hitler and the Japs, no family's property would be secure, and no man's life or woman's chastity would be safe. A few people back there do not seem to realize that we are in danger, but in all sincerity we are. That is why we men of the Armed Forces are here and not in the homes we love so well. Of course we all hope to return home, and the hope is perhaps more dear to us than any we ever had before, but we know that all of us will not have that happy privilege. But if it takes my life, (as it will take the lives of some of us,) I had rather die a thousand times than have my wife and little boy at the mercy of a Gestapo agent or a Japanese soldier. I know there are others who feel as I do. We have a bloody, fearful job to do. It is not a hopeless undertaking, for which thank God for the heroism of the Russians. With your help we will get the job done as soon as possible. Is your shoulder to the wheel and are you doing all you can?

To the names of Carroll Smith of Dutton and Claude La Fon of Huntsville, killed in action, may be added the names of Charles Rankin and Henry Rankin of St. Paul, officially listed by the War Department as missing in action in the Philippines. This means that they were either killed in action or taken prisoner by the Japs. While home on my brief furlough I saw Ted Rankin of Japton, brother of the boys, and he gave me the above information. Both boys were school mates of mine at St. Paul.

I am also informed in a letter from my grandmother, Mrs. J. W. Nelson of Tahlequah, Oklahoma, that her stepgrandson, J. D. Nelson, of the Navy was lost in the battle for the Philippines. It is probable that he went down with his ship, but there is a possibility that he was rescued by the Japs and is being held prisoner. I knew J. D. quite well, and will always remember a very pleasant month that I spent with him some years ago while visiting my grandmother at Tahlequah. He is a nephew of L. A. Nelson of Huntsville, former assessor of Madison County, and of W. L. Nelson and Mrs. Sallie Thornsberry of Combs.

I wonder if anyone at home has ever heard anything definite of Sidney Marcum of Combs, an old school mate of mine, who was in the Philippines when the Jap attack came.

Well, when I wrote to the Record last time, I expected to be gone from Camp Wolters very shortly. However I am still here, one of four members of my class still being held. Two of them are fellow Arkansawyers, one of whom is my good friend B. M. Willbanks, the ex-mayor of Plummerville whom I mentioned before. Five more of my Arkansas friends are just leaving for Fort Benning, Ga. I expect my shipping order at any time, but one never knows in the Army. Because we don't know we sometimes suffer inconveniences, but the advantage in such a system lies in the fact that if we don't know the enemy doesn't know, which is the reason for us not knowing in the first place.

I received a nice letter from Leon E. Ogden, son of Mr. and Mrs. Earl Ogden of Pettigrew. He is stationed at El Paso, Texas, and like me he is thrilled at any mention of the Ozarks. He read my letter in the Record and writes that he is very familiar with the K. P. and the guard duties I mentioned. Well, what doughboy isn't? It certainly isn't pleasant while doing the work, but it doesn't make such bad remembering when it is all over with.

Best Wishes to All.

Cpl. Orval E. Faubus
Co. B, 55th Bn.,
Camp Wolters, Texas

MADISON COUNTY RECORD
October 22, 1942

FROM ORVAL E. FAUBUS

Fort Benning, Ga.
October 11, 1942

Dear Home Folks:

I have only time for a brief message at present. My first week's training at this school has just passed and with only a brief Sabbath pause we continue into the second. I was never busier in my life. They throw work to us here like pitching hay into the barn to avoid a sudden shower.

There are men here from all points of the compass; every state is represented and many foreign countries. There are men here who have already seen action on all the fronts, and men who fought with the Chinese and the Spanish Loyalists before World War II brought death and destruction to every part of the globe. There are men from every walk of life, farmers, mechanics, store clerks, teachers, lawyers, publishers, and public officials. There are any number of college graduates many of them from the best known college institutions of America. In my company are five service men who are professional baseball players (one of them from the Cardinals) and a professional boxer who was once a champion in his class. Today while in the day room writing letters I sat at a table and chatted with a service man who wrote a history book and is the owner of a publishing and printing business.

This evening while sitting in the mail room I heard service men put in long distance calls to their home folks in Massachusetts, New York, New Jersey, Florida, Arkansas, Nebraska and California. Most of them, when they feel low in spirits and want a break in the monotony of constant drill and training, attempt to call some loved one for a few cheerful words from home. However telephone service, like transportation service, is not at all good.

In time we will all get acquainted and have some very pleasant associations, but so far we have been too busy. All other considerations take secondary place to the one great aim of licking the Axis.

Two of my comrades of Camp Wolters are still with me here, Craig of Nebraska [Don C. Craig, North Platte, Nebr.] and Ben M. "Shorty" Willbanks of Plummerville, Ark., whom I have mentioned previously in my letters. "Shorty" is a good fellow, friendly, affable, helpful, honest and intelligent, an excellent combination of good qualities.

I know the Ozarks are most beautiful now. I think of them every day and long to be there, but we must set the Rising Sun before I am again free to watch sunsets in the Ozarks.

About five minutes ago I made the acquaintance of a fellow named Herb Moore, who played professional ball for Siloam Springs in the Missouri-North Arkansas League in 1940. He is well acquainted with my friend, Russell Elrod of Siloam Springs, and also has a close acquaintance with Freddie Hawn, a relative of the editor of the Record. Everywhere

I go it seems there is some incident which calls to mind the expression, "It's a small world."

Candidate Orval E. Faubus<br>
Co. 15, 3rd Bn.,<br>
2nd Student Tng. Regt.,<br>
Fort Benning, Ga.

## MADISON COUNTY RECORD
### November 26, 1942

## FROM ORVAL E. FAUBUS

Fort Benning, Ga.
November 15, 1942

Dear Home Folks:

I take time to write rather hurriedly to you again. There are perhaps more interesting things here of which to write than at my former station, but as I am undergoing what is perhaps one of the most intensive training courses now being given to many members of the Armed Forces, I haven't much time for writing.

In this course one must constantly be "on the ball" or expressed in another way "on the beam." It has the same meaning to me as when my Dad used to say "walking the chalk line." A few days illness, absent from one formation, missing at bed check just once, and the unlucky candidate is on his way out of the school and back to his old organization. Also a few failures of the weekly tests which we get, or a display of nervousness at a critical moment, may mean the difference in a non-com's stripes or an officer's gold bars.

I really feel sorry for many of the boys that fail for it means a lot to some of them. As for me, I would like to be an officer, of course, because I feel that I can do more as an officer, but I realize that men of the ranks are just as important, and that it is just as great an honor in every sense to be one. As long as each one does his part, and we get the awful war finished, what does it matter what that part is? Realizing this I now understand fully the oft quoted expression, "Let not ambition mock your useful toil" which I once did not clearly understand. And realizing this it will not be with great regret that I continue to serve as a man of the ranks, nor with great joy should I graduate. The great joy for me will be the coming of peace and the day when we all can return home, and the great regret will be for those who lost their lives and will never return.

Two Sundays ago I was sitting in the day room writing when a quiet, friendly voice said, "Hello, Faubus!" Thinking it was one of my company mates I returned the greeting without too much interest. I glanced up and noted the name "Grigg," and knowing we had no one in the company by that name, I raised my eyes higher and found myself looking into the friendly face of Kenneth Grigg of Kingston. I guess he thought strange of me for I was so surprised that for some time I hardly found words to greet him. Kenneth is also an officer candidate here at Fort Benning, and if the fates and the examining officers are kind, he will make a good officer. I know he will be a good soldier in whatever capacity he serves, but I sincerely hope he gets the gold bars.

Looking at Kenneth's friendly face as we talked, my gaze wandered beyond him and back to Madison County, and I could see again the green hills around Kingston as they looked when I made my first campaign in the county. I walked from Kingston up by the Bunch home, on up by the Weathers farmstead, up Dry Creek, thence across the mountain and back down Sweden Creek and to Kingston again. Then I footed it across the mountain by "Doc" McCollough's place and down Dry Fork by Kenneth's home to the Carroll County line, thence back across the mountain westward. I was lost for some time in that thinly settled section, but after running and walking rapidly for some 8 or 10 miles I came out of the woods at Tom Lane's place just as the thick darkness of the summer night was settling down. Then next day up Kings River to Loy I hiked and thence across the mountain and came out at night-fall in the vicinity of the Camp Ground School (Lower Camp Ground if I recollect the name correctly). I remembered how the friendly people of that section had invited me into their homes and given me food and drink and lodging and listened kindly while I told my story, and would not think of taking pay for any service which they rendered to me. As Kenneth and I talked the scenes, the names and faces passed in review through my mind, Weathers, Bunch, Wright, Stamps, Bowen, Parker, Cook, Fancher, Mitchell,

Maxwell, McCollough, Lane, Holt, Grigg, Sanders, White, Fields, Cline and all the others. I will always remember with amusement how, when I came to Fred Berrys' place he took one look at me and without further words, took up the telephone and called his wife saying, "We'll have company for dinner." [noon meal].

Another Kingston boy, Bill Cline, is a member of a regular infantry unit somewhere in Fort Benning. I have also heard that a Johnson boy of Wesley is located here somewhere. I met him while home on furlough but cannot at this moment recall his first name.

Recently I received a card from an old camp mate of Camp Wolters, Texas, Charles L. McCoy of Clifty, bearing the postmark of Angel Island, California, and an address which indicates that he is now located somewhere in the vast Pacific.

Clyde Davis, St. Paul, is now at Camp Polk, La., and writes me that our buddy of Camp Wolters, Jim Rowlett, also of St. Paul, has gone across the Atlantic. If true he might now be in the fighting in Africa as well as my cousin, Shirley Thornsberry of Combs who has been in England for some time. The last word from Marvin Haskins, St. Paul, and George Corbitt, Drakes Creek, they were at Fort Sam Houston, Texas, and Marvin was soon to go north as a part of an airborne unit. A former pupil of mine, Oscar Dunaway of Thorney, has for some time been far out in the Pacific.

Soon our boys from Madison County will be, perhaps even now they are, scattered all around the world.

Life here at Benning is very interesting, would be very much so if we had time to take close notice. However things outside our work can be noticed only briefly in passing. Every day, up and down, go the marching columns of men, and from some point always can be heard the crackling rifle fire, the chatter of the machine guns or automatic rifles, and the heavy explosions of mortar and artillery shells. The airplanes of many types, observation, pursuit, bombers and transports, criss cross the sky, and often we can see, blossoming out in the sky behind the transports, the white flower like 'chutes of the paratroopers as they plunge out of the planes into the clear Georgia skies. They appear to come out faster than one per second, and even when you are watching closely they appear as if by magic behind the huge sky birds, and float gently down to earth.

As I told you before there are people here from almost everywhere. On my one trip to town I saw a great number of Canadians, who are here for training as parachute troops, mingling with the great numbers of our boys from every state in the Union.

The other day while firing the heavy machine gun on the range, I had on my right an officer of the Chinese Army. He was learning how to manipulate the gun so that he could go back and teach his own people on the other side of the world. Watching his slight form as he so intently bent to his task, I thought of the six years of hell his people have undergone at the hands of the Japs, and I could not but conclude that we were much more lucky than they.

On last Thursday it fell my lot to lead a rifle squad in action, before a visiting British Officer, two officers of the British Indian Army, Gen. Allen, the camp Commandant and other dignitaries. The Britisher made us a brief talk after the demonstration. He spoke highly of the Americans already in England and stated that they had gotten along famously, and that he sincerely hoped they could make us feel welcome should we come their way. Everyone thought he was very nice.

As I may not write again soon I wish to acknowledge letters from the following: Pfc. Arvill Shipp of Camp Hood, Texas, who speaks longingly of the wooded hills of the Ozarks but says he is getting along fine. Arvill used to tramp through the woods a lot and I know that, like me, he could not help being lonesome for them this fall. J. A. Tucker of Wharton writes and sends a religious paper containing letters from men in the service. Maurice Johnson sends me some religious papers from Los Angeles, California, and Mrs. Nettie Stevenson, also of Los Angeles, (formerly Miss Nettie Brandenburg of Combs) sends literature of the Technocrats. L. S. Dunaway of the Conway Advertising Agency of Conway, Arkansas, writes "I'll be glad to help elect you Secretary of State when you return." Thanks also to my friends in Madison who have written and to whom I have not replied. I'd like to mention all of you, but I have burdened the kind editor of the Record too much already. Remember he is as much entitled to thanks for news of the boys far away, as me or any one else.

Sincerely, Orval E. Faubus

P. S. Today, Nov. 18th, I received a nice box of candy from the H. D. Club of Combs, Mrs. Marie Thornsberry, Secretary. It helped to cheer me very much. Many times we have the feeling so aptly expressed by the author of the hymn, "Lead, Kindly Light" when he wrote: "The night is dark, and I am far from home, lead Thou me on."

Such thoughtful acts of kindness help to drive away the loneliness, and are appreciated very much by the men of all the Armed Forces.—O. E. F.

## THE INFANTRY SCHOOL (OCS)

### FT. BENNING, GEORGIA

Training in the Infantry School of Ft. Benning, Ga., where all trainees were known as candidates (candidates for commissions as officers), was as concentrated and intense as any I have ever experienced. The day began with getting properly dressed, including a shoe shine, cleaning the barracks, making up your individual cot, and properly arranging books, equipment and clothing. A candidate could get a demerit if any one of these things was not done to the satisfaction of the inspector, and inspection was constant and strict.

The accumulation of ten demerits by any candidate could result in his disqualification for further training and expulsion from the school. In the first few days I got three demerits because my cot failed to pass inspection. This came about because a neighboring candidate, in making his bed and sweeping underneath after I had finished mine, had accidentally touched my cot, leaving a small wrinkle in the blanket, or had fanned a few pieces of blanket lint underneath.

I learned to re-check my cot and the area underneath, the last thing before leaving the barracks. I received no more demerits in this field, but did get another for failure to check the bulletin board some time during the first week.

The knowledge to be gained at the school included many things. A candidate must be able to name the parts, acquire the skill to assemble or set up, and to describe the functioning of all weapons, as mortar, light; mortar, heavy; machine gun, light; machine gun, heavy; rifle, MI; and carbine, M-something-or-other (now forgotten). The training included close order drill, which any candidate might be called upon at any moment to direct. We marched or rode from point to point on the huge reservation to classes or demonstrations in the proper use of scouts, infantry units, artillery, tanks, tank destroyers, camouflage, chemical warfare, communications, etc. No candidate will ever forget the huge, comfortless motorized vans, or the small, open railroad cars, which operated on the rail and highway transportation systems of the reservation. And then there were the obstacle courses. A cartoon, a favorite of the trainees, which appeared in the 15th Regiment camp paper, The Pine-Bur, showed a monkey in uniform nimbly going over a high wall, which was a part of all such courses. Said one tactical officer to another as they observed, "Best candidate I've had so far."

There were imaginary and mythical problems of all kinds involving Army units and weapons. After a certain amount of training, candidates were called upon, always without foreknowledge, to give solutions to these mythical problems. There was always a "school solution." Even if the chosen candidate didn't hit upon what was considered to be the proper solution, if he showed ingenuity, and knowledge of the units and weapons involved, he could make a passing grade. The school solution gave rise to another favorite cartoon which appeared in The Pine-Bur. It showed a prostrate school officer in a dead faint and the students cheering with the caption, "He hit the school solution."

Training was not finished with the ending day. After evening chow (meal) we fell out and marched in formation to a class room for two hours of study, always in charge of a tactical (school) officer. The study period always ended with a five-minute address by one of the candidates.

For the first ten days of our camp training, a candidate was selected for the address by the camp officers and his name posted on the bulletin board well ahead of the time to speak. We were told that at the end of ten days, no further notice would be given. A candidate to make the speech would be selected at random by the officer in charge. We all knew what was required, we were told, and all should be prepared.

I seldom studied the dry, lusterless military manuels at these study periods. A description of the mechanical functioning of the BAR, MI, etc. bored me almost to distraction. After the period of instruction and some study, I read a magazine or book, made notes and occasionally wrote letters. On the eleventh night I had the thought, "Not much chance to select me out of 208 class members. But, just in case, I'll make some notes." Then I outlined a brief speech, laid it aside and began reading.

In charge that night was Lt. Berger, an officer of excellent military bearing, a charming, irrepressable manner, and with one of the keenest minds I have ever encountered. At the proper time he called the class to attention, restated the previous announcement about the speeches, and selected a candidate.

The candidate arose, plainly ill at ease, and attempted to speak. At the end of a minute and a half, he gave up and sat down. "Well", said Berger, "We have time for another" and called a second candidate. He couldn't speak at all, apologized and sat down.

"In that case," said the personable lieutenant, "We'll have another." Jabbing the roster with his finger he exclaimed, "Eenie, meenie, minie, (pause) Fay-bus!" (A common mispronunciation of my name).

I looked startled, but was not as taken aback as I appeared. I already had some good buddies in the outfit and spontaneously they began to applaud and call my name. The two previous failures had created a situation where the students were looking for some one to "carry it off" in the speech making. Responding to the situation I arose, began gathering up books and papers as if I had been waiting for the call, and stepped into the aisle with an air of complete confidence. (I wasn't all that assured). Lt. Berger, noting the developments, quickly fell into the spirit of the occasion. As I walked forward he dashed back stage to secure a table, a pitcher of water, and a glass. He filled the glass from the pitcher and set them on the table as for a dignitary.

The applause was thunderous before I reached the lectern, and I felt successful before I opened my mouth. I have lost the notes on my speech and don't recall much that I said, but my remarks, mostly humorous, literally brought down the house three or four times. I closed on a serious note of what we had to defend, how the country was depending on us, and our responsibilities to the men who would be in our charge if and when we became officers. Then I gathered up my papers and walked off the stage. Again there was tremendous applause. As I went down the aisle I looked back. Lt. Berger was shaking his head in amazement and slapping his thigh.

He bent double with laughter two or three times before he could dismiss the class.

That brief speech was probably the most successful small event of my life.

As Thanksgiving approached, the class was told that we could prepare a program to be given in connection with the evening meal. As a result of my speech, the committee for the program asked me to be master of ceremonies. An excellent Thanksgiving dinner was served and in addition to the candidates and class officers, the battalion commander and the regimental chaplain attended.

I have found in my files a copy of the remarks I made on that occasion. It was an opportunity to say things about our training and circumstances, and to our officers and about them, which would have been difficult otherwise. The remarks were greatly enjoyed by all those present, but will, I realize, have much less meaning to others.

Major Johnson, Officers, Fellow Students,

Having been for some time now, since the date of my induction to be more specific, unaccustomed to such meals as we have had the pleasure of enjoying tonight, I am forced to labor at a disadvantage. I think it is customary to expect of a toastmaster a display of a certain amount of humor and wit. Well, there was once in my life, as there was in yours, a time when I was accustomed to thinking and acting, with a stomach well filled with good food. But as I said, having been unaccustomed to such conditions now for six months, 1 week, 5 days, 11 hours, 44 minutes, and—well we'll not mind to be exact,—I'm afraid it will have an adverse effect to that which one in my position should feel. Therefore you must not expect much, other than the presentation of the entertainment and the speakers of the evening. However let me warn you right now, that all the tactical officers are here, and if anything like as many of you go to sleep as do in the classes over in building B-19 and B-12, somebody is going to be disappointed. And if I get as sleepy here as I sometimes do over there, naturally there'll be need of a new chairman.

Having told the only good joke that I know that would be suitable for an occasion of this kind, the night that Lt. Berger called on me for a speech over in study hall, if I were to attempt to tell you any humorous stories, they would have to be about the strange folklore of the hills with which I am most familiar. As that is a distinct sort of humor, which is appreciated most by the type of people among whom it has its origin, people who live in quiet places, who have much leisure, and to whom a strange face is something to be noticed and remembered, I'm not quite sure it would be fitting for such a cosmopolitan audience as we have here; frank and argumentative "Downeasters," reserved Northerners, gay Southern Blades, and the quiet friendly men of the West. And there are also the Texans of whom it is said that they think they have a nation of their own and whose newspapers would lead you to suppose that they were fighting the war with Uncle Sam as merely a secondary helper.

So with due respect to all parts of our great union, and every part is a valuable part of the union, and every part is as dear to its own native sons as my home is to me, with that thought in mind I think, for the most part, I'll just call on the entertainers and present the speakers this evening.

So at this time we'll have Candidate Davis [Michael Davis, Winston-Salem, N. C.] play some musical numbers for us.

(A slow number was played)—That is the cadence to which our mess hall table waiters usually perform while we're waiting for the biscuits or the liver and onions.

(A fast number was played)—That is the cadence to which they perform when removing the dishes from the table, after or slightly before we've finished a meal. I jabbed at the last bite the other day and stuck my fork into the table. I might have got him, but you know the old saying, "the hand is quicker than the eye."

We will now have a skit by Candidates Marto, Lippincott, Loos and Levkoff. [A comedy skit by Candidates John P. Marto (address unknown); Howard E. Lippincott, Marlton, N. J.; Edward C. Loos, Victoria, Texas; and Bernard H. Levkoff, New York, N. Y.]

Fellow Candidates, I think among the many things which we here tonight have to be thankful for, that shouldn't be overlooked, is our good fortune in having been stationed at Ft. Benning for this course of instruction, under the leadership of such commanders and instructors as we are privileged to have. All my life, since I was a barefoot boy back in the hills, with a head full of dreams and visions of what the great outside world beyond the mountains was like, on up into manhood when I learned something about that outside world, I have heard and read of many great men. Strong men of endurance, wise men, men with vision and patience, fighting men, such men as I read of in the Bible, like Samson, David, Job, Solomon, Daniel, Jonah, Moses, and the warrior, Joshua, who had the sun to stand still while he fought a battle. Men of history with whom you are as familiar as I, and more modern characters like Superman, Popeye, Mandrake and Tarzan, and the mythical characters like Hercules, Zeus and Apollo.

But I never knew, until I came here to begin training, that such men existed, and could be found in great numbers in one place in these modern times, as are found here at Benning. To those people who have not been privileged to be here and to see and hear, that might sound a little far-fetched, but if we could relate to them some of our experiences here, it would surpass even their wildest expectations.

These men here, leaders and instructors, have but to gesture, and whole armies spring into being on the ranges using the most modern weapons of warfare, mortars, machine guns, artillery; deployed riflemen, snipers, descending paratroopers are produced simply by the waving of the hand. They point with their fingers and battalions and regiments march by, tanks roar across the landscape, or artfully concealed observers rise from the earth at our very feet. They have but to speak and war planes appear as if by magic to bomb and strafe troops and gun positions. They speak into a microphone and a voice replies, "Yes, I see you. That man on the extreme right is Brooks." And then in a tree on a nearby hill a form magically takes shape and clambers down to the ground.

We know, that among these men, are many as wise as Solomon, or they couldn't possible know all the solutions to all the school problems. We know there are many with the patience of Job or they couldn't stand their own lectures, nor could they ever possibly answer with courtesy all the $64.00 questions asked by some of the students.

And when some of these instructors walk out before a class like O. C. 138 and say with a straight face that they expect us to receive and retain as knowledge all the information they fling at us in 50 minutes, we know that they, like Daniel when he went into the Lion's Den, are displaying more courage than good judgment.

And when another, after completing a lecture asks, "Any questions? No? Good! you've got it"—then we know that he has more blind faith and is getting "took in" even worse than Jonah when he was swallowed by the whale.

And, as already recalled, such feats of Moses as striking a rock and bringing forth water, have been equaled here many times over, and the renouned accomplishment of the warrior, Joshua, when he halted the sun in its journey through the heavens, is here at Benning almost an every day occurrence. For the purpose of the problem, they make not only the sun perform, but the moon, the stars, the earth and the O. C. [Officer Candidates] students as well.

One incident in particular I recall which occurred some time ago on the rifle range. A rifle squad was ordered to go into position for a dawn attack upon the enemy, which the instructors were, of course, to produce at the proper time. For the purpose of the problem it had to be done at night, so the instructor gestured, the light faded, darkness sped in as if on the wings of the wind, and it was night. After giving the squad what he thought was ample time to reach its positions, the instructor announced, "All right, daylight is coming." "Sir," spoke up squad leader John Doe, "we're not ready yet." "Very well," replied the instructor, "I'll have it to wait." And then he did what Charles Boyer in his most dramatic role was unable to do, "Hold back the Dawn."

Many other superior qualities, too, these men have. There are engineers the equal of Goethals; Medical Corps men comparable to Mayo Brothers; demolition men that must love destruction as much as Nero; orators that could have vied successfully with Mark Anthony or Daniel Webster; scouts that could have marched with Boone and Carson, and many others.

Naturally, we, as students, cannot help but gain some of the knowledge and acquire in a small way, at least, some of the qualities of the men who lead and instruct us. It is with that purpose that the course is given, and it is hoped that the training, together with the mode of living, will make supermen of at least a part of us. I think the hope is well founded, for anyone who can survive the dust and smoke and fumes of these hauling vans in which we ride, can live and fight successfully in any desert dust storm.

And anyone who can endure the bone and marrow penetrating chill of these cool Georgia mornings, without contracting pneumonia or some other fatal affliction, is ready for service in Iceland, Alaska or Northern Russia.

Anyone who can shave every day in this southern atmosphere, using the water available, which ranges through the whole field of temperatures, to mention a few, ice cold, cold, cool, tepid, lukewarm, warm, hot and scalding hot, and suffer no permanent injury to his complexion, is ready for service in any climate or clime so far as his skin is concerned.

A further aid to toughening in respect to climate, is the turning on of the heat in the barracks on warm days, and keeping it turned off on cold days and nights.

Futhermore the innumerable, dry, dull lectures we have received, which most of us have learned to sleep through so successfully, have now taught us sufficient patience so that we are well prepared for duty in the dreary realm of the months-long Artic night, or the lonely watches on the tiny, isolated atolls in the seemly unlimited reaches of the Pacific.

On the other hand the rapidity with which we have been compelled to make changes, as for example, map reading to obstacle course, from individual instruction to field orders, from bayonet fighting to overhead fire with machine guns and mortars, from voice and command training to the silence of night patrols, or from a member of a squad to regimental commander, has adequately fitted us to cope with the swiftest strokes of Hitler's blitzkrieg type of warfare.

Other things, too, which we encounter, that will help teach us patience, endurance, bravery and other qualities which we should cultivate. As for example—at home in civilian life, we were likely, on Sundays especially, to exercise our rights to Life, and Liberty, in the pursuit of happiness, while here in camp on Sundays we find that it takes other magazines along with copies of Life and Liberty, to keep us in reading while in pursuit of a hair cut.

And so, although most of us are yet far from being the perfect type of superman they would have us be before those gold bars may grace our shoulders, I'm sure that we will agree that we have greatly benefited from this course. We have probably learned more in the short space of time we have been here, than during any other period of equal length in our lives before.

We are pleased to have with us tonight, some members of this superior type of men of whom I have just spoken, and whom I will present to you now.

It is said in the Holy Writ that the first shall be last and the last shall be first, so tonight the last shall be first; you understand I said last and not least, for far be it from me to say who is the greatest or the least among this class of people.

I present to you now the leader of the 4th platoon and company supply officer, who, we all know, must have some of the magic of Mandrake about him or he couldn't produce supplies for all of O. C. 138 as efficiently as he does.

Students: Lt. McKee. [1st Lt. Gregory T. McKee, Supply Officer]

We now have the assistant 4th platoon leader, who is also the mess officer. Of all the great men I can think of I know of none he more closely resembles, than that strong, rock-like character of the protruding jaw and rasping voice, Popeye the Sailorman. I know that a short time ago the resemblance was much more striking than now, but he still has many of the admirable qualities never-the-less.

Candidates: Lt. Klinger. [2nd Lt. Harry F. Klinger, Jr., Mess Officer]

We now have the 3rd platoon leader, who must be something in the nature of a genius, for he is partly responsible for the smoothness and efficiency with which our training program progresses, he being also plans and training officer. I am at a loss to say just what great man he resembles most, but because of his pleasantness and smiles, and jolly air, he reminds me often of Santa Claus. Of course we haven't received any gifts since being here but I do hear that the most of the students are looking forward with great hope, to the presentation of a certain paper or document or commission along about Christmas time. However, it would never do to compare so young and handsome a man as Lt. Bryant with a fellow so old as Santa Claus. And too, judging by his great interest in certain of the fairer sex which we sometimes see with him about the post, I'm afraid that if he were Santa Claus the presents would be very unevenly distributed.

Students: Lt. Bryant. [1st Lt. Clyde A. Bryant, Plans and Training Officer]

We now have the 2nd platoon boss, with whom we have had no difficulty in observing a striking resemblance to a certain famous character. We've no doubt that some time his exploits will be almost as well known as those of his well known counter-part, the handsome, swaggering, daring, adventuresome pilot of the rocket ships and space ships, Buck Rogers.

Students: Lt. Berger. [1st Lt. Robert E. Berger, Administrative Officer]

I'd like to see him on some of his adventures and learn what Alura looks like.

We now have the leader of the 1st platoon and executive officer of the company. To the casual observer he might appear to be just an ordinary person going about his work, but such is not the case. If you observe closely you will soon learn that he knows just what he is doing, that he says little, hears much, and sees all that goes on about him. (If you watch closely you can see him writing part of it down in a little note book) He perhaps resembles most closely another great military executive known to all of us, our country's first such official, George Washington.

Students: Lt. Ginder. [1st Lt. Grove R. Ginder, Executive Officer.]

We have now our company commander whose strong determined and efficient ways and methods are well known to all of us. Along with those qualities he also carries always the admirable traits of friendliness, courtesy and helpfulness. He has so many good qualities that he could be said to resemble many great men, but the outstanding one of whom he most reminds me, is the famous cartoon strip character, Daddy Warbucks. Perhaps the strongest resemblance of the two is the ability of each to inspire unswerving loyalty, and that we all know they are able to do.

Students: Capt. Leland. [Capt. Alanson T. Leland, Commanding.]

And now, fellow students, this man, whom few of you had seen before tonight and therefore unknown to most of you, but whom almost all of you should have seen at least half a dozen times since being here, is a man who represents, to us, the power to whom the wise and the humble voluntarily turn at some time in their lives, and the power on whom all men voluntarily or involuntarily call when confronted with situations in which the puny hands of man are powerless longer to help.

This is our chaplain, of the 2nd Student Training Regiment, Chaplain Wilson. [Edwin C. Wilson.]

Now students, in presenting this next, and last man, it is needless to say more than, that he is the superman of the supermen of the 15th Company, our battalion commander, Colonel Johnson.

[Lt. Col. Frederick E. Johnson, Battalion Commander, Cambridge, Mass.]

Roster of

## OFFICER CANDIDATE CLASS
## FIFTEENTH COMPANY

Second Student Training Regiment
Infantry School Service Command

### FORT BENNING, GA.

Of the 208 original members of class No. 138 there were 163 graduates, on Dec. 30, 1942.

Adams, Robert W., Canton, Illinois
Anderson, Herbert L., New York, New York
Andrews, Howell L., Tuscaloosa, Alabama
Aque, Victor S., Rochelle Park, New Jersey
Arnett, James E., Jr., Knoxville, Tennessee
Arnold, Cecil B., Hillsboro, Texas
Barnett, Paul W., Seminole, Oklahoma
Barraclough, Donald F., North Platte, Nebraska
Boyd, John J., Long Island, New York
Breeding, Frank M., Jr., Hillsboro, Texas
Broadley, William H., Endicott, New York
Broderick, John M., Brooklyn, New York
Brooks, Wilson D., Pensacola, Florida
Brunetto, Anthony, Montclair, New Jersey
Burbidge, Robert K., Peoria, Illinois
Byerly, George W., Lima, Ohio
Cade, Robert D., Dallas, Texas
Cadieux, Clarence J., Detroit, Michigan

Carver, Henry W., Farmersville, Texas
Chase, Lawrence R., Bristol, Connecticut
Christie, Lewis W., Dallas, Texas
Civalier, Joseph J., Watervliet, New York
Connelly, John T., National Park, New Jersey
Conrad, John, Long Island, New York
Craig, Don C., North Platte, Nebraska
Culpepper, Carroll W., Geneva, Florida
Daniels, Harrison W., St. Paul, Minnesota
Davis, Michael, Winston-Salem, North Carolina
Deadwyler, Warnock C., Cincinnati, Ohio
Decker, Sidney B., Orange, New Jersey
Dibella, Louis J., Glenridge, New Jersey
Diggs, John E., II, Norfolk, Virginia
Dizon, Daniel D., San Antonio, Texas
Dooley, Joseph S., Cos Cob, Connecticut
Dunnahoo, Jack R., Temple, Texas
Eckenrode, Donald M., Lilly, Pennsylvania
English, William R., Oklahoma City, Oklahoma
Faubus, Orval E., Huntsville, Arkansas
Fehlis, William W., Ottine, Texas
Flater, Noel H., Pikesville, Maryland
Fritz, William G., Rio Dell, California
Gage, Robert E., El Paso, Texas
Garthwaite, Harry, Roselle, New Jersey
Gee, Edward W., Coleman, Texas
Georgi, Joseph E., North Bergen, New Jersey
Gniffke, Paul G., Tracy, Minnesota
Golding, David A., Revere, Massachusetts
Goshorn, Robert A., Ossian, Indiana
Gray, Charles A., Dallas, Texas
Grundy, Daniel,, Volant, Pennsylvania
Hammill, Charles P., White Plains, New York
Haney, Arthur W., Jersey City, New Jersey
Harster, Arnold C., Rochester, New York
Healy, Martin J., Philadelphia, Pennsylvania
Henson, Thomas J. L., Harrisburg, Pennsylvania
Hill, Benjamin H., Hillsboro, Texas
Hinski, Eugene V., Haddonfield, New Jersey
Hoagland, Melvin J., Wind Gap, Pennsylvania
Holt, James M., Ballinger, Texas
Houston, Hubert E., Temple, Texas

Howard, Richard T., Somerville, Massachusetts
Hrubec, Anthony J., Rochelle Park, New Jersey
Hughes, Barney W., Jr., Brownwood, Texas
Inman, Harold L., Greenwich, New York
Jakunskas, Bernard F., South Boston, Massachusetts
Kenny, Edward C., Stephenville, Texas
Kirk, Gerald C., Locke, New York
Kisslan, Michael E., Linden, New Jersey
Koeller, Richard H., La Crosse, Wisconsin
Leah, Louis D., Chelsea, Massachusetts
Ledford, Lark, Jr., Galveston, Texas
Levkoff, Bernard H., New York, New York
Lewis, Richard M., Long Island, New York
Lippincott, Howard E., Marlton, New Jersey
Long, Richard M., Stapleton, S. I., New York
Loos, Edward C., Victoria, Texas
Lyons, Joseph D., Amarillo, Texas
Mackenzie, Clifford, Brooklyn, New York
Mallon, Robert K., Los Angeles, California
Massey, Eddie A., San Diego, California
Matheson, Glenn E., Highland Park, Illinois
Matthews, Henry E., Hingham, Massachusetts
McAuliffe, John J., New York, New York
McClenahan, Henry I., Palo Alto, California
McCoy, William A., West, Texas
McDonald, Martin H., Jr., Grafton, Massachusetts
McDonald, Walter T., East Boston, Massachusetts
McDowell, Donald E., Oakland, California
McGinley, John E., Montclair, New Jersey
Meadows, George E., Lake Wales, Florida
Mellen, Charles W., Stanhope, New Jersey
Meyers, James L., Kane, Pennsylvania
Miller, Richard A., Gary, Indiana
Moore, Herbert S., Petersburg, Virginia
Morton, Darrel A., Santa Ana, California
Myers, William S., Elizabeth, New Jersey
Naegele, William C., Cleveland, Ohio
Newell, Donald L., Des Moines, Iowa
O'Brien, Robert E., Roxbury, Massachusetts
Ogren, David M., Jamestown, New York
Olenick, Michael W., Cleveland, Ohio
Orr, Edward F., Kittanning, Pennsylvania

Pantsari, Eric W., Garwood, New Jersey
Pappin, Richard, Englewood, New Jersey
Perkins, Duncan G., Houston, Texas
Perry, Roy W., Bahama, North Carolina
Peterson, Walter J., Fort Sam Houston, Texas
Pettijohn, Willis T., Stephenville, Texas
Petty, William C., Washington, New Jersey
Prestifilippo, Anthony C., Glenridge, New Jersey
Reeb, William A., Oak Park, Illinois
Reeves, Roger E., Newark, New York
Reiber, Keith E., Chicago, Illinois
Reischel, Eldephone C., Glidden, Wisconsin
Retherford, Bob, Lockhart, Texas
Reynolds, Victor D., New Brunswick, New Jersey
Robinson, John L., Krakow, Wisconsin
Robinson, William A., Dunellen, New Jersey
Ross, Fred J., El Paso, Texas
Rowe, Marion W., Louisville, Kentucky
Rowland, Oliver L., Jr., Forrest City, Arkansas
Schlachter, George E., West Haven, Connecticut
Schneider, Robert A., Roslindale, Massachusetts
Schumacher, William F., New York, New York
Sedmak, Michael P., Jr., Sheboygan, Wisconsin
Senerote, Leonard A., Brooklyn, New York
Settanni, Michael O., Brooklyn, New York
Sharp, William L., Dallas, Texas
Sicher, Mario, Brooklyn, New York
Simmons, George E., Paterson, New Jersey
Slaughter, Chester C., Meyia, Texas
Smelley, Marion L., Fort Worth, Texas
Spector, Jean S., Belmont, Massachusetts
Spendlove, Bernard, Sanford, Maine
Stagnaro, Francis W., Springfield, Massachusetts
Stauffer, Willard F., Cheyenne, Wyoming
Stearns, Vincent J., Poughkeepsie, New York
Stern, Hubert B., New York, New York
Suttmeier, Victor H., Bay Shore, New York
Sutton, Foster J., Des Moines, Iowa
Szares, John W., Portchester, New York
Talley, Arthur L., New Boston, Texas
Tang, Lloyd G., New York, New York
Tatem, Earl W., North Vernon, Indiana

Theriault, Gerald E., Salem, Massachusetts
Thomas, William N., Jr., Lupton City, Tennessee
Thompson, Hubert A., Jr., San Antonio, Texas
Timmerman, William H., Bynbrook, New York
Tisinger, Louis H., Houston, Texas
Vasu, Claude F., Youngstown, Ohio
Voninski, Peter, East Syracuse, New York
Warren, Seymour, New York, New York
Watson, Charles W., New Lebanon, Ohio
Watts, Robert W., Troy, Texas
Wehs, Edward P., Bellevue, Pennsylvania
Weissman, Harry, New York, New York
Wells, John W., Kingsbury, Texas
Welsh, Lloyd, New York, New York
Wilhelm, Linwood G., Richmond, Virginia
Willbanks, Ben M., Plumerville, Arkansas
Williams, Leland L., Assumption, Illinois
Willis, Andrew H., Jr., Erie, Pennsylvania
York, Ikey, Columbus, Georgia

## CHAPTER II

SERVICE AS OFFICER PRIOR TO COMBAT

MADISON COUNTY RECORD
March 18, 1943

FROM ORVAL E. FAUBUS

Camp San Luis Obispo, Calif.
February 14, 1943

Dear Home Folks:

As I begin this letter I note that this is St. Valentine's Day. And immediately my mind is off on a train of memories. It is with an effort that I force myself to push these memories into the background, so that I can give my attention to the tasks at hand.

I find that thoughts of other service men from the Ozarks run much as mine do. Our trains of thought bear much the same relation to home as do the spokes of a wheel to the hub. When at home, our thoughts could go out in many different ways on various trails we had traveled, but when out on one of those trails (as we are now) our memories all run, like the spokes in the wheel, back to the hub of our existence, that which is in fact the center and basis of all human life, the home.

I quote from a letter received recently from Pvt. Shirley Thornsberry of Combs who is now somewhere "across" in the Eastern theater of operations. The letter was written Dec. 6, 1942, was sent to me at Ft. Benning, Ga., forwarded to Camp Robinson, and then followed me here. (When you see this, Shirley, you will understand the long delay in answering). He says, "I have been reading your letters in the Madison County Record; that is the first thing I look for when I pick up the paper, and I like them fine. I always think of the time when we left Huntsville together. There is one boy with me that left Huntsville with us, Loy E. Vanbrunt (of Delaney). He is a fine boy and we sure have had a good time together. There is also a boy from Siloam Springs and another one from the south part of Arkansas. Sometimes we get to talking about the old Ozark Hills with those beautiful leaves of all colors, falling early in the autumn morning after old Jack Frost has paid them a visit; and the jay birds knocking the chinquapins out of the burrs that used to stick in our bare feet while we were picking up the chinquapins and robbing the little squirrels."

So you see how some of Shirley's thoughts run. I have received letters from other boys which sounded much the same. It does not mean that we are always thinking thus. Most of the time we are too busy. But it is only natural that our thoughts are more of home when we sit down to write to those still there.

When I left Camp Robinson at the end of a two-weeks stay, the area was covered with ice and snow. It was much the same at home where I spent three days in winding up my business affairs, and preparing for the trip out here. However after the first day's travel the weather became rather pleasant, and much of the time it was "shirtsleeve" weather even outside the car.

The traveling party besides myself, Alta and Farrell, consisted of my sisters, Connie and Bonnie Faubus of Combs, and Basil Crawford of St. Paul. Therefore, the whole trip was like a family reunion and visit with old friends. Basil, aside from being a good driver, is in many ways a very pleasant companion and proved very helpful on the trip. He has a keen mind and is a well educated and well read young man. I found his conversation and views very entertaining and interesting. Our views on politics, both national and international, had such great similarity, that I could not help thinking that a stranger would be amazed to learn that we were members of opposing political parties.

On one problem, which will soon face our country and likewise most of the other countries of the earth, Basil and I found ourselves with a mutual desire and a mutual fear.

The desire is that the Allied nations and the few remaining neutrals (if any at war's end) set up a workable plan for maintaining peace after the war. The fear is that the Isolationists of this country (both Republicans and Democrats, right now mostly Republicans) will prevent full American participation and thus wreck the plan's chances of success. This problem I have discussed and heard discussed many times among the men of the Armed Forces, and I am fully convinced that any politician preaching the silly doctrine of having America "crawl into a hole and pull the hole in after it" will have a hard time getting the votes of the veterans of this war, no matter what political name he bears. They may call themselves Republicans, Democrats, Progressives or Socialists, but if they preach the doctrine of isolationism you can be sure they are "Know-Nothings" and are as out of date politically as the bow and arrow are in a military sense.

Speaking again of the trip, the chief joy and interest of the journey to me was the privilege of being with my little boy for 24 whole hours each day. Naturally he has grown considerably since I left for the Army last spring, and most of his quaint and interesting mannerisms have changed somewhat. Others he has lost entirely, and some new ones have been formed. The grasshoppers he now calls by their right name and not "hopperdrasses" as he once did. Now he can remember the name honeysuckle and not become confused as he did after I had shown him the first blossoming vine he had ever seen, and tell his mother they were "suckle-blooms."

Nevertheless, his ever interested and excited prattle during the trip, of "twains" "engins," "box tars," "towboys," "stweet tars," "wivers" and the like, was very enjoyable to me. I know that in the transformation of my body when leaving this life for the next, my ears will have to be much more keenly attuned if angel voices sound any more beautiful to me than his happy laughter or his childish attempts at song.

At present we are rather well situated here at Camp San Luis Obispo. We found a place for Alta and Farrell to stay on a ranch some three miles from camp. [A small residence with barest necessities converted from a chicken house] At present married officers are not required to stay on the post during off-duty hours, so I can be with them almost every night and almost every Sunday. I am now instructing and drilling troops more than nine hours each day and attending school one hour each night, which does not leave much free time.

The weather here is usually very pleasant (above 90 degrees the past two days) except for the occasional fogs. Flowers are blooming beside the buildings, in the meadows and along the banks of the brooks; the wheat fields are a smooth, bright green; some fruit trees in the orchards are covered with blossoms, and as Farrell walks about the ranch house yard the wild mustard reaches above his knees. Friday while on a hike I lay on the ground in the warm sunshine during the ten minute rest period and searched in the wild clover for a stem with four leaves.

I have in my platoon a number of boys from Arkansas, but none from Madison County. They called for volunteers in the company for the weapons platoon, and all the Arkansas and Oklahoma boys immediately came forward when they found that I was to be the leader. There are several boys from Tennessee and others from North Carolina, New York, New Jersey and Pennsylvania.

One day last week I was very pleasantly surprised to encounter Pvt. Hugh Fritts of Thorney on the street here in camp. He had been inducted at Camp Robinson while I was there, and shipped to this camp, arriving about three days ahead of me. He is in the same regiment as myself. He said another Madison Countian from Hindsville was with him but did not remember his name.

I had planned to go to the induction center while at Robinson to see the Madison county boys who were inducted on Jan. 21, but was prevented from doing so.

All of you boys in the service, no matter what branch or where located, I'll be glad always to hear from you. Don't for a minute think that because your former fellow private and KP has now become an officer that it makes any difference in his attitude, for it doesn't. It is just that I have a little more to do and a great deal more responsibility in the job of licking the hateful Hitler and the detestible Japs. And the sooner the better for us, for then we all can have again the wonderful privilege of being private American citizens at home.

As it is now the hour of midnight, the camp has grown quiet. The croaking of the frogs along the brook can be heard quite plainly. At times the muffled roar of the surf upon the beach is borne in upon the ocean breeze, but it is not loud enough to disturb the sleeping soldiers as they dream of home. The ocean's sound causes to arise in me a vague uneasiness and concern when I think of those now sleeping forever in its dark depths, and I feel a great hatred for those who caused them to be there.

Good night!

Most sincerely,

Lt. Orval E. Faubus
Co. F, 320th Infantry,
Camp San Luis Obispo, Calif.

## ORIGIN OF THE 35TH INFANTRY DIVISION AND THE 320TH INFANTRY REGIMENT WORLD WAR II

Almost a full year before America was plunged into the war by the Japanese attack on Pearl Harbor, the 35th (Santa Fe) Infantry Division was ordered into Federal Service by the War Department. Executive Order 8605 of Dec. 23, 1940, federalized the National Guard units of Missouri, Kansas and Nebraska which made up the 35th Division.

The units assembled in early January 1941 at Camp Joseph T. Robinson, Arkansas (on the northern outskirts of North Little Rock and the larger city of Little Rock) for what was scheduled to be a year's training. After that the National Guardsmen of the three states could return home.

According to all reports these "Citizen Soldiers" of Kansas, Nebraska and Missouri, liked the people and the area in which they were training. And according to all reports this feeling was reciprocated in full by the people of Greater Little Rock and the State of Arkansas in general.

The year of training, which included maneuvers in Louisiana, was drawing to a close. The men and officers were looking forward to getting back to their homes and civilian pursuits and had started to count the days until their "time was up." Then when only 16 days remained until the period of service would end, the radio brought the dismaying news of the bombing of Pearl Harbor.

These men of the Mid-West, which constituted the original 35th Infantry Division, were then, like all other men of all the Armed Forces, "enlisted for the duration."

Soon word came that the Division, already trained and combat ready, had duties elsewhere. The men of the Division, who had won the respect and admiration of the people of Greater Little Rock and Arkansas, instead of going home must continue on duty.

Among the many acts of appreciation by the people of the state was the issuance of an official proclamation by Gov. Homer M. Adkins, declaring all members of the Division to be honorary citizens of Arkansas. Among the many festivities of farewell was a street dance in Little Rock for all division personnel.

Commanding the 35th during its Arkansas training period was Maj. Gen. Ralph E. Truman of Missouri (first cousin of then Sen. Harry S. Truman, later vice-president and president) from Dec. 23, 1940 to Oct., 1941. He was succeeded by Maj. Gen. William H. Simpson who commanded until April, 1942.

After Pearl Harbor, the Division's first assignment was the defense of the Southern California Sector of the Western Defense Command. Spread along the lengthy California coast the 35th maintained its unity and again quickly won the respect and admiration of the people. The Californians called it their "adopted Army."

In March 1942 came re-organization, by War Department directive, to the standard triangular division. Two infantry regiments, the 138th and 140th, were detached and sent elsewhere, leaving the 134th and 137th. Under the triangular setup, another infantry regiment was required.

All remaining units of the Division were assembled at Camp San Luis Obispo, California in Jan., 1943. There on Jan. 14, 1943 was activated the 320th Infantry Regiment, which with the 134th and 137th filled the infantry requirements of the 35th division.

It was to this new infantry regiment, the 320th Infantry, that I was sent from BIRTC (Branch Immaterial Replacement Training Center) at Camp Joseph T. Robinson by Special Order No. 23 on Jan. 23, 1943. The order contained the names of 89 officers, six captains and 83 second lieutenants, to staff the new regiment. They were as follows:

## CAPTAINS

Walter B. Fowler
Henry H. Hare
William C. Huey

James A. Leach
Henry B. Leighton
George B. Probstfield

## 2nd LIEUTENANTS

Marvin E. Shipp
Curtis H. Alloway
McKeen E. Brimhall
Charles P. Brochu
George W. Byerly
Thomas V. Camarda
Nicholas C. Demetrulias
Dave E. Ferris
Joseph R. Fitzgerald
Melvin V. Fritts
Morton (NMI) Kligerman
Roman W. Knopke
Robert W. Adams
Edward H. Mietlicki
Riley P. Shirley, Jr.
John M. Van Deusen
Louis G. Xintas
Lauren A. Burton
Audra M. Cowan
David J. Dunn
James D. Harney
Stanley F. Klimuszka
Homer W. Kurtz
William H. Leitch
Glen (NMI) Mooney
John A. Pitts
John J. Pulgin
Maynard C. Ragan, Jr.
Leonard W. Rogowski
Philip H. Shaffer, Jr.
Jack (NMI) Sternstein
Reinhard A. Stumpf
John L. Van Winkle
Arley D. Adams
Thomas S. Aschoff

David H. Barthfield
Walter V. Demkowski
Melvin L. Larson
Eugene J. Lenar
Dominick J. Lostumbo
Paul E. Mossey
Vernon W. Nichols
John B. Platt
Francis L. Prall
Eugene S. Ridenour
Stephen J. Rutkowski
John S. Skowronsky
John R. Soyke
Edward S. Wilson
Abraham D. Ziegelbaum
Walter E. Anderson
Elbert (NMI) Cammack
Ralph G. Carpenter
Arthur E. Christiansen
Rudolph C. D'Amico
Robert E. Gage
Milton (NMI) Ginsburg
Charles L. Harmon
Fred A. Kreml
Albert G. Kudzia
Arthur J. Manzi
Spencer M. Shoemaker
Farris C. Simmons
George J. Stahl
Ernest L. Strasil
Leo E. Thomas
Harold C. Thompson
Kenneth E. Birkett
Thurman H. Deskins, Jr.
Arthur J. Desroche

Pierce (NMI) Earle
Orval E. Faubus
James (NMI) Fisher
John W. Keith
Peter J. Loveless
Edward F. Orr
Thomas F. Potter

Norman C. Shepard
Stanley S. Underwood
Howard S. Warnock
Gilbert (NMI) Wilson
Ernest H. Zielasko
Edmund J. Zimmerman

By Command of Brig. Gen. Mallon

W. H. KcKee, Lt. Col. Inf., Adj.


Gen. Simpson was succeeded as commander of the Division by Maj. Gen. Maxwell Murray in April, 1942. Gen. Murray was succeeded in Jan. 1943 by Maj. Gen. Paul Baade, the commander we came to know so well during succeeding months of training and combat. Gen. Baade remained in command until the Division was deactivated after the war.

From Jan. through March, 1943, the Division remained at Camp San Luis Obispo undergoing further reorganization and training. The 216th Field Artillery Battalion, which supported the 320th Infantry Regiment in training and combat, was activated there on Jan. 6, 1943. On April 1, 1943 the entire Division moved to Camp Rucker, Alabama for advanced training.

At the time of the move to Camp Rucker the component parts of the Division and their origin, were as follows:

Hq. & Hq. Co., 35th Inf. Div.

134th Inf. Regt. - from 134th Inf. Regt. of 34th Div., originally 5th Nebraska Infantry.

137th Inf. Regt. - formerly 1st Kansas Infantry.

320th Inf. Regt. - activated Jan. 14, 1943 at Camp San Luis Obispo, men from everywhere.

127 F.A. Bn. - formerly 127th F.A. Regt. from Eastern Kansas.

161st F.A. Bn. - formerly part of 1st Bn., 161st F.A. Regt.

216th F.A. Bn. - organized Jan. 6, 1943 at Camp San Luis Obispo with initial cadre of officers and enlisted men from the 161st F.A. Bn., other men from everywhere.

219th F.A. Bn. - activated Jan. 12, 1943 at Camp San Luis Obispo with a cadre of officers and enlisted men from the 130th F.A. Bn. originally of the Kansas National Guard; other men from everywhere.

60th Engr. Combat Bn. - activated Jan. 29, 1943 at Camp San Luis Obispo, men from everywhere.

110th Med. Bn. - organized from the 110th Sanitary Train, Nebraska National Guard Med. Regt. of 35th Div., and the 117th Sanitary Train of 42nd Division.

35th Qm. Co. - part of the 110th Qm. Regt., Nebraska National Guard.

35th Div. MP Plat. - activated Dec. 23, 1940 at Garden City, Kansas.

35th Cav. RCN Troop - activated March 1, 1942 at Camp San Luis Obispo, men from everywhere.

735th Ordnance Co. - activated Nov. 15, 1942 with men from Kansas and Nebraska.

35th Signal Co. - activated Dec. 24, 1940 with men from Kansas City, Kansas.

## MADISON COUNTY RECORD
### April 1, 1943

## LIEUT. ORVAL FAUBUS GOES TO CAMP RUCKER

Lieut. Orval E. Faubus has been transferred from Camp San Luis Obispo, Calif., to Camp Rucker, Alabama, and he and his family visited homefolks here and elsewhere in the county Friday, Saturday and Sunday while enroute to their new location.

Nevertheless, the following letter from Lieut. Faubus, written before he knew he was to leave California, will attract the usual interest with which his communications are read.

[The Editor]

Camp San Luis Obispo, Calif.
March 14, 1943

Dear Home Folks:

Today, as last Sunday, we were scheduled to work, but just as I had gotten my class organized for instruction a runner came down from headquarters with the welcome tidings that classes were dismissed for the day. The men cheered the news, I gladly dismissed the class, and now I am taking advantage of the rare opportunity to do some writing.

On this Sabbath day we have what has been the usual weather since we came here. The sky is overcast with grey clouds and a light cold rain is falling. On last Sunday we worked all day in such weather, and the sticky mud, our damp and wet clothing and the chilly rain made it very unpleasant. It was not bad; no one suffered; it was just unpleasant.

However, when the sun shines it is really beautiful weather and a beautiful country. Such a day was Sunday, Feb. 28. On the preceding day when I came out of the company orderly room, two soldiers were standing by my car and looking it over. When I approached they saluted and one of them said, "Sir, it looks like you have the car I used to own." In the conversation which followed I learned that the one who spoke had owned the car which I had bought from his mother at Fayetteville before starting out here. He was Pvt. Charles Townes of Fayetteville and his companion was Pvt. Henry Hyden Jr. of Springdale. On Sunday I had them and Pvt. Hugh Fritts of Thorney out for dinner with us, and in the afternoon we went down to the beach at Morro Bay. It was the first time Fritts or Hyden had ever seen the ocean and the first time Townes had seen the Pacific.

It was a pleasant event for all of us. Fritts' first reaction was that he had "never seen anything like this," and his next was that he wanted to get to the water and dip up some and see how it smelled. Farrell and Alta pulled off their shoes and walked in the sand, splashed in the edge of the surf and fled from the breakers as they came rolling in. We went out on the pier and watched the waves as they were thrown shoreward by the great ocean as it heaved and moved like an uneasy bosom. We watched the ducks swimming in the water and the sea gulls floating in flight over its glassy surface; the little ducks paddling in the smooth stretches and diving under the breakers as they rolled over them. Also we saw the patient fisherman on the pier hook some fish out of the briny deep.

The real heartfelt pleasure and joy of such a meeting perhaps cannot be appreciated by you who have lived always with friends and loved ones, because never having really missed them you have never truly felt their need. Nor do I think such an occasion can be appreciated to the fullest extent except by those who live thus [among friends and loved ones] and are then cast out alone into strange places among strange people. Then do they realize, perhaps for the first time, the real worth of the things for which we are fighting; the house we call home, weather-beaten or fine it makes no difference; the folks who live there and the neighbors who live nearby; the little school house and the country church by the cross-roads, and all the other things which make up the life you know and which we have known. If our enemies should win, all these things would lose their true meaning to us, and the good and the pleasure which they now give to all would be given no more to anyone. When I think of the few "slackers" in America it is usually with profound pity that their ignorance is so vast or their cowardice so great that they will not do their part in the great struggle to preserve these privileges which they enjoy along with the rest of us.

My father has written that my old school mate and playmate, Sidney Marcum, is now a prisoner of the Japs. Perhaps we shall learn later, if not already, that Charles and Henry Rankins (high school friends) of St. Paul and Blake Vanlandingham of Thorney, all listed as "missing in action," are also prisoners-of-war, and were not killed when the flames of war first burst over the Pacific. However it has been confirmed that J. D. Nelson, nephew of L. A. Nelson of Huntsville, went down with his ship in a naval battle in the Pacific.

Most of the men in my outfit are firing on the range this week. The morale of the whole outfit is very high and the men are very cheerful. A great deal of friendly rivalry is evident among the men for shooting honors. There is rivalry between the groups, between the platoons and companies, and also between the men from different states. I expect the Tennesseans or the Arkansawyers to lead, but that is not certain. There are some Mexicans from along the southern border who are excellent shots, (a Mexican had high score yesterday) and there are some boys from Ohio and a few from Brooklyn who show promise of becoming good riflemen.

We are all hoping that the Americans start something in Europe soon and we are working hard to be ready to do our part when the time comes.

Sincerely, Lt. Orval E. Faubus

\* \* \*

[During my stay at San Luis Obispo while driving on the highway one day, I picked up two soldiers hitchhiking. They were Pvt. Chester Robinson of Parks, Arkansas and Pvt. Gately Daniel of Prescott, Arkansas. They were most happy to see another person from their home state.]

## MADISON COUNTY RECORD
May 20, 1943

### FROM LT. ORVAL E. FAUBUS

Camp Rucker, Alabama
May 9, 1943

Dear Home Folks:

Only a short time ago I returned from church here in the camp chapel, which had today a special "Mother's Day" program. I had three good reasons for attending church today; first, my mother would have wanted me to be there; second, I felt the need of spiritual help; third, I have found that you always derive some good from attending church whether or not you feel the need at the time.

It is truly written that "man does not live by bread alone." No doubt Hitler's labor slaves are fairly well fed, as are the inmates of his homes for unwed mothers and also the unfortunate women of the conquered countries whom he has forced into houses of shame for the use of his troops. Reports which tell us that thousands of them are dying daily or are killed seeking escape, show that life without liberty or the chance to pursue happiness is not worth the living. Religious liberty, denied to all whom Hitler and the Japs rule, is the greatest factor in the pursuit of happiness. That is why we all should be willing to die if need be rather than have our enemies win.

Recently I have been given a new assignment with duties and work with which I was not very familiar. As a consequence I have had another very busy period and have written only two letters during the past month. [Secret work from which I was relieved after leaving Camp Rucker.]

I noted after my arrival here that the usually reliable "Record" erred slightly in stating that we visited friends and relatives in the county from Friday to Sunday when we passed through there in March. I wish it could have been true, but my party which consisted of my wife and boy and Mrs. Wallace B. Cull of Kentucky, arrived in Huntsville about dusk on Friday and at the same time the following day we were well on our way to Alabama. Of the approximately 24 hours spent there, most was devoted to business and even then I did not get to see the driver of my school bus nor the students as I very much wanted to. Nor did we get to see my father and other members of the family or my wife's family all of whom live very close to our route of travel. Sunday we spent crossing southern Arkansas, the corner of Louisiana and central Mississippi. Monday afternoon we arrived at our destination here in camp.

We visited longer with Madison Countians in Fullerton, Calif., than we did at home. We spent Sunday, March 21 there visiting three of my sisters, Connie, Bonnie and June Faubus, and Arch Brandenburg and daughter, Ottilee, and a host of others too numerous to mention. However I want to name the servicemen I saw there who were Pvt. Ray Bolinger of Huntsville, Pvt. Paul Couch and Pvt. Everett Glenn of Asher, and Marine Private Verle Hall of Combs. They all looked fine in their uniforms especially Pvt. Hall who looked much like the picture on the Marine enlistment posters.

Also Virgle Ledford had a telegram from Pvt. Roy Drain of Asher who is on duty somewhere in the Pacific.

A number of Madison Countians are doing good work there in the war plants. Troy Ledford who is working in an aircraft factory said, "I have never been absent from the plant a single day and was a half-hour late only once and that caused by driving 40 miles out-of-the-way because of high water." Dora Beth Dixon of St. Paul has been working for over a year in an aircraft plant. After a year's work she made application for leave of absence in order to go home and visit her folks, but later when she thought of the boys at the fronts and on the seas who could not come home she withdrew her application and apologized for having submitted it. To me that shows a wonderful sense of duty. Two of my sisters work in an aircraft plant on the swing shift. Arch Brandenburg, who is old enough for an old age pension, is working in a vital war job. The Pharrises, Bill Stewart, and a number of others are doing their part in the vital war plants around Fullerton.

In thinking along this line I recall the time one year ago last April when we were still living in the pleasant hills of the Mountain Grove community, and our good friends and neighbors, George Neal and family, were preparing to go to the West Coast to work. Some people tried to discourage George by warning him that the coast might be bombed. To which he replied in that slow, friendly Arkansas drawl which made me like him so well, "Well, now, somebody has to do the work. And if there's any bombing, I'm no better than anybody else."

To all those named above and others who are doing likewise, I say that yours is a wonderfully fine example of patriotism and service when viewed in any light. Your example truly stands out when compared to the actions of some others, who, when the first anti aircraft shells burst over the coast cities, left their jobs and fled like scared rabbits back to the hills of Madison County and other places. It is also in wonderful contrast to another shameful spectacle now being seen in America, where ablebodied men with a few or no dependents have left important jobs to start running a "one gallus" farm in an obvious effort to escape the draft. Some of these "newly-turned" farmers may mean well, and if so, well and good. The farm produce is needed. But if they are doing a "one-mule job," arising at 8 to 10 o'clock a.m. to begin work, foxhunting two or three nights a week, and quitting work every Saturday at noon to go fishing, it will lead many to doubt their sincerity.

We are just now getting into this war up to our necks. Up to this time we have just been wading around the edges while the British, the Russians and the smallest conquered countries wallowed in the deepest blood. Our Navy, the Air Force and the Merchant Marine have been in, yes, but the Army is just now getting started. For example in the fighting in Africa the Allied troops faced far less than a dozen Axis divisions while on the Russian front there are 240 divisions with others scattered around Europe yet unengaged in fighting. All these must be overcome, and after that the Japs. Even the most optimistic observer cannot foresee a victory before 1944 and many think it will take longer. Our casualties will become higher and higher as the war continues, and even now many people in Madison County have received that saddest of all messages.

Faced with these serious facts, that thousands of our boys have yet to die before victory is won; it will be years before others can come home; many at the front are still praying for arms, planes and ammunition; we in the camps are still training with 50% of the equipment we need; and thousands of helpless people are being starved and slaughtered in the conquered countries, is it any time for you, an American, the most privileged of all peoples, to evade YOUR duties, or to do an excessive amount of pleasure seeking of any kind?

I hope these questions need go to but a few. Surely most Americans are doing their duty.

Since coming here I was very happy to contact Pfc. Hugh Bunch of Kingston. His outfit had been on maneuvers when I arrived and was still camping out. Consequently he was very hard to locate but after asking man after man for several days I finally found one who knew him. I sent him my address and the next night he came to see me. He was looking fine; had a nice tan from being out in the open so much. We couldn't make arrangements for the weekend because his unit was scheduled to move to a new post. However on the following Saturday as I was driving to town I stopped to pick up two soldiers and who should one of them be but Hugh. Of course we again had a nice but brief visit. He said he was to leave the following morning. He gave me Frank Cannaday's address but I haven't yet written to him. If I remember correctly Paul Corlett is at the same post with him which isn't far from here. I sure would like to see them, but it is a bit too far for a weekend drive with rationed gasoline.

Recently received: a V-Mail letter from Pvt. Charles McCoy of Clifty who is somewhere in the Pacific. Letters from Sgt. Marion "Cotton" Murphy in the North Pacific zone of operations; Pvt. Willard Bohannan of Clifty who is in Florida; Lt. Robert W. Hughey, of Combs, another Madison County man who has been made a commissioned officer and is now with the Signal Corps at Ft. Monmouth, N. J.; Pvt. Harold N. Harris of Huntsville at Ft. Laredo, Texas; Pvt. Glenn Officer, formerly of Huntsville, now at Oklahoma City, Okla. News that Doyle Haskins, son of Mr. and Mrs. Cal Haskins formerly of Ball Creek, is now in the Marines and has already "sailed" for foreign duty; that Bruce Faubus, son of Mr. and Mrs. Eli Faubus formerly of Combs, is now at Keesler Field, Miss.

Congratulations to: Prof. Henry Burke of the State Vocational School for his voluntary service and upon being commissioned in the Air Corps.

Sincerely,

Lt. Orval E. Faubus,
Hqs. Co., 320th Inf.,
Camp Rucker, Alabama

RESTRICTED

SPECIAL ORDERS)              WAR DEPARTMENT
NO.         167)          WASHINGTON, 16 June 1943

EXTRACT

15. Announcement is made of the temp promotion of the following-named officers to the grades indicated in the AUS with rank fr date of this order:

2D LT TO 1ST LT

Arley Donald Adams          Orval Eugene Faubus
Gordon Hunter Bryan         William Campbell Fessenden
Victor Hutton English       Riley Pillow Shirley, Jr.
              Robert George Walker

By order of the Secretary of War:

G. C. MARSHALL,
Chief of Staff.

OFFICIAL:
J. A. ULIO,
   Major General,
   The Adjutant General:

## SILVERMAN, TRASK AND CULL

Shortly after arrival at Camp Rucker, Sidney Silverman joined the Regiment. He was assigned to Co. F where he joined me, Gene Trask and other officers and men of the company. By chance Silverman, Trask and I found quarters for our families in the same large plantation-type structure in nearby Newton, Alabama. Since we lived in the same building while off base, often rode together in going to and from camp, and worked together almost constantly in training, we became very close.

Also in Co. F was Sgt. Wallace Brent Cull of Harrodsburg, Ky. I first met Sgt. Cull at Camp San Luis Obispo when he was assigned to the Regiment as a private, a trainee like most of our men. Only 17 or 18 years of age at the time, he was newly married and his wife soon followed him to the camp from Kentucky.

Cull was one of the most courteous, cooperative young men I have ever known. When we were to leave for Camp Rucker, I remarked one day in his presence that I was looking for some one to help me drive to our new station. Diffident and hesitant, he approached me later, explained that he needed transportation for his wife, and asked if she could go with my family and help with the driving. I agreed, and from then on the association of our families was quite close.

Sgt. Cull, like all soldiers, had great pride in his home state. He was especially proud of Kentucky's success in basketball, and of the fame and ability of the state's great political leader, Albin Barkley. He believed in the cause for which we were fighting and wanted to be a good soldier. He was an excellent soldier, an idealistic patriot and one of the finest men I have ever known.

I can never recall my Army experience without a memory of Sgt. Cull. It is much the same with Silverman, Trask, Ginsburg, Brochu, Kelly, Glatzer, Byrne, Jamison, Northam, Gardner, Talcott, Braffit and many others.

## FROM LIEUT. ORVAL FAUBUS

Camp Rucker, Ala.,
June 27, 1943

Dear Home Folks:

I noticed today that Alta, in heading a letter, had written "Hot Spot, Ala." That describes the climate of the place, except that the heat is not just in this spot but extends over the whole state and most of the South. However the heat is not the most unpleasant feature of the climate. Personally I much prefer heat than cold. The most unpleasant feature is its conduciveness to sleep and lethargy. In fact it is the sleepiest, laziest climate I have ever experienced. Now, I can well understand why people of the southern countries like a "siesta" in the afternoon.

There is nothing very spectacular to write about here, where we are still in training. The boys having the high adventures are those in Africa, the Pacific, India, and those in the planes which now almost constantly fill the skies over enemy territory. But though they have the greatest adventures they also have the greatest dangers, heartaches and suffering, as witness Guadalcanal, New Guinea and Attu. I send my best wishes to Leon Ogden, wounded in the African battle and now in a Pennsylvania hospital, and to all the other boys who have reached any of the various fronts.

I have two copies of the picture which appeared in the May 17 issue of Life Magazine, in which is seen the boy thought by some to be Keith Anderson of Witter. The soldier on the extreme right really resembles Keith, but anyone in the Armed Forces sees so many others who resemble people he knows, that it is sometimes difficult to be sure. However, if his folks say so, it must be Keith. If so he now has a rating, for the soldier in the picture is wearing a sergeant's stripes.

The training period is not without its hazards. Recently the crews of some of the new armored tank-destroyers were firing the big guns, with which they are armed, in target practice and the shells were landing in the bivouac area of some foot troops. Luckily radio communication halted the firing before casualties resulted.

A serious accident occurred some time ago when one of a group of soldiers in training in the field picked up a "dud" (a dud is a shell that has been fired but failed to explode when it landed). While the soldier was tinkering with it the old shell exploded, blowing out his life and the lives of two others, and injuring six more enlisted men and one officer. Subsequent investigation revealed that the soldier had been in the Army for more than two years; that he had been instructed a number of times never to touch a dud, and that his act was in direct violation of his instructions and orders.

These incidents are rare exceptions. It is surprising how few injuries occur among the men while in training, fewer even than would occur to the same number of men in civilian life. One reason is that for every act which results in injury or danger to the men some officer must pay dearly if he cannot prove that he took every safety precaution.

I find that, without question, the boys from the hill countries and those from the plains of the West make the best field soldiers while in training. The fact is that they already know much about caring for themselves that the others have to learn the hard way. Many of the boys from the sidewalks, when they first come into the army, actually don't know which end of the gun the bullet comes from, and on a lot of other subjects they are just as ignorant.

The other day one was wondering where milk came from, and it developed that he really hadn't the faintest idea. They know nothing about the production of food, and even less about the woods. They wouldn't know oats from potatoes or peanuts from popcorn if they saw them before they were prepared for eating. Remarked one of them when we were out on bivouac, "Krist, it's a wonder we don't take all kinds of bed-bugs back to our barracks, sleeping out here among all these rotten logs." They talk continually of "jigger (chigger) stings," "fly stings" and "bee bites" as if they thought anyone should have at least honorable mention for enduring such hazards and hardships for even a few days. So you can understand why most outfits are in training for a year or more before they are ready for combat. It takes quite awhile to teach such men how to live in the open, not to mention how to fight successfully under trying conditions. (Question of a soldier's New York wife to her landlord, "What kind of trees do peanuts grow on?")

You must not interpret the above as meaning such men are not smart in many ways, or that hillbillies and plainsmen have a corner on all the courage or fighting ability. Such is not the case. By the time they have finished training, you can scarcely distinguish between the different groups. The city boys also have some decided advantages in learning and education. Modern warfare has become a game which can be played to the best advantage only by experts, and it has become so complex that a man must have a good education before he can master the most of it. The illiterate in war, as in civilian life, is relegated to the more menial tasks with little or no chance for advancement.

As to the war itself, we are now approaching midsummer and still no big gains by Hitler or the Japs. In fact both have suffered set backs. At least the Axis partners are doing the guessing [now] instead of the Allies. My guess is that Hitler has passed the peak of his power. Instead of fighting and breathlessly hoping as we did at the beginning, we can now fight with the glorious assurance that victory in the end will ride upon our banners, if we resolutely push ahead both on the war fronts and the home front.

There is no relaxing of the effort on the war front, but I am sorry to say that I, like most other service men, think that things could be better on the home front. I feel that the actions of the misguided strikers, the profiteering of many business men both big and little, the unjustified race riots, the bullheadedness of some labor leaders and the isolationist ideas of some of our political leaders, all constitute a profound disgrace to the country. Each act is very near treason to the men at the front.

It is not time yet to turn from the war effort to personal interests. Great efforts and great sacrifices must yet be made before victory is won. Hitler still has the most powerful war machine in the world except one, the Red Army. The Russian losses of 10,000,000 soldiers and civilians, compared to our losses of 90,000 shows the smallness of our sacrifice in the struggle. If the British and American storm of invasion will overcome the Western ramparts of the Nazi fortress, the Red Army will roll in from the Eastern front, and there will come to a timely end the most powerful and brutal regime the world has ever known. To open that Western (or Second) Front the fighting men must have the products of

American farms and factories. That is why the victory depends on you who work as well as on those who fight. Are you working?

Sincerely,

Lt. Orval E. Faubus,
Hqs. 320th Inf.
Camp Rucker, Ala.

\* \* \*

R E S T R I C T E D

HEADQUARTERS 320TH INFANTRY
APO 35

Camp Rucker, Alabama

SO 130                                                12 July 1943

E X T R A C T

1. A SCM is aptd to meet at Hq 320th Inf at the call of the president thereof, for the trial of such persons as may properly be brought before it.

DETAIL FOR THE COURT

LT COL WILLIAM F NORTHAM, President
CAPT JOSEPH L VIGNES,
CAPT WILBUR T DAVIS,
CAPT GERALD K ULM,
1ST LT MARK C SHEALY,
1ST LT MALCOLM W McLEOD,

2D LT MILTON GINSBURG, Trial Judge Advocate
2D LT CHARLES P BROCHU, Asst. Trial Judge
Advocate

1ST LT ORVAL E FAUBUS, Defense Counsel

Unarraigned cases in the hands of the Trial Judge Advocate aptd by par 1 SO 104 this Hq 12 June 43 will be brought to trial before this court.

By Order of Col. SCOTT:

McGREW HARRIS
Capt 320th Inf.
Adj

NEWS OF OUR BOYS

All news of Our Boys gathered the past week, including
the mention of those at home now or those who have returned to their stations, is being carried over till next week, and
we are giving you instead the following good, long letter
from Lieut. Orval E. Faubus, which we know you will enjoy
equally as much as the regular news in this column, all of
which will appear later.

-V-

Camp Rucker, Alabama,
August 11, 1943

Dear Home Folks:

I came into my room to read today after the work was
done. First and foremost in my interest was a copy of the
Record received today. And so for some time my thoughts
have been quite a long ways removed from my present location as I alternately rejoiced and sorrowed with the news
from home.

I cannot help thinking now after reading everything,
including even the ads and legal notices down to the last line,
of how the thoughts gleaned from the printed page of the
home town paper range through the whole field of human
emotions. There is the pleasure brought by good crops, business success, picnics and social gatherings, and the disappointment brought by drought, business failure or political
defeat. There is the genuine joy of a family reunion or a
soldier home on furlough, and there is the heartbreak of
goodbyes. The lines read up to the starry-eyed happiness of
newly-weds and down to the despairing grief of those who
have known the death of a loved one. To us who wander and
work in distant places it is a reflection in the mirror of memory of the life we left to answer the call of duty.

Perhaps most "home town" papers do not say so much
or say it so well as ours. I remember once that my father and
I, who have seen a number of such publications in our knocking about, decided after a business like analysis that

— 106 —

"Hawn's" paper was the best of its kind we had ever seen. That was some time ago, even before I got into Madison county politics, and even now after the paper published all the things my opponents wanted to print about me in the campaigns, I still think that Dad and I were right.

Of chief interest to me now is the column "News of Our Boys" and the letters from the service men. (I must admonish the editor now never to let any unworthy letter of mine interfere with the column). I have wondered and wondered who "Uncle Mc" can be, but I must say that he puts out a side-splitting brand of humor and some sound philosophy. Although we all know that Ruby V. Hughes is a successful farmer and the champion apple-grower of Madison county, there is another field in which he could be just as successful, for his writings are always enjoyable. Another source of real pleasure in the Record is the "War Eagle Clarion" so ably edited by J. D. Easley of my own White River country. His selections to start off a column each week are real gems of poetry, and many of the writings in the column show great promise. I also read with interest the letters of Reynolds, Roberts, Dr. Wentz and others. Neither can I fail to mention the local items and the community columns which are the backbone of any country newspaper. I wonder whatever became of Vernon Stenzil? I also often wonder why the most gifted writer of all has ceased to function, referring to the "Sage of Hock's Creek," Sherman Clark.

When I had finished reading the dusk of evening had settled down. On looking up from the paper I saw through the westward window the most beautiful sunset that it has been my pleasure to see since I left the Ledford home on Pinnacle Mountain some years ago. Instead of switching on the lights as I had intended, I felt compelled to sit and gaze at the intermingled and glowing colors until they had faded to the last dull streaks of red. Here on the vast coastal plain of the South the field of color of the sunset had much greater depth and faded more slowly than those of the mountains. As I sat gazing out into what was at the time literally the "Golden West," I thought of the boys I know who are far out in that direction, that the sun which for me had just set, was just then rising on their activities. To name a few: Sheridan Crowder who a little more than a year ago was riding the Japton school bus with me; Ray White a friend of St. Paul high school days; the Robbins boys, Oscar Dunaway, Roy Drain and Paul Couch who spent some happy days as students of mine on the Pinnacle mountain; Cecil Ogden, the Drake brothers, Doyle Haskins and others. Some have gotten below the equator in lands like Australia, New Zealand and the South Sea Islands where they will soon be having spring while we have autumn. I cannot help thinking that those who were once pupils of mine will learn more of geography during this war than they ever learned in the school room with me.

And far off to the northwest of the many-hued field of glowing color, my little boy at this hour has probably fallen asleep after a day so filled with activity as only a little boy of four can fill one. The dimpled little hands and fingers which once clasped the small colored marble which I now carry in my pocket, are now relaxed, the little brown legs which moved so ceaselessly throughout the long summer day are now still, and the melodious, happy voice so often raised in childish glee is now quiet after the sandman's passing. Thank Thee, Oh God, and brave men and women everywhere who have kept the bombs from ever falling near, [him] and greater thanks still when the death-dealing missiles cease to fall on little children anywhere.

August 29.

The above I penned some time ago, and not having time or the inclination to revise or re-write, I send as is. I have just returned from a week's maneuvers in North Florida. For a whole week we lived in the field without any of the so-called luxuries. It was the first week in a long time that I did not read even one word of news about the outside world. When we came out of the woods the Russians had taken Karkhov and were pushing on toward Germany; the Quebec conference had ended, and a candidate by the name of Bailey had defeated an Anti-Newdealer for the governorship of the State of Mississippi. The world moves whether you keep in touch with it or not. (I wish the Isolationists would learn that lesson).

A short time ago I looked up Bill Stafford of Clifty who is a member of a medical unit here in Camp Rucker. Recently I saw Hugh Fritts of Thorney for the first time since we came from Camp San Luis Obispo, Calif. He will probably be home on furlough by the time you read this. Pvt. Harmon of Elkins was for a time a member of the 320th Inf. here and attended a class which I instructed. He made himself known to me one day (I knew him before but had failed to recognize him. One sees so many soldiers that look like some one you know) and in course of our conversation he showed me a photograph with the remark that he guessed that I knew the party. I took the picture and found myself looking at the fair countenance of one of my former pupils of the Pinnacle school, Miss Geraldine Ledford. Pvt. Harmon volunteered to join the paratroops and has now gone to Fort Benning, Ga., for training.

I am now a staff officer (Intelligence Department) of one of the battalions of the 320th Inf.

It looks like the big push might be on soon for us in Europe. I hope so for the sooner we get started the sooner we will see the war's end. A number of officers and men have been going from my unit. Since being at Camp Rucker I have had three different roommates, and have lost all of them to overseas duty.

Best wishes,

ORVAL E. FAUBUS
Hqs. 2nd Bn., 320th Inf.
Camp Rucker, Alabama

[Room mates at Camp Rucker who shipped out: Lt. Pierce Earle, Pittsfield, Mass.; Lt. Arthur J. Manzi, Worchester, Mass.; and Walter V. Demkowski, Chicago, Ill. Also Lt. Irving Krieger, East Orange, N. J., who was co-defense counsel with me in the courts martial proceedings, shipped out on Aug. 30, 1943.]

\* \* \*

Camp Rucker, Alabama
20 September 1943

DETAIL FOR THE COURT

LT COL WILLIAM F NORTHAM, President
CAPT JOSEPH L VIGNES
CAPT WILBUR T DAVIS
CAPT GERALD K ULM
1ST LT MARK C SHEALY
1ST LT MALCOLM W McLEOD

— 109 —

2D LT MILTON GINSBURG, Trial Judge Adocate
2D LT CHARLES P BROCHU, Asst. Trial Judge
Advocate

1ST LT ORVAL E. FAUBUS, Defense Counsel
1ST LT SPENCER M SHOEMAKER, Asst. Defense
Counsel

By order of Col. SCOTT:

JOSEPH SZABO
Maj. 320th Inf.
Adj.

[Col. Don M. Scott commanded the 320th Inf. Regt. for most of its training period at Camp Rucker, Ala. Shortly after the date of the order above, he was relieved of command. After the war he retired and lived for several years at Little Rock, Arkansas before his death.]

\* \* \*

Camp Rucker, Alabama
12 October 1943

DETAIL FOR THE COURT

MAJ PHILIP W BURNS, President
CAPT JAMES P FORSYTH
CAPT ALBERT C FREDERICKSON
CAPT HAROLD S B BASS
1ST LT HAROLD C THOMPSON
1ST LT MORTON KLIGERMAN

1ST LT MILTON GINSBURG, Trial Judge Advocate
2D LT EDWIN H WHITE, Asst Trial Judge Advocate

2D LT SAMUEL G O'BRIEN, Defense Counsel
1ST LT ORVAL E FAUBUS, Asst Defense Counsel

By order of Lt. Col. UNDRITZ:

JOSEPH SZABO
Maj 320th Inf
Adj

[Lt. Col. Undritz succeeded Col. Scott in command of the regiment, until Col. Bernard A. Byrne joined the unit as commander. Undritz, a Texan, was well liked. He remained as Ex O of the regiment until shortly before the end of Tennessee maneuvers, when he received orders for duty in the Pacific Theatre of War.]

## COL BYRNE TAKES COMMAND

Some time after Oct. 12 and before the regiment left for Tennessee maneuvers, Col. Bernard A. Byrne, a Regular Army officer, was given command. A light complexioned Scotsman with close cropped sandy hair and twinkling eyes, he was tall and, by his own description, "the thinest man in the Army." Always affable, pleasant and friendly, he was, after close acquaintance, very talkative. Strangly enough for one so voluble, his talk was always interesting and never boring in the least.

He was quietly observant after taking command of the regiment, until he had learned its inner workings and something of the personalties of the officers and men with whom he must deal. Then he welded the regiment into a unified, efficient force without factions, discord or dissent. Without demanding, he had the complete loyalty, devotion and respect of the officers and men of his command, because every soldier felt that Col. Byrne was just as loyal to him, as he was to the colonel himself.

To those of us who knew him well, he had one peculiar habit which I have never seen before or since. When busy scribbling notes or handling papers while pondering a problem, he would place his lighted cigarette over his ear in the same manner as some place a pencil. Among those who observed this unusual practice there was always the thought that in his concentration on a problem, oft times a battle order, that he would forget and be burned. But our fear never materialized. He was never burned. He always removed the burning cigarette, although often, it seemed, just in the nick of time.

Every man always willingly carried out the colonel's orders. He felt that the order would not have been given until the colonel had considered all angles, and based upon honest evaluation, deemed the order necessary.

In all the months we worked with him, I never heard a single expression of ill will toward Col. Byrne.

MADISON COUNTY RECORD
Nov. 25, 1943

## FROM LIEUT. ORVAL E. FAUBUS

Camp Rucker, Ala.,
Nov. 12, 1943

Dear Home Folks:

It is principally due to some of my friends at home who urged me to do so that I attempt these few lines tonight. I find writing a most difficult task when not in the mood for it.

It is now 11:20 and there is quite a rush of work still going on around the headquarters. I am the duty officer tonight, so I will have to wait until it quiets down before I can get any rest.

As we will already have moved and be using our new address by the time you read this, it will not be disclosing any military information to tell you that our training at Camp Rucker has ended. We had a division review Thursday marking the close of the period. It is a grand sight when approximately 18,000 trained men with their banners and colors and battle equipment pass in review to the stirring strains of the band. When you stop to think of the number you find that is more people than there are in all of Madison county.

We also had an air show, principally to aid officers and men in the identification of our own aircraft when we get to the fighting fronts. Some of our bombers look very deadly and efficient as they have proven themselves to be to our enemies. Our latest type fighters are actually so fast that when they fly straight at you from a low altitude they reach you and pass ahead of the sound of their own coming.

The progress of the human race in the field of travel, and all the fields of invention, is truly amazing. In the time that it once took to go from Arkansas to California, one can now go around the world a number of times. Man's progress has been so rapid and the peoples of the world have been drawn so closely together in recent times that we must of necessity work out some means of keeping the peace, or we may all be destroyed.

Today as part of a test in the work of the Intelligence Department I went up in an artillery liasion plane for a flight over the camp and the reservation. I have studied aerial photographs so much lately that it hardly seemed like a new experience. I was surprised at the smoothness of the ride, and the slight jar when we landed was nothing like as severe as those I used to experience while riding a farm wagon or hauling timber to market. A landing strip such as that from which the plane took off and landed could be easily fixed in almost any field in Madison County. Which means that some day such planes may be almost as common as was once the well-known model T.

My recent leave among the people in the county I love so well, was enjoyable beyond expression. I especially want to thank my old friends and neighbors of my home community for the fine supper they set for me while I was there. That supper, as well as the fine Sunday dinner with the Ledfords, is the kind of meal a soldier many times dreams about in his lonelier hours. There are many wonderful cooks in the Ozarks and I name three whose food I have eaten and enjoyed many times—Mrs. Maudie Ledford, Mrs. Carrie Thornsberry and my aunt Julia Joslin. And, too, I must mention the fried chicken prepared by Aunt Mary Nelson.

I was hardly away from my little boy at all during my leave. He is getting old enough now to be quite a companion. Since our return to Alabama I have not seen him cross even once, which really does my heart good, for if there is anything I admire in any person it is good humor. He picked up some typical hillbilly expressions while he was home that he had not used before and which are amusing to some of my friends (and which I also enjoy).

He and Alta are now at Lebanon, Tenn., where I hope to be able to see them a few times during the next training period. The officers and men of my unit will not have any pleasant time during the next few weeks. Living in the open in winter can be anything but fun.

I want to thank all the service men who have written, and if I have not answered and you see this I want you to know that I am thinking of you. My most recent letter from a service man was a V-mail from Pfc. Denver Samples who is now overseas.

Lt. Orval E. Faubus
Hqs. 320th Inf.,
APO No. 35, c/o Postmaster
Nashville, Tennessee

* * *

RESTRICTED

## HEADQUARTERS 320TH INFANTRY
Tennessee Maneuver Area
APO 35, c/o Postmaster
Nashville, Tennessee

26 November 1943

### DETAIL FOR THE COURT

MAJ HAROLD V HUGHES, President
CAPT JAMES P FORSYTH
CAPT DWIGHT D BONHAM
1ST LT FRANK W GARDNER
1ST LT HOMER W KURTZ
1ST LT LAUREN A BURTON

1ST LT MILTON GINSBURG, Trial Judge Advocate
2D LT FRANK X SPERL, Asst Trial Judge Advocate

1ST LT ORVAL E FAUBUS, Defense Counsel
2D LT ERNEST H ZIELASKO, Asst Defense Counsel

By order of Col. BYRNE:

KENNETH H FRAZIER
WOJG                          USA
Asst Adjutant

[During the winter maneuvers in Tennessee, trials were often held in the open using a stump for the witness chair. The proceedings seemed rather awkward, with all participants bundled in heavy clothing including overcoats and gloves.

As the makeup of the court indicates, Lt. Ginsburg and I were most of the time pitted against each other in these proceedings. Ginsburg disliked discomfort so much that under such circumstances he was disgruntled and hard to deal with. However we got the work done. On one occasion in a full

— 114 —

day's proceedings we used a damp cold stump as a witness chair in 17 different cases.]

\* \* \*

Nashville, Tennessee
14 January 44

DETAIL FOR THE COURT

CAPT JAMES A LEACH, President
CAPT WILLIAM WALTON
CAPT GERALD K ULM
1ST LT HOWARD M KISER
1ST LT FRANK W GARDNER
2D LT SAMUEL G O'BRIEN

1ST LT MILTON GINSBURG, Trial Judge Advocate
2D LT JOHN P KELLY, Asst Trial Judge Advocate

1ST LT ORVAL E FAUBUS, Defense Counsel
2D LT EDWIN H WHITE, Asst Defense Counsel

By order of Col. BYRNE:

KENNETH H FRAZIER
WOJG                                 USA
Asst Adjutant

\* \* \*

MADISON COUNTY RECORD
Feb. 3, 1944

FROM LT. ORVAL E. FAUBUS

Camp Butner, N. C.
Jan. 27, 1944

Dear Home Folks:

Well, at last the winter maneuvers in Tennessee, with their ever-present mud, rain and cold, are over and by now a large part of the unit is here in Camp Butner, North Carolina. And only those who have lived for a time in the open without benefit of a house or a settled place of residence, and such items as chairs, tables, beds, stoves, a floor to keep one out of mud, and such like items, can realize what a wonderful change it is.

Most of us never realized before that four walls could encompass such a heaven as they do enclose.

But we learned a lot more than that while on maneuvers, not alone of military matters such as movement and supply, but of what men can endure and still remain healthy and well. If anyone had told me before that men could live in the cold and rain of winter as we did without becoming ill, I would have scoffed at the idea. But we did, having as little if not less illness than while in garrison.

The city boys and those who were formerly office workers possibly learned more. We who knew something of outdoor life learned that those who did not know how to build a fire in the rain, or strike a match in the wind, far outnumbered those who did know such things.

We learned, too, that the maneuvers proved a testing ground for men as well as equipment. For example the captain who dressed neatly and looked like a "softie" while in garrison, proved quite the contrary. He had a very difficult and trying job, and although his face chapped and his lips became swollen and cracked and his hands sore and stained, he went about his duties calmly and seemed to smile as often as before. Too, he shaved and washed more often than most, although the pain must have sometimes been severe. I watched him one day, stooping by a smoking fire and wetting his face from his helmet. By the time he could smear on the lather the cold wind would chill it and the razor would slide over most of the tough beard. After using three blades he finally concluded but it sure was a botched up job.

On the other hand there was the sergeant, a big shot with a lot of authority while in garrison, who turned out to be almost helpless in the field. He spent most of his time looking for opportunities to avoid unpleasant tasks and situations. Instead of taking care of himself and helping and directing others as he should, he whined about like a lost kitten. At the end of one dismally wet and cold day he was wandering around with no tent, his blankets sodden in the rain, with not even a place to sit down. Finally a private disgustedly took him into his dry blankets and sheltered him throughout the long winter night.

Yes, we learned who could take it and who couldn't regardless of past experience. We learned whom to admire and whom to despise. We learned the value of men who could chop wood and build a fire, or find their way in the dark, or read a map, or drive long hours without falling asleep. We learned who could crawl from his bed when he was awakened and brave the freezing wind of the winter mornings while accomplishing his assigned tasks. We learned, too, who could not do these things but had the courage to learn; and we learned who was worthless because he neither knew nor had the fortitude to endure and learn. (Of the latter there were fortunately very few).

Some things which stuck in my memory:

Soldier-crowded Lebanon on the weekends with standing room only in the barber shops for those waiting for baths and haircuts and dozens turned away. There was the time I held my place in line for two and one-half hours for a bath. I finally gave up on the hair cut and returned the following morning at opening time.

The long lines of those waiting to eat in the cafes and restaurants which extended out the doors and curved for some distance down the sidewalks. In one line was every rank from privates on up to a lieutenant colonel who had a place just outside the door and was hanging right on to it.

The swift pursuit planes strafing the river crossing and a full colonel lying in the mud along with the rest of us.

At 2:00 A.M. the surprise and capture by our leading troops after a 22 mile hike, of an enemy force blocking our route of march. The tired men again wearily formed their lines and we continued not yet having reached our objective.

Eating in the blackness before the dawn of a winter day, when you sometimes got your wool glove in your mouth along with the bread, because it was so cold you could not eat bare-handed, and so dark that you ate by feel alone and could have done almost as well with your eyes closed.

One of many bivouacs where it was so sloppy around the mess (army term for place of eating) that you had to step with care to keep from splattering the food with mud while it was being served, and if you dropped anything as fork or spoon, apple or bread, it was lost in the watery substance which covered the whole area.

The homesick look on the faces of the men on Christmas Eve when maneuvers continued and there were no furloughs. The tears in the eyes of one still smiling young fellow who was away from home for the first time on that [Christmas] day.

The thunderous cheers of the same men when the Colonel spoke to them on Christmas night, as they stood in a sea of mud with a misty rain coming steadily down.

The somehow touching appearance of the slight, youthful sergeant (who lived where we did) when he came home one weekend unshaven, unwashed and uncombed, his apparel muddy and weather-stained and carrying on his back a beaten barracks bag filled with dirty clothes. His young wife took one look at him and broke down and wept.

Christmas Eve with my wife and little boy (I missed the last one) when he sleepily pulled off his footwear, replaced his boots and had me to help him hang up his stocking. Then he turned innocently to his mother and said, "Mamma, where's my other stocking?" When I laughed he was abashed and hid his face in his arms. He was not greedy; just an innocent little boy who did not want to miss out on anything from a fine old fellow like Santa Claus.

How utterly luxurious seemed to me the one room with a bed, a dresser, a table and two chairs for which we paid $40.00 per month, and extra for fuel, etc.

Remember with disgust:

The landlady who had apartments until she saw our little boy and then was just out; then in sharp language tried to excuse herself to my discouraged but silent wife as if she had spoken what the landlady knew must be in her thoughts; finally the lady said she didn't care.

The old "Scrooge" who nailed up the doors to his dilapidated and vacant barn to keep young American soldiers from taking shelter therein against the cold, wet, winter weather, and opened them up again after the soldiers had gone.

Our grasping landlord and landlady (the only bad ones we've had) who during the last week charged all the tenants extra for electricity, use of radio and coal, and one quiet little mother from Detroit "50¢ for talking."

Memories that restore Faith:

The kind lady (a widow with one son in the army) who took my family and Mrs. Cull into her home after the house they had rented burned to the ground destroying a large part of their possessions. Others present offered to do likewise.

The unknown Air Force officer who encountered my wife and little boy while they were telephoning me of the disasterous fire, and offered them $25.00, all the money he had, and said he could get more from his friends if that wasn't enough. They did not need the money but we shall never cease to bless the fine fellow whoever or wherever he may be.

Oh, Yes! One more I shall set down. I can never forget the pained look of surprise on my wife's face when she found out that such people as the "Scrooge" and the landlord and landlady mentioned above, do actually exist.

But with all the memories of the maneuver period, I probably shall have some more pleasant and almost certainly some more poignant and painful, for we have not hit the real thing yet.

Just a word from two of my friends who have. Pfc. Doyle Haskins of the Sixth Marines, son of Mr. and Mrs. Cal Haskins, formerly of Ball Creek, writes from the Southwest Pacific, "I know what war is like; I was at Tarawa." (One of the bloodiest battles in Marine history). Those few words say more than I could in many pages.

Pfc. Oscar G. Dunaway, son of Mr. and Mrs. T. A. Dunaway of Pinnacle community, a former pupil of mine for five terms of school, also writes from the Southwest Pacific and I just got his letter today. He says in part, "Just saw your address in a clipping from Madison County Record, Sept. 25 issue." He has been a number of places including Guadalcanal and was there when the battle was finished. "I can't say much of my experience there, but I will say it was just plain hell."

And now in closing: May God and good luck be with those in the battle zones. We, who are not there should be able to take care of ourselves and help take care of those who stand between us and the enemy.

Best wishes to all,

Lt. Orval E. Faubus,
Hqs. 320th Inf.,
Camp Butner, N. C.

Camp Butner, N. C.
3 February 1944

DETAIL FOR THE COURT

MAJ WILLIAM J HOEFLER, President
CAPT CHARLES W BAER
CAPT KENNETH F TROSSEN
CAPT EDMUND R CASEY
CAPT MALCOLM KULLMAR
1ST LT VICTOR H ENGLISH

1ST LT MILTON GINSBURG, Trial Judge Advocate
2D LT JOHN P KELLY, Asst Trial Judge Advocate

1ST LT ORVAL E FAUBUS, Defense Counsel
2D LT SAMUEL G O'BRIEN, Asst Defense Counsel

By order of Col. BYRNE:

ROBERT N EKSTRUM
Capt. 320th Inf.,
Adj

\* \* \*

MADISON COUNTY RECORD
March 30, 1944

FROM ORVAL FAUBUS

Camp Ritchie, Md.
March 4, 1944

Dear Home Folks:

I write this from the rugged, snow-covered hills of Maryland. We arrived here yesterday, a beautiful sunshiny day, much reminded of spring in the Ozarks. We found a place to live and I signed into camp and my duties.

Early this morning sleet and snow began to pelt from a heavily overcast sky, whitening the class-room and barrack roofs and bouncing from the hooded storm-coats of the hurrying, rosy-faced WACS and the helmeted heads of the soldiers. All day without let-up it has continued, and no matter how often my gaze strayed from my studies toward the nearby hill where my wife and little boy were sheltered, it could not be seen. Now at nightfall the camp and surrounding forest-covered hills are well-blanketed in white and I, fearful that my car wouldn't make the steep, icy mountain road, am spending the night in camp. Apparently the heaviest fall is now over but as I look from my barracks window I can see a sleety mist still flying through the gathering darkness.

It is quite a change from the weather of North Carolina. There the atmosphere was becoming quite springlike and many trees were already budding. Although the temperature here is much lower than anything I experienced in Alabama or Carolina, the cold does not hurt so much. It does not have the penetrating damp quality which is so insufferably unpleasant in the deep South. I'm not comparing the climate with that of Tennessee because that would not be normal. There we were often out in the cold for a week at a time without fire and little shelter. The comparison would not be fair.

On the way up here we drove through Richmond, Va., second capital of the Confederacy, and then crossed the Potomac river into crowded Washington City. I thought the movies had over-emphasized the crowded conditions of our war-time capital but after driving through, I decided not. We thought of Paul Corlett and wondered if he was still stationed there.

I wanted to stop and tell FDR that he is right about the soldier-vote bill.

A short time before leaving Camp Butner I had a letter from my old friend, Woodrow Ledford, formerly of Pinnacle community. He is in a medical unit at Camp Bragg which was about 100 miles south of my post. We tried to arrange for a meeting but his duties just then would not allow him off duty long enough to come to Butner and, as there is no gasoline for pleasure driving, we could not go down there.

Pfc. Hugh Fritts, Co. I, 137th Inf., Camp Butner, formerly of Thorney, stayed all night with us Saturday, February 26, the night I wanted Woodrow to come see us. As we all three used to play basketball together in South Madison, we were going to have a small Madison County Reunion with the help of Alta and Farrell. Well, we had a good visit with Fritts and talked over old times and bygone incidents, including some of yours, Woodrow. Some other day maybe we can have the visit, along with many other Madison County soldiers and homefolks.

I can't say much of the camp here [restricted area] except that it is very picturesque, perhaps the most beautiful I have seen. It is set back in the hills which are as rugged and wooded as some of the Ozarks. Alta and Farrell live up on a rugged ridge in a former summer resort about two miles from camp. They buy their groceries at the little station of Pen-Mar, just across the Mason and Dixon line in Pennsylvania. It is what might be called just a whistlestop, a combination station, postoffice and grocery much like the old home town of my youth on White River.

As I write tonight I hear a train whistling through the Maryland hills. It calls to mind the days of my early boyhood when the train we knew as the B, M and E would come whistling through the late evening darkness down Mill Creek Valley from Cass to its home station of Combs. That train wove itself into my life, so that since I never hear a locomotive whistling through the hills without it recalling a train of many memories.

Recent V-Mail has brought news of Pfc. Denver Samples in Italy, Pfc. Everett Hill in England and Pfc. Arthur Tice in Greenland. If Sgt. Earlis Lawson who wrote from Foley, Alabama, and Pvt. Bohannan of the Signal Corps who wrote from Lebanon, Tenn., will write again, I will answer. I got your letters while on maneuvers and I did little writing then.

Best wishes to all,

Lt. Orval E. Faubus
Sec. B, 1st Student Trng. Bn.,
Camp Ritchie, Md.

[Another officer from the 35th Div attending the school at Camp Ritchie, Md. was 1st Lt. Ernest B. Allen, Jr. of the 216th FA Bn.]

\* \* \*

Camp Butner, N. C.
11 March 44

DETAIL FOR THE COURT
MAJ EDWIN C MOMM, President
CAPT ALBERT C FREDERICKSON
CAPT SHELDON P LOOMIS JR
CAPT KENNETH F TROSSEN
1ST LT ALBERT R WAKEHAM
1ST LT RUPERT L WHITTINGHAM

2D LT LEO K WILLIAMS
1ST LT MILTON GINSBURG, Trial Judge Advocate
2D LT JOHN P KELLY, Asst Trial Judge Advocate

1ST LT ORVAL E FAUBUS, Defense Counsel
2D LT SAMUEL G O'BRIEN, Asst Defense Counsel
By order of Col. BYRNE:

KENNETH H FRAZIER
WOJG                    USA
Asst Adjutant
\* \* \*

MADISON COUNTY RECORD
May 4, 1944

## FROM LIEUT. ORVAL FAUBUS

Atlanta, Ga.
April 9, 1944

Dear Editor:

I wish to express my appreciation for the friendliness and hospitality shown me and my family during my few days leave in Madison County, and for the wonderful dinner set for me by some of my neighbors at Greasy Creek and Combs.

The last day of leave was somewhat marred by the rainstorms, which forced me to wade White River in order to get started on the return journey. My brother, Elvin C. Faubus (who helped me) and I were almost washed away in the crossing and most of my clothing got wet. Also I am sore in almost every muscle today, as a result of helping my brother and one of the Ball boys push and pull my car out of the Ritchie Branch when the motor was drowned out by the high water.

I am now in the USO lounge in the huge R.R. station at Atlanta, Ga. It is a welcome place for travel weary service men and women to rest while waiting to begin the next lap of their journeys. Refreshments are served free of charge by volunteer workers, mostly young ladies, who work so many hours each week without pay. To many tired and lonely service personnel it is a very welcome service indeed.

One can brush elbows with many different people in such a place. Most of these here now are of the army and represent many different units and branches. Across from me sit two sailors, barely more than kids, one sleeping in his chair, the other turning through a magazine. Behind me is a lady marine and to my left a young wife faces her youthful sailor husband while he fondles a tiny baby.

Talk among the officers and men on the train had broadened geographically in recent months. While it used to be of the various camps in the U. S. and outlying possessions, it now includes camps in England, towns in Italy, cities like Cairo, Casablanca and Algiers, places in India and the South Pacific, and on around the world. On the shoulder of a young marine from Fayetteville, Ark., was a patch and on his breast a service ribbon of the Pacific Theater and three battle stars.

Although this great effort in which service men and women are engaged, is sometimes hard and lonely and to some a thankless task, I would not for anything miss having a part in it. Because it is necessary, just and right and, of course, must be done. To me and almost every service man a slacker is the most detestable creature on earth.

Although there are many interesting things to see and hear, this trip has been very dull to me. In my other travels during the past year I had my family with me and a childish, golden voice was questioning and exclaiming about many things along the way. Therefore, on this trip I was remembering more than I was seeing, such as when Alta and I were looking at the map for a highway we had mentioned, and a small hand reached over my shoulder and a voice says proudly and gladly "Ars (there's) highway number six." So I keep seeing a little finger slightly soiled with a tiny stained nail pointing to highway No. 6 on a road map.

Of the many interesting things I learned of service personnel while at home, I will here mention only three. I saw Sgt. Leo Sisemore of Drakes Creek with whom I was inducted two years ago. [Apparently an error on my part. It was Arlis C. Sisemore in the group with which I was inducted.] He was home on furlough. Shirley Thornsberry of Combs, also inducted at that time, was home. He was given a medical discharge after being hospitalized for some time in Iceland and New York. He was flown back to the U. S. from Iceland, and a passenger on the plane with him was Capt. Clark Gable of the Air Force. The Caler twins, Dessie and Bessie, former students of mine in the Pinnacle community, have enlisted in the Women's Army Corps (WAC). Dessie is now married to Pfc. Frank Stevens who is serving in India. They also have a brother in the service, Pfc. Roy Caler, who is overseas. We should be especially proud of the women in the services for all are volunteers.

My train is about due, so I must shove off. With no mishap I should be back with my unit tomorrow night. As I close this letter I notice a new day is beginning. It is now 12 minutes past midnight.

Don't forget your donation to the Red Cross and the U.S.O. They are many times helpful to your men and women in the services.

Sincerely,

Lt. Orval E. Faubus,
Hqs. 320th Inf.,
Camp Butner, N. C.

\* \* \*

## MADISON COUNTY RECORD
### April 20, 1944

### NEWS OF OUR BOYS

#### From Pfc. Charles Samples

Editor Madison County Record:

This is my first attempt to write an article for your paper. I have read the Record for years and have enjoyed every line of it. In fact, it is the only link I have with most of my friends in the county, as it is impossible to get much news from personal correspondence.

I especially appreciate the articles written by Dr. Wentz, J. S. Faubus, W. H. Burton, and others. I have always put Orval Faubus in a class by himself.

My thoughts for the past year, and I'm sure I'm speaking for thousands of G.I. boys all over the world, have been mostly concerned with what kind of a world we will find when this war is over. I realize that some of our most brilliant men have begun to elaborate on the subject but, as far as I know, no one has offered a fool proof plan. I don't intend to offer a plan but give you a few facts that I think are worthwhile.

The sooner that we realize that the boys and girls of today will be the men and women of tomorrow, the sooner this plan can be started. We must depend upon them. The positions that men and women are holding today will have to be filled by these boys and girls. How they fill these positions and regard their duties is up to the people.

These young people must be trained today, to take over tomorrow. Beginning with the grade schools, games of all kinds should be organized. Also public speaking should be encouraged.

We might say that there are three important elements that go to make up the early life. Broad mindedness, physical fitness, and a sense of fair play. Have any one of these three things and you are likely to have them all.

Our boys and girls must be physically fit if they are to take over our duties in the post war world.

Christianity is absolutely necessary for a happy home and also the other small things that lead to happiness with mutual respect for each other.

It is up to the people to take charge of this work, and encourage it in every possible way. The boys that are scattered all over the world have every right to expect the best of the people.

We must see that we don't lose the war at the peace table, or the boys will have lost all they fought and died for. If we avoid the chaos that followed the last war we must begin now. Remember, the price of Freedom is eternal vigilance.

Sincerely, Pfc. Charles Samples

Note—Pfc. Samples is in New Guinea and has seen some combat service.

[The above letter by Charles Samples is included because it shows the serious thinking of the rank and file participants in the war, of various faiths and walks of life. Samples, a countryman, a Republican, returned from the war, ran successfully for office, served for a time as a county official, and is now a businessman at Huntsville.]

# OFFICERS
## of the
## 320th Infantry Regiment
## Camp Butner, North Carolina
## April 22, 1944

On April 22, 1944 at Camp Butner, N. C. a photograph was taken of the regimental officers present for duty as of that date. According to a list of names identifying those pictured, as well as a list of the names of those not present, the following constitutes the names of the officers of the 320th Infantry Regiment of the 35th Infantry Division and the units to which assigned at that time.

### 320th Regtl Hqs & Hqs Co

Col. Bernard A. Byrne, CO, Bradenton, Fla.
Lt. Col. William F. Northam, Ex O, Columbia City, Ind.
Maj. George W. Jamison, S-2, Oakland, Calif.
Maj Edwin C. Momm, S-2, Irvington, N. Y. (trfd to 1st Bn Hqs as Ex O before combat)
Capt. William L. Haley, Jr., Com O, Sioux City, Iowa.
Capt. Donald J. Hoag, Chap, New York, N. Y.
Capt. Alfred H. Stone, Chap, Elgin, Ill.
Capt. Herman V. Tarpley, Chap., Daisy, Tenn.
Capt. James P. Forsyth, CO Hqs Co, Little Rock, Ark.
Capt. Wilbur T. Davis, S-1, Wyanet, Ill.
Capt. Thomas P. McElroy, Jr., S-3, Grand Forks, N. D.
1st Lt. Orval E. Faubus, Ln O, Huntsville, Ark.
1st Lt. Frank W. Gardner, Ln O, Arlington, Mass.
1st Lt. Milton Ginsburg, Ln O, St. Paul, Minn.
1st Lt. William H. Quillin, Ex O Hqs Co, Texarkana, Tex.
1st Lt. Sidney Silverman, I & R Plat, Detroit, Mich.
2nd Lt. Ward Talcott, Asst S-3, Lebanon, Oregon (trfd to Co E before combat)

### Hqs Hqs Co, 1st Bn

Maj. Harry A. Beckley, CO, York, Nebr.
Maj. William J. Hoefler, Ex O, Unknown
Capt. Joseph L. Vignes, Hqs Co CO, New Orleans, La.
Capt. William Walton, S-3, Newton, Kan.
1st Lt. Henry G. Morgan, Jr., Hqs, Birmingham, Ala.

1st Lt. Arthur E. Christianson, Com O, Matapan, Mass.
1st Lt. Ralph G. Carpenter, Hqs Co, Mt. Sterling, Ill.
1st Lt. Eugene A. Duffy, Hqs Co, Batavia, Ill.
2nd Lt. Albert Statuto, Hqs Co, Revere, Mass.
2nd Lt. Earl F. Scheinost, Hqs Co, Creighton, Nebr.

## Co A, 1st Bn

Capt. Malcolm Kullmar, CO, Lake Worth, Fla.
1st Lt. Kenneth E. Birkett, Chicago, Ill.
1st Lt. Stephen J. Rutkowski, Atlantic City, N. J.
1st Lt. Riley P. Shirley, Jr., Louisville, Ky.
2nd Lt. Charles W. Bell, Valentine, Texas
2nd Lt. Leo K. Williams, Atoka, Okla.

## Co B, 1st Bn

Capt. Robert N. Ekstrum, CO, Minneapolis, Minn.
1st Lt. Kenneth H. Brown, Puente, Calif.
1st Lt. David H. Barthfield, Unknown
1st Lt. Winston C. Coleman, Valdosta, Ga.
1st Lt. Grover C. Roberts, Pine Bluff, Ark.
2nd Lt. Raymond W. Brafitt, Watertown, Mass. (trfd to
    1st Bn as S-2 before combat)

## Co C, 1st Bn

Capt. Charles W. Baer, CO, Frederick, Md.
1st Lt. Raymond P. Brauch, Rockford, Ill.
1st Lt. Joseph R. Fitzgerald, Hartford, Conn.
1st Lt. Alfred H. Harrison, Unknown
2nd Lt. Charles H. Dalton, Madison, N. C.
2nd Lt. Carlton C. Thornblom, Paris, Texas

## Co D, 1st Bn

Capt. Gerald K. Ulm, CO, Maywood, Ill.
1st Lt. Roman W. Knopke, Crookston, Minn. or Kansas
    City, Mo.
1st Lt. Albert R. Wakeham, Dumont, N. J.
1st Lt. Louis G. Xintas, Baltimore, Md.
2nd Lt. Kirksey O. Looney, Crane, Texas
2nd Lt. Francis E. Oden, Ukiah, Calif.
2nd Lt. Jack M. Sabata, Des Moines, Iowa

2nd Lt. Frank X. Sperl, Flushing, N. Y. (trfd to Pers Sec Serv Co before combat)

## Hqs & Hqs Co, 2nd Bn

Maj. Vincent Keator, CO, Thoenicia, N. Y.
Capt. Thomas A. Swanson, S-3, Corvallis, Oregon
Capt. Henry H. Hare, Hqs Co, Los Angeles, Calif.
1st Lt. Larry D. Gilbertson, S-2, Alma Center, Wisc.
1st Lt. William G. Kuh, Hqs Co, Montgomery, Ala.
1st Lt. Garth C. Ramsey, Hqs Co, Lakewood, Ohio
2nd Lt. Charles V. Litherland, Hqs Co, St. Francisville, Illinois
2nd Lt. Henry O. Tietjens, Hqs Co, Carrolton, Mo.

## Co E, 2nd Bn

Capt. Edmund R. Casey, CO, Los Angeles, Calif.
1st Lt. Stanley S. Underwood, Bland, Mo.
1st Lt. Roupert L. Whittingham, Marshfield, Wisc.
2nd Lt. W. E. Ramsay, Unknown
2nd Lt. Donald A. Scott, Unknown

## Co F, 2nd Bn

Capt. George M. Hodson, Jr., CO, Brookline, Mass.
1st Lt. Wilbur A. Gotter, Louisville, Ky.
1st Lt. Thomas F. Potter, Meriden, Conn.
1st Lt. Eugene F. Trask, Washington, Iowa
2nd Lt. Felix M. Gangemi, Freeport, L. I., N. Y.
2nd Lt. Clark F. Palmer, Montgomery, Ala.

## Co G, 2nd Bn

Capt. Melvin V. Fritts, CO, Fort Valley, Ga.
1st Lt. Charles G. Bell, Binghamton, N. Y.
1st Lt. Franklin C. Cech, Cleveland, Ohio
1st Lt. James H. McCoy, Walla Walla, Wash.
2nd Lt. Alvin H. Hamrick, Unknown
2nd Lt. George T. Ramsden, Oceanside, N. Y.

## Co H, 2nd Bn

Capt. Harvey A. Smith, CO, Denton or Forsan, Texas
1st Lt. Thomas V. Camarda, Brooklyn, N. Y

1st Lt. Arthur L. Coil, Enterprise, Ala. or Overland Park, Kansas
1st Lt. Howard M. Kiser, Unknown
2nd Lt. David J. Dunn, Mt. Vernon, N. Y.
2nd Lt. Roy W. Preston, Seneca, Mo.
2nd Lt. Vernon A. Vagts, Annomosa, Iowa
2nd Lt. Edward G. Walsh, Detroit, Mich.

## Hqs & Hqs Co, 3rd Bn

Lt. Col. Clarence W. Docka, CO, Seattle, Wash.
Maj. Joseph Szabo, Ex O, Anderson, S. C.
Capt. Albert C. Frederickson, Chicago, Ill.
Capt. Robert B. Tobin, Hqs Co, Pistol Point, Texas
1st Lt. Homer W. Kurtz, S-2, Collinsville, (or Troy) Ill.
1st Lt. Harold E. Peterson, Com O, Lynnwood, Calif.
2nd Lt. Carl Ermelbauer, New York City, N. Y.
2nd Lt. William Perkowsky, New York, N. Y.

## Co I, 3rd Bn

Capt. John F. Hardy, Jr. CO, Chester, S. C.
1st Lt. Clifford M. Head, Topeka, Kansas
1st Lt. Charles P. Brochu, Cleveland, Ohio
1st Lt. John F. Hermanspan, Jr., Yonkers, N. Y.
1st Lt. John J. Pulgin, New York City, N. Y.
2nd Lt. Meyer O. Berman, Unknown

## Co K, 3rd Bn

Capt. Kenneth F. Trossen, CO, Chicago, Ill.
1st Lt. Edmund J. Zimmerman, Houston, Texas
1st Lt. Glen Mooney, Ozark, Mo.
1st Lt. McKean E. Brimhall, Salt Lake City, Utah
2nd Lt. John P. Kelly, Broken Bow, Nebr.
2nd Lt. Clifford J. Rainford, Chicago, Ill.

## Co L, 3rd Bn

Capt. Hilton M. Lynch, CO, Unknown
1st Lt. Curtis Alloway, Kansas City, Mo.
1st Lt. Robert H. Hoffman, Indianapolis, Ind.
1st Lt. Ernest L. Strasil, Fall City, Nebr.
2nd Lt. Ernest T. Hayes, Unknown
2nd Lt. Leo E. Thomas, Lima, Ohio

## Co M, 3rd Bn

Capt. Dwight D. Bonham, CO, Table Rock, Nebr.
1st Lt. Victor H. English, Portland, Oregon
1st Lt. Dale O. Britt, Unknown
1st Lt. Lester L. Remley, Kansas City, Unknown
2nd Lt. Samuel G. O'Brien, Des Moines, Iowa (trfd to
    Regtl Hqs before combat or soon thereafter)
2nd Lt. W. E. Rounsavell, Unknown
2nd Lt. Travis R. Rowe, Unknown
2nd Lt. James R. F. Woods, Palo Alto, Calif.

## Cn Co, 320th Regt

1st Lt. William C. Fessenden, CO, Long Beach, Calif.
1st Lt. Melvin L. Larson, Unknown
2nd Lt. John R. Orr, Unknown (thought to be Texas)
2nd Lt. Leslie A. Lakeness, Unknown

## A/T Co, 320th Regt

Capt. Arthur D. Wilson, CO, Pacific Grove, Calif.
1st Lt. Don L. Wright, Muncie, Pa.
1st Lt. Ernest H. Zielasko, Ohio
1st Lt. Robert W. Adams, Canton, Ohio
2nd Lt. Kenneth I. Botton, New Brunswick, N. J.
2nd Lt. Ernest J. Jones, Unknown
2nd Lt. Warren F. Prescott, San Francisco, Calif.

## Serv Co, 320th Regt

Maj. Harold V. Hughes, S-4, Oakland, Calif.
Capt. Paul H. Heil, CO, Dennison, Ohio
Capt. James A. Leach, Davenport, Iowa (trfd to 3rd Bn
    Hqs before combat)
Capt. Sheldon P. Loomis, Asst S-4, Unknown
Capt. Richard J. Shamla, Regtl TO, Glenco, Minn.
Capt. Gerard T. Armstrong, Pers O, Baton Rouge, La.
1st Lt. John W. Keith, 3rd Bn S-4, Detroit, Mich.
1st Lt. Morton Kligerman, Poughkeepsie, N. Y.
1st Lt. Raymond W. Mody, 1st Bn S-4, Detroit, Mich.
1st Lt. George W. Byerly, 2nd Bn S-4, Lima, Ohio
2nd Lt. Charles E. Scovel, Battle Creek, Mich.
CWO Kenneth H. Frazier, Wichita, Kansas
WOJG Edwin K. Stearns, Tucker, Ga.

WOJG Milford W. Boll, Asst S-4, Scribner, Nebr.
WOJG Raymond S. Patterson, Hutchinson, Kansas
WOJG Glenn Wells, Asst S-4, St. Louis, Mo.

### Med Det, 320th Inf

Maj. Lloyd A. Smith, Regtl surgeon, Tyler, Minn.
Capt. John H. Shumate, Jr., DC, Georgia
Capt. Forest A. Rowell, Jr., Hastings-on-the Hudson,
N. Y.
Capt. Joseph J. Cacioppo, Unknown
Capt. Albert E. Chiron, Unknown
Capt. Thomas E. Havel, Unknown
Capt. Morris Himmelstein, DC, Unknown
1st Lt. John E. McKeigue, Cambridge, Mass.
1st Lt. Theodore R. Struhl, Unknown

Of the list above, I can find no record to indicate that
the following officers accompanied the regiment overseas.
They may have been transferred from the unit before we
sailed on May 12, or before the regiment was committed to
the battle lines in Normandy.

Maj. William J. Hoefler, Ex O of 1st Bn
1st Lt. Alfred H. Harrison, Co C
2nd Lt. W. E. Ramsay, Co E
2nd Lt. Donald A. Scott, Co E
2nd Lt. W. E. Rounsavell, Co M
Capt. Sheldon P. Loomis, Asst S-4, Serv Co
Capt. Thomas E. Havel, Med Det
1st Lt. Theodore R. Struhl, Med Det

There were changes in assignments for other officers
before we reached France. I have noted a few in the original
April 22 list, which I can recall. After we hit combat, the
changes came rapidly and were almost a daily occurrence. I
served in three or four different positions during the combat
period as did Ginsburg, Gardner and Silverman.

A few officers may have been added to this list of 156
before we left the states, to cross the ocean and the channel
with us. Anyway, after we hit the battle lines, the changes
often came with great rapidity. There was a turn over of more
than 400% in officers in some line companies during the combat period.

## NEWS OF OUR BOYS

### "FAREWELL TO AMERICA"

Location Unknown,
Undated

The soldiers file on to the train with dispatch and precision. Scarcely are we in position and seated when the highball signal sounds and we begin to move. I glance out the window and someone is waving madly a good-bye to a girl in a red dress. As it gathers speed the locomotive gives a long and mournful whistle which called to me like a voice from the past. If many men before now had felt no trepidation, I think that now even they felt some tightening of the cheek.

We began to speed through green woods, still fresh with the newness of spring. Flowers are blooming along the tracks, their bright colors waving gaily in the gentle breeze. Soon the unfolding panorama reveals a path leading off through the forest which borders the fields. The pale green waves of wheat undulate in the warm wind with rhythmic grace. From a farm house set on a gentle knoll three little children wave wildly at the now flying train.

It is already past mid-afternoon, and as we speed along there flashes through my mind the wonderful music and snatches of the song "So Little Time." But the train, like time, does not wait for either music or farewells. Yet no matter how swift the speed, it cannot carry me away from my thoughts or my memories.

There comes into view, silhouetted against the sky, a motherly woman holding her hat in place with both hands. Beside her a younger woman of shapely form, the breeze ruffling her dress about her knees, stands shading her eyes against the sun, while both gaze fixedly at the speeding troop train. A farmer sits motionless on his plow and stares, while his weary sweat stained team, thankful for the brief respite from their labors, stands with drooping heads. The workman in the shop has momentarily forgotten his hammer and looks while the iron remains unstruck. There are more children including a little round headed boy in horizontally striped sweater and a little girl with flaming red hair. Still smaller ones just able to wave tiny hands, and others larger shading their eyes with closed fingers as they gaze in wonder at the entrained troops speeding to an unknown destination.

Almost every human activity, it seems, is stayed for a time as there goes by the soldiers destined for battle.

We pause briefly in the city. Friendly people continue to wave and smile. A middle-aged lady comes as near as permitted to the coaches and, as if her entreaties would somehow aid us, she urges, "Please get there, and hurry back."

The eventide sets in as we continue through the country. I see little groups talking leisurely in the villages (typical of my homeland). The shadows lengthen across the landscape, and again the song: "So little time, And there's so much to say." The children are finishing up their day's play. Some people pause from their evening chores to watch us go by, but many are now sitting leisurely about their dwellings enjoying the cool of the evening, or are just coming back to the rest, the peace, the security and contentment of their homes.

The shadows fade as the evening sun westers and leaves the land bathed only in the soft colors of twilight. As the train slows for a siding I can hear a bird singing its evening song in a cottonwood near the track. The pale, mild green of white oak floats by, and I know its foliage, now being dampened by the early dews, would feel so soothing to my feverish brow. Nothing brings back quite so vividly to me the recollections of home as the sight of white oak trees.

A little boy on a tricycle stops pedaling to hold high one tender hand and wave. Again we stop and a group of play-stained urchins gather near the cars, among them one little fellow with neck so small that it seems it could with difficulty hold up his tousled head.

A very pretty girl attempts to maintain her poise and dignity while walking past half the length of the train. She fails and turns away her head, smiling and blushing furiously. Those who are frankly friendly have no difficulty, but haughty dignity is something not recognized or permitted by troop train soldiers.

One car of men toss coins to the gathering of bare-footed boys as the train pulls away.

I am very tired and now have grown sleepy, but I do not want to miss even one last look at this beautiful country we are now departing. The light is now fading and I can see only dimly the friendly faces along the countryside. A girl in a white waist is raking new mown grass on the lawn. Another sitting on the steps of a house is waving both hands as if to say "hello" and "good-bye" to all.

Now a few of the houses are lighted. A mother stands on a porch and looks longingly (perhaps she sees in her mind's eye another who has already gone away). A patch of woods, shadows darkening within its depths, and I know that somewhere out there in the hills a whippoorwill is beginning to call.

There now fills my ears, grown louder with the stillness of approaching night, the roar of the train and the lonely, urgent call of the whistle. The lights on the train come on, or I could no longer see to write. The cinders drift in through the open window and grime my face and hands and blacken my paper (and I think of some one whose hands are soft and warm and tender. I strain to drive away the thought because it is too painful).

Soon will be the last look, and again the song: "With heaven so near, And so little time." In the last light of the fast fading day I see the wonderful soft green of a meadow, and my desire to stroll slowly through its coolness and beauty is as sharp as a pain. And now some one is waving, waving, from a house on a green hillside, and all at once it hits me— that weakness I have fought and tried to keep from me—and suddenly I am so lonely, so lonely, that I want to lay my head on someone's breast and weep. For a moment the feeling is overwhelming, but with bitter fight I put it from me.

When I again look up, the twilight is still lingering as if it knew my longing and was reluctant to draw the curtains across the last light of day. Now the woods are dark, and have grown fearsome to little boys. (Why did I have to think of a little boy; as if he were ever entirely out of my mind). The white dogwoods are barely distinguishable; a country road gleams lightly as it leads off across the country. On the far western horizon there is the faintest tinge of pink, the last gesture of the now departed day.

The farmers have now "lighted the lamp within the house." The cows are bedded down; the chickens are upon their perch, and the wild birds have flown to a safe resting place; the lights of the cities are shining brightly. Throughout all the land, both bird and beast, and our fellow human beings, our loved ones, have sought the peace and safety of their respective homes or the pleasure and companionship of friendly, lighted places.

Yes, heaven is very near; just out there beyond my touch. The green fields, the pleasant woods, the rose trellis by the wall, the farmer with his weary team, the frolicking puppy with the waving children, the girl in the white waist, the mother preparing the evening meal, the cars upon the highway, the lights of the city (never yet dimmed by blackout or shattered by bombs; how thankful we should be), all that is heaven to us. It is so near, and yet for us so far away.

I can see no more. The thick mantle of darkness is spread over the land. The train rocks and reels as with clang and clatter and urgently calling whistle it plunges onward into the night. I close the window to shut out the flying cinders, and pray for sleep and the peace and rest that can come with repose.

The sands of time have run out. Ahead lies work and loneliness and danger in strange and far-away lands, and perhaps a rendezvous with battle and with death. Someday, we hope, the hour glass of time will again be filled; but for the present, my comrades and I have said our farewell to America.

> Lt. Orval E. Faubus
> Hqs. 320th Inf.,
> APO 35, c/o Postmaster, N. Y., N. Y.

P. S.

Thousands before me have said their farewell to America. I cannot say if their farewells have been so fraught with loneliness and longing as mine or if they were more so. I can speak with certainty only for myself. But from what I have seen in the faces and eyes of my comrades and from what I have heard them say, I am convinced that it would be difficult to over-emphasize the anguish of these good-byes. On the other hand, the voyage and the battle is an adventure, but anyone who thinks of it as a pleasant one is a fool. I think all soldiers look upon the war as a desperately dirty and dangerous job which we have to finish, and its end will bring such relief and joy that I would not even attempt to express it. — O.E.F.

\* \* \*

[The above was written while traveling on the troop train from Camp Butner, N. C. to Camp Kilmer, N. J.

At Camp Kilmer the final preparations were made for going overseas. From there we went to the Port of New York for embarkation.]

## MEMORIES OF THE VOYAGE

We reached the harbor during the night and assembled in the giant piers by the ship side. The last people we saw, other than the members of our unit and ship's personnel, were the uniformed lady Red Cross workers as they passed out hot coffee, hot chocolate and doughnuts to us before we went aboard. Presently we walked the gangplank we had talked so much about, and were directed to our positions by guides who had already gone aboard the ship for that purpose. As it was already late at night (or early morning as reckoned by the clock) we bedded down, and, overcome by our weariness, were soon asleep.

I had thought that by morning we might be at sea, but when I awakened in the dawn we were still in the harbor. However it was not long before the announcement "All ashore who's going ashore" sounded over the loudspeaker. The engines began to throb and presently we moved out from the dock. Tug boats nosed up to the side of our ship, looking like mice beside an elephant, turned it about and pushed us out into the channel. Our great ship picked its way through vessels of every type and description, a great number flying the flags of many nations other than our own. Its great whistle called hoarsely now and then to warn of its coming. Soon we cleared the harbor and with silent farewells in our hearts, we took our last look through the smoke and the haze at the city and the receding shores of our homeland. Many, perhaps all, were, like myself, seeing far beyond the fading sight of land to other scenes and happier times, among which were vaguely recollected faces and half-remembered voices, and my greatest wish and my most earnest prayer were for their safety and well-being.

After a few days we grew accustomed to the sight of the vast blue ocean. The ships of the convoy rarely changed formation and each in its place became a familiar part of the pattern of every day life. Their prows threw out a white spray as the vessels plowed along and each left a brief trail in the constantly changing water like the momentary streak of a shooting star in its path across the night sky. When the sun shone warm and the surface was broken only by the light ripples, the sea did not appear unfriendly. But when the wind blew cold under a drab, gray sky, and the waves constantly rose and fell in ever-changing, unresting turbulence, it offered no comfort to the bravest heart and was as lonely as the calling of wild geese lost in a fog.

Only once during our voyage did the wind and gale approach storm proportions. Then it was interesting to watch the billowing waves rise high and the wind whip the tops from them in foaming white spray. Great troughs would appear in which a small boat would be for a time completely hidden, or rising on the crest would briefly be outlined above the level of the ocean. I thought that if the heaving mass of water could suddenly be solidified, the depressions and hollows would make excellent shelter from the rain-laden gale. This reminded me again and again of how, as a small boy, I used to seek shelter from the raging March winds in just such land formations in the Ozarks as I accompanied my father at work in field or forest.

The ever changing shape of the ocean's waters goes on relentlessly and the motion is as constant as time itself. Any idea that one could rest quietly and still on the sea is an entirely erroneous conception. One might rest peacefully, in life or in death, on the vast heaving waters, but the quiet and stillness of rest on the land would never be found on the surface of the rolling sea.

After settling into the routine of life on the transport, the days seemed to run together. I sometimes could not remember what day it was and I noticed that others had the same difficulty. There was a great deal of time that was our own. Much of it was spent in reading. (The ship had a well stocked library and almost everyone had brought along books and magazines). Many wrote letters almost every day although they knew that the messages could not be mailed until after completion of the voyage. I consciously avoided writing of any kind, because to write to some one was to think of them, and when thoughts were painful and could in no wise help the situation, I thought it best to avoid them as much as possible.

The monotony was broken by certain duties which had to be performed, meals twice a day, strolls on the deck, drill and inspections, but even this left much time in which one could not always read or sleep. Even the church services, the occasional movies, the special service programs as boxing matches, music by one of the bands, etc. still left time. So we filled in by discussions, arguments and card games. We discussed almost every subject known and sometimes the talk grew heated. Occasionally a participant would grow eloquent in the presentation of his views. Witticisms and humor were constantly injected and sometimes a better than ordinary joke would break up a hot argument in a roar of laughter.

The stateroom which I occupied along with five other officers became somewhat of a center for such discussions. It contained two lawyers (one each from Minn. and Wisc.), a genial Irishman with an excellent sense of humor (Conn.), a Harvard man with a cheerful Boston accent (Mass.), a former Ford worker, perhaps the most sincere one of the lot (Calif.), and myself. As to religion of the six, three were Protestants, one a Jew, one a Catholic, and the other I don't remember. In politics three were Democrats, two Republicans while one called himself an Independent.

[With me in my stateroom during the voyage were Lt. Milton Ginsburg, St. Paul, Minn., Lt. Frank W. Gardner, Arlington, Mass., Lt. Joseph R. Fitzgerald, Hartford, Conn., Lt. William C. Fessenden, Long Beach, Calif., and Lt. Larry D. Gilbertson, Alma Center, Wisc.]

I might add as an aside, that if the general opinion expressed in the discussions is any indication, regardless of the avowed politics, that if the president will run again there will be no change in the presidency until the war is over. One Rebublican, a former farmer of Mo., said he had never voted for the president before but would this time. The Republican from Calif. said he had voted for him once and against him the last two times but would vote for him this time because we needed him until the war is over.

The ship's rules forbad gambling aboard the vessel but there were all kinds of card games from solitaire and two-handed gin rummy to as many as a dozen participants in a game of "Black Jack." Also to relieve the tedium of the voyage many men made small bets on anything from the turn of a card to which side of the ship a sea gull would fly while passing. When one submarine alert would be over they would bet on the time the next would occur.

Up on deck one night I was watching and listening to the spray as it spread in gleaming white from the prow of the ship. We were passing through an area in which the water contained a great number of phosphorescent bodies. They appeared to be about the size of silver dollars and shone in the water along side the vessel as it plowed forward. Two soldiers were standing by, and one said they reminded him of his boyhood as he used to sit on the shore at night and watch the objects in the water (on the coast of Maine). He said according to fable the gleaming white bodies represented the ghosts of all the people who had ever been lost at sea.

As Air Watch Officer for the voyage my duties often took me up on the sun deck. I happened to be near the bridge late one grey afternoon when there was considerable activity there. One of the accompanying warships far out in front was flashing back a message to the other ships and to the convoy. I could not see the war vessel itself but only the flashing of its signal lamp as, with the rapidity of a skilled typist, the seaman sent back the message. I overheard the Transport Commander tell the General, who was on the bridge, that they had contact with submarines up ahead. Our own ship was busy sending messages and carrying out orders which would enable the convoy to avoid Hitler's sea wolves who sought our destruction.

The most comforting impression of the whole voyage was the presence of the accompanying warships, which, no matter when one looked from port hole or deck, were always there by our side, ever watchful, ever on guard for our safety. Sometimes the DEs moved more rapidly and great plumes of white spray would rise in the air from the depth charges they were throwing to ward off enemy submarines.

Once when gazing over the vast, trackless ocean there came into my mind the thought, "In the hands of God and the ship's crew." But on thinking more clearly of the situation I concluded it would be more correct to say that we were "In the hands of God and the U. S. Navy." For our ship's crew alone would have been helpless to save the thousands aboard from the lurking undersea raiders without the aid of the Navy. And when I thought about the part that God plays in the situation I knew that he could save all physically by a miracle, but that the days of miracles are past. I realized then that only by our own efforts (of all) would we come through, for a "faith without works is dead" and the old adage "God helps those who helps themselves" was truly spoken.

My bunk was near the side of the ship where I could hear the gentle lapping of the waves when I retired at night. The rocking of the ship as we plowed steadily onward was somewhat restful and lulling, and would have been conducive to peaceful rest had it not been for the thought of the lurking subs in the cold sea outside.

There was no outward sign of worry or concern during the whole voyage, and possibly there wasn't a great deal of concealed worry. Our Navy has been very successful in guarding the convoys which are constantly going out to all parts of the world.

However I have chuckled quite often at the way the lieutenant, who slept above me, tumbled out of his bunk and grabbed for his clothes, when the first real "Stand by to Abandon Ship" signal sounded. He sure didn't lose any time.

Later the grapevine had it that ours was the largest convoy to cross the ocean up to that time.

Our ship was the Edmund B. Alexander.

* * *

[We sailed from the Port of New York on May 12, 1944.

The ships of the convoy which carried the men of the 35th Infantry Division, and the units aboard each vessel, were:

## SS EDMUND B. ALEXANDER

| | |
|---|---|
| Hq. & Hq. Co., 35th Inf. Div. | Special Troops Medical Det. |
| 320th Infantry Regt. | 127th F. A. Bn. |
| 35th Reconnaissance Troop | 216th F. A. Bn. |

35th Signal Co.

## SS GENERAL A. E. ANDERSON

| | |
|---|---|
| Hq. & Hq. Btry., 35th Div. Arty. | 60th Engineer (C) Bn. |
| | 134th Infantry Regt. |
| 35th Div. MP Platoon | 161st F. A. Bn. |
| 35th Div. Band | 219th F. A. Bn. |

## SS THOMAS H. BERRY

| | |
|---|---|
| 137th Infantry Regt. | 735th Ordnance Co. |
| 35th Quartermaster Co. | 110th Medical Bn.] |

## IKE AND PATTON VISIT THE TROOPS

In England most of the 320th Infantry Regiment found quarters at Topsham Barracks near Exeter. Quarters were found at Newton Abbott for Anti-Tank Company and the Third Battalion, less Company L and Company K, which were at Bovey Tracy and Bishopsteigton. Cannon Company was at Okehampton, where the 216th Field Artillery Battalion was also quartered.

The 60th Engineer (C) Battalion was distributed as follows: Headquarters and Service Company at Wadebridge, Company A at Padstow, Company B at Trevone Bay and Company C at Harlyn Bay.

The 110th Medical Battalion was quartered at Poor Law Institute, the Kendall Building and Town Arms, the last two on Fore Street, and the Methodist Church on Pool Street, all in Bodwin.

The 35th Division Headquarters was quartered at the old town of Tavistock. Other units were scattered throughout the area in Camborne, Land's End, Redruth, Penzance, St. Ives, Hayle, Prah Sands, Lizard Point, Penrose Estate, Launceston and Bere Alston. The 137 Regiment Headquarters was in the old structure that formerly housed the Duke of Cornwall. Other units of the Division lived in the home of Sir Conan Doyle, creator of Sherlock Holmes.

Here in this beautiful, historic region of Old England, with even greater history in the making, the Division received an inspection visit on June 25 by the Supreme Commander of the Allied Expeditionary Forces, General Dwight D. Eisenhower. Among those who accompanied him were Gen. George S. Patton, soon to lead the American Third Army on the Continent, and the Supreme Commander's son, Lt. John Eisenhower.

It was a typical day in England, lowering gray skies with misty rain, the drifting mist making wet and dripping the green grass, red roses and grey stone walls of the countryside, and bathing in heavy dampness the helmets and trench coats of the massed troops. The General made his appearance with his party at Exeter at 0910 where the 320th Regiment was assembled in the quadrangle at Higher Barracks.

After greeting the 320th's commanders, Eisenhower walked among the troops, shaking hands with some, chatting *briefly with others and questioning still more. With his warm smile and friendly, interested, down-to-earth manner he set everyone at ease. In a sense, the General made the group "feel-at-home." He conveyed to the men the feeling that he, the Commander, was interested in their welfare.*

*A visit from the Supreme Commander with his son was a signal occasion, but we were also interested in getting a good look at Gen. Patton. Unlike Eisenhower, who wore the customary long trench coat over a dress uniform which was accompanied by the visored cap and tan shoes, Patton was dressed in a close fitting jacket of regulation dark green, with riding breeches and overseas cap of the same color. He strode about in highly polished boots of a darker hue, at times without a coat as if in defiance of the rain, the stars of his rank on both jacket and cap glistening more brightly than usual because of the gloom of the day. In his hands he carried a short staff or riding crop.*

*We had heard much of Patton and his previous exploits and of the incident in which he was reported to have slapped a soldier in a hospital in Italy. Our impression of him at that time, gained from press reports and soldiers' gossip, was not too good. This not-too-good impression of Patton, which we later decided was erroneous, explains our amusement at an occurrence which happened as Eisenhower, after his visit in the ranks, mounted an improvised platform to speak to the troops. Looking about for his son, the Commander could not spot him. We saw him turn to Gen. Patton and heard him exclaim, "Georgie, where's John? Go and find him for me."*

*To hear the great Patton addressed so informally and sent on such a small errand, was in such great contrast to the spit and polish and military formality the General was reputed to demand of all subordinates, that it delighted all of us who saw and overheard. Naturally, the story of the incident spread throughout the regiment afterward to those who were not close enough to hear, and they were equally pleased.*

*In his rather brief speech to the troops, General Eisenhower still further generated the friendliness and warmth he had begun to build in his trip through the ranks. He was from Kansas, he recalled, in the Midwest, and it was good to see some men from home. But he was proud of all the men from every state and section. Together, we had a great job* to do. *He was counting on us to do our part, and he knew we would do it well.*

*As I listened to his remarks, the whole scene enveloped in the all-encompassing misty rain of the British Island, I noted even more closely his demeanor and its effect on those he addressed. About his attitude there appeared no trace of the arrogance of power which causes people to fear a figure of authority. Instead there showed the humility, which, when apparent in a figure of great power, draws people to a leader in a bond of faith and respect. The human attributes of warmth and a sort of shy friendliness seemed to emanate from the man as invisible waves, which could be felt going out to his hearers, drawing them to him in an intangible bond of understanding and fellowship.*

*The Supreme Commander concluded his remarks with a smile and wave of his hand, almost as if apologetic and half sorry that we had to be there to hear him, a gesture which still further cemented the bond of comradeship he, unconsciously it seemed, had created between himself and his listeners. As he left the stand followed by his retinue, I turned to a trench-coated fellow officer standing by my side and said, "That man will be president some day."*

*As the General departed he left behind no strong exclamations of "Go get them! We will win!" Nor had he uttered any highsounding phrases about duty in a great cause. The justice of our cause was taken for granted by all. To mention it was unnecessary. Rather the Commander left with us the quiet confidence that we had a good leader, who wanted to do his best for us, and wanted us to do our best for him in the difficult task in which we were all engaged. There was no claim of infallibility. Although no such words were spoken, we understood that, at times, he could be at fault, as sometimes we might be at fault. Nevertheless, we had a leader on whom we could depend for all possible assistance in the great struggle we must continue to wage to finish the job that must be done.*

*This unusual quality of Eisenhower to draw people to him in an unspoken bond of fellowship, I heard described years later during his presidency, in unique but appropriate words by former Governor Thomas E. Dewey of New York.*

*It was at a meeting of the Executive Committee of the National Governor's Conference to which I was host in 1958* at Hot Springs, Ark. Gov. Dewey was not then a chief executive, but as a prominent Republican leader and friend of President Eisenhower, he had been sent to the meeting for a purpose.

Beginning with Arkansas during the so-called Little Rock crisis in 1957, the Eisenhower administration had federalized several National Guard units, without permission of the Governors of the states involved, and without transmitting the orders through the chief executives. Prior to that time such a method was considered unconstitutional and had never been used. Always before in the history of the Republic, National Guard units had been called into federal service by notifying the state governor, who then conveyed the orders to the proper officials in the Guard.

A short time before the Hot Springs meeting some National Guard units in Illinois had been federalized by President Eisenhower and the Secretary of Defense, without notifying the chief executive and without transmitting the order through him. The then Republican Governor of Illinois, Phillip Stratton, who was also Chairman of the National Governor's Conference and likewise Chairman of the Governor's Executive Committee, was very displeased by the action. Consequently Stratton had drawn up a very strong resolution opposing such procedure as unconstitutional and illegal, and made known that he would present the resolution to the Governors' Executive Committee for consideration and approval at the meeting.

The national administration, desiring that no such resolution should be considered or adopted by a group of governors, had, according to information I received, sent Gov. Dewey to the meeting to look after the matter. Although Gov. Stratton apparently felt strongly about the resolution, and informally discussed it with me and other governors present, I can only assume that Gov. Dewey was successful in his mission. The resolution was never officially presented to the committee nor was the matter discussed at any official session. Anyway, whatever the reason for Gov. Dewey's presence in Hot Springs, he was a prominent figure at the gathering.

Late one evening during the committee meeting after official sessions had ended, a small group of us fell into an informal visit. The group included Gov. Dewey, Gov. Johnson *of Vermont, Gov. Edmund Muskie of Maine and myself. When by chance one joins such a gathering, he never knows how long the discussion will continue or at what point the group will break up. On that occasion Gov. Dewey was in a loquacious mood and proved to be a most pleasant, informative and interesting conversationlist. The other three mostly listened, each unwilling to break the spell of what grew to be a pleasant interlude with his peers, a pleasure seldom enjoyed by public figures without interruption.*

*The informal discussion extended into a talkfest that lasted until 4 o'clock in the morning.*

*During the course of the discussion, the conversation somehow got around to President Eisenhower. We discussed Eisenhower, the man, the soldier, the public official. Said Gov. Dewey of him, "Ike has his own private, personal pipeline to the American people."*

*I think Gov. Dewey's expression was very appropriate. During the war Ike, as we all referred to him, had his own private, personal pipeline to the American soldiers. It was especially well established to those with whom he met and chatted informally. From those who saw and heard him, and from the news media, the pipeline was extended to all those of his command. Because of this feeling of fellowship with Ike, the man, there was seldom, if ever, any criticism of Eisenhower, the General. We, of the rank and file, had the fullest confidence in his sincerity and good intentions, and never during the conflict did we have reason to question his military competence or ability.*

*To the American soldiers of the ETO, Ike was a good man and a great general.*

## THE CHANNEL CROSSING & LANDING

Lt. Braffit, myself and other officers and men of the 35th Div were recalled from the school at Shrivingham, England, before the completion of the course of study.

[Officers from the 320th Inf. Regt. ordered to the American School Center for the Military Intelligence Course were: 1st Lt. Homer W. Kurtz, Collinsville, Ill., 1st Lt. Larry D. Gilbertson, Alma Center, Wisc., 2nd Lt. Raymond W. Braffit, Watertown, Mass. and myself.]

We all knew what the early recall meant,—the division was destined for the Normandy beachhead.

Rejoining our respective units, we soon made ready. We loaded on the small compact cars of the English trains. As they moved out with whistles calling, we took our last look at the quaint, ageless, gray stone walls and the beautiful roses of Devon. At that season the scenes of that attractive section of Old England will always be indescribably beautiful, but they were even more appealing for battle-bound soldiers who knew not what their fate would be.

Reaching the port area we saw damage wrought by German bombers in a foray the previous night. The bombers returned again in the darkness and the mournful wailing of the English air raid sirens can never be forgotten.

Next morning, July 4, we loaded on vessels and set out across the English Channel in a "bridge of ships" that reached from coast to coast. The crossing would be termed uneventful. (Later I learned that the dock troops who loaded our equipment, stole from the vehicles practically all the stationery, toilet articles, candy, chewing gum and other such items belonging to the battle-bound GIs. Also, two or three days later a vessel carrying troops of another division was torpedoed by a German submarine with the loss of 400 American soldiers.)

The course seemed to be eastward and then south. It was a warm day of bright sunlight. Some of us gathered by the superstructure on the sunny side of the deck and basked in the warm afternoon sunshine. I gratefully soaked up the warmth on my sore head. My sinuses had been bothering me a great deal.

We joked, argued, discussed various subjects and made small wagers. Among those present I recall Lt Xintas, the Greek with the pleasant crooked smile. He was still feeling glad and proud because of news received only three or four days before, that he had become the father of a son. There were the idealistic Lt. Silverman; the labor union advocate, Lt. (CIO) Peterson; and two of our fine chaplains. Present also were the big brave officers, Capt. Swanson and Lt. Talcott and others.

[Our chaplains then were Capt. Alfred H. Stone, Elgin, Ill., Capt. Herman V. Tarpley, Daisy, Tenn., and Capt. Donald H. Hoag, New York, N. Y. Other officers were 1st Lt. Harold E. Peterson, Linwood, Calif. (There were a number of Petersons.—This one we called "CIO Pete" Peterson because he was such a vocal advocate of the labor group, Congress of Industrial Organizations of which he was a member. He and I played gin rummy for hours on the voyage across the Atlantic. He was communications officer for 3rd Bn.) ; Lt. Louis O. Xintas, Baltimore, Md. (another CIO man) ; Lt. Ward Talcott, Lebanon, Ohio; Capt. Thomas A Swanson, Corvallis, Oregon; Lt. Sidney Silverman, Detroit, Mich.]

As we approached the coastline of Normandy with the hundreds of ships scattered over the water, a storm approached from the southwest. The cloud obscured the sun and an early, unnatural darkness settled over the scene. As we anchored a chill wind speckled the sea with white caps. The forest of barrage balloons, flying at the ends of strong cables tied to ships and anchors as protection from the German dive-bombers, surged in the wind. A few broke loose and were rapidly bourne away by the gale toward the coast of France to the northeast. Jagged streaks of lightning flashed from the dark cloud followed by the roll of thunder. Some of the balloons were hit by the lightning. They burned with bright orange flashes, and trailing black smoke, settled slowly into the turbulent waters.

The early, unnatural darkness with the chill wind filled me with a nameless, vague, uneasy forboding of evil to come. I could not rid my mind of the troubled thoughts.

Later, when the wind had quieted and the light gray natural darkness was settling over ships and shore, the men gathered along the shoreward rail where they stood silent or conversed in subdued tones. We watched in the distance the flickering lightning and listened to the deep roll of thunder which was not of the heavens. It was the battle front near Caen, held by the British and Canadians, where the fighting then was the heaviest. Soon the grey light had merged into darkness.

From an airstrip on shore a plane took off and then, reportedly hit by lightning, fell in glowing flames to its death.

In the darkness the German planes came in their nightly raids. Unseen in the dark sky their drone sounded like the angry buzz of bumble bees. The ack ack and machine guns opened up, filling the heavens with streaks of fire and rosy bursts like the transitory trails of falling stars and the brief blooming of red flowers.

After retiring the men constantly tossed and turned uneasily in their swinging canvas cots. The constant squeaking made by their turning gave me the thought of creaking saddles on many horses, treading on soft ground as silent men ride through the still night.

I spent a wakeful night and re-called many times riding my saddle horse through the Ozark Hills.

The next morning we went ashore at famed Omaha Beach, wading the last few yards through the surf of the ocean's edge. We marched to an assembly area near the village of St. Clair, and shortly afterward entered the battle lines. Soon many of the men, who had tossed so uneasily on their cots the last night on shipboard, were as silent and still as only death could make them.

CHAPTER III

THE NORMANDY CAMPAIGN

Official Dates

June 6, 1944 to July 24, 1944

*WE ENTER THE BATTLE LINES*

*On the morning of July 5, we climbed down the landing nets on the sides of our ship and clambered into landing boats which took us the short distance to shore. The boats did not beach sufficiently to put us on dry land, forcing us to wade the remaining distance through the ocean's surf. Then we climbed the now historic and oft photographed sandy slopes of Omaha Beach, and marched to an assembly area near the village of St. Clair where the regiment awaited further orders.*

*While the regiment waited Maj. Jamison and I were sent on ahead to gain any information possible that would be useful. Taking a jeep and driver, we made our way into the battle lines to a regimental command post of the 29th Infantry Division where we spent the time, questioning, listening and learning from the battle experienced troops, until the 320th Infantry was ordered forward.*

*On the night of July 9, Gen. Baade, Commander of the 35th Division, issued Field Order No. 2 which directed the 320th Infantry Regiment to relieve the regiment of the 29th Division where Maj. Jamison and I were situated. At the same time the 137th Infantry Regiment was ordered to relieve elements of the 30th Infantry Division to our right. The men of the 320th moved into the lines on the night of July 9, effecting the relief before daybreak of the 10th. The troops remained in place the next day, familiarizing themselves as much as possible with the terrain, their own positions and the positions of the enemy. The units relieved by our two regiments merely moved over so that the 35th Division was now in the battle lines with the 30th Division on the right and the 29th on the left.*

*According to the 35th Division History of World War II, the first round of artillery was fired at 2051, July 9 by B Battery of Col. Reed's 216th Field Artillery Battalion. The Division received its first casualty, according to the history, on the night of July 10. About 1920, while Co H of the 137th was moving into position, eight rounds of 88mm artillery fire were poured into the area. One was a direct hit into the foxhole occupied by Pvt. Owen J. McBride, an ammunition bearer. He was killed instantly.*

*The 320th Regiment and the Division did not have to wait long for further orders. In response to a Division directive, Col. Byrne gathered his staff members and battalion commanders in the stone house command post in the Norman orchard on the night of July 10 to issue his first combat order. The format and procedure was the same as we had experienced in training on Tennessee maneuvers. But no longer were we playing games of war. It had already become apparent to us from the V-1s on England, the sunken ships along the shore, the battered French countryside and the awesome sound of artillery all around us, that this was the real thing. Not only were we faced with real combat, but we were up against an already battle-wise enemy in our German foe.*

*The 35th Division was a well trained and, for the most part, a well led military force. Perhaps we were as ready for committment to the battle lines as training could make us. Still, it seems to me now, it is most unlikely that any man, or group of men, can ever be completely prepared by training for actual combat. Men do not become battle-hardened and combat-wise until they have experienced the first few days or weeks of actual fighting. This initial combat experience is called the baptism of fire. No really good combat units exist until the men of those units have received their baptism.*

*I was more of a realist about actual combat than many of my comrades. There were many expressions of horror and amazement by some of my buddies at the wounds, death and*

— 151 —

destruction which occurred during the next few days. I can remember thinking, without expressing the thought, "Well, what did you expect? This is war!"

It takes some time to devise and transmit a battle order. When the Colonel's order was completed, the battalion commanders then returned to their posts, summoned their company commanders, if they had not already done so, and conveyed to them the order. The company commanders then did likewise with their platoon leaders, who then did the same with their squad leaders. The squad leaders then made known the orders to the members of their squads. When this transmission of the order had proceeded through the entire chain of command, all the men of the regiment were then advised and ready for the attack.

The ultimate objective of the Regiment and the Division in the attack was the Vire River south of St. Lo. I recall that after completing the order the Colonel, by way of dismissal and goodbye to the officers present, remarked, "I'll see you all at the river."

As the sober-faced commanders and staff members departed quietly into the dark night, bearing uneasily their heavy burden of leadership, I had the somber thought that in all probability we would not again gather in unbroken ranks for the next order as we had been privileged to do after training problems in the States. The thought was all too prophetic. Before the Regiment reached the Vire, some had come to another stream, - that river toward which we all journey and which we all must cross, leaving their surviving comrades to carry on.

At 0500, July 11, the Division and supporting Corps artillery opened fire on the enemy. Over 200 guns smashed at the German-prepared positions for one hour. Then at 0600, H-hour, the first of many for the Regiment, the Santa Fe doughboys "jumped off" in the attack. For the men of the 320th Infantry Regiment, the 35th Division and supporting units, actual combat had begun.

Camp Pittsburgh, France

27 January 1946

I must say that in the beginning I had no intention of writing the following, which may be termed a journal or diary. I just began to write one night, and kept it up at brief moments, during the many days of combat that followed.

Needless to say that now, since the writing is finished, and the men, the many, many men who made up the 320th Infantry Regiment, have reached the end of the trail as a unit, the writing is invaluable to me. Not for any amount of money, or anything like fame or fortune, would I sell the following words, if it meant taking from me the memories which they alone can help me to accurately recall.

I had thought that long before now, I would have made additional copies of the original to better insure that it would not be lost. However I have been so exhausted since the end of the war that I have been unable, up to now, to force myself to begin the task. Just recently a fire destroyed a building near by and scarcely anything was saved from the flames. It was a forceful reminder to me of how uncertain is the salvation of this one record, so long as I keep it with me in its present form. I am very often away from my quarters and the papers could so easily be lost from fire or other causes. Should that occur, it would be to me an irreplaceable loss and a life-long regret.

So now, although still tired and very listless and lacking in ambition, I begin, with a great deal of dread, the making of three copies of the original record.

\* \* \*

*I finished making the three copies with the help of a civilian stenographer at Camp Herbert Tareyton near Le Havre, France my last station in Europe before returning home. I mailed separate copies at different times to different individuals, and carried the original writing with me on the return voyage to the States.*

*After a delay of 25 years the writing is now being published.*

\* \* \*

# THE JOURNAL
## THE RECORD BEGINS

Normandy, France,
St. Lo Front,
July 11, 1944,

Time - 0120.

On duty in CP. The rest sleep around me. The telephone gets quiet, so I munch a D-ration and write. The arty thunders, both distant and near. Now and then are bursts of German MG fire from front, distinguished by a higher pitch and great rapidity of rate of fire. Our patrols are out, and I wonder if they have been unfortunate enough to fall in front of the deadly hail of fire. Now and then a mortar speaks —like a baby's cough compared to the thunder of the big stuff.

Two "Long Toms" belch near by, shaking the blackout curtains and causing vibrations in this house of solid stone.

The three young birds in the nest over my head are now sleeping quietly, quite some contrast to their noisy feeding during the day. They have been reared in strange circumstances and surroundings. I wonder if they will miss the thunder when the storm of war has passed on.

(This D-ration grows less tasty and takes lots of water)

The "Long Toms" speak farther back and I hear them [the projectiles] whispering in their flight overhead on their journey of death.

I wonder how many will fall tomorrow. Someone I know perhaps. (Today is now. I had forgotten the other day passed away at midnight). Certainly some one who has loved ones and wants to go back, even as I, or the ones I know.

[Where I wrote today I meant to write tomorrow. I began writing shortly after midnight on the morning of the 11th, but I was thinking of the time as July 10th in relation to the attack on July 11th.]

\* \* \*

Today I saw some pictures which a member of a friendly unit (29th Inf Div) had taken from the body of a slain German soldier. One of them showed ten Nazis (or Germans) holding a young girl on the ground while another snapped pictures of her "private parts." Her dress was up around her breast and all her lower person was bare. A German was holding each leg firmly, her arms were pinned to the ground by others, and another pressed her waist. There was every indication that she was struggling, but her body was twisted but slightly. They held her firmly and in good position for the shots. One photo was a close up. The other pictures showed her to be a shapely lass, apparently 15 to 17 years of age, dark-haired. Not much of her face could be seen as she had turned it from the camera. Those who held her were rather youthful, some only partly dressed, one having on only a pair of abbreviated shorts, and all highly amused at the sadly discomfited situation of their victim.

[The circulation of the pictures among our GIs had a beneficial effect. To them it confirmed the feeling that we were on the right side in opposing those who would commit such an offense. To subject an innocent person to such an indignity was completely foreign to the thinking of our idealistic young Americans. When they thought of such an act in relation to their loved ones at home, they were angered and became more determined in their opposition to the Nazis.]

* * *

WOOSH* - Barely had time to write the above. The Jerrys really threw in their stuff and from 2 o'clock to 5 they shook things all through our sector. The old house really vibrated a few times, and have I been busy keeping up with the situation. You can bet there were no drowsy moments. Some of the people I talked to weren't too steady.

Now 0540 - Going up to a good position to see attack jump off.

Our arty began at 0500. It's going good now, and boy! it sounds good.

0840 - Went up to front - got there about 0600 and jump-off had started. The lead was flying in every direction. They "whammed" and "whinned" by me in the road. I had to stop and deficate, so got Christofoli to watch one way and another man another until I had finished. [Using an abandoned excavated gun position]. A German with a machine pistol (judging by sound) was firing from woods and bushes and the bullets were flying over my head and over the road. I watched through the hedge but could not observe anyone. Lt Head[1] had some men and we thought of taking it out, but mortar fire began falling around the position [ours] and we got out.

1   1st Lt. Clifford M. Head, Co I, Topeka, Kans.

It was a job for light mortars, and after meeting the Colonel,[2] I took Maj Szabo[3] and Lt Kurtz[4] back and showed them the position. A platoon with light mortars from the reserve was to come up and clear it out. A German MG on right was firing viciously and some of the bullets whipped down the road we were using. Mortar fire was falling behind and eighty-eights were crashing beside the road as I came back. At one point, one hole was in the road as I went up; three holes were there as I returned. Miraculously no one in that vicinity had been hit while I was there.

I recall now how each man would duck quickly when a bullet would whiz close by or smack into the high bank of the road. Once when I ducked involuntarily as a bullet zipped into the road bank beside me, a soldier standing in the shelter of the opposite bank said calmly, "It ain't the ones you hear that hurt you." I agreed laughingly, a rather sickly laugh it must have been. I don't remember too certainly. But the ducking was not of one's own volition. It was an involuntary reaction from the angry whine of the close flying lead.

One PW had been brought in when I returned. A Yugo-Slav, he gave up and wanted to quit fighting.

Our forces have suffered casualties. One plat is reported down to 14 men. Reports are not very clear as yet. It is a beastly country for offensive, and the almost ever-present Normandy rain is falling.

I began to fall asleep when I returned, being up all night, and now the let down as the high pitch of the excitement of the morning begins to wear off. I am very tired now.

I can hear a German MG firing, and we curse the sound. The day's experience is putting hate and iron in the blood of those who survive. It may be costly, but we will lick the sons-of-bitches, and it may be we will wipe the Huns out. I hope the Russians do it if we don't.

Maj Jamison[5] has gone out. Lt Silverman[6] is helping run the CP. Perhaps the major will learn how bullets sound

---

2   Col. Bernard A. Byrne, CO of 320th Regt. Bradenton, Fla.
3   Maj. Joseph Szabo, 3rd Bn Ex O, served also in 2nd Bn Hq, Anderson, S. C.
4   1st Lt. Homer W. Kurtz, 3rd Bn S-2, Collinsville (or Troy) Ill.
5   Maj. George W. Jamieson, Regtl S-2, Oakland, Calif.
6   1st Lt. Sidney Silverman, I&R Plat comdr, Detroit, Mich., often referred to as Sid.

whipping by. I wonder, hope and pray that Lt Trask,[7] Sgt Cull[8] and Pfc Hugh Fritts[9] are having good luck. My thoughts are the same for all, of course, but war does not allow all to survive.

Two more PWs brought in by C Co. Sid and interpreter busy with them.

They keep lobbing 80mm mortars at us.

It is a world no civilian can ever know. Civilians can hide from the storm and wait and pray for its passing. We must go into the hell and finish the job. With sickened souls, despairing hearts and hate in our minds we must stick it out to our finish (in one way or another) or the war's finish. There must be a hell hereafter for men who wilfully make such hells here for us.

We have air and arty superiority, but weather does not permit fullest use of air. It is damned good to have.

Report from Lt Ginsburg[10] with unit on our left; says Germans have been captured in American uniforms. Also reports looting of bodies by enemy.

Now 0945. - Damned Huns throwing quite a lot of stuff into our troops just up front. Those mortars have a slamming concussion.

The bird still flies in and out feeding the young, but I fancy the day is a little worse than usual for them.

I am very tired, but I am a damned sight better off than the boys who are taking out the MGs and mortars.

Cpl Ostapczuk[11] just asked if I was still saving or collecting patches (insignia). I replied with a laugh that I hadn't much time or interest here.

1000 o'clock - I got sweaty this morning and now I shiver.

1008 - The two men who brought in PWs return and report they can't get back for snipers. They say one man killed by sniper about 150 yards from here. "We shoot the next prisoner," they remark. The iron creeping into their blood.

---

7  1st Lt. Eugene F. Trask, Co F, Washington, Iowa, often referred to as Gene.

8  Sgt. Wallace Brent Cull, Co F, Harrodsburg, Ky.

9  Pfc Hugh Fritts, Thorney, Ark., a home town friend even before the war.

10  1st Lt. Milton Ginsburg, Ln O, Regtl Hq, St. Paul, Minn., often referred to as Milt. He was liaison that day with 29th Inf. Div.

11  Cpl. Edward W. Ostapczuk, 320th Hq, Elizabeth, N. J.

I hear a sniper up the road now, and it sounds like a German rifle which has fired 5 times just across the road. Sid has taken his gun and gone out to investigate. The sons-of-bitches are making it hard on themselves.

Yes, snipers about. They killed one of our guards as reported above.

1045 - Maj Jamison just returned. He was under arty fire and shot at by snipers.

1100 - Battle with snipers just outside door and bullets are whiging about. Have learned Lts Coil[12] and Dunn[13] are casualties and also Capt Eckstrum;[14] Dunn seriously, others slightly.

1940 - Lay down at noon - slept soundly until 1630. I faded completely from the war and was dreaming of looking at shiny new articles as if I were going to set up a store; a little hard to come back to the world we are living in.

Have eaten my one meal of the day.

Two more PWs making a total of 11 today; Mostly foreign elements, Poles, Czechs, Slavs, etc. They say they want to surrender whenever possible but German officers and non-coms prevent. Only one German among our PWs.

* * *

Lt Zintas,[15] the pleasant, talkative, mustachioed Greek of 1st Bn, has been killed, and another officer of 1st Bn, Lt Braugh.[16] Lt Brown[17] and Morgan[18] are wounded. Zintas was a father not long ago and was as proud as could be. Now his son will never see him and he will not see his son. A very pleasantly argumentative fellow, a Democrat and a labor union man.

Father Hoag[19] just came by; dirty, bearded and tired. Having it better now, he says. They were very busy this

---

12  1st Lt. Arthur L. Coil, Co H, Enterprise, Ala., or Overland Park, Kans., seriously wounded, out for several months.

13  2nd Lt. David J. Dunn, Co H, Mt. Vernon, N. Y., evacuated, never returned.

14  Capt. Robert N. Ekstrum, CO of Co B, Minneapolis, Minn., seriously wounded, out for several months.

15  1st Lt. Louis G. Xintas, Co D, Baltimore, Md., KIA by arty shell July 11.

16  1st Lt. Raymond P. Brauch, Co C, Rockford, Ill., KIA July 11.

17  1st Lt. Kenneth H. Brown, Co B, Puente, Calif.

18  1st Lt. Henry G. Morgan, Jr., 1st Bn Hq, Birmingham, Ala.

19  Capt. Donald J. Hoag, Catholic Chaplain, New York, N. Y.

morning and got a lot of arty fire also. A Catholic and truly a man of God. I just remember now that he told me on the boat that he wrote something about me while back in training and would show it to me some day. "Father," I said, "If I get bumped off send it to my wife." "All right, I'll do that," he said.

2030. - Our arty really whistling over now.

2135 - Quite busy for some time now. G-2 paid us a visit; said the General[20] was quite pleased with our conduct; was quite happy with our situation so far. I did not like the expression "happy." How can anyone be happy over this bloody business. I don't guess the General is happy - just not disappointed over our conduct in battle.

While talking to Lt Braffit[21] over telephone, who was up in his OP, I heard shots and an involuntary curse from him. Presently he said, "That was not meant for you, Judge. (Judge is my nickname with many of the officers). There are some damned snipers about." Braffit is our newest S-2 and the best; a wonderfully fine fellow.

Talked with Capt Swanson[22] of 2nd Bn. Co G withstood a counterattack and four officers are casualties (none killed) and several men.

Lt Palmer[23] of F Co was wounded. Other officers okay. So Lt Trask is yet all right and hope Sgt Cull is also. If Margaret[24] and Evelyn[25] knew where their true loves were now, how their hearts would bleed. I wonder about my wife too (when not too busy) and my little bright-eyed inquisitive boy with the round head and so fair face. Perhaps all of them have spent a pleasant day.

\* \* \*

The French Lieutenant (American officer specialist assigned to us) got a native to take some laundry for Maj Jamison. On his way out he was picked up by one of our boys and marched in, and the Major had to get him released. Later I heard him asking the French Lieutenant to apologize for him, as he didn't know enough French. Amusing things amid the horrors of the battle.

20  Maj. Gen. Paul W. Baade, CO of 35th Div, Ft. Wayne, Ind.
21  2nd Lt. Raymond W. Braffit, 1st Bn S-2, Watertown, Mass.
22  Capt. Thomas A. Swanson, 2nd Bn S-3, Corvallis, Ore.
23  2nd Lt. Clark F. Palmer, Co F, Montgomery, Ala.
24  Wife of Sgt. Cull.
25  Wife of Lt. Trask.

Some one says that Maj Smith,[26] chief med officer, is a very tired and a very horrified man tonight. He is a good and pleasant man. It seems, so far today, that the enemy has not fired on our first aid and medical men.

The Comdr[27] of regiment on our right has been wounded (we learn) and evacuated.

Three more PWs making 14 today in the worst kind of terrain for such work. One of them today was an unshaven youth of 18 who has been in the Army for three years, Czech nationality, probably forced in German Army after fall of Czecho-Slovakia.

Some of the PWs look up when our arty shells are going over, and express the hope that we will give the Germans hell, as they made them fight against their will.

However as long as those soldiers, no matter how unwilling, sit out there spraying lead with those amazingly rapid MGs with a German NCO behind them with a pistol, they can kill about as many American or Allied soldiers as a bad SS man.

1130 [2330] - I am going to lie down and sleep now. Maj. Jamison will be on duty tonight. Stuff is plenty active now.

Wednesday Morning,
July 12,

0905

I had lost track of time until I "figured up" and determined the day of the week. [Wednesday] I remembered it was Sunday when we moved up because the French civilians were walking home from church as we came through the villages and the beautiful Normandy country-side.

I slept well during the night. I understand the Huns did not throw so much last night. Guess we knocked out some of their stuff yesterday. Just learned from our PW interpreter

---

26   Maj. Lloyd A. Smith, Regtl Surgeon, Tyler, (or Balaton) Minn.

27   Col. Grant Laying (of Conn) CO of the 137th Inf., evacuated, did not return. Gen. Sebree, Asst Div Comdr took over the regiment until Col. Harry R. Emery reported for command of the unit. The 137th Asst S-2, with whom I trained at the Mil Int School in England and whose name I have forgotten, had an arm blown off, was evacuated and did not return. Lt. Col. John W. Wilson, Comdr of the 219th FA Bn, was killed as was Capt. John R. Kerr, Arty Ln O. Maj. Claude N. Shaver assumed command of the 219th FA Bn.

that the Germans are using their "foreign element" troops as their outpost line. Behind them are Germans.

This morning we used a loudspeaker in an attempt to induce them to surrender. A number started out with their hands up but were fired on by their own forces from the rear. They jumped back in their holes and are now being shelled by arty from both sides.

Correction of yesterday. The guard at our CP was not killed by a sniper. The medics found he had been hit by shrapnel (we think from an air burst). He was not yet dead, and was evacuated to hospital.

\* \* \*

Both the old birds are inside this morning, and I think they intend to induce their off spring to try their wings.

\* \* \*

Capt Baer[28] and Lt Fitzgerald[29] of C Co missing. Hope they turn up okay, for Fitzgerald is one of the finest fellows I have ever known. He was in my stateroom coming over; a genial Irishman with a brand of humor appreciated by all who knew him. We had a lot of fun. He was always asking Lt Ginsburg, "Say, Milt, what is that thing I see sticking up out of the water that looks like a gas pipe?"

\* \* \*

100 - Our attack which started at 0800 has advanced about a hedge row on the left. This damned hedge row country is tough for advances. Perhaps while we engage the enemy here, our forces are advancing elsewhere (They are as we have learned). [At the beginning of this paragraph the time must have been 10.00 rather than 01.00]

\* \* \*

Maj Jamison returns from front, plastered with mud from falling into holes and ditches to escape mortar and arty fire. I guess Lt Gardner[30] got a pretty good baptism as he was with him.

---

28  Capt. Charles W. Baer, CO of Co C, Frederick, Md.

29  1st Lt. Joseph R. Fitzgerald, Co C, Hartford, Conn., a roommate on the voyage. Listed as MIA July 11. Later we heard that he was killed.

30  1st Lt. Frank W. Gardner, Ln O, Arlington, Mass.

# STORY OF THE RUSSIAN P. W.

A Russian PW was taken or gave himself up one night, to the unit we relieved, shortly before we came into the lines. He offered to lead a patrol back to enemy lines. He was given arms and American uniform and guided a patrol which took prisoners and knocked out positions. He is proud and glad to work with us, and has been assisting the Rcn element of the unit which took him. He said, "You do not have to feed me. Give me arms and ammunition and I will get my food." He said to a lieutenant, "You take one man and kill 20. I will take one man and kill 20. That will be 40 of the so-and-so."

He was taken prisoner by Germans at Minsk in first days of Russian war while wounded. He was forced into Nazi army and his papers show that he had never taken the oath of allegiance to the Germans.

He was very happy when told of the liberation of Minsk by the advancing Russians. He hates the Germans and is very glad to help us kill them.

*  *  *

We have secured other PWs who are willing to help, but have not made use of them.

Sgt Smith[31] of Chicago writes to his wife but doesn't say much of the war - principally he says not to worry that he is coming home.

*  *  *

Our arty going out with a wheeooo, wheoo, one after another. Now the arty close by goes off with a succession of whams.

*  *  *

1100 - I write this with ineffable and unforgettable sadness. Sgt Wallace B. Cull[32] of F Co has been killed. He fell in the first attack yesterday morning. He was young and brave and was leading his squad in the attack. No one told me before, perhaps because they knew he was my friend.

Sgt Koch[33] told me as he went by with his unit on the way back to the front. I went to talk to him and inquired how he was and then inquired of Sgt Cull. "Hadn't you

31  S/Sgt. William "Muscles" Smith, I&R plat, Chicago, Ill.
32  Sgt. Cull listed as KIA July 11. Sgt. Allen D. Hill, Clay Center, Kans., another sqd. ldr. in Co. F, got a projectile through the helmet which split the top of his head, but survived.
33  Sgt. Don A. Koch, Co F, Lima, Ohio.

heard?" he said. I shook my head, "No." "I hate to tell you this," he said quietly, "But they got him. He was the only one that was killed." I found it hard to believe. I asked if he was sure that he was dead. Did they have the body; could he still be alive. He told me, yes, that he was sure he was dead, that Cull was in the push; he went over the hedge leading his men; he was hit in the hand or arm and was trying to get back when they shot him in the back and killed him. Koch said the men dragged his body back part way but had to abandon it. He did not know if they had yet recovered the body, but it will be recovered and cared for.

0300 - July 13 - I now remember writing that if Margaret [the wife of Sgt. Cull] could know where he was how her heart would bleed. If she could have really known, that her true love was no more, and that his body was lying in the wet fields of No-Man's Land in far-away Normandy, perhaps even her life would have bled away, as would certainly have all the light and cheer and happiness in her tender being.

Perhaps the little son, Wallace Brent, Jr., who was born to her on the day that his father saw the last of America, [May 12] will be some consolation to her.

Nothing worse can happen to me now. He was like a brother to me. To lose my life would perhaps not be so painful. How I dread the news for Margaret, and it will also be inexpressably sad to Alta. He is another father who will never see his son.

July 13, 1944 Time: 0315.:

Terribly busy today after I learned of Sgt Cull's death, for which I am thankful, (for being busy). I could scarcely see for my tears at times, and at other times I cursed my troubles and at still others laughed mirthlessly at the strange and incongruous things which occur.

\* \* \*

We got 17 PWs so far tonight by our psychological warfare. Sgt Donovan[34] with guards brought them to CP in two bunches. The interpreters are now working on them in hope of getting something useful [information] for tomorrow. They are literally loaded with stuff, [matches, cigarettes,

---

34  Sgt. Richard A. Donovan, with 3rd Bn RCN unit, Baltimore, Md.

lighters, knives, watches, can openers, corkscrews, etc.] having enough stuff in their pockets to fill a small sack. I wish I had time to relate all their stories for they talk plenty and tell all they know. One old-like fellow, an Austrian, not too bright, says, "That guy Hitler has really been feeding us a line." Some are just kids with baby-like faces still unshaven.

The one new, a Pole, very intelligent, was only a rifleman, because they would not trust him with anything else. He is giving us a lot of information that will be useful.

One more PW making 18 during night.

The time is H minus 12. The arty barrage is going over and soon, in 12 minutes, the troops will again go forward and some will die.

\* \* \*

Oh, yes. My judgment of the birds activities was correct. The fledgings flew for the first time and all returned before nightfall to spend the night at home. Home what a wonderful word. The birds are going out again now. [mid-morning as I recall].

\* \* \*

Yesterday Lt Barthfield[35] was killed. A bullet went through his head from side to side piercing helmet on each side, and he dropped where he stood. A good officer and a brave man gone West.

\* \* \*

All sorts of wild rumors float around but here are a few things that have happened. One man hit in the breast by a mortar shell and his life blown out in one blast. Another practically cut in two by a burst from the amazingly rapid and deadly German MG. One officer is sitting with others. An officer is killed on one side and another seriously wounded on the other and he escapes unscathed. He has already had enough narrow escapes to fill an ordinary life time but carries on apparently unruffled. Lt Gardner picks up a man at the gate who can't even remember his name and we send him to medics to be treated for battle shock. A young lieutenant stands by the door, a strained look on his face, and suddenly gives way to uncontrollable sobbing. Major Hughes[36] and myself take his weapon and send him to the aid station.

---

35  1st Lt. David H. Barthfield, Co B, address unknown, listed as KIA July 12.

36  Maj. Harold V. Hughes, S-4, Oakland, Calif.

Lt Braffit comes in with his cheek swollen from a shrapnel wound, blood on his hands, begrimed and sweaty from doing the work of three men. There is nothing but praise from all who work with him. The calm voices of Capts Walton[37] and Frederickson[38] when I talk to them personally or on the telephone, as if they were talking of common place things, yet their tones weighted with fatigue and great weariness. Capt Hodgson[39] as excited as a fresh-kissed school girl, apparently expecting the worst and would perhaps get it if there were not cooler heads about. Perhaps he had good reason as he said Capt Swanson[40] was killed and Lt Talcott[41] missing. Lt Gilbertson, scared (almost as badly as I) and weary, and with a great longing to be out of this, but going up again to the front as one who knows his duty.

Sgt Donovan bringing prisoners in and Lt Kurtz bringing information, still calm and cheerful. Those of us who are about are heartily amused at the antics of the PWs and then I think with horror, (remembering Cull and the others killed) "My God! how can I laugh?"

\* \* \*

I keep the work of the CP going and hurriedly scribble in this and have neglected to write to my wife. Others have not written and for better reasons.

\* \* \*

Yesterday a war correspondent was here with a major from Corps getting the story of our psychological warfare or propaganda activity. (which secured for us the 18 PWs last night). The second time they were in the CP, the major remarked during the course of our talk and activity, "I believe I know you." He looked familiar to me, and we soon found that we were fellow Madison Countians. He was Maj Woodrow Anderson, son of Tom Anderson of Crosses. We used to play basketball on the same court, he with Crosses and I with Combs. We recalled many mutual friends and

37  Capt. William Walton, 1st Bn S-3, Newton, Kans.
38  Capt. Albert C. Frederickson, 3rd Bn Hq, Chicago, Ill.
39  Capt. George M. Hodson, CO of Co F, Brookline, Mass.
40  Capt. Swanson was listed as KIA July 13. It was said that he would have been coach at Oregon State if he had returned home.
41  2nd Lt. Ward Talcott, Co E, Lebanon, Ohio, listed as KIA July 12. According to my information, Talcott and Swanson were killed in the same engagement, but Swanson's body was not recovered until a day later. Talcott was a big man with fine bearing, highly intelligent.

acquaintances. Strange that after 15 years without seeing each other, we two from the quiet, peaceful hills of our homeland, should meet on a bloody battle field in far-away Normandy. We did not have much time for reminiscence and it is not much of a situation for that. [The war correspondent was Ira Wohlfert who wrote a story, "How a Nazi Quits" based on his visit to our lines.]

\* \* \*

0925 - Arty continues to roll and thunder. The enemy mortar shells slam into our lines and reach around our CP. The chatter of our MGs is answered by the deadly purr of the German weapon. Somewhere in the fight is Lt Trask. May God take care of him for sometimes a man cannot do much for himself here. But the sound of battle no longer disturbs Brent Cull and the other gallant ones who died with him. May they know the peace in the other life which was not theirs in this one.

\* \* \*

1515 - Capt Bonham[42] reports Capt Swanson as almost certainly killed as well as Lt Talcott. Also Lt Fessenden[43] reported hit, and dead when he arrived at the aid station. This not confirmed but fairly certain. Fessenden was a wonderful fellow; was in my stateroom on the way over.

Lt Fitzgerald, who was reported missing, turned up again. (rumor) The enemy shelling our forces pretty heavily now. He knows this terrain so well that he has every advantage on the defensive.

Said Lt Kurtz, "Another Casino," and I think he is right.

\* \* \*

2220 - The casualty list includes the name of Henry Hyden, seriously wounded. He is an acquaintance of Springdale, Arkansas.

\* \* \*

Captains Ulm[44] and Trossen[45] and Lt Oden[46] are wounded.

\* \* \*

---

42  Capt. Dwight D. Bonham, CO of Co M, Table Rock, Nebr.
43  1st Lt. William C. Fessenden, CO of Cn Co, Long Beach, Calif., listed KIA July 11, hit by white phosphorus shell.
44  Capt. Gerald K. Ulm, CO of Co D, Maywood, Ill., listed as LWA July 12, evacuated, did not return.
45  Capt. Kenneth F. Trossen, CO of Co K, Chicago, Ill., recovered and returned.
46  2nd Lt. Francis E. Oden, Co D, Ukiah, Calif., LWA on July 12, evacuated, did not return.

Must get some rest. I am about to fall over.

* * *

[Casualties[47] not mentioned in the Journal.]


July 14, 1944
St. Lo-Front
Normandy

Time: 2240 - Back on duty tonight while Maj Jamison gets some rest. I slept rather soundly last night after about 40 hrs of duty.

The Germans are shelling the Red unit's positions right now with mortars. I certainly feel for the fellows on whom they are falling. Shelling really puts the fear into a man.

Most of our casualties have been from shells. Comparatively few have been shot.

A few moments ago there was brought in the metal tail of a shell which was a dud. It had hit a soldier squarely piercing his body and killing him. The shell had to be blown to prevent others being injured should it explode. The tail metal piece is sent in for identification to aid intelligence.

* * *

Last night 18 men of B Co, who went forward on the first push on Tuesday morning, returned to our lines. They had pushed into the enemy lines and were cut off and pinned down by enemy fire during the whole time. It was on this push that Capt Baer and Lt Fitzgerald were lost. The rumor that Lt Fitzgerald had returned was false as he has not yet been found. Capt Baer visited this group each day and was to return early last night, but when he did not, the group of

---

47 Chaplain Hoag, evacuated as sick July 12, did not return. Father Hoag had a light heart attack during the voyage and when the ship docked was carried off on a stretcher. He recovered during the six weeks we were in England and insisted on remaining with the 320th. On the second day of the push, he suffered another heart attack.

1st Lt. Franklin C. Cech, Co G, Cleveland, Ohio, listed SWA July 11, did not return.

1st Lt. Eugene C. Levi, Co K, Phoenix, Ariz., a replacement, listed SWA July 13, did not return.

Capt. Albert Chiron, Med Det, address unknown, listed LWA July 10, did not return.

18 under Sgts Moen and Sullivan[48] made their way back to our lines.

*   *   *

Had some mail from home today. Was the first letter from Alta since she had heard from me after the sailing. Seems strange and out of place to get a letter from home in such an atmosphere.

*   *   *

One of the Regt medics was killed yesterday. He had too much nerve and would go anywhere for a wounded man. He was the fellow who liked to talk with me and "kid" about Arkansas when we were on Tennessee maneuvers. I learned to admire him then because he was so resourceful and so handy at building fires, cutting wood and such like chores. He and another aid man were after two wounded who fell up front. A mortar barrage was falling and he rushed out to get his man before the barrage could catch him. As he went over the hedge row a shell exploded in front of him and the shrapnel almost cut him in half. The concussion of the same shell knocked the other aid man on his butt. Another shell hit beside him and blew him over the hedge just where he wanted to go. He grabbed his wounded man and got back un-injured. The body of the dead aid man is still out there for the ground is controlled by enemy fire.

*   *   *

0037 - (July 15 now) I have just been outside for awhile. The night is as still as the death which is coming to so many. The trees standing in the quiet darkness, the damp dew on the grass and the gentle murmuring of the stream makes one think how nice it would be to walk with someone you love through the peaceful looking orchard. But the momentary flashes all around the horizon, like lightning before a coming storm, and the crashing thunder of the exploding shells makes one realize how far away is such a possibility. Two tracer bullets flash across the horizon shining out from the stream of deadly hidden bullets streaming from a MG position. Then "Jerry" cuts loose with a "moaning minnie" and it wheeeooo's its eerie arc across the sky and lands with a terrific wham within our lines.

*   *   *

---

48  Sgts. Moen and Sullivan were evidently from Co C; I have no further information on them.

Capt Baer returned to lines tonight.

From the details given by Capt Bonham there is small chance that Capt Swanson or Lt Talcott have survived.

* * *

Sgt Donovan and Lt Kurtz are displaying exceptional skill and courage in carrying out their duties in the lines. Yesterday Sgt Donovan brought in a wounded man of F Co who had lain wounded in front of our lines since the Tuesday morning push. How I wish it could have been Sgt Cull, but from all evidence there is now and was never any hope that he survived. I find myself wishing that he could have been wounded and could have recovered as the war ended, to go safely home. But thoughts and wishes, words, hopes or prayers are now to no avail. Thoughts of him bring only a depressing sadness and the pangs of what will be a life-long regret. Do the brave go first? Certainly it seems so, for he, Swanson, Zintas and Talcott were among the bravest of the brave.

* * *

Eight more PWs last night and one today. Our artillery is driving them in.

* * *

Lt Silverman and I and R men doing good work. Three casualties, none serious, among his platoon.

* * *

0555 - Jerry sure catching hell now from our arty.

Just spent some time censoring mail. A tedious unpleasant job, but the men here deserve every consideration, and anyone knows the Co officers are busy enough.

A comparatively quiet night. Got four PWs. Bet they are glad they are out of that barrage.

* * *

1000 - Second Bn has advanced with aid of TDs. TDs withdrawn but more going up. 2nd Bn fighting like hell. Gilbertson[49] calls for interpreters saying they had nine PWs at their CP. Maj Jamison, Lt Silverman and interpreters gone up.

---

49  1st Lt. Larry D. Gilbertson, 2nd Bn S-2, Alma Center, Wisc.

Major Szabo came down and got information from PWs taken last night on positions in front of Col Docka's[50] Bn.

Lt Braffit and three others, including one of the new officers, were in the enemy lines last night. They were fired on point blank at about 15 ft by a MG but escaped unscathed. They were pinned down for some time and fired on at other times but returned with valuable information. They found a wounded man who has been for two days in No-Mans-Land but were unable to bring him in. An attempt was to be made today. The new officer, a replacement who arrived yesterday, really got an initiation to the front. They were out in the salient to the right where Baer has been isolated and where Swanson and Talcott were lost.

\* \* \*

Capt Haley[51] says he just heard the radio news from London and they say there are eleven German Divisions in the St. Lo Sector, but that they almost all were understrength. No wonder we are having such a battle. But if it was not for this hedge row terrain we would soon have them licked. This about the worst possible terrain for an offensive, and, of course, admirably suited for either holding or delaying type of defensive warfare.

\* \* \*

1410 - The battle rages. Twenty PWs taken this morning. I saw Sgt King[52] who had brought in a bunch of them. He was haggard and weary. He said one of their medics and Sgt Woszniak[53] were killed this morning as well as others and two platoons of F Co pretty well cut up in the advance. The TDs helped them go forward.

Lt Trask was hit in the leg this morning but is still in the line with his men. May God take care of him.

The Huns are throwing their hellish mortar fire into our men now. We are throwing back artillery again and again but it does not seem to silence all their mortars. Almost all

---

50 Lt. Col. Clarence W. Docka, CO of 3rd Bn, Seattle, Wash.

51 Capt. William L. Haley Jr., Regtl Com O, Sioux City, Iowa.

52 Sgt.      King, Marion, Ill., a staff sergeant of Co F, close friend.

53 Sgt.      Woszniak, Chicago, Ill., plat. sergeant of Co F, a good friend.

Pvt. Birch Houseal, Co F, Memphis, Tenn., an acquaintance, wounded at the time Woszniak was killed.

day they fell on our troops and every burst was like the beating of a hammer in my brain. Now, 1920, the shelling has slackened and I hope the bastards let our boys rest. But we are not letting them rest.

Kurtz and Donovan, who are as cool and collected as anyone in the field, were in this evening and they were visibly shaken by the shelling they had undergone. Pvt Porta,[54] big, strong fellow, now wearing a fierce looking beard and handling a rifle and a bare bayonet as though they were toys, was in briefly. He was up in the sunken road today, the chief enemy strong point in front of 3rd Bn, but was driven out. He reported three direct hits today on fox holes in K Co, which means three fatalities. Captains Bonham,[55] Fritts[56] and Hodgson hit and Bonham evacuated. Others back in line. Lt Kuh[57] was hit but is back in line. I heard Lt Trask[58] was evacuated with a wound in the leg. Perhaps the war will be over by the time he is well, and he can go home to his wife, Evelyn. I can't help but feel thankful for him even though every man is needed. It is a very faint ray in the many clouds of darkness.

Capt Thomson from G-2 was down. [to our Hqs.]

I learned from Lt Kleigerman[59] that Sgt Cull's body was brought out and taken to the cemetery. I feel a little better that it was recovered and not left in the open fields of Normandy.

The front is relatively quiet now, and I must get some rest.

Time: 2000.

[A casualty[60] not mentioned in the Journal.]

---

54 Sgt. Louis A. Porta, Broderick or Sacremento, Calif., Hq Co, 3rd Bn. I instructed Porta in RCN and intelligence work at Camp Rucker and recommended him for promotion to Sgt but he was not promoted. Within a week after we hit the battle lines he was promoted.

55 Capt. Dwight D. Bonham, SWA, evacuated, returned in November.

56 Capt. Melvin V. Fritts, CO of Co G., Fort Valley, Ga., treated at aid station and remained in the lines.

57 1st Lt. William G. Kuh, Hq Co 2nd Bn, Montgomery, Ala.

58 Lt. Trask seriously wounded, did not return. My record lists him as SWA July 11. He was probably lightly wounded on that date, and received the serious wound on July 15.

59 1st Lt. Morton Kligerman, SV Co, Poughkeepsie, N. Y., responsible for removal of bodies from battlefield to collecting points for the military cemeteries.

60 1st Lt. Glen Mooney, Co K, Ozark, Mo., listed as LWA July 15, did not return.

St. Lo Front, Normandy
(SW of Village of St. Clair)

July 16, 1944

Time: 2345.

On duty as it nears midnight. Tonight it is rather quiet with even the arty falling momentarily silent. Braffit reports enemy sending up red and yellow flares, and Kurtz reports firing of tracers into the air.

Spent some of the little leisure time in talking to Lt Edmond de L'Cluse, the former French officer who is with us as a member of our MII team. He is very useful, not alone in getting information, but other things, as some French bread, butter, and the alcohol we are now using in our lanterns. [We used Calvados also].

Last night I slept almost like a log after I fell asleep. Just as I had lain down I heard someone calling, "Faubus, Faubus." It was Braffit bringing in some PWs who had given up. He wanted them questioned before he returned so he could get information on positions to his unit's front. They got some very useful information. That boy really works, and I would certainly hate for anything to happen to him. He has been through one war already (Guadalcanal in South Pacific) as an EM which should be enough for any man, but now he is here in this one. One war for a lifetime, I say, is enough, so I certainly hope he is lucky.

Some times I have this thought: If the human race does not find enough sense and Christianity in its make up to prevent war, it should be wiped from the face of the earth and leave it to the birds and beasts. But I do know that Isolationism, Republican or Democrat, will not help to find a solution.

\* \* \*

Had nine PWs last night. Lt Silverman talked to some of them. One bunch of five had made up to come in and surrender. They came in to our lines in three groups and when they all met in our CP inclosure it was really a happy reunion. One told Sid it was the happiest day of his life. (They chattered to each other like a bunch of happy chickens).

Some of these enemy soldiers are really in unfortunate circumstances. They are shot by the Nazis if they try to surrender and shot by us if they don't. Sgt Donovan actually saw two trying to crawl to our lines with white bands on their heads, who were fired upon by their own forces and forced to return. Many of them are ignorant and weak and easy to control. If they had more guts they would shoot some Germans and then come on over. But I guess it takes a lot of guts anyway as they have been told that we do not take prisoners but kill everyone. And a number have lost their lives trying to come in because some of our boys are jittery about things that move in the night.

\* \* \*

Our Red Cross man (Charles Glatzer)[61] talked to a Czech who was from the same town as were his parents.

Saw Sgt Parker[62] of F Co today. He dropped by to see me and to tell me of Cull and Woszniak[63] and others lost in his company. He is quite shaken and very hard hit at the loss of his friends. In such a case what consolation can one offer. What consolation can anyone offer me for the loss of Sgt Cull? There is none. None of our friends will be restored. There is only the prospect of further losses. So war is all that Gen Sherman said except there is more of it. But it is not us who need consolation. It is those who are near and dear to those who died.

I saw Capt Shumate[64] of the medics. He says Capt Bonham and Lt Trask are hit seriously enough that they will not be back. Both will survive all right if there are no complications. I am thankful, trusting Evelyn, that Gene will return to you.

\* \* \*

---

61 Charles Glatzer, Cleveland, Ohio, field representative for the Red Cross with our regiment. Each Inf Regt had a Red Cross representative whose duty was to convey messages to and from the relatives at home and the soldiers in times of emergency. A field representative could be helpful in many other ways to the soldiers. Glatzer became known as "Red Cross Charlie" or the French version of "Croix Rouge Sharlee." Of Czech descent, he was short, comical in attitude and appearance, and invariably cheerful. He was liked and respected by every man who came to know him. We couldn't have had a better Red Cross man.

62 Sgt. Parker of Chicago, Ill., (now Arcadia, Calif) was a long time friend from training days; full name unknown.

63 Woszniak, plat Sgt of Co F, Chicago, Ill., long time friend; full name unknown.

64 Capt. John H. Shumate of Med Det, of Georgia.

Today saw Lt Underwood,[65] the Missouri boy, bearded and haggard but carrying on. Saw Lt Garth Ramsey,[66] another soldier who is fighting his second war. He was still going great.

Lt Gardner just left to go back to Division. He is cheerful and shoots the bull as if he were on maneuvers. However liaison from here to higher headquarters is not as tough as holding the front lines or making an attack. However I think he has plenty of guts and can do any of it if it comes his way, which it may any time. He was caught in barrage up front the day we made our first broadcast to the enemy. (I can't remember what day as I lose all track of time) He, Maj Jamison, a war correspondent (Ira Wolhfert) and others were flat in the mud and water of the ditches. The shells were whizzing over and landing. One whizzed over, failed to explode and Gardner stuck his head up and exclaimed, "A dud!"

Lt Ginsberg seems depressed and goes about dejectedly and he has not seen nearly as much as the company officers.

Lt Kurtz was in this evening. Mail was delivered yesterday and he finally got around to his about 4 a. m. Among his letters was one from Veterans Administration telling him he had no insurance due to some technicality or "paper work" error. What a hell-of-a-communication to get under such circumstances. Said Kurtz, "Boy, if I had known that I would have been scared to death."

I don't know how Col Byrne[67] feels inside but he still goes about apparently calm and cheerful. However I wish he would settle down a bit and not be so prone to accept as news every good rumor that floats in. He is nice to everyone and is well liked and respected as any commander I have ever seen.

Lt Col Northam[68] is the same methodical fellow. I really think he would make the best combat commander. I hope we never need another but if we do, I hope he is the new CO.

There is not enough detailed planning in these operations. It's no use throwing men against these prepared positions

---

65  1st Lt. Stanley S. Underwood, Co E., Bland, Mo.

66  1st Lt. Garth C. Ramsey, originally Co H, now Hq Co 2nd Bn, Lakewood, Ohio.

67  Col. Bernard A. Byrne, Regtl CO, Regular Army Officer, Bradenton, Fla. He was well liked and known to all as Col. Byrne or Ben Byrne

68  Lt. Col. William F. Northam, Ex O of the regt, Columbia City, Ind. A Regular Army Officer, he was efficient and known to be fair in his dealings with all.

without a well laid scheme of attack and thorough preparation. I've been so busy doing my job that I don't know just where the fault lies. I am convinced that costly mistakes have been made needlessly. I think Swanson thought he was leading his troops still behind our lines when he fell to enemy machine guns. In the first push, troops on our right had orders to attack south when their lines were facing west. Had this been known perhaps Lt Fitzgerald would not have been lost and the troops with him. Some one failed to read a map correctly. [The Red Bn showed on its map that the enemy salient jutting into our lines on the right had been taken by our forces when it had not. The White Bn, acting on this information, walked into the German lines, resulting in the deaths of Swanson and Talcott.]

But all of us, at times, learn only in the school of experience, and every operation can't be perfect and we can't all go home from combat. However in this game the stakes are the highest and when the cards are down the loser cannot borrow to get back in the game. Therefore when others bet their lives on your hand, you should certainly know what cards you are playing. Whether it is good enough to win or not, is a risk we all take. Nobody should bet on his partner's aces and find he is holding deuces.

Two men from L Co, Pvts Shettleroe and Hale,[69] bring in a PW who gave up into lines. (I have been busy for some time.) They report an officer,[70] a replacement who had been with them only a few hours, was killed today while on patrol. The body was not recovered so it is not confirmed as the two men with him got away very quickly.

Capt Lynch,[71] L Co Comdr, was wounded last night and evacuated.

\* \* \*

0800 - [July 17] - Lt Braffit came in with a PW about 0645. Right now the Red Bn is in the attack and all the fury of the battle can be heard as we work here. We are spotting

---

69 Full names and addresses unknown. Wayne J. Shettleroe of Hamtramch, Mich., is listed in the roster but I do not know if he is the same as the soldier who was with Hale.

70 2nd Lt. Durwood L. Lott, Co L, McClinny, Fla., listed as MIA July 16; lost the day he joined the outfit as a replacement, was KIA.

71 Capt. Hilton M. Lynch, CO of Co L, address unknown, listed LWA July 16, did not return.

enemy gun positions from PWs and pass them on to the unit in the line or have arty fire brought on them.

The work now takes my time . . . . .

* * *

Only one Co Cmdr remains in Blue Bn, Capt English.[72] Capts Hardy,[73] Trossen and Lynch have been wounded and evacuated.

The battle has been fierce most of the time. Pvt Porta distinguished himself more in the lines. One company has assaulted one hedge row on the left sector six times only to be thrown out each time. All in the line begin to show the strain. A number are cracking, called "battle exhaustion" known as "shell shock" in World War I.

Even Kurtz and Donovan are showing the strain and Jamison and Silverman are looking haggard.

The White Unit is getting some rest today. The Red and Blue Units were pinned most of the day, but had small losses.

Eight more PWs taken during the day. Total to now, 91. I'm falling asleep, don't know if I can stay awake to chow time or not.

[Casualties[74] not mentioned in the Journal.]

St. Lo Front,
Normandy,

July 18, 1944

Now 1153 - Man, oh man . . . did I sleep last night. I awoke only once at 0230 when they were bringing in PWs. There were 11 more during the night. Total 102.

The enemy seems to have withdrawn during the night. They were driving in on his flanks using tanks. They would never give us any support of that kind or we would have gone on through. We have given the Huns hell anyway. Our Blue and Red Bns now advancing. The White now attached to Corps. We may move CP any minute.

---

72  1st Lt. Victor H. English, at first Ex O and then CO of Co M, later CO of Hq Co 2nd Bn; Portland, Ore.

73  Capt. John F. Hardy, Jr., CO of Co I, Chester, S. C.

74  1st Lt. Rupert L. Whittingham, Co E, Marshfield, Wisc., listed LWA July 16, did not return; 2nd Lt. Clark F. Palmer, Co F, Montgomery, Ala., listed LWA July 16, did not return; 2nd Lt. Claud D. Bell, Co B, Jamesville, N. Y., a replacement, evacuated as sick July 17, did not return.

Just heard that Sgt Englander[75] of 2nd Bn Hqs was killed last night by one of the German's infernal mines, and two others badly injured at same time. Also heard that Lt Kuh[76] has been evacuated with a shot in the knee.

At the Stone House CP,
St. Lo Front,
Normandy,
July 19, 1944

Time: 1150.

Just got this paper from Sgt Kearns. I think this is Tuesday. One finds it difficult to keep track of time. The days and nights seem to run together into one period. In a way this battle period seems like an eternity, and in another, only a brief time. But it does seem a long time since Sgt Cull was killed on the morning of the first push.

Just found out this is Wednesday, so it really is difficult to keep oriented as to time. So it was a week ago yesterday morning that Sgt Cull led his squad into battle in an assault on the enemy's prepared positions, and went out bravely to his death.

\* \* \*

Yesterday Lt Silverman with three I and R men were on reconnaissance with Capt Davis[77] for a new CP location. They were looking over an area. Capt Davis led the way down a path followed by Lt Silverman and then Sgt Ferran.[78] Pvt Reidel,[79] who was following Ferran, set off an S-mine. It sprang up to about the height of his head and exploded. He received head wounds from which he shortly died in spite of prompt aid by the medics. Sgt Ferran was seriously wounded as was Pvt Campbell[80] who was following behind Reidel. Lt Silverman was wounded in the hand, one of the balls passing through his fingers. All were evacuated.

---

75  Sgt. Englander, full name and address unknown, was a friend of training days.

76  Lt. Kuh recovered and returned after this wound.

77  Capt. Wilbur T. Davis, CO of Regtl Hq Co, Wyanet, Ill.

78  Known as "Big Buddy" Ferron of Mt. Shasta, Calif., a sgt in I&R plat., listed on regtl roster as Raymond P. Ferron, Palo Alto, Calif.

79  Donald F. Riedel, I&R plat, Cleveland, Ohio, listed KIA, July 18.

80  Bruce E. Campbell, a replacement for I&R plat., Mattoon, Ill.

So Reidel, the little fellow with the innocent blue eyes and fair face, is no more. His young bride of so few weeks, whose happiness with him was so brief, will wait in vain for his return until she receives the message so weighted with sorrow. Then she, like many others, must solve her problem as best she can.

Reidel was such a nice kid and reminded me, always, more of an innocent school boy than of a soldier. But he was a good soldier and was as useful here as anyone. The platoon will certainly miss Sgt Ferran who was one of the best we had.

\* \* \*

Just had a call (from the hospital) from Lt Silverman who calls for us to come bring him back. He could stay in hospital for 10 days but wants to return to the unit.

The war has rolled a little way from us today. The Division on our right and left converged on St. Lo squeezing us into a narrow sector, and we are to be pulled out I think. Probably be committed elsewhere.

But anyhow the men are getting a chance to relax today who have suffered hell for a week and more. The German defenses, from which they were forced to withdraw, are reported to be most complete and very strong. Two CIC men came by yesterday and went over to the German CP which fell into our hands. They report the system of defenses to be the most intricate and complete they had ever seen.

I think the General, after looking at the defenses of the enemy and the number of enemy dead, was completely satisfid with the effort we made in this sector.

Now that the thunder of battle has grown faint to us, it seems quite peaceful here. Some one out back is playing the same tune over and over on a harmonica. The ground is dry, but under gray leaden skies the burying squads are gathering the dead of both armies from the fields, hedges and ditches of Normandy.

At the Front,
Normandy,
July 21, 1944

Time: 0050.

On the 19th we moved and again today. This evening it was raining with some thunder and lightning. The evening was dark and forbidding, like that eventful one when we approached the shore of France before landing on the beach.

The vegetation is all wet and dripping and the Normandy soil is muddy and sticky. It is very dark, so there must be some doughboys who are very lonely and miserable tonight. The short darkness could be very comforting and protective to lovers if it were peaceful here. Instead it is very fearful and the awful stench of the dead animals and dead soldiers, completely overwhelms that [the fragrance] of the few roses and yard flowers which survive in the shattered villages and beaten country-side.

\* \* \*

The engineers are completing the sandbagging of some of our CP installations. They are plenty noisy and I'll be glad when they get away. There is the sound of a skirmish, slightly south of east, so I judge there is a raiding party in or behind our lines.

The "Bosche" are throwing over a bit of stuff. Some of the moaners go overhead and Sgt Kearns[81] says, "That Son-of-a-bitch sounds like it is not over 10 feet high."

Some of our own arty is firing from back of us and we hear the crack of the shells as they pass overhead before we hear the report of the gun.

\* \* \*

The Huns did some bombing and strafing last night, and also smoked a road over which one of our Bns was marching. After communications had failed, Sgt Gatchell[82] delivered a message to the Bn Cmdr personally after others had reported that they could not get through and the Colonel has awarded him the Combat Infantryman's Badge.

\* \* \*

Several "Moaning Minnies" coming in now and they are hitting not too far away. They sound weird and fearsome

81  M/Sgt. Kearns, in charge of Regtl CP operations, keeping daily journal and records. I worked with him many days in training maneuvers and combat. Older than most of the troops, he had received his training for administrative work in the CCC Camps of the Great Depression era, and was as steady and dependable as a well-ordered clock.

82  John E. Gatchel, Memphis, Tenn. He once rode to Memphis with me when we both were going on leave from Camp Rucker. All combat infantrymen were awarded the Combat Infantry Badge, but Gatchel was the first to receive it officially.

when everything else happens to be quiet. But the purr of their [German] MGs is to me the most hateful sound I have ever heard.

* * *

Lt Silverman is back on duty, his wounded hand encased in bandages. Pretty courageous and dutiful thing to do when he could have had at least 10 days rest and safety. He is living proof that a Jewish lad can make a good soldier. (Too many forget that Christ was a Jew).

* * *

We got indications from many PWs that something big was to be initiated by the Nazis on the 20th. The 21st is now almost 2 hours old and I have not heard of anything big by them.

The heroic Russians continue their onward surge, and we and the British and our allies are knocking the hell out of the German Army here in Normandy.

Our Division got a very nice commendation for its part in the capture of St. Lo (which I am making a part hereof as of this date). It was hell beating the Nazis out of their prepared positions but we finally did, and found heaps of dead Germans and abandoned equipment when we advanced. The few news reports I have seen, describe the fighting "as intense as that on the beaches on D-day" and on our sector it was.

But the commendation comes too late for Swanson, Talcott and Cull and the other brave who have fallen. While we who have so far survived are glad to receive the credit due us, I can say for most, it is small comfort. A few it seems are quite interested in promotions, medals and such, but they usually are those who already carry quite a bit of "brass" and spend most of their time in the comparative safety of a well-dug-in CP. I must say however, that there are no safe spots on the battle front, but there are places that are safer than others.

* * *

Last night I watched the troops of the line as they marched single file in the darkness, already footsore and weary after days of battle, up to the front in this new sector we have taken over. I thought as I have thought before, that there is no lot in the world any harder than that of the foot-slogging Infantry. I felt and prayed for my comrades in this situation as I never had before. The officers of the line really look beaten and haggard. One of them, Lt Head, has a wound in the thigh but is carrying on in the line. [He soon took over command of a company].

There is a "Bosche" plane up, and its hum reminds me of an angry bumble-bee. That reminds me still further that I am pretty far removed from the vari-colored holly-hocks in which I used to trap bumble-bees and which will soon be blooming in the peaceful door yards around the farm houses of the Ozarks. Or perhaps they are blooming now. One forgets so much. The war is our world and our life and the other one we know fades away. We remember most strongly when we write or receive mail. I'm sure it is best that we do not remember too much. Perhaps it is nature's way of protecting us from a memory that would be too painful because of its remoteness and inaccessibility. As for me, I have put my pictures and mementos away and may possibly not look at them again until this business is well over with. This I do know, that if an angel from heaven should appear in our midst at home, that it would be no more astounding than if some one dear to us should suddenly appear here among the carnage of the battlefield.

In such conditions as these, or even of the garrison or field life before battle, the wife or sweetheart or loved one assumes, to a great extent, the aspects of a perfect ideal or of a heavenly being. All of which John Steinbeck realized when he wrote, "Never, never again, will women seem so fair," to these men of battle. Women should (and do) personify all that is soft and warm, tender and kind, friendly and companionable, and these [qualities] a soldier craves and desires above all things and greater than any other. Those things are the opposite of what predominates on the battlefield. For the enemy there is hate and cruelty and sometimes fear. Among your own, duty and fortitude counts for more than love or kindness. If one cannot or does not perform his duty, he is useless to his buddy no matter how great his love for him. If he cannot endure the hell of the shells or the strain of the struggle, he be of no help, no matter how kindly disposed. [For the combat soldier] compassion, pity and niceties he must largely put aside, [control] for often he will talk with a buddy who will the next minute be dead, or a friend will have to be left wounded to die because enemy fire prevents his rescue, and sometimes the soldier will eat his food in the presence of and with the odor of the dead.

The higher leaders in any conflict do not always have to endure such. For many of them, life remains quite pleasant. Many enjoy more privileges and prestige because of a war. Because this is so, they perhaps do not dread or dislike conflict so much as the men who do the actual fighting and the work closely connected with it. Therefore I would suggest as a deterrent or preventive of war, the execution of all officers, both civil and military, of the losing side. Then men like Hitler, Mussolini, etc., all who start wars for conquest and glory, would hesitate before embarking on such adventures, and lesser fry would hesitate to serve them. It would not deter the leaders in the cause of freedom for usually they fight for a cause or an ideal for which they would be quite willing to die and which they would not want to live without.

\* \* \*

Now - 0347. - Occasional firing as if patrols were clashing. It is cold and I shiver.

\* \* \*

Two messengers from a friendly arty unit came into the CP a short while ago without ever being challenged by a guard. The security of this unit is damned poor. I just hope the damned Germans don't get through to raid the place.

\* \* \*

In "Stars and Stripes" of Monday, July 17, 1944, printed "Somewhere in France" there is the heading - "Yard-by-Yard Fight for St. Lo," "Battle Typified in Report: Took 3 Hedge Rows." I copy below the two paragraphs pertaining to our sector.

"United States forces at St. Lo held positions southeast, northeast, north and northwest of the town and needed to capture ground to the south and southwest to complete the ring. German guns from wooded hills to the south poured heavy fire on the advancing Yanks and threw in long-range fire in support of Nazi paratroop defenders.

"Advance Three Hedgerows."

"St. Lo was under its sixth successive day of seige yesterday. The fighting was as hard in its way as the first landings on the toughest beaches on D-Day, one field dispatch said.

The dispatch added that the whole story of the bloody battle could be summed up in one report which reached a command post outside St. Lo, 'Advanced Three hedgerows,' a sizeable bitterly contested advance in this kind of fighting."

The report, "Advanced three hedgerows," originated with the 2nd Bn of our unit. The advance was made with the aid of TDs. The report was sent in by me in the S-2 periodic report written for Maj Jamison. It is likely that S-3 also sent in such a report but anyway it came from our unit where the fighting was as tough as stated by the dispatches quoted above.

[A casualty[83] not mentioned in the Journal.]

The Division could well be proud of the following commendation:

## HEADQUARTERS XIX CORPS
## OFFICE OF THE CORPS COMMANDER

France
A. P. O. 270,
c/o Postmaster
U. S. Army
19 July 1944

SUBJECT: Commendation.

TO:        Commanding General, 35th Infantry Division

A. P. O. 35, c/o Postmaster, United States Army.

1. The capture of St. Lo climaxes an operation of major importance to the American cause, and brings to a successful conclusion the initial combat action of the 35th Infantry Division.

2. It was marked by repeated instances of personal and group heroism of the highest order and has earned for your division a place among the great organizations of American military history.

---

83 1st Lt. Robert H. Hoffman, Co L, Indianapolis, Ind., listed LIA July 21; did not return.

3. Please convey to the veteran officers and men of your division my pride in their achievements, and my sincere congratulations on a job well done.

> /s/ Charles H. Corlett
> /t/ CHARLES H. CORLETT
> Major General, U. S. Army
> Commanding

This letter General Baade indorsed to the units of the division, adding his own "sincere personal appreciation, satisfaction and congratulations" to each member of the command for his fine performance in this brilliant victory.

When a copy of this letter reached the United States, President (then Senator) Harry S. Truman, a Captain in the 129th Field Artillery Battalion of the 35th Division during World War I, asked for and received permission to have it inserted in the Congressional Record.

General Baade also sent a message to his men on the same day through the medium of the "Santa Fe Express," the Division newspaper, as it published its first overseas edition on French soil. In the paper the General said:
"Men of Santa Fe:

"You are now combat veterans. You have proven yourselves capable of taking your place in the line with the fine soldiers of our own Army and the Allied Nations. As we continue on the positive path to victory, I congratulate you for the glorious start you have made."


At the Front,
Normandy,
July 22, 1944

Time: 1040.

Have just come over to IPW Hqs, along with Lt Ginsberg, to shave. I have been working with them [the IPW team] and they extend me every courtesy. Yesterday I secured for them the services of an engr squad to clear up a more or less shattered French bldg for their hqs. They found one room with four walls still intact although the windows have been shattered. It leaked very much so they have shelter-halves stretched overhead. Lt Tischi, who headed the team, has now left us, but Sgt Martin Selling[84] and Sgt Leo Camp are still here along with Lt de L'Cruce. Capt Dolan is the CAC man attached to us.

\* \* \*

1625: Have just returned from a trip through the area. The villages lie in ruins, blasted, burned and crumbled. The area at the front lines has not yet been cleared of dead, and the cows, hogs, dogs and Germans lie dead and stinking, scattered indiscriminately along the roads and hedges and in the rubble of the ruined villages. One might adequately photograph the scene for others to see, but no one could ever fully grasp the horror and awfulness without actually being on the ground, not only to see, but to feel the presence of and to smell the sickening stench of the dead. Such has been this front from one arm of the ocean to the other, along the sectors held by the Canadians, the British and the Americans - but on this front perhaps a bit worse right now.

\* \* \*

This sector is relatively quiet at this time. In fact the rain has halted practically all operations throughout Normandy. The men have dug in and live in their dug outs like animals. An occupied area makes me think of a prairie dog village or a ground hog colony. The men come out for chow and to do the necessary work, and slither about in the mud as the Normandy rain or mist gathers on their net-draped helmets and falls in droplets on their raincoats or perchance down their collars. Occasionally some one falls in the mud and arises with one side well plastered with the sticky substance. A change of clothes is not easy or sometimes not possible, so the unlucky one goes about until it washes off, or if he gets inside, until it dries and then a part can be brushed from the clothing.

Our training during maneuvers in the mud and cold was certainly well suited to qualify us for life on the battle fronts of this region.

[A casualty[85] not mentioned in the Journal.]

---

84  Sgt. Martin I. Sellings, IPW team, Newark, N. J. He and Sgt. Camp were from Germany and one or both had been imprisoned in Hitler's concentration camps. They escaped to America, joined the U. S. Army and returned with us to Europe. They questioned the PWs for information of military value.

85  1st Lt. Francis J. Schrey, Co B, address unknown, a replacement, evacuated as sick July 22; did not return.

Now 0105 - So it is early Sabbath, July 23. I am on duty tonight, and all alone in this CP tent. The night resounds with the noise of shelling and counter-shelling. Except for the sounds of war it is quiet as only the night in the country can be. The Bosche have been sending over considerable stuff as if searching for our CP. Right now I hear the sound of a motor as some damned fool is charging a battery or more likely warming his feet. If I could get to him right now, he would know some one had handled him. I'll search him out tomorrow. Such a sound is a dead give away for enemy listening posts or patrols. Some people never learn by observation but must have an experience, and in this game the price of a lesson may be a human life.

My feet are cold and damp, so I have lighted a candle and placed it on the ground and by placing my feet over it in a chair I get some warmth. These deep fox holes the men have dug are fairly warm. If it is possible to get into one with fairly dry clothes, one is fairly comfortable.

\* \* \*

The Hun planes are up. I hear their peculiar, angry buzzing.

\* \* \*

Capt Leach[86] just called from Blue Bn and reports all fairly quiet.

\* \* \*

Capt Haley calls to say the recent shelling cut two of our telephone lines but we still have communication.

\* \* \*

I hear some one whistling along just as if there was not a war on. Some of the Hqs boys need a little initiation to the front lines. But some of them may get too much before it is over. Lt Gardner has been given Command of Co B. He will get his captaincy now if he is not unlucky. Lt O'Brien[87] is now LO.

\* \* \*

Saw Capt Hare,[88] Capt Fritts, Lts McCoy[89] and Gilbertson when at White Bn today. Lt Col Keator[90] seems a little

86   Capt. James A. Leach, now with 3rd Bn, Davenport, Iowa; transferred from SV Co.
87   2nd Lt. Samuel G. O'Brien, Des Moines, Iowa, now Regtl LO.
88   Capt. Henry H. Hare, Hq Co, 2nd Bn, Los Angeles, Calif.
89   1st Lt. James H. McCoy, Co G, Walla Walla, Wash. Short and red headed, he became known as "Fighting James McCoy."
90   Maj. Vincent Keator, CO of 2nd Bn, Thoenicia, N. Y.

the worse for wear but others seemed fine. I never thought Capt Hare would stand up so well as he is a bit more aged than others, not much of an outdoor man, and back in garrison seemed as excitable as an old hen with a brood of ducklings that had jumped into the water. Here he carries on fine and seems more settled and calm than others, and his unit has had plenty of hell. One cannot always tell who will stack up in combat and who won't.

A 2nd Lt[91] there, (I know him but can't think of his name) who has the job of helping to collect the battlefield dead, was complaining angrily that someone had stolen his trailer which was filled with German bodies. "And," he added "they didn't even bother to dump out the dead Krauts."

\* \* \*

Over on the road some guard halts the vehicles and calls out the sign and gets the countersign in answer, loud enough to be heard here clear across the draw. The distance is more than 100 yards, so a Nazi soldier with an understanding of English could easily pick up those vital words at quite some distance. I reckon some people are born dumb and stay that way. Hear that motor running again. Guess his feet are cold once more. If his fool luck runs out and a German gets a chance at him, his feet will never be warm again.

Hear a MG suddenly speaking in the night. One of ours. So some one is jittery or a German patrol is active.

On duty all night - very cold and damp . . .

Normandy Front.
July 23, 1944

Time: 1010.

This Sabbath has been relatively quiet. Except for an occasional salvo, the artillery of both sides seems to have been observing the day by remaining silent. There has been quite a little activity on the front, perhaps indicative of renewed attacks by enemy, or perhaps he was seeking information.

There was a flurry of activity about an hour ago when some Jerry planes came over.

---

91 Probably 2nd Lt. Charles E. Scovel of Sv Co, Battle Creek, Mich.

\* \* \*

I have come over to S-2 tent where Cpl Ostapczuk, Pvt Bock[92] and myself have been kidding Sgt Smith. Lt Silverman was an interested on-looker. He is trying to get Sgt Smith "on the ball" as we say, but he will have a time and is certainly an optimist to even attempt it, or so we told him in Smith's presence. Smith says he is only 24 years old, but is slower than I am, if that is possible. I often tell him I don't know how he could have gotten so slow in 24 years.

\* \* \*

Have written a few letters today; kept thinking of Sgt Cull and the others who were killed. Some more of us will go in this next push.

[A casualty[93] not mentioned in the Journal.]

Normandy,
24 July 1944

Time: 0850.

No rain yesterday, or today as yet, but skies are heavy and grey. The ground has dried somewhat. I am writing in S-2 tent again where I can continue my kidding of Sgt Smith. He is going to bed now.

A new officer has joined us, assigned LO, Lt Clark,[94] who has been to Fayetteville a number of times while stationed at Camp Gruber, Okla. His home is up-state New York.

\* \* \*

Last night Lt Kurtz, Blue Bn S-2, and Sgt Porta (recently promoted because he showed up good in combat) were visiting Co I CP while sending out patrols. They, along with Lt Head, Lt Brochu,[95] Sgt Stein[96] and a Bn runner had taken shelter in the dug-in, sand-bagged CP when the Huns be-

---

92  Pfc. Richard J. Bach, Regtl Hq, Little Rock, S. C., who came to America from Germany.

93  2nd Lt. Grover C. Roberts, Co B, Pine Bluff, Ark., listed as MIA July 22. He did not return. I heard much of Lt. Roberts but never knew what actually happened to him until the publication of this book.

94  1st Lt. Glen L. Clark, a replacement, assigned as Ln O, Regtl Hq; Potsdam, N. Y.

95  1st Lt. Charles P. Brochu, plat ldr, Co I; Cleveland, Ohio.

96  1st Sgt. Leslie R. Stein, Co I, address unknown, who joined the 320th at Camp San Luis Obispo.

gan shelling their positions. The CP sustained a direct hit on the roof from a 80 mm mortar shell and not a single occupant was injured. Kurtz said all that came through was the flash, the smoke and the roof. It was evidently a contact fuse shell which exploded as soon as it struck. Had it been a delayed fuse type, it would have pierced the dugout and exploded inside, and all would probably have been casualties.

Said Kurtz, "That's as close as I ever want to come to getting squibbed" and then he added "Lt Head immediately grabbed his helmet and began looking for a new CP." Sgt Porta seemed only amused by the incident.

\* \* \*

Quite a bit of shelling during the night but pretty quiet now. Fortunately they have not zeroed in on our present CP as yet.

\* \* \*

Time: 2400 - On duty again tonight. Have just talked to White Bn. Lt Underwood[97] was killed a short time ago by mortar fire. He was a rather close friend of mine, being from Missouri, and we had some mutual acquaintances. One was James Farrar of Springdale, Ark. Underwood was a practical, down-to-earth fellow, a real good useful officer of the line.

Have been listening to a MG duel. God, how I hate the sound of that Jerry gun.

Those damned mortars keep ringing out in the still night.

\* \* \*

Heard that same motor again tonight. Finally found out who was running it, so I think the Colonel will have it silenced.

\* \* \*

Went back to shower room set up in the rear areas today, had a bath and a change of clothes. First clean clothes in three weeks; made me feel both good and bad. If you happen to get a touch of the comforts of peace and civilization, it brings back a longing for them that hurts and hurts. Otherwise one seems to be reconciled to the conditions and danger until it becomes quite bearable.

---

97 1st Lt. Stanley S. Underwood, plat ldr in Co E, Bland, Mo., listed KIA July 24. He joined the 320th when it was activated.

The shower installations were being run by a Negro unit. Men were being brought in from units in reserve and in rest areas. They were let in, so many at a time, were given about 3 to 5 minutes and then when a whistle was blown, stepped out to make room for the next bunch. I don't guess Lt Underwood ever got a chance to go there for I think they started only yesterday.

* * *

The linemen were stringing wire along the road to St. Lo on new poles just set up to replace those cut down by the retreating Germans. The lines go forward before the area is cleared, for I noticed a dead Kraut still in the ditch beside the road.

It is very cold and damp in this CP tent.

I am trying the field expedient of two candles underneath a chair again tonight to keep my feet from freezing.

* * *

A mortar shell on this CP would not see us with the luck of Lt Kurtz and company, for there is only the tent overhead, and the sandbags reach only part way up the walls.

* * *

I have written several letters today, the rather quiet front giving me more leisure. The radio news tonight reported the quietest day on the Normandy front since D-Day. I think of the story, "All Quiet on the Western Front" [a story of WW I]. I remember it said of the principal in the story, "He fell on a day in which there was so little activity that the newspapers reported the front with the line, "All Quiet on the Western Front."

So fell Lt Underwood, [in this war] perhaps our only fatal casualty of the day.

* * *

The bath and change of clothes and writing so much has made me think of home. Hope Aunt Ada [McChristian] takes care of mother's grave in that lonesome little cemetery on the Ozark hillside. But I know she will, for she is a very helpful and tender hearted person.

* * *

Now 0054. - Firing and shelling in the night continues.

* * *

While going through the Red Bn's lines today with the Colonel, Lt Braffit accompanied us. As we went along he told me something more of his experiences, when we had so much hell in the other sector. He virtually led the attack of that Bn on the occasion of which we talked. A BAR man, Mike D'Rrico,[98] advanced with him. Said Braffit, "He was just about ripped open by a machine gun and fell near me when we were all pinned down. He said to me, 'Lieutenant, can't you do something for me?' There was nothing I could do. Then he began to say his prayers and died there beside me. Faubus, when you hear a man say his prayers like that and die, you just can't forget it."

Braffit said also that he had been thinking about "Old man Barthfield." Certainly Barthfield was a good officer and one of the bravest of the brave. I can remember well when I first got to know him, a long time ago, it seems, at Camp Rucker, Ala.

\* \* \*

Now working with Maj McElroy[99] as assistant S-3, a change of two or three days ago. My NCO help, Cpl Bridgewater[100] of Tulsa, Okla., and Sgt Kearns.

\* \* \*

Lt Silverman making a good asst S-2.

Those damned Huns really throw a lot of mortar fire tonight.

\* \* \*

Had a letter from Mrs. Ledford today. She told me of all the boys who were teaching at the schools where I once worked, etc. Her talk of crops, canning and frying chickens [broilers] made me somewhat homesick. (Wish those damned mortars would stop. They bother me sitting here alone). Also had a letter from one of my former pupils of Pinnacle Community, Oscar Dunaway, who is now in South Pacific.

\* \* \*

98 I could obtain no further information on Mike D'Rico and am not even positive of the spelling of his name. The regimental roster, published after the war, was incomplete and so mixed up that it was of very little help in research.

99 Maj. Thomas P. McElroy, (a captain at Camp Butner) Regtl S-3; Grand Forks, N. D., who joined the 320th when it was activated.

100 Cpl. Odie H. Bridgewater, S-3 section of Regtl Hq; Tulsa, Okla.

Mention of the South Pacific reminds me of what Lt Braffit said of that area. He was through the Guadalcanal Campaign and others. He said the fighting there did not compare to this. According to him the Japs do not approach the Germans in the use of any weapon and also the German weapons are much better. They had some tough spots there of course, but it was much easier to lick the Japs there than the Huns here.

Of course the terrain here has been one big obstacle to us. These stone and dirt hedge rows with their tough hedge growth are really hard to get over. The fact that we can get over and lick the Bosche at the same time, is proof that Hitler's army is nearing its end.

* * *

Time: 0250 - Have just been out and looked around. The night, so far as nature is concerned, is as still and quiet as one could ever see. The sky is clear, the stars looking down, and the Big Dipper now hanging low over the northern horizon. Some night insect in the brush of the ravine close by was calling lonesomely, but I could barely catch his small voice once in awhile, for the horizon is lit by the flashes, and the night echoes and re-echoes with the reverberations of the big guns and of their exploding shells of death and destruction. Some, because of weariness and exhaustion, sleep in spite of the noise; others stir fitfully in their fox holes or sandbagged dugouts, and think of home and pray. Others stand on guard, watching uneasily the fitful, momentary shadows revealed by the cannon's lightning, ever faithful and vigilant that their buddies may be secure from surprise if not from danger in their uneasy rest. Others, like my friend, Lt Underwood, have joined the ranks of those who sleep the long sleep, silent and undisturbed, unconscious of the quiet stars as of the fury and noise of the raging man-made hell, to wake no more until the trumpet blast shall call them all from their long rest into that other world.

[Losses[101] not mentioned in the Journal.]

---

101 Near the end of the Normandy Campaign Lt. Col. Harry A. Beckley, Comdr of 1st Bn, York, Nebr., left the Regt. He did not return. About the same time Capt. Charles W. Baer, CO of Co C, Frederick, Md., was evacuated and did not return.

S/Sgt. Archie L. Jones, Co F, Haynes, Ark., joined 320th at San Luis Obispo, wounded and evacuated in fighting at St Lo, later returned.

[This letter was written to my hometown newspaper on July 24, but did not reach it until much later.]

AT-THE-FRONT, NORMANDY
July 24, 1944

Dear Home Folks,

As our lines are static today and somewhat quiet, I have a bit of leisure - and thus these lines to you.

I said it was rather quiet, but I can remember times when I would have considered it noisy. For there is still the drone of the planes overhead; the roar of our artillery and, what is of more concern, the thunder of the Bosche shells coming in; and along the front lines the wham of the mortars and occasional bursts of machine gun and rifle fire. But it doesn't sound like much after the terrific battles of the past several days of which the taking of St. Lo was a part.

Shall I write to you of Normandy? To speak of it now would be but to tell you of war, for it wholly prevails in the sections I have seen. One of my fellow officers while gazing with solemn face and sad eyes at the scarred countryside remarked, "To appreciate the beauties of Normandy one must close his eyes and think of peace."

That is true. For the once quaint and ancient stone villages are now blackened, shattered wrecks. The buildings that remain standing have great gaping holes, the windows shattered to bits and the walls scarred by the marks of many bullets. The fields and gardens are crisscrossed with the tracks of war vehicles, trucks and artillery and the heavy tread of tanks, and pockmarked with the craters of exploding shells. The apple trees of the once picturesque orchards are smashed by shells or their branches clipped and scarred by the flying shrapnel. Here and there in the woodlands a tree has sustained a direct hit and toppled crazily to the ground. Along the many fences and hedgerows are numerous holes, where men have burrowed into the earth like animals to escape the hell of fire which wrought all the havoc with the formerly peaceful and beautiful countryside.

And instead of the sounds of peace, as the cackling of hens and the quacking of ducks about the farmyards, or the lowing of cows from the pastures, or the calls of urchins playing along the paths and hedges, there reigns over all the sounds of war. Along the zone of action one can no longer catch the scent of the clover or the fragrance of the few surviving roses, for overwhelming all other odors is the awful, horrible stench of hogs, cows, dogs and men lying dead together, all alike slain by the bursting shells and the flying bullets.

I'm sure that if any of you could see this war ravaged country, you would be thankful that you are an American, and that the war is being fought over here instead of our own country. And that reminds me that in my few brief thoughts of other things, I noticed in a clipping received from home, that Congresswoman Clare Booth-Luce made the statement at the Republican Convention that, "G. I. Joe need not have died had it not been for Franklin D. Roosevelt." That statement is idiotic in the extreme. No matter who had been president or what party had been in power, we would have had to fight Hitler. I think we should have started sooner, and certainly if we had waited much longer we would have been fighting in America instead of over here. Any criticism of the President because we went to war is entirely misguided or malicious, and no doubt he has made as great a war leader as we could have found.

I hope our good Congressman, Bill Fulbright, goes to the Senate. I guess that will be decided by the time this reaches you.

It seems queer to be thinking of other things out here in the battle lines. But after being here and realizing the awful things Hitler and his henchmen have done, it gets under my skin to hear of any unjust criticism of anyone who is fighting or working against the Nazis. They have practiced every atrocity known on the unfortunate peoples they have conquered. I have heard the stories from these French people whose sons and daughters have been taken away for whatever purpose the Germans saw fit. I have heard the tales of the prisoners-of-war whom I have helped handle by the dozens and scores; unfortunate Czechs, Poles, Austrians, Yugo-Slavs and Russians who have been impressed into Hitler's army to fight against us and their own people. We have actually seen them being fired upon by the Germans while trying to escape to our own lines. Last night's report is typical: "Took one PW and seven Russians escaped from the Germans into our own lines." You can guess of course that such prisoners are very useful to us.

We also get good evidence of their barbarities from real Nazis, as letters, orders, photographs, etc. One in particular I remember, a photograph taken from the body of a dead German, showing ten of them holding powerless a young French girl who had been stripped of her clothing, while another photographed her nude form from various angles.

Of course you know what the Japs have done to our men and women, so I need say nothing of that. However I guess some hair-brained Isolationists will say that we started the war with them at Pearl Harbor.

I say to you in all sincerity, as one who has seen enough of war, that there must be worked out some international plan to keep the peace, so that the next generation will not have to go through a man-made hell like this in which we are now living. Any person or any party who works to bring about such a plan will be a friend of humanity. Anyone who opposes it because he wants to live alone or for any other reason, will be as the blind leading the blind to destruction.

As to the war with Germany, the powerful surges of the Red Army, the bombings and unrest in Hitler's domain, our gains in Italy and our successful invasion here in Normandy, all are rapidly spelling out the Nazis' doom. I have bet just about all my money that this war will not go beyond November 11. I feel confident of winning, but it is sometimes a little questionable whether the loser will be around to pay or the winner to collect. The major with whom I work made bets with three officers, of whom I was one. The other two have been killed in action.

As for me, I am well and healthy, but I don't think I could have been hurt any worse if I had been hit, than when the enemy killed my nearest and dearest friend on the morning of our first push. He was young and brave and was leading his squad in an assault on the enemy's prepared positions. He was so young and fair and gentle and loved his wife so much, that it doesn't seem right that he should have died. My heart breaks when I think that he is gone and that his lonely wife will wait with such longing until she receives the messages so weighted with sorrow and despair. His little son, born on the day we saw the last of America, and named for him, will never see the man who would have been such a wonderful father to the little boy.

Other good men, many of them my close friends, have gone West since we actively entered into the conflict. Scarcely a day passes without some face is missing that will not be seen again. But we are beating the hell out of the Bosche. The prisoners taken far outnumbered our killed and we advanced over a battle field strewn with his dead.

We have lots of equipment, but perhaps if we had a few more tanks or planes, we might have saved some of our lost. Did you report for work today, or buy a bond? Or is the war loan drive lagging? Or are you grumbling because the debt is too large (as I heard when there) and it will take some of the filthy lucre from your pocket to pay it? Give your answer to us on the battlefield, not in words, but in deeds and results. This war is not yet finished and there is another one to win. The whole damned debt, enormous as it is, does not equal the destruction being wrought in this country or Russia, and does not equal the life of my fair young friend who now sleeps forever in a soldier's grave in Normandy.

Best Wishes,
Lt. Orval E. Faubus

### LT. JOHNSON OF SWEDEN

*During the combat period in Normandy, a Swedish officer was attached or assigned to the 35th Div Hqs. Sweden was a neutral country but when the Nazis occupied Norway it became apparent to many Swedes that the residents of their country would have only the limited freedom which Nazi Germany permitted them to exercise, and that their sovereignty as a nation might be completely destroyed if Hitler won the war. With this realization many Swedes fled the country, some joining the Allied forces to help fight the Nazis. Among the latter was the officer attached to our division. A part of his duties was acting as liaison officer from 35th Division Headquarters to other units and to the regiments. In this capacity we saw him frequently at the 320th Headquarters.*

*As a youth I had often read the jokes in the farm magazines from the midwest, jests which often spotlighted the mispronunciation of English words by the Scandinavian residents. The most common was the sounding of J as Y which I had never heard, and consequently often wondered if it was an exaggeration. My experience with the Swedish officer, apparently a fine fellow in many ways, removed the doubt.*

*The code name of Division was Justice, the Regiment, Juniper, and the Swede's name was Johnson. As he reported by telephone to Division, on his visits to our headquarters, I was often amused to hear the following.*

*"Hello, Yustice! This is Lt Yohnson. I am over at Yuniper."*

## NORMANDY CAMPAIGN ENDS,
## NORTHERN FRANCE BEGINS

*July 24 officially marked the end of the Normandy campaign. St. Lo, at the center of an important road network, had fallen. Other troops farther west had driven to the sea on the southern coast of Normandy and then mopped up the German forces cut-off in the Normandy Peninsula. Allied forces now controlled good seaports, and beaches other than Omaha and Utah for the landing of men and supplies.*

*During the 320th regiment's more than two weeks of combat, some of us who survived had begun to become familiar with the upper echelon of command, with other units of the Division and the organizations which supported us.*

*The figure of our division commander, Maj. Gen. Paul W. Baade, with his ever present carved walking stick which he used to point and direct as he gave commands and instructions, became more and more familiar. We grew accustomed to the sight of our assistant division commander, Brig. Gen. Edmund B. Sebree, who became known as "The Doughboys' General" because he was so well liked and respected by junior officers and enlisted men.*

*Many of us came to know well the voices, the figures and the mannerisms of the following: Col. Maddrey A. Solomon, Div. chief of Staff; Lt. Col. Don Ashlock, G-1; Lt. Col. John T. Hoyne, G-2; Col. Walter J. Renfroe, Jr., G-3; Lt. Col. Delbert C. Lefler, G-4; and other staff members.*

*Brig. Gen. Theodore L. Futch commanded our Division Artillery. The 216th FA Bn. supported our regiment. Its commander, Lt. Col. Kenneth H. Reed of Horton, Kans., and* all his officers and men soon came to seem almost a part of our own outfit.

Col. Butler B. Miltonberger of Nebraska, Commanded the 134 Infantry Regiment. We had come to know him and some of his officers and men as Lt. Col. Alford C. Boatsman, commander of his 1st Bn, and Lt. Col. Alfred Thompson of Omaha, Nebr.

Col. Layng, commander of the 137th, was lost the first day of the attack, July 11, and was succeeded by Col. William S. Murray. Two of the 137th Battalion Commanders were Lt. Col. Albert M. Butler, Hastings, Nebr., the 3rd Bn, and Lt. Col. George T. O'Connell, Emporia, Kans., the 2nd Bn.

The 60th Combat Engineer Bn was attached to the Division to build and repair roads and bridges. This the men of the outfit often did while helping our 320th Infantrymen fight off the enemy. The battalion was commanded by Maj. Edwin C. Pumroy.

The 448 AAAW Bn moved always with us to protect against German aircraft. It was commanded by Lt. Col. James Floyd Eason of Roanoke, Va.

Then there were other units moving with us in support when they weren't being used elsewhere, and whose men and officers soon seemed like a part of our own outfit. They were the 737th Tank Battalion, the 784th Tank Battalion and the 654th Tank Destroyer Battalion.

In my work I became familiar with Maj. Clarence E. Woods, Asst Div. G-2 and other figures, mostly by telephone and official records and correspondence.

In the Normandy Campaign the 35th Division was a part of the American First Army. But another army was being secretly formed of both armored divisions and infantry divisions to engage in an intense "blitzkrieg" type warfare the like of which no American Army had ever before known.

That army was soon to become more widely known than any other, and its commander to attain fame unique in American military annals and world history as well.

It was the American Third Army commanded by Lt. Gen. George S. Patton, Jr.

By the taking of ports and road networks in Normandy, and the widening of the beachhead, the stage had been set for the introduction of this army and this commander on the military stage. All the might of the Allied military forces of

Europe, ground, air and sea, were to be brought to bear to
break the German lines. Then the Third Army under Patton
was to plunge through the breach, and carry lightning warfare
into the heart of France cutting behind organized German
lines of resistance.

The 35th Infantry Division was made a part of the Third
Army. Our depleted ranks were filled with replacements of
new men and officers. The time was appointed. An important
H-hour awaited. Patton and his tanks, trucks and men were
poised and ready. The stage was set. Newsmen and high
military officials, including McNair, General of all American
Armies, came to see the curtain lifted. The campaign was to
begin on July 25th by breaking the German lines south of
St. Lo.

Then Patton's armor and men were to move through the
gap.

## CHAPTER IV

## NORTHERN FRANCE

At the Front,
Normandy
July 25, 1944

A quiet day on the front. Only occasional shelling, mostly mortar, and sporadic small arms firing. The highlight of the day was the bombing attack in front of our lines by 3,000 bombers, half of which were heavies. We could not see it all of course, but what we could see coupled with the thunder of the bombs was indeed impressive. I marvel at the ability of anyone to survive such an ordeal, for the ground shook here and the bombs were falling some distance away.

Lt Braffit called up and was tickled as could be over the hell raining on the Germans. He said, "Judge, I have got your money laid out and will pay you now if you'll come up here."

I have a bet with him that the war will be over by Nov. 11.

Wonderful news from Russian front. If events continue the same there, my bets are secure.

A quiet day here, but still not for some. Two artillery linemen for the forward observer were casualties, one killed the other seriously wounded. There were others wounded by mortar shells. Even now are the wheeooo of shells going over.

So to bed, and some rest tonight.

### THE GREAT BOMBING RAID

*July 25, 1944*

*The bombing raid mentioned in the entry of July 25th was, up to that time, the largest in the history of the world.*

*The record still stands. The raid was to pulverize the German lines on about a three-mile front south of St. Lo, preparing the way for an advance by the infantry. When the breach in enemy lines was made by the foot-sloggers, Patton's armored divisions were then to move through the opening for a massive break-through and fan out behind the German lines.*

*There was a most tragic occurrence in connection with the bombing raid. The first waves of bombers dropped their missiles in the designated area. As each succeeding wave dropped its load, a great cloud of dust and smoke arose. After a time the bomber pilots could no longer see the ground and the bombs were released into the cloud of smoke and dust. A slight breeze was blowing from the enemy lines toward ours, and the cloud drifted slowly over our positions.*

*As the cloud floated toward our lines, each succeeding wave of planes dropped its bombs closer and closer until they were falling on our own troops. Desperate efforts to reach the planes by radio were finally successful. Perhaps the message had to go all the way to England where the planes were taking off. When the message got through, the bombers got back on target by dropping their loads into the forward edge of the dust cloud or just beyond its edge.*

*The 35th Division's position was just to the left of the bombing area and thus the Division personnel escaped damage from the bombing error.*

*Among the American casualties that day from our own bombs, was Gen. McNair, Commander of all the American Armies in the ETO. He was watching the raid from a forward position.*

*The famed war correspondent, Ernie Pyle, was an observer. He almost lost his life in the raid. One of his columns, quoted in part from Stars and Stripes, said the following:*

### BOMBING BY THEIR OWN PLANES
### FAILS TO BREAK UP YANK ATTACK

#### By Ernie Pyle

*Normandy-With our own personal danger past, our historic air bombardment of the German lines holding us in the Normandy beachhead again became a captivating spectacle to watch. By now it was definite that the* great waves of four-motored planes were dropping their deadly loads exactly in the right place and by now two Mustang fighters flying like a pair of doves patrolled back and forth, back and forth, just in front of each oncoming wave of bombers as if to shout to them by their near presence that here was not the place to drop their loads.

And then we could see a flare come out of the belly of one plane in each flight. Just after they had passed over our heads the flare shot forward leaving smoke behind it in a vivid line and then it began a graceful downward curve. That was one of the most beautiful things I've ever seen. It was like an invisible crayon drawing a rapid line across the canvas of sky saying in gesture for all to see: "Here, here is where to drop, follow me." And each succeeding flight of oncoming bombers obeyed and in turn dropped its own hurtling marker across the illimitable heaven to guide those behind.

### Three Planes Down

Long before now the German ack-ack guns had gone out of existence. We had counted three of our big planes down in spectacular flames, and I believe that was all. The German ack-ack gunners either took to their holes or were annihilated.

It seemed incredible to me that any German could come out of that bombardment with his sanity.

When it was over even I was grateful in a chastened way I had never experienced before for just being alive. I thought an attack by our troops was impossible now, for it is an unnerving thing to be bombed by your own planes.

The leading company of our battalion was to spearhead the attack 40 minutes after our heavy bombing ceased. The company had been hit directly by our bombs. Their casualties, including casualties in shock, were heavy. Men went to pieces and had to be sent back. The company was shattered and shaken.

And yet Company B attacked, and on time to the minute. They attacked and within an hour they sent word back that they had advanced 800 yards through German territory and were still going.

## GIs Can Be Majestic

*Around our farmyard men with stars on their shoulders almost wept when word came over the portable radio. The American soldier can be majestic when he needs to be.*

*There is one more thing I want to say before we follow the troops into France in the great push you've been reading about for days: I'm sure that back in England that night other men - the bomber crews - almost wept, and maybe they did really in the awful knowledge that they had killed our own American troops, but I want to say this to them. The chaos and bitterness there in the orchards and between the hedgerows that afternoon have passed. After the bitterness came the somber remembrance that the Air Corps is strong right in front of us.*

\* \* \*

*It will be noted from the Journal that our unit did not begin driving until the second day after the bombing raid. We widened the breakthrough gap by attacking German positions on the left flank or eastern edge, which had not been bombed, and continued for several days to push the enemy back to the southeast. Then we were pulled from the lines to catch up with Patton's armored spearheads to the south.*

*The Germans had by then devised a counter strategy. Mustering their available crack troops including Panzer units, paratroop and SS Divisions, they attempted to cut off Patton's tank columns by driving behind them to the sea at the nearest point - Avranches. The 35th Division, hurrying south, was, in the words of Col. Byrne, "Literally thumbed off the road" and thrown in front of the German advance. Our Division with the 30th Infantry Division met the German thrust headon at Mortain astride the main highway leading to the sea. In some of the most confused, desperate, bloody fighting of the war, we blunted the SS and Panzer-led drive and turned it back as other forces pressed its flanks.*

*Then the 35th, needed to re-inforce and assist the armored spearheads, was again pulled out of the lines and sent to join the pell mell drive with Patton's armor across France. The 35th was on the extreme right flank. As we drove for-*

*ward we had also the task of protecting the right flank of
the whole American Army from the thousands of German
troops cut off in Southern France. We were making the
famous "end run" with the Third Army. Read about that,
the Mortain battle and the preliminary fighting in the entries
which follow.*

At the Front,
Normandy
July 27, 1944

Time: 0500

A rather quiet day on the whole. A delegation of officers
from another unit [28th Infantry Division] came in to look
our lines over. First visit to the front for most, if not all of
them. Tragically one of them, CO of AT Co, was caught in
a mortar barrage with Capt Wilson[1] and Lt Prescott[2] and
seriously wounded if not killed. Thus some go through much
at the front and remain unscathed and others are killed in
the first hour. An M Co man was also hit at the same time.
Wilson, Prescott and another man, an EM, dragged the
wounded to safety at their own risk.

Among the visiting officers today I recognized a familiar
face. He was my platoon leader when I was in basic training
at Camp Wolters, Texas, Lt Dilts, now a captain. Also he
happens to be a classmate of Capt Forsyth[3] of our Hqs Co.

\* \* \*

*[The 28th Infantry Division was to relieve the 35th so
that we could join Patton's spearheads in the breakthrough
to the south. For some reason plans were changed, we remained in the lines and continued to push on foot for several
days.]*
Word received today that Sgt Ferran[4] died of his wounds.
Lt Silverman was pretty much "cut up" by the news. "Judge,
how long is this slaughter going to continue?" he said. We

---

1  Capt. Arthur D. Wilson, Pacific Grove, Calif., CO of AT Co.

2  2nd Lt. Warren F. Prescott, San Francisco, Calif., AT Co.

3  Capt. James P. Forsyth, Little Rock, Ark., a West Point graduate, CO of Regtl Hq Co.

4  Sgt. Raymond P. Ferron, I & R Plat, had shown such cool judgment and ability that he had been recommended for a battlefield commission before his wounds and death.

sat down and talked for some time, and I pointed out how good the big picture looked; that the slaughter can't continue too much longer. Then I helped him censor mail and he seemed to feel much better. We can't any of us live forever and all must die. So it is better to die here in war than that we all live as slaves, if so it must be. And that is the way it is right now.

\* \* \*

The past day was very pretty for Normandy and our troops had pretty easy going. But the units on our right and left were pushing so they were the ones who reaped the hell today.

\* \* \*

Last night two German paratroopers, members of the Luftwaffe, came into our lines and surrendered. They talked not quite so freely as the others, but they told quite a bit. I think that it is a significant sign that even Hitler's best is beginning to crack.

\* \* \*

Now 0530. - Think I'll sleep about an hour. Been on duty all night.

Oh yes, we were strafed about midnight by German planes. Makes you get down into the dirt.

From

## MADISON COUNTY RECORD

[This letter arrived at the same time as the one written on the 24th. Both were published in the same issue of the paper.]

AT-THE-FRONT, NORMANDY
July 27, 1944

Dear Home Folks,

It was a day some time ago when the fighting was furious and hard when the following incident occurred. Sweat-stained runners were dashing about on foot or whizzing by on jeeps; the ambulances were hurrying back and forth evacuating the wounded; loads of ammunition were rushing up, and prisoners were coming back toward the rear. The thunder of the shelling was without let-up by either side, but ours much the heavier.

While we were busily engaged in taking care of our part of all this, there came into the command post a major from higher headquarters and a newspaper correspondent. Introductions were brief of course; we gave them the information they wanted and they went out to look around while we continued our work.

Some time later they returned to the CP and as things had slowed down a little, we were discussing the difficulties of the operations in that sector. I remarked that I had spent a large part of my life in the woods and hills but that this was the worst terrain I had ever seen for offensive action.

It was then the major said, "I believe I know you" and haltingly, as if reaching far back into his memory, he called my name. I was almost dumbfounded to learn that he was formerly a boy from the old home county whom I once knew quite well and with whom I used to play basket ball, Woodrow Anderson, son of Tom Anderson of Crosses. (Nephew of Jim Anderson, former representative, and of Dave Anderson of Huntsville). He is now a major in the Signal Corps of the U. S. Army.

We had time to briefly recall a few of the things we both remembered, principally some of the games in which we both played. Each of us was the smallest member of his squad at that time and consequently were usually paired off in the contests. Some participants in the games we played up and down White River were Elmo Ritchie, Bill Stewart, Mark Guinn, Burrell Smith, the Buck brothers, the Barrons, Eversoles, Bells, Lloyd Cornett and Dick Gilstrap. There were others no doubt, but we had not much time and the circumstances were not conducive to memories.

We expected to meet again but that was some days ago, so it may be that we shall not. Nonetheless, it did seem passing strange that after 15 years break in our acquaintance, we two from the pleasant, peaceful hills of the Ozarks, should meet again in a shell-shattered stone-house command post on a battle field in France.

———

Received two copies of the Record today and a glance at their pages brought back such a flood of memories as to be almost overwhelming. I could not possibly enumerate them to you and I must not release my thoughts to them.

One memory though I could not quite forbid was brought on when I read the poem "Milking Time" in Easley's department. For a brief moment I could again see the sunset glow as the "shadows climbed the bars," feel the soft coolness of the twilight, hear again the "katy-dids begin to trill" and my father's voice as he cared for the stock, and the drumming of the white stream into the tin pail as my mother milked the gentle cows. I even fancied I could again catch the scent of the fresh, warm fluid as it overflowed the shining vessels and the snowy foam ran down the sides, and remember quite clearly how I wrestled with the insistent calves, being often thrown for a loss, and grew quite angry at their senseless plunging. Then on the leisurely walk to the farmhouse when the milking was done, with the friendly watch dog frolicking about, the fragrance of the flowers perfuming the air, and the whip-poor-wills beginning to call, my anger would melt away and my heart be as peaceful as the quiet hills.

---

A far, far cry from my present circumstances are the scenes back there, and my prayer is that you who read these lines may never know how great the difference in the two worlds.

Some very interesting letters in the Record from servicemen, and especially good was the one from Pfc. Charles Samples about our good ally Australia.

Thanks to Ruby V. Hughes for his good wishes to all U. S. servicemen and I think he means that for all who fight for freedom everywhere.

Thanks to the Huntsville American Legion for its much needed and well appreciated service to those who are going away to do their duty to their country and to humanity.

Good luck and best wishes to all at home, and to those who serve in the far-away parts of the earth.

Sincerely,

Lt. Orval E. Faubus
Hqs. 320th Inf.,
APO No. 35, c/o P. M.
N. Y. C., N. Y.

At the Front,
Normandy
July 27, 1944

Time: 2000

On duty all night, [didn't get the hour's sleep] up all day, so I'm very sleepy. Our forces are now pushing. Blue Bn has reached its objective, but Red Bn meeting resistance. Last report had three wounded in field they were trying to get out before shelling the place. Later a PW was taken so the Bn is making progress.

Another I & R man was lost today - only wounded, not thought to be serious. He was one of the new men brought in as a replacement.

Capt Hardy[5] came back from hospital after treatment for battle exhaustion. He still could not take it and had to be sent out again and probably will be unfit for combat from now on. He jumped like a rabbit every time artillery went off, even our own.

He said there were many cases back there being treated for battle exhaustion, some of them really bad. One fellow had lost all his memory, couldn't even remember how to feed himself and had to be showed how to do everything.

\* \* \*

Forces on our right have made appreciable gains west of St. Lo. If their progress continues we will soon have "Le Bosche" out of Normandy.

The Russians are bridging the Vistula and the men of Hitler's Eastern Army are running out. God speed the Red Army. So to bed in my fox hole.

[Other casualties[6] not mentioned in the Journal.]

At the Front,
Normandy
July 28, 1944

Time: 0213

On duty now. Le Bosche has been putting on quite an aerial show for us tonight. His colored flares, mingled with

---

5 Capt. John F. Hardy, Chester, S. C., CO of Co I, evacuated as sick July 27, did not return.

6 2nd Lt. Richard H. Thurow, Co D, address unknown, a replacement, evacuated as sick July 27; and 1st Lt. Thomas V. Camarda, Co H, Brooklyn, N. Y., listed LWA July 27; neither returned.

The beachhead area with troops landing from the ships and marching up the slope - from a drawing by Olen Dow.

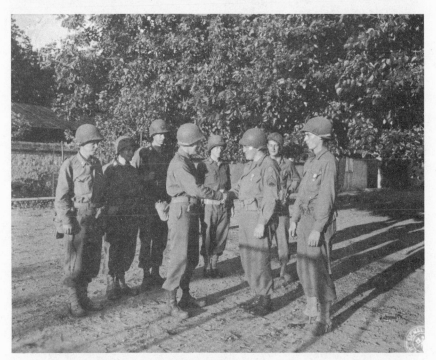

S/Sgt. Louis Porta, Sacremento, Calif., and Pvt. Johnson, full name and address unknown, each awarded the Silver Star for heroism and gallantry in action at St. Lo. The ceremony was held in Montargis after its capture by the 320th. In the back row, left to right, Lt. Keith, Capt. Trossen, Capt. English, Capt. Leach and Lt. Kurtz. Front, Lt. Col. Greer making the award to Porta as Pvt. Johnson observes after receiving his medal. (photo by Signal Corps, from Kurtz).

Faubus, the jeep driver, a well known buddy then but the name now forgotten, and Lt. Sid Silverman on the visit to the Chateau near Bonneval Aug. 19, 1944. (photo by Mr. Ide, obtained from Silverman)

A roadside battle conference somewhere in France. Col. Byrne, center, facing camera and Lt. Col. Northam on left. Others unidentified. (Photo from Red Cross Charlie)

Faubus at Lening, Al-sace-Lorraine, Nov. 25, 1944. We had just arrived at a new CP and I had removed my overshoes, jacket, trench coat and headgear, when Red Cross Charlie urged me outside for a moment to snap the picture. The tanker over-alls, purchased for the winter weather, were worn over the regular wool trousers and "long-handl-ed" underwear. (photo from Red Cross Charlie)

Red Cross Charlie on the road to Bastogne, snaps a picture of the road sign and his jeep. Note the chain on the tire and the downed communication lines. (photo from Red Cross Charlie)

Kraut prisoners of war in background with American captors in foreground, somewhere in Alsace-Lorraine. (Photo from Red Cross Charlie)

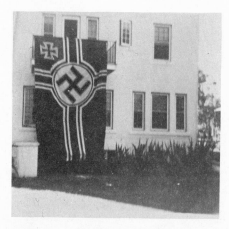

The Nazi battle flag captured by Lt. Braffit in Bar-sur-Seine, France, Aug. 30, 1944.

A real French gendarme, Monsieur Bazin, left, Red Cross Charlie in his disguise, center, and Lt. Silverman at Mazerulles, France on Sept. 18. (Photo from Red Cross Charlie)

Cpl. Edward W. Ostapczuk, Elizabeth, N. J. with whom I worked many, many hours during training and combat in the 320th Infantry.

Col. J. D. "Alex" Alexander, Chicago, Ill., CO of 3rd Bn, 320th (photo from Kurtz or Glatzer)

our tracers and ack-ack is quite a display. The bombs did not fall close enough to be dangerous, (to me) but shrapnel and bullets whizzed by occasionally.

I couldn't see enough from the tent. Everyone was hunkering behind the sand-bags, so I went out and got in my hole and stuck my head in the uncovered portion where I could watch. The ack-ack looked like big stars blossoming in the clouds and then winking out.

* * *

Three I & R men were hit by bomb fragments when the Germans bombed a RJ south of here, - Sgt Harris,[7] Pvt "Red" Rhodes[8] and Pvt Smith (Smithy).[9] Makes a high rate of casualties for the platoon.

Four men of 2nd Bn were wounded by a teller mine today, one probably fatally.

Several casualties in other Bns as they pushed forward today. Sixteen PWs so far tonight including one officer, an egotistical little "oily," quite smug, with "Iron Cross" and other decorations.

Too sleepy now. Think I shall lie down.

At the Front,
Normandy
Sunday, July 30, 1944

Time: 1700

Have moved up and again in full contact with the enemy after he was driven back. Now just north of town of Torigny. The enemy is on high ground and can "look down our throats" as we advance. As he is constantly driven back, as he will be from now on, he can always choose his ground. Therefore he has every advantage of terrain, but we will beat them anyway although not all will survive. I hope the Russians and the European underground exterminate every damned Nazi and German militarist. I am afraid that we Americans will be too lenient, for after they are beaten they can appear very humble as I have already seen.

The English people, with whom I talked while in that country, felt as I do. They all wanted the Russians to get

---

7 Sgt. Joseph Harris, Chattanooga, Tenn.
8 Pfc. Robert R. "Red" Rhodes, Elkins, W. Va.
9 Pvt. Raymond "Smitty" Smith, Cleveland, Ohio.

into Germany first, because they were afraid we and the British would not "wind up" the Nazis as should be done.

\* \* \*

A small brown bird, with yellow breast, hopping about in the thick bushes beside the bank where I have dug my "hole," reminds me briefly of my boyhood and how I enjoyed watching them. I say briefly because any memory here will be brief for there is too much war.

I went out to the latrine (a slit trench dug in the ground) short time ago and just as I got set the Bosche slammed a shell into the field above me. About the time I finished he slammed down a pair a little closer, which threw dirt over the bushes into the low ground where I squatted. Except I was not squatting when they hit. I thought of what Maj Smith said last night. He was telling a story when Jerry sent over a bunch of his stuff. We all jumped in holes and the only break in the story was the major's interjection, "Damned annoying, y'know it?"

Looks like somebody might get hurt around here, [more shells came in] for luck does not hold out forever.

\* \* \*

The Huns lost men even after they broke contact in the withdrawal. Their dead was along the road as we moved up. One corpse beside the road looked like he had a dozen holes. Must have been hit by shrapnel from a close shell burst.

We had about seven wounded Krauts night before last. They were given the same treatment as our wounded. German planes were over at the time and they were kept in the hospital tent until it quieted somewhat. Some of our aid men who speak German talked with them, and were impressed that some of the wounded PWs were pretty nice fellows. Most of the Germans, in fact I think all of them, now thought they would lose the war. Asked why they continued fighting, they would give an expressive shrug and a spread of their hands. No PW has ever offered a reason why they continue.

Which goes to show the blindness of the Nazi Doctrine, or is it German blindness of the natives of that country. Germans in our country seem open minded as Wendell Wilkie and others.

The German officer was curious as to where he was to be sent. One of our officers told him we were sending them all back to Russia. "Oh nein, nein," he said, "anything but that." It seems he hoped to be sent to the States (he speaks fair English and has a relative there). Almost all of them hope to go to the States. The bastards have been fighting to destroy our way of life, our kindness, our generosity, our willingness to forgive, and have criticized us for those qualities. Yet they are the first to take advantage of them [American qualities] when they can be useful to them. Like a heartless criminal who gives no mercy in the commission of his crimes but is the first to cry pitifully for mercy when he is caught.

The Germans have shown no mercy to those they have conquered. I hope the guilty scoundrels get none when they are finally finished.

\* \* \*

The evening sun breaks out and shines beautifully through the foliage where I sit with my feet in my fox hole. Overhead the planes glint as they wheel and dive. Jerry throws over a shell which whispers and whispers in its flight and lands with a bam on the slope behind. Soon another follows - seems he is zeroing in on a target nearby. The next one is closer. May be us. Later: Well if it was us, he didn't succeed but he may have gotten something on the road behind. But he keeps feeling and feeling for us for now they come quite close in front.

\* \* \*

Just in front of me is a field of grass and clover, just right for cutting. It is fully ripe and waiting for the scythe. Magallanes,[10] the boy with the peculiar, soft Mexican accent, replies to my comment that the field is ready to be cut, "But I would like to see the man who would cut it. He would be a brave one."

However if we are successful, and we probably will be, and push on, next week some Norman farmer will be harvesting the fresh smelling hay. Most of us will be pushing on after the retreating Huns; many will be back in the hospitals and some will be sleeping the long sleep along the way, mayhap even beside the now gently waving grass and clover.

---

10 Pfc. Santiago B. Magallanes, Regtl Hq Co., Las Cruces, New Mexico, the colonel's orderly.

The brown bird with the yellow breast flits silently back to the bushes beside my sand-bagged refuge, and a timid little mouse looks from a hole in the bank, his whiskers moving nervously.

* * *

Sunday! The word sounds peculiar out here and how different our activity from that of Sabbath Days in the past. Different as heaven from hell? The expression does not seem to carry enough meaning. I wonder just now where the ministers I know were today, what they said. Certainly they didn't hear any whispering [rustling sound of shells overhead] like I hear, and the dead they saw were dressed as beautifully as possible and laid away with tender care, and the coming of night holds only peace and quiet and comfortable rest. What the night holds for my comrades is too much to say.

* * *

Now 0350 - (July 31) and except for occasional shelling the night is quiet. The men need a good night's rest.

Just had a call from Maj Gillis[11] who says British tanks are to our left front after a break through on their sector. That is very good news.

Col Byrne has a very bad cold. I have heard him coughing very frequently during the night. He is so hoarse he can hardly talk which is really a handicap for him. I can remember only one man among my acquaintances who could equal him (Chas S. Cook of St. Paul, Ark.) in rapidity and continuity of speech. However he is a very interesting and always entertaining talker. His pet peeve is the Air Corps with their double pay for flying, while the Infantry, with the hardest lot of all gets nothing extra no matter what they do.

* * *

Capt Tobin[12] of 2nd Bn, tells me they lost nine men last night from an 88 shell. It hit the top of a hedge, giving

* * *

11  Maj. William G. Gillis, Jr., a West Point graduate, Cameron, Texas, a replacement, who later commanded 1st Bn.

12  Capt. Robert B. Tobin, Pistol Point, Texas, originally with 3rd Bn, now with 2nd Bn Hq.

it the effect of an air burst, hitting some of the men in their holes. It killed a Lt Newlin, the [216th] arty forward observer, 2 men of Co E and wounded six others.

Strangest death was that of an AA man attached to Col Reed's arty unit. A German bomber dropped an extra fuel tank and it fell on the man while he was sleeping in a fox hole. It crushed and mangled his legs, but his immediate death was thought to have resulted from the fumes from the fuel which came from the burst tank. He had moved into that particular fox hole only that night because it seemed a little better than his own and the former occupant had moved away. The one he left is still undamaged.

\* \* \*

I'm glad the shelling is not heavy tonight for there is no protection at all around this Cp tent. All others are fairly secure in their dug-in positions. Sgt Coyne[13] is on duty with me tonight.

\* \* \*

Just had a call from Lt Braffit, who wanted to know if I had anyone who could bring Lt Gardner to their CP for the order for tomorrow. Seems Gardner is here by mistake and no one at msg center knows the way to Red Bn CP. Braffit was somewhat "pissed up" that no one knew the way, and justly so I guess. He will have to come get Gardner. That fellow certainly works hard and takes chances, and I hope his luck holds out.

I hear Lt Gardner is doing a good job as Co cmdr. I can't place Lt Alloway[14] in my mind right now, but I hear much praise of his work and also Lt Head. Sure hope Head can go home to those twin boys of his at Little Rock, Ark.

\* \* \*

I'm almost certain I broke a rib today when I fell into a slit trench during some shelling. Certainly sore enough. [The rib was broken, as shown by X-rays after the war.]

\* \* \*

---

13  Sgt. Ralph H. Coyne, Sv Co, Alhambra, Calif.

14  1st Lt. Curtis H. Alloway, originally Co L, now with Co K, of Independence (or Kansas City), Mo. On July 28 in command of 120 men of Co K, his force engaged 150 Germans of a parachute company, killed or wounded 45 of the enemy and captured 30 others.

Lt Kurtz and Sgts Donovan and Porta continue to do exceptional work. They were shelled out of every OP they set up today. Porta brought in a MG today. He is getting quite a collection of special German weapons, - a paratrooper's knife, a flash light of three colors, etc.

* * *

The shells certainly have a wheeoo and dreadful whispering at this time of the morning (0440).

[Other casualties[15] not mentioned in the Journal.]


Normandy Front,
Near Torigny,
August 1, 1944

The enemy fights delaying actions. He retires in the night to prepared positions of his own choosing where he has every advantage as our troops advance. We can break his lines with armor and artillery but it is practically impossible with infantry alone. We have had very little tank support, so our boys have really had tough going.

Yesterday the Red Bn ran into a hot fight. Lt Hermanspan[16] led his platoon in an assualt on a French village, firing his carbine as he advanced. They took the village, but a burst of MG fire caught him in the head. So part of the price paid for the French hamlet was his life and the lives of others who fell with him. He was a smiling happy fellow invaribly jesting with someone. Tragic it is indeed that the lives of such pleasant, happy fellows as he, should be lost in beating the beastly Nazis with their super race ideas.

---

15  2nd Lt. Albert Statuto, Hq Co, 1st Bn, Ft. Devens, (or Revere) Mass., listed SWA July 31; 1st Lt. Albert H. Buerck, Co E, address unknown, a replacement, listed LWA July 30; Capt. George M. Hodson, CO of Co F, Brookline, Mass., listed SWA July 31; 1st Lt. Thomas F. Potter, Ex O of Co F, Meriden, Conn., listed SWA July 31; 2nd Lt. Joe Lafferty, Co K, Roanoke, Va., a replacement, evacuated as sick July 31; 2nd Lt. Ernest T. Hayes, Co L, address unknown, listed LWA July 30. Of these six officers none returned. Lt. Col. Alfred Thompson, Omaha, Nebr., of the 134th Inf., mortally wounded on July 31.

16  1st Lt. John F. Hermanspan, Jr., Co I, Yonkers, N. Y., listed KIA Aug. 1. Co I was a part of the 3rd Bn. Hermanspan may have been transferred to another company, or the 3rd Bn took the town.

Capt Frederickson[17] was lost yesterday to us. He was seriously wounded but it is thought that he will live. He, Lt Kurtz and Sgt Porta often operated together, and were many times far in advance of their troops. The last two were quite grieved at the breaking up of their triumvirate.

Porta continues to bear a charmed life. He was shelled by 88s yesterday which hit so close that his big body bounced on the ground with every concussion. They chased him through a village with MG fire which was ripping at his heels as he ran. Today he captured a PW which had been by-passed and brought him in. "A damned Jap," he said and was itching for him to make a false move. The PW certainly looked Japanese all right. He was Oriental Russian from the Asiatic portions of the Soviet Republic. He had been wounded while fighting with the Russian Army, captured by the Germans and later impressed into their army. When asked if he would like to be back with the Russians, he was overjoyed at the thought. Another PW this morning was a First Aid man and a priest. Among the effects of one Nazi, a paper showing he had visited a prophylatic station for the prevention of veneral disease while in Italy. It contained the name of the place, the madame who ran it, the name of the prostitute with whom he had relations, the time of his visit, and also the time he had preventive treatment. Also the name of the soldier and his doctor. Rather peculiar document to carry around.

\* \* \*

Capt Hodgson,[18] comding F Co, was wounded yesterday and evacuated. He is not likely to be back. One of Maj Smith's medics lost a foot yesterday, blown off by a "shu" mine. Sgt Porta reported that a sergeant in K Co was wounded by another such mine this morning. Had a foot blown off and his testicles almost blown away. Diabolically cruel, these Nazis.

\* \* \*

17  Capt. Albert C. Frederickson of Hq, 3rd Bn, Chicago, Ill. He sometimes led attacks, part of the time riding our supporting tanks. He was seriously wounded and evacuated. Later we received word of his death, listed DOW Aug. 16.

18  Capt. Hodson's loss already reported. Now only two of the original officers remained in Co F, Lts. Gotter and Gangemi.

A hazy sky results in a sort of half-sunlight over the hedgerowed, uneven Normandy landscape today. The big guns thunder as our troops relentlessly pursue the enemy, with a cool breeze gently rustling the green foliage of the orchards and causing slight undulations in the ripe grain fields. It is quite chilling when one is quiet. Scenes of natural beauty which look unmoved upon the scenes of death.

In America, the news of today's successes will be hailed gladly when people read the papers or listen to the radios. But for many here it will be their last look at the blue sky, the fleecy clouds and the green of the orchards. The old strange mixture of joy and sadness, laughter and tears. Too often good news for one brings sorrow to another. But the great tragedy is that the sorrow and heartbreak brought to the peoples of the earth by this conflict is all so unnecessary and could have been avoided. I don't mean we could avoid it now, for the Bosche must be beaten. But prior planning and forethought on a Christian basis with stress placed on the unruly can prevent any such conflict as the one in which we are now engaged.

\* \* \*

Lt Keith[19] weeps when he discusses the loss of Capt Frederickson, as did Chaplain Stone[20] when he talked with Lt Silverman of Sgt Ferran's death, even as I wept when Sgt Cull was slain. Lt Silverman is very low in spirits again after the loss of two more of his men. Pvt Smead,[21] newly promoted to sergeant, and Pvt Kromula[22] were wounded when the wall of a burning building fell on them as they were passing in a jeep. Kromula not serious but Smead may have a broken back.

More and more, emotion seems to leave us and we function more as machines. The Bn comdrs Col Docka, Col Keator

---

19   1st Lt. John W. Keith, Sv Co, S-4 for 3rd Bn, Detroit, Mich.
20   Capt. Alfred H. Stone, Protestant chaplain, Elgin, Ill. The other Protestant chaplain was Capt. Herman V. Tarpley, Daisy, Tenn.
21   Sgt. Fred Smead, I & R Plat, Yakima, Wash. We learned later his back was broken and he remained paralyzed from the shoulders down.
22   Pvt. Joseph "Scott" Kromula, a replacement for I & R Plat, Detroit, Mich. Outcome of wounds unknown.

and Maj Waring,[23] and all the men of the lines look haggard and worn. All the weaklings have long since been weeded out and only the strong and the brave continue in the lines.

Saw Lt Brochu last night for first time since we entered the lines. More than three weeks now, - three weeks today since Sgt Cull was killed. I wonder if Margaret has yet received the news that well break her heart.

\* \* \*

My information is that Lt Fitzgerald was killed. His body was found after our advance. The body of Lt Talcott was not found, and there is a rumor that he might have been picked up by the enemy and, if he lived, is a prisoner-or-war. None of this is confirmed by any reliable source and it is unlikely that he was saved. [He was killed.]

\* \* \*

Aug. 1 (5 min. to Aug 2.)
Now 2355

Moving out soon on night attack, on advance to river to south, ordered by two 2-star generals. My only regret is that they are not going with the troops they have ordered out on this foolish mission. A night attack should be planned. I don't see how the generals can have a clear conscience in their safe dugouts.

We're off.

Normandy Front,
On River So. of Torigny,
Aug. 3, 1944

0515:

The above few words, about our night mission, may sound resentful. Certainly everyone resented the nature of the order, which was in the nature of a reprimmand because the general did not think our unit had made satisfactory progress. It was given just at nightfall, perhaps without any forethought whatever, and prior planning or reconnaissance was

---

23 Maj. Frank S. Waring, a replacement, Holyoke, Mass. He commanded 1st Bn for a short time until Maj. Gillis took over. Records indicate Waring headed the battalion when it took Torigni sur Vire on July 31.

impossible. The troops were already dog-tired after marching and fighting all day.

Whether I live or die, I shall never forgive Gen. Gerow[24] for such a thoughtless act which might have cost unnecessarily the lives of many good men. I do not know if Gen Baade was in full agreement with the order or if he had no choice in the matter.

*   *   *

We marched all the balance of the night, winding about and around over the hedgerows, streams, ditches and banks. It was killing work on the men with heavy loads of ammunition and the heavy weapons. Contact was often broken and men temporarily lost. I hurried up and down the column, directing, re-establishing contact and occasionally helping on a reconnaissance to the flank. When daylight came we had made no appreciable progress, except to lose sleep and wear down still further the weary men. The units pushed on to the river and gained their objective.

Then came an order to cross the river and continue the attack. Maj Docka got his Bn over and established on other side. About one platoon of 1st Bn got across but were driven back by the Germans with the use of a half-track. Lt Bell[25] killed three of the enemy with his carbine, got his men out and back across the stream with MG bullets spatting the water around him. He had bullet holes in his clothing but not a mark upon his skin. The 1st and 2nd were unable to cross during the day. The Germans from high ground south of the river rained shells on our men on this side. The 1st Bn lost three vehicles, and the aid stations were pretty busy. The men were so tired that they no longer dodged at the shell fire and neglected to dig in. Men at the rear of a column slept while the point was being fired on. They staggered when they walked and when they lay down it was often necessary to move their legs in order to drive by in a jeep. [On more than one trip that day I had to get out of my jeep, move the

---

24 Maj. Gen. L. T. Gerow, Comdr of V Corps, of which the 35th was now a part. The order was given by him accompanied by Gen Baade.

25 2nd Lt. Charles W. Bell, Co A, Valentine, Texas. (There were also 1st Lt. Charles G. Bell, Co G, 2nd Bn, Binghamton, N. Y., wounded on July 11, now hospitalized, and 2nd Lt. Claude D. Bell, Co B, Jamesville, N. Y.)

legs of a soldier who never noticed, so my driver could get the vehicle by the temporarily sleeping men.]

Then another order to attack, and, without fail, take hill 203 during the night. Col Northam's face was drawn and his voice shaking after receiving the order. Lt Braffit stood by a tree crying, not for himself but for his men. I tried to comfort him but there was no comfort to offer. I felt the same as he.

And now, as I am on duty, I get the reports that the troops of our 1st and 2nd Bns have crossed the river and with the 3rd have occupied the hill. Our arty drove the Germans out during the early hours of the night.

Now another order to attack to the south at 0800. I must wake Col Byrne, who is so hoarse he cannot talk except to whisper.

* * *

If my luck ever goes bad I will get hurt doing a bodily function, which puts one in a very awkward position. Yesterday while I squatted on one side of a stone house, the Huns slammed down three shells on the other side. They were 88s for we did not hear them until they exploded.

Thrice in a short space of time the lieut (from V corps who accompanied me) and I had barely moved from the places where the shells landed. Most of them you could hear and have time to crouch by a hedge or fall into a ditch, and hear the shrapnel buzz and zing over head.

* * *

This afternoon Lt Braffit brought in two PWs. He was much cheered up as the troops are advancing rapidly to the south mopping up pockets of resistance. Success has probably lent them the extra energy to carry on over the miles they have covered today. It is reported we will meet the British at the town of Vire.

* * *

Yesterday the sun was hot and burning, the first day I had ever sought shade in Normandy. Today has also been warm and mostly dry. Showers wet certain portions of the front. When nature's thunder broke out I had difficulty at first in distinguishing it from our own. It didn't sound fierce enough for the man made kind, so I watched in the dark cloud to the south and discovered it was not artillery.

* * *

SCENES OF WAR.—

Near where I sit now. - Three pretty little red and white calves lying dead in the farm yard, slain by the flying jagged pieces of shrapnel.

* * *

As we moved up the other day - Four half grown ducklings playing in a water filled shell crater about 4 feet by 4 feet in the hard surfaced road, and the jeeps and other army transport driving around them.

* * *

As we moved up on the night march - the hastily dug holes along the hedges where the White Bn had their hot fight, the stretcher bearers still bringing out wounded after the hour of midnight and three big, fine cows lying dead in the grass, their heads and necks outstretched and twisted by their last agony.

* * *

[A casualty[26] not mentioned in the Journal.]

## MILLER OF 137th WINS DSC

*Capt William C. Miller, Athens, Tenn., Commander of Co B, 137th Inf., was awarded the Distinguished Service Cross, reported to be the first in the Division, for wiping our two MG nests and coordinating the attacks of both Cos. B and C on August 1st.*

* * *

## CORPS LT TOURS FRONT WITH ME

*On Aug 2 a lieutenant from Fifth Corps was sent up to the 320th Regiment to check on the situation. Since I had to carry a message to one of the battalions in the advance I invited him to accompany me.*

*We went by jeep to a point near the 1st Bn Headquarters, then left the vehicle to walk. It was the first time I had seen dust from vehicles along the front. The road toward the headquarters went part way along a ridge line, which was under observation by the Germans who were firing artillery at the dust clouds raised by passing vehicles.*

---

26  1st Lt. John M. Griney, Co D, address unknown, a replacement, listed as LWA Aug. 2, did not return.

We found the battalion headquarters sheltered from enemy fire behind the ridge crest. Maj Momm[27] was in charge. Lt. Braffit was there.

The Colonel wanted to know if the troops had reached the stream at the foot of the hill to the front, and if a crossing had been effected. Division and Fifth Corps also wanted to know. They didn't have the information at the battalion headquarters, which they should have as their troops were in the advance. So the Corps lieutenant and myself set out down the slope, which was in plain view of the Germans stationed on the hill tops beyond the stream. We could be seen as we moved across roads and through openings between the trees in the apple orchards.

Several times the enemy fired on us with artillery and fortunately we had always moved just beyond the shells' impact area. The rounds still landed so close that the fresh foliage, little green apples and twigs, cut from the trees by the flying shrapnel, dropped down on us as we lay in the dirt.

Finally I had to answer the call of nature. Seeking shelter at an abandoned farm house, I got on the far side from the German guns and squatted in an L formed by the building. My selection of the spot I'm certain saved me. The enemy must have had the structure under observation for they laid in a number of shells, some of them air bursts, which luckily exploded over the building or on the opposite side from me.

The lieutenant had taken shelter in the house. When the firing stopped he came outside to see about me, and we proceeded back up the slope to the battalion headquarters. As we moved along a road the Germans again followed us with artillery fire. A number of times as we plopped in the roadside ditch the little green apples, leaves and twigs showered down on our helmets and backs.

We reported to the 1st Bn that their troops had reached the river and some were across. Returning to regimental headquarters we gave the Colonel a report and the lieutenant returned to Corps with his report. It was one of the few times, if not the only time, that I saw anyone from Corps up that close to the leading elements of an attack.

\* \* \*

---

27  Maj. Edwin C. Momm, Ex O of the Bn, Irvington, N. Y. (another listing gave his home address as Union, N. J.)

Normandy Front,
North of Vire
Aug. 4, 1944

We moved up again and established our CP in a group of farm buildings. Last night I slept on the stone floor of a combination dwelling and barn, formerly used by the Germans. The place stank only slightly less than the smell of death at the front lines.

Our troops have made rapid progress this morning and portions of them have already reached their objective for the day, (Now 1145). There are rumors that we will be pinched out by forces converging on our right and left, and get a rest.

\* \* \*

Saw Lt John P. Kelly[28] of 3rd Bn in the column the other night. In garrison he did not impress me as a very rugged soldier, but now he looks very rugged with many days' growth of black beard on his face. He is the only officer left in his company (L) of the group who first entered the lines.

Also spoke again to Lt Gangemi[29] for first time since England. Saw Lt Head, a brave one he is, and others not seen for some time.

Kelly still has his peculiar short laugh. He said, "Gees, how would you like to be back to Butner?"

\* \* \*

Time: 1530. - Half amused, half angry, more sick with disgust as I write these few lines. I have been left at rear CP today to look after all matters. There is no communication with the CO [Col. Byrne] or with the staff who are forward. Things have really been pretty hectic here and I have dispatched as many as three motor messengers forward with urgent communications to the Colonel. At three different times had the General [Baade, Div Comdr] on the line in person. Then in the midst of an urgent message, which must be expedited, which concerns mix-up of our troops with others

---

28 1st Lt. John P. Kelly, Broken Bow, Nebr. He was assigned at Camp Butner to Co K but was now with Co L (if my memory was not at fault when I made the entry). We were long associated in training and courts martial proceedings and were close friends.

29 2nd Lt. Felix M. Gangemi, Freeport, L. I., N. Y., a friend and fellow officer of my original Co F.

and a possible attack by our tanks on friendly troops, he takes time to reprimand me for not "Siring" him enough. And honest-to-God, I thought I was over doing the courtesy a little, for scarcely a phrase or sentence passed me without a "sir." Then he takes time and interrupts my efficiency to demand a few more "Sirs." Sometimes I think that many of these Generals are much more (if not wholly) concerned with their own prestige, reputation and position than they are with winning the war or saving lives, and the human beings who serve under their command are no more to them than are the soulless and feelingless trucks, tanks and guns which they command.

[Other casualties[30] not mentioned in the Journal.]

## HEADQUARTERS V CORPS

APO 305, U. S. Army
Office of the Commanding General

201.22                                                                5 August 1944
SUBJECT:      Commendation.

TO:              Commanding General, 35th Infantry Division

1. Upon the relief of the 35th Infantry Division from attachment to the V Corps, I desire to express to you, and through you to the officers and men of your division, my thanks and appreciation for their excellent performance while under my command.

2. The 35th Infantry Division was attached to the V Corps two days after the beginning of operation "COBRA." They were ordered to make an immediate advance without all of their organic motor equipment, which could not be made available due to traffic priorities. During the eight days which your division fought under this corps, from 28 July to 4 August 1944, it advanced approximately 27 kilometers, took the town of Torigni Sur Vire on the afternoon of 31 July 1944, and later effected a crossing of the Vire River. Despite the fact that it fought continuously against heavy delaying action and over difficult terrain, the 35th Infantry Division reached all of its immediate objectives and its final objective.

---

30 2nd Lt. Christy Labhart, Co G, Evansville, Ind., a replacement, evacuated as sick Aug 4, did not return.

3. The foregoing is an achievement of which you and every member of your division can be justly proud. My personal thanks and best wishes for continued success go with each and every one of you.

/s/ L. T. Gerow
/t/ L. T. GEROW
Major General, U. S. Army
Commanding

To which letter General Baade indorsed the following message to his troops:

201.22                    1st Ind.                    PWB/mla

Hq 35th INF DIV, APO 35, U S ARMY, 15 Aug 44

TO:   All officers and enlisted men, 35th Infantry Division.

1. Again a Corps Commander has seen fit to commend the Division for an achievement of great magnitude. It is just praise and I am exceedingly proud to transmit this commendation to you who have contributed your full measure of hard work and devotion to duty in making the Division so successful.

2. Please have every officer and enlisted man of your command fully informed of the contents of this letter to which I add my own gratitude and congratulations for a job well done.

/s/ Paul W. Baade
/t/ PAUL W. BAADE
Major General, U. S. Army
Commanding

Normandy Front,
Aug. 5, 1944

Time: 0140

They were shelling us just after dark (around 2230), so I told Maj McElroy to call me when he wanted me to take over and lay down in my hole. Our White and Blue Bns were already in position and Red was attacking on the left toward village of Le Neufbourg. Shells were roaming the heavens in their eerie whistling way, searching for human lives, seeking to blast forever the hopes and happiness of someone. The roar of the guns echoed and reechoed and the reverberations of the explosions rolled back and forth across the moonlight bathed Normandy country side. Some exploded in empty places injuring only the foliage of the trees and the soft green vegetation. Others slew the innocent cows and calves, the uneasily sleeping fowls, or struck down the frightened and bewildered watch dog. Others found those for whom they were intended, blasting away their lives and hopes, and denying to many waiting loved ones the answer to their prayers.

Along the front of the Red Bn I could hear the sound of the machine guns, some fast, some slow, some German, some American. One often wonders after a blast whether someone is lying in mortal agony who a moment before was whole.

The moon tonight is bright and beautiful, - one of the most wonderfully beautiful nights I have ever seen. Such scenes of death, destruction and agony as it witnesses here; but somewhere it looks down on lovers walking through its romantic light and shadows, on lonely wives and sweethearts who rest uneasily and turn and silently pray into their pillows for those here with me; and a little boy murmurs "Daddy" in his sleep and in the morning asks, "Mamma, when is Daddy coming home?" Somewhere is peace, but here the moonlit night is made continuously thunderous by the sounds of war and the only consolation is that contained in a poem I used to like very much, "Even This Shall Pass Away."

Today Maj Waring,[31] in command of Red Bn, was evacuated to the hospital by the medics. He was too concerned for his men and worked too hard for them. A good man and a good commander. Maj Momm is presently in command of the Bn. I have been very uneasy that Lt Braffit would break as he is a good and kind fellow and often works like one possessed. As I have said before, one war is enough for any man and this is the second for him.

\* \* \*

There is a terrific bombardment right now, sounds like a mortar barrage into our lines. It beats terrifically on my heart and mind when I think it is falling on our men.

\* \* \*

---

31 Maj. Waring after hospitalization returned to the 320th.

Our artillery caused explosions and fires in the village of Le Neufbourg just at nightfall, which continued for some time. Must have set off a German ammunition dump.

*  *  *

A thunderous barrage is now rolling and a rain of hell is falling on someone.

*  *  *

The war is rolling swiftly through parts of France now. There is not time enough for the Germans to evacuate all the civilians. Lt Kurtz and Sgt Porta told of being kissed on both cheeks several times today as they passed through newly liberated villages. In a village here they found a French girl, age 20, who was shot through the stomach last night. She was taken to our medics for treatment. The Germans looted the village before leaving, so it is likely she was shot because she objected to their pillage or refused to submit to them before they left.

In the town of Torigny, which we captured and have now passed, the Germans had herded the inhabitants out of the town to the southwest, but as they [the Germans] withdrew, allowed the civilians to return. When our troops entered the Huns turned their artillery loose on the village, and French men, women and children were strewn dead and wounded about the streets along with our own men. They were in the act of greeting some of our troops shouting "Viva Americans" while they threw flowers into the jeeps and embraced our men in the streets. We soon evacuated them from the town to a refugee center until the war has rolled far enough away for them to return.

Last night in the gathering darkness, as I was on a mission to a neighboring unit, I saw a whole group of small children beside the road, waving and shouting and giving the proverbial V-sign to the Americans who were passing. Artillery fire was falling just up the road and sometimes over ranged them.

Today as I moved up from the rear CP a little French tot stood by the road and handed me a beautiful flower as I drove by. It was a beautiful lavender cluster of blossoms and was reminiscent of the lilacs in the dooryard of the old homestead far away.

*  *  *

The thunder of the artillery makes the candle flame jump and flicker casting wavering shadows on the tent walls.

* * *

Strange, strange sound of peace I hear just now (0325), the crowing of a cock in the distance heard faintly in the so brief intervals between the artillery's roar. I think of my boyhood and the early morning crowing of the fowls. My father use to rise by their sound and I can well remember of sleepily hearing my mother's voice as she said to him, "Sam, it's time to get up. I hear the rooster crowing."

The sound (now passed) also recalled another memory, when late at night one could hear suddenly the early morning crowing of the cocks in the neighboring farm yards. It seemed they [the roosters] had a strange custom of suddenly waking in the night. One would send out his clear challenge ringing faintly in the still night and the others on adjoining farms would answer. For a time there would be challenge and reply one after another until the calls ceased as suddenly as they had begun. This always caused me to note the time, when away from home, and I would traverse, sometimes with heavy feet but usually with a light heart, the miles I had to travel home. The most pleasant trips however were when I had my fast stepping filly, Queen. After standing hitched during most of the day and far into the night she would be very impatient. On the homeward journey her fast clopping hoofs, echoing in the still night as she sped through the shadowy draws, over the lighter flats and by the quiet farmsteads, was not unlike the passing of a whirlwind.

A wonderfully clean and pleasant memory, so strange when recalled by the crowing of a cock amid the strain and horror of the present situation.

* * *

Planes have droned overhead all during the night but many have sounded like our own. I have heard no bombs fall near.

* * *

An explosion near by almost upsets the candle. Not enemy, thank heaven, but a new battery of our big stuff opening up.

* * *

I note that several of the men and officers have been able to secure this potent drink, Calvados, and other beverages. Some drink rather freely it seems, perhaps to relieve the strain or to give the courage which we all so desire. I have not felt the need of its use for that purpose, but I do not think I have been subjected to as great a strain as many others. I want to keep my head as clear as possible, but I make no attempt to judge the acts of others under such circumstances as surround us. If almost anything helps anyone to bear these awful burdens, I think it would be justifiable.

\* \* \*

Rumors that we will be pinched out tomorrow by convergence of American forces on our right with Canadians and British on our left, and that we will get a two to seven day rest. Well we can certainly use it. This coming Sunday will make a month in the line for us and our regiment has not once even been reserve. We have constantly been in the line since our first committment.

\* \* \*

News from all war fronts is good. Our armored forces [Patton's] are now running pell mell through Brittany, and the Russians cannot be stopped. Maj McElroy says the radio had a report that Hitler's Baltic Armies of 30 divisions had surrendered. If that report is true, the end is nearing rapidly.

\* \* \*

It seems the nearer I get to the end the easier I am to become frightened. It would be a sad fate to survive until the last days and then get killed, yet such will be the fate of many.

\* \* \*

Another thunderous barrage is descending on the enemy. Good enough for them since they will not cease a hopeless struggle for a cause now lost, and end this fearful slaughter.

\* \* \*

We got a Polish prisoner yesterday who had hidden from his German masters when they withdrew and waited until our lines came to him. He was a young kid, not yet having shaved, who was orderly for the regimental officers. Because he could barely speak German and for other reasons he was often beaten by his masters, and was a virtual slave for them. His brother had been killed because he would not serve in the German Army. He saw the Nazis cut his head off and he does not know what has become of the rest of his family, but most if not all are very likely dead.

* * *

The [next] story not personally seen by me, but came through channels. Our forces at the capture of Rennes liberated two Russian girl slaves, still in their teens and taken by the Germans in 1941. They worked for the Germans during the day and were forced to submit to them at night. A Russian-born American officer told them the Germans were being driven from Russia and their armies cut to pieces, and that they could soon go home. To which they replied that their parents had been killed, their property destroyed and they had no one to go to. They asked only to be allowed to work in a safe place.

How different has been the lot of the Russians and others to that of the people of America.

* * *

Saw Lt Orr[32] yesterday looking his old rugged self. He personally killed three enemy soldiers in a fierce fight in the push this week.

Normandy, France
Sunday, Aug. 6, 1944

Now in assembly waiting to move. Sounds strange to hear the thunder in the distance and not all around us.

Principal pastime and occupation seems to be eating. The men gather in little groups, heat their rations on the little gas stoves or small fires, "shoot the breeze" and eat. Some have secured "Calvados" and are quite argumentative.

I have never seen one who enjoys food like my friend Lt Ginsberg. He is always engaged in enjoying food or in the

---

32 2nd Lt. John R. Orr, Cn Co, address unknown, but I seem to recall he was from Texas. At Camp Butner near the time of our departure, a soldier of his unit had approached Lt. Orr with a plea to avoid going overseas. I have never heard such a patriotic lecture given so eloquently and vehemently, as the soldier received from Lt. Orr. The time was late evening after training hours and they were not aware that I overheard from my room nearby.

pursuit of food. He is very unhandy at preparing rations, - evidently had no training whatever as a Boy Scout, - and I am always amused at his attempts to make a fire or to keep one going. But he is certainly persistent if his efforts result in something to eat. I can remember only one other person who was so obsessed with the idea of eating as is Milt. That was an old fellow by the name of Phillip Climer who stayed with my family when I was a kid. We used to ask him quite often, as a sort of means of passing the time, "Phillip, do you eat to live or live to eat?" His reply would always be a sincere "I jots, I live to eat."

I think that if the Germans should succeed in keeping food from Milt for awhile, that he would go out and attack them single handedly. Milt is a very sincere and conscientious worker and really a noble fellow. Contrary to Nazi notions he is one Jew who is an all-around good fellow.

* * *

We are to move tonight, perhaps to join another and a new army which I hope is to drive right on through France. [We had been driving and holding the left flank of the break-through as the armored spearheads advanced and fanned out behind the German lines.]

Normandy Front,
South of St-Hilaire
August 9, 1944

Time: 0510

Quiet day yesterday, but suddenly aroused from sleep this A. M. at 0300 to move to the front. We don't know how hot it will be until we get there. I've been busy until this minute.

I was back to personnel section in rear yesterday to see my friend, Lt Frank Sperl.[33] Sure was glad to see him. I left a few items in his care including the earlier portions of this journal. There were too many chances of my losing it while moving about.

* * *

---

33 2nd Lt. Frank X. Sperl, Sv Co, Flushing, N. Y., mentioned in the introduction, and who took care of the finished portions of this journal as they were gotten to him from time to time.

Quite a lot of activity by the Luftwaffe last night. Some were shot down and one fell into the area of one of our artillery units. I saw one shot down in flames the night we moved to this area.

Rubble was strewn all about the streets, and part of the town of St. Hilaire was burning as we passed through it on our way here. The bombing was just before our column entered it.

I was caught at a RJ some distance from the town at the time. The Hun's planes lit up the area with flares and then circled about with the ack-ack banging away at them. Pieces of shrapnel were falling about. I found a nice nook back from the road between a stack of wood and a hedge. Clark and Ginsberg piled in on top of me without hesitation, and in doing so Clark slapped a big bunch of nettles in my face. I also got on to them with my hands and my skin had not stopped stinging by the next day. Ginsberg also got stung and complained almost as much as I.

The column was miles long and stopped along the road. Bombs fell near the RJ and planes continued to drone overhead for some time. I couldn't help but be amused when Ginsberg said "Jesus, Faubus, it looks like they want to get us killed." Upon my laughing he remonstrated, "Well, it does." A little later we were cursing the absence of our Air Corps and wondering why we did not have some night-fighters. I remarked that they were probably in England courting some English Tommy's wife or girl friend while we were over here taking this s--t. Then Clark and Ginsberg were amused.


At CP West of Mortain
August 10, 1944

Time: 0105

Things have been pretty hectic during the evening and night. For a time L Co was completely cut off and surrounded by Germans who were calling on them to surrender. Tanks and infantry [German] cut the company off when it advanced ahead of the others. Later on the tanks drew off to the south and now the men of the company are regaining contact with the Bn. Lt Kelly is with that unit and I hope he is all right. Lt. Orr[34] of Cn Co, attached to Blue Bn, fell in the fight tonight. A contact patrol from Lt Head's Co is now trying to reach him to bring him in. Not known yet the extent of his injuries or if he is still alive.

The others around this CP have finally gotten to bed. The attack continues tomorrow and they must have some rest. Sgt Coyne and myself are on duty.

* * *

The situation on this sector is very fluid or I might say uncertain now. A great deal of the enemy to our front are practically cut off, and within their lines are units of ours cut off, some for three days now. In fact there are some more "Lost Battalions" here. The German troops with which we are in contact are SS troops, panzer units and parachute troops, the elite of Hitler's army. In most cases they resist fiercly and the fighting is furious.

(According to the big picture, Hitler's armor grows less each day and our armor is now cutting behind his entire army here. But that thought is not very comforting to a Bn cut off from help or an individual waging a battle for his life).

I can understand now why all the French refugees were streaming by us yesterday. They could foresee the battle here and [were] trying to get out of range. If one had not grown quite used to suffering, hardship and death, he could not help being touched by the plight of the refugees. They were hurrying desperately along the hot, dusty roads, all ages, condition and sizes, either carrying, pulling or pushing, on all sorts of carts, buggies and bicycles, a miserable mite of their earthly possessions. Each bore his burden from the smallest, weakest tot to the oldest and most feeble person. Only those who were ill or were so feeble they had to be supported, or those heavy with child, carried no load of goods. For the most part their faces bore a strained look. They neither paused nor hesitated for one moment but pushed relentlessly on, their forms becoming dust stained and fatigued. Now and then they glanced at the sun as if anxiously noting if there was yet enough time to get far enough from the coming battle. Almost everyone threw us a fleeting smile and if they had a free hand, raised it in the "V-for-Victory" sign. Most touching sight were the little babes, most of whom

---

34  Lt. Orr fell in the advance. He was listed as KIA Aug. 10.

were being pulled or pushed in their small jouncing carriages along the rough roads by their worried mothers, their little weary forms becoming covered with dust. There were almost no young or middle aged men, and few women. [young or middle aged] The very old and the very young predominated. An example which explains this - the two young women who did laundry in the stream near by. The husband of one had been killed by the Germans in France, the husband of the other was a prisoner (slave) in Berlin.

* * *

The town of St. Hilaire is a wrecked mass of rubble. One who has not seen such cannot imagine the destruction. Because it is an important cross roads the Germans have bombed it almost nightly since we captured it. But the roads and bridges are still working.

* * *

Getting pretty sleepy as I've been up since 0300 yesterday for our morning move. The thunder of battle rolls back and forth, mostly our artillery. But that is no longer any deterrent to sleep. In fact it would seem a little strange without it. The Hun planes were out again tonight. I heard a few bombs fall but none near.

* * *

The weather continues hot and dry, but it is still very cold and damp in the early morning hours. A bad time indeed to be lying wounded in the damp, open fields of Normandy as some certainly are after the battles of yesterday and tonight.

* * *

The barnyard cocks have suddenly taken a spell of crowing (0210) answering each other as I once used to hear them in America, then suddenly fall silent. The country is not so beaten here, and there are many fowls and farm animals left on the farms. We find many places untouched by war here.

Time: 1800 - By reading the headlines of the 8th, 9th and 10th, one can get an idea of the vital role our unit is playing in Allied strategy right now.

(Newspaper story - Nazis Drive to Cut off U. S. Spearheads)

This Division with the 30th Inf Div on our left is setting squarely athwart the German counterattack route to Avranches and the sea. Should they, the Germans, be successful it would spoil the whole Allied plan of action. So we are beating off the Nazi thrusts by the elite of Hitler's Army, - SS troops, Panzer Divisions and parachute troops, plus remnants of units we helped to drive down from the north before [ourselves] moving down here. More than that we are advancing and re-taking ground from the Germans in bloody and uncertain fighting, as witness the "cut off" of L Co last night and its subsequent reunion with its Bn.

On our left, the 120th Inf has a Bn, less one Company, which has been isolated in Mortain for four (or more) days with no contact at all. Supplies have been dropped by plane to some of those troops.

On our right one Bn of the 134th has been cut off and greatly decimated. Contact has been made with parts of the unit; other segments are lost. And still today the fighting continues with unabated fury.

From near the town of St. Cyr on the right flank of the 137th, through the 134th sector, on through our unit's front and north through the zone of the 30th Div, the tide of battle rises and falls as there is mingled together the desperate struggles of the infantry, the fierce engagements of the armor, the thunderous bombing of the air forces, and the concentrated, all encompassing barrages of the artillery.

Many heroic deeds today will be unknown and unsung for both the doers and the observers may well perish in the struggle.

\* \* \*

Saw Lt Gardner at about 1400. His company of infantry (Co B) were to ride a tank Bn past the town of Mortain and take a hill just beyond which lies in the center of the zone of contest. A desperately dangerous mission, and I couldn't help but pause in my thoughts a moment to say a prayer of God-speed for those brave men and their leader. Gardner's men were to consolidate positions and hold the hill if they reach it. Other units were to attack supported by other tanks, TDs, planes and artillery at about the same hour. [Men of Co C rode the leading tanks in the charge].

\* \* \*

Last night at about 0400, Capt Hayes, Regtl Chaplain for the 134th Inf, came into the lines of one of the companies of our Blue Bn. He had been sent back into our lines by his German captors with an offer to exchange 53 medical personnel and wounded of ours which they hold, for seven PWs which we have of theirs. The personnel of ours, which is mostly 134th and 30th Div, include two doctors from each and Father Hayes. He is to return into the German lines tonight about 2200 with the Allied reply. He had a list of the PWs the Nazis want in exchange which includes one Lt Col who is not a non-combatant. This may prevent the exchange even if feasible. I expedited his mission by securing transportation for him from the company to this CP and thence to Division hqs.

He reported that the Germans had taken quite a number of our fighting men as PWs (mostly from the cut up and isolated units we presume) and that they were being evacuated on to the German rear. He said also that the enemy had plenty of stuff. While blindfolded he could smell the armor and hear it moving by. When the blind was removed he could see tanks and armored vehicles parked under camouflage nets, trees and other natural cover.

The 53 non-combatants and wounded were being held there for possible exchange and had had a tough time. They were bombed once and strafed twice, along with their captors, by our air force.

He said he was to go back tonight. I have learned nothing further today about the strange case but I am very interested to learn the outcome if possible.

\* \* \*

Yesterday one of our arty liaison planes was shot down by the Huns. It got over the lines a little too far and the ack-ack got it. It managed to maneuver so as to fall just in front of our lines and our men rescued the two fliers. Both were badly shaken up and injured but no one killed.

A German plane was shot down the other night over us at too low an altitude for the fliers to jump safely. Both jumped but were found dead by the collecting co personnel, their chutes still unopened.

\* \* \*

The sky is now well filled with our planes, some diving through the German ack-ack on enemy targets and others flying high, out bound or home bound, to or from other missions.

Our 320th needs all the assistance possible now, as all units are committed and no reserve at our control to back them up. The Germans still hold the town of Mortain and the high ground to the east. Tanks also committed and objective not fully attained. We are holding what may well be the last strong German offensive effort.

*    *    *

Lt Orr not recovered. His radio man, who shot the German who shot Orr, left him for dead as also did a non-com who was near them. He was pierced through the middle and fell on his back and lay as if dead. It is reported that the area was reached and his body could not be found. It is barely possible that he revived somewhat and may have been evacuated and given medical aid by the Germans.

Everyone who knew him regrets keenly his loss as he was one of our best and bravest officers.

*    *    *

Picture in my mind as of yesterday. The foot soldiers slogging forward to the battle lines in the warm bright sunshine, their feet leaving brief imprints on the green grass of the orchards and meadows, and plucking green apples from the low hanging boughs of the apple trees and chewing them as they tramped along.

*    *    *

The slow flying liaison plane up there now buzzing along, its wings and fuselage bathed in the rays of the setting sun, while the landscape is already wrapped in the purple of evening and the twilight damp is already settling on the cool grass. (2135)

*    *    *

Jerry's stuff is coming in, crump, crump of mortars and wham of shells. May be a tough night for all. I know it will for some.

*    *    *

I try not to think of the end of the war but to live from day to day and be thankful, as each day dawns, that I have

survived thus far. But the constant strain causes me to long
for the end sometimes, more than I can ever say. Sometimes
more for the sake of others (it seems) than for myself.

At-the-Front
Mortain
Aug. 11, 1944

Time: 1335

Still hot, dry and clear today. Good for the air and our
armor.

Reported today that Lt Orr's body found where he fell,
so previous reports that they were back to the spot were
false. Sgt Conley[35] also was killed yesterday. He had already
been recommended for a decoration and for a [battlefield]
commission as an officer.

* * *

Our tank column got into the town of Mortain yesterday evening with about a platoon of our infantry. Several
of our infantry who rode the tanks were casualties, shot from
the tanks as they rode into enemy positions. Most of our Red
Bn now in the town and other two moving up. So looks as if
we had successfully blunted the enemy spearhead which was
to reach for the sea and thus split our forces. [Cut off Patton's armor and the infantry with the tank forces.]

At-the-Front
Mortain
Aug. 12, 1944
Forward CP.

Time: 0825

Right now I snatch a moment to write as I sit at our
advance CP on the hill above the battered and ruined town
of Mortain. It would be a beautiful scene in peace, but with
the smoke and dust of battle obscuring and limiting my vision, with the sickly odor of the dead in my nostrils and the
sounds of battle all around, it is no pleasant scene.

---

35   T/Sgt. Irvin F. Conley, Co K, Iona, W. Va., was one of our
original non-coms whom I had known for months. He was awarded
the DSC for gallantry displayed on July 13 in singlehandedly wiping
out an enemy MG nest.

Looking back from here over the country we have traversed, I marvel that we were able to take this position at all. From here I can see over the country over which we fought as if looking at my open palm. The Huns really could look down on all our movement as we maneuvered our forces against them.

Just to mention a small part of the cost of the hill which I saw as I came up.

Burned out tanks and TDs, both German and American, all along the road up to the town and to here. Most were blackened, burned ruins which had seared the road way and roadside. Many of the crews had been cremated in the fiery flaming infernos.

Rear area crews were cleaning up some of the tanks. From one they had removed an American body which appeared to be in good shape except the head had been blown completely away and only a black hole remained where his neck should have been. I noticed that his shoes [as well as coveralls] were nice and clean and worn scarcely any at all. Near the crossroads just south of the town were numbers of American dead, some partly in and some out of their foxholes. One soldier with red hair reclined on his stomach and face on the road bank almost as if in the attitude of prayer. There were German dead too, and the ever present, swollen, dead cows.

A soldier came off the hill side with his shirt bloodstained and dirty and nursing his arm, having been wounded by a German MG. I took him back to the Aid station and then continued. A German came hurrying out of a field to the road [his hands on his head,] jabbering excitedly and surrendered to the Colonel's party. [about 50 feet to my front]

"My first PW," says the Colonel.

The men frisked him of weapons and I sent a guard with him to the PW coll pt.

* * *

Today the AT Co lost two trucks from mines in road and four men were wounded including Lt Adams,[36] one of my Ft. Benning class mates. Yesterday Pfc Peterson's[37] I&R

---

36   1st Lt. Robert W. Adams, A/T Co, Canton, Ohio. A Ft. Benning classmate, he was one of the original 320th officers. He recovered and later returned.

37   T/4 Arnold Peterson of Minneapolis, Minn., one of the I & R originals. (not certain of first name).

vehicle had two tires shot off and a bullet went through his rifle holder right by his head. They all escaped. Today they lost three vehicles in an arty barrage and luckily only one man wounded. Another received a burn when grazed by a MG bullet.

Last night four men of C Co, part of the troops who had gained the town by riding on the tanks, returned into our lines. The tanks had been so decimated that they sought cover and when daylight came the troops had no supporting force. The Germans either killed or took prisoner, with tanks and MGs, what few [Co C] did not escape. No definite number may ever be given but will merely be totaled as dead, wounded and missing. Lt Gardner was wounded in the action, the seriousness of which I do not yet know. The charge on the hill was made by 54 tanks. The Germans knocked out 30 of them. There was not proper co-ordination of tankers and infantry after the objective was reached.

The above action, coupled with last night's and today's in which the Blue Bn under Lt Col Northam and the Red Bn under Maj Gillis, drove forward and took this high hill, and reached and relieved the isolated battalion of the 120th Inf is one of the epics of this war. The Bn of the 120th had been cut off completely since last Sunday and today is Saturday. They had intermittent communication by radio and some supplies were dropped to them by air. But they were really in a bad way, after constant harrassment and attack from all sides, especially their wounded of which there were about 50. Prompt relief was not possible and was delayed for three or four hours because mines, shattered tanks and other debris of the battle had to be removed from the road before vehicles could come up. They were one thankful bunch to see some friends again.

[News story - Long Toms Fire Medical Aid to 'Lost Battalion'].

Our Inf Regt, to take this hill and effect the relief, attacked on a front as broad as that of the whole division on our left and over the most difficult terrain. I wonder yet how we succeeded. But we expended a number of men, vehicles and tanks in accomplishing the task.

I talked to one lad who was first to be relieved, [from the Lost Battalion] a Pvt Reynolds of Illinois, member of an AT Platoon of the 120th. Almost his whole unit was surrounded and captured, vehicles and all. He and two other men escaped as they were being evacuated to the rear. He hid in holes along a stream in the midst of the Germans for the entire time. He said many of the Nazi troops were drunk much of the time, did much shouting and moving about at night, that they had plentiful supplies of liquors and had a number of girls or women for the entertainment and use of the troops. He stated that it seemed that this state of affairs was the only reason of the Nazi troops for continuing to fight.

I know that will sound unbelievable to many but the report is bourne out by another report which comes to light in the following story.

Pvt John Dudley,[38] now known as the "Mad Medic" because of his escapades, went out yesterday morning and got himself captured. In the afternoon Col Hoyne and Capt Thomson from Div G-2 were at our CP with correspondents from Yank magazine checking on the story of Father Hayes and the strange offer he had brought from the Germans. At that time who should come into the CP but this Pvt Dudley with a Nazi soldier, they having entered our lines under a white flag. Dudley had been released to guide the Nazi to our lines with a repetition of the offer bourne by Father Hayes. As it happened I again was the first officer encountered. The German clicked his heels and gave the Nazi salute in the most approved Hitler fashion. (I have sometimes returned regular German Army salutes, one does it automatically, but I did not and I will not return Nazi salutes).

So the Yank correspondents and photographers got their story, much embellished, pictures and all.

Father Hayes had returned to the point where he was to enter the German lines but found the Germans gone and the ground in the hands of our troops. The German offer of exchange had to be declined because the officers called for by them were not available to us. The Nazi was sent back with a written reply but Pvt Dudley was not allowed to accompany him.

Dudley said that he had gone all the way back to a main German hqs where there were many German officers sitting around tables in nicely furnished, paneled rooms in underground caverns and dugouts. He stated that they had un-

---

38 Pvt. John D. Dudley, Morristown, N. J. Before the war ended the exploits of Dudley would have filled a book.

believable stocks of fine liquors (I smelled some on his breath) and considerable numbers of girls acting as orderlies and clerks. He was blind folded while traveling to and from the German rear to the front lines.

* * *

Statement of Pvt Reynolds, who hit the beaches on D-Day, "This was much worse than D-Day."

Statement of a 1st Lt, a replacement, who viewed the tank wreckage of this battle along with me, "I was three months in Africa and I never saw anything as bad at this."

* * *

Word has just come that we are to be relieved. Maj Jamison and I are to remain here until about 2200 (now 1950) to orient the incoming units on the situation. So if my luck holds out a bit longer perhaps we will get that long needed rest.

The damned Huns have been shelling this hill all the time I have been hurriedly writing and I'm sure they'll bomb the place as soon as darkness comes. The sun is now dropping into the thick haze on the far western horizon (and I think briefly of a little round faced boy waiting way out there under the sinking sun, a dark red sun here in the haze of battle; out there a beautiful sunset glow in a peaceful America.)

The shells now land so close that shrapnel is dropping around.

* * *

The Hun planes were very active last night. They have some flares which light up the night as if it were day. They shook the earth around us last night with their bombs. Some fell in the first Bn causing casualties. The planes swept back and forth over us looking for targets. For some reason I am not much afraid of them but most of the men are. Every drone of an enemy plane overhead gets a curse from some of the men for our Air Force because they do not put up night fighters. Last night our ack-ack did not seem at all effective. While most are afraid of the aerial bombs it is the arty which I fear. I shake in my boots every time the damned stuff comes in, and that is pretty often.

* * *

The General [Baade] was up and looked over the battle-field and our positions. He was exceptionally well pleased today. He seemed quite happy. It is difficult to see how one could be happy after seeing this battlefield, and the red haired soldier in death as if in prayer. Perhaps it is the attitude of the professional soldier who must needs look upon death with as little compassion as a doctor looks upon suffering.

\* \* \*

All sickness cannot be avoided (much of it could) but all wars could.

[Maj. Jamieson and I with a few enlisted personnel held the forward CP. The stench of the dead was constantly all about us. Others were killed, wounded or captured to our rear in the confused fighting.]

From The

## THE STARS AND STRIPES

### LONG TOMS FIRE

### MEDICAL AID TO

### 'LOST BATTALION'

---

Shells Filled With Drugs
Hurled to U. S. Outfit
Surrounded by Nazis

---

MORTAIN SECTOR, France, Aug. 13 (AP)---An American Long Tom gun, sending over life instead of death, fired shells containing blood plasma, morphine and sulfa drugs to a "lost battalion" fighting on a hill behind the German lines. [A Bn of the 120th Inf Regt, 30th Inf Div.]

For five days this American battalion caused great havoc and refused two demands to surrender from Hitler's crack SS troops until it was relieved by a regiment which fought its way to the hill position. [The regiment was the 320th Infantry]

They were supplied with food by divebombing planes and received medical supplies by Long Tom shells.

The problem of getting medical supplies to the wounded was solved by clearing out the insides of smoke shells and stuffing them with medical suppplies packed in cotton wool. The shells were then fired to the hilltop.

All except the morphine arrived in good shape, even the blood plasma in glass containers.

\* \* \*

### PVT. JOHN DUDLEY

*Pvt. John Dudley, Morristown, N. J. had been heard of throughout the Regiment before his capture by the Germans at Mortain. At first he was a member of the Medical Detachment. He wandered away from his place of duty one day, picked up a rifle and went alone through an enemy roadblock from which the Germans had been firing only a few moments before. Beyond the roadblock he "liberated" a French village*

*before returning. Shortly afterward he was made a rifle-
man - he said he wanted to fight - and put in a line company.*

*On the day he was captured he walked down the main
highway leading to Mortain and into the German lines. Before starting off down the road which had been hot with
fire, both friendly and enemy, he said to the soldiers with
him, "I'm going down that road. When I reach the crest (of
a slight rise several hundred yards away) I'll turn and wave
to you if everything is all right. If I do not wave, you'll know
the Germans are still there."*

*His comrades watched Dudley until he reached the crest.
There he was seen to pause, as if listening to someone near-
by, then turn and walk off the road. He had been captured.
Later that day or the next, he returned to our lines with the
Nazi soldier with the German offer of exchange of prisoners.*

*Dudley and the German soldier came first to the Third
Battalion Headquarters of Col. Docka, who immediately
brought them to Regimental Headquarters. I was in charge
at the time and was the first to receive them. Naturally this
information was a decision for higher authority. Fortunately
Division G-2 personnel with correspondents from Yank Magazine, were at the 320th Headquarters at the time and the
matter was referred by Col. Byrne to them.*

*In bringing Dudley and the SS trooper to our head-
quarters, Col. Docka had unfortunately forgotten to blind-
fold the German. After he was permitted to return to his
lines, we moved our command post in a hurry. We knew the
Nazi would report its location and it would be shelled by artillery and that night bombed by the Luftwaffe.*

*Later Dudley was courtmartialed for one of the times he
wandered from his post of duty. I was the Trial Judge Advocate who handled the prosecution. Dudley was given a light
sentence, returned to duty, - he was a good soldier in many
ways and seemed without fear - and later assigned to Service
Company. We became friends, I saw him occasionally and he
sought every opportunity to do something for me.*

Back-to-rear-CP
Mortain
Aug. 13, 1944

This Sabbath Day is bright and sunny. When someone
mentioned that it was the Sabbath Col Docka kept asking

incredulously, "Is this Sunday? . . . Is this Sunday?" The weather continues dry and warm and the ground firm and I hope our offensive is still rolling.

We were relieved last night, but the troops did not get to the rear assembly areas until well after daylight. A night relief is very difficult, especially without previous reconnaissance by the relieving unit. Also our troops were still driving, and as Maj Gillis said, he "had to catch them by the shirt tail and bring them back." A platoon of K Co was cut off by the enemy and could not be brought out. An effort was to be made to gather up stragglers and lost today, and perhaps the platoon will be reached and relieved. Maj Jamison and I did not get back to CP until this morning.

\* \* \*

This morning Capt Davis, Capt Forsyth and their driver, McCartney, were still missing after going on a reconnaissance for a new CP location yesterday. Today Capt Wilson found the body of his platoon leader, Lt Prescott[39] and the bodies of two of his men. About 200 yards farther along the road was the corpse of Capt Davis,[40] shot through the head by a burrp gun. Of Capt Forsyth[41] and T/5 McCartney[42] there was no trace, and neither of their vehicle or equipment. Therefore they are "missing in action" and it is hoped by many of us that they are captured, rather than something worse, but it is only a hope for there is no definite indication.

\* \* \*

[Other casualties[43] not mentioned in the Journal.]

---

39  2nd Lt. Warren F. Prescott, AT Co, San Francisco, Calif., an original and close friend, listed KIA Aug 12.

40  Capt. Wilbur T. Davis, S-1 of Regtl Hq, Wyanet, Ill., an original, listed KIA Aug 12.

41  Capt. James P. Forsyth, CO of Regtl Hq Co, Little Rock, Ark. an original with whom I was closely associated in training and combat, listed MIA Aug 12. We later learned he was a POW.

42  T/5 McCartney, Regtl Hq Co, driver for either Capt. Forsyth or Capt. Davis. He was listed as MIA Aug 12. I never heard of him again.

43  2nd Lt. Roger R. Heroux, Co E, address unknown, listed LWA Aug 12; 2nd Lt Samuel E. Belk, Co B, address unknown, listed as LIA Aug 13; both replacements, neither returned.

## FIGHTING AT MORTAIN
### (From 320th Inf History)

*Tanks of the 737th Tank Battalion rammed through a hail of artillery, Nebelwerfer, mortar, anti-tank, machine gun and sniper fire with infantrymen of Co C like perched ducks riding the tops. S/Sgt Julius E. Cardwell of Social Circle, Ga., Pfc. James E. Buchner of Nebo, N. C., and Troy E. Stricklen Jr. of Sutton, Mass., rode their tank 600 yards into the Nazi lines. They then dismounted, deployed and protected it until soldiers farther behind could reorganize and fight their way up.*

---

*2nd Lt Warren F. Prescott of San Francisco, Calif. was ordered to move his platoon 400 yards to the front. He reconnoitered the route, returned and led his men forward. Half the way up, when the lead vehicle was in front of one concealed machine gun and the last vehicle in front of another, the enemy opened up from ambush.*

*Many men were immediately wounded. The platoon had little chance but those who could, fought. Jumping from his truck Pfc. Carl Ash of St. Louis ran along a hedge row behind which the Germans were hiding. He fired his pistol at them, yelling and cursing, which gave his buddies a chance to organize.*

*Lt Prescott pumped clip after clip from his carbine until he was killed. Sgt. Paul Clevenger of Marion, Ind., fought until riddled with 24 bullets. He was captured twice in the wild melee and both times succeeded in killing his captors and fighting on. Finally the 24th slug which entered his body rendered him unconscious, but later he recovered and crawled to safety.*

---

*In rescuing the Lost Battalion, Pvt Murray H. Watnoffsky of Bronx, N. Y., a 2nd Bn medic, discovered a wounded soldier pinned in a ditch under a huge boulder which had been rolled on him by a shell burst. Some one had given him water but had been unable to lift the stone. Watnoffsky and three others just managed to free the soldier. Then he smiled, said, "Hello. I guess I'll be all right now. Got a smoke, please."*

## NORTHAM AND GILLIS WIN SILVER STAR

*In the assault on Mortain hill and the push beyond, Col. Byrne sent Lt. Col. Northam to lead the 3rd Battalion, while Maj. Gillis led the 1st Bn. Later I talked to an enlisted man who was one of those assigned as runner and protection for Col. Northam. He thought his assignment would be relatively safe, he related to me, but he soon found his commander moving with the forward elements as he urged them on, crossing roads under fire and sometimes ducking enemy bullets in his temporary command post.*

*The surge forward by the two battalions as a combined attack force led by Northam and Gillis was eminently successful. For their leadership and bravery in the attack both officers were later awarded the Silver Star.*

---

*Lt Kurtz and Sgt. Porta with a patrol were the first to reach the "Lost Battalion" on the hill.*

---

CP South of Le Mans
Aug. 15, 1944

Time: 0730

In the midst of the above writing I was ordered to Div Hqs as the head of our Regtl billeting party. We were given orders to proceed to a point south of Laval in vicinity of Agente and reconnoiter for assembly areas for our regts. Upon reaching that point word reached us by rumor that plans had been changed. Then a signal officer showed me a written message, "Proceed to Le Mans." So we fell in column and took off toward that town.

The leader had made a very "negligent" error in not officially informing us of the change and giving us a rendevous point. Before long the column was broken up, and in seeking the area of our leader some of us went through Le Mans. I guess we would have been near Paris by morning if a rumor had not started from somewhere that the route beyond the town about 6 miles had been cut by the Germans, and the MPs turned us back. We went back west of the town and bivouaced for the rest of the night while keeping a watch on the road for any of our vehicles coming through. We found the area here yesterday morning and I barely had the bivouac sites selected before the troops began to arrive.

We are still in the same positions, part in assembly and part in outpost battle positions, here in an area of soft sandy soil and groves of pines. When I finally got a chance to lie down, I looked up through the waving pine boughs, smelled the pungent odor of the needles and had a momentary feeling of nostalgia.

The change from one day to the next, from the grim and terrible scenes of Mortain Hill to the pretty villages and towns and beautiful country-side; from the ghastly mutilation and horrible death to wonderfully clean and beautiful little children, lovely women and friendly people of all ages; from the stench of the battlefield to the fragrance of flower gardens along the roads; from the feelings of fear and hate, grief and despair, to that of victory, cheer and triumph, was, and is yet, almost more than I can realize. The French people stood in groups along the highways and lined the streets of the towns, cheering and waving. The children and maidens tossed flowers into the vehicles or handed them to us as we rode by. Many stood with pitchers and glasses ready to serve drinks of cider and wine, whenever we briefly paused. Some GIs, who passed out gum and cigarettes when we briefly stopped, were given kisses on both cheeks. They [the French civilians] swarmed around the vehicles to shake our hands and reached out to touch us as we drove by, all smiling and waving and giving the V-sign. My arm was actually tired from replying as we rolled and rolled through liberated France in pursuit of the retreating Nazis.

And here around the assembly area we have enjoyed such hospitality as I have never known, and I come from a region noted for its friendliness and hospitality. They give of their liquors, wines and ciders, their vegetables, bread and eggs, some until they have no more, and we have to force pay upon them. They gladly accept gum or cigarettes but often they stick the proffered money back into some part of our equipment or into the jeeps and we have to deposit the money some place about their house and depart.

If ever I have seen a sincerely happy and grateful people, it is these liberated French. Our propensity to have things our own way, the oftentimes rude manners of some of our drinking GIs and officers, and the inclination of some of us to abuse their generosity, may somewhat cool their friendly attitude. But aside from this I see no obstacle to the continuance of most friendly relations so far as the masses of the French people are concerned. Such things produce a highly satisfactory state of feeling after the many days of almost ceaseless fighting we have gone through.

To the above there is a bitter afterthought. Lt Kurtz led a patrol back to where the platoon of Co K was cut off. They found two dead bodies of our men, and scattered on the ground a dozen steel helmets and some American arms, indications that the whole platoon was either killed, wounded or captured. So at the last minute, fate denied to them, as well as to Lt Prescott and his men, and Capts Davis and Forsyth and others, the opportunity of seeing some of the results of the hell which we have endured for so long. Results which were purchased by the labor and sweat and endurance of those of us who yet survive, by the blood of the wounded and by the lives of Swanson, Talcott and Cull, of Zintas, Conley, Orr and Underwood, and all the others who so bravely died.

\* \* \*

Lt Kurtz and Sgt Porta were the first to reach the isolated battalion on the hill by Mortain. Porta is already recommended twice for decorations and Kurtz once.

\* \* \*

We have several French speaking soldiers who have talked much to the French people. I have asked them how the French like the Germans and what the Nazi attitude was toward the conquered. Lt Silverman summed it up thus. "They don't like the Bosche because, briefly put, they took their food, their liquors and their women and paid them nothing."

Lt De L'Cruce, "Yes, there was some collaboration with the Germans, mostly among the higher classes, and some voluntary association by the women, also mostly of the same class. Many of the rich, in order to protect their property, had to, let-us-say, play ball, and the German officers could offer many comforts and conveniences to the "nicer" women for their association. For the poorer classes there was no choice. The Germans merely took a girl by the scruff of the neck as you would a puppy and made her come along. When the girl became pregnant as a result of the association, willing or unwilling, or a prettier one was spotted more suitable to the "Superman's" taste, the former unfortunate female was simply discarded to fend for herself or to be grabbed by another Nazi. If a girl was unwilling there was always punishment for her, up to being shot. Sometimes the powerful rather liked the art of overcoming resistence of unwilling females. And there was always the more powerful persuasive force of the threat of punishment to the unfortunate's family."

Again: The French people are overjoyed at being liberated.

Rothschild Chateau, Chateaudun
August 17, 1944

Time: 1045

Our White Bn, after fighting which lasted all yesterday, finally occupied and secured the town of Chateaudun this morning. The little sawed-off, smiling, fighting Lt McCoy[44] was finally hit and wounded in the first advance on the town. It is reported his wound was serious so I guess his services are lost to us for the duration.

Lt Litherland[45] of Hqs Co of same Bn was also seriously wounded in the same action. So two more of my friends of long standing have passed from the picture. It is getting somewhat difficult to see many of the old faces.

Lt Ginsberg took over the duties of S-1 and Capt Casey[46] (formerly commanding E Co) as hqs commandant, after the loss of Capts Davis and Forsyth. Lt Ginsberg is as crabby as a setting hen because he has a lot of work to do and some of it isn't in good order.

\* \* \*

We got orders to move from our other assembly area late on the afternoon of Aug. 15. We got organized and stood by for orders to move out which came just at nightfall. Rain had been falling and with no moon and an overcast sky,

---

44  1st Lt. James H. McCoy, Co G, Walla Walla, Wash., an original, listed LWA Aug. 16, did not return.

45  2nd Lt. Charles V. Litherland, Hq Co, 2nd Bn, St. Francisville, Ill, an original, recovered and returned.

46  Capt. Edmund R. Casey, Regtl Hq, formerly CO of Co E, Los Angeles, Calif., a close friend from early in 1943.

blackout driving was really difficult. Parts of the column were lost at different times, and Lt Silverman and Sgt Donovan with the I & R platoon did a wonderfully good job keeping all the column on the right route. We were far along on the way at day light. Many, or perhaps all, of the French people along the route were much surprised to awaken and find the Americans rolling through their villages and along the roads.

As soon as they realized what was going on, they piled hastily from their beds, wiping the sleep from their eyes, some still in their night clothes and gowns and others dressing as they came, and as before, smiling, waving, laughing and some shouting, "Viva la Amerique." Some were weeping for joy, or perhaps it was they remembered some loved one who had been taken away or killed by the Nazis and could not be present for the "Great Liberation."

Those in the villages set back from the road did not become aware of our presence so soon. At times I could see the first ones who had risen hurrying and running toward the highway followed by twos and threes and then larger groups until the populace of the whole village had streamed across the fields and gathered by the road. Then many began to hurry back and bring up food such as eggs, butter, bread, apples, and whole bottles of cider and wines which they gave to the battle worn and trench-stained occupants of the jeeps and trucks.

They would accept no pay but would accept, with many thanks, our own gifts of cigarettes, candy and lumps of sugar which come from our K-rations. Some brought great pitchers of wines and cider which they served in glasses to those who happened to be near when the column paused. And always, during the stops, they swarmed around the vehicles, young and old, shaking our hands, wishing us Godspeed and talking at the rate of twenty-to-the-dozen even though we couldn't understand their language.

* * *

We now have our CP, by invitation of the caretaker, in an old French chateau, property of the Rothschild family. I understand it was a magnificent place when well kept, and is still quite luxurious. There are full length mirrors in large airy rooms, big comfortable beds, pieces of furniture, as tables, chairs and desks of intricate design of rare materials which must have cost hundreds of dollars for each individual piece when new. There are bath tubs and a water and light system, but unfortunately out of working order at present. But to have such rooms, and chairs and tables to use in carrying on our work, is quite a contrast to the dug-outs, the dirt, and the general all-around hell of the hedgerow country of Normandy.

\* \* \*

Here the country is generally level with only slight rises and shallow draws. It is a grain country with great stacks of wheat and barley and herds of cattle. It reminded me constantly of the grain sections of Oklahoma and Kansas. I stood out north of our CP yesterday by a hay stack and watched our artillery shells landing in the edge of the town as our White Bn rooted out the German pockets of resistance.

\* \* \*

This morning upon awakening (from the first good night's sleep in five) I noticed upon a trellis by the caretaker's doorway a magnificent array of Morning Glory blossoms, deep purple, lavender, dark red, and a bright shade of pink. Beaded with silvery droplets of dew the blossoms glowed in the early morning light. It was the most typical and reminiscent scene of the door yards and fields of home of any I have yet seen in France.

\* \* \*

I now understand why all German PWs carried pocket knives with corkscrews attached. They were used to open all the many bottles of cider, wines and liquors found in France.

\* \* \*

We have PWs taken this morning. The news of the operation on the Mediterranean Coast of France is very heartening indeed. The battle of France is moving rapidly toward a climax.

[A casualty[47] not mentioned in the Journal.]

---

47 2nd Lt. Otto Wilrich (or Willrich) Co G, LaGrange, Texas, a replacement, listed KIA Aug 17.

Chateau de Touchaillou
August 18, 1944

Time: 2130

Moving from this location to a new CP north of the town. Many very interesting and odd experiences yesterday and today, but must move now, and the darkness prevents writing.

But the shaven heads of the female collaborators, the parades of the FFI, the joyous greetings of the French populace, all are interesting angles of the two days' adventures.

Chateau de Touchaillou
August 19, 1944

Time: 0045

We are now set up in our new CP in the woods by a stream. There is quite a bit of aircraft activity overhead now which sounds like Jerry planes. Some night birds or animals are breaking the night stillness with loud, raccous screams and complaining. Some of the guards who are not familiar with night noises, will keep an uneasy eye and keenly tuned ear turned in their direction.

*   *   *

This morning Lt Silverman and I with one squad of the I & R went to the town of BONNEVAL on a combined mission of Rcn and sight seeing, and to pick up some PWs reported as being held there by the FFI. We found no evidence of the enemy and the FFI reported the town and vicinity as clear. Being among the first Americans to enter the town, we were hailed as real "Liberators" and treated accordingly. There were the usual crowds, handshaking, kisses on both cheeks and the gifts of wines. Mothers brought their children to have a look at, and to shake the hands and kiss the cheeks of the respected "Freedom soldiers" from the great country across the sea. After four long years of oppression and darkness it was naturally a great day for them and the populace as a whole was simply overjoyed. Parents were so proud when we occasionally found time to hold a bright youngster in our arms and many wanted to be photographed with us.

The FFI simply fell over each other in their attempts to aid us. Their principal help was in giving information and acting as guides. While we were there the FFI brought in a captive who we learned was a Russian who had escaped from the Germans.

There were a great number of women and girls working around the French hqs, many of them strikingly beautiful. They offered us food but we did not then have time to eat. Lt Silverman speaks French so we had no great difficulty in dealing with the FFI or others of the civilian population.

When a remark was made about beautiful women some members of the FFI seized Sid and me by the arms and said they would take us and show us "a beautiful woman." They led us down the uneven stone-paved street to a building formerly used as a German Hqs and up a flight of stairs where they kicked open a door which had been partially barricaded from within. A middle-aged lady retreated to the far side of the room and a member of the FFI pulled a blanket from over a figure, which was huddled in the corner, and stripped a cloth wrapping from its head. I looked into a face which appeared to be frightened and feverish but soft and well kept with large eyes and arched and darkened eye-brows. The face was made to look grotesque by a closely cropped head. It was with difficulty I could tell it was a woman except by noticing the full breasts underneath a pale blue waist. I wanted to see what she looked like standing but I did not ask them to have the cowering, silent figure to rise.

This is the punishment being meted out to the women of France who consorted, lived with, or otherwise collaborated with the German conquerors. The punishment can be said to be mostly humiliation, which is pretty mild for the friends of the enemies of freedom as compared to that meted out by Hitler to the friends of those who opposed his tyranny.

Yesterday Lt Col Northam was a sort of semi-official at the proceedings in the town of Chateaudun in which between 60 and 70 such women were rounded up by members of the French Underground (now FFI) who then cropped their heads as closely as possible and then paraded them through the streets before releasing them. Some were weeping, some white-faced and silent with fear, while others were somewhat defiant. The attitude of the crowds was not so much one of hate and abuse, but more of derision, scorn and amusement. There was much laughing and pointing of fingers as the strange parade of women collaboraters walked or stumbled along the stone streets around the town square. None of them were very pretty even before their hair was shorn away. From the best information we can obtain many, if not the great majority of them, were common prostitutes or women of questionable character.

The Underground Forces at first requested permission to shear their heads, strip them of clothing and march them nude through the streets but Col Northam got them to stop at the hair-cropping and parade. They are also holding in custody a number of male collaborationists, nine of which they requested permission to shoot. This was not given of course. Those matters they can attend to after we have moved on as the military does not wish to interfere in any way in any of the French's internal affairs or civil matters.

Sgt Porta and Lt Kurtz were present when two of the first women were brought in. One was protesting and a French civilian booted her in the rear with such force as to lift her six inches off the ground. Sgt Porta was very amused because the woman thought Lt Kurtz had delivered the kick. She directed her invective at him until she was forced into the building.

A major (doctor) of the medical corps viewed the scene and his impression was a room filled with women with white and fear-strained faces, and the atmosphere tense and filled with hate. One of the women begged him to intercede. But he could do nothing and turned away "literally sick" (This was before a final decision had been reached as to just what would be their punishment). The major's conclusions were that he could see the French point of view and realize the justness of the punishment. Occasionally one would try to break away but menacing weapons on every hand forced her back. If one objected on approaching the shears the cold and deadly guns silenced her (and that is quite something to do).

There were five German prisoners at Bonneval, all in the hospital, four members of the German army who were wounded and a member of a labor battalion who was ill. We did not think it wise to move them but send an ambulance back for them later.

At the hospital as elsewhere we were greeted joyfully in the customary way, the nurses, attendants and doctors hurrying from all quarters to see the AH-MER-I-KANS. There was a nurse or attendant who spoke very good English. She said there was one of their workers, who had been wounded by a bomb sometime ago, who would like very much to see us if we could come to his room. With one of the men I visited him and spoke to him briefly through the English speaking lady as an interpreter. Strange that he should be so glad to see us after being injured by one of our bombs.

* * *

Back in the town square some member of the FFI told us that there were eight PWs a short distance from the town, and that they had been sent for and would be delivered to us very shortly.

Then a young man says in very good English that there is a gentleman who wishes to present me with a bottle of wine in the name of victory. Accepted of course, and no use to offer pay as it will be refused.

The young English speaking gentleman then says that there is a chateau very near, the owner of which speaks very good American and who would be glad to have us visit him if we have the time. As the young man was very insistent, Sid and I decided to pay a brief call while we were waiting for the delivery of the PWs, and thus we encountered the most pleasant experience of our stay in France.

The chateau is 3 or 4 kilometers from the town and, as we drove out, learned that the young gentleman is a tutor for the owner's children, teaching them languages (English for one) history etc. When we approached the estate we observed that it is surrounded by a high wall and fence with entrances like the medieval castles of old (This one is 15th century). As we drove in the gate the young man said, "You may claxon now."

The driver did not understand of course, but as we passed other establishments on the place our English speaking guide again said, "You can claxon now." The driver still did not understand so I explained "You can blow the horn." To please the young teacher (or comply with what may be a custom of the lord and master) we gave the horn a few toots as we passed the houses and drew up to the marble steps in front of the chateau.

First to appear was the young son who burst through the door with an American flag and embraced each of us hailing us as "Liberators." Then appeared two young ladies, one very pretty, the other strikingly beautiful, followed by the owner and all greeted us very effusively. The owner spoke very good English but the ladies or the son could not converse freely in that language. They informed us, "We have been waiting four years for this."

After some moments of talk the owner informed us that we had arrived just as his wife was about to give birth to a child, and asked if he might have the use of our vehicle (a jeep) to send for the doctor. Naturally (no enemy being in sight) we dispatched our driver with one of the young men who had accompanied us, post haste, and they returned in such a short time that I am sure the doctor had one of his wildest rides.

In the meantime our host ushered us though a sliding paneled door into a large room, broke out a bottle of fine champagne, at the same time conveying to us the regret of the lady of the house that she was unable to welcome us personally, and insisted we drink a toast to victory and the liberation of Europe. Later when our host had again filled the glasses, Lt Silverman, with his good command of French, offered a toast to the ladies which must be customary for it seemed to meet with general approval. The conversation and visit were most pleasant, not alone because the owner could converse freely in English but because he was a very friendly, well-educated, well-informed man. Everyone appeared so genuinely glad to see us. The owner insisted we return for another visit if we had the opportunity, and gave us his Paris address to which he intends to return as soon as it is liberated, and asked us to visit him there.

I find it hard to forget the reaction of the boy who seemed to be so excited and so remarkably thrilled. For him the coming of the Americans was an event of once in a life time, perhaps so for all of them.

My hasty glances of that part of the estate which we saw, revealed a beautiful forest through which ran picturesque winding roads and bicycles paths, with here and there gardens and houses for the tenants or workers. In front of the chateau was an open space covered with flowers and green lawn bordering the drive way. My brief look at the structure itself does not enable me to describe it except to say that it is like the castles in the story-books of my youth.

After we had mounted our jeep and were about to take our leave, our host suddenly exclaimed "Wait, wait, we must have a photograph" and dashed after his camera. Whereupon all grabbed their cameras except the two girls and the boy whom we got on the vehicle with us. For several moments we were "shot" from all angles.

I noticed that while we were there, that though the tenants came out where they could see, they all kept their distance. Yet when we went by them they waved and smiled and seemed as genuinely happy to see us as those with whom we visited so briefly. I had a fleeting thought of how wonderful it would be if America could always deserve and keep the good wishes and respect of all classes of good and sincere people everywhere. Place visited—

DOMAINE DE MEMILLON
Joseph Ide, Proprietaire,
St-Maur-sur-le-Loir-par Chateaudun
(Eure-et-Loir*)
Telephone: No 4 Bonneval

\* \* \*

On the evening of the 17th I saw the FFI parade through the streets of Chateaudun. They were led by girls, most of them young and very beautiful, carrying the French colors. They had no musical instruments of any kind but sang at intervals their stirring national song the "Marseillaise." They were a motly looking aggregation of forces in all sorts of uniforms and armed with all sorts of weapons. About the only things they had in common were, their purpose, the elimination of le Bosche, and their arm bands of the French colors bearing the Blue Cross of Lorraine signifying the Fighting French. They were divided into sections, each having a chief, and their march discipline was good. Many members of the Force look very experienced and tough and no doubt they are. Some have been carrying on against the Germans here for many months.

After the parade they broke up into groups for work and some went out on missions that night.

The following letters and indorsements were received by Gen. Baade.

## HEADQUARTERS
## THIRD UNITED STATES ARMY
Office of the Commanding General

APO No. 403, U. S. Army

19 August 1944

SUBJECT: Commendation.

TO: Major General Gilbert R. Cook, Commanding XII Corps, APO 312, U. S. Army

Please accept for yourself and express to the officers and men of your Corps congratulations and thanks for the magnificent performance of all of you as evidenced by your rapid advance and capture of CHATEAUDUN and ORLEANS.

The manner of performance by all concerned is superior and you are hereby highly commended.

/s/ G. S. Patton, Jr.
/t/ G. S. PATTON, JR.
Lieutenant General,
U. S. Army
Commanding

## HEADQUARTERS XII CORPS
Office of the Commanding General

APO No. 312, U. S. Army

21 August 1944

AG 330.13

SUBJECT: Commendation.

TO: All Commanders and Units, XII Corps

1. I regret that General Cook is not present to transmit to you the Army Commander's commendation of the XII Corps.

2. I take great pleasure in forwarding it to you, and I request that it be brought to the notice of all members of the Corps.

/s/ M. S. Eddy
/t/ M. S. EDDY
Major General, U. S. Army
Commanding

1 incl: Copy of ltr of commendation.

To which General Baade made this indorsement:

330.13                1st Ind.                PWB/mla
HQ 35th INF. DIV. APO 35, U. S. ARMY, 25 Aug 44

TO: All Officers and Enlisted Men, 35th Infantry Division.

Your glorious achievement in capturing Orleans and Chateaudun will forever be extolled in the history of World War II. Again it is my honor to say to all of you: Well Done!

/s/ Paul W. Baade
/t/ PAUL W. BAADE
Major General, U. S. Army
Commanding

On-the-Move
France
August 21, 1944

Time: 0906

We have reached a village within sight of Pithiviers, and the deployed troops are going forward through the wet wheat stubble toward the town. The country is as flat as the wheat country of Kansas or Nebraska, and must be very remindful of home (as it is to me) to many of the advancing soldiers as they plod through the sticky mud, the wet woods and the clean stubble to engage the enemy. A giant smoke stack, a church spire and one large building can be seen rising high above the rest of the city. They are good vantage points for the enemy's lookouts, and certainly they can already see us and have us under their guns if they have not run away at the news of our coming. There are no shots as yet, and our rcn has already entered the outskirts of the town. But it is their policy to remain hidden, if possible, while our rcn units go by and then catch our main body with their fire. There are beautiful flowers at the edge of the village where we wait; and bright green cabbages. From amid the broad leaves of the vine there gleams the golden yellow of a pumpkin brightly polished by the preceding nights rain. And we shall soon see what we shall see about "Le Bosche" in the town.

* * *

0955: - We move in closer. Our rcn reports the town clear. The overjoyed inhabitants are streaming out to meet us and Maj McElroy is encoding a msg which says in effect "Liberated." We shall now proceed to secure the place against counterattack.

Pithiviers, France
August 22, 1944

Time: 0550

On duty all night and for once I was too busy to write anything. The night has been rainy and pitch black, and very difficult for runners and msgrs to get about. At home it would have been a good night for peaceful rest in a warm room with the gentle rain pattering in subdued tones upon the roof. Here we have been busy preparing for further advances and battle as we pursue the disorganized enemy forces.

East of Montargis, France
August 23, 1944

Time: 1250

We met opposition along the network of canals and rivers between us and Montargis and have been waiting for further orders. Our units with others have the enemy forces in the town surrounded and Lt Col Hoyne [of Div] has gone into the city to ask them to surrender. The Div Chief-of-Staff, Col Solomon, is here waiting word of the outcome. We attack in ten minutes if they do not choose to give up.

* * *

We got a number of PWs yesterday and last night and more today. One was a woman member of the German forces

— 261 —

taken yesterday. I could not get the details of her capture but questioning disclosed that she was born in Yugo-Slavia, is a citizen of Russia and was working in France at the time it fell to the invading Nazis. Some time later she was placed in a concentration camp where she remained for nine weeks before being impressed into the German forces, where she has been serving for more than two years by doing general chores and nursing. Our PW Sgts, Seiling and Campbell, questioned her in regard to military matters only, and appeared to me to be somewhat prejudiced toward her and somewhat skeptical of her answers. However our Free French officer talked to her in his language which she spoke fluently as well as Polish and German in addition to those of her native country (Yugo-Slavia) and the one of her adoption (Russia). She told him she had escaped from the Germans and was fleeing toward our lines at the time she was taken, that she was an unwilling servant of her Nazi masters and was very glad to be away from them and in our hands.

It was just after nightfall when I went to the PW Hqs where she was being interrogated. The light cast by the wavering gas lamp and the flickering candles revealed a very womanly figure with features that were strictly feminine. Her brown eyes seemed never to rest but to wander constantly so that it was very difficult to meet her direct gaze. Her attitude was neither defiant nor pleading; only troubled.

She answered all questions freely and in the manner of most Europeans gave most of the meaning to what she said by tones and gestures, except that hers were more subdued than most.

She was neither large nor small but might be described as buxom with strong arms and hands which I imagine would be very cabable with whatever work she might be doing (She was a farm laborer before falling into the hands of the Nazis). She was somewhat dirty and disheveled and her face slightly sunburned from the past few hours experiences. When the interrogators had finished she was sent away to Div Hqs along with eight male PWs.

The one word I can think of to describe her best is womanly, and it is the opinion of all of us that she was made to serve her "supermen" masters in more ways than one. Perhaps she is one of those characters with not enough fortitude to withstand the forces of circumstances brought to bear against her, but like the weaker branches of a tree, bend with the storms, but is glad to resume the former positions when the pressure is relaxed. Of that and many other things I could not judge. Certainly she is one more of the unfortunate victims of Hitler's evil forces, which spread like a scourge over Europe and but for the grace of God and the Red Army would have engulfed the world before the forces of liberty could have been mustered against them.

* * *

Lt Col Hoyne was able to enter the town but could find no one in charge of the German forces. Our arty opened and our troops jumped off at 1300. They are already reaching their objective. One hundred and ten PWs have just come back on foot in charge of Sgt Donovan. Others were sent by truck and still others are being taken.

On this front and other fronts the great Battle of France is rapidly developing into one of entrapment and rout for the German forces.

Just East of Courtenay, France
August 26, 1944

Time: 0027

On duty tonight and so sleepy I can hardly hold my eyes open. Our CP is set in a thick woods and it is so dark outside that you cannot see your hand if you hold it before your eyes. Lt Gilbertson accompanied by Lt Byerly[48] came into the CP at 2340 for their Bn order. They had difficulty finding their way, and Lt Gilbertson was bitching as usual and voicing numerous complaints, at which Byerly was most of the time amused. Byerly is a classmate of mine from Ft. Benning and certainly is one swell, pleasant fellow.

While driving through Montargis on the 23rd I encountered another classmate whom I had not seen since graduation, Lt Kohler.[49] He was in charge of our group when we went to the [Ft. Benning] school from Camp Wolters, Texas. Another classmate joined the regiment sometime ago, Lt

48 1st Lt. George W. Byerly, Sv Co, S-4 for 2nd Bn, Lima, Ohio, a Ft. Benning classmate, along with me ever since.

49 1st Lt. Richard H. Koeller, Co I, address in Ft. Benning roster as La Crosse, Wisc., given in unofficial list as Six Mile, S. C., came to 320th as a replacement.

Eckenrode,[50] now assigned to I Co. He was in my platoon at Benning and we were quite close friends. I've been wanting to visit with him ever since he joined us but there is so little time for anything but business. Lt Reischel,[51] whom I saw recently, Lt Barraclaugh[52] and Lt Garthwaite[53] are others with the Division. Barraclaugh had been wounded and just returned to service. I have not heard from Garthwaite since we entered the lines.

\* \* \*

I had Charley Glatzer, the Red Cross Man, check on Pfc Hugh Fritts for me. He reported he could find no record of wound or death so he must still be alright.

\* \* \*

In today's operations mopping up east of Montargis our unit got 61 PWs and the 134th got about 1,500. At that rate the war should be over soon.

\* \* \*

Well, I'm so sleepy that I cannot see and my senses keep fading. So am forced to stop and snatch a few moments of sleep here beside the telephones.

East of Courtenay, France
August 28, 1944

We are still at the CP in the woods just east of Courtenay. Our unit as a whole has had more leisure since we arrived here than at any time since we landed in France. It has been my misfortune to be ill most of the past two days and still today. I have a very severe sore throat, caused by my sinus trouble, which is always much aggravated by damp weather. Right now my neck is sore clear down into my shoulders, both ears are painful and I have difficulty swallowing. I am developing into a real "'sorehead."

\* \* \*

Yesterday our 1st Bn went east to secure the town of Troyes. The armor had already been in the town but it

---

50  1st Lt. Donald M. Eckenrode, Co I, Lilly, Pa.
51  Lt. Eldephone C. Reischel, 35th Div, North Platte, Nebr.
52  Lt. Donald F. Barraclough, 35th Div, North Platte, Nebr.
53  Lt. Harry Garthwaite, 35th Div, Roselle, N. J.

seems the only troops who can really secure, organize and control a place is the hardworking, hardfighting Infantry. Maj Gillis's unit had reached the town and report, "Situation well in hand."

Col Northam and Maj Jamison visited the town and report it one of the largest our troops have yet controlled. The people were wild with the joy of their liberation. While there they learned that the Fighting French had helped in the liberation. The armored forces had a German general among their PWs. The French forces had also taken a general, whom they stood against a tree and shot because he had allowed his forces to kill some French wounded. A considerable number of the female collaborators had been taken into custody, their heads shaven and then painted black, after which they were stripped and marched stark naked down the streets of the town.

The happy inhabitants were clustered about each American vehicle showering flowers and gifts of wine and food on the occupants. The hand of each soldier would be shaken as much as if he were the most popular candidate at a political rally in the States. And instead of seeking babies to kiss, one often had to submit to being kissed by everything from babies to beautiful maidens and on up to old wrinkled men and women. Truly this "Liberation Campaign" is in strange contrast to the heartbreaking task we had in Normandy.

\* \* \*

Lt Gardner and Lt Shirley[54] returned to the unit during the night. Both had been released from the hospital and placed in a replacement center where they were awaiting reassignment. They ran off from the replacement camp and hitch-hiked their way back to our regiment. It speaks well for them that they sought to rejoin us even though it meant an earlier return to battle. Lt Shirley was wounded during the first week of battle north of St. Lo.

Gardner was hit twice during the fierce engagement for the hill at Mortain. Both have been reassigned to their old units, Gardner as cmdr of his Co.

\* \* \*

---

54  1st Lt. Riley P. Shirley, Jr., Co A, Lewisville, Ky., returning with Lt. Gardner, both having recovered from wounds.

Lt Parrish[55] is our new liaison officer and now takes his turn at night duty along with Clark, Silverman and myself.

\* \* \*

Chatted a little while with Lt Gotter[56] today, now in command of Co F, and the only officer remaining of the old originals in that unit. He is having a little difficulty because an aid man in his Co was caught entering a French house to do some "souveniring" without the permission of the owner. The great majority of our men are all right, but some can cause a great deal of trouble and create some bad impressions by their lack of discipline.

Some men have heard from Lt Trask, who did not mention his wounds, so it is thought he is doing all right. I learned from 1st Sgt Larsen[57] that Lt Potter's foot was amputated above the ankle and one of his testicles was removed. Result of his injury by a German mine. Capt Hodgson, injured at the same time, was doing all right.

\* \* \*

I have heard from Alta that Margaret has heard of Sgt Cull's death on July 11. She notified Alta by telegram, who was, needless to say, stunned by the news. I spent some time yesterday composing a letter to Margaret, as she had requested that I write to her. A very difficult task weighted with sadness and regret.

\* \* \*

(Letter of Aug. 28, 1944 to Mrs. Margaret Cull).

Somewhere in France
August 28, 1944

Mrs. Margaret Cull
Junction City, Ky.

Dear Margaret,

Now that I know that you have been officially notified of Brent's death, and Alta has sent me your address, I am

55 1st Lt. Donald B. Parish, LO of Regtl Hq Co, a replacement, Portville, N. Y.

56 1st Lt. Wilbur A. Gotter, CO of Co F, Louisville, Ky. Lt. Gangemi was out with wounds but returned later.

57 Larsen, first sergeant and old friend of Co F, no other information.

writing to you. It is with the deepest sadness and regret that I attempt these few lines to you, but since I know that you want to hear from me, I am writing them.

I know that no words of mine, nor anything else, can be any comfort or recompense to you for your great loss, but since you request it, I think I can tell you some things which may lessen your anxiety as to the circumstances of Sgt Cull's death. As you will already well know in your own mind, he died bravely. He was leading his squad in the attack on the morning of our first assault on the enemy lines. He was struck by small arms fire and killed. There was no suffering. His body was recovered and is now buried in an American cemetery on the northern coast of Normandy. Should I survive the war, I will visit it before I return so that I can describe it and tell you just where it is when I see you again.

Margaret, I know your grief will be great, and there is no use for me to try to tell you of my sympathy, for in doing so my grief would creep in and perhaps but add to yours if that is possible. There are some things I want to point out to you, of which you may be proud, and which may give you courage to carry on.

First: I know that Brent felt the same as I do about the war. It had to be fought and won, and it was his own free, willing choice that he have his part in it. Among other things, he was fighting for the right of his little son to grow up in a free country, with all the opportunities he had known, and the right to love and marry the woman of his own choice, just as he had done before him. Without fighting and winning the war this would not be possible.

Second: Do not forget that death must come to us all, and no finer, braver, or more glorious death could come to any one than that which came to him; fighting bravely for God and country in the defense of freedom and the rights of humankind. He is already across the dark river, which we all must cross, and has entered into the portals of that country which waits for the good and the brave.

Third: We must now consider things in the light of present circumstances. As they now exist, what would Brent want? We know that his first concern would be the welfare of you and his little son. So you must do the things that would be best for you, in order that you can do the things that would be best for the little boy. He would want him to have the best care and guidance possible and you know that Brent would think you are the one to furnish that care and guidance. It could not come from a woman broken and embittered with grief. We know that it could not, so you must remain the same cheerful, lovely, friendly person to the little boy, that you were to Brent when you were together, no matter what the cost to you in effort and determination.

Let me say, Margaret, that I do not doubt that you will. I just want to let you know somehow that I understand the terrible load you will have to bear. I wish that somehow I could reach out my hand and help you in some way, but I know that the burden of grief is one that must largely be borne alone. I know that you will not fail but will bear up bravely until the greatest sorrow is past and then carry on as Brent would have you do.

Will you please convey to Brent's parents and other relatives and friends my deepest sympathy. And if there is any way at all that I can be of help or comfort to you, you have but to let me know, and I will make every effort in my power to comply. As for me I could not have felt his loss more keenly. He was like a brother to me. His untimely passing will be one of the greatest of my lifelong regrets. As long as I live the memory of our association will be with me, and I know that I shall never know a finer, braver person than Wallace Brent Cull.

Most sincerely,

Lt. Orval E. Faubus
Hqs. 320th Inf.
APO No. 35, c/o P. M.
NYC, N. Y.

Outskirts of Troyes
August 29, 1944

Late in the afternoon we got orders to stand by ready for move on half-hour notice from our CP near Courtenay. We moved out at 2040 from the woods and got through the town about nightfall. The people were sitting about their dwellings or gathered in little groups on side walks and the roadsides. They waved at us, gave the V-sign and some shook our hands if we paused. From many came the few English phrases they had picked up, mostly "good night" and "goodbye." Some seemed to say it with feeling as if wishing us God speed in clearing the remaining Germans from their beloved France.

The journey took most of the night over a countryside bathed in dim moonlight. Sometimes when I looked out, I could see there were far vistas that would enable one to see great distances if there had been enough light. Most of the time I spent with my head covered with my coat or a blanket to protect it from the chill wind. My skull is sore enough this morning even with what care I could exercise. Now that my rib is sufficiently healed that it doesn't bother much anymore, my sinus gets bad.

We closed in our new area at 0200 this morning and spent the remainder of the night in a park here on the edge of the town. I notice there are a number of bomb shelters and the green lawns are crisscrossed by trenches and their appearance somewhat marred by the piles of dirt.

The French are going up and down, old, young and the youthful beauties. I have seen just about every shade of hair ever worn by women in the little time spent here this morning. Many of the GIs are having considerable amusement, shaking hands, some being kissed, and attempting by sign language and the use of the little French language books to converse with the beauties. A very few of the soldiers are a bit forward, bordering on rudeness, especially one fellow who is trying to break the style of greeting. Their kisses of greeting or friendship are placed on the cheeks, never on the lips. I think I shall have to go speak to this fellow before he impairs friendly international relations. (I have always thought and now I am convinced, that a subject much needed to be taught in America is good manners.) This group of fellows across the street are engineers who seem to show a decided lack of training and discipline.

Just across from me is a large stone building, some of the windows shattered, now standing empty. It is a former German headquarters.

Some children come by and beg for chewing-gum. They certainly learn to say those words quickly enough.

Many of the vehicles in the streets are big high-wheeled wagons drawn by big horses with little tingling, musical bells on the hames of the harness. I think they would be very interesting sights to Farrell.

The Free French are much in evidence and seem to be better uniformed here. Col Bryne was here yesterday and saw a procession of 30 small caskets in a funeral procession. They contained the bodies of children killed by the Germans when they shot up a children's sanctuary before their withdrawal from the town. It is reported the FFI executed some German soldiers as a result of this and other indiscriminate killings by the Huns before our troops and the FFI won the town.

*　*　*

An old fellow is going about over the area and in a cup, fashioned from a piece of paper, he is putting all the discarded cigarette butts he can find. [The cigarette butts were unrolled and the remaining tobacco used to make other cigarettes. We observed this practice throughout Europe all during the war.]

CP SE of Troyes
August 30, 1944

Seems like it should still be "today" but it is now "tomorrow" for it is now 0409 on another day. Light rain fell from about noon until nightfall and the night has been cool and damp. The bones of my legs have dull rheumatic aches and the dampness is no good for my sinus. I think sometimes I'm a bit old for this sort of life. It takes youth to stand this and keep springing up fresh again. And then someone might ask, "How do the generals and other high officers, who are older, stand the hardships?" I can answer "By going to bed in a warm dry place while lieutenants and enlisted men stay on duty." But everyone, both young and old, have their troubles. It has been my observation in this war that the older ones are doing as well as the others. Certainly I have no cause for complaint.

*　*　*

We are settled now in positions SE of Troyes. So far as our intelligence can determine there are about 15,000 Germans within the next 12 miles and orders have been issued to attack them in the morning. We are doing it with one regiment (about 3,000) and an armored division whose strength I don't know. However we have plenty of artillery, so it will be a rough day for Jerry, and maybe for us. The orders were completed about 0200 and I have been on duty since then.

I did a little writing to friends at home tonight. Not being in the mood I found it very difficult and gave up the attempt.

* * *

I see Lt Braffit occasionally now. He is very cheerful, and hardworking as ever. He went out on rcn the other day and returned driving a fine German staff car. Col Byrne suggests that the government should not be paying him now as he is having too much fun out of the war.

* * *

Amusing incident. Pvt Brickman, recently a Sgt, arguing with Pvt Davenport about who outranks who. Brickman claims to rank his fellow private because he was more recently a sergeant, as Davenport was busted some time ago. Davenport says not, that he ranks Brickman because he has been longer in grade.

* * *

A few days ago Col Northam and Maj Jamison were out together and having a few moments to spare and needing a hair trim they dropped in at the coiffeur's (barber shop). Col Northam, with his hesitant French, which he thought was plenty good, told the barber to cut it short in the GI style which he has been wearing. Evidently his French was not so good. The barber seized the clippers and sheared a strip right down to the skin half way across his skull. There was then nothing to do but have it all clipped that way. Maj Jamison was almost in convulsions from laughing at "the expression on Col Northam's face" when he saw in the mirror what had happened. The Colonel did not deny that he was chagrined, "Yes, God damn it," he swore, "He had run them half way across my head before I could stop him." "Then he held up the clippers and said 'Surbonne?' (Good?), and when I saw what had happened I just nodded my head, 'Yes, yes, Good', and had him clip it all off."

It was funny enough to hear about but if I had seen it I guess I would have been as well tickled as the time I saw my old friend, Arch Brandenburg, fall off the rostrum in the cafe at Okanogan, Wash.

For the past few days every time I look at Col Northam's gleaming skull, I think of the female collaboraters with their closely sheared heads. But I have not dared tell him so.

* * *

Interruptions are quite frequent during this writing with last minute plans and details for tomorrow's operation. Right now Maj Gillis is trying to make sure of getting food for his men before the jump off. Bn and Co Cmdrs certainly have tough jobs in this war. We are having difficulty finding Maj Hughes in the dark. Right now I must send for special unit Cmdrs and give them the instructions for the day.

Villy-en Trodes
August 31, 1944

We are now set up in the above village with our CP and quarters in the village school and other public buildings. The inhabitants welcomed us joyously. The pretty young school ma'am swept out the buildings while others began to bring in chairs, lamps and other articles for our use. Everyone came out into the streets, the old, the young, the pretty and the ugly, some of them clean but most of them dirty, for this is a farm village and it was a rainy day with its attendant mud.

After awhile some of them got together (asking the assistance of Lt de L'Cluse, our French officer) and arranged a sort of committee to present a wonderfully beautiful bouquet to the Colonel and tender to him and his command the thanks of the villagers for their liberation. They were led by the pretty teacher, now looking very sweet and chic in a nice grey suit, and her assistant likewise very nicely dressed. They presented the bouquet, somewhat shyly as is the way with all country people, and then each pretty lass bestowed kisses on the Colonel's cheeks. I imagine some of the observers found themselves wishing for promotions at that moment.

As we drove into the village yesterday I could hear the church bells ringing to herald to the inhabitants their liberation from "Le Bosche." When we entered the villages some of the bells rang for the first time in over four years. I do not know if all the bells are silenced all the time throughout France.

Oh, yes! I surreptitiously slipped the red, white and blue silk ribbons from the Colonel's bouquet and mailed them home for a souvenir.

* * *

Much to our surprise the Germans pulled out and ran away yesterday as we advanced. We occupied our objectives, including the towns of BAR-sur-SEINE and VENDEURE-sur-BARSE and the hwy between. Lt Braffit got another nice souvenir in the first named town, a big red German battle flag with the black swastika in the center.

Lt Jones[58] of AT Co found seven members of the FFI who had been tied with rope by their German captors who then slit their throats while they were helplessly bound. Their bodies were turned over to the French for care and burial.

* * *

Lt Braffit brought to the CP this morning a Frenchman who was picked up yesterday by members of D Co in their advance. He is a member of the British Army having escaped from France when it was occupied by the Nazis, and continued his opposition with the English. He was dropped behind the lines by parachute before the Invasion to engage in sabotage. Sometime after our troops entered France he contacted an American rcn unit and with the permission of his British Cmdrs had been working with them since.

On Sunday his rcn element of two jeeps and crews were in a village to the east of our lines. A German regiment entered the town and caught them unawares. He escaped into a garden and attempted to make his way to where the jeeps were concealed in a woods. He was pinned down by MG fire and could not move for about half an hour. He then managed to crawl about 30 yards away so the Germans did not find him when they came up to look. He remained hidden but could not get away. The Nazis set up their defense all around him with a Bn on each side. He concealed himself in a bush during the day and several times the German officers discussed their positions within his hearing. On Wednesday the Germans withdrew before our advance and he was relieved by our men after three days without a bite of food or a drop of water. According to his story he had very little concealment

---

58  2nd Lt. Ernest J. Jones, AT Co, address unknown.

while among the Nazi soldiers. "They could have seen me at any time during the day if they had looked closely." he said.

* * *

There were the British man and woman, who had been parachuted behind the lines to gain information of the enemy, whom we encountered on the morning of our advance on Chateaudun. They certainly had plenty of courage for theirs was a most dangerous mission. We helped them on their way back to higher hqs with their information.

* * *

Gen Sebree, who is in command of our task force at present, visited our hqs this morning and then went to see the Bns. My first impression of him at Camp Rucker, Ala. was most favorable and it has not changed during our weeks of combat. My only unfavorable impression was when he wanted to demote Sgt Donovan for double timing some German PWs at Montargis. I'm sure Col Byrne will dissuade him on that score for they are old cronies and Sgt Donovan is such a good man.

Yesterday I saw a most beautiful flower garden in BAR-sur-SEINE. The many different flowers of all sizes and colors made a pattern which was truly fascinating. There are many flowers of many varieties throughout this section of France, but the great, gorgeous, many-hued blossoms of the dahlias predominate everywhere.

[Other casualties and losses[59] not mentioned in the Journal.]

---

59 Somewhere, sometime in the latter part of August we lost Lt. Col. Vincent Keator, Thoenicia, N. Y., Comdr of 2nd Bn; Lt. Col. Clarence W. Docka, Seattle, Wash., Comdr of 3rd Bn; and Maj Edwin C. Momm, Irvington, N. Y., former Comdr and Ex O of 1st Bn. We now had lost all of the original Bn Comdrs, and several more of the higher Bn officers. One of the three chaplains was gone, and at Regtl Hq, the S-1 and CO of Hq Co were lost. Some line companies had lost all the six original officers, and others were down to only one. Several of the original officers remaining were casualties who had recovered and returned to duty. Nearly every line company had a new comdr and some had had three or four. Later I heard of Col. Docka leading a Bn in another Div., but I never heard more of Col. Keator or Maj. Momm.

Brienne-le-Chateau
Sept. 1, 1944

Another jump along the road to Germany, but our primary task to guard the right flank of the army while forces
far to the north of us continue to forge ahead. Right now we
are set up in a great chateau on a hill overlooking the town.
The word goes round that it is one built by Napoleon which
he used for pleasure and relaxation on visits from Paris.

In the gathering darkness two EM and I were hunting
a place to sleep in the ground floor rooms of the great building. We discovered and captured a German soldier hiding
there.

It is certainly a magnificent place, or was, as it is now
somewhat in disrepair and much in need of care. The main
building faces to the west with a cleared area in front large
enough for a football field which is flanked by rows of trees
set on tiers or benches which slope away progressively step
by step. Each bench has a tree shaded driveway so there is
ample space to conceal our vehicles. Any number of horses
with vehicles could have been tethered there in the past. I
imagine those were used for walks by the lords and ladies
who sought relaxation here in the by-gone days, and the
horses were placed in the immense underground chambers
which can be entered through two great swinging doors from
the west. On each side is a great fireplace and from the high
ceiling still hangs a great "chandelier," and swinging from
it many glass chimes which tinkle musically at any movement.
To a newcomer the many rooms and cubby holes, hidden
closets and stairways seem complex indeed. I walked until
I got tired trying to find my way to the top of the structure
where the Germans had constructed an OP during their occupancy. Before I could find my way up, I finally had to
accept the services of an I & R man who had been acting as
a lookout.

From the position atop the ancient castle one has a magnificent view of the country for miles in every direction.
From the main entrance on the west a road leads straight
as an arrow until it fades from the sight and likewise to the
east a road leads away into the distance. From high above
the green rounded crowns of the trees, I could look down on
the red and gray roofs of the houses in the town, which was

settled around the base of the hill on the southwest. Radiating out from the town like the spokes of a wheel are the picturesque, tree-lined roads of France, bordered by grain fields now filled with the shocked wheat, pastures dotted by grazing cattle, the regularly patterned gardens, the great barns and faded houses of the peasants, patches of woodland and orchards. Interwoven through all were the regular fence rows and the winding green fringed streamlines. Along the highways move some of our military convoys and a few vehicles manned by the desperate killers of the French underground. After four long years of secret, furtive work they are now fighting in the open with flags flying from every vehicle. Nearer the town the roads are dotted with cyclists or footmen all converging on the town for the liberation celebration. Flying gaily from the church, the highest building in the place, is the red, white and blue colors of the French Republic.

As I stand looking out at the scenes stretching away on every side, [I am] trying to fix in my memory a few of the things I see, and thinking what an amazing number of stories the castle walls could tell if they could only speak, - of the young Napoleon going to school and drilling on some of the soil I could see below; of Napoleon the Conqueror returning in triumph up the tree lined driveway; of the gay celebrations within the walls, of plans and intrigue; of the generations that have come and gone since that time, their hopes and ambitions, their successes and failures, their loves, their joys and heartbreaks; the late coming of the invading Germans with their deeds of shame and woe; and now the unrestrained wave of joy and happiness which sweeps over the land with the coming of the Allied Armies. And as I watch, five shells land in a brown field about half a mile away. They came from over to the east where the disorganized and beaten Germans, fleeing for their lives toward the Fatherland, fired them as a sort of token of resistance. As I turned to leave I noticed that one of the would-be conquerors from the north had scratched his name upon one of the red-tiled smokestacks that stand ceaseless, silent watch above the castle walls.

[An American GI had carved his name beside it]

Brienne-Chateau
Sept. 2, 1944

Now at 1445, we are sitting in our chateau CP waiting orders for a further advance toward Germany. It rained last night and this morning and now it is cold, with the breeze fanning the moisture from the browning crowns of the trees. Harbingers of approaching autumn.

We have been sitting ready to move for over four hours now. There is a hitch in supplies from higher hqs. I think our army on the whole has advanced so rapidly that the supply service is having a hard time to keep up.

\* \* \*

Yesterday afternoon, on a moment's notice, I had to go back to BAR-sur-SEINE to investigate charges of rape placed against two soldiers of C Co. A most unpleasant, distasteful and regrettable task, as well as the incident. One of them appears to be guilty and the other very little better. They were admitted to the house because they were Americans, and their conduct has done much damage to the good will existing toward all Americans. [I learned later the soldier was acquitted in a courts martial trial. It seemed the woman in the case had been a German collaborator. The towns people came to the defense of the soldier]

These French people are so glad to see us that it is actually touching, and our opportunities for creating and extending good will toward us are unlimited. What these people have suffered at the hands of the Germans is incredible and unbelievable to most people.

The most amazing and interesting stories I have heard of the French resistance and the hardships of the people, came from two English lads which reached our CP at VILLY-EN-TRODES on Aug. 31. They were shot down over France on May 3 and parachuted from their flaming bomber into the darkness of a woods at "5 minutes to 12 midnight." One landed in a lake but got out all right. They have been living and fighting with the French Resistance since that time. The advance of our troops gave them an opportunity to start back to England. They were moved about from one home and one woods to another by their French friends. "Everyone knows French men cannot keep secrets from each other." and (to quote) "Every bloody one of the blokes always knew

— 277 —

our whereabouts and not a blooming one ever gave us away."
This, more clearly than anything, demonstrates the loyalty
of the French to the Allied cause and their opposition to the
Germans. For if anyone of their French helpers had been
caught aiding them [the two English airmen]the whole family would have been executed on the spot, their property con-
fiscated and their home utterly destroyed.

A most amazing thing that one of them told me, was
that "intelligence" had instructed them that when shot down
to seek help or sanctuary from the poorest houses, that they
were almost always friendly and that the rich were more
apt to be collaborators.

According to the version of one of them he really picked one poor enough, a one-room affair inhabited by a Pole
and Russian, where he was flea bitten and otherwise uncomfortable for a time. But they were friendly and their hearts
loyal and kind. This flyer, a dark, keen-eyed, mustachioed
little fellow, told his story with a wit an humor that "bowled
over" his listeners. Never let it be said that there are no
humorous Englishmen. I have seen living proof that there are.

[He must have been a Scotsman]

The other fellow was a keen chap also and between
bites and sips of the food and drink we had given them, they
collaborated on a few of their adventures. Incredible tales
they could tell and I would have paid anything to have the
humorous fellow's story in the manner in which he told it
there in the straw and manure-strewn, stone barn where
they were eating.

Outstanding. - Favorite trick of the White Russians
(anti-Soviets), to cut out the balls and the eyes of captives
and then run over them with tanks while still alive. "We saw
four of your chaps (American Aviators) done that way,"
they related.

The German soldier who lobbed a grenade over the door
and killed an old Frenchman because his feeble trembling
hands could not turn the lock quickly enough.

[*It seems the common people are always the most loyal
to their country. After the war while working in Little Rock,
Jim Malone Jr. told me of landing with the American forces
on the coast of Okinawa in the Pacific.*

*In the countryside they encountered cold, unfriendly
looks from the people. As soon as the troops got into the*

*cities and large towns, the more prosperous business people began to appear, exhibiting friendly glances, "bowing and scraping, rolling out the welcome mat," as Malone described their attitude, and inviting the Americans into their places of business.*]

Joinville, France
Sept. 3, 1944

Today our CP is set up in a former German Hqs in this town. We made the jump over to this place in the bright light of a full moon, taking off from the chateau formerly used by Napoleon just at nightfall.

There is no organized resistance here, only isolated individuals and groups in hiding which are easily mopped up.

Word comes from Lt O'Brien that the 80th Div on our left passed through a town yesterday in which the Germans had killed all the inhabitants, men, women and children.

We will soon have them back into Germany where they can no longer engage in brutality on the conquered. In fact, I think we would be entering the Fatherland right now if we had gasoline for our vehicles.

* * *

Unforgettable sight; Yesterday as we stood in the misty rain by our vehicles waiting to move out, the setting sun broke through a rift in clouds to the west and there appeared to the east, glowing beautifully in all its varied colors, one of the most perfect rainbows I have ever seen. It continued to show in the sky for some time, forming a glowing archway over the road we were to travel to the eastward. It reminded Col Byrne and Col Northam of similar scenes in Hawaii. I remembered the rainbow colors which appear so often in the spring and summer skies of the Ozarks, and the Ledford boys of Pinnacle Mountain singing "Rainbow, Beautiful Rainbow."

* * *

Had a letter from my Aunt, Mrs. Ussa Wheeler of Tahlequah, Okla., in which she said her boy, Pvt. Leslie Jones, was with the 319th Inf in England. She may not yet know of it but if he is still with the unit, he is about as near Germany as any one. They fought along side us for awhile but are now some distance ahead of us to the north and very near the German border.

* * *

This great stone building has running water and electric lights. The Germans certainly did not do much wrecking in many places. They had to get out in too much of a hurry.

Joinville, France,
Sept. 5, 1944

We are still in the great stone building, Le Chateau du Grand Jardin, and no orders to move as yet. Things have grown so quiet that today I saw the first card game among the staff officers since we landed in France. Maj Jamison and Lt Col Northam are engaged in a game of gin rummy. Those two are the best friends to each other, I think, that I have ever seen, and seem to get as much pleasure from their friendship as anyone possibly could.

Finally, after all these weeks in France, an American movie (You know, those shows which are supposed to follow so closely behind the front line troops) has finally caught up to us. It will begin showing for the men at 0900 tomorrow. That is if we do not get gasoline and orders to move.

Chief recreation, for the staff and headquarters group, is listening to the news and plotting on our situation maps the progress of the Allied armies which are moving with amazing rapidity.

* * *

From the<br>MADISON COUNTY RECORD<br>Oct. 5, 1944

NEWS OF OUR BOYS

From Private Hugh Fritts<br>[Thorney, Ark.]

Somewhere in France,<br>Sept. 6, 1944

Hello, all you readers of the Madison County Record. As I have a little spare time I'll write you a few lines. To me, the Record is almost as welcome as letters from home, but by the time it gets to me it is usually two months old.

Like many other boys from Madison county, I have been in France about two months and the going has been very rough. We hit the front lines as soon as we came over and have been in two major battles and a number of small ones which were usually a lot more dangerous than the larger ones. One of the larger ones was the Battle of St. Lo, and the other one I cannot mention at this time as military secrecy does not permit. But we are lucky that we were not chosen as part of the invasion army on D-Day. Right now we have "Hitler's Silly Goose Steppers" fighting for their last chance to get back to Germany.

We soldiers over here and in the Pacific really appreciate the bond drives in America but we really get mad when we hear of a strike back there. If a person, who is low down enough to strike in war time, could be at the battle front only one minute, he would never strike again.

I have a brother who had been in England about a year, and the last time I heard from him he had been sent over here. I believe he will be pretty safe though, as he is in a non-combat unit. [The brother, Paul Fritts, survived to return home.]

As for the country of France, I think it is a lot more like America than England. But of course, there is no place to be compared with the "Good old U.S.A." The French people are very tickled to see us. Those who have been lucky enough to get arms and form the FFI are a great help to us. They are usually busy cleaning the snipers out of the cities by the time we arrive. But once in awhile there is a civilian who is a Nazi sympathizer. These are soon rounded up and are dealt with severely. I will close, hoping it will not be long until Germany is whipped and has enough war to do her for 1000 years.

Pfc. Hugh Fritts 38446431
Co. I 137th INF.,
APO No. 35 c/o P.M.,
New York, N. Y.

Joinville, France
Sept. 7, 1944

We are still in the great stone chateau which is fortunate. It has given the men an unexpected rest and the staff an opportunity to catch up on paper work. Very little leisure for me as yet. Yesterday I helped run the theaters and also prepared schedules for all units and notified them of same; the day before [I prepared] an information and historical record of the past month for S-1; the day before that, court martials. Wonder what will come today.

* * *

Had a letter from Elmer Oliver [Huntsville, Ark.] yesterday with pictures showing his appearance before and after four years service as clerk of the local draft board of Madison County (Pictures entered as a part of this record).

* * *

A misty rain is falling steadily today and everything is wet and dripping. News comes that Patton's Army (ours) is driving again, so I do not expect the lull to continue much longer.

* * *

Today, as the trucks drive by, slinging out filmy mud from the whirling wheels and the men huddle in their pup tents or go about wrapped in their rain coats, the wind has risen and is blowing the mist from the trees as they wave in the great gusts of air. The unfastened shutters of the old castle started banging as if being slammed by the invisible ghosts of the long dead past. We had to fasten them before continuing our work or our pleasure. During such times I almost invariably remember my boyhood on the old farmstead, with the wind sweeping in from the south over Mill Creek and White River Valley, bearing with it the first pattering gusts of rain and giving always its warning of the discomforts of the approaching winter.

Joinville, France
Sept. 8, 1944

Another day at the chateau. The blazing fire in the fireplace has been good. But now we have orders to move at dawn to vicinity of Nancy where fierce fighting is reported.

So, "take rest while ye may, for strife comes with manhood, and waking with day."

*  *  *

From the
MADISON COUNTY RECORD
Sept. 28, 1944

LETTER FROM ORVAL E. FAUBUS

Somewhere in France
Sept. 8, 1944

Dear Folks,

Quite some time has elapsed, and we have covered some distance since I last wrote from Normandy. I did not know until just recently that the letters had ever reached their destination.

For over four days now we have not moved, and have been out of contact with organized resistance, an unexpected and much appreciated opportunity to rest out of range of enemy guns. We have continued to pick up prisoners, but the only disturbance was the occasional strafing by a few aircraft from the fast dwindling Luftwaffe which luckily caused no casualties. Even the much publicized movies, which, according to reports, follow so closely behind the front line troops, have finally caught up with us, and the old men of the unit have had a chance to see a show for the first time since we landed on the beaches several weeks ago.

Our command post has been set up in a great stone chateau (or castle) which we are told was built in 1542. It is a former German headquarters (for four years) and has Nazi symbols and drawings on the walls. One notice, in small print stuck tightly to the wall, warned of the danger of foreign broadcasts, forbade anyone to listen, and further warned that the violation of the rule was a crime punishable by death for anyone guilty of such disloyalty to "der Fuhrer."

The "supermen" cleared out just before we arrived, and left a good set of office furniture and a number of very dirty mattresses and pillows. There are also electric lights that work and, best of all, wood for the marble framed fire places. The blazing fire during these cool, rainy days is the most cheerful thing I have experienced since landing in France.

— 283 —

I am entranced by the leaping flames and glowing embers and find my mind wandering far away, and sometimes far back over memory's trails through by-gone days. (Need I say more?)

Oh, yes! A not-to-be overlooked luxury was my fourth bath in more than two months.

But this unusual comfort of war is soon to end. Even now I should be getting some rest for we are to be off at dawn, and our destination happens to be right at this moment one of the hottest spots of the battle front. And it is no comfort to know that the closing battles of the war can be just as furious, and just as tragic to the people in them, as the first ones. And to those [at home] who receive the little notices, the casualties can cause just as much heartbreak.

The war as a whole is going surprisingly well. I would not be surprised if I am some distance into Germany by the time you read this. Hitler's forces are hopelessly beaten, and every day he continues the war is but prolongation of a useless and purposeless slaughter. This fact, along with the barbarities of the Nazis toward the conquered peoples, is building a hatred toward them that did not exist in the last war.

For example, we found seven members of the French Underground forces who had been tied with ropes and their throats slit by their German captors while they were helplessly bound. In another town, the day after we liberated it, there was a funeral procession which contained thirty small caskets. In their last drunken reprisals before they left, the Germans had shot up a home or sanctuary for children, killing 30 of them. Many others were wounded.

Let no one tell you that the French aren't fighting, and they are certainly a great help, too. With their assistance we can always learn just where the Germans are in any locality. [Also] we picked up two British aviators on Aug. 30, who were shot down on May 3 and had been hiding and fighting with the French resistance forces ever since. (What stories they could tell!).

Well, I must warm my hands by the fire and get some sleep. We may not have such comfort again until the war is over. Besides, writing makes me think and remember, which isn't so good now. Every recollection of the battlefield is marked with the memory of a friend's face whom I shall not see again. Yesterday I was with a truck load of officers from one of the battalions and only four of them were old friends. Once I had known all the officers of that unit.

Many, many thanks to all of you that wrote to me.

Yours for victory,

Lt. Orval E. Faubus
Hqs. 320th Inf.,
APO No. 35 c/o P. M.,
New York, N. Y.

West of Nancy, France
Sept. 10, 1944

Time: 1125

Today we have the chilly weather of autumn. The sky is a clear blue and only once have light fleecy clouds blemished its wide expanse. Everyone is seeking the bright patches of sunlight here in the forest. Woodcutters have been at work here during the summer, clearing away the trees and slender poles and converting them into piles and piles of wood cut into three-foot lengths. A few choice trees and saplings have been left standing so that the cleared area is like a grove or orchard with the trees casting over the cleared ground an irregular pattern of sunlight and shadows. The uncleared portion of the woods is so dense that only an occasional ray of sunlight succeeds in penetrating the thick overhead cover of boughs and foliage. To look from the lighted clearing into its depths is almost like looking from a lighted room into outer darkness.

At present I have sought a bright patch of the warm sunlight with a wood pile for a backstop in order to gain as much of the precious warmth as possible. I am seated on my coat, writing, but the chill wind does not permit one to become really comfortable. I have been chewing a couple of pieces of this K-ration candy, and it attracts the most active and numerous of the autumn insects, the yellow jackets. They come buzzing around, very irritating, seeking one more last sweet meal of the year before the cold of winter puts an end to their activities. Every now and then some one suffers a "bite" from one of them, as it is more often expressed. Many of these former city boys have not yet learned the difference between a sting and a bite.

Incident of most interest this morning, the sight of bombers passing overhead, their silvery sheen glistening beautifully in the sunlight, and a little later earth-shaking rumbles heard in the direction of Nancy. They are making an "air-strike" on the German positions around the city.

Our regiment is in reserve today, a somewhat rare occurence it seems, while the others advance. Silverman has just returned from one of them and they have advanced to their first objective, a stream west of the town, without opposition except some artillery fire. Very likely we shall see action before the city falls. The Germans will likely defend as it is the last strong barrier before the German border and also is protecting the left of the last escape route for the German troops trying to get out of France and home to the Fatherland.

Yesterday we moved up to this place without incident. It was a cool ride, was cool here, and most uncomfortably cool during the night. I was certainly glad that duties did not keep me up during the night. I crawled into my blankets with the coming of darkness (2100) and did not arise until breakfast call at 0800. I have been so miserable with my sinus troubles that I have been wondering how I will be able to stand operations should the war continue for long. I'm afraid I won't be able to do so, but I hope that I shall.

Me for a warm climate when this damned struggle is over.

* * *

Lt Col Northam was awarded the "Silver Star" on Sept. 7, for his part in the action at Mortain. Maj Gillis also got the same award for his part in the action. Those two certainly deserve plenty of credit for the success of that action. But a lot more Silver Stars are due to others, who participated in that battle, if justice is done.

However, of one thing I am now convinced, and that is the extreme difficulty, if not impossibility, of awarding medals and decorations with justice to all. Perhaps it can be said, truthfully, that all who received medals deserved them. (I think certainly that Northam and Gillis also Porta and Donovan who have received bronze stars). But there are others who had just as high a sense of duty and performed just as courageously and usefully their assigned tasks. Sgt Cull led his men out bravely as ordered and lost his life in the first hours of combat. Capt Swanson was leading his Bn when he was cut down by the deadly German MG. He could just as easily have had someone else in the lead and have been in a safer place himself. Lt Talcott went out to attempt a rescue, even against the urgings of other officers, and died along with him. Lt Fitzgerald and Lt Bell[60] (of G Co) advanced far ahead of the others that first day. Lt Bell crawled back, shot through both legs, and Fitzgerald has never again been heard of. Eight men who were with Bell were left far ahead of our lines fighting desperately against great odds. To my mind Lt Zintas was one of the bravest, yet a white phosphorous shell blasted him into the next world before he had really had a chance to prove himself. Lt Trask stayed in the line and led his men, although each hour was torture, visibly shrinking each day, until he was cut down by enemy fire, being very severely wounded. There may be belated medals for a few but not for all. For example how can we ever know how much heroism Talcott displayed before he fell in the darkness or what Fitzgerald did after he passed beyond our lines and knowledge. What about the eight men still fighting when left by Bell; the lost platoon of L Co, cut off and lost along the dark fencerows among the SS brutes beyond Mortain; or Gardner's men of Co B who rode the tanks toward the town of Mortain in the face of the fiercest fire, were cut off among the hedgerows and fought until they were wiped out.

Most of those men, if not all, are yet without medals. Many of them will never be heard of again, and the bodies of some who died in the tanks were never recovered.

Yet a division staff has, to my knowledge, awarded medals to all its members and some have perhaps not even yet heard the whistle of bullets.

I guess it is very difficult to deal out perfect justice.

Bois d'Orme
Sept. 12, 1944

The Bois d'Orme is a woods SW of Nancy. We moved to this point early this morning and have been waiting for committment on Division order. It is a very nice woods but living in the woods is getting unpleasant because of the increasing chill in the autumn air.

---

60 1st Lt. Charles G. Bell of Co G, Binghamton, N. Y., an original wounded at St. Lo.

The other two regiments are doing the fighting at present. The 134th had a tough time crossing the Moselle River and the Canal. The Germans resisted fiercly, blew up a bridge and shot up the assault boats. Some men were pinned in the water by MG fire as much as 10 hours. The story of one incident is that the regt found a bridge that was not blown and got one Bn across. The enemy then shelled the bridge and blew it up; then counterattacked the troops across the river and drove them back with heavy losses. The Krauts still fight fiercly, and sometimes very skillfully, even though their cause is now hopeless. Perhaps all of them do not yet realize that the war for them is lost.

[Other casualties[61] not mentioned in the Journal.]

Across the Moselle River
Sept. 13, 1944

Time: 0830

Just as I was writing last night in comes the Generals [Baade and Sebree] and party with plans for today's action.

By dawn this morning the 1st Bn, with atchd tks and TDs, was across the river. We followed and behind us came the other Bn.[62] I was riding with the Colonel and we went up front to find Maj Gillis. Upon reaching the crest of the hill, we found the light we could see from across the river was a village burning. It had been shelled, burned and ruined. A few bedraggled old women and others were poking forlornly through the ruins. The Germans had just vacated the hill where Gillis had his OP. While we watched the Huns threw a dozen shells into the ravine in front of us. They were trying for our advance troops. The bursts sounded like large mortars but some whistled "like 77s," said somone.

Just now Lt Kurtz brought in a PW. He was sitting out on the hill with a good MG, but he walked in and gave up.

---

61  1st Lt. Robert D. Overfield, Co H, Poplar Bluff, Mo., a replacement, listed KIA Sept 11; 1st Lt. George A. Thomay, Co C, Salt Lake City, Utah, a replacement, evacuated as sick Sept. 12, did not return.

62  The 3rd Bn led by Lt. Col. Joseph D. Alexander of Chicago, Ill. This is the first time I recall seeing Col Alexander, a replacement to the 320th, formerly with the 137th Regt until wounded. The 2nd Bn was then attached to an armored outfit where Overfield was killed, probably the 4th Armored Div with which we fought all across France.

He is a jaunty cuss, excellently equipped and clothed. He smiled said, "Good morning" and "Deutchland Kaput" (Germany all finished). He is veteran of five years, not an SS man, and does not like them. He said his mother had written that she would not be happy until he was a PW. Quite an interesting character. He could have done a lot of damage with his deadly MG if he had chosen to fight. No doubt the Colonel and I walked and rode within its field of fire.

* * *

In entry of Sept. 13, 1944
[The following is from a news item from The Stars and Stripes.]

## QUOTES FROM PRISONERS

"There's a shortage of men in Germany. My mother was forced to give my father written permission to visit other women because there weren't enough Aryan men at home . . ."
(Sgt in parachute division)
This German PW gave us the above information in the news item about his mother. He said she was very unhappy about this situation.

* * *

The mortars are falling on Gillis's advance troops as they push forward. Some shells are reaching out to the ridge above us as we work here. The war is so near over in Europe, but still men continue to die. The days are full of might-have-beens.

This Moselle River Country is, to me, the most beautiful of any over which we have yet fought. The high ridges, with orchards, green pastures and cultivated fields, offer excellent observation over the draws and valleys. Both the enemy and us seek shelter in the woods. Danger for each lurks around the curves of the winding roads. The apples and plums are now ripe or ripening. They were little green balls when we entered the conflict. I picked up some pale yellow plums from the ground this morning that were delicious. They had been shaken from the trees by the blast of shells. Only a short time before the Germans had been eating them for there on the ground was a German cigarette wrapper, recently dropped, and other signs of their late occupancy.

* * *

Now (0922). As we stalk around the CP and carry on our work the Colonel finds a four-leaf clover growing in the green sod.

* * *

Word reaches me that Capt Hare of 2nd Bn was wounded yesterday in his unit's action with an armored unit. Not confirmed.

Word comes of first wounded in today's action. Not strange. It is to be expected. We always wait unconsciously for the word but never mention it to each other. It is a subject "taboo" among us. We speak only of those who have already been killed or wounded and then very infrequently.

* * *

Moselle! It is pronounced exactly the same as Alta's middle name, which she spelled Mozel. I shall think of her often until we fight beyond this stream and region.

* * *

Can't write much now; work to do.

* * *

## MOSELLE CROSSING

*In the crossing of the Moselle elements of the 134th got across at night on a captured bridge, but were thrown back the next day and the bridge destroyed by the enemy. The next day Capt. Joseph Giacobello, Mt. Union, Pa., crossed with a small contingent of Co. F, 137th Infantry. They were given up for lost when the remainder of the battalion were forced to abandon the crossing. Three days later when a crossing had been effected in fierce fighting by the entire regiment and elements advanced along the east bank, they were greeted by Capt. Giacobello and his men.*

* * *

## PATTON VISITS OUR FRONT LINES

*The situation was fluid, we moved rapidly and many things happened in the period Sept. 13th to 16th. I was so busy that my entries in the Journal were limited and consequently a number of note worthy occurrences were not mentioned. One of those was the visit to the front line positions of the Third Army Commander.*

— 290 —

It was on Sept. 13th that Gen. Patton made an appearance with the 320th Infantry Regiment while it was in the attack. He continued forward to the CP of Maj. Gillis's 1st Bn and then still further to a forward observation post.

It was one of those days when the advance went according to the military book. The troops of the battalion were deployed in the advance with scouts in the lead and the forward squads deployed as skirmishers. As Patton watched and listened the advancing infantry made contact with the enemy.

At first there floated in the sound of the German MGs and rifles as they opened fire on our forward elements. There followed almost immediately the sound of our own small arms as our troops returned the fire. There followed the explosions of German mortars which were soon overwhelmed by the reply of our own. Our mortarmen, with long experience, had become most skillful and could in a few minutes time, lay hundreds of shells on enemy targets. Patton listened with evident approval as he heard and observed this display of skill with mortars by troops he commanded, coupled with the sound of our own MGs and rifles.

Then as the word came back giving enemy positions and targets, our cannon company opened fire accompanied by our highly competent artillery (216th FA Bn). Very shortly our attached tanks were moving forward to assist in clearing stubborn pockets of German resistance in buildings or woods. Shortly prisoners and wounded were coming back as the German positions were overrun, or outflanked and enveloped. The enemy resistance crumbled and the advance continued.

Those present at the CP, both men and officers including Maj. Gillis, naturally observed closely the military leader who had already become the most famous general in the American Army with the possible exception of the Supreme Commander. They related to me (I was not present, being elsewhere on duty at the time) that Gen. Patton listened quietly and intently, seldom speaking. When he had observed sufficiently, he spoke a few words of commendation and good wishes to those present. Then, on his face a slight smile with an expression of complete satisfaction and approval for what he had observed, he turned and made his way back down the slope toward his vehicle.

*The Germans used a number of tanks and anti-tank guns that day as well as a lot of big stuff. Three times in three hours 88s blasted Pfc. Charles J. Rose of Scranton, Pa. clean out of his hole.*

\* \* \*

Sept. 14, 1944

[After a move forward, and a new CP]
[Damelevieres]

Very hectic around the CP now. The bns are crossing the Meurthe River; foot elements are already over and marching north toward Nancy; the engineers are bridging and making fords; reports are coming in; there is much activity to be coordinated so Col Bryne and Maj McElroy are very busy and usually keep me active. We are now in a temporary CP near village of Damelevieres. Last night we spent at the CP at the base of the hill which we established before the battle yesterday. It rained all night and I know the troops must have been miserable. I got Milt to [help me] pitch a tent just before the rain began, so [we] managed to sleep in comfort. [A small pup tent. Two men were required as each soldier carried one-half of each tent.] Almost all activity ceased during the night as it was pitch black.

About noon we moved up to a woods and set up. The mud was almost as bad as that of Tennessee last winter. Later we moved on down here. Soon we shall cross the Meurthe as we intend to set up on [the] opposite bank for the night. No more time now. Perhaps more later.

[Casualties[63] not mentioned in the Journal.]

### DOMBASLE
#### (From 320th Inf. History)

*In the fight at Dombasle on Sept. 15 in the 1st Bn. sector, Lt. Braffitt captured an unblown bridge with a jeep*

---

63  2nd Lt. Franklin C. Gough, Jr., Co C, New Orleans, La., a replacement, listed KIA Sept 13; 1st Lt. Albert R. Wakeham, Co D, Dumont, N. J., evacuated as sick Sept 12; 1st Lt. Charles C. Coker, Co G, Athens, Tenn., evacuated as sick Sept 13; 1st Lt. John A. O'Donnell, Co B, address unknown, evacuated as sick Sept 15; 2nd Lt. Clarence A. Edsell (or Edsall), Co C, address unknown, listed LWA Sept 15; 2nd Lt. Harold R. Shenk, Co F, address unknown, listed LWA Sept 15; 2nd Lt. Michael A. DeFeen, Co M, address unknown, listed LWA Sept 15. All officers were replacements except Wakeham; none returned to duty.

*and one MG, but heavy enemy fire prevented a crossing. Finally, men of Co C secured a bridge head in another location by crossing in boats found in the canal. Maj. Gillis, directing the attack, swam and waded the waterway several times.*

*It was in this engagement that Sgt. Walter Newman of Detroit, Mich., a 1st Bn cook (later mess sergeant for Cn Co) came up to the forward advance with Lt. Christianson. There he unjammed an abandoned light MG and with its fire silenced an enemy strong point. Later he picked up an MI and helped capture 21 Germans.*

\* \* \*

Across the Rhin [Rhin-Marne Canal; Le Sanon River]
Sept. 16, 1944

I now sit on high ground, where we have temporarily paused in a tin shed as full of shrapnel holes as a sieve. Our troops are advancing. [The CP remained here for the night.]

On Sept. 14 we crossed the Meurthe in the night and set up in some buildings near village of Rosieres. Next day the French ganged around like a Fourth of July picnic. They wanted to look at Americans and also to see in defeat the many German PWs we handled yesterday.

Last night I was on duty in town of Somerviller as control officer for the crossing. The Krauts shelled the hell out of the place. One shell hit the building in which I worked with 3rd Bn CP group, shattering the glass and plaster about our ears. Crossings quite successful in spite of the Hun shells, and we are now pushing on.

\* \* \*

Saw Lt Gilbertson a few moments ago as the 2nd Bn rejoins us today. He confirmed the report of Capt Hare's wound. The shell hit quite near Gilbertson and gave him quite a shock. Also Lt Alloway of 3rd Bn was wounded yesterday and Lt Jones of AT Co. Three more of the old originals. Lt Kiser[64] has returned to 2nd Bn from hospital.

\* \* \*

The shell which came so near last night wounded slightly Sgt Manning, who some time ago was recommended for a commission. Two other men were wounded seriously. After

---

64 1st Lt. Howard M. Kiser, Co H and the 2nd Bn Hq Co, address unknown.

the terrific blast of the hit, Sgt Porta jumped up and ran out and returned carrying a wounded man. The medics hurried in and by the dim light of the flickering candles and blackout flashlights, cut away his bloody clothing and dressed his wound. "Robert Green" I heard them get his name from the tag which is always attached to a casualty. And all the time the shells kept coming in to the surrounding buildings and for some time thereafter before there was a lull.

\* \* \*

Lt Zielasko[65] just visited our forward CP. He is always asking if I have my money ready to pay off the bet to him. (I bet him the war would be over on or before Nov. 11). He told me he heard Bing Crosby and accompanying feminine attractions sing for some of the Division troops yesterday. "Now don't feel bad," he said, "I thought about you." I guess that is about as close as such shows can get to real front line troops. Silverman just came in and told me he saw Bing at Div Hqs this morning while there on a mission.

\* \* \*

The damned Huns are shelling us now, mortars I think. So enough writing for now.

\* \* \*

Much later:

Some days ago we captured a German storehouse and among other things there was a great quantity of fine liquors, champagne, etc. Naturally we appropriated a great deal of the stocks as our rightful spoils of war and placed a guard over the remainder.

Thinking we might have a possible chance of returning this way some day, we arranged through good offices of Lt de L'Cruce to store some in the cellar of a friendly French civilian. We stored as follows: 6 cases of Champagne, 3 cases Cointreau, 1 case Benedictine, 5 cases Cognac (large) and 4 cases Cognac (small). One liquor connoisseur ("expert" I should say because I can't spell the big word) estimated it to be worth $2500.00.

\* \* \*

---

65  1st Lt. Ernest "Ernie" H. Zielasko, originally A/T Co, now LO for Div Hq, from Ohio, a 320th original officer.

# INCIDENT AMONG THE FRENCH AT ROSIERES

*At one point during the brief time at Rosieres before being sent to Somerviller to control the stream and canal crossing, I was chatting with Lt. Quillin in the barnyard area. The area was between a huge barn and the building in which the CP had been set up, and a number of French civilians were about, all of them talking excitedly. Observing them Lt. Quillin remarked, "Just look at them damned Frenchmen. Watch them!" he exclaimed, nodding his head toward a particular group as they gestulated in animated conversation. "If you'd cut their damned hands off they couldn't say a God-damned word."*

*I watched the gestulating civilians, as much amused at Quillin's remarks as at their antics. Quillin's apparent cynical attitude was recognized by all of us, but to those of us who knew him well, we considered it a "front." He was diligent about his duties and worked as hard, and many times harder than anyone to do all he could for all the troops. We knew him to be as compassionate and warm-hearted as anyone. Therefore his outward cynicism was always somewhat amusing.*

*"Well," I replied to his remarks, "It is a time for excitement among these people, although I'm inclined to agree with you." I had thought many times that a Frenchman would have difficulty in expressing himself if he could not use his hands while speaking.*

*As Quillin and I conversed there presently entered the farmyard alone a rather tall Frenchman of slightly more than medium size. He was bareheaded, his sandy pompadored hair in disarray, and as I recall, wearing a short leather coat. He came up to us and began a conversation in limited English. He had a strained smile on his face, and about him there was an air of uneasiness. As I recall, he did not gestulate as much as was customary, but kept running his hand through his stringy hair brushing it back from his face.*

*Shortly a group of Frenchmen arrived, approached us in an agitated manner, and took in charge the first arrival. We couldn't fully understand their inquiries, but finally determined that their questions concerned the tall Frenchman, who now wore a sickly look and had become silent.*

*Quillin and I referred them to the headquarters where there were French speaking personnel. A delegation went* inside the CP while others remained with the tall man, now apparently their prisoner. Presently the delegation returned and spoke and gestulated to the others. Then the whole group departed the farmyard dragging with them the unwilling sandy-haired man they had taken in charge.

Moments later a short distance away in the direction the Frenchmen had gone, a shot rang out. Quillin and I looked at each other, both somewhat puzzled, but each suspecting what probably occurred.

I then learned that the delegation had inquired at the CP if the man were our prisoner, saying that he was a notorious German collaborator. Those in the CP at the time of course stated that we had no such prisoner; that all our prisoners of war were sent to the rear upon capture. Finding that the alleged collaborator was not in custody of the Americans, the members of the group hustled him away and, so we were told, summarily executed him as soon as they were out of our sight.

Other information indicated that as soon as the Germans were driven from the area, the collaborator had probably fled to the Americans hoping for protection by them from the wrath of those against whom he had worked for his German masters. Of course Quillin and I knew nothing of these circumstances during the time a part of the drama was unfolding in our presence.

Since combat troops could not concern themselves with such matters, perhaps the best course for the German collaborator would have been to hide until he could contact the Civil Affairs Officials or until the French government authority was re-established. Then, at least, he might have obtained a trial before being dealt with so severely.

## THE RHINE-MARNE CANAL AND
## LE SANON RIVER CROSSING

Shortly after nightfall of Sept. 15 orders came from Div down to the Regimental CP at ROSIERES for a night crossing of the Rhine-Marne Canal and the Le Sanon River. Our troops had advanced to the waterway and it was now the demarcation line between the opposing armies, except for the small bridgehead established by the 3rd Bn where the engineers were constructing bridges.

* * *

*Col Byrne designated me to carry the orders to the forward battalion, deliver them to the battalion commander, then stay on the ground to control the crossing. Engineers of the 4th Armored Division were to install and maintain the bridges which had to be built. 320th Infantrymen were already across in the bridgehead protecting the engineers and the bridges. The order directed all of Col Alexander's Battalion to cross, followed as rapidly as possible by the attached armored units of the 320th, 137th and 134th Regiments, then finally by the 4th Armored Division.*

*To assist me I took a squad of the I & R Platoon in charge of Sgt Smith. We reached Col Alex's[66] headquarters late, perhaps 2100 or 2200 at night. I instructed Sgt Smith to find shelter for his men from which they could operate and went in to deliver the orders to Col Alexander.*

*Naturally all his men and officers were dog tired. It was the end of the third day of fighting and advancing by the Regiment, a part of which Gen Patton had observed earlier. Col Alexander's men had already found shelter, dug in and bedded down with communications established. Avoiding the language of the front, I will say the colonel was unhappy with the order and vented his anger on me.*

*I finally told him, "Colonel, I didn't originate the order, I'm just delivering it. I can't help the situation any more than you can."*

*Sgt Porta, bless his brave heart, was there. He had already become the colonel's (Alexander) right arm. He got a chance to say to him quietly, "Sir, I know this man," referring to me, "and he is all right." The colonel wearily sat down on the floor, leaning his back against the wall and summoned his staff and company commanders. Working by the dim and flickering candle light on the situation map, he outlined the maneuver to them when they had gathered.*

*"Men," Col. Alex asked, seeking any suggestions, "Will that work?"*

*They agreed that the plan was alright, and departed to carry out the order. With Sgt Smith I had already reconnoitered the bridges, one across the stream and another the canal which ran along side. I had to keep up with every de-*

---

66  Lt. Col. Joseph D. Alexander, commanding 3rd Bn, called Alex by close friends and referred to in that manner by almost everyone.

*tail because I was in charge and would be blamed for any mixup.*

*I was prepared to go with the first contigent to cross, when Sgt Porta said, "Lt, I'll guide them over. I've already been across." Away he went, his huge frame with the slightly hunched head and shoulders, giving confidence to everyone with whom he worked. Shortly he was back, reporting everything went well. At other times during the night whenever he could be helpful he was available, catching brief naps between times, or conversing in low tones with me or the colonel.*

*I used the I & R men as runners to inform each unit when its time came to move out and to inform me when each crossing had been completed. By runner also a message was sent back to Regiment that the order had been delivered and first movements were going well. We heard no more from them (regtl hqs) during the night.*

*No doubt enemy observers reported the activity for it could be detected by the sound of moving vehicles if for no other reason. The Germans began shelling the place from gun emplacements behind the ridge to our front, the rounds arching over the hill and into our positions. My post remained at Col Alex's CP which was in a stone building adjacent to the main crossroad in the town. Naturally it was a prime target because of its location beside the road where all the traffic was moving.*

*Apparently a business building, now empty, its glass front faced the street and the enemy lines. A safer location would have been across the street in a stone building with the back toward the enemy, which was where Sgt. Smith had located his squad. Every time a shell came over the hill that night I could picture it coming through the glass front.*

*Dozens of tired men were sleeping in the large room, including Col Alex and his staff. My post was in the back right-hand corner where I could look through the glass front and to the left at the doorway.*

*An experienced combat man can tell from the scream of a shell when it is headed directly for him. In that split second before it strikes, the soldier must duck. There is no time to move, just go down. Finally one came over the hill that was tagged for us. I foolishly ducked behind a stove beside which I was sitting (which would have been little or no protection), instead of flattening out on the floor. There is so little time* to think. The screaming round missed our room by about four feet, striking the front wall of the next room and entering it just on the other side of the partition beside which I sat and beside which men were sleeping.

The piercing scream and the deafening explosion followed by flying debris and falling fragments of stone, aroused the men. As they arose, scrambling almost in panic, Sgt. Porta was already on his feet. Calming the men immediately with reassuring words, he dashed out the door. Almost immediately, before others could think, he was back inside carrying a wounded man in his strong arms. Then out he hurried again to look for other injured.

The medics were summoned. By the dim red glow of their blackout flash lights they dressed the wounds of the stricken soldier. A recent replacement, he was known only as "that new man." I heard one of the first aid men call his name in the darkness as they read his dog tags, Robert Green, and it stuck in my memory forever. He was sent out with other wounded in an ambulance along the road being used by the incoming armored columns.

All night the shelling continued. I counted 14 duds which came into the buildings in our vicinity. A dull thud could be heard at the end of the screaming flight with no consequent explosion. I had the thought that the duds might be the work of sabotage by slave laborers in the munitions plants of the Third Reich.

Reports of casualties continued to come in but there was no serious disruption of the crossing. Fortunately most of the shells overranged those who had crossed the stream, and, for the most part, the bridges. There was one lucky ironic result of the move. The message center of the 3rd Bn was already dug in with telephone communication established when I came with the order. Of course the men were unhappy to be disrupted and very displeased with the move in the darkness. Some time after they had moved, an enemy artillery round scored a direct hit on the hole they had vacated.

Lt Zielasko, then an aide to Gen Wood, Commander of the 4th Armored Division, accompanied the general to the area of the crossing that night. Amidst the shelling the general remarked to Zielasko, so he reported to me, "This is no place for us" and they got out.

As dawn was breaking, the last of the attached armor was crossing. Some one, perhaps Sgt Porta or Sgt Smith, reported to me that the engineers had abandoned the bridges because of the shelling. Just after daylight, alone, I walked the some 200 yards to the bridge to check. The structures were still intact and passable but no maintenance troops or others were about. The approaches to the first span had been worn away by the tanks and other vehicles. I picked up a shovel lying nearby and filled in the depressions as the Germans dropped mortar shells over the hill into the bridgehead area.

Finishing the work, I walked back to my command post and arrived just as a 4th Armored tank roared up. The turret opened and a Lt Col stuck his head out and inquired, "Where can I find the 320th CP?"

"Colonel," I replied, as I stood in the roadway, "It's in the town of Rosieres about 3 miles back. But, if it's any help to you, I'm in charge of this crossing."

He gave me a momentary, intense look, then with a snappy salute he said, "Lt, that's good enough for me. What are your orders?"

"Sir," I replied, "the last of the other units have just cleared the bridges. The structures are still intact. Your units (4th Armd) can begin crossing in 15 minutes." At least 20 minutes time had been allowed for each unit to disperse after crossing during the night.

"Thank you, Lt" he said, and without further ado picked up his radio transmitter and his messages and orders began to crackle through the air.

Soon the 4th Armored tanks were roaring by. The sight and sound of an armored division in full movement is one of the most earth-shaking, awe-inspiring spectacles in the world. The iron behemoths roared by on the narrow road in single file, shaking the earth where I stood, and in rapid succession crossed the bridges. As they dispersed beyond the stream and charged up the hill into the enemy positions, I continued to stand by the command tank listening to the messages.

"Objective A taken at 0715" from one column. "Objective B occupied, what are your orders?" from another. I'd like very much to know the name of that tank officer, and if he survived the war. He knew his business and how to respect responsibility in others regardless of rank.

As the tanks took their objectives, Col Alexander's infantry moved forward to wipe out the pockets of enemy in the draws and in the fox holes. Some bayonet engagements occurred that morning as the slopes were taken, and later on as the advance continued, one of the few times for such fighting for the men of the 320th, and one of the few times during the war in Europe.

Sgt Porta, as usual, was active. During the advance a German shot a lieutenant (whose name I have now forgotten) and was then captured by Sgt Porta. With one strong arm, Porta shoved the PW into the presence of Col Alex and the General who had come up - Baade and Wood both may have been present - with the exclamation, "Here's the son-of-a-bitch that shot Lt. _____.

As the 3rd Bn continued its advance under Col Alexander it approached the town of Buissoncourt several miles farther on. A German battalion held strong positions in the town and along the road to the north. Cos I and K secured a ridge in front of the town but were pinned down by heavy enemy fire in the open beyond. With practically no cover a further advance or withdrawal threatened heavy casualties. The weapons platoon of Co I under T/Sgt. Saul Joseph of Chicago, Ill., fired 26 boxes of MG ammunition and 850 rounds of 60mm mortar. The platoon was supported by Co M's heavy MGs and mortars, but the deadlock between the opposing forces still held.

It was then Col. Alexander directed the bayonet charge. Two platoons of Co L were brought up and passed through the Co I positions followed by the reserve platoon of Co I. Overhead fire from tanks, TDs, the MGs and mortars kept the Germans in their holes as the bayonet chargers dashed about 300 yards to the German positions, firing as they advanced. When the fire slackened, the Krauts looked up, the bayonets shining in their faces. Most of them immediately surrendered, but, in the words of T/Sgt. Raymond Sneade of Worcester, Mass., "a few had to be stuck." About 40 of them took off through a cornfield on their hands and knees but a few shots into their rumps brought them to a halt and surrender.

Among the prisoners taken were the battalion commander and eight of his staff. The bayonet charge was led by 1st Lt. Leo Thomas who still further added to his battle *laurels and his title of "Fighting Leo." Sgt. Sneade was awarded the Silver Star for wiping out one of the MG nests.*

*The above action began on the night of Sept 15th and went forward on Sept 16th. The journal entry of the 16th was made in the afternoon of that day, as we paused on a crest above the slopes and the waterway where the crossing and advance had occurred.*

*I can remember so clearly watching from the crest, where we established a temporary regimental CP, our artillery firing from the valley behind us, the shells passing just over our heads bound for targets beyond. Their terrible whispering in their flight overhead is unforgettable.*

*I must add that Col Alexander's attitude when I delivered the crossing order that night was due to battle weariness. He had been with the Regiment only a short time and had not yet come to know many of us. He is a wonderful man, and was one of the finest commanders of the Division. He apologized to me many times afterward, although I never felt that any apology was due.*

*   *   *

Remereville, France
Sept. 17, 1944

We are paused now in a French General's home as our temporary hqs. The owner has taken off with the FFI. The Germans have been using his house as hqs and now us. It is a magnificent place with a piano in almost every room, and clocks, book cases, mirrors, etc. that must be priceless.

We moved out of our area on the hill above the river we recently crossed. The only shelter we had there from the rain was a tin shed as full of holes as a sieve, made so by our artillery. There were numerous leaks and small protection from enemy shelling but many of us slept there any way. Many of the men pitched their pup tents, others slept under vehicles.

For others in the lines there could not have been much shelter, and today in the attack there was none. Almost everyone is wet and miserable. Yet the fighting goes on, in the steady rain and the sticky mud. The tanks roar lustily as they drive forward, their guns belching flame, the artillery booms and crashes, the mortars begin their coughing and follows the stunning crash of their shells exploding, the MGs start their chattering and other automatic weapons bu-r-r-p, bu-r-r-p, in bursts of fire. When all of this has sufficiently quelled enemy fire, the wet miserable and defenseless (so far as bodily protection is concerned) infantry start forward to take the positions. Always enough enemy fire remains to take its toll, and take its toll it does, of the intrepid foot soldiers who display a courage unexcelled by any other branch or group of warriors who ever fought and died in this, or any other age.

The light is growing dim now at 1630 (4:30 P.M.) and outside the rain continues steadily. Lt Clark has kindled a fire in the fireplace, which only increases my thoughts of those outside, their wet clothing plastered by the sticky mud, plodding steadily on, or hovering in muddy holes from enemy fire; and of those who lie by the roads or in the fields who feel not the pelt of the rain nor the chill of the evening, nor hear any more the guns firing or the vehicles going by, nor see the gathering gloom settling about the wet fields and the dripping orchards. They will look no more at the pictures carried in their pockets nor read again the letters from their loved ones,—pictures and letters now being soaked and blurred by the cold rain.

I guess I think too much of the more unfortunate. No one can bring back those who have died, and all that can be done is being done for the wounded and those who continue in the conflict.

* * *

Soon we move on to new location, - if plans do not go awry.

A moment ago Maj McElroy sat down to one of the pianos and played a few bars of some beautiful music. Sounded so strange and out-of-place as if some one had opened slightly the door of heaven and let a few strains of that music slip out to unsuspecting and incredulous hearers.

* * *

The report about Lt Kelly[67] being wounded is true. He was hit in the arm which was broken in two places. Reported as hit by fire from friendly troops. He is out for duration now, and I hope he is O.K.

---

67 Lt. John P. Kelly, Broken Bow, Nebr., recovered and returned.

Sgt Miller of 2nd Bn killed by Germans who tricked him by speaking English.

Yesterday our 3rd Bn, with the aid of artillery and attached units, completely decimated an enemy Bn. Total PWs last night, 136 including 9 officers. PWs on preceding day approximately 200, mostly taken by 1st Bn.

\* \* \*

A short time ago a tank in which Lt Braffit was riding was knocked out in an assault on a town. Chalk up another close one for him.

Today Sgt Porta drove through a woods on rcn and reported it O.K. A following vehicle was blown up by a mine. A short time later he and Lt Kurtz had stopped on the road near a jeep. A large tree, which had been hit by shells, suddenly, without warning, fell between their vehicle and another. I saw him a short time ago, with not even a raincoat, his 220 lb frame soaked and his bearded face all dark with the dirt and grime of combat.

\* \* \*

The Huns have jammed the radio waves today and prevented us getting news. As the Siegfried line is now broken and the Russians are on the offensive at Warsaw, there may be great news which the Germans do not want us to receive.

\* \* \*

[Casualties[68] not mentioned in the Journal.]

Mazerulles, France
Sept. 18, 1944

Yesterday Lt Braffit was killed. A short time after his escape from the tank, his Bn was moving up to by-pass the town. Finding that four men of the mortar platoon were unaccounted for, he went to look for them. [Braffit was S-2 for his Bn. "Hell," he said, "S-2s are expendable but we need those mortar men!"] His driver came back, wounded, and said that Lt Braffit had sent a message by him, to send him

---

68 1st Lt. Stephen J. Rutkowski, Co A, Atlantic City, N. J. an original, listed SWA Sept. 16, did not return; WOJG Glen Wells, Regtl Hq Co, St. Louis, Mo., an original, evacuated as sick Sept 16, did not return; 1st Lt John R. Reed, Co G, Antomba, Minn., a replacement, listed as KIA Sept 17.

(Lt Braffit) help. They found him dead, full of holes from a mortar burst. That is the story as near as I could get it from different parties. His driver had been evacuated, and it may be that his, Braffit's own lips were the only ones that could have told the true story, and they will speak no more earthly words. His body had been brought into the Regtl Aid Station and as we were moving out from the French General's premises the priest,[69] surrounded by a group of men with bared, bowed heads, was saying the last rites over his broken body. [I had no time to write them.]

Never have I seen a braver, more energetic man than Lt Braffit, nor one more devoted to duty. He did whatever he found to do that needed to be done, whether or not it fell within his field of duty. He was sincere, kind and helpful, and so considerate of others that often his heart was breaking for those who were carrying a burden almost too heavy to bear.

I have many pictures of him in my mind; his harried look when we were together at the American School Center in England where they were feeding us dry, text-book stuff which bored us to death. He would look at me, I would shake my head and grin, he would shake his head and smile back, and we would endure.

I remember his righteous, Irish anger when some Lt Col in one of the other regiments "bawled him out" for reporting something to him which Braffit thought he should know, as it was near the sector boundaries and concerned both units. I'm sure this Lt Col, a son-of-a-bitch if I ever heard of one, was simply chagrined that his rcn had not already found the item reported by Braffit.

I shall never forget his sunny smile and cheery greeting, almost always present, even in the face of all the danger and hardship and hell which he endured. And I can never erase from my mind the memory of him, worried and worn almost to the breaking point, standing by a tree one dark evening, weeping silently for his men, who, then already exhausted, had been ordered to cross the Sur-Vire River that night and take the high ground beyond.

Let no skeptic ever say to me again, "I do not believe in heaven and hell," for there must be a heaven to reward

69 Probably Capt. Elwyn A. Bierie, Catholic chaplain, St. Louis, Mo., who succeeded Father Hoag.

men like Braffit, and a hell for those like Hitler and his brutal minions.

God rest his brave and kindly soul and grant him peace in the next world which was to him here denied. [Braffit won many decorations. Later I had the satisfaction of writing the citation for his award of the Croix de Guerre by the French authorities.]

* * *

Word reaches me that Lt Overfield [see footnote No 61] was killed last week while his unit was engaged in helping the Fourth Armored Division. He had been with us since three days after we entered the lines. Two other officers killed, one in F and one in H, and three others wounded. They were all new replacements, whom I had not come to know. Also a good friend of mine from F Co, Sgt Heidelbrink, whom I have known a long time, was killed by a mortar shell which hit on the edge of his fox hole. Sgt Koch, one of the last of my good friends among the EM, is still okeh.

* * *

Just as I finished writing the above Maj Jamison asked if I wanted to go get a bath. I went with him and Col Northam and had a good hot shower (have just returned, and am greeted by two shells which just landed). The shower was found by one of our French speaking men. It was certainly good, but such things remind me too much of the good things left behind and bring to me sometimes a desperate longing for this business to be over.

* * *

Had a letter from Lt Trask today, who is in hospital in England. He says he is now able to walk with a cane. Hope this business is over before he has to come back.

* * *

We are in assembly area today at Mazerulles, but because we are so far out to the front our troops have to set up defensively. Our Cn Co, AT Co, mortars and some MG's have been defending us from Germans just to the NW. The damned Krauts have shelled us all night and day and our arty has not yet been able to stop them. Just now a Frenchman came in and gave us some positions of enemy cannon and troops, so perhaps the arty can get something done now.

* * *

No mail from the States in four days now. Seems to come in bunches.

\* \* \*

Two men from our company were hit by the shell a moment ago. Both are in a bad way. The medics are giving plasma to one of them now. Later. Have just returned from Aid Station. Four men were hit, one of them Zachary from Locksburg, Arkansas. I remember that he went home on furlough from Camp Rucker, Ala., at the same time Alta went home from there. They rode with Capt Shealey to northern La., and from there on the train. Alta could not speak too highly of him for his helpfulness to her in taking care of Farrell on the trip. I recall that she remarked of how anxious he became as he neared home. He is in a bad way, both arms broken (the medics said the left one would be lost, the other would probably be saved), a slight chest wound and another wound. Another who was hit was Lt Kohler of Co I, a class mate of mine from Ft. Benning, not seriously. Another was T/5 Roberts of our Regtl Hqs Co.

\* \* \*

*The casualties mentioned above came from one of those mixups, or lapses of thought, which occur in battle.*

*Our arty was setting up to our rear after a move. The btry called their forward observer with us in the town in which we were situated, and asked for a target on which to fire in order to establish range. The F. O. with us, observing a town to our front still held by the enemy, replied, "Try the church steeple in the next town up," meaning the town beyond our location. Looking at the map, the arty btry picked out the next town up from where they were located, which was ours. The btry aimed its guns and fired a salvo of four rounds. The range was calculated so well that the salvo rang the bell in the church steeple. Therefore the four casualties were from our own arty - a lapse of thought which should not have occurred but which was quite understandable, and just one of the errors in the great confusion of war.*

*Years later while campaigning for governor in SW Arkansas, I met a young man with an artificial limb, the other shrunken shoulder padded and built up, and with impaired use of the arm.*

*"Do you know me?" he asked.*

*"You're Zachery," I replied.*

*I had not known how he fared from his wounds until then. He had employment with the Employment Security Division of my administration, a job which I hope he still holds.*

\* \* \*

Saw Lt Christianson[70] of 1st Bn a short while ago. He seems to hold up as well in combat as otherwise. Must have a strong faith of some kind. Saw also Lt Coil[71] of Co H.

W/O Frazier[72] has been up forward with us for some time now. He can out talk anyone except Col Bryne. He is always cheerful and a hard worker. That makes him okeh by me.

\* \* \*

Lt Brimhall[73] was wounded seriously today, just five days after returning to duty from hospital where he had recovered from wounds received previously while in combat with us.

\* \* \*

I am copying below a letter which I got from Capt Casey. My reason for doing so, is that I think it contains in its simple sincere lines all the pathos, longing and heartbreak of a casualty in war. [The letter was to Capt Casey from the widow of Lt Underwood] It is addressed:

Capt. Casey (Co Comm) Serial No. unknown)
320th Inf., Co E, c/o Postmaster
New York, New York

Dear Friend,

Since I received the message of Stanley's death I've tried almost every way there is to learn something about what happened etc. Today I heard from the Whittinghams. Mrs. Whittingham wrote that you are supposed to write to me. I realize you're awfully busy but I sure would be glad to re-

---

70  1st Lt. Arthur E. Christianson, Com O of 1st Bn, Mattapan, Mass., an original officer of the Regt.

71  1st Lt. Arthur L. Coil, Co H, Overland Park, Kan., an original, returned after recovery from wounds suffered July 11 at St. Lo.

72  CWO Kenneth H. Frazier, Pers Sec of Sv Co, Wichita, Kans. an original.

73  1st Lt. McKean E. Brimhall, Co K, Salt Lake City, Utah, an original officer of the Regt. His second wounds proved fatal, listed KIA Sept 20th.

ceive a letter from you if you were suppose to write one to me. I want to know what its all about.

It does not seem possible he could be gone, it's so hard for me to believe. Did you talk to him or see him? Was he killed instantly or not? Did he make it to a hospital or not? Were there any last words? Did he tell anyone anything to write to me? The message said he was killed July 24 (Monday). The last letter he wrote was on that day. He said he was O. K. This may seem strange to you but it would be a relief to me to know where he was hit. If he thought he was going to be a cripple for life I know he didn't try to live. You don't know how bad I wanted him to come back under any condition he could make it back to me. When a woman loves a man like I did him its so hard to give him up. My heart has suffered a thousand deaths since I received that telegram. I would like to believe there was still hopes of a mistake but don't suppose there is.

Please write me all you know about him.

Your friend,

Mrs. Stanley S. Underwood
Owensville, Mo.

*    *    *

Capt Casey told me that on that day, it being a quiet one, Lt Underwood had gone back to the Aid Station for something; he had washed, shaved, written his wife a letter and then lay down and fell asleep. Capt Casey called the medics and they replied he was asleep, so he told them to let him rest until the latest hour possible. He awoke and went back to the front lines just before nightfall. He was out to check some new men who had come in, to see if they were properly dug in and protected for the night. On the way he stopped by some of our mortar positions. Two enemy mortar shells fell, the second one killing him almost instantly.

*    *    *

Charley Glatzer, our Red Cross man, was returning to our CP today after an absence of a few days, part of which was spent in Paris. Someone directed him to Champenous, which we by-passed yesterday on the way up, and was not cleared of the enemy. As Charley approached the town he passed a burned out tank (American, the one in which Bra-

— 309 —

ffit was riding yesterday I think) and noticed three Germans standing near by. Thinking they were already PWs, or by-passed individuals who would give up, he pointed his finger at them and called on them to surrender. There was no reply and sensing that something was wrong, he speeded up his jeep and took off down the road, zig-zaging to make himself a difficult target. The Germans fired on him with a bazooka but luckily missed. He passed three more [enemy soldiers] and stuck out his hand, "no, no," and got by without them shooting. By this time he was well into the town and darted his vehicle into a garage. The French civilians, seeing what was wrong, immediately shut the door, hid Charley's stuff (about $800.00 worth of goods bought in Paris for the men and officers), buried his uniform and had him disguised as a French peasant in no time at all. He then strolled out in sight of 18 Germans and walked nonchalantly down the street to another house, where they dressed him in the blue uniform of a French gendarme. He stayed in the town for some time; our artillery shelled targets nearby; when some American tanks approached the German soldiers withdrew. The Krauts then shelled the city and killed 5 civilians and wounded four. The French then asked if they could have an ambulance and a doctor to care for the wounded. By this time Charley had learned where we were and volunteered to come through if a tank would come through with him. The tankers could not send one of their vehicles, so it ended up by Charley and some of his brother gendarmeire coming through on his jeep under the flag of the Red Cross.

Charley was certainly glad when he got here. He was so funny looking in his suit and in the manner of telling his story that we were all amused in spite of the gravity of the situation. The suit looked as if it had been tailored for him, and Col Northam remarked that he looked "more like a Frog than a Frog himself" ("Frog" - slang for French).

His story disclosed how glad the French are to see us come. He said they had their flags all ready to hang out and a number of them were armed, ready to assist our infantry when it approaches the town. Some actually cried for joy when they learned the Allies were on the way, and were so near. They are also hiding, or have been, one of the tank crew members who escaped when it was hit.

The FFI has such a hatred for the Germans that when they get arms and get going, the Huns fear them more than us. They are sometimes glad to surrender to us to escape the FFI.

* * *

Well, I'm so sleepy I cannot keep my eyes open. If I can stay awake to hear the midnight news, then I shall awaken Sgt Coyne, and see if I can snatch a few winks here by the phones. The German guns have so far been pretty quiet tonight. Ours are firing at intervals.

The 1st Bn has left to join the 4th Armored. Maj Gillis said they [the 4th Armd] told him they were all set to go to Germany when they took off. We follow tomorrow or soon thereafter.

Well, I must stop.

[Casualties[74] of Sept. 17 and 18.]

## THE GREAT DEBATE

*At this time in the High Command, we later learned, a great debate was going on. Up to this time all armies had been driving and now supplies had run low. Also lines of supply had been greatly extended by the advance of Allied armies, especially Patton's Third. Consequently, transportation difficulties had developed to such an extent that all armies could not be adequately supplied for continued full scale offensive operations. A choice must now be made as to which armies would receive adequate supplies and keep driving, while others would receive limited supplies and hold.*

*The British and Canadian armies had advanced north along the coast, and were now on the extreme left flank (north and west) positioned in Holland. The American Ninth Army and the American First Army had reached Northern France and advanced into Belgium and Luxembourg, and were*

---

74  1st Lt. Raymond W. Braffit, S-2 of 1st Bn, Watertown, Mass., an original, listed KIA Sept 17; 1st Lt. Riley P. Shirley, Co A, Louisville, Ky, an original previously wounded, evacuated as sick Sept. 18; 1st Lt. Howard M. Kiser, Hq 2nd Bn, address unknown, an original, evacuated as sick Sept. 18, only a few days after returning from the hospital; 1st Lt. Donald N. Eckenrode, Co I, Lilly, Pa., a replacement and Ft. Benning classmate, listed LWA Sept. 17; Maj. Joseph Szabo, Hq 2nd Bn, Anderson, S. C., an original, listed LIA Sept 18; none returned.

*now holding the center, the Ninth next to the British. Patton's Third Army had made the great end run across France and advanced into Alsace-Lorraine. Its armored spearheads were now reaching for the German border. Still further east the Seventh Army, after landing on the Mediterranean Coast of France, had advanced up the Rhone Valley to a junction with Patton's forces.*

*To supply the Seventh Army for the major drive was not strategically feasible, and evidently the First Army was not considered. Therefore the subject of the Great Debate was whether to send the supplies to Patton's Third Army or to the armies on the north and west, which included the British, the Canadian and the American Ninth.*

*It appeared, at first, that the plans were to supply Patton's Army and order it forward in the big push. It was about this time that I personally saw the secret orders which had come from the 35th Division to the 320th Headquarters calling for an advance across the remainder of Alsace-Lorraine, over the upper Rhine River and into southern Germany. The major cities in that region of the Fatherland were circled on the map as our major objectives. This was the basis, no doubt, of the word from Fourth Armored Headquarters to Major Gillis that they were "all set to go to Germany when they took off." At one time, pursuant to the secret orders in our hands, we in the 320th were loaded on trucks ready to take off eastward with the armored divisions. Then the orders were changed, we detrucked and continued our advance on foot.*

*Then orders came late in September to establish defensive lines, get under cover and hold. At this time I was in Gen Wood's headquarters with Col Byrne where he visited with the commander of the 4th Armored. In full battle dress the famed general paced up and down in his huge tent like an angry, caged lion and chafed at the orders he had received. "Hell, Byrne," he ejaculated, "I can't set down. This in an offensive unit." (At another time Gen Wood was in our headquarters). Even then he was pulling back his farthest advanced forces. While we were there a weary, battle-stained lieutenant, commander of an armored infantry force, reported to Gen Wood. His unit, which had been almost in sight of the German border on the eastern edge of Alsace-Lorraine, had pulled back in response to the latest orders.*

*We heard later by the grapevine that Gen Wood had raised so much hell about the decision that he was relieved of his command and sent back to the States.*

*It became apparent to us later that those who favored a push by the armies on the north and west had prevailed in the debate. The final decision had been made to supply the British and Canadian Armies and the American Ninth Army for an effort to cross the lower Rhine, where it had three definite branches, and push into North Germany. We later learned that those who favored that course had argued that Allied armor could operate more effectively on the plains of North Germany than in the mountainous region of South Germany.*

*As those familiar with the war will know, the effort on the north was made by three air drops of parachute troops to secure and hold bridges across the three branches of the lower Rhine, - at Eindhoven, Arnheim and Nymagen. Armored and infantry forces then drove forward to connect with the pockets of paratroops. Once the junction was effected, the last bridgehead was to be enlarged for the mass crossing.*

*The Germans resisted fiercely, shooting the Allied tanks off the high, embanked, narrow roadways. Junction was made with the first two bridgeheads held by the parachute troops, but the third could not be reached. Finally the remnants of the third force had to be withdrawn. The effort to breach the lower Rhine had failed. From the standpoint of the "Big Picture" of the war, that was the saddest day for me. The effort to bring the conflict to a conclusion in 1944 had faded away in the German success at Arnheim. I knew then that the war would last all winter.*

*The reader will note farther along in this book the terrible campaign for Alsace-Lorraine which began on Nov. 8. During the five or six weeks that we were holding in place, the Germans had re-occupied the region, including Metz, in force. They established a strong defense line reaching all along the front. By the use of slave labor and impressed people of the region, defense works had been prepared, including gun positions, extensive mine fields and anti-tank ditches. One hugh trench, dug by slave laborers, stretched for miles across the flat, muddy plain.*

The reader will note that rain prevailed and the area was a vast sea of mud. The armor was unable at any time to effect a major break-through. The brunt of the fighting in the advance fell on the weary, foot slogging doughboys, who occupied the region, fighting for every foot of ground, mile by mile, town by town, in a campaign which lasted from Nov. 8 to Dec. 21.

I believe those who advocated the southern offensive, including Patton and Gen Wood, were right. The divisions in the Third Army knew how to advance. We had already moved farther and faster, captured more prisoners and occupied more area than any other force in Europe on the Western Front. Some time in September we had jeep patrols in Metz which then had only light occupying forces. The great fortress could easily have been taken by infantry or armored forces if we had received sufficient gas to get the trucks or tanks to the city. We could not move fast enough on foot.

Gen Wood's Fourth Armored Division was undoubtedly one of the finest, if not the finest offensive outfit of the war. With patrols of armored infantry in sight of the German border across Alsace-Lorraine, they had to be withdrawn. There were other battle-wise divisions under Patton as the 26th Infantry, the 80th Infantry and the 6th Armored Division. If the Third Army had been turned loose, it could have taken in a week's time, the two oft disputed provinces and occupied that part of Germany west of the upper Rhine. We might then have continued all the way into South Germany - and taken the major cities outlined on the battle map as our objectives. If not, we would at least have avoided the terrible campaign of Nov. 8 to Dec. 21, and the cost in casualties, supplies and equipment would not have been as high. The Germans were disorganized in September. By November they had reorganized and, while they could not hold the ground, staged planned withdrawals to previously prepared positions as they inflicted maximum casualties on our advancing forces. For every mile of ground given up, the enemy exacted a heavy toll from the attacking infantry and armor and those who accompanied them.

Late in the Alsace-Lorraine campaign a company commander was gathering the remnants of his unit for a move. His platoon leaders were reporting. Noticing a lone NCO he inquired, "Sergeant, where is your platoon?"

*"Sir," replied the Sergeant, "I am the platoon."*

*I am unalterably convinced that had the Third Army been permitted to continue, it would have reached the Rhine about six months before the Allied forces finally effected a crossing. We would have occupied hundreds of square miles of enemy territory before reaching the river, probably would made the crossing and might have ended the war in 1944. Even if success had not been so extensive, Patton's forces would certainly have over-run all of Alsace-Lorraine and German territory up to the Rhine. The delayed campaign for those provinces in the snow and the rain, the muck and the mire, through numberless prepared German positions, would, without doubt, have been prevented. And, who knows, perhaps the Battle of the Bulge in the Ardennes, the most costly in history to Americans, would have been avoided. However, the failure of the armies on the north and west to attain their objectives, had now set the stage for both bloody campaigns, in which the 320th Infantry was destined to participate as a part of the 35th Division and the now famous Third Army.*

*I don't know why the decision was made to attempt the crossing on the Lower Rhine. Some observers now say the decision was based more on political factors than on strictly military considerations. Others speculate that it may have been professional jealousy of other general officers, both British and American, toward Patton. The thought has occurred to me, as it has to others, that the decision for the effort on the north by British forces might have been at the urging of Churchill, to which Roosevelt acceded. Then Eisenhower was persuaded to this course in order to continue the spirit of harmony and cooperation between the British and American high commands, which, up to that moment, the Supreme Commander had so successfully maintained. Anyway, whatever the reasons for the final directive, there is little doubt in my mind that Gen Eisenhower changed his mind, and revoked the first order, which was directed to Patton and the Third Army. Perhaps some day, when all the records are opened and scanned, and all the memoirs are written and read, we will know the real reasons for the final decision to attempt the breach of the German lines on the north. At the moment we can only speculate as to what they were.*

*I do know the terrain of the northern region was most unsuitable for such a drive as was contemplated - a decisive breakthrough to bring the conflict to an early end. The roads of Holland were built-up structures standing high above the low lying fields which were scarcely above sea level. To stall an offensive drive, the German gunners had only to force the tanks, other vehicles and men off the highroads into the mud and water of the surrounding fields where they were bogged down. That was exactly what happened to the British forces as they attempted to drive forward. Consequently the attempt to link up with the brave paratroopers failed.*

*No such problem existed in the Third Army sector. In the first place there was only one branch of the upper Rhine River in South Germany, and that not so wide as the lower branches in Holland. Secondly, the terrain of Alsace-Lorraine was similar to that of Central France over which Patton's Armor and Infantry had already operated so successfully. Also at that time the ground was firm enough for movement of tanks, both before and beyond the Rhine River. None of these favorable factors for a rapid offensive existed in the lowlands of The Netherlands.*

*There were other factors, intangible though they may be, which we, who came to know combat and the combat forces so well, cannot overlook as we view in retrospect the Great Debate, its final decision and the ultimate results. Those factors involved such intangibles as attitude, spirit, confidence and the willingness to drive regardless of other considerations.*

*We had great respect and admiration for the British forces, both officers and men. They believed as fully as we in the justice of our cause. They had borne for a long time the brunt of the battle, as a nation, a people and a military organization, while we still remained non-belligerent and free of the conflict. The stand of the English people under the leadership of Winston Churchill, almost alone for a time against Nazi tyranny, I consider one of the greatest examples of heroism in the history of the world. That stand constituted, perhaps, in the words of the Prime Minister himself, "their finest hour." They had every reason to want to win, and the members of the British Army could and did, fight and die bravely when the need arose or the occasion demanded.*

*Still, having said all this, there was something about the British forces which we Americans had difficulty in understanding. It seemed to us there was the failure at times to* "strike while the iron is hot," to "ride while in the saddle," - in other words the failure to drive with all the dispatch and power available, sacrificing all other considerations, when there was an opportunity for greater success or more decisive gains.

For example, the British would stop in the midst of a roaring tank battle to have tea, as they were seen to do in the engagements of Falaise Gap at the time the 35th Division was helping to stop the German offensive at Mortain. For a time at Falaise Gap it appeared the Allied armies would entrap large segments of the engaged German forces. But the gap was not closed and the enemy forces withdrew. No one will say, least of all I, that the German forces escaped because the British tankers stopped for tea. But because they did stop for tea, or for other causes on occasion, at what appeared to be inopportune times, the thought developed among up that they did not always go as far and as fast as they might have. Perhaps the British Army had been at war so long that there did not, at that time, exist in its ranks, as in the American Army, the overwhelming desire to "get it over with" as quickly as possible and "get back home."

Also in the Third Army we had a commander in whom we had the greatest confidence. Patton's "God-dammit, to-hell-and-gone, go-get-em" attitude suited us to the fullest degree. He became known to us as "the Combat General." He knew how to push an army on to victory and the combat experienced divisions in his army had learned how to drive. We had learned well the great advantage of hitting the enemy when his forces were disrupted and off-balance. We had come to know how much more hell there was in going up against his prepared positions as we had in Normandy and at Mortain. We believed Gen Patton understood these things and would exercise his power of command accordingly. Our confidence in him was still further enhanced when we learned from questioning hundreds of German prisoners-of-war that the enemy had the greatest respect for Patton as a commander. We further learned from the captives that the Germans feared Patton more than any other general and his forces more than any other army on the Western Front.

Therefore the matter of command of the forces which were to make the effort to achieve a major breakthrough was important. The effort on the north was to be entrusted to the most famous and perhaps the best British General, Bernard Law Montgomery. With the British Eighth Army, Monty, as he was known, had won a great victory over Field Marshall Irwin Rommel's Afrika Korps at El Alamein but Patton had been equally successful against the forces of the Desert Fox farther west in Africa. Later when both commanders had landed their forces in Sicily, Patton's Americans had decisively outgained the forces of Montgomery in the conquest of that Italian Island.

In the great invasion of Europe, Montgomery's Army again faced the forces of Rommel at Caen, the hinge of the Normandy effort, and the German Field Marshall's Army fought the invading British to a standstill. When Patton was permitted on the scene and given command of the American Third Army, he drove through the break in the German lines made by the infantry after the great bombing raid, and in typical hell-for-leather style began to overrun enemy territory, killing and capturing thousands of the same German forces.

In the decision to be made in the Great Debate it seemed that these intangibles, with the other factors involved, weighed heavily in favor of Patton and the Third Army over the more conservative, steady British under Montgomery. Both great leaders had reputations as vain glorious generals. Yet, in the choice of a commander for an undertaking of the kind under consideration, - a quick hard drive to obtain decisive results at a most critical point, - we would have placed our bets on the personality universally recognized as "Old Blood and Guts" Patton rather than the highly esteemed general known as "I-am-God" Montgomery.

In the future when men study the campaigns of the Western Front as they now study those of the Civil War, the decision to make the breakthrough on the north instead of the south will be debated, much as Pickett's Charge at Gettysberg is now discussed. Based on my knowledge of the circumstances, I am fully confident the first decision for the effort on the south with Patton should have been permitted to stand. However, considering the fate of individual men in war, if the course had not been changed, I might not now be writing these lines. Still, this does not alter my conviction that Patton would have been successful where Montgomery failed. The great conflict might well have been brought to an earlier end, thus saving thousands of lives.

*There was an interesting footnote to the great contro-*
*versy some time later in the conflict. In the closing days of*
*the war or shortly after it had ended, I saw picture post cards*
*of Gen Patton, which circulated, to what extent I do not know,*
*among the American troops. The post cards showed a picture*
*of the famous general standing on the bank of the Rhine*
*River, "taking a leak" (urinating) into the waters of the*
*stream. Below the picture were the words, "If they had turn-*
*ed me loose I would have done this six months ago." Barring*
*the possibility of becoming a casualty, he would have done it.*

Mazerulles, France
Sept. 19, 1944

Time: 1120

Still in our CP in the school building. The night was
quiet but the Huns are laying the shells around us this morning. We had 41 casualties from artillery fire yesterday.

The Colonel has gone up to Div Hqs now for orders. Perhaps we will be off soon. It is better to be moving and killing
Germans than to be sitting out front as we are, receiving
enemy shells. Quite a number of our boys in regtl hqs are
somewhat nervous. Some of them (new) have not been subjected to very much fire.

The damned Germans should all be turned over to the
French and Russians, who will deal with them in a way which
fits their crimes. It is possible to understand why they should
keep on fighting, evil though their intent, when they had
a chance to win. But now one of their worst crimes is the
continuation of the hell and the slaughter after the issue
has been decided. I think they shall regret the increasing hatred which their madness is creating.

* * *

2200 - Well, we move tomorrow.

This afternoon a very pretty French girl from the town
of Campenous, bringing Charley's money belt, shoes and some
other articles, rode up to our CP on a bicycle. She almost hug-
ged Charley's neck when she saw him. Because she was so
young and pretty, the Colonel says he is beginning to wonder
about Charley's story of how he came to be wearing someone
else's clothes. And the second thing he wonders about after

seeing her, is why Charley came back at all. The Colonel nearly always sees the humor in every situation. But anyone who
sees Charley does not need to look farther for humor. It is all
about him and a part of him. Every man in the regiment
knows him, and I think I have never seen anyone more universally liked. He fits the part of a Red Cross man like Santa
Claus fits Christmas.

He is a sincere and industrious worker, and if every man
loved his neighbor as he does, half the minister's work would
already be done. He is Czech nationality and speaks a number
of languages.

\* \* \*

Some how I keep looking for Braffit to come through
the doorway or drive up in a jeep. Then I remember that he
will never appear again. Lt Kligerman says his wounds were
from MG bullets. Now we may never know.

Arracourt, France
Sept. 20, 1944

Time: 2208

Our CP is in this town tonight while our two Bns are
facing to the south and east. We joined the 4th Armored today, and tonight there is enemy on almost every side. The
war as a whole may be going good, but the fight is furious
where we are. There are something like 200 enemy tanks
facing us. We shall take care of them, I am sure, but at what
cost we don't know.

Our CP for awhile was at Juvrecourt today but we
shifted back here to be more centrally located for our Bns.
At that place some of our AT men captured 3 PWs, one of
whom was an officer. The officer refused to talk until Sgt
Seillers threatened to send a photostatic copy of his diary to
Germany. Then he answered all questions. Another striking
proof that Hitler rules even his own by terror. One of the
men who participated in the capture remarked, "We were
looking for roasting ears and these turned up," indicating
the PWs, who were taken in a cornfield. (If I were back on
Pinnacle Mountain at the Ledford home there would be plenty
of late fall roasting ears, red, ripe tomatoes and cornfield
beans. I wonder if I am going to get through to enjoy all
that again. A man has only so much time here, and the odds

are against a long stay in this business. Only eight officers of all the originals left in the 2nd Bn).

Even our service trains are now up where there is shelling and fighting. Now they are in a woods not far away. Capt Heil[75] told Silverman, "I saw a German in here this afternoon and I shot at him too." Whereupon Maj Hughes dryly remarked, "I'm going to have to take that cognac away from those boys I guess."

It just happened that after our CP was set up tonight, we gathered in a group for awhile and had about an hour's "bull session." Col Byrne told a few of his many funny and varied experiences, and others had some to relate. I might say that we were almost cheerful for awhile. But there is always in my mind those who are not so well situated, those who have gone on to the West and those who will go in the continuing struggle.

Unfortunate incident of the day, - our own artillery threw some shells into our 3rd Bn causing 3 casualties.

Sgt Porta is now S-2 of that unit and has been recommended for a commission. Lt Kurtz now has a company and will be recommended for a captaincy.

Arracourt, France
Sept. 21, 1944

We have not moved today. The 2nd Bn, in conjunction with the tank sweep of a part of the armored division, helped clean out an area just north of the Rhin Canal. Otherwise the day has been fairly quiet. Our Air Force came over and bombed and strafed on a small scale. Just now a gun off to the south is throwing shells at us but so far none have hit too close. I can hear the gun fire, then the shells come whistling in and explode near by.

\* \* \*

Received word today that Lt Jones'[76] wounds were fatal. Another nice fellow and a good officer is bivouacing across the Divide tonight.

\* \* \*

---

75 Capt. Paul H. Heil, CO of Sv Co, Dennison, Ohio, had been with us all the way.

76 2nd Lt. Ernest J. Jones, A/T Co, address unknown, one of our original officers, listed in unofficial record as DOW Dec. 28, evidently in error. In the journal entry of Sept. 16 I find the note that he was wounded on Sept. 15.

Had some mail from home today, and one of the letters is from Farrell. He "dictates" to Alta and she writes his message to me. "Tell him that Golda bought me a tank"

"Tell him I took a shower bath about dark."

"Tell him I got a broken winged airplane but it's a toy."

"Tell him I saw a tank just like weal (real) but it was made out of wood and was a toy."

"Tell him its dark now."

"Tell him I saw Snow White and the Seven Dwarfs. Tell him an old woman changed into a witch and made Snow White go to sweep (sleep)"

(Then he asks, "How much is that wrote?")

"Tell him I've been outside playing with my tank."

"Tell him you bought me a twuck and Golda bought me a funhie (funny) book."

"Tell him we live right by a motorcycle garage and we hear lots of noise, that it makes lots of noise in it."

"Tell him I'm aim to put the stamp on and put the letter in and seal it."

"Tell him we went to the park and took pictures and Grandpa bought us some ice cream."

"Tell him, Oh, (I'm trying to think of something to tell him)"

"Tell him that sometimes we go over to Grandma's and Arvis's both."

I must say that such a letter is to me infinitely touching. No more powerful or forceful reminder could be brought to me of the love and tenderness left behind. Such things one puts away in the back of the mind until something like the above brings them again to the fore. And then the fear, the longing and the sorrow wells up in the heart and is for a time overwhelming.

Occasionally I think of him when the shells are going over; of his tender little body, weight about 25 or 30 or 40 lbs. (I wonder how much he does weigh).

The little warm brown hands, the nails usually play-stained; his so-round head with the definite crown in his hair; his sparkling dark eyes, always pleasure bent or adventure seeking, until the sand man dims and closes their sight. Many times long ago (it seems) when he would fall asleep in my arms or by my side, his tender loveliness would bring an uncontrollable lump in my throat. I would go and tenderly put him to rest and keep my face from Alta until the mist had cleared from my eyes. I wonder why I had to love him so much?

Sometimes in the hell of the conflict I think that one 50 caliber bullet would make his features unrecognizable; a mortar shell would blow him apart; the cannon shells, which weigh more than he, or the great 90 lb projectiles of the heavy artillery, which whisper so terribly overhead, would not leave even one tiny piece of him to be found. May God grant to the peoples of this earth the willingness and judgement to prevent him from ever coming within hearing of the roar of guns of war. This, I pray, not only for him, but for all little children everywhere.

War can be prevented. Courts for mankind can settle international disputes just as our national courts settle national disputes or local courts mediate small controversies. They must be backed by international forces for peace just as local forces for peace (police) back up the lesser courts. If there is another great war it may well destroy our civilization.

Now 2250; and so some sleep.

Arracourt, France
Sept. 22, 1944

Time: 2310

Another quiet day, one in which there were no casualties in the two Bns for which I feel a deep and heartfelt thankfulness.

Now, as I write, there is a program of good music on the radio we have managed to keep with us. There has just concluded "Long Ago and Far Away" a tune which I have always thought inexpressably beautiful.

There are still sitting around the table as I begin to write these few lines, Maj McElroy, Lt Silverman and Capt Scherer[77] (FA). Lt Ginsberg and Maj Hughes have just said "Good night" and retired.

77  Capt. James B. Scherer, Regular Army officer of Oklahoma, at Regtl Hq as FO for 216th FA. Another FO for the 216th was 1st Lt. Thomas M. Miller of Oklahoma City, Okla. Miller was a very small, youthful officer, stationed with 3rd Bn Hq, who sometimes made decisions and commanded the Bn when other officers were not available. He and Capt Scherer seemed more a part of the 320th than the arty.

Lt Frank Sperl, my good friend (but a hard-boiled Republican), is with us tonight. Very glad to see him as he works in the personnel section which remains with Div Hqs and I don't often get a look at him. He is a very cheerful fellow and when we can forget the war long enough he kids me about voting for Dewey.

* * *

Received a copy of the "Madison County Record" today in which appeared my letters of July 24 and 27. Several read them and said they liked them. Maj McElroy asked if I got more than one copy of the paper; said he liked the writing very much and would like to have it. I thought when they started to read it that he would be the one least apt to like the letters. One cannot always tell what is in the heart or the emotions that well therefrom. A calm exterior often hides a flood of feeling.

If it is true that we are all brothers under the skin (and I think we are) we can find a way to curb the ruthless ambitions of power-mad people, both political and economic, and prevent the man-made hells which we call wars.

* * *

Today I learned that Capt Frederickson had died of his wounds after reaching the hospital. Word reached us through a letter from his wife to one of us, saying she had received the death notice.

* * *

Magallanes, the New Mexican boy with the Spanish accent (today I heard him saying "deeper" for dipper), came into the CP room tonight when we were getting the nine o'clock (2100) news to listen with the rest. He is a likeable lad, yet very amusing in his serious way, and one of the most polite and courteous people I have ever known. I shall never forget when we were at the dug-in CP by the lake about the 2nd week after entering the conflict, when one night the Krauts were strafing and bombing our positions. The ack-ack and MGs were going like mad, making a terrific din, punctuated now and then by the heavier explosions of bombs or salvos of artillery. I had crawled into my covered hole, more afraid of shrapnel from the ack-ack than anything else, and stuck my helmeted head out to watch. The Colonel was just going to bed in his dugout and Magallanes, who had just prepared his sleeping bag, was still there. The sky was all lit up by multi-colored flares and gun flashes and streaked with tracer bullets. The Colonel remarked "Gosh, Magallanes, it's just like a Fourth of July picnic." Replied Magallanes, "Yes sir, only more serious, sir" That reply in his fast, soft, Spanish-accented English was as funny as could be in spite of everything.

He and Checci[78] are quite a pair. A couple of days ago two shells landed quite close to them while we were on the move. Checci described the incident in emphatic language and concluded that "it looked pretty serious for awhile." I am always amused at him when he attempts to tell Maj McElroy how to find his tent or sleeping bag after he has prepared them. He never says to go right or left but directs "you go this way, you turn here, and then there and you'll find your bed here" turning his hands about and up and down to illustrate. He reminds me of some of the hill people of home giving road directions. One is often more confused at the end than at the beginning.

Moving his hands about also reminds me of the gestulating French and what Lt Quillen says about them. Lt Bill Quillen,[79] a slim, flint-eyed, tanned and leathery Texan, is executive officer of Regtl Hqs. It is his hard, practical, horse-trading ability that usually keeps our mess well supplied with eggs, fresh vegetables, fruit, French bread and other products of what ever land in which we happen to be fighting. He is the most cynical man in his expressions I have ever heard talk (I don't think he means half of it), and there is not an ounce of idealism in his make up. He watches the natives talk awhile with their innumerable gestures and then remarks "These God-damned Frenchmen. If you'd cut the sons-of-b_____'s hands off they couldn't say a single damned word."

I might add that in spite of his extreme practicallity and apparent lack of sympathy, that he is no exception to the rule, that to know a Texan is to like him.

\* \* \*

___
78   Pfc. Joseph A. Checchi, Crosshill, N. J., orderly for Maj. McElroy and Maj. Jamieson.

79   1st Lt. William H. "Bill" Quillin, Regtl Hq, Texarkana, Texas, an original 320th officer, and originally from Arkansas.

In spite of the fact that our Bns did not fight today, the force with which we are working [4th Armd] repelled two tank attacks by Hitler's forces. Some of the greatest tank battles of the Western Front have raged around us the past few days. At least 68 German tanks have been knocked out in this sector of the front. Our losses were very small. Today the cavalry lost five vehicles but the Nazis lost five tanks in the same vicinity. We had some air support doing a limited amount of strafing and bombing of enemy positions and vehicles. It seems that Hitler (who is reported as now being in personal command in the West) is recklessly throwing in a big part of his last reserves in this sector in an attempt to halt us. More of his intuition I guess like at Stalingrad.

What a blessing if he would die suddenly from any cause. Then I think the Germans would cease to drag out an already lost struggle and so many lives and hardships would be saved.

* * *

Occasional artillery, some distance away, in the damp still night, seems to almost push the glass from the windows. The sudden rattle of the panes sometimes startles me but I have long since become accustomed to the sound of the big guns.

* * *

A memory. The musical tolling of the church bells in this French village here near the closing of the day.

The first time I heard such bells was in a small village near our assembly area before we entered the Battle of Mortain. It was early evening and I inquired the reason. The French lieutenant smiled and said, "The Lee-ber-ray-shun." (liberation) "They ring every day now since the Americans came."

I can also remember the look of pure joy I saw on the faces of the people there as they watched our planes going over to bomb Germany even though it would smash and damage parts of their own country.

* * *

It is now 1615 o'clock, and the rain or mist has not let up all day. It has kept our Air Force grounded and makes it difficult for tanks or anything else to move.

"Kraut weather," mutters the Colonel, "made in Germany." It is a better defense for them than they can put up with their men and their weapons. Our positions have remained the same and there has been little activity.

Just now as I write the sun breaks through momentarily, but it will not be long enough for a strike on the Huns.

* * *

This sitting in the dry with some leisure to read, write, talk, and listen to the news on our little battery radio, gives me an anxious longing for the conflict to end. The news on the whole is very good. It gives me that "so near and yet so far" feeling like the time I lost the Democratic nomination for the House of Representatives by four votes. However that did have a finality about it which I could accept, and make plans accordingly, but this does not. It keeps one on tenter hooks, so to speak, unless kept busily engaged. Then the hope and the longing is always with me subconsciously. So the staff arouses, opens a case of cognac, drinks, talks, and tries to keep from remembering too strongly the hardship and horrors of war.

* * *

Today we received news of the lost platoon of K Co in the Battle of Mortain. I have copied the letters below.

Somewhere in Belgium
Sept. 14, 1944

Hy Sarge,

I'm still alive and kicking. . . . Do you remember when we started down the mountain at Mortain? Well, after we got pinned down on the road, three of our boys tried to get back but they didn't have a chance to cross the road. About 20 Krauts made an assault and then the inevitable happened. They had us surrounded. Sgt Myers spoke in German and off they took us. Sgt F. Oliver was wounded in the chest by a machine shot and was taken away in an ambulance. For seven days they marched us around the pocket. [Falaise pocket where American forces almost surrounded the German Army that drove for the sea and were stopped at Mortain.] At the seventh day we neared Chambois. We could hear the Bren gun all day. We figured that the English were pretty near. A barrage opened up and the Krauts started to run wild. It was every man for himself. A lieut, Morabito, me and a Kraut hid in the river for three hours. When it started to get dark we made for what we thought were the English lines, only to find the Canadians, which was a welcome sight. The Kraut that was with us gave up to us.

A series of interrogations followed and then we tried to make for 3rd Army Hqs. We came around Chatres when we could not get any more transportation. So we stuck with the 703. As soon as we can hit a stragglers train we will get back.

We escaped from the Krauts on the 19th of Aug. Ever since the 23rd of Aug. we have been with the 703 Rec Co.

So until we meet again, give em hell. Morabito sends his regards also. [Pfc Jerome A. Morabito, Co K, Punxsutawney, Pa.]

> My regards to all,
>
> Gus
>
> Pfc K. A. Petkanas, 32617379
> Rec (RCN) Co, 703 TD Bn
> Apo 230, c/o P. M. N. Y., N. Y.


(the second letter)

To: 1st Sgt James D. Kennedy
   Co K, 320th Inf, Apo No. 35

> From: Pfc K. A. Petkanas, 32617379
> Rcn Co, 703 TD Bn
> Apo No. 230, c/o P. M.

Hello Sargent,

Writing you the few lines to let you know I am still alive. Did you hear of any of the other fellows getting away from the Germans. I would like to know what you did with my personal equipment. I had some pictures and papers in my bag. I suppose their are only a few of the old boys left. Have you heard anything about Sgt Oliver? He was shot and the Germans took him away. I am writing you this letter somewhere in Belgium. Well, Sgt, if you get time I would like to hear from you. Good luck. I hope to see you in *Berlin*.

> Jim

(third letter)

To 1st Sgt Co K, 320th Inf

I can certify that these two men from your company have been with this outfit since 23rd of Aug. and I'll have a certificate of service ready for them when we contact your straggler lines. Our Adjutant, Capt Beacham, has been trying to contact the straggler lines but cannot seem to do so. I have not picked them up on my M/R as yet except for rations. They're well taken care of and certainly needed a rest after their experiences. If you want any additional information write to me.

> 1st Sgt Geo C. Boyce
> Rcn Co, 703 TD Bn
> Apo No 230, US Army

This is the only information we have had of the lost platoon. The letters speak for themselves so any comment of mine would be superfluous.

* * *

Intelligence has reached us that the Germans plan to attack our positions in the morning. All units have been alerted to be ready for them in the early dawn.

There is furious fighting in Holland around the furthest area occupied by the airbourne army. It seems the Germans are making a last desperate stand. To me the fighting has the appearance of the same kind of effort as was made to take Moscow, to hold at Stalingrad and the counter - thrust which we helped to stem at Mortain. It is a final act of desperation before the inevitable collapse. In the end it will avail Hitler and his henchmen nothing, but will drag a lot of good men down in the final struggle.

[Casualties[80] not mentioned in the Journal.]

Arracourt, France
Sept. 25, 1944

There was no attack yesterday on our lines but the armored units which we support sustained some thrusts by

---

80  1st Lt. Elmer (L) Buxton, Co L, Syracuse, N. Y., a replacement, listed NBI Sept 22; 1st Lt. Morton Kligerman, Sv Co, Poukeepsie, N. Y., an original, listed NBI Sept 23; 2nd Lt. Selby G. Benton, Co B, Cornelia, Ga., a replacement, listed SWA Sept 23; none returned.

enemy armor. Our forces were quite successful in beating them off. It was another day of rain, with a break in the clouds just before nightfall. Our air support was out just at the right time and caught some enemy columns just as they were attacking Maj Gillis's Bn, and broke up the assault. Our Bn had an outpost of eight men wiped out.

Gen Wood [John Shirley Wood, Monticello, Ark., star West Point football player, CO of 4th Armd Div] was in our CP yesterday. He was pacing up and down like a caged animal because we have been ordered to assume defensive positions here. He stamped and swore and said he had a fine offensive outfit but not suited for defense, but finally concluded that he would "have to get under cover."

Today has been the same, rain and mud, counterattacks by the enemy in which they have suffered heavily, and considerable shelling of our positions. The enemy has been perhaps more heavily shelled.

One story (by Col Reed of his [216th FA] unit) was that 140 Germans were digging in along a ridge SE of our positions. They were under observation and a Bn of arty was laid on them. After it lifted, four were seen to start away and they were cut down by fire from a TD unit. All are reported to be left on the ridge, dead or wounded.

* * *

Today in the rain I was on a mission to higher hqs. The vehicles were slinging their filmy mud and, with the speed of the jeep, the drops of rain felt like hard pellets hitting the face. [In combat the tops and windshields are down to prevent casualties from flying glass or metal in case of a hit]. In peace and sunshine the beauty of the country would be easy to appreciate and enjoy. Most of the roads are lined with trees, planted at regular intervals, one such section being lined with apple trees now covered with fruit, some rosy red, some golden. From the high ground excellent views of the surrounding country reveal smooth green meadows and pastures, brown grain fields and the closely grouped houses of the villages. At present the scenes are marred by the signs of war; the big guns tearing up the smooth turf as they go into position; the convoys making ugly tracks in the sticky mud of the fields; burned out tanks and other vehicles along the roads; the fox holes and the shell craters; the branches smashed from the trees by shell fire; the dead cows and hogs, their forms puffed and swollen with legs sticking grotesquely in the air, lying in the fields where they were felled by shell fire. I saw ten fine black and white cows and two calves lying in one group in a field west of Champenoux.

Some day, if ever I have the opportunity in peace time, I am coming back and drive over the same route I traveled today just to see how beautiful it is without the mud, rain and war. The villages, I know, will never be too nice until they have some new sanitary rules or laws. The compost (manure) piles made of dung, straw and other materials, which they have in their door yards and streets, we would hardly have in our barn lots.

The route - Arracourt, SERRES, HOEVILLE, REMMEREVILLE, ERBERVILLE, CHAMPENOUX, LANEUVELOTTE, LAITRE, AMANCE. There is a wonderful view of the country from the latter. It was here the enemy delayed our advance for some time because of the wonderful observation and fields of fire afforded by the heights.

\* \* \*

Today Lt Gotter[81] of F Co was a casualty. "Hit in the foot and leg by a stray 88" it was reported. He was the last of the original officers who came over with that company.

[A casualty[82] not mentioned in the Journal.]

Foret de St. Jean Fontaine
Sept. 27, 1944

Time: 0100

Today we spent at Arracourt still with the armored unit. It was wet with low hanging clouds, as the past few days have been, with the rain descending steadily on the dripping forests, the wet fields and the slippery, slimy roads. Orders were given and countermanded throughout the day as the situation fluctuated. The men who did not understand it all, who started to obey one order and then were told to do something else, must have been pretty disgusted, especially in the discomfort of the clinging mud and the dreary rain.

---

81 1st Lt. Wilbur A. Gotter, CO of Co F, Louisville, Ky., an original, listed LWA Sept. 25, did not return.
82 1st Lt. Walter H. Williams, Hq Co 1st Bn, address unknown, a replacement, listed LWA Sept 25, did not return.

And finally when the armored units, which were to relieve us, got around to accomplishing their mission, they made such a stir and hubub that the Krauts shelled the place and even attacked. One company had to stop and fight and could not get out until well after dark. There were several casualties from the shelling. Four dead were reported whose bodies had to be left. After all had been reported out of position and on the way, we started. Then the 3rd Bn called for an ambulance for more wounded. Ours [ambulance] had already gone but we managed to get an artillery unit, that was just moving in, to send theirs. Lt Silverman went to guide them and has not yet reported in to us. We left there at about 2100. It is now 0100 and I am a bit uneasy about him. He gets a lot of missions during which most anything could happen to him.

A lot could happen to all of us tonight if the Huns threw shells into this forest. We arrived, after dark, of course, driving always without lights, and felt our way into these woods. No one has troubled to dig-in in the dark and the wet. So there won't be much protection from the shrapnel if it comes.

Sgt Coyne and I are on duty. Already he sleeps, sitting on his chair his chin sunk on his chest, while I write. Everyone else is now rolled in their blankets or sleeping bags. The artillery is making the otherwise still night thunderous with its sound. When I step outside the blackout tent and watch, the flashes light up the whole horizon like lightning from summer storms. A few moments ago MGs were barking at each other.

Our unit finally wound up the day by being attached to corps. They have given us a mission for tomorrow. It seems we are to relieve or help a portion of the 80th Div. That is the unit in which my cousin, Pvt Leslie Jones, is fighting. We have reports that their losses have been very high, and I wonder if he is still all right. The odds are against his being okeh for an infantryman's days of combat are strictly numbered. Our 2nd Bn has only seven of the original officers remaining, and the losses of the old original [EM] members of the units have run well over 50%, not to mention casualties among the replacements.

\* \* \*

[*Pvt. Leslie Jones, my first cousin of Tahlequah, Okla., was severely wounded by MG fire. I got the information from a 320th man, also wounded, who was in the same hospital with him. Jones asked about me and asked our 320th Infantryman to give me the news about him. Jones recovered from his wounds, survived the war and returned home.*

*In total casualties the 80th Div, although in combat a shorter time, suffered more casualties than the 35th Div. For the duration of the war the 80th was 8th and the 35th was ninth in total casualties, as shown by statistics I read in Europe after the war. The Order of Battle reports show different figures.*]

* * *

Col Northam and Maj Jamison went to corps hqs, which is in Nancy, to get information on our new assignment. Their CP is in a big building in the town. They have snappy MPs, with shoes all shined, as orderlies around the place. Rear echelon troops have passes to the town and could be seen in stores, cafes, the shows and the like. But the poor doughboys are out here in their muddy fox holes and, instead of the sounds and sights of comfort and gaiety, there is the roar of the deathdealing artillery and the flash of its lightning breaking the blackness of the lonely night. Truly no lot could be harder than theirs.

Maj Jamison said, "Gees! It looked good to see people doing civilized things again." I replied that I did not want to see any of it, as it depresses me to see anything that reminds me of peaceful pursuits until I can be free for a time at least from the duties and hardships of war. Col Byrne and Maj McElroy were inclined the same way and the Colonel remarked, "Yes, I want to get this shindy over with and go home."

Looks like we may have a tough time for awhile in the war, not that it has ever been easy at any time.

One would have to be here with us to ever actually realize the misery of the situation.

The dark and the wet, with the chill creeping into your bones, no warmth or light to seek, and no safety or haven from the danger. If the war recedes from us, ours is the heart breaking duty to get up and seek it out again and go forward into the hell. The prayer, "Let this cup pass from me" is not for us. The bloody cup we must find and drink to its last bitter sorrowful dregs, until our part of the work is finished, either by death or by wounds, or the completion of the task.

* * *

Luckily we have some liquor tonight, Benedictine and Cognac. Neither Sgt Coyne or I like it but a few sips keeps the chill from penetrating too deeply.

Foret de St Jean Fontaine
Sept. 27, 1944

Time: 1910

We have remained in reserve today except the 1st Bn which has been attached to the 137th. They are now fighting as night falls. The Germans, in rather heavy attacks today and early this morning, had penetrated behind the Jury unit with two companies in front of our positions. Did not look so good for a time but everything was taken care of.

The Germans are throwing in their tanks in what is proving for them suicidal missions. One entire force was wiped out this morning in an attack on our positions.

* * *

Every one here dug in today, good deep fox holes, most of them covered. Lt Silverman and I almost built a house. We dug a place wide enough for both of us beside a log and then covered it over with poles and these big bundles of sticks which some French woodcutter had stacked in the clearing. A piece of shrapnel would have a hard time getting to us in here, and besides it is warm. As to a direct hit, it does not matter where you are if you get one of those.

Right now we have a candle lit inside and Sid is reading as I write these lines.

* * *

Last night Sid got back all right but could not find us in the forest in the dark. So slept near by and found us this morning.

* * *

The battles here are developing into struggles as intense as those around St Lo. I can't see what the Germans mean by throwing in so much of their stuff, but we are really helping them to get rid of it. Artillery from both sides has been fierce all day. Some came whining in just up ahead of us as I brought up a last load of bundles of wood after we had eaten supper. One of the men on the same mission said, "That's pretty close, lieutenant." "Not too far away," I replied, "but I only hope it stays that far." "Yes," he answered, "but you can't trust those German PFCs. They're liable to mess up."

* * *

There has been much discussion of who could and would be released to the point system, since the news of the plan was released. Almost everyone has been counting his points and voicing his complaints (if any) if he did not have enough. Recently the men around the kitchen were discussing the subject and someone was kidding Dionesi[83] (called Dominees by everyone) about not having enough points. Someone said, "Oh, Dominees does not want a discharge. What he wants is a trip around the world." Said Dominees seriously as he moved a large can of food, "Yeah! and it looks like I'm gonna get it too. I've only got 30 points."

[Casualties[84] not mentioned in the Journal.]

Still in the Forest
Sept. 28, 1944

Time: 1445

We were very gratified to find the sun shining this morning when we arose. Not alone does it relieve the discomfort but it allows the Air Force to operate, and dries the ground so we can begin rolling again. The sky is not fully clear as light, chilly-looking clouds, flying from the northeast, often obscure the sun. At such times the air is so cool that my hands become numb if not actively engaged, and I have difficulty stopping the shivers.

We are still in reserve, except the 1st Bn, and therefore don't have much to do. Today the CP platoon has been digging in the CP and most of the men are improving their fox holes.

---

83  Pvt. Frank A. Dionesi, cook's helper and worker at Regtl Hq, Brooklyn, N. Y., called Dominese, liked by everyone.

84  2nd Lt. John P. Smith, Co A, Berkeley, Calif., a replacement, listed MIA Sept 27, not heard of again; 1st Lt. Cass B. Speasmaker, Co K, London, Ohio, a replacement, listed KIA Sept. 26.

If they needed any incentive the artillery the Krauts let loose last night was enough. There was as much thrown at us as at St Lo, but not so accurately. Most of the "stuff" landed in unoccupied areas.

Up front the troops are busily engaged in fighting off continued attacks by the enemy. A short time ago word reached us that the motor-pool of the 3rd Bn of Jury unit fell into enemy hands. Our 1st Bn is hemmed in on three sides by attacking Germans. But the enemy suffers heavily and is only whittling down his own strength by his, so far, futile efforts. The Air Force has just concluded a bombing and strafing run on the German positions.

\* \* \*

This forenoon the General [Baade] paid us a visit and bestowed on the Colonel the Bronze Star for "meritorious service." When we were being lined up for the ceremony, I at first thought we were in for a reprimand for some unknown offense. It turned out to be something pleasant for a change (if anything about war could be termed pleasant).

Incidentally perhaps I had better add that three days ago orders came through awarding me the "Bronze Star." But, as I have written home, I feel there are many who deserve decorations more than I.

\* \* \*

I think the failure of the gamble for the bridge and crossing at Arnheim has lessened our chance of shortening the war. It was a brilliant undertaking and I'm sure would have succeeded if bad weather had not hampered the operation. Only military men know how much the weather influences the carrying out of military plans. We shall succeed in the end anyway but the cost and time will be greater. [The phrase, "the cost and the time will be greater" was truly prophetic.]

\* \* \*

Had a letter yesterday from my friend, Elmer Oliver, who fought through France in the First World War.

\* \* \*

It is so cool I must stop writing. I'm beginning to wonder how I am to endure the cold and discomfort.

\* \* \*

The CP platoon is having difficulty getting an excavation made large enough for the CP tent. They have reached ground so hard that it can hardly be chipped with a pick. They are digging small holes in the bottom and blowing it loose with blasting powder.

* * *

I have read about bull dozers and graders being up to the front in carrying on their work, but today is the first one I've seen. A huge grader is working on the roads in and around the forest here. They are not close enough to the lines to be shot at but the shelling can certainly reach them here. However it is safer during the day than the night. The German artillery does more firing at night when their positions cannot be spotted by our "flap-flaps" (arty liaison planes).

One of Col Reed's flap-flaps had an unusual escape the other day. One of our own arty shells grazed it while in flight, creasing its side. Contact was not quite sufficient to explode the shell which would have blown the plane to bits in the air.

[A casualty[85] not mentioned in the Journal.]

Bioncourt, France
Sept. 29, 1944

Time: 1910

We moved into this place late yesterday evening. The CP platoon was still digging on the place for the tent, the medics had just finished an excavation for theirs, the men had good covered fox holes all prepared for the night, and then orders came through to move.

The 3rd Bn moved without eating. It has gotten to be SOP (so everyone says) for us to get orders so late that they cannot be executed in day light.

Last night the AT platoon of the 3rd Bn got on a different road (whether by their own mistake or misleading information I was unable to determine), than the one taken by their column and ran into enemy MG positions. They were shot up in the darkness. Lt Perkowski[86] was wounded and ordered his men, including four wounded, to fight their way

---

85  1st Lt. Edward M. Carroll, Co C, Chicago, Ill., a replacement, listed as KIA Sept. 28.

86  2nd Lt. William Perkowsky, Hq Co 3rd Bn, N. Y., N. Y., an original, listed SWA Sept. 29, did not return.

back to the lines. Two trucks with AT guns were lost and two jeeps. The Bn, in clearing the woods today with aid of TDs and tanks, got back to the spot about 1600.

They found Lt Perkowski lying on the ground, his leg and foot badly shot up. The body of the platoon Sgt was near by. The Germans had left Perkowski when they pulled back, taking three of our men prisoners one of whom was wounded but able to walk (Sgt Porta's driver). The trucks burned but the guns and jeeps were recovered in good condition.

I'm certainly glad Lt Perkowski was only wounded and was brought in okeh. At the staging area [Camp Kilmer, N. J.] before sailing, when things were finally in order for the voyage and passes were available for 12 hour visits to New York, then he and I were sent along with about 600 others to a rifle range some distance away for some firing. He and I were to zero our carbines, about a 10-minute job for each of us. We were there all day and did not get back to camp until well after nightfall. Then we learned that all passes would terminate at midnight; that we were sailing on the morrow. His home is in New York City, and I remember how heartsick he was that he would not get to see his "old man" (as he called his father) and his family. I urged him to go anyway telling him he would get to see them for an hour. But he lay down on his bunk resignedly and said he would let it go.

I saw him often on the voyage over, and quite often since we've been in combat. He is the sort of fellow at whom everyone laughs good naturedly and whom everyone likes. I am very glad he still has a chance to see his "old man."

So another of the old originals has dropped out of the picture along with some veteran EMs. Gradually, one-by-one and sometimes faster, our numbers grow less and less. Someday, if the war continues long enough, we will all be gone. Then the old regiment will be like Pa Perkin's old razor, "Good as new" but which had had 3 new blades and five new handles since he had been using it alone.

Lt Kliegerman, another of the old originals, our special service officer whose principal duty in combat is to care for the bodies of the dead, went out recently in a truck accident. It is reported that his injuries were slight so he may return to us shortly. [Evacuated Sept. 23, did not return.]

* * *

Shelling of the Bn positions is quite heavy. There have been about 30 casualties evacuated in past two or three hours, including some quite serious concussion cases. The men say they do not hear the shells come in but the concussion is terrific. We are sure it is from the German 120 mm mortar which has a range of 6,000 yards.

* * *

As to weather, today has been beautiful. The ground fog cleared rather early and our Air Force was working by 1000 in a clear blue sky under a bright sun. One of those nicest of autumn days when the air is neither cool nor warm but just brisk enough to make one feel zestful and glad to be alive.

By the back door of our CP, a house of thick concrete walls, a tree of late fall peaches is ripening. In the garden near by are pears, russet colored, late fall vegetables, and others of the summer season which have outlived their usefulness, as the vine full of ripened yellow cucumbers. In the valley and the curving slope beyond, the trees and fields are wearing for the last few times, their dress of bright green. Already in a few places can be seen tinges of brown and yellow, as on the vineyards' leaves, which guard the deep purple of the ripened grapes.

I plucked a mellow white peach from the tree and for the first and only time this year, tasted the delicious flavor of the fruit. That simple act recalled a hundred memories to my mind in spite of the artillery thunder and the war vehicles going by. If I had been so inclined I could have recalled hundreds or perhaps thousands more. There was the tree of "October peaches" which grew in one corner of the door yard during my youth and tasted so good when eaten on cool frosty mornings; the many varieties and colors we had in the orchard, the firm clingstones, deep golden yellows, the blood red Indians and the big juicy Albertas. There was the one tree of delicious June peaches of which, after a day of hard labor in the fields, I once ate 30 at one sitting. Dad never did believe the story but I know I made a correct count for I piled the seeds together and made a recheck after I had finished. I also remember when Arvil Ledford ate 35 peaches as we walked the five miles from Thompson to his home on Pinnacle Mountain. We had played two games of basketball that day. The noon meal had been light and he had no supper at all. He topped off the 35 peaches with a hearty meal when we reached home that night. I have told that to many people who did not believe it. Sedentary people, usually of the city, have no idea of the amount of food that can be consumed by those who lead a truly strenuous life. Is it not truly written that "one half does not know how the other half lives."

And so as I stood eating the peach and recalling more pleasant times and scenes, others were being killed or maimed and broken in mortal combat. Many in despair and unutterable longing were looking for their last time at a beautiful day.

* * *

Lt Silverman and Pvt Bock are on duty tonight. They are warming a can of water by the heat of the little fireplace for a rag bath after things quiet down. "A whore's bath" is the universal army terminology for such a cleansing.

[Casualties[87] not mentioned in the Journal.]

Bioncourt, France
Oct 1, 1944

Time: 0040

The last day of September has slipped away, discolored with blood and tainted with the acrid smoke of hell. Such a day we hope we shall never see again. But still they continue and will until the war is won. This day has been the worst for our unit. They have been shelled heavily and continuously in their woods positions.

This morning Maj Gillis[88] was killed while visiting the command post of Co B. His loss is great for he was the most

---

87 1st Lt. Charles D. Lower, Co L Plat Ldr, address unknown, on Sept 29 with his plat went to the aid of Co L of 137th when its hqs was being attacked. Later his plat formed a square for reception of his own company, holding off the enemy as the company assembled. Lt Lower's plat suffered 29 casualties that day. 1st Lt. Arthur L. Coil, Co H. Overland Park, Kansas, an original, wounded, recovered and returned to duty, listed SWA Sept 30; 1st Lt. Charles R. Hale, Co C, address unknown, a replacement, listed NBI Sept 30; Capt John F. Larsell, Med Det, address unknown, a replacement, evacuated as sick Sept 30; last three did not return.

88 Maj. William G. Gillis, CO of 1st Bn, Cameron, Texas, a replacement, West Point graduate, listed KIA Oct. 1 in Gremercy Forest; his death occurred on Sept 30.

practical and level headed officer in the regiment as well as brave and considerate.

Twice today, while in the woods on missions to the Bns, I was caught in the shelling. The first time at the 1st Bn CP was not too bad although they dropped them in pretty heavily. It was pretty hard for my driver (Pvt John Skender of Hamburg, Ark.) to get back in the jeep and get it out of the ditch, but he finally made it and we got back okeh. In the dugout into which we dived were two of the oldtimers, Lt Christianson and Capt Vignes.[89] Also several enlisted men. I don't see how those two stand it so well.

My driver told some officers (Clark & Parish) when he returned that I was a man without fear. He does not know how mistaken he is. I don't think I could ever hold up like some of the men on the line do.

The second time, Skender with me again, they shelled us into a ditch as soon as we approached the woods. [Old WWI trench where we saw Lt Carpenter[90] the first trip] Later we were able to get out and proceed. When we approached the RJ I left the driver and jeep at a place where they would not obstruct the passage of other vehicles along the narrow muddy road. Also there was a pretty good hole already dug that Skender could use. That hole probably saved his life.

I went to the crossroads in the midst of the woods and stayed while I checked elements of the 2nd Bn as they passed, moving to block or fill a gap on the right flank. In the meantime the Huns laid battery fire on the road I had just traversed, and walked right down it to the crossroads. For a small target it was the most terrific and concentrated artillery fire I have yet encountered, St Lo and Mortain not withstanding. It was both time fire and contact, fired in battery. Several men were hit as I watched from the road-side, men of F Co. Safely by were E and G. When my mission was completed I broke from cover and dashed for the jeep. I could see where the mud had been scarred away by the great jagged pieces of shrapnel, leaving hard white spots in the road. I reached the jeep and flopped in the hole as the next salvo crashed on both sides. Skender was praying and crying

---

89  Capt. Joseph L. Vignes, Hq 2nd Bn, New Orleans, La., an original, formerly 1st Bn Hq Co.

90  1st Lt. Ralph G. Carpenter, Hq Co 2nd Bn, Mt. Sterling, Ill., an original.

in the hole. I saw big tears on his cheeks when I got him out to turn the vehicle about. He did not quite get it turned in time so we flopped while the next ones exploded. Then, with my urging, he got it turned and we flopped again. The shells bracketed us perfectly but we remained untouched. This time when the shrapnel stopped whizzing I said, "Now," and without urging Skender piled in and we sped away. The trees along the road had literally been scorched with the fury of the barrage. A shell crater loomed in the roadway but it was too late to slow down. The jeep leaped it in full flight, careened, righted itself as we sped on out of the woods.

When we came out of the woods, along the road ahead of us was the smoke of shell bursts. So we were going towards as well as away from it. Perhaps we timed it right that time, one never knows whether to go or to stay, whether to run or to walk, whether to hurry or to wait, for there is no predicting where the awful death-dealing missiles will land.

Tonight the Motor Transport Officer of the 2nd Bn, who was there at the crossroads near me, (I can't think of his name now) told me that the next salvo plowed into the hole I had just left, showering them with dirt.

On reaching the CP and reporting to Col Byrne, I found there was quite a bunch of the High Command gathering for a conference. There were Maj Gen Baade and Brig Gen Sebree, our Div Comdrs; Maj Gen [Manton S.] Eddy, XII Corps Comdr; Maj Gen [Robert W.] Grow, CG, 6th Armd Div; and Maj Gen. [Hugh J.] Gaffney, Chief of Staff of the 3rd Army. Also Col Solomon, Div C of S, the three regtl Comdrs [Byrne, Miltonberger and Col Robert Sears] and many lesser staff officers. [including Col Northam, Maj Jamison and Maj McElroy]

They were clearing the room of junior officers in order to hold their conference on operational plans. Reporting briefly to Col Byrne I had just stepped out the back and was talking to Capt Smith, Gen Baade's aide, when the Krauts got our range. A salvo came in, one shell striking the yard wall by the front door. The first man I saw who was hit was Sgt Millican[91] who was suddenly lying at my feet. There was great confusion momentarily. All the brass were being herded to-

---

91 Sgt. Millican, Regtl Hq, full name and address unknown, SWA, never learned results of his wounds, did not return.

ward the cellar so they could get on with their war plans. One of them stopped and said to take the wounded man below. I helped to carry him down. Sgt Pohl[92] got there some way with a shrapnel wound in his knee.

The dust and flying glass, the heart-rending cries of some of the wounded, the red stains and the sickening smell of blood, all form an awful picture not easily forgotten. The flesh and blood of the guard, who was standing by the gate, were splashed all over the steps and walls by the door. The leg of another man was blown clear up into the hallway and there was also a finger lying there. Another man's leg was almost severed and dangled when someone attempted to drag him to cover. One of the men killed was Gen Eddy's driver, and his [Gen Eddy] aide was wounded as was Gen Gaffney's aide. Pvt Dorf had a slight wound in the hand and arm. Gen Baade's jeep was wrecked but the driver, who had momentarily left the vehicle, escaped. Gen Sebree received a slight shrapnl wound in the leg. I was the last to speak to the guard at the door. He suffered almost a direct hit and his flesh and blood were splattered over the front of the gray-walled building. There were 14 casualties from one 4-shell salvo of artillery.

More shells came in during the afternoon and tonight but so far no damages. There were quite a few casualties in the Bns.

Two more of the oldtimers I encountered today while the going was hot and heavy were Lts Ermelbauer[93] and Carpenter.

\* \* \*

Today I could not help but notice, as I have noticed before, the tired, strained faces of the troops as they streamed out from their shell ridden assembly to a mission of battle and death. And I thought that if, in future years, a veteran should say that he was in the war, or relatives should say that they had men in the war, one should find out in what capacity they served. If they served in the QM Dept, the Air Corps, the Engineers, the artillery, or any other branch besides the Infantry, give them full credit for what they did.

92 Sgt. Pohl, msg ctr chief, Regtl Hq, full name and address unknown, wounded, evacuated, never returned.

93 2nd Lt. Carl Ermelbauer, Hq Co 3rd Bn, N. Y., N. Y., an original.

But if you find that a man marched and fought with the Infantry, take off your hat, say him a blessing, and a prayer that he may have a home in heaven for he has already had his share of hell.

May God be with us! If I live to see another October I shall never cease to be thankful.

\* \* \*

## GERMAN SHELL NARROWLY MISSES JACKPOT

*[On Sept. 30 the big situation map of Europe showed a fairly even line for the battle front reaching from the North Sea to the Mediterranean, except for one place where a salient extended into the enemy lines like the point of an arrowhead. That point was just east of Nancy and was occupied and held by the 320th Inf. Consequently we had enemy forces to the front and on both flanks and were being shelled from all three directions.*

*Communication between regiment and the battalions by 193 radio failed that morning and I had to deliver messages personally. I took a jeep and a driver, (John J. Skender, Hamburg, Ark) and we set out along the winding road through the open fields and into the woods where the troops were situated. Our jeep proved to be the only moving object in the area. Other vehicles were under cover and the men were in fox holes and covered dugouts.*

*At the edge of the woods Lt Carpenter popped out of a deep WWI trench and hailed me. I told him where I was going and he shook his head with a wry grin as if to say, "I'm sorry, good luck and most likely farewell." We visited a moment, then Skender and I continued.*

*After passing the main RJ in the woods, the enemy shells came into the tree tops. Halting the jeep we headed for a hole on our left about 50 yards from the road and dived in head long. It was here I encountered Capt Vignes, Lt Christianson and a few other old acquaintances. It was a rather large dugout covered deeply with poles and earth to protect from tree bursts, and filled with men and officers.*

*While we waited for the enemy artillery to subside, some of our TDs started to withdraw along the narrow road. Wearily and with tight face, Capt Vignes checked his .45 revolver, went out to stop them and ordered the huge vehicles with their big guns back in place. If German armor should attack the positions, the TDs would be necessary to repulse them. Otherwise the German tanks would rout our men out of their holes and destroy them. The TD withdrawal stopped, Capt Vignes returned to the dugout.*

*The artillery slackened and Skender and I had to go. I led the way with Skender following by 10 to 20 paces. He would stop, his feet apparently rooted, and as I urged him on he would lean toward me, then back toward the dugout, like a tall slender tree in a fluctuating gale. I finally got him to the jeep. "Skender, come on," I urged, "We can't stay here all day! We must go! We have to get back to headquarters." I stood by while he tediously backed and wheeled the jeep on the narrow muddy road until it was headed back in the right direction. Then we returned to regimental headquarters and reported to the Colonel.*

*Later in the day with a German attack under way, the 2nd Bn was ordered to move from a position on the left to a position on the right to fill a gap in the battle line. I was directed back into the forest to report progress and developments and Skender and I were on our way again.*

*Finding a small space just before reaching the RJ, where the jeep could be parked off the road and a hole for Skender's protection, I left the vehicle and driver. I proceeded alone on foot to the RJ, crossed it, found a vantage point for observation and a hole nearby where I could take shelter.*

*There were loaded ammunition trucks under cover in the trees. Knowing that the movement of a battalion would attract the German artillery, and that the RJ would be a prime target, I advised that the ammo trucks be moved out of the area. They got out just in time.*

*The enemy laid a barrage in marching fire on the road which I had just traversed, coming down the road step by step to the junction. The 2nd Bn came from the left and therefore was not caught until the barrage reached the RJ. I stood by the roadway and looked at the weary, strained faces of the muddy, battle-stained GIs as they slogged along in the mud. One slithered and fell. From weariness he hesitated about rising and a comrade called out, "Are you hit?" He struggled to his feet and slogged on.*

*Company F, my old unit of the 320th, was caught in the artillery fire with the column extending across the RJ.*

I saw 14 casualties right before my eyes. One man was severely wounded and the aid men placed him on a stretcher to be evacuated. Before they could get away another shell caught all of them, killing the wounded man and killing and wounding the aid men. Some old originals who had survived for three months were lost there. Finally, to my great relief, the last men of Co F had gone by.

I was in and out of my hole as the Germans kept a steady fire on the RJ. I timed the shelling, and determined that battery fire was coming in at 40 second intervals. The whole battalion finally cleared the RJ and was in place. It was now time for me to report. I broke from my cover, running through the mud for 30 seconds and then getting down in ditch, depression, hole or whatever cover was available while the next salvo of shellls exploded.

Reaching the jeep I found Skender crying and praying in his hole. I piled in with him and after the next shells exploded I said, "Skender, what's wrong? You have a good hole. Others had to be out in this."

Wordlessly and tearfully he pointed to a stack of ammunition beneath a tree beside the hole. If an enemy shell had hit the ammunition dump, there would have been left no Skender and no jeep, only a bigger hole.

I then told him I had timed the enemy fire, and when I said the word, he was to jump out of the hole, work at turning the jeep, then jump back in the hole on my command. I climbed out of the hole and stood each time he worked the jeep for 30 seconds, then we both would jump back in.

Three times he worked with the jeep, always leaving the motor running while we crouched in the hole for each group of exploding shells. Finally it was turned, pointing in the right direction. "Now, Skender," I instructed, "When we hit that jeep this time we must be out of here before the next shells hit."

We waited for the next salvo. It bracketed us perfectly but we and the jeep miraculously remained untouched. We jumped out, hit the jeep and took off. Skender pushed the accelerator to the floorboard. We discovered a fresh shell hole in the narrow road too late to stop and no way to avoid it. We cleared the hole and teetered on two wheels for some distance before the vehicle righted. The momentum kept us *from overturning. With Skender it was the farther the faster, until I had to reach over and jerk his foot from the gas pedal.*

*We were away from the RJ by then, and I said, "Skender, don't you know you can't run away from a shell. You're just as apt to run into one." As the words left my mouth a shell burst blossomed with mud and smoke from the roadway just in front. "See there!" I exclaimed as we noted the burst. If we had not been slowed slightly, perhaps three to five seconds, by the new shell hole in the road, the round to our front would have been on target.*

*We made it back to the CP where I found the concentration of generals and staff officers. In the face of the German attack, they were concerned about the gap in the lines. Since there was no radio communication they were awaiting my return. In about a 30-second report I told the Colonel the Second Battalion had successfully moved, suffering casualties, and plugged the gap. Col Byrne stepped back into the conference room where the generals waited and I walked to the rear of the building. At that moment a salvo of enemy shells fell on the command post, one shell hitting the gate and walkway a few feet from the front door. Immediately there were the cries of wounded and the strong smell of cordite and freshly spilled blood as troops scurried for shelter. I was the last to speak to the guard near the door who was blown to bits, and had just passed the message center chief who was hit.*

*After a few moments the generals moved to the basement to continue their deliberations. A decision was made to withdraw from the arrowhead salient and straighten the line for a better defensive position. Such a withdrawal, although small, would not have been considered, had not orders already been received from the High Command for all units of the Third Army to establish holding positions.*

*The battalion commanders were notified and began their plans for the movement to be made during the night.*

*Gen Sebree was walking about after the shelling subsided. He said to me, "You know, I'm scared worse than I thought I was, or I've been hit. Something is running down my leg." He had been hit in the upper leg by a small piece of shrapnel and blood was trickling from the wound.*

*And what of Skender after letting me out of the jeep? He dashed a few yards away, parked the jeep and took shelt-*

er in the corner of a stone building. Looking for better shelter he spotted an opening in the floor. He ran and dived into the basement as a German shell knocked in the corner of the building where he had been crouching.

The council of war over the generals and staff members dispersed, Patton's Chief of Staff returning to Third Army Headquarters at Nancy where he informed General Patton of the withdrawal decision. The General immediately countermanded the order. "Not a foot of ground will be given up," he directed. The new order cancelling the withdrawal was called to Gen Baade, either by telephone or radio who in turn called it to Col Byrne.

The Colonel immediately sent for me to transmit the change in orders to the battalions. Again I called for a jeep and driver but before leaving I went to the 193 radio crew to see if the message could be transmitted by radio. The crew tried diligently for some time without success. I finally gave up and started for my jeep. Before I reached the vehicle, the radio operators called me back. Contact had been made. I stood by until we had a "Roger" and "Wilco" from all the battalions. Then I breathed a sigh of relief, reported to the Colonel and went to my quarters.

Several junior officers, including me, used for sleeping quarters the room the generals had vacated during the shelling. It almost became a historic spot, for here the Germans just missed the jackpot of the war. Had the shell which struck near the door been four feet higher and eight feet to the right, it would have entered the room through the window before exploding. In that stone building it would, without doubt, have made casualties of five generals, several colonels and majors, and staff officers of lesser rank, and most of them would have been fatal.

Even then the score for one shell was not bad from the German viewpoint. It had wounded one general, two generals' aides, killed a general's driver, wrecked another's vehicle, and killed and wounded a number of men of the 320th Headquarters including the message center chief. There were still more casualties in the area from other shells.

Incidentally, the Colonel and I both would have been certain casualties where we conferred in the doorway if we had not moved only seconds before the shell struck.

Darkness was falling as I went to my room. It had been a hectic day, but I continued to work for sometime. It will be noted from the Journal that I did not begin writing of the day's events until after midnight.

And what of Gen Patton's countermanding of the order for the line straightening maneuver? At the moment we cursed him as a callous, hardhearted military leader who had no compassion for his troops. However subsequent events in the Alsace-Lorraine Campaign which began in November proved the famed general to be exactly right. If we had given up the positions as planned, it would have cost far more in every way to retake them later, than it did to hold them at that time. Patton did send elements of the 6th Armored Division in a sortie around our advanced positions the next day, to clear out and drive back the enemy artillery emplacements which were shelling us from three sides. After that our positions proved to be fairly tenable.

That night at regimental headquarters I talked to a lieutenant, the motor transport officer of the Second Battalion, who was at the crossroads. He related that just after I left my observation point there, a shell from the next salvo made a direct hit on the hole I had been using and in his words, "plowed it under."

\* \* \*

Another fatal casualty in the fighting on Sept. 30 and Oct. 1 was T/5 Harold J. "Doc" Lange, a Co. B first aid man (medic) of Chicago, Ill. Lange and "Chief" Snyder had become legendary as aid men from the time of St. Lo. In writing of "Doc's" death, Pvt. Whitney Hanson had this to say.

"His almost fanatical desire to help his "boys" had made his performance from St. Lo to Gremercy one of almost continuous heroism.

Short, slope-shouldered, awkward, and well in his thirties, Doc had been a beloved laughing-stock in the States where he was attached to C Company. He was afflicted with a lisp and the lisp became a stutter when he was excited. During a drill or a hike he was always out of step. His trousers bagged like Sad Sack's and his spectacles seemed always about to slide off his nose. His boys ribbed but respected him, for Doc neglected looking

— 349 —

*after himself until the last Joe had been cared for, the last blister bandaged.*

*Stories of his self-sacrificing zeal are innumerable. In Normandy Doc's boys scrawled their names on a piece of paper: they wanted their aid man's bravery officially recognized. The day after he was killed he was to have been presented the Silver Star for an action on July 12 when he crawled through a hedgerow and into a machine gun swept field and administered first aid to and then evacuated a wounded rifleman.*

*On the day Lange was killed he went forward against the advice of his platoon officer into open terrain in the face of artillery, mortar, machine gun and sniper fire that had caused many casualties. His brassards could be seen plainly by the enemy machine gunners. But as he knelt by a wounded man, Nazi machine gunners gave Doc a burst. Soldiers saw him pick himself up, continue his work. But the Nazis didn't like that.*

*Next day Lange's body, riddled by machine gun bullets, was found among the dead, many of whom wore first aid dressings which Doc had applied."*

*Sgt. James A. Burzo of Brooklyn, N.Y. was another who lost his life in the fierce forest fighting. When his Co L platoon was ambushed from the front and both flanks Burzo pushed forward alone against the Nazi positions. A MG mortally wounded him but he continued. He threw a grenade at the spitting MG and then closed with the crew, killing four and routing the remainder. Then he collapsed from loss of blood and died in the position he had captured.*

Bioncourt, France
Oct. 2, 1944

There has been some sunshine today, through breaks in the chilly clouds, which revealed a sky of topaz blue. Some of the clouds were low and dark and from them the first sleet rattled down on the roof of our damp, thickwalled house.

The men in the fox holes and gun positions have had it easier today. Yesterday the thrust of the 6th Armored Div chewed up or drove back enemy units near our positions. We have cleaned out the Krauts in the woods and the increase in our artillery fire seems to have silenced or quietened some of the enemy batteries. Occasional shells still fall around us here but none have hit on our positions.

Talked today to Pfc Bush[94] an old friend of F Co. They suffered several casualties [14 which I saw] yesterday from the same barrage which caught me at the cross roads.

My friend, Sgt Sanders,[95] was severely wounded and Sgt Coghorn[96] was killed.

* * *

Today Lt Gen Patton, Comdr of 3rd Army, visited our CP. He pinned a medal (Bronze Star) on Col Byrne and complimented him and the men of the unit on the fine job done in the war.

He seemed very well pleased and was very mild and considerate in his manner. I remember one remark, "The more of them we kill, the sooner we can go home." I must say his actions here certainly belied his reputation. Gen Sebree came with Patton and, as they entered the yard, showed him where the shell landed in front, the marks of the shrapnel and the blood of the slain soldiers splattered over the grey walls of the house.

* * *

Yesterday Gen Lenz, XII Corps Arty officer, visited our CP.

I have seen my share of generals since being overseas from Eisenhower (seen in England with Patton) on down. I saw Gen Gearhart of 29th Div just after St Lo. Gen Futch our own Div Arty officer often visits our CP.

If that shell (on Sept. 30) had been eight feet to right and six feet higher it would have hit the biggest jack-pot of the war, - five generals, four colonels, two lt cols, a number of majors and lesser fry.

Yesterday while visiting the regiments Gen Baade was wounded slightly in the chin by a small piece of shrapnel. [Gen. Baade was out one day for treatment before returning to duty.]

---

94 Pfc. Don Bush, Co F, Alma, Mich, one of those now becoming known as the "old originals," - a member of a unit who came overseas with it.

95 Sgt. Clay Sanders, Co F, Van Nuys, Calif., outcome of wounds unknown. Sgt. Hill says Sanders survived.

96 I could find no other information on Sgt. Coghorn of Co F.

* * *

I spent most of today making reports on past month's action. I dictate the report to Sgt Coyne who takes it down in shorthand and then types it for submission to S-1.

\* \* \*

Tonight Col Byrne made some awards of bronze star medals including mine, Capt English and Maj Jamison. Then Col Northam called Capt Haley and directed him to gather his communication chiefs and "report to the Colonel without hesitation." Very shortly they came in and lined up, apprehension in their glances and every attitude, and concern plainly visible on their faces. Then Col Byrne presented Capt Haley with the Bronze Star. Their relief was visible and audible as they sighed, thanked the Colonel and filed out.

[A casualty[97] not mentioned in the Journal.]

From The

## MADISON COUNTY RECORD
Nov. 23, 1944

### FROM LIEUT. ORVAL E. FAUBUS

France, Oct. 2, 1944

Dear Home Folks:

This is my favorite month and, with nostalgic longing, I think how wondrously beautiful it will be in the Ozarks when the hills have put on their "cast of many colors." It will not be so pleasant here. The weather is oftimes discouraging, with slippery, slimy roads, sticky fields and dreary dripping forests. Today the first sleet rattled off the roof of this damp, thick-walled house.

We had a fairly comfortable room with furniture and a nice little fireplace, but the Krauts knocked in the door and shattered out all the windows with a well placed salvo of artillery, so now we operate in the basement without benefit of heat. And those of us who still operate are glad to carry on without complaint.

Recently our army commander visited us, pinned a medal on our regimental C.O. and complimented the men of the unit (through the commander) on the fine job they have

97   1st Lt. Melvin V. Love, Co I, address unknown, a replacement, listed LWA Oct 2, did not return.

done. The compliment was well deserved for only once, and that for a period of about four days, at a time when the going was light, has an infantry unit been ahead of ours, from St. Lo to here, which has been a long road. However, there is nothing about the war (except the end) which can ever give me pleasure; not even medals and compliments. There are too many of those who earned them who can never reap the rewards. They are now out of our reach beyond the Great Divide.

The enclosed extract shows my recent award. I must say that many others deserved it more than I. Recently I heard from Cpl. Joe F. Baker (of Huntsville) who reports that he was in the battles around St. Lo. I last heard from Pfc. Hugh Fritts (of Thorney) on Aug. 28. He is with the same infantry division as myself and has participated in all its engagements.

Best wishes to all,

Lt. Orval E. Faubus,
Hqs. 320th Inf.
APO No. 35, c/o P.M.
New York City, N. Y.


Bioncourt, France
Oct. 3, 1944

Today has been quiet. The enemy did not attack us and neither side molested the other in this sector except by arty fire.

I went into Nancy with Lt Ginsberg and Clark for a bath. There was a long line and when I finally got to the shower it barely had the chill taken from the water. But now I have clean clothes again, which feels a bit queer.

It was also very strange to see civilization again. The many people on the streets, some automobiles, women in nice clothes and attractive hair-dos, the stores with civilian goods, little children being wheeled about or playing in the streets; all signs of a softness, comfort and tenderness which has become foreign to us. To see such things for a brief time and then return to the front, with its hardness, cruelty, hardship and death, is too much of a contrast. It depresses me very much.

Tonight, myself, Capt Casey, Lts Quillen, Silverman, Clark and Parish, and M/Sgt Kearns sat around the fireplace in the room from which the CP moved after the shelling and argued and scattered the "bull." Maj Jamison and W/O Frazier are playing gin rummy. Others have retired, and so to bed myself. 2205.

Bioncourt, France
Oct. 5, 1944

Today I saw a fellow officer of Co F during the San Luis and Camp Rucker days, Lt Warnock.[98] He had learned we were here and came to visit us. Naturally he didn't find too many of the old timers.

Last night Lt Head returned to us from hospital and is given command of Co K. He looked very well and did not seem to mind being back (but it is sometimes hard to tell from the contenance what is in the heart).

* * *

Some time during the past few days Lt Coil was seriously wounded and has been evacuated. So we have lost another officer and another of the old originals.

Today Capt Fritts[99] was wounded for the third time; this time by a mine which exploded beneath his jeep. Again it was not serious and he is still with the company.

* * *

The Huns have been throwing some heavy stuff at us, reported to be from a II-inch Ry gun. The explosion leaves a hole that would bury a truck and one big oblong piece of shrapnel was picked up 600 yds from point of the shell crater. So far (and I knock on wood) none have landed on any of our troops. [A number of the shells fell in our area.]

* * *

Today, as is so often the case now, the clouds are low and gray. From the leaden skies the falling mist has made everything wet, cheerless and miserable. Yesterday they said it was a beautiful day in St Louis where was played the first

98  Lt. Howard S. Warnock, address unknown, with 320th in training at Camp Rucker, then in combat with another division.
99  Capt. Melvin V. Fritts, CO of Co G, Fort Valley, Ga., an original. Continued in the line only one day after wounds, then evacuated; listed as LIA Oct. 5, did not return.

game of World Series. October the beautiful! It is that in the Ozarks I know. Here . . . perhaps it is still a long way from peace. It is far from spring, I know, and springtime is far away in my heart.

[A casualty[100] not mentioned in the Journal.]

Bioncourt, France
Oct. 6, 1944

Time: 0918

Late yesterday evening there returned to us Maj Waring, Lt Ramsden[101] and Lt Lakeness.[102] They have recovered from their wounds and returned to duty. Maj Waring will again take over the 1st Bn to replace Maj Gillis, whose death made a place for him shortly before he got here. However the officer, who was the greatest help to him before, is not now present to lend him that assistance. Lt Braffit was cut down by the German MGs at Champenoux.

Lt Hammrack[103] also recovered from wounds and returned to duty at the same time as Lt Head.

\* \* \*

Lt Ramsden was wounded in the first engagement north of St Lo. He had a pretty severe wound, a piece of shrapnel through his back into his kidney. He has been out ever since in hospital in England and replacement centers in France until he finally got back to the unit. His wound still bothers him some. He is slightly older (now 35) than myself. I guess he and I are the two oldest officers of grade of lieutenant in the regiment. There are many senior officers younger than we. I was at one time the oldest officer in the regiment except the commander.

---

100  2nd Lt. Melvin L. Larson, Cn Co, address unknown, an original, listed NBI Oct 5, did not return.
101  2nd Lt. George T. Ramsden, Co G, Oceanside, N. Y., an original, wounded at St. Lo.
102  2nd Lt. Leslie A. Lakeness, Cn Co, address unknown, an original. wounded, recovered, returning to duty.
103  2nd Lt. Alvin H. Hamrick, Co G, address unknown, an original. When Capt. Fritts was wounded on Oct 5, all officers of Co G had become casualties. Ramsden and Hamrick had now returned to duty.

Bioncourt, France
Oct. 7, 1944

Time: 1400

This is a beautiful fall day filled with antumnal sunshine. There are warm spots on the southward side of the houses by the grey stone walls, but by the northern walls the damp still lingers. Trees yet filled with their green summer foliage cast cool shadows. High in the cloudless azure sky, the silvery planes gleam brightly as they wheel in flight. Somewhere over Germany, I know they engage in mortal combat. But here they rule unchallenged in the daylight hours.

It is such an ideal day that one almost enjoys it at times. But the ever-recurring sound of the artillery keeps bringing back the uneasiness which is so hard to lose up here. The military vehicles keep going by. Our patrols, outposts and observation posts remain active. Occasionally there can be seen a jeep, filled with medical personnel, their red crosses on white background shining in the sunlight, a stretcher perched above their heads, dashing out to bring in a casualty.

\* \* \*

Now 1605 and I have just finished talking to my good friend, Sgt Koch of F Co. The sight of him touched me deeply. He has faded away until he is almost a shadow. His clothes hang loosely on him. His face is seamed and lined deeply with the many tragedies he has witnessed. His voice is somewhat broken and it is easy to tell, when you hear him speak and look into his eyes, that he is near the breaking point. Yet he goes on bravely and cheerfully, although we know full well (as he told me) that sooner or later it will be his time if he continues at the Front. If there is anything upon the lowly earth which can touch one, and make him pray with all the earnestness of his being, it is such a situation.

I know there are many who would not know whereof I spoke if I attempted to describe the conditions here. Strong men can stand almost anything for a time. But when one is compelled to go on day after day in this uneasy and uncertain hell, it finally becomes too much to bear. Ninety-one days now since we had a chance to relax, not to mention the four or five days of crossing the channel, landing and moving up to the front lines.

There is Sunday for the workers and rest for the Air Corps after 25 and 50 missions. But for the tired, hard-living, bloody-fighting Infantry there is often no relief. The workman can go home to rest, the air man (brave fellow though he may be) can return to his base, the rear echelon trooper has after duty hours for rest and relaxation, but for the front line soldier there is no surcease from danger and hardship.

His sleep may be fitful and uneasy, disturbed often by the eerie scream of the shells seeking out his hiding place, or the roar of tanks moving into position for attack. He may awaken to the rattle of gun fire and the explosion of grenades as the enemy raids his lines. And when in his dark and lonely fox hole he lets his mind wander from the hell of which he is a part to that remote and unattainable heaven which was once his home, it is to think of it with despair and painful, inexpressible longing.

\* \* \*

Koch told me: The barrage that caught F Co the other day, of which I saw a part, took the life of Sgt Born.[104] This casualty in addition to the others I knew. Koch threw off his coat and pack and luckily found a hole. A tree burst left five holes in his overcoat.

Just recently on this front the first platoon of F Co ambushed about 30 Germans and wiped out all but seven.

One young German remaining, who was wounded, dashed over to a tree before they could get to him and hanged himself with a belt. Of the remaining six, the four unhurt carried the two wounded and they were sent back to our rear as PWs. Sgt Koch said they cut the self-executed soldier down from the tree, as they were afraid others might discover him and think we [Americans] had done the job.

He also told me that my friends, the Arkansas boys, Lane,[105] Lindsey[106] and McCormic,[107] were now the NCOs in the weapons platoon and were doing an excellent job. Lane has been wounded once, recovered and returned to duty.

[A casualty[108] not mentioned in the Journal.]

---

104  Sgt. Roy E. Born of Wisconsin, Co F, KIA Sept 30.
105  Sgt. Lensy P. Lane, Co F, Garfield, Ark.
106  Sgt. Lindsey, Co F, of Tennessee.
107  Sgt. Claude Michael McCormic, Co F, DeQueen, Ark.
108  Capt. Alvin (or Aline) Fishelman, Med Det, address unknown, a replacement, evacuated as sick Oct. 8, did not return.

Bioncourt, France
Oct. 9, 1944

Yesterday, one Bn of the 134th attacked to a limited objective on our left. The whole 80th Div attacked on their front still farther to the left. The 134th reached its objective without too much difficulty but the 80th Division's situation is still confused. It is reported fighting continues. There are many stories of the confused and "mixed up" way in which that unit operates. So far it is not noted for successful and efficient operations but quite the reverse. The truth or falsity of the reports I have not been able to determine.

I talked to a soldier yesterday who has a brother who recently joined the 119th Inf (part of 80th) as a replacement. That is the same unit in which my cousin, Pvt Leslie Jones, is serving. It has been so severely mauled that I fear for his safety.

[Jones was severely wounded by MG fire. He was in a hospital with a 320th man who brought me the information. Jones recovered and returned home.]

The Germans have been active on our left today. They almost invariably attempt to regain ground that has been taken from them unless they are in full retreat, and they are not that anymore on this front. They lost some tanks today and yesterday. The PWs our neighboring units took amounted to almost 2,000. Our own unit's activities have been mainly patroling and ducking into fox holes to escape the occasional shells which come in.

\* \* \*

Yesterday a "club mobile" came to our CP and handed out doughnuts and coffee to those around here. One girl went up to one of the front line positions. Boxes of doughnuts and large cans of coffee were sent up to those in the forward fox holes and gun positions. It was good for most of the men to hear again a feminine voice that could be understood. It has been more than ninety days for most of the old-timers.

\* \* \*

Last night I was on duty. There was enough activity so that I did not get to sleep. Today courts martial proceedings kept me occupied most of the time. Now my eyes are tired and the lids are heavy. The day has been gray and dull with heavy mist. Already at 1630 (4:30) the gloom of night was settling down over the fields and woods as the mist still swirled around the gray-walled buildings and over the dark entrances to the small underground "homes" of the soldiers. And now, as I write, the dark day has ended (1820) and the prayer in everyone's heart is for days made brighter with the lights of peace. The mail just came and I see a letter from my father. Now to read it and then to bed.

* * *

There is an article in Yank, the Army weekly, entitled "Montargis," covering first three pages of the Sept. 24, 1944 issue. The writing deals entirely with incidents which occured to our Division when it captured and secured that town. My journal of that date mentions some of the happenings dealt with in the story.

I remember very well that we discussed at our CP the advisability of offering surrender terms to the garrison and some of us expressed a willingness to carry the offer of surrender terms to the Germans. Later we learned that higher hqs had attempted to transmit terms to the German Commander in the manner described in the story mentioned above.

### GENERALS VISIT 35TH

*On 10 October, General George C. Marshall, Chief of Staff of the United States Army, in company with Lieutenant General Thomas T. Handy, Lieutenant General George S. Patton, Jr. and Major General Manton S. Eddy, visited the 35th. General Marshall asked many questions, but appeared to be especially concerned with the condition of the enlisted men, and whether they had adequate clothing and supplies for their comfort. —From 35th Division History.*

Bioncourt, France
Oct. 11, 1944

The news, now heard over the radio or as read from the "Stars and Stripes" and the commentaries by the news casters, does not indicate an early end of the war. The failure to connect with the airborne troops at Arnheim has definitely lessened the chances for an early victory. The Germans now hold the river line. It may be difficult to cross because from now on the weather is likely to be unfavorable. The main hope now for an early victory is the success of the Russian Armies from the east but the Germans have the bulk of their armies opposing them. If the mud settles down soon they may not be able to achieve a breakthrough.

One month from today my bets will be due unless someone "bumps off" Hitler or our armies get going soon. But such things are of small concern. In fact they are but minor things through which we attempt to relieve our minds from the constant discomfort and strain. Things which we prized highly in civilian life, as wealth, power, prestige, etc., have very little value here, or none at all. It gripes the front line soldier no end to read in the paper some complaint from soldiers still in the States or in rear areas, about promotions, pay, furloughs, discharges and like things. One that set everyone on fire was a complaint by some Air Force ground personnel that they could not "compete socially" with the flying personnel because of the latter getting flying pay. When I see such I want to swear and curse and wave my hands. I seek to find words to express my utter, contemptuous disgust but there are no words or expressions that seem to fit. They are all too weak.

Then I feel slightly sick and a wave of nausea comes over me. I push the thought from me, as we push away the thoughts of death and danger, of the cold clinging mud, of the awful smell of warm fresh blood and flesh when a body is splattered to bits, and the sickening stench of bodies beginning to decay where they lie in the fields and the ditches.

We are thankful merely to survive from day to day, glad when the shells come over only occasionally, and glad indeed when a hot meal can be had even if eaten under conditions mentioned above. A bath and clean clothes once in a month is a windfall. A chance to spend your pay? Social competition? A dress uniform? The sight of a woman whose soft voice can at the same time be understood? They are not of the world of which we are a part. And those who are not of this world should be constantly thankful of that fact, and [should] have but one main guiding thought, to do their duty to the fullest extent while enjoying their happy conditions, and keep their God-damned, measly, insignificant, inconsequental, asinine, morale-damaging complaints to themselves until the world of combat ceases and we can all again enjoy the things about which they complain.

Our greatest and ever present desire, the war's end, and with it the destruction of those we oppose. Secondary - relief so that we can rest and reorganize before carrying on with the struggle. Another of small matter to us, but about which we sometimes think, we would like for others to understand us and the job we are doing. But I, for one, know that is impossible.

Only those who have lived in this world can ever know what it is like. Our greatest individual hope is, of course, to return home well and sound, and our greatest hope for the future is that some plan will be worked out whereby the future will be free of wars.

\* \* \*

Yesterday was a miserable rainy day which covered all the earth with sticky, slippery clinging mud. Today the sun broke through only at very brief intervals. So the mud is in no way lessened.

\* \* \*

Sgt Koch was here again. He told me when the First Platoon lined up for chow yesterday an 88 shell came in and wounded Sgt Schemmel, the platoon leader. This First Platoon has lost three platoon sergeants killed, two acting platoon sergeants wounded, and now Sgt Schemmel[109] wounded. Says he, "Looks like a jinxed spot."

Capt Casey was talking to his old mess sergeant of E Co. He reported the veteran Sgt Dezinnick[110] of that unit wounded yesterday for the fourth time. Two wounds were light, one caused by shrapnel which pierced his helmet through and through and caused a head injury, and two serious, including this last one. When evacuated to England, because of the first serious wound, he had a chance to stay in England and instruct in the use of German weapons but refused it and returned to the unit.

Capt Shumate, one of our Medical officers who was evacuated for illness (sinus trouble), has returned to our regiment.

\* \* \*

---

109 Sgt. George Shemmel, Co F, Gary, Indiana, the sixth plat sergeant of 1st Plat, Co F, to become a casualty, 3 killed and 3 wounded.

110 Sgt. Dezinnick, Co E, no other information, wounded the fourth time on Oct 10.

I notice "Stars and Stripes" reports a "mystery" gun as shelling in Third Army area. We, of course, have known about it for some time. In fact we have a big iron fragment from one of the shells in our CP which was picked up near one of our Battalions. Division reports that nine shells from the gun fell in Nancy last night. No report of damage.

[One of the shells knocked down a building one block from Gen Patton's Hqs.]

The last issue of "Yank" carries the news, finally made official, that the 35th Div is in France.

Perhaps we shall no longer be the "ghost forces" as we have been up to recent date.

Attiloncourt, France
Oct. 16, 1944

Yesterday we moved to this new location which is very little better, if any better at all, in relation to the positions. So far as any of us are able to determine it must have been made merely to satisfy the whim of the CG, or else to make room for some other headquarters to move into the place we vacated. Well, either one is a sufficient reason, so that is that.

Our situation here compares favorably with the former. There is a big cellar for the operations room; there are rooms and beds for the ranking members of the staff; the men can all sleep in shelters in the houses of the town and most of the vehicles are parked under cover. Capt Casey found a cellar across the street which, with straw spread over the floor, makes a fairly safe and comfortable place to sleep. Besides Capt Casey and myself other occupants are Lieuts Parish, Clark, Quillen and Silverman. [Lt John Keith of Sv Co occasionally spent a night with us here] We have a very nice room upstairs, where I now write, which has a combined use of work and pleasure during the day, but may be given over at night to the indulgence of that dubious past-time, which is termed by some a sin, regarded by others as a pleasure, and engaged in by some as if it were a useful form of work. [Poker game] The failing of this room, compared to the one we just left, there is no fireplace by which to warm my feet. Quite a drawback to me for, as a rule, when most people are comfortable in weather moderately cool, I am miserable, or to say the least, very uncomfortable.

(A moment ago), I ask Lt Parish if he spelled his name with one r or two. "Only one," he replied, "There used to be two but there were some Scotch in the family and they cut out one of them to save the ink."

I think of that as an example of the admirable American quality of the ability to tell and enjoy a joke at one's own expense. I remember another illustration of this near the beginning of the campaign when we were fighting the desperately tough battle of Normandy. Our gains were in yards while the advance of the Russians was several miles per day. We were briefly discussing the matter one day with an officer from a neighboring unit. "Yes," he said, "We're already instructing our men in the identification of Russian uniforms so they won't shoot our Allies when they get here."

Those of us who are acquainted with the Nazis know that it is impossible by any stretch of the imagination to ever visualize our hardheaded and arrogant enemies either making or appreciating a joke at their own expense.

*   *   *

Just outside the window one of the village inhabitants is busily using a pitch fork to pile the mixture of straw and dung on the great stack already accumulated. He is dressed in heavy brown trousers, blue vest and corduroy jacket, and on his head a billed cap. A cigarette dangles from his lips. As he slops about his legs are protected from the mud by leather puttees. He is skillfully piling up the messy mixture, watched constantly by his faithful, black, wooly-haired dog. During my observation I decide that he and I have some things in common. We both know the smell of the barnyard and how to use a pitch fork. It has now been some time since I grew tired from the use of one. I used to think there was nothing more distasteful in the way of work and the sight of the smoothly worn handle looked very discouraging to me. But right now I would gladly trade these tools of war, my pistol and carbine, for that friendly symbol of peace and plenty, the lowly pitchfork.

*   *   *

Now a tank goes roaring by on the road beside the house. Lt Parish is just finishing his industrious cleaning of the room. He is the son of corporation parents from upstate New York, who I understand are quite wealthy (and therefore, as is generally the case with wealthy upstate New Yorkers, are anti-Roosevelt). But he certainly isn't afraid to take hold and do his part of the ordinary, menial tasks. Certainly a very likeable fellow, this pleasant, laughing, friendly, young Republican from the Empire State.

* * *

The 137th, after some time in reserve, has relieved the 134th. Those men will now get some rest. Perhaps it will be our turn next for relief from the front lines. Some of the men are near the breaking point. Each day the area suffers some shelling. Yesterday B Co had a man killed and others wounded.

Attiloncourt, France
Oct. 21, 1944

We have word now that soon we will go in reserve, which means we can move back a short distance from the front. If not out of artillery range, the front line troops will at least be out of reach of small arms and mortars. Tonight they are receiving some arty, mortar and small arms fire.

Yesterday the fighter-bombers burst a dam farther up the stream and we expected a flood by this morning. It has not yet materialized as the water is traveling much more slowly than expected. The waters chased some Krauts out of positions in the low ground where the air force and artillery could get at them.

* * *

One day recently three Air Force men (P-51 pilots) came up to visit the front lines. We had our usual mud and, while they were present, the Huns obligingly threw over some mortar shells. They had to dive into muddy fox holes. The pilots said they had given up a leave to Paris to come up and see how we live. They then remarked that they had heard stories of how the Infantry lived, but none of the stories were as bad as they found. They further said that they no longer needed to be told who was winning the war. They knew it was the Infantry.

Their visit was a very fine gesture on their part, and the last mentioned remark was possibly more in the nature of a tribute to the hardliving doughboys than a truth. For we in the Infantry do not claim to be winning the war alone or to be the most important, but we do know that we, and those who live with us as medical aid men and arty forward observers, endure the greatest hardships and suffer the greatest casualties. No other branch lives in such danger and hardship so continuously.

\* \* \*

Today we got information that we can send 40 men and 4 officers on 48 hours leave to Paris. Because of our stabilized situation, we can repeat the leaves every three or four days. Some of the men and officers are very interested. I am not. I do not think I would go if I could. Perhaps I should be more interested in such things as a means of helping me to endure. But nothing interests me except the crushing of Germany and the ending of the war.

Two or three days ago I went into Nancy for a bath. While there I walked through some of the stores and shops and went into a cafe and a hotel. The hotel and cafe were crowded by pleasure seekers; there were drinks, music, light, soft voices and laughter. The contrast was so sharp, no one could ever clearly express the difference. I was so greatly depressed that I have not yet fully recovered. I know there were some there who had seen combat in all its horrible forms, but there were so many who knew nothing of it, part of them in uniformed rear echelon jobs. There seemed to be a difficulty or lack of understanding. It seemed to me there were those who had seen the "world of combat" and longed to be understood. The others may have tried to understand and thought they did. But they did not and never will. For no one will ever understand this world who has not lived for a time therein.

I bought some toys for Farrell. Sid and I found a photographer's shop and had a picture taken. If mine is good that will be my yuletide present to Alta. It is too difficult to attempt to find anything else.

\* \* \*

News today of the fall of Aachen to First Army troops and of good progress on the Russian front. I guess the biggest news at home is the invasion of the Philippines. If that operation goes well perhaps they will not need survivors of this struggle to go to the Pacific Theater.

\* \* \*

Two of our field grade officers had passes in Nancy for a few hours. A friend had fixed them up with dates but they could not speak each others language. Said one of the officers very perplexed and disappointed, to his date, as they walked along the sidewalk to a cafe, "Can't you speak a word of English?" Evidently she did not for she still couldn't understand his question.

\* \* \*

## COL. BUTLER M. MILTONBERGER

*On one occasion I recall being in the headquarters of the 134th Infantry commanded by Col. Butler M. Miltonberger. It may have been while his unit was relieving ours on Oct. 24. Enemy shells had inflicted casualties on one of the forward units and a runner had just brought the news. Col. Miltonberger abruptly stopped his work and inquired of the runner, an NCO, about the casualties. The messenger gave the details and, evidently aware of the main source of the Colonel's interest, explained that the casualties did not include any of the old original Nebraska troops.*

*The 134th was originally constituted of Nebraska National Guardsmen who had been federalized about a year before Pearl Harbor, as a part of the 35th Division. Col. Miltonberger had commanded the 134th Regiment all the way in both training and combat. Many of the original troops had been lost along the way by transfer, casualties and other causes, and the commander was naturally quite interested in the welfare of those who remained.*

*In February 1945 Col. Miltonberger was promoted to Brigader General and became deputy commander of the 35th Division. He replaced Brigader General Edmund B. Sebree who went to the 28th Division. Lt. Col. Alford C. Boatsman of 1st Bn, took over command of the 134th Infantry Regiment, replacing Miltonberger.*

*After the war Gen. Miltonberger was appointed Chief of the National Guard of the United States a position in which he served for some time with offices in Washington, D. C.*

\* \* \*

## PATTON ENCOUNTERED IN NANCY

While in reserve at Brien-sur-Seille or in the lines three or four miles farther eastward, the 320th Infantry Regiment was permitted to send its members to Nancy, 15 to 20 miles distant, almost at will for baths and supplies at the military facilities, or on leave. Gen. Patton's Third Army Headquarters was located in the city and sometimes the famed commander was encountered by our troops.

Patton had a reputation as a "spit and polish" officer. We constantly heard rumors and reports of his rules for the subordinates of his headquarters, and of how tough he was in enforcing them. In fact, he had a set of well publicized rules and regulations for the entire Third Army. They concerned us very little for we were almost constantly in the front lines, but a combat soldier had to beware of transgressions if he had occasion to be in a rear area.

Patton's regulations gave rise to one of the famous "Willie and Joe" cartoons of the war. Willie and Joe were portrayed as typical frontline GIs, dirty and unshaven with disheveled clothes and battered equipment, their overloaded transportation piled high with all manner of articles. Actually combat vehicles were loaded to full capacity with gear, equipment, weapons, captured goods and sometimes souvenirs, piled on a piece at a time, until we sometimes wondered how all the material had been loaded at all. In fact if a vehicle had been unloaded and then reloaded immediately, it would have been very difficult, if not impossible, to get all the material back on the jeep, truck, half-track or other military conveyance. Therefore the situations and comments of Willie and Joe, most of the time so appropriate for the front, were a delight to combat troops.

In this particular cartoon Willie and Joe were portrayed as part of an army other than Patton's. They had their typical disheveled, bed-raggled appearance, driving a battered, mud-smeared, typically overloaded vehicle. They had stopped their truck before a huge sign on a road leading into Patton's Army area. The sign read, "Boundary of Third Army Area" and underneath was a list of rule violations and fines, "$30.00 Fine for Being Unshaven, $25.00 Fine for Shoes Not Shined, $20.00 Fine for Blouse Unbuttoned, $50.00 Fine for Vehicle Overloaded" and a number of others.

*One character at the wheel was saying to the other seated beside him holding a walkie-talkie radio, "Call up Headquarters and tell them we'll be 48 hours late. We've got to make a detour."*

*We all knew Patton to be a strict disciplinarian, but some of the combat troops had opportunity to see him in a different light. We lived in the all-encompassing mud and the unrelenting hardships of the forward positions. Our commander, Col. Ben Byrne, was a good disciplinarian, but most understanding and kind. We wore clean clothes and washed our vehicles whenever possible, but it wasn't often possible for either. Coming from foxholes, dugouts and other front line positions, our troops naturally were not always spic and span on their trips to Nancy.*

*One day a lieutenant of the line with some of his soldiers encountered the Third Army Commander while on a trip to Nancy. Patton stopped the lieutenant and his men, pointed out their deficiencies as to dress and gave the officer a dressing down for his condition and the condition of the soldiers. The lieutenant listened patiently in a proper military attitude.*

*Then Patton inquired, "What is your outfit?" The lieutenant identified his unit as a part of the 320th Infantry of the 35th Division.*

*Immediately the attitude of the famed general softened. "That's a damned good outfit," he said. Then with the kindest attitude, he concluded, "All right, son, go ahead. But the next time you come in, try to fix up a little better."*

Village of Brin, France
Oct. 26, 1944

At noon on the 24th our relief was begun by the 134th Inf and was completed in the last hours of darkness on the morning of the 25th. Two of our Bns, 2nd and 3rd, have moved back a short distance across the stream and are here in reserve in vicinity of Brin. The 1st Bn, under Maj Waring, moved just back of the front to Gremercy and constitutes the reserve for the 134th.

It is good to think that our haggard, worn, and weary men with bearded faces and dirty, mudstained clothes, are now getting some rest from small arms and light mortar fire at least. However we must still be ready for action at any time and we are not out of range of enemy artillery. Some 88s came in to our right this afternoon.

The first night we were here the Germans used their railway guns and threw 17 shells over us into Nancy about 12 to 15 miles farther back. It is reported that one hit about a ½ block from Gen Patton's house. Also a rhobomb hit just north of Nancy one night recently.

Troops of rear echelon units coming up from the town report, "They threw everything at us but the kitchen sink." That was only a light taste of what front line troops have to take. That many shells fell in less than 3 minutes on the crossroads the day F Co was caught marching by. Chaplain Stone told me that on the morning of the 28th (or 29th) in the Gremercy Forest the Germans began a barrage, and for an hour and a half the eerie, menacing whine of the shells did not cease. The crashing explosions awoke them and they could not go back to sleep. One of the men with the chaplain counted 596 shells, grew tired and stopped counting. Luckily most of them were falling in an unoccupied area to their rear.

On Sept. 29 when the 3rd plat of L Co, commanded by Lt Charles Lower, was moving up to plug a gap in the lines of the 137th and throw the enemy from their rear, they ran into strong opposition. After a hard fight they drove the enemy back and started to dig in. Before they had succeeded in digging in completely an arty barrage fell on them inflicting 27 casualties in the one platoon. [A platoon has 36 men, 5 NCOs and one officer.]

\* \* \*

In an old barn near the edge of the village a rough stage has been improvised and Lt Quillen, our acting special service officer, has secured some shows for the men. By running them three or four times a day it has been possible to give a little entertainment to an appreciable number of the men. It is hoped we can get to all of them by the time our period of reserve duty is over. At most of these shows I have been giving a brief orientation lecture and bringing them up to date on the news. I find that it has been truly said that those who make the news have little time to read it. Most of them actually do not know of their place in the news of the past weeks. I must say that I would not know myself were it not for the opportunity to hear of events over the little battery radio which Maj McElroy fortunately (or thoughtfully) brought along with him when we came from England to France.

* * *

Tomorrow makes 110 days in combat for our Division which, I understand, equals the record established by it in World War I.

* * *

Yesterday Don Rice, with a small supporting cast, gave two shows for some of our troops (he is really a one-man show himself). He remarked to me of the difference in the attitude and behavior of these troops and those of the rear echelons. The troops behind the lines, who have not seen combat, are very noisy. They troop into the theaters with shouts, much loud talking and laughter, much back slapping and horse play. The audience is very noisy and has to be called to order before beginning the show. Those troops are having a lot of fun (if you discount their longing for home) and to them the war is a great adventure, some times an enjoyable one.

These combat troops come trudging wearily in carrying their stained weapons. They splash almost unknowingly through the dirty muck of the door way and sit down on the ground, on their helmets or the rough wooden seats, completely heedless of dirt, dust, mud or discomfort. There is absolutely no horse play or joking and only now and then the sound of a subdued voice. They proceed directly to a selected place and without further ado sit down and wait without impatience. One could scarcely find an attitude of more quiet decorum at a funeral in the States. The light on them reveals that some have bearded faces, a few have red-rimmed eyes and all have a strained and weary look that touches me to the core of my heart. It is not enough to say that these men have walked through the Valley of the Shadow of Death. They have been through the Valley of Death itself, more than one of those Valleys, and have seen the Grim Reaper gathering in his chosen ones from all about them. They have taken and held hill tops which were, for a time, a part of raging hell itself. At other times they watched and waited in the night, while the sheet lightning of the artillery flashed along the horizon, and the shells moaned overhead. Again, they just watched, when things were quiet and still in the lonely, heavy darkness of their forest positions. Or they

— 370 —

went out on patrol through No-Mans-Land toward the enemy positions, stepping carefully and slowly, with a prayer on every breath, that they do not walk into the lanes of enemy fire or upon any of his mines and booby traps.

So, I do not think it strange that some of them just sat quietly staring at the skilled showman for sometime after he had begun his performance. They looked as if they did not comprehend this strange thing they were (seemly) seeing for the first time, or as if they had forgotten how to laugh. But somehow laughter is contagious, even to men such as these, and before the performance ended I think that all had once more had a brief moment of pleasure.

* * *

The light is bad [as I write] and causes my eyes to hurt. We are having a light plant constructed that we can take along with us but it is not ready yet. My head and throat are sore from my sinus trouble and, for three days, one jaw has been so sore that I cannot yawn without a sharp pain. My writing tonight has been difficult, slow and laborious. Midnight has now stolen up on me.

I am placing in the record here, a poem written by Sgt Coyne. He has been transferred to Personnel Section, Div Rear and today mailed it back to me. I had asked him for a copy sometime ago.

(This poem was inspired by the sight of a dead soldier lying in a cross studded cemetery in the vicinity of St. Lo, France)

### VALLEY OF THE VANQUISHED

#### By Ralph H. Coyne

Black hangs the veil of night around thee,
Softly now the wind rushing o'er the graves
Bearing the darkness of decadent stone,
Shall cool thy troubled brow no more.
No heroes here - all joys allayed,
Gone the zest of life and living -
Only the black pinions of death shall fly this night,
Stealing low through every valley,
Leveling all that lies before him,
Smothering all with his heavy cloak.
Too weary thou to strive against him,
In peaceful resignation see thy comrades fall,
Though some may sickeningly writhe beneath his stroke,

Low, a gangrenous pallor they now acquire.
How many souls this night shall breach the valley of the deep
And join the multitudes on high?
No roll of earthly organ here greets thine ear,
Or chants of harmonious choirs offering up thy final dirge;
No cast of bereaved with mournful tears,
Or words of solace from thy brothers here emerge;
No coffin decked with ancient laurels
To shelter now thy twisted lifeless being,
But to the elements herewith committed,
Bared to the wind and rain and swift decay.
No epitaph thy past good deeds recall,
Only the silence of thy earthly tomb,
In blank submission slowly sinking into the great abyss,
To dwell forever within the bosom of ages past.

(The voice of a spirit speaking to and pointing the way to the fallen
    soldier)


## CONQUEST

Arise, and in thy parting from this lowly vale
Let not revenge which all around thee lieth,
Your companion be or bring to thee the visitation of travail,
Or command thee into existence as an endless wraith.
But rather by His blood exonified,
Ascend unto the star strewn heavens aglow,
And there beyond the terrestrial heights abide.
Cast not your eyes back upon the murderous plot below,
But cleansed by waters of the Sacramental Fount,
Leave behind the foolish foils of selfish men -
See their cheap and tawdry garnished medals now they count,
Who even now do quaff the victor's stolen chalice,
That all may see and hear their perfidious boast,
And filled with the earthly vintage of evil design,
Their minds fermenting slowly on the fiendish toast -
Contented for the moment as the freshly drained kine.
But lo, their greed and lusts do wreathe 'round their souls as filial
    fetters,
Preventing them from passing through the rented veil,
And grasping the reward long promised in the Holy Letters,
Barring them forever from the great communal rail.
Outcast into eternal darkness as were the foolish virgins five,
Their names now from the parchment of life swiftly fade,
And meaningless they hide among forgotten governmental archives,
Forgotten forever, ere their bodies in the grave are laid.
Cast off now the yoke of their parasitical association,
Who e'en before thy blood has cooled stalk out new prey;
Come forth and join the multitudes in the great reformation,
Await with Him now the coming of the Great Victorious Day.

Brin Sur Seille, France
Friday, Oct. 27, 1944

Today Lt Silverman and I with Sgt Smith and Cpl Hollo-way[111] went by jeep back to Visziles and brought up the cognac. I don't like the Cognac, I've never drunk but a few sips and that very infrequently, so I got a few bottles of the champagne for myself and the party.

We got a fair meal at a local cafe (45 francs, 90c each) and there consumed a bottle.

The scenery along the way was the chief interest of the trip. Some of the trees are now becoming quite barren. Almost all remaining foliage has some color. There are splotches of color in the woods, along the fence rows and in some of the fields; just enough to be a quite painful and forceful reminder of the glorious autumn now in its fullest in the Ozarks.

There kept running through my mind over and over the words of a poem, I used to teach each fall to the students in the country schools. It was entitled, "October in Tennessee," but so aptly fit, in almost all its meaning, October in the Ozarks, that it was very appropriate for the season.

Some of the words were -

"Yet still amid the splendor of decay
The chill winds call for blossoms that are dead;
The cricket chirps for sunshine passed away,
The lovely summer songsters that have fled.

And then November like a conqueror comes
To storm the golden city of his foe,
We hear his rude winds, like the roll of drums,
Bringing their desolation and their woe."

It might be said there is sometimes a sort of splendor in destruction as the poet says there is in decay. The mighty, belching flame of the big guns as they hurl their lethal loads of destruction into the burned and battered cities does not fit my definition of the word splendid or splendor. The thunderous roll we hear is not that of rude winds and neither of drums. It denotes death by violent and destructive means

---

111 Cpl. John "Honest John" Holloway, I & R Plat. address unknown. He and Sgt. Smith were two of the few remaining original I & R men. William "Bill" Dickson, Barnesville, Ohio was another.

which causes every heart to murmur and a prayer to spring unspoken to (or perhaps whispered by) the lips. With the sound comes much desolation and woe.

At Nancy, Sid and I picked up the pictures we had taken a few days ago. I thought they were very good and so have sent mine back across the ocean to relatives with the warning that they may be the only Christmas gifts that I will this year be able to bestow.

\* \* \*

Have learned that Lt Ramsden fell ill after his return to us and has been again evacuated.

Lt Kuh, wounded at St Lo, has returned to duty and received his old assignment as 2nd Bn communications officer. Warrant Officer Glenn Wells,[112] who for a time filled the job, has gone to hospital because of illness, and is reported to be in serious condition.

Word has reached us that Capt Fritts, who was evacuated the day after his third wound, would possibly not return. His hearing has been impaired and he has otherwise suffered injuries of a permanent or semi-permanent nature. Well, he has done his part, and I am thankful to know, turned out lucky at last. When we were at Camp Butner he was a very happily married man. The last time I had a chance to talk to him, he told me he was expecting to become a father. I hope he can return to his family.

A brief note from Mrs. Margaret Cull in which she wrote, "The last words Brent said to me were 'keep smiling' and I'm doing my best. I say a special prayer for you every night." Poor Margaret! It does not seem possible she is a widow.

Three officers around the CP who like to talk of their families are the Colonel, Maj Hughes and W/O Frazier. Of course it does not have to be the family for Frazier. He'll talk about anything. (But he is a good gin rummy player. I can't beat him enough to stay even). Sid will always talk about his wife and show her picture. I remember Maj Hughes's family at Camp Rucker and also Lt Col Northam's beautiful wife and very pretty children. He and Maj McElroy seldom mention their families but I'm sure they think of them as much as anyone, as well as Maj Jamison.

112  WOJG Glenn Wells, Sv Co, Asst S-4, Com O for 2nd Bn, St. Louis, Mo., an original, did not return.

[Casualties[113] not mentioned in the Journal.]

\* \* \*

*When we stored the liquor with the French civilian we*
*gave him the signatures of a dozen or more officers, any one*
*of whom would be authorized to pick up all or a part of it.*
*If only a few had such authorization, they might all become*
*casualties and thus no one would be able to claim the beverage.*

*After obtaining a part of the stock on Oct. 27th we*
*never had time or the need to get the remainder until the war*
*was over. Then, after the Regiment had moved to assembly*
*area in France, a party was dispatched for the balance of*
*the liquor. Unfortunately for us the name of our French*
*officer, de L'Cluse, who had long since left our unit, was on*
*the authorized list. Our detail was informed that he had re-*
*turned some time before and obtained the remaining liquor.*

*The French civilian, a school teacher, was evidently most*
*trustworthy. After our division moved on eastward with the*
*advancing front, the rear echelon troops occupied the area.*
*The civilian could have sold the liquor for a substantial*
*amount, but he kept it faithfully in his charge for our return.*

\* \* \*

The following letter, while commending the 35th Infantry Division for its valiant part in the liberation of France,
indicated the shape of things to come:

HEADQUARTERS XII CORPS
OFFICE OF THE COMMANDING GENERAL

APO 302, U. S. Army
14 October 1944

Major General Paul W. Baade
Commanding, 35th Infantry Division
APO 35, U. S. Army

Dear General Baade:

The fighting of the last few weeks has punched home
to us one point so obvious and so clean cut, that I want every

---

113  2nd Lt. Marc T. Finn, Co M, address unknown, a replacement, evacuated as sick Oct. 28; 1st Lt. Charles E. Scovel, Sv Co, Battle
Creek, Mich, an original, evacuated as sick, Oct 28; 1st Lt. Alvin H.
Hamrick, Co G, address unknown, an original, evacuated as sick Oct.
30; none returned.

soldier and every officer in the Corps to realize its full significance. That point is this: *The Germans, even the best and most experienced are visibly frightened of us.* They are frightened by your superior equipment, frightened by your more skillful tactics, and above all, frightened by your magnificent courage and will to win.

Since the beginning of your memorable drive from Le Mans through Chateaudun and Orleans, the 35th Infantry Division has met its assigned tasks with distinction. It seized Pithiviers and Montargis, and assumed the prodigious task of protecting the south flank of the Army and the XII Corps from Orleans to the east. Despite vigorous enemy counterattacks it has played a major part in the establishing, defending and enlarging of our bridgehead across the Moselle. All members of the Division have conducted themselves in a manner of which they may well be proud.

We are now between rounds of a fight to the knockout. The last round saw you stagger the German back into his corner. While we are now gathering our strength for the kill, he is hanging on the ropes. He cannot last another-he is bound to go down. I am confident when the next round comes up that the 35th Division will continue to show him the same courage, the same skill, and the same driving determination that have won for it its successes to date.

I congratulate the 35th Division on its past—I wish it Godspeed and early victory in its future.

Sincerely yours,

/s/ M. S. Eddy
/t/ M. S. EDDY
 Major General, U. S. Army
 Commanding

Hq. 35th INF. DIV., APO 35, U. S. Army, 17 Oct. 44

TO: All Officers and Enlisted Men, 35th Inf. Div., same address

1. No one knows better than each of you how true the Corps Commander's words are. Each individual in this division has given his best—the proof is the record. As we prepare ourselves to continue on our march to victory against the inferior enemy, I urge every officer and enlisted man to inventory his knowledge of his job and his weapons—Train!

Practice! Ask questions! Let's go in for the kill with every ounce of strength, knowledge and determination we have.

2. I desire that every commander insure himself that all members of his command receive full knowledge of this letter to which I add my sincere appreciation and heartfelt congratulations for your splendid achievements.

/s/ Paul W. Baade
/t/ PAUL W. BAADE
Major General, U. S. Army
Commanding

Brin-sur-Seille, France
Nov. 6, 1944

We have gotten to stay here in reserve longer than we expected, which leads me to think now we may get a tough assignment. Most of the men have been able to see some shows and have gotten baths and clean clothes. Some have been to Nancy. Most are more rested than for a long time. We have still been under shell fire, especially the 1st Bn which is the reserve for the 134th and situated at Gremercy. Maj Waring called us today from the cellar while they [enemy shells] were landing. Pvt Rosen[114] asked him how many rounds, as a matter of information, and he said "Say, when those things are falling, I don't stand up and count them."

\* \* \*

Have heard that Lt Morgan,[115] Capt Eckstrum,[116] Capt Guilford[117] and others are at replacement pool on their way back to us.

\* \* \*

Capt Dolan, our CAC officer, is now a major. He came around yesterday with his bottle of gin receiving the congratulations. He seemed very happy and pleased.

And it is no longer Lt Kurtz, but Capt Kurtz.

\* \* \*

Recently we came across a document, taken from captives, Germans in the German Army, which, would be ample

---

114 Pvt. Rosen, Regtl Hq, Jersey City, N. J.

115 1st Lt. Henry G. Morgan, 1st Bn Hq, Birmingham, Ala., wounded, returning to duty. An original, he was assigned to Co B when Lt. Braffit became S-1 of 1st Bn, before we crossed the Channel. Later Morgan was transferred to 1st Bn Hq.

116 Capt. Robert N. Ekstrum, Minneapolis, Minn., wounded at St. Lo as CO of Co B, returning to duty, was made CO of Cn Co.

117 Capt. Charles F. Guilford, CO of Hq Co, 1st Bn, Dearborn, Mich., a replacement, wounded, returning to duty.

proof for all those who doubt the utter depravity of the German people under Nazism. I have made a copy and herewith include it as a part of this record. It is addressed to "Dear Front Line Soldier" and signed "League of Lonely War Women."

Dear Front Soldier,

When will you come back on leave?

When will you be able to forget the hard duties of a soldier and exchange them for a few days of joy, happiness and love? Back at home we know of your heroic struggle; however, we do understand that even the bravest gets tired and that he needs a soft pillow, tenderness and healthy pleasure.

WE ARE WAITING FOR YOU!

For you who have been compelled to spend your leave in a foreign town; we are waiting for you whom the war has robbed of his home, waiting for you who stands alone in the world without a wife, without a fiancee, without a flirt.

WE ARE WAITING FOR YOU!

Cut out our badge on this letter. Display it visibly on your glass in every tea room, in every bar which is in the vicinity of a railway station; soon a member of our League of Lonely War Women will take charge of you, and the dreams you dreamt in the front lines and the longings of lonely nights will find fulfillment. . . . It is you we want, not your money, therefore ask for our membership card at once. There are members everywhere, since we German women understand our duties towards our country and towards those who defend it.

Naturally we are not unselfish - - for years and years we have been separated from our men folk, surrounded by all these foreigners; naturally we long to have again a real German boy to press him to our bosom. Don't be shy; your sister or your sweetheart is also one of us.

We think of you, but we also think of the future of our country. He who rests, rusts.

LEAGUE OF LONELY WAR WOMEN
(VEREIN EINSAMER KRIEGERFRAUEN)
* * *

The execution plant at Lublin, Poland should destroy or nullify the Nazis last claim as being human but I guess there are those who will yet defend them. They will be voting for Dewey for President next Tuesday, or tomorrow it is now, time having rolled around to 0210 Monday morning. There will be a lot of good people vote for Dewey, too, but the fact that Hitler hates Roosevelt so much should make him a strong favorite with people who love decency and hate tyranny.

\* \* \*

Even though I'm duty officer guess I'd better get a few winks if not impossible, as I have three courts martial cases to try tomorrow.

\* \* \*

Lt Peterson,[118] the CIO Dem of 2nd Bn, still going strong and kids very much, Maj Leach,[119] an ironclad Rep.[ublican]

### ORIGINAL OFFICERS LOST

*Somewhere along the way, most likely long before the end of the Northern France Campaign, we had lost a number of the original officers of the Regiment not mentioned as casualties up to this point. Some of these went out, for what particular reasons I do not know, in the first few days of combat. Others lasted longer. They had trained with the Regiment in the States, came overseas and entered combat with it. Among these original officers lost to the unit were:*

*1st Lt. Winston C. Coleman, Co B, Valdosta, Ga.*
*1st Lt. Earl F. Scheinost, Co C, listed also in Co B and 1st Bn Hq, Creighton, Nebr.*
*1st Lt. John J. Pulgin, Co I, N.Y., N.Y.*
*2nd Lt. Myer O. Berman, Co I, address unknown*
*1st Lt. Ernest L. Strasil, Co L, Fall City, Nebr.*
*2nd Lt. Clifford J. Rainford, Co K, Chicago, Ill.*
*1st Lt. Dale O. Britt, Co M, address unknown*

---

118  1st Lt. Harold E. Peterson, Com O, 3rd Bn, Lynnwood, Calif., an original.

119  Capt. James A. Leach of Sv Co, Davenport, Iowa, an original, trfd to Bn Hq, later promoted to Major.

## CHAPTER V

## ALSACE-LORRAINE CAMPAIGN

*It may seem strange to the reader, as it does to me now, that fewer entries were made in this diary during periods of quiet. It will be noted there is only one entry from Oct 27 to Nov 8. One of the reasons was because of other writing - thousands of words in reports, administrative matters and courts martial proceedings, but more important, perhaps, there was not so much activity and therefore not the urge to record events.*

*During this period Gen Patton visited the 320th and spoke to the assembled officers. He said he had asked us to do many difficult things in the past and we had done them well. He praised all of us as patriots and good soldiers and said he must soon ask us to perform even more difficult tasks. It was then he wept as he spoke.*

*The 320th remained in reserve until Nov 7, the day of the General Election in the States. On that day I had gone back to Nancy where I got a bath and clean clothes in a military facility. Afterward I visited with Lt Kenneth I. Botton, AT Co, New Brunswick, N. J. and other friends in the outfit. It was the last bath and the last quiet visit in many days.*

*Upon my return to Brien-sur-Seille, arriving in the last light of day, expecting to find my friends in what had become familiar surroundings, I was faced instead with silent, empty rooms. Almost everyone was gone. Among the few who remained there was cheerless, intense activity as they prepared to leave also. The 320th, I found, had been directed back to the forward positions with orders to attack in the darkness of early morning.*

*I think that never before or since have I been so disconsolate and comfortless, nor had a feeling of such unutterable loneliness and despair. In the brief period in reserve we had quickly grown accustomed to the relative quiet and a little more comfort. Now we must go back to the hell of fierce combat, back into attack after attack with the attendant casualties and heartbreak. Winter had come on and the weather conditions would be far worse than we had known before. (According to French authorities, the heaviest rainfall in 200 years).*

*Quickly I gathered my gear, weapons and papers while the jeep driver found his equipment, and we hurried to rejoin our already departed comrades. As darkness settled over the battered, rutted countryside we set out along the narrow, muddy road which led to the forward positions. Wordlessly I watched the gathering gloom engulf the shell-pocked fields of purple cabbage and the bomb-cratered expanses of sugar beets, all the holes now filled with water, and thought of the discomfort of the night and the misery of the morrow.*

*We were moving up to begin Gen. Patton's Third Army drive across Alsace-Lorraine, for us the worst campaign of the war. In the days to come we were to learn how truthfully Patton spoke when he said he would ask us to perform more difficult tasks than we had previously done. And, recalling his emotion when he spoke, we were soon to realize more clearly why he wept.*

* * *

Gremercy, France
Nov. 8, 1944

We moved to this place last night in darkness and mud. The artillery barrage this morning was one continuous thunder along the whole front. The buildings trembled and the dark, cloudy sky of the pre-dawn hour shimmered with the red flashes of the guns and exploding shells. The men were attacking this morning in the awfulest mud I have ever seen. Every man must be wet and miserable. I don't see how they could be otherwise.

What miserable, dreary and cheerless conditions in which to fight and die.

* * *

Capt Eckstrum, Capt Bonham and Lt Tedder[1] returned to us yesterday, just in time to get set for the jumpoff. Eckstrum was hit the first day at St Lo and Bonham about the third.

\* \* \*

Snatches of news on the radio (BBC) tell of Roosevelt's victory. I caught enough to know that Fish and Nye were defeated and that the Democrats had gained some seats in the House. I am glad because it gives us a better chance to make a lasting peace. I don't want my little boy to have to go to war, ever. Nothing worse than war can happen to the world, and seldom if ever can anything worse happen to individuals than to participate therein.

\* \* \*

I guess some of the boys will die this morning without ever knowing whether the man for whom they voted was elected or defeated.

\* \* \*

I have to break off sometimes in the middle of a sentence, to come back, minutes or hours later to finish it.

\* \* \*

Lt Col Northam was very gratified at the Dem victory, and especially so at defeat of the Isolationists, Fish and Nye. Lt Silverman is very pleased. We would have a lot of pleasure kidding the Republicans if the times were not so serious.

\* \* \*

Our 3rd Bn has Fresnes; the 2nd has been thrown back from the edge of the woods in fierce fighting. There have been numerous casualties and about 50 PWs have been taken. Four of our [attached] tanks have been knocked out by mines around Fresnes.

Capt Eckstrum, who now has Cannon Co, just now returned from Bn OP where he could see one of the damaged tanks.

Fighter-bombers are aiding our attack and the artillery keeps shaking the building by thunderous blasts.

---

1  2nd Lt. Donald W. Tedder, Co C, address unknown, a replacement who had been wounded, returned to duty.

Capt Casey[2] has fallen ill and went to hospital this morning. Lt Quillen was also sick but came up to Co this morning.

Capt [Elbert B.] O'Keefe of the 134th has been with us as liaison from that unit. He is an old acquaintance of the American School Center [in England] when Braffit and I, with Gilbertson and Kurtz, were there.

* * *

Now 2030.

With the early darkness came the cold pelting rain, as if the poor doughboys were not already miserable enough. The hope of receding mud for tomorrow's activities has vanished. Maj Smith came back from the Bn aid station riding the hood of a jeep to make room for casualties. He was soaking wet and muddy to his hips. Of the conditions [he said,] "Terrible!" and he is a modest man.

This has been one of our worst days for casualties, almost 200 for the two Bns, and in such awful conditions.

I have never had much fear of dying if I could be warm and dry. Under such favorable conditions, I think I might, quite tranquilly, say my last silent farewells (if given time and opportunity) and breathe my last. But under such conditions as today and tonight, I can think of it only with an attitude of the greatest dread.

I am thankful that at least a few of us are dry tonight and hope that all can find sufficient shelter.

* * *

Heard that Capt Alloway[3] got it again today; fortunately was only wounded and has been evacuated.

Our medical personnel have managed, by laboring hard and constantly, to take care of all wounded. Any MD or aid man who has worked on the front with the Infantry has thrice earned a blessing and forgiveness for any fault or sin.

W/O Frazier got out his precious bottle of brandy to give Maj Smith a drink. And so, as I do not know what the morrow may hold of strife or trouble, I think I shall take a

---

2 Capt. Edmund R. Casey, formerly CO of E, then CO of Regtl Hq Co, a close friend as far back as Camp Rucker, evacuated as sick Nov. 8, did not return.

3 Capt. Curtis H. Alloway, originally 1st Lt, Co L and Co K, Kansas City, Mo., wounded and evacuated the second time.

nip to drive away the chill before I sleep, and heed the poet's advice to "Take rest, while ye may."

\* \* \*

The total PWs for today were 68 subservient, blind and thickheaded members of the Hitler Army. Their thoughts and expressions are but reflections and repetitions of the Nazi propaganda. They seem to have no sympathy or compassion for one another. Each seems to care only for himself.

If they could only but think, or had only but thought, for themselves, how much misery might have been avoided. I am reminded of what Minister Matthews once said at Newton, Ala., "It makes all the difference in the world what you believe."

[Other casualties[4] on Nov. 8.]

Gremercy, France
Nov. 9, 1944

Now 1240.

This morning at 0600 we attacked again. The 3rd Bn completed the cleanup of Fresnes and sent in 31 more PWs. The rain had stopped when it was good light but everywhere is mud and more mud, sloppy, so that it splashes and soaks the men when they try to avoid the shell fire; slick and slippery so that they slide about and sometimes fall, and move always with difficulty; and yet it clings, making leaden and heavy the cold, soaked feet of the Infantry. The air was cool, seemingly with a hint of fairer skies, and for a time the clouds were light and broken, revealing fleetingly a distant sun.

It was then (1000) the bombers were passing over, flight after flight, with deep-throated and resounding roar, with their protecting fighters weaving rapidly around and above them, appearing with their vapor trails, like tiny fleeting comets. We could glimpse them through the breaks in the gray overcast, passing through the patches of pale, cold blue. They were both going and coming. Some additional part of Germany must now be devastated.

---

4 2nd Lt. Walter R. Harrington, Co F, address unknown, evacuated as sick Nov. 8; 1st Lt. Jesse (M) Beene, Co L, Las Cruces, N. Mex., listed LWA Nov. 8; 2nd Lt. Rodney D. Baber, Co L, Memphis, Tenn., listed LWA Nov. 8. All replacements, none returned.

Capt Zurman[5] lost five to seven of his tanks yesterday, blown up by mines. One explosion was so violent that it blew up the engine and one man was killed by a piece of it passing through his body. Other tanks were disabled by having the treads blown off. They were out in open under enemy fire, and the crews were killed trying to get out and get back to our lines.

Lt Bosley[6] of the 2nd Bn was shot through the head while walking behind Capt Bonham along the railroad bank which runs between Fresnes and the woods where the enemy is entrenched. Capt Bonham got assistance and carried him back to a point where he could be evacuated. He still showed signs of life when taken back.

Capt Bonham came to Regtl Hqs this morning, soaked and miserable. He got by the fire and Lt Quillen got him some dry clothes. He has been made Hqs Co Comdr in place of Capt Casey.

Sgt Walsh[7] of Cn Co reports two men of his unit killed this morning by a tree burst from a German arty shell.

Shortly before I began to write the sky became dark. A few minutes later snow was flying thickly, melting as it settled gently upon the wet earth. And so another means of bringing discomfort to the men is added to their manifold miseries.

\* \* \*

Gremercy, France
Nov. 9, 1944

Time: 2015

Our CP still in this little collection of stone and concrete buildings. Lt Silverman left at dark to set up a forward CP in Fresnes.

---

5 Capt. Zurman, Stanford, Conn., full name unknown, commanded a battalion of tanks attached to the 320th. He directed the tank charge at Mortain. Sometimes Capt. Zurman and his tanks were sent elsewhere to support other forces before returning to our unit. They were a brave outfit and worked well with us.

6 1st Lt. Albert E. Bosley (listed also as William E.) Co E, Wichita, Kans., a replacement, listed DOW Nov. 9. He died of his wounds after being carried from the front lines. Had participated in the battle of Mortain and all engagements since.

7 Sgt. Walsh of Cn Co, no other information available.

After the flurries of snow today, the weather brightened somewhat. At one time the sunlight fell momentarily through the westward windows. But, as during last night, the rain came with the darkness, and everything is dripping and sodden. The night is as dark as a blackboard.

Today our 2nd Bn, with the aid of the 1st Bn and one company from the 3rd, got through the German defense system along the edge of the woods. When they got back behind the wire the medics followed and sorted out the wounded from the dead where they had lain since yesterday, all through the dark and rain-dreary night, just where they had fallen when they advanced into the fire lanes of the German machine guns. The defense line has now been broken and our troops are now well into the woods.

Mines are strewn thickly all about the town of Fresnes, in the fields and all along the roads, along the entire enemy front. Two TDs have now been added to the nine wrecked tanks and also the tank retriever of the tank unit.

Mine clearing details have been at work but only small areas have been partially cleared. There are all kinds of stories of miraculous escapes, and then there are those who did not escape.

Those who have followed the infantry and tankers in the area find plenty of evidence of the fierceness of the struggle. There is a Lt Cooper[8] here, as Comdr of the TD unit, from N. C. (Henderson), and with the accent of those from that region. One of his TD crews and a mine clearing crew reported to him that the dead Krauts were lying around "like watermelons in Georgia." Also that there were many Americans dead but only about one third the number of the Germans.

If we had good weather, we could push through [the enemy positions] them and on to the Rhine with much smaller losses.

\* \* \*

Tanks, TDs, trucks, even whole regiments of men, continue to move in the dark and wet. I think I would find it difficult to believe if I had not seen such things for so long now. There is always confusion, the constant struggle against

\* \* \*

8 1st Lt. Scott Cooper, of the 654th TD Bn, attached to 320th, Henderson, N. C.

it, the eternal "straightening out" and correction of errors. It is a part of war.

I once read that "the human mind is so constituted that it can become adjusted to any situation, else grief would often cause death." I know it is true, for here one can see as much horror and struggle, death and injury, as would fill many, many ordinary life times at home.

* * *

Capt Saddler of the 134th, an acquaintance of the American School Center in England, has been with us today as liaison from his unit. [1st Lt Glenn W. Saddler when at the school, now a captain.]

* * *

Tank incident. — It hit a huge box mine with each tread. The explosions lifted the huge vehicle into the air, throwing the driver clear and the commander to the floor, without injuring either of them.

* * *

S/Sgt Martin Seilling was interrogating the PWs today and as always was interested in information as to the identity of the enemy units opposing us. He found one prisoner who, as a runner, might have such information. He talked willingly enough as almost all of them invariably do. He was sent out, he said, to contact and report to a motor transport sergeant but could not find him. "That's him over there," he added, pointing to another PW. The one indicated had preceded him to the PW collecting point and had already been questioned by Sgt Seilling.

A German lieutenant being questioned, replied that he had 15 or 20 more men other than those taken but did not know their whereabouts. At this point guards came marching in another bunch of captives. Upon observing them the lieutenant said, "There they are. Those are the rest of my men."

Another German officer, when his interrogation had been finished, requested permission to ask a question. It was granted. He then said he had a friend, who had been captured in Africa, who wrote he had been sent to America where he was allowed to continue his studies. The officer wanted to know if he could be sent to America and allowed to continue his education, as his friend had been.

It is a typical German attitude. They wish to take advantage of us in every way, of our kindness (or softness), our mercy and our methods of fair play. But nowhere, in the record of Nazi policy, can we find any evidence of like treatment from them toward others. Instead we find the slave laborers, enforced prostitution, and execution centers like Maideneck. I am convinced their partial practice of the rules of land warfare, as laid down by the Geneva Convention, is only for selfish reasons.

* * *

I have the election figured out, except I don't know whether Dewey carried Oregon or Colorado to get his 118 electoral votes.

* * *

Must go down to the cellar to the CP center, as I am duty officer for tonight. Our attack continues tomorrow. I hope and hope the advance is not so costly.

[Other officers[9] not mentioned in the Journal.]

Fresnes, France
Nov. 10, 1944

We are situated tonight in the shell-shattered and shell-pocked town of Fresnes. The streets are littered with debris and not one single building is whole.

The troops have had difficulty all day, and into the night. The mud has remained as bad all day. On my way to the 134th today, I noticed by the roads, fox holes filled with water. Some, which had overhead cover, were filled up to the top. [With water flowing out as if from a spring.]

Our CP tonight is the cellar of a building which the Germans used as a strong point in defending the town. They had a machine gun in a window which covered the draw to the west.

It is very chilly tonight. For the first time in a great while, I glimpsed the stars when out in the night a few moments. I don't see how some of the troops stand the combined damp and cold. The pale, distant stars are looking down upon a lot of misery and heart break tonight.

* * *

9    1st Lt. Dale D. Meese, Co I, Decatur, Ill., previously with Co K, wounded, returned to duty about Oct. 28, became Ex O of Co I on Nov. 8. Capt. Clarence E. Stephens, Jr., Stafford, Kans., now CO of Co H.

Another old friend of F Co was seriously wounded yesterday, Sgt Curry.[10] Eight men of that Co were killed yesterday and a much greater number wounded.

I think Lt Gilbertson, S-2 of 2nd Bn, has broken under the long strain of combat, 125 days now.

I think Capt Zurman, Comdr of our tank support, is one of the bravest men I have ever seen. Another is that imperturbable North Carolinian, Lt Cooper of the TD unit. Capt Zurman was in the tank charge at Mortain and in many other tight places with us. He is from Conn.

\* \* \*

The Colonel [Byrne] has a cold and is hoarse. The strain seems to be telling quite a bit on him and Maj McElroy. Col Northam and Maj Jamison seem to bear up well. Capt Bonham seems the least disturbed. However he had only three days at St Lo before he was wounded and has been back only three. It takes about two weeks for the strain and uncertainty to begin to tell on most individuals.

Tonight Capt Zurman was telling me of things he did the first two weeks which he would not do now. He mentioned Lt Braffit as being one of the most notable men of combat that he had seen.

(Now this Kraut radio, tuned to an English program, is playing, "In the Good Old Summer Time." My God, how far away!)

This afternoon Lt Clark went to the hospital. He has some ailment which would not clear up and Maj Smith sent him back for diagnosis and treatment.

Lt Parish is doing fine, as are Silverman, Quillen and Donovan. W/O Frazier looks ghostly but Maj Hughes seems unchanged.

\* \* \*

Word just phoned in to Maj McElroy that Capt Gardner[11] (formerly Lieut) had been killed. And so to the West beyond the Great Divide has gone another of the bravest of the brave.

I recall that coming over on the boat there were six of us in one little stateroom, Gardner, Fitzgerald, Fesenden,

---

10  Sgt. Wilbur Curry, Co F, Troy, Ohio, an old original, a friend since Camp Rucker.

11  Capt. Frank W. Gardner, CO of Co B, Arlington, Mass., an original, listed KIA Nov. 10.

Gilbertson, Ginsberg and I. The first three are gone. Gilbertson I think has broken, which leaves two of us. I remember that at Camp Butner and coming over there were three liaison officers, Gardner, Talcott and I. Now there is only one of those three.

Well, for the Infantry and those who go up with them, as Aid men, Tankers and TD men, [and arty FOs] it is only a matter of time.

\* \* \*

News released tonight of V-2 over England. With little improvement that weapon can reach and destroy any part of the earth. A plan to maintain a lasting peace becomes each day more imperative. Success to you, Roosevelt, Churchill, Stalin, Tito, Eden, Joe Ball, Fulbright and others.

\* \* \*

The radio plays, "I Had a Little Talk With My Lord." May the Spirit care for those who are beyond the reach and help of all others.

There comes to my mind, as there has so often come, the meaningful words [of an old religious hymn] "The night is dark and I am far from home." "Lead thou me on." "I was not always thus."

[Three more original officers[12] lost.]

Fresnes, France
Nov. 11, 1944

Twenty-six years ago today, the world was made deliriously happy by the return of peace. Today this war continues with unabated fury.

On that happy day so long ago, I can remember as a little boy, listening wordlessly and quietly to the talk of my parents and the few others I saw. There was no special celebration by them; they just went to bed a bit later at our isolated farm home, but feeling a great relief, and a greater happiness than for a long time. I listened, with awe and wonder,

---

12  1st Lt. Larry D. Gilbertson, S-2 of 2nd Bn, Alma Center, Wisc., sent to rear on Nov. 9 for assignment to other duties; 1st Lt. William J. Kuh, Hq Co, 2nd Bn, Montgomery, Ala., previously wounded and returned to duty, evacuated as sick Nov. 10; 1st Lt. Kenneth E. Birkett, Co C, Chicago, Ill., formerly Co A, listed NBI Nov. 10. All originals, none returned. 1st Lt. Travis E. Hendren, Co G, Cleveland, N. C., a replacement, wounded and evacuated Nov. 8, recovered and returned.

to the distant explosions of dynamite charges set off by happy celebrants at farm houses and at the villages along winding White River, far into the night.

Peculiar, but as I started to write this, distant explosions recalled that event to my mind, which I had not thought of for many a day. Too many of the explosions here are not distant enough and there is a great difference in the feelings they produce. Then, the muffled thunder brought a vague wonder and a sense of extreme joy because something bad had been brought to an end. Now the explosions are no longer muffled by distance and a feeling of security, but their violence and destruction stir up an oft recurring feeling of dread.

* * *

Casualties have not been so heavy today but the going has been tough. The conditions have been so miserable, and are now, that I don't see how the troops endure them. They can't for long that is sure.

A lieutenant [a new officer, one of our many replacements] from B Co (can't think of his name now) was back to be treated for slight wounds suffered from a German grenade. He pulled off his shoes and socks which had been sodden for three days. He put on some dry socks and sat by a stove in the staff drivers section and fell asleep. When he awakened his feet were swollen and painful and could not get his shoes on. [Lt Quillin took care of the officer.]

He was with Capt Gardner when he was killed. They were ambushed and pinned down by fire just before night fall, he, Capt Gardner, Maj Leach, Lt Col Walker[13] and others. They could scarcely move because a MG was fanning fire over their backs and riflemen were firing. One of them heaved a grenade which struck a bush and rolled back. It was a dud or they would have been killed by their own grenade. They heaved another, whose only effect was to incite the enemy to use theirs. They [the enemy] threw over three but no one was injured except him. [the lieutenant]. Then Capt Gardner got up to look around and see what could be done and was cut down. When hit he exclaimed as so many others have "Oh, my God!" and fell to the ground. When they could get to him later, he was dead.

---

13 Lt. Col. James T. Walker, a replacement, address unknown, took over command of 1st Bn. Maj Waring was injured on this date.

Darkness saved them from a prolonged stay in the positions. This morning the Krauts were gone.

Some men of B Co and C Co killed a German captain who refused to surrender. Also captured was a "boy of about 14" driving a beautiful pony hitched to a cart on which was a wounded Nazi soldier.

We are now opposed by troops of the Eleventh Panzer Division, slightly better troops than those whom they relieved or replaced. Most, if not almost all [in] the other unit, were killed or captured.

\* \* \*

There is only one officer left in B Co. Our casualties have been worse than at St Lo.

\* \* \*

Incidentally, today I lose my bets. But money here is as dirt. No matter how plentiful, it cannot buy one moment of pleasure, peace, or relief.

\* \* \*

I am duty officer tonight, but do not feel like writing. With Clark gone and Lt Silverman again establishing a forward CP, Lt Parish and I have alternate nights.

\* \* \*

Heard a part of the Notre Dame - Army football game, and thought of Maj Gillis. Some one said he was Co-Captain of the Army team when attending West Point.

[Other casualties[14] on Nov. 11.]

Forest de Chalins
Nov. 12, 1944

Our troops pushed on to the NE edge of the Forest de Salins today while the other two regiments came up on either side. There was scattered resistance. There were killed, and we took a few more PWs. Our troops are now out to the edge, and except for a few Germans who might have been

---

14  Maj. Frank S. Waring, CO of 1st Bn, Holyoke, Mass., an early replacement, listed LIA Nov. 11, did not return; 2nd Lt. John F. Miller, a replacement, Co B, Baltimore, Md., listed NBI Nov. 11, did not return; 1st Lt. Earl D. Fisher, Co I, Flint, Mich., a replacement, listed KIA Nov. 11; 2nd Lt. Granville P. Brundage, Co I, Strafford, Conn., a replacement, listed KIA Nov. 11.

missed, the forest is clear. Shells are falling on the troops in the new positions.

The sky was leaden and gray throughout the day. There is still some late greenery, and enough late autumn color to give the forest a sort of subdued golden glow. It is a rather nice forest, where it has not been damaged too much. As I came up there was just enough snow fall on the ground to give the whole a sort of "white necklace trimming of old lace" effect.

Just as we arrived at this farm house CP, on the edge of a clearing near the center of the woods, the snow began again to fall. Sometime later when I glanced from the window it was still sifting silently and softly down. The scene, framed by the window on a back drop of motionless trees etched against a gray sky filled with the drifting flakes, was all at once a picture of home and boyhood, and snow fall in the Ozarks. I remembered briefly, with a pang, the thrill always brought by the first snow storms of the year in that region, and thought of what disappointment and misery it was bringing here.

The thoughts kept bothering me, so I told Parish where I was going and stepped off into the quiet, fast whitening woods for a short walk (no work at the time being urgent).

I wanted to see if it could bring me a touch of the peace of mind which I once could gain from winter woods. But it was no use. This section of the forest was littered with twigs and tree tops blasted down by the shells. Besides there was always plainly audible the thunder of the big guns. There were dim roads which might be booby trapped, or used for fire lanes by by-passed Nazis. At one place some German soldier had built a shelter by re-arranging a stack of wood. Peeking inside I saw a folded grey blanket which had been left behind. At places the blast of the shells had blown away the leaves, laying bare the torn earth, and here the snow melted more rapidly leaving dark scars in the expanse of white. Looking closely I could see smaller scars where the jagged pieces of shrapnel from the bursts had plunged into the ground through the leaf covering. And all about on the trees were lighter scars, where the flying hot shrapnel had torn away the bark and into the white wood beneath. They were not smooth, even cuts, but jagged with splinters, and of many odd and uneven shapes. I thought of the bodies which had been and would be torn by the hard, cruel, unmerciful splinters of steel, and of the times they had come so close to me and others who had not been struck down.

I returned to the CP, my boots much cleaner from the walk in the leaves and snow, but there was not the peace of mind I sought.

\* \* \*

The 2nd Bn [Hq group] is in this same building, so I happened to see today some old acquaintances of that unit. They included Lt Litherland who has returned to duty after recovering from wounds received at Chateaudun. There were also Capt Smith,[15] formerly of Cn Co, Lt Byerley, Capt Tobin, Lt _____ and others. [The last name could not, at the moment of writing be recalled; now it is completely forgotten.]

\* \* \*

The air is very chill; the candle flickers; my fellow officers snore upon the floor. Outside some trucks on night missions grind along the deep mud of the roads. Far and near is the intermittent roar of the artillery. Near the door a guard challenges those who slosh up to the CP through the muck and mire. Out in the damp cold forest and along the wet fields are many doughboys who cannot find a shelter inside, who must be terribly wet and miserable. Some of those who rest near me stir uneasily and cough with an annoying harshness; results of their exposure to the unfriendly elements. Nearby an artillery piece shakes the entire establishment and the contents, including my paper, with every blast.

\* \* \*

This evening Sid and I opened two bottles of champagne and a bottle of Scotch. We junior officers passed the bottles around and said, "Eat, drink and be merry, for you know the rest." We called it in honor of Roosevelt's victory, but did not leave out the Republicans. They didn't like the Democrat victory, but they did like the liquor, so everyone joined in and, while the little bit lasted, we drank and argued the matter with joke and banter and laughter.

---

15  Capt. Harvey A. Smith, formerly CO of Co H, now 2nd Bn Hq, Benton, (or Forsan) Texas, an original.

But now the transient, fleeting smiles have passed from the uneasy faces. The brief laughter, which for a passing moment lightened a heavy heart, is silent. And I think, as I have so often thought in many late and lonely hours, "the night is dark and I am far from home."

\* \* \*

It is planned that we get one day of rest tomorrow. Then we must be ready to "'load up and roll," which means we take off with the armor on motors and push rapidly far into enemy territory. The one day's respite from attacking is so the men can dry their feet to stop so much "trench feet," which is causing a considerable number of non-battle casualties.

So into my bed roll on the floor. Incidentally I have not slept in a real bed since leaving the States in early May.

The new day is one hour old. 0100, one a. m.

Forest de Salins, France
Nov. 13, 1944

Now: 1240:

The 2nd Bn moved into this building on morning of Nov. 11. On night of Nov 11, Lt Silverman, with a group of the I & R, moved here to set up an advance CP for regt. We followed yesterday, and last night every nook and cranny was filled with sleeping men. We are now fixing to move.

Five minutes ago some GI, taking down the stove pipe up in the attic, found a Kraut who had been hiding there all the time. He was well armed with rifle and grenades.

Said some one, "Just goes to show that anything can happen in the ETO."

\* \* \*

Capt Vignes, Lt Bell [Charles W. Bell, Co A, Valentine, Texas] and Lt Morgan of 1st Bn were here this morning. We shoved back from the stove and let them sit down. They pulled off their sodden shoes and socks and dried their feet. Some how, as sometimes does, they got to telling experiences. Lt Bell of A Co has been in the lines continuously since St. Lo, and I guess the experiences of that youthful officer would fill two or three ordinary volumes. For example, just now the strap that carried his shovel is hanging loosely, almost cut away by shrapnel. Lt Morgan has a dent in his helmet made by a sniper's bullet and another burned his chin.

Other incidents gleaned from their conversation:

One man had his field jacket ripped open by MG bullets but his body was not touched.

Another soldier, carrying out a wounded comrade, got in line of German fire. The MG bullets drummed off the shovel strapped on his back, sending sparks flying, but he was not hit.

Capt Kulmar[16] back at Mortain, was seated reading a map and transmitting a message on the radio. A German MG cut down on him shooting the radio out of his hands, cut his sleeve open, and perforated his map, but he was wounded only slightly by one grazing bullet.

Once their whole Bn was pinned in a sunken road, automatic fire whinging over head and the 88s shelling them. Along came an old Frenchman, a young lady and a little boy, hurrying along amidst the fire. They had to hold them because if they passed on, they might tell the Germans of their situation, who could not see how many there were in the road. The old Frenchman became frightened at the shelling, ran across from one bank to another, huddled under a tree, pulled a branch down over his face and sat there as if hidden. His actions were so funny that the men and even the young lady were laughing at him. The little boy toddled over to Lt Bell and sat between his legs, trembling with fright at the whizzing bullets and the crashing shells.

* * *

They told of the misery and the fighting of this last action; directed "Smokey,"[17] the GRO Sgt, where he could find bodies of their men who fell along the way; in matter of fact tones they said there were four at one point, three at another, six at still another and so on along the way to their objective. Capt Gardner's body had been carried out to a place easily found, and at other points, bodies of the slain had been carried from the woods to the open. But for this there was not always time or men to spare. Most of their platoons are now skeleton strength and one platoon had a single sergeant left. This morning there were 20 men with

---

16  Capt. Malcolm Kullmar, CO of Co A, Lake Worth, Fla., an original.

17  Sgt. "Smokey" Dodd, Sv Co, North Carolina.

frozen feet. [In answer to the query of his Co Comdr about the platoon the Sergeant replied, "Sir, I am the Platoon"]

In the course of the action men had died in many ways. One was killed by a shell but not a mark was made upon his body. He bled at the eyes, nose, mouth, ears, everywhere that blood could come from the body without breaking the skin. The terrific, stunning detonation of the missile had simply wrecked his internal organs and blown the life from his body.

There was the case of the medic, who walked out to treat a loudly crying wounded German, and was killed by sniper fire. There was the case of "Old Chief,"[18] as he is called, an Indian first aid man, who follows the men right out to the front. One young kid soldier was fired upon and fell out [in front of] before the others. The Indian walked boldly out to get him, and this time the Germans held their fire. The kid was not wounded, but pinned to the ground by the fire. Said "Old Chief" without hesitation, "Play like your dead," tossed his rifle and helmet to one side and carried him to safety.

\* \* \*

Now we are fixing to move. Hope all the men can get dried, for they can't hold out if they don't. I'm afraid those further back do not realize fully the seriousness of the conditions.

Vaxy, France
Nov. 14, 1944

Yesterday we moved off the hill from the farm house CP to this town. It's almost as badly battered as Fresnes. Every building leaks. I'm on duty tonight and there's no dry place on the floor where I can spread my bed roll to catch a few naps beside the telephone as I can sometimes do on quiet nights.

Our 2nd Bn is at the disposal of the 134th Inf today. The other two Bns are in recently taken towns getting a little rest, and trying to dry and reduce the swelling in their water soaked feet.

---

18  S/Sgt. John E. Snyder, Med Det, Irving, N. Y., now Silver Creek, N. Y., an Indian first aid man, whose exploits became legend in the 320th from the time of St. Lo, and was known throughout the Regt as "Old Chief."

One of our TD platoons ran into trouble today. Had several men killed; one had his head blown off by fire from an enemy tank. The 2nd Bn suffered some from shelling. Only occasional shelling has been reported around us and the other two Bns.

I think there were 31 officer casualties in the last action. Lt Thomas,[19] an old-timer, was wounded. Lt Fisher was killed and another whose name at this time I cannot recall. [Probably Birkett of same Co as Fisher.]

\* \* \*

There is a bomb crater near our CP about 35 feet across and 10 to 12 feet deep. Probably made by one of ours which fell before the place was captured.

I feel very miserable, caused by a severe cold. Hope I can get better for I have a lot of work to do in the matter of courts martial proceedings.

The weather continues very bad. The mud, if possible, grows worse with the long continued daily rain and snow. It seems the main action is aimed at Metz. Perhaps they are waiting for its fall before trying to push our armor forward very rapidly. It would be difficult, if not impossible, to make rapid progress now.

The sinking of the battleship Tirpitz is good news.

\* \* \*

Most amusing incident of the day was listening to Dominees telling of all the rackets in New York. He used to be a taxi-driver there. His knowledge of the city, its people and their clever schemes, is very extensive. . . . "Well," he said, "some of them ask for it. You have to be clever if you live there. Sometimes a guy walks out to a cab and wants to be taken to an express station when there is one right beside him with a big sign on it."

Pause: "So what?" says someone.

Replies Dominees in unhesitating seriousness, "So, you take him a couple of U-turns and charge him a buck." Roars of laughter.

19 Probably 1st Lt. Leo E. Thomas, Co L, Lima, Ohio, known as "Fighting Leo," as he was an original. There was also 1st Lt. Arthur E. Thomas, Hq Co, 2nd Bn, Pawleys Island, S. C., or Fayetteville, N. C., a replacement.

He has an eccentric habit of batting his eyes, the action of which involves the brows and skin of his forehead as well as the lids, which is often amusing to me to watch. I never observe the action without recalling an expression I often heard my father use during my youth, "Batting his eyes like a toad in a hail storm."

In Dominees' work with Checci and Magallanes around the officers' mess, he calls them, "My junior staff."

The Italian cook[20] (born in Hot Springs, Arkansas) looks on laughingly while they work and carry on their disputations. The other cook is unperturbed until there seems to be more play than work and then gives directions which do not go unheeded.

*  *  *

*Lt Col Warren T. Hannum Jr., Commander of the 2nd Bn, and Capt Robert B. Tobin, the operations officer, won praise for dedicated leadership of their men in the campaign immediately following the Nov. 8 attack. They endured to a great extent the mud, rain, snow and waterfilled foxholes of the forest fighting along with all the men of the battalion.*

## COL. ROBERT SEARS

*On the last day of October, Colonel Sears, who had so capably led the 137th since 25 July, received orders which took him from the regiment. At midnight the command (of the 137th) was taken by Col William S. Murray, Nogales, Arizona, formerly of the 5th Infantry Division—35th Div. History.*

*Col Robert Sears, well known to the headquarters group of the 320th, briefly commanded a battalion in our regiment. I have forgotten the exact time but it was possibly during the Alsace-Lorraine Campaign.*

*I saw Col Sears often and became well acquainted with him in the early days of combat. In the fighting for St. Lo, Col Sears, then without a command, played the role of a scout and sniper. Using an M-1 rifle he spent much time with the most forward rifle troops, where he was reported to have shot a number of German snipers in their positions in trees and other hiding places.*

---

20  S/Sgt. Audo E. Soncini, Regtl Hq Co, Woodside, L. I., N. Y.

## AXIS SALLY AND LORD HAW HAW

*By this time in the campaigns, we had for many days and nights been subjected daily to the two most famous or, to us, infamous, of the English propagandists for the Germans. Those of us who often worked late at night and had access to a radio, had grown most familiar with the soft, soothing tones of the English traitress, known as Axis Sally. Equally familiar was the resonant, appealing voice of the English traitor, who broadcast from The Fatherland under the radio psuedonym of Lord Haw Haw.*

*As we advanced across France and neared the German border in eastern Alsace-Lorraine, the BBC from England and the Armed Forces radio from Paris grew more distant. Often those stations were difficult to reach on our small radios while the Nazi broadcasts came in loud and clear as we steadily advanced toward the Fatherland. We tuned in the German broadcasts because at times we could get no other, and at other times listened by choice. We were interested in what the propagandists had to say, Axis Sally had a program of good American music, and we liked to hear Lord Haw Haw's German version of the news. The thought that we would be influenced by the German line of propaganda was as remote as the stars.*

*Axis Sally used an excellent selection of American songs and music, better even than those used by the American Armed Forces radio. She was well versed in American tastes or had an expert technical adviser. While we liked the absence of commercials on all the British broadcasts, neither were there any commercials on the German programs.*

*Axis Sally intersperced her musical numbers with subtle propaganda which was mostly talk of home (America). Mainly she tried to leave the thoughts that we shouldn't be in the war; that we were doing a dirty job for others; and of how nice it would be to be back home. Her programs were expertly done; there was seldom an error that would detract from the propaganda line, and she had an excellent voice. As a whole the propaganda was altogether amusing to us and never in the least effective.*

*Still, there were times when Sally's propaganda given in soft, soothing tones, or Lord Haw Haw's slanted version of the news, related matter-of-factly in faultless English, did get under our skins. A few times I saw Lt Silverman be-*

come furious, resulting in brief but vehement lectures to all in general and no one in particular, on the falsity of the entire Nazi doctrine. He knew he had no need to convince us who agreed with him fully. It was merely a way to get the matter off his chest. Not given to profanity usually his strongest expletive was "Those no-good bastards." Lt. Ginsberg was sometimes upset, and occasionally Capt Scherer was sufficiently provoked to exclaim, in his more educated way, "Those traiterous sonofabitches." When in need of expression I was more likely, in unguarded reversion to my less cultural language, to refer to the propagandists as "Them dirty sons-a-bitches."

The Axis Sally and Lord Haw Haw programs were limited, especially the latter as it was confined to news casts. Therefore we listened many hours to the regular German programs which invariably had excellent music. The thought often occurred to me that things could have been vastly different if the German nation had been as talented in peace making as its people were in the field of music.

Most of those who listened, like myself, knew nothing of the German language. We learned to recognize only one statement in the Teutonic tongue, which was made for the benefit of the German populace, usually late at night when the Allied bombers had returned home or during bad weather when they couldn't operate. It was, "No enemy aircraft are reported over the Third Reich."

## SPURRIER WINS MEDAL OF HONOR

The capture of the town of Achain may be credited to one man - S. Sgt. James J. Spurrier, Bluefield, W. Va., a squad leader of Co G, 134th. In the attack on Nov. 14, the 22-year old sergeant entered the town alone from the west while his company approached from the east.

Spurrier shot the first three Germans with his M-1. Then picking up BARs, American and enemy bazookas and grenades wherever he found them, he began to clean out the town. He crumbled one strong point with bazooka shells, killed three more Nazis with a BAR, captured a garrison commander, a lieutenant and 14 men. He silenced another defense point by killing the two occupants. Out of ammunition and under fire from a house by four enemy soldiers, Spurrier threw a German grenade into the building, killing the four defenders.

*Later that night Spurrier, now known as the one-man army, had charge of an outpost. While checking security he heard Germans talking in a barn. He set fire to a supply of oil and hay and captured four enemy soldiers as they ran out. Still later he spotted a figure crawling toward a sentry, killed a German when there was no reply to his challenge.*

*According to his battalion commander, Lt Col Frederick Roecher, himself only 25 years of age, Spurrier killed 25 enemy troops and captured 20 others. In March, 1945, Sgt. Spurrier for this engagement, was awarded the Congressional Medal of Honor.*

## THE GERMAN ROCKET BOMBS

*At about 1300 on October 21, 1944, the Santa Fe encountered its first robot bomb. It landed in a forest south of Lay St. Christopher, [near Nancy] but did no damage—35th Div. History.*

*A robot bomb was also known as rhobomb, buzz bomb or V-1. The long, angular missiles were launched from concealed ramps deep in Germany. After launching, the bombs were propelled through the air by a motor in the rear. The range was determined by the amount of fuel placed in the missile to run the motor.*

*We saw and heard many of them pass overhead aimed for targets far behind our positions. At night the flames from the exhaust glowed like a red tail as the projectile sped along at a steady pace. We learned that as long as we could hear the sound of the motor and see the red tail from the exhaust, we were safe from the bomb. When the sound ceased and the red tail vanished, those below scurried for shelter. The fuel had run out and the bomb was coming down.*

*These robot bombs were used extensively on England with especial concentration on London. In fact they were falling on the capital city before we crossed the channel to begin the invasion. Later they rained in large numbers on Antwerp and Liege, Belgium, after those cities fell to the Allied armies.*

*Later in the war, the exact time I have now forgotten, we heard of a new rocket bomb falling on London. The new projectile, more powerful and with a speed faster than sound, was launched by a new rocket fuel straight up into space above the atmosphere where it then took its direction and range from an installed aiming device. Unlike the buzz bombs,* the new projectile traveled with such speed that it struck its target with devastating force without any warning of its approach.

As the men of the infantry and armor with their supporting troops steadily moved forward in battle after battle, we constantly heard from German prisoners-of-war and other sources, rumors of the impending use by Hitler of some devastating new "secret weapon." With the knowledge of the German rockets in our minds, we could not discount completely the thought, that some time the information we obtained might turn out to be fact instead of rumor.

## PVT JOHN DUDLEY AGAIN

Some time during late 1944 Pvt John Dudley again came forcefully to my attention. I had the unpleasant task of investigating preliminary charges of desertion brought against him for absence from his place of duty. The charges, if substantiated, would subject him to trial before a General Court which could sentence him to prison, or even death. Possibly the investigation was made during the time the Third Army was holding in October. I still have the statements, unfortunately undated, of Pvt Dudley and a witness, 1st Sgt John S. Laskowski of Service Company, who could testify only to the time the accused was absent from his company which was from Sept 15 to Oct 11, almost a month.

The accused told a wild but coherent story of going out to secure eggs, vegetables, etc. from French civilians. (I knew he was prone to such activity for on two or three occasions when Dudley discovered me in the Sv Co area, he attempted to provide me with fresh tomatoes, fruit, or beverage he had "scrounged" from civilians).

According to his story, Dudley encountered two Frenchmen who said they knew where such supplies could be obtained, but French currency would not be accepted in payment. Dudley returned to his company area, obtained a supply of rations, chocolate and cigarettes to trade, and accompanied the two civilians to a village some 200 yards distant. Arriving at a house the Frenchmen offered Dudley a drink of wine which he accepted. The drink must have had "knockout drops," according to the soldier, because he didn't know anything more until he woke up in a cellar during the night.

Upon waking Dudley called and three civilians appeared, one of them holding a pistol. The armed man waved Dudley to one side and when he didn't move fast enough struck him with the gun on the side of the head. It was then the soldier realized the civilians were unfriendly. They took Dudley to a dark woods, gave him his empty carbine and indicated for him to go. In the darkness Dudley was lost and wound up spending the night in a haystack. Next day he returned to the area of Service Company to find everyone gone.

After much inquiry for his unit, which Dudley related in detail, he eventually wound up with Troop B of the 2nd Cavalry. The unit gave him a lift across the river and up to the front, passing several units but none of them a part of the 35th Division. He bivouaced with the cavalry unit, and during the night it received orders for a mission and had to move out before daylight. The officers gave Dudley the choice of remaining there alone or accompanying the unit on its battle mission. The accused chose to go with the cavalry outfit.

From then on during most of his absence, according to Dudley's story, he fought with the cavalry force. The fighting in which he participated included the battle of Lunneville, and at one time Troop B, a reconnaissance platoon, was within 3/4 kilometers of the German border. (This information corresponded with the advance of Gen Woods' 4th Armored Division and the subsequent withdrawal for the Third Army holding operation).

Dudley said a Lt Langley was in charge of Troop B and a Lt Cameron was second in Command. The battalion commander was a Lt Col Eastern or Easterling, and other officers were Col Mansfield and Col Reed. He said Lt Langley was wounded and evacuated while he fought with the unit and Lt Cameron was now in command of the troop. Finally, when opportunity afforded, Warrant Officer Grovie of the 2nd Cavalry accompanied Dudley to the MPs in Nancy where he reported to them to be sent back to the 320th. A letter, he said, was on the way from officers of the Second Cavalry to the 320th which would substantiate his story.

Having dealt with Dudley before and knowing something of his personality, I believed his story of combat with the cavalry unit. However I had no opportunity to find and *interview any of the men or officers of the outfit. I strongly urged the Division authorities to allow some one the opportunity to further investigate before final charges were preferred. Evidently this was not done, and with no corroborating testimony for Dudley's statement, he faced a General Court on charges of desertion because of the month's absence from his company.*

*Before the court convened his defense counsel, after reading my statement and hearing Dudley's story, made a successful effort to contact the members of the Second Cavalry, and was able to obtain them as witnesses at the trial. Not only did the witnesses testify to the truthfulness of Dudley's story of combat with their unit, but praised him as one of the finest soldiers they had ever seen.*

*Dudley was completely exonerated, and returned to duty with Service Company. Afterwards he sought me out to thank me for my fairness in the investigation and my efforts to corroborate his story which, no doubt, aided somewhat in his acquital.*

*The thought occurred to me that Pvt Dudley should have been in charge of a tank in an armored force. He would have given the German Panzers a hard time. Still, he might have "took off" again as he had done before, and headed his armored vehicle for Berlin. In the light of events in the years since the war, that might have been a good idea, if the American Army had gone with him.*

\* \* \*

Vaxy, France
Nov. 16, 1944

No writing yesterday because I felt so tough that I could hardly hold a pen. I have a very severe cold and so some temperature. At home I would have stayed in bed. "Doc" Smith gave me eight large pills to take this afternoon and nine now before going to bed, [total of 17 pills and capsules] which I have just swallowed. I was amazed at the number, but he just said in his good-humored, abrupt way, "You'll wake either well or dead." Guess I'd better leave this, go crawl into my bed roll before they knock me out. [Years later at a 35th Div reunion I reminded Maj Smith of the incident. His reply, "Gees, I wish I could remember the prescription!"]

— 405 —

All the Regiment quiet today, and neither did the Division advance. Action will be resumed soon I'm sure.

News of Ninth and First Armies going into the offensive sounds good to me. Perhaps it means we still aim for victory this year.

\* \* \*

Col Bryne was awarded the Silver Star Medal today. Gen Baade came down from Div Hqs to bestow it.

\* \* \*

The Corps Hqs has been shelled. It is seldom they get that close to the front.

\* \* \*

Hope our next job is not tough. Clearing that forest (Chateau-Salins) was a bloody and hard task.

[Casualties[21] not mentioned in the Journal.]

Morhange, France
Nov. 17, 1944

It is now really 0206, Nov 18. There is more artillery tonight, both coming and going, than I have heard for some time, for such a sustained period of time. Ever since I arrived here (in jeep with Parish and Silverman with Morgan[22] driving) our heavy stuff has really been sending it out. The Krauts have been throwing it back, and some of it is too close for comfort.

\* \* \*

"Doc" Smith's pills really fixed me up last night, and during the day I have felt much better. Conducted three investigations of courts martial charges and attended to some other matters.

The ground was frozen this morning. Saw plenty of ice when I arose at 0900.

\* \* \*

At last we got a good story on the 320th. It appeared in the "Evening Standard" of London. Capt White, public

---

21 1st Lt. Carl E. Peterson, Co F, Duluth, Minn., a replacement, evacuated as sick Nov. 16, did not return; 2nd Lt Clifford (or Clifton) Martin, Co G, address unknown, a replacement, listed LWA Nov. 16, did not return.

22 It may have been Pvt. Robert F. Morgan, Cn Co, Detroit, Mich.

relations officer of the Division, called me about it, and also thanked me for the letter I sent him about the clearing of the Chateau-Salins Forest. He said it helped him in getting the story over. I will make copies of the article and get them to the men, as they will be gratified to know they are getting credit at least for a part of what they do.

*　*　*

## EVENING STANDARD, LONDON, ENGLAND
### Monday, November 13, 1944

---

### PANTHERS WERE LEFT: NO PETROL

From
Philip Grune
Evening Standard War Reporter

WITH THE US THIRD ARMY, CHATEAU SALINS, Sunday Night — Driving ahead in bad weather conditions, elements of General Patton's army today gained up to four miles advance in certain sectors of the front.

The most important gain has been an advance of three miles by tanks of the 4th Armored Division, supported by the 104th Infantry Regiment, to the northeast. They are now one mile beyond the town of Rodalbe, which is 25 miles north-east of Nancy.

But in the 12th Corps sector there were also valuable strategic gains. The *320th Infantry* cleared the Forest of Chateau Salins and are now 1000 yards beyond the village of Chateau Brehain at the north-east tip of the forest.

It had been thought that the forest would be difficult to capture because the enemy had concentrated a large force of men with a plentiful supply of small arms and light artillery.

### Now It Is The Mud

This shows a four mile advance during the day, and in the operation our troops entered the village of Oron.

They also captured four hundred prisoners in this area, as well as five tanks which had been abandoned and were undamaged.

Americans fighting out here now recalled the stories they heard of the last war. Most of the roads have been turned into quagmires, great showers of oily, black mud being thrown to each side as the tanks churn through.

During the Normandy and Brittany campaign we complained of dust. Now it is the mud.

Today it was impossible to travel more than a few hundred yards before the windscreen was covered so thick that it was impossible for the driver to see his way.

I tell of this to give some idea of the difficulties our tank men are facing, and why an advance of three miles in one day is a remarkable achievement.

The *35th* Infantry Division reached the town of Bellange today, and liberated many villages and hamlets including Vaxy, Gerbecourt, and Fonteny. It was the *320th Infantry Regiment* which did most of the fighting, smashing back Germans in house-to-house fighting in several villages.

### 4836 Prisoners

At Fonteny our troops found the abandoned tanks. They were not damaged but found to be out of petrol. All were latest type Panthers.

In some parts of this sector today, our troops found unwillingness among the Germans to fight.

There appears a desire to withdraw eastwards, and more and more are giving themselves up as prisoners.

* * *

We push on tomorrow with the 320th again in the attack. We have not yet missed a tough job. I hope this one tomorrow is not tough, but they're surely using that artillery on something. It continues to roll with terrific thunder and the great lightning flashes light up the whole horizon. The near ones light up everything around. The Jerry's incoming stuff continues to shake the ground occasionally. Must be pretty good size artillery he is using.

News of the attacks up north leads us to be hopeful. Maybe it all means more than we dare to hope without being too optimistic.

In talking to Capt White today I learned that Lt Manzi,[23] my old friend of San Luis and Camp Rucker days, is back at Army Headquarters. Has an assignment there, the lucky cuss. If there is ever a lull I hope to go back to see him as I can go with Capt White. Manzi, Lts Warnock, Trask, Silverman, myself and Lt Wright[24] (now of AT Co) were all together in F Co at San Luis and later at Camp Rucker.

\* \* \*

Well, I must get a lantern, and then turn off the motor for our light plant so it can rest. Guess I'll have to break up a card game for four night owls.

\* \* \*

Had quite a time getting up here tonight along the slimy roads with columns of trucks, half-tracks and tanks going both ways in the darkness. We caught up with Jamison and Northam who had left almost an hour before we did. Lt Quillin and others have not yet arrived.

Don't know if they're waiting to come up in the morning or had difficulty on the road.

There is always the possibility of getting to a certain place just as one of the Hun shells arrives.

\* \* \*

Now 0435: Shelling quite heavy for past few minutes. Some just hit close by. A badly frightened sergeant, with E Company's chow, just checked in at the CP. He went on his way with the food as the Co can not eat unless he gets there right away. I just checked with the Bns (they are right near us) and both have been getting shells. So far no casualties are known.

Mighty good to sleep through something like this. Then if you don't get hit you are okeh, and if you do, well at least you missed the fright.

[A casualty[25] on Nov. 17.]

---

23  1st Lt. Arthur J. Manzi, Worcester, Mass.
24  1st Lt. Don L. Wright, A/T Co, Muncie, Pa.
25  1st Lt. Maxwell Kamm, Co H, Clinton, Ind., a replacement, listed LIA Nov. 17, did not return.

Morhange, France
Nov. 18, 1944

Now 1640:

All the CP group has now gone forward to the next site except me. I wait to direct any late comers (just gave directions to Capt Waters of the Engrs) and for transportation.

I write this with my pad lying on the broad window sill of the stone building, on the thousands of pieces of shattered glass. Not enough light remains within the room to see how to write. The day has been partially clear. Just a few brief moments ago the cold, distant, winter sun sank from view and the last orange tinges of sunshine have faded from the low hills and the sides of the red brick buildings. All about the town square before me are men and vehicles, some fixing to move out, most preparing to spend the night. The artillery just outside the town thunders and thunders, sometimes with deafening detonations. All sorts of Division, Corps and Army groups are moving into town. Now that the cold of winter has set in, buildings and shelter are at a premium.

Some Kraut planes were over about an hour ago and there set up an uproarious racket of firing as dozens of MGs and AA guns opened up on them. A red hot piece of shrapnel or a bullet fell with a sizzle in front of me where I stood watching from the door way. Some men just watched, others dived under trucks.

Must go. Here's Morgan for me with the jeep. Want to get there before light fails completely.


Rocrange, France
Nov. 18, 1944

Now 2045:

Our CP now in some shattered, dirty, stinking buildings in this town. A dead cow, beginning to smell to high heaven, lies broken and muddy in the edge of the road right in front of the door. There is sporadic shelling in the area and these buildings do not offer much protection.

The Bns did not have much success today. They have had tough going. The 2nd Bn could not take the town of Bermering and is still fighting there. The 1st Bn took Vallarenge but was stopped on the high ground beyond. A few days ago Maj Waring was again evacuated. Lt Col Walker,[26] who took command of the Bn in his place, was hit today, a serious shoulder wound, and is now lost to the regiment. Lt Litherland just came in with Lt Col Hannum.[27] He told me Lt Votts[28] or (Vaughts) of H Co was killed today. Lt Garth Ramsey of H Co was wounded in the foot and evacuated.

In the 3rd Bn Capt Brochu was knocked out by the detonation of a mortar shell. For some time he could not hear but is now regaining his hearing and may not be lost to the Co.

Sgt Koch just told me that Sgt McCormic[29] of F Co was killed yesterday. He was struck in the back by a mortar shell and I guess it killed him instantly. I remember him when the 320th was activated at Camp San Luis Obispo. He was one of my first acquaintances in the Co and he and the other Arkansas boys volunteered for the weapons platoon when they found I was to lead it. He was then just a "rookie" as were the others; just a friendly homesick boy with a wide grin, from some rural section of my home state. I recommended him for his stripes then, but we filled up with old men transferred from another unit. He did not get his stripes until he proved his worth in combat soon after we entered the lines at St Lo. The last time I saw him was when we were in reserve at Brin. He had the same wide infectious grin, only slightly dulled by the long strain of combat.

I am deeply saddened that he cannot now ever return to the home he loved so well, and to which he wanted to go back so badly.          *   *   *

There are many stories like his. Just a good, clean, friendly American boy, called from his home to a war he did not want to fight and all because of selfish aims and a lust for power by some one we have never seen. Every day, every

26   Lt. Col. James T. Walker, address unknown, took over command of 1st Bn, lasted only a week as CO, listed as LWA Nov. 18, did not return. Capt. William Walton, Newton, Kans., assumed command of the 1st Bn.

27   Lt. Col. Warren T. Hannum, CO of 2nd Bn, a replacement, San Francisco, Calif. (or Denver, Colo), a West Point graduate, joined the 320th and took command of 2nd Bn on Aug. 28.

28   1st Lt. Vernon A. Vagts, Co H, Annomosa, Iowa, an original, listed KIA Nov. 19, his death was Nov. 18.

29   Sgt. Claud Michael McCormic, Co F, DeQueen, Ark., KIA Nov. 17. S-Sgt. Allen D. Hill, Co F, Clay Center, Kans., recently returned, SWA by same shell, said it was an 88.

night, every hour that this war lasts, sees many, many sad endings to lives like his. But they go on and on through the hell, because there is a duty and a belief that our cause is just.

Tonight the stars are shining, dim pale points of light far, far away. And the longing in our hearts for this war to cease is as great and unutterable as the stars are distant and unattainable. But I think the loneliness and longing, which at times wells from our hearts, would fill all that space and well out beyond the silent stars.

Harold A. Reinert,[30] 1st Sgt of E Co now commissioned a 2nd Lt, today took over command of a company in the 2nd Bn.

\* \* \*

[On Nov. 18 I wrote a letter to the Madison County Record which was later published. It is omitted because it is repetitious of Journal entries.]

\* \* \*

## CAPTURED EQUIPMENT IN ALSACE DRIVE

*From the Chateau Salins Forest to Morhange the 35th Division captured the following enemy material:*

| | | | |
|---|---|---|---|
| 150mm arty pieces | 6 | Anti-tank guns | 44 |
| Rds. bazooka ammo. | 500 | Anti-aircraft guns | 13 |
| Rds. arty. ammo. | 5,005 | Mortars | 18 |
| Rds. small arms ammo. | 100,000 | Rifles | 893 |
| Truckloads ammo. | 2 | Rds. 120mm mortar ammo. | 30 |
| Ammunition dumps | 3 | Barrels rifle ammo. | 10 |
| Wagon loads barbed wire | 1 | 20mm AA guns | 6 |
| Tanks | 28 | Chow wagons | 3 |
| Half-tracks | 15 | Hand wagons | 15 |
| Cargo trucks | 10 | Rds. 88mm ammo. | 510 |
| Motorcycles | 6 | Command car | 1 |
| 105mm guns | 6 | Grenades | 15,096 |
| 88mm guns | 15 | Pistols | 47 |
| 75mm howitzers | 4 | Automatic rifles | 19 |

30  Harold A. Reinert, 1st Sgt. of Co E, assigned to Co F as a 2nd Lt, Dodge City, Kans. For exceptional combat leadership he was awarded a battlefield commission. Numbers of NCOs won such commissions. Because of experience and proven ability they were superior to many officer replacements we received because of the latter's inexperience in combat.

| Mines _____ 274 | Panel body truck _____ 1 |
| Rds. 20mm ammo. _____ 600 | Ambulance _____ 1 |
| Personnel carriers _____ 2 | Jeeps (U.S. recaptured) __ 2 |

In addition to this, close to 2,000 prisoners were captured.—From 35th Division History.

Rocrange, France
Nov. 19, 1944

Now 1100:

M/Sgt Kearns said they had just got a message that Bermering is now clear.

There was plenty of artillery last night going both ways. Our own is really supporting us in force. A few moments ago I could see six "flap-flaps" in the air at one time.

\* \* \*

One of the best stories I've heard on the interrogation of PWs. An interrogation team was questioning two prisoners. One of them talked but the other refused. When the interrogator finished he hung a tag on each one as is customary. On the one who talked the tag read, "Send to U.S.A." On the stubborn one, "Ship to Russia." Upon reading the tags the [second] prisoner immediately broke down, began to cry and told the IPW man everything he knew.

Almost all PWs talk freely, but there are a few reluctant ones. On those [the latter] our own IPW team has used the same angle at different times but not quite the same way.

\* \* \*

There is quite a bunch of civilians staying in the cellar of this house, where I slept with Capt Bonham and Lts Quillen and Parish. A few come out to milk, care for their stock which they have housed in the stone barns as much as possible, get fuel, and other like chores. They then get back with the others in the cellar, which is their underground refuge until the storm of war has passed away from them. This morning I heard a child crying; it was a strange and unreal sound in these surroundings.

On the surface everything here seems German. The Nazis began the Germanization of the province shortly after the fall of France in 1940. All the signs, maps, publications, etc, are in the German language. Most, if not all, the inhabitants speak both that tongue and the French, and many, no doubt, are French in sympathy.

Bermering

Now at Bermering - 2245:

We moved to this place in the late afternoon. We are short on transportation and I was left behind. I caught a ride up to the new CP with Lt O'Brien as he came from Division with new orders. Darkness was beginning to fall, causing the fires in the burning towns and buildings to glow brightly in the gathering gloom.

While standing around in the last town waiting to move up, I noted the new outfits and men moving in. Some seemed to be closer to the front than usual. One [soldier] was complaining about the dead cows (three were lying near by) and wondering, "Why in the hell couldn't they bury them," "They" meaning the preceding troops, namely, us. I had difficulty in keeping myself from asking him who had time to bury them. Did he expect us to employ our time burying cows, when sometimes we could not always care for our wounded and very often [had to leave] our dead unburied.

Some more [soldiers] had not found as much room as they wanted. One was grumbling because he had to sleep in a room with some person toward whom he seemed to have a pronounced dislike.

Others were moving about without helmets, without arms, and in shirt sleeves. They shouted at each other, indulged in pranks, horse play, and many seemed in high good humor. What a difference in their attitude and that of our men. It was easy to see that the hell our men had come to know had some how escaped these troops. [A Lt of a long range arty unit told me in kindly tones, "I cannot do you any good unless you're out there at least five miles."]

Also after our doughboys had pushed on ahead and the CP had followed them, the civilians could some how sense that the war was receding from them, and they came out from their hiding places. The fear which we had seen in their faces had given way to smiles. I saw more of them in the last 30 minutes there, than I had in all the previous time. Many were talking with the soldiers, and both they and the troops were "getting on" quite well.

* * *

We are having some trouble with civilian evacuees now. Maj Dolan[31] and Sgt Frankel are very busy getting them out of the freshly occupied towns. Maj Smith and his medics took care of some tonight who had lost their shoes and otherwise suffered from shock and exposure.

They fled from the town which we can see burning up ahead. They lost their shoes when they fled from the roads into the fields and ditches to evade the fire of the charging tanks as they entered the town today. I went over to the aid station to get some more pills for my cold and got there just in time for the hand shaking as they were leaving.

\* \* \*

Capt Brochu has been evacuated and may not be back. I hope not anyway. He has been in the front long enough. Lt Stonesifer[32] was lost today as were Lts Martin, Patrick,[33] Humphrey[34] and Lang.[35] We are badly in need of new officers now, but replacements are not to be had at once. The drive continues relentlessly and the non-coms will lead the platoons in the battle. Very often they lead any way. Sgt Shupe[36] of G Co has been given a battlefield commission and is now an officer in his company.

\* \* \*

It is sometimes difficult to get to the wounded who fall in an advance in this open country. Also Maj Smith is short a number of trained medical personnel and cannot get replacements. Yesterday about 16 men fell who could not be reached until this morning. Some were perhaps lost because of this. Tonight the aid men and litter bearers are searching in the darkness for those who could not be reached today.

\* \* \*

31 Maj. Dolan and Sgt. Frankel were Civil Affairs Corps officials, attached to our unit, who set up laws, rules and regulations for the civilians in the areas we captured.

32 1st Lt. Glenn L. Stonecipher, Co M, Patterson, Calif., a replacement, later returned. (Lt. Martin lost on Nov. 16, see 21).

33 1st Lt. John R. Patrick, Co G, Central City, Pa., a replacement, wounded Nov. 18, later returned. He had joined Co G on Aug. 8.

34 2nd Lt. James K. Humphrey, Co H, Washington, D. C., a replacement, later returned.

35 2nd Lt. Ray T. Lang, Co A, Concord, Mass., a replacement, listed LWA Nov. 19, did not return.

36 2nd Lt. James R. Shupe, Co G, Freeman, W. Va.

My cold, which was better yesterday, is much worse today. [Other casualties[37] not mentioned in the Journal.]

## THE ARMY RUNS OUT OF INFANTRY

*Not long after the entry of Nov. 19, which mentioned the shortage of trained front line medics and our need for replacements, a directive was promulgated by the higher echelons of command to transfer to the infantry five per cent of the personnel of all other branches of the American Armed Forces. This included troops of the quartermaster, signal, medical, finance, and legal divisions, as well as engineers, artillerymen and all others. The replacement pools had run out of trained infantrymen with which to fill the depleted ranks of the infantry combat divisions. Gen Patton may have been the first to issue the order for transfers as a means of securing replacements for his infantry units, but the directive soon became general policy for the entire American Army.*

*The planners had miscalculated. Proceeding on the assumption, based on the use of armored forces, the more effective weapons of the chemical mortars and artillery, the great fleets of bombers with their destructive missiles, and the fighter bombers with both machine guns and bombs, that there would not be the same need for foot soldiers in this war as had existed in past conflicts, the planners had drawn up blueprints for the training of a certain percentage of men for all services, including the training of replacements for casualties. Before the war for American ground forces in Europe was six months old, the projections of the planners had proved to be erroneous. Casualties among the footsloggers as compared to losses in other branches of the Service were far heavier than had been anticipated. Not enough trained infantrymen or combat medics were available to fill the gaps in our units even during the Alsace-Lorraine Campaign.*

---

37  1st Lt. Carlton C. Thornblom, Co C, Paris, Texas, an original, saw action at St. Lo, Mortain and all the way - listed LWA Nov. 20, did not return; 1st Lt. James C. Goodchild, Co C, Saco, Maine, joined as a replacement July 13, slightly wounded Nov. 8 but remained in the line, wounded and evacuated on Nov. 18, later returned; 2nd Lt. Charles H. Dalton, Co C, Madison, Wisc., an original, wounded and evacuated Nov. 20, later returned; 2nd Lt. Harry H. Chevalier, Co L, Ozone Park, N. Y., a replacement, listed LIA Nov. 19, did not return.

During the fighting in the Ardennes the need for combat infantrymen, both men and officers, had become so critical, that infantry replacements were being flown across the North Atlantic from America in mid-winter, an action that would not have been undertaken except in dire emergency. Other replacements were sent by the fastest ships, as the Queen Mary and Queen Elizabeth, which took only six days from New York to the British Isles, where the troops disembarked, rushed across the Islands and up to the front, sometimes taking less than two weeks from home to combat. An entry in the Journal during that period makes note of replacements being received who had not been in the Service as long as we had been in the front lines.

Still the number of new trained men was insufficient to replace the infantry losses, and the transfer policy was put into effect to further meet the need.

The orders for transfer of personnel applied even to our own artillery - a component part of the Division. Long before this time experienced members of the military knew well which branch was suffering the greatest losses of killed and wounded. We heard many stories about our artillery units, of how the men who received the orders for transfer, realizing the greater danger they would face, checked their insurance to see it was in proper order, wrote letters home, and had farewell parties with their buddies before coming up to our lines. While in the hospital at Liege, Belgium, I heard some terrible griping from medical corps GIs who had received their orders to join the infantry.

After the war was over statistics revealed that 75% of all casualties during the war in the European Theater of Operations, was borne by one branch of the Armed Forces, - the infantry, thus still further confirming its title of "Queen of Battles."

\* \* \*

## CAPTURE OF FREYBOUSE

The Germans strongly defended their garrison and supply town of Morhange but it fell to Division attacks on Nov. 16th. Ten other towns were taken in the next three days with the capture of 1,500 enemy troops.

At Freybouse Lt Thomas R. Travis with 20 men of Co K, 137th, took the first house killing 15 Germans and cap-

*turing eight others. In the second house captured by Lt. Travis and his men, the Germans threw phosphorous grenades on the roof setting it on fire. As the roof collapsed, the 137th doughboys moved downstairs and continued to fight until the flames seared their window positions.*

*The group fought its way back to the first house, keeping the prisoners, and held out all night against automatic and bazooka fire. Next morning the enemy called on them to surrender or be burned. Lt Travis yelled, "Go to hell!" Stormtroopers set fire to the roof. The group was entirely surrounded when the lieutenant spotted a friendly TD edging into the outskirts of the town. Travis gained its attention and pointed out German strong points with tracer fire. The TD knocked out four enemy MG nests, forced a withdrawal of other enemy MG and bazooka teams, and the town was occupied and held.—From 35th Division History.*

Linstroff (linsdorf)
Nov. 21, 1944

It is now 0130 of the 21st. We moved to our new location and got settled just before nightfall. The wind was high, driving the rain before it, and the big drops, somewhat unusual here, struck the face with stinging force and made splashes in the pools and puddles along the road. The smoke from the burning towns did not rise as yesterday, but lay flat along the country side, leaning low with the winter wind over the shell-scarred and track-marked earth. The trees along the roads and in the orchards waved wildly in the gale, and the wind moaned through the cracks and the holes in the battle-scarred buildings. It was of such a time Robert Louis Stevenson was thinking when he wrote, "Windy Night."

The wind has quietened somewhat now, but the rain continues to turn everything without into a vast expanse of muck and mire.

\* \* \*

It was a dismal day (Nov 20) on which to come to the end of life's journey, as did Lt Christianson,[38] the communication's officer of the 1st Bn. His jeep hit a mine as he was directing the laying of wire in the late afternoon. He was

---

38 1st Lt. Arthur E. Christianson, Com O of 1st Bn, an original, Mattapan, Mass., listed KIA Nov. 20.

killed and the driver injured. I know his disposition was sunny and cheerful to the last. I never saw him any other way. He was one of the finest men I have ever known.

We used to visit each other in barracks at Camp Rucker and talk philosophy, religion, morals, politics, etc. Lt Christianson was an inspiring man with whom to talk and a most useful and helpful individual.

Three other officers out today, Brundage,[39] Wilson[40] and [unknown did not get his name]. The redoubtable Sgt Porta was finally hit today; shell fire inflicted a wound as they were advancing through an open field toward a town. It is reported he is back with the unit, but that report not yet confirmed.

* * *

Today a letter was returned to me which I had written on 23 Sept to Pfc Hugh Fritts, [with the 137th Inf] my hometown friend from Thorney, Ark. It was marked "Deceased" which can mean only that he was killed in action. I know of no words to express, or any way of showing, my regret and sadness that he cannot return home. Of that I cannot now say more.

* * *

There is news that the armies in the north make progress; the French have reached the Rhine; Metz is about to fall, and I know of our own progress. Tonight our 3rd Bn is in Francaltroff and the 1st is in Erstroff. The attack continues tomorrow. So we draw nearer to victory over an embittered Hitler who keeps throwing in his forces like a madman without regard to human life or suffering.

* * *

I have now quite a bit of this journal on hand. I think I shall send it back to Lt Sperl for safe keeping. One unlucky hit up here would mix it irretrievably with this black, sticky mud.

---

39 2nd Lt. Granville P. Brundage, Co I, Strafford, Conn., listed in an unofficial record in my possession as KIA Nov. 11. I do not know whether the record is in error, or I just did not hear of his death until this date.

40 This was probably 2nd Lt. Warren Wilson, Co L, Stillwater, Okla., a replacement, as he was listed LWA Nov. 19, and did not return.

Lt Ginsberg has learned his brother is back near Nancy and has gotten permission to go back and see him. I can send it by him.

There has been sporadic shelling throughout the night.

* * *

On duty with me tonight is Pvt Bock of Little Rock, South Carolina. He is a native of Germany. He had to flee because of Hitler, going to America while his sister fled to Sweden. He hates Hitler and Nazism as much as anyone, but otherwise seems to be a very kindly and tolerant lad.

I know he is mighty faithful in his duties as a soldier in this war and is liked by all who know him.

* * *

Today is my anniversary. Twelve years ago Alta and I were married [it was 13] by preacher [S. P.] Eden on Ball Creek. Now gone by are some more pleasant times. I cannot help but wonder about her and the little fellow tonight. The little bright-eyed interesting lad. What a joy to be with him again.

Today also was the wedding anniversary of Brent and Margaret Cull. They will never have another and were never permitted one really happy celebration. Shattered and vanished are our plans to all celebrate together some happy time when opportunity afforded.

Maj Smith told me recently that today was also his marriage anniversary.

* * *

What a cost in dreams and hopes and plans and happiness, that goes into the crushing of his monstrous thing called Nazism and Junker militarism.

* * *

Outside is the steady, incessant patter of the rain.

Lindstroff
Nov. 21, 1944

Now 1145:

We are fixing to move on up. Everything from the rear is piling in here on us.

Sgt Porta had a pretty bad wound in his big leg up near the buttock. He was evacuated and will be gone a long time. [Seriously wounded; reports that he was still with the unit were false] I figured he'd get it sooner or later and I'm glad he was not killed.

The Huns really throw stuff at us from the high ground. They are fighting a shrewd delaying action, but they are getting the hell beat out of them.

[Casualties[41] on Nov. 21].

Erstroff (Ersdorf), France
Nov. 23, 1944

Today was Thanksgiving, but I would never have realized it if some had not said it was, and the cooks had not prepared a good turkey dinner for the evening meal.

Many of the men did not get their turkey today. They were too busy fighting. The cooks will prepare it and, if possible, it will be served tomorrow. Until late in the night, one company had not yet gotten any food, and of course had only their emergency K-rations.

It has been a comparatively light day of battle so far as combat goes. We lost no officers but, in this Thanksgiving Day, I note from the casualty report that two [EM] were killed in action, thirteen were seriously wounded, there were 12 non-battle casualties and a number missing in action. "Smoky" was here with his crew [GRO Personnel] and from this little battered Lorraine village picked up the bodies of two fallen and all-but-forgotten soldiers. There is no time to remember the dead, when we have difficulty in caring for and keeping up with those who yet live.

Tonight, just without the command post, the big guns, with great belching tongues of smoke and flame, are throwing heavy shells into Germany, into the Siegfried Line and the cities just short of the Rhine River. Soon, all along the front, we will be closed up to the border and German cities and buildings will be destroyed. German civilians, men, women and children, will be cowering in cellars or fleeing along the roads to escape the battle as others have done in other countries.

---

41  2nd Lt. Herman Menke, Co D, address unknown, a replacement, evacuated as sick Nov. 21, did not return; 2nd Lt. Harold A. Reinert, Co F, Dodge City, Kans., a sgt newly commissioned a 2nd Lt. didn't last long as an officer. He is listed LWA Nov. 21, did not return.

— 421 —

Good news, - the armies to the south have broken through all German defenses and reached the Rhine.

My cold clings to me almost as tightly as the ever-present dampness, mud and mist cling to this battered Lorraine countryside.

A few heavy enemy shells fell in our area tonight.

Lening, France
Nov. 25, 1944

Tonight, when outside for a few minutes, I could hear enemy shells whine overhead and explode in Francaltroff. This being a small village, they were passing it up for a bigger target. From the looks of all these towns, there are plenty of soldiers and vehicles in any of them to make a good target. We seem to encounter more artillery as we push closer to Germany in this drive.

Yesterday I caught a ride down to this place with Red Cross Charlie when he came by. The battered country, with deep, marred tracks, shell craters, wrecked vehicles and dead livestock, would make an awful and awesome picture to one unaccustomed to war. I saw seventeen dead horses and mules on the way down. [Many were farm animals but it appeared some horses had been used to pull German arty] One had a rope lying beside it as if the owner were on the point of haltering it when the shell fell, and had dropped and gone (or been carried) away. In one spot were a dozen dead sheep.

Most of the fallen soldiers had already been removed. Some were still being felled, of course, by the shells that came in.

* * *

Tonight is clear for the first time at night since we started this push. The moon is very pale and high.

[Co F loses another commander[42]].

### NEBRASKANS WITH THE 320TH INF. REGT.

*Lawrence Youngman, correspondent for the World-Herald, Omaha, Nebraska, was assigned by his newspaper to*

---

42 Capt. Carl Zech, Co F, address unknown, evacuated as sick Nov. 25, did not return. A replacement, Zech was another of a half dozen or more commanders of Co F since entering combat. The company had now lost four officers since this drive began on Nov. 8.

*follow the exploits of the original Nebraska National Guard unit with the 35th Division - the 134th Infantry Regiment. He wrote almost exclusively of the 134th because his paper wanted news for its readers of soldiers from the home state of Nebraska.*

*During the Alsace-Lorraine Campaign Youngman came to the 320th and wrote a story of our Regiment's experiences and explained it as follows:*

*"With the 35th Division there is another regiment which has a special claim on the interest of Nebraskans and other people of the Middle West.*

*It is the 320th Infantry, youngest unit among the three in the division, but with a splendid record.*

*Here is the reason it holds special interest for our area: When the regiment was constituted at San Luis Obispo, Cal., in January, 1943, it started out with three thousand new men. To put it on an equal footing with the other two regiments in the division - the 137th from Kansas and Nebraska's 134th — it was decided to take one-third of the men from each of the other two regiments and "swap" them for an equal number of men in the new regiment.*

*Consequently, a substantial number of Nebraskans and Kansans soon were members of the new regiment. And each regiment then had one-third new men and two-thirds older, more experienced men.*

*From that time, through maneuver areas in the states and from the Normandy beaches across France to Lorraine the route of the 320th has closely paralleled that of the 134th. But the day-by-day chronicle of events is entirely different."*

*Mr. Youngman then chronicled briefly the exploits of the 320th in the war beginning at St. Lo, including the relief of the "Lost Battalion" at Mortain and the capture of major French cities in the various campaigns up to the time he wrote the story. He wound up his news report, which was published in the Sunday, Nov. 26th issue of the World-Herald, by listing the names and addresses of the enlisted men of Nebraska still remaining with the 320th.*

*SV Co - M Sgt Gerald D. Harding, Beaver City; T/5 Alvin Lueders, Gibbon.*

*A/T Co - Pfc Charles J. Henderson, Omaha; Pfc Laverl E. Miner, Wakefield.*

Cn Co - T/5 Wayne Byron, Auburn; Pfc Troy L. Doty, Weeping Water; First Sgt Clyde R. Fleury, Blair; S Sgt Carl J. Lindmier, Omaha.

Med Det - T Sgt Guy J. Lovell, Jr., Scottsbluff.

Hq Co 1st Bn - T/5 Sidney C. Cohn, Nebraska City; Pvt Wayne W. Hart, Belgrade; Sgt Alfred C. Koontz, Auburn; Pvt John D. Kvech, Lincoln; T Sgt Orr T. Nichol, Jr., Omaha.

Co A - T/4 Elmer E. Vonderohe, Madison.

Co B - S Sgt Anton L. Hubl, Lawrence.

Co C - Sgt LaVern E. A. Faber, Alliance; Pfc Walter G. Sillik, Omaha.

Co D - Sgt Melvin J. Marshall, Brock.

Hq Co 2nd Bn - Pvt Edmond T. Whalen, Lincoln.

Co E - Sgt Carl H. Benson, Hordville; T Sgt Monte V. Totten, Elgin.

Co F - Pvt Virgil D. Skalberg, Wausa; S Sgt Roy E. Cunningham, McGrew.

Co G - S Sgt Donald L. Giles, Nebraska City; T/5 Louis F. Maly, Wahoo.

Co H - S Sgt Floyd D. Engdahl, Norfolk; Pfc Donald L. Leutzinger, Omaha.

Hq Co 3rd Bn - S Sgt John L. Dillworth, Lincoln; T/4 Charles S. Young, Ansley; Pfc William J. Butler, Purdum; Pvt Thomas A. Kretz, Columbus; Pfc Charles A. Post, Omaha; Pvt. Fred D. Lewis, Omaha.

Co I - T/5 Charles R. Altschuler, Madison; T/5 Salbadore G. Chavez, Nebraska City; T/4 Everett W. Else, Elm Creek; Sgt Allen C. Johnson, Newman Grove; Sgt Verrol R. Keyser, Sargent.

Co K - T Sgt Royal A. Offer, Adams. [Awarded a battlefield commission.]

Co L - Pfc Ernest J. Meyer, Otoe.

Co M - Corp Herman A. Janssen, Franklin; Pfc James N. Knudson, Newman Grove; Pfc Glen W. Meyer, Princeton; Pfc Robert W. Stavo, Rosalie; S Sgt John J. Towey, Loretto; Corp Leland E. Thompson, Burwell.

Insming, France
Nov. 26, 1944

Today we moved here in the morning hours. We expected to stay two or three days, but already tonight we have orders to move to another assembly area. All but the 1st Bn is being

— 424 —

assembled. It will join us later. There is no telling where or what our next mission will be. We may be used to exploit a break through somewhere on the front.

I am duty officer tonight. Just now some enemy shells are falling just short of our location. This hqs group has been very lucky about being hit by shells. Whenever anyone mentions that they always knock on wood. No one would think of mentioning our luck without doing that. Funny how superstitions develop.

\* \* \*

Charley [Red Cross Charlie often referred to as "Croix Rouge Sharlee"] was with us tonight, I got to telling him about the characters and the customs in the hills of Arkansas, and got pretty homesick. There just are not any words to tell how wonderful it would be for the war to be over and for us to be home again.

My cold hangs on and on and I really feel tough.

Insming, France
Nov. 27, 1944

Time: 0750:

This morning the whole world about here is white, quiet and brittle in the frozen grip of an all-encompassing frost. The many frost resistant plants, as cabbage, etc, in these Alsacian gardens are as crisp as fresh chilled head-lettuce. Some, which up to now have withstood the first mild attacks of winter, will soon blacken and wilt with thawing upon the coming of milder temperature after this severe onslaught. The many beer and wine bottles, scattered in plentiful profusion around this former German headquarters, have glistening white sides. The little neatly stacked pile of garden stakes, the ugly warped planks near the back entrance, the smudged fence, the dirty, beaten road, and the torn earth, each, this early morn, has a lacy white, intricately woven decoration. In the midst of the garden, the shell crater has a frosty edge, deeper inside [the crater] mushrooms of ice have pushed up from the mud, and the puddle of water in the center has an ice covering.

There is enough air movement to waft away the steam from the Bronson heater where the cooks are heating water for the preparation of breakfast. Smoke floats gently upward from the chimneys of some of the soldier occupied houses. But the strung wires are motionless and the bare trees stand solid, "still as death."

I hear a somewhat familiar sound, and, looking up, perceive a solitary raven, or European Crow, flapping forlornly across the dark gray heavens uttering his plaintive call. It is then I notice the sky is solid with clouds moving toward the east and I recall the saying of the hill folk of my homeland, so often spoken by my Dad, "clouds over a frost, a sure sign of snow." In the east is a tinge of pink, growing slightly deeper in color with the breaking dawn, and I remember words of my mother, "Red in the morning, the sailor's warning."

But I know that Infantrymen need no signs or harbingers to forewarn them of stormy and bloody times. They know for a certainty that their lot is, and will be, difficult until the war is ended.

\* \* \*

Our Headquarters has now come to life and breakfast is waiting. Charley has found a nice collection of Nazi pictures, many showing various poses of the arch-fiend and certain of his chief henchmen.

Pontpierre, France
Dec. 1, 1944

We have been here since the 27th. I came over in the C & R Car about 0900 of that day. During the day all units moved to this vicinity and set up in this or neighboring towns. We have been in Corps reserve since, and the survivors of the recent campaigns have had a chance to rest.

For me the days have run together for I have been ill most of the time. Some days I stuck to my bed roll, usually without eating, in an effort to wear out my cold or grippe. When able, I have worked on courts martial trials and investigations, and the monthly "after action" reports. [I lay in my bedroll, fully dressed as always except for overshoes and trenchcoat, alone in a damp upstairs room for 3 days and nights. The men brought me food which I could not eat. I sipped periodically from a quart of Scotch.]

Just a few minutes ago finished working five investigations handled during the day. Worked from 0900 to 2330 with only one brief pause of about 15 minutes for supper.

Now, after a letter to Alta (only two written since being here), I am scribbling these few lines (now 0015 Dec 2) before going to bed. My cold sure hangs on, with sore throat, sore neck and head caused by aggravated sinus.

There are no outside clothes lines in this country. Clothes would never dry outside. There has been water on top of the beer barrels outside our CP ever since we came here. I have noticed it every time I stepped outside to blow my nose or visit the latrine.

* * *

Lts Silverman and Parish and Cpl Fieldsteel[43] are the only ones besides myself who have not retired. One of the officers and the corporal are on duty for the night. Sid has been listening to a German broadcast and does he get "burned up" at their subtle line of propaganda. Then they play American recordings - as I pen these words, "Goodnight Wherever You Are," very beautiful to a lonely homesick soldier (as myself). That pleasant upstate New York Republican, Lt Parish, has just now generously bestowed upon me a sizeable piece of delicious fruit cake sent to him by the Portville Victory Club (his home town). So after eating that, to my bedroll for much needed rest; still feel pretty miserable.

We move tomorrow it seems.

[Co F gets a new commander[44] after losing another[45]].

Uberkinger, France
Dec. 2, 1944

We moved to this location today, which is back near where we concluded the drive on Nov 25. Soon we jump off in another attack. Wonder who will go this next time.

Received word today that Sgt Porta[46] had died of his wounds. Doesn't seem possible that that big, lively, brave and smiling fellow could now be still and silent forever.

---

43  Cpl. Robert J. Fieldsteel, New York, N. Y., worked at Regtl Hq, later promoted to M/Sgt.

44  Co F has a new CO, Capt James F. Watkins. My unofficial list gives his street address as 309 Jefferson St., but omitted the town and state.

45  1st Lt. John M. Roberts, CO of Co F, New Haven, Conn., a replacement, with the Co at least since Oct. 1, hospitalized in Nov., recovered and returned Feb. 15, later promoted to Capt.

46  Sgt. Louis A. Porta, 3rd Bn Hq, Broderick, Calif., wounded, evacuated, died of wounds.

Last time I saw him, he was showing me pictures of his wife and baby, who live in California near the place Alta is now staying. He was going to give me their address so I could send it to Alta and let her write them. But that, like many other things that have been planned, was not to be.

Last time it was Christianson, Vaughts, [correct spelling - Vagts] McCormic, Porta, Gardner and others. Yes, I wonder who it will be this time.

The artillery [German] grows worse as we approach the Seigfried Line.

Plans have been made and orders already given for the attack in the morning. The troops will start moving well before dawn. The enemy has already been encountered. It seems every foot of ground must be fought for now.

* * *

And so, I will get what rest I can. This cold is wearing me down. I am not writing to Alta so often now, and to almost no one else. I have to force myself to scribble the few lines which keeps this record up to date. It is with great effort that I push myself to perform the necessary duties that are mine.

* * *

## SGT. LOUIS A. PORTA

*Sgt. Louis A. Porta was undoubtedly one of the greatest combat soldiers it was my privilege to know during the war. It may seem strange to many, that in all our contacts and experiences together, I never knew his first name. It is likely also that he never knew more of my name than Lt. Faubus. To us it was not strange. The military men of training and combat knew each other by titles and last names, or as "the oldtimer," or "that new man" as the soldier was known, whom Porta carried, wounded, into the room the night of the Rhyn-Marne Canal and Le Sanon River crossing at Somerviller.*

*In searching my records for more information on Porta, I find he is possibly listed at least four times in the mixed up roster of 320th members published after the war. His name and address is given as Louis Porta, 418 1/2 10th St., Sacramento, Calif., and then Louis A. Porta at the same address, then Louis A. Porta, 426 3rd St., Broderick, Calif. and Louis*

A. Porta, Box 371, at Broderick. I feel certain all these listings are for one and the same person.

At Camp Rucker, Alabama I trained Porta, along with the reconnaisance members of all the battalions, and the members of the Intelligence and Reconnaisance platoon of regimental headquarters company, in patrolling, reconnaisance and combat intelligence. This training along with his natural ability, qualified him to be of great assistance to all commanders in combat. Porta, then a private, did not do too well in the tests given by other officers. Like me, he did not think it necessary to describe or relate the obvious such as the correct military answer to the question, "What is the proper action to take when fired upon by the enemy?" The answer sought was "Take cover." The big fellow usually ignored such an answer as being completely obvious to anyone and was thinking about the proper action to be taken to get out of a situation and what to do farther along.

I never learned his background or ancestry and therefore never knew what led him to instinctively do the right thing when the chips were down. Anyway, for the most part he did know intuitively what to do in almost every situation and the rest he learned in a short time.

From my experience with him in training I was convinced he was a natural leader and would make an excellent combat soldier. As has already been related, I recommended him for promotion to sergeant then, which was not approved. My judgment was proven correct when, in less than a week in the battle lines before St. Lo, he had demonstrated his ability and received his promotion.

In rough, tough situations in combat, such as we encountered so often, I regarded Porta the equal of twenty ordinary men. In the face of the greatest danger and at great risk to himself, he seemed always to act quickly and accurately without regard to his own personal safety. How many close calls he had before finally receiving his fatal wounds only God would know, for I'm sure Porta lost count long before the end.

At the time of his death he was serving as S-2 under Col. Alexander on the 3rd Bn staff, a position which calls for the rank of first lieutenant. He had already been recommended for a battlefield commission which he would have shortly received if he had lived. He had already been decorat-

*ed for bravery a number of times and other recommendations were pending.*

*From my personal experience and observation, I can name many brave men, heroes of the front lines, tried and true in every way. But whenever any time or place such men are mentioned there are always two which immediately come to mind as outstanding, - Lt. Raymond W. Braffit of Massachusetts and Sgt. Louis A. Porta of California.*

\* \* \*

Uberkinger, France
Dec. 3, 1944

Made a trip back to Division Rear today, a round trip of a little more than 70 miles. A very cold and unpleasant journey (but much better of course than attacking through the mud and wet). While there, had an interview with Lt Col Williamson, the JA, who is a former prosecuting attorney from the southwestern edge of the Missouri Ozarks. His speech had the old familiar home town ring and it gave me a slight feeling of nostalgia to talk with him.

While at the personnel section, talking to Lt Sperl,[47] I encountered Capt Haire (Hare), [Henry H. Hare] who was returning to the regiment who will be up a little later. This mud, discomfort and danger seems to me to be a very shocking situation to which to come back after a rest in a nice hospital.

\* \* \*

I have learned that Lt Gilbertson has been reclassified and sent to Corps Hqs. There was nothing wrong with him, except he just couldn't "take it" anymore. He is very likely just as well physically as many men who have remained at the front.

Oh well, "C'est la Guerre."

\* \* \*

47  Lt. Frank X. Sperl, Pers Sec of Sv Co, Flushing, N. Y. Others with whom I visited on trips to personnel section at Div Rear Hq were, M/Sgt. Robert E. "Ted" Woods, Sv Co, Helena, Ark., and Capt. Gerard T. Armstrong, Baton Rouge, La., Personnel Officer in charge of the section.

## CHARLES W. BELL, VALENTINE, TEXAS

*1st Lt. Charles W. Bell, CO of Co A, personally led a surprise dawn attack across a flooded stream to take the town of Uberkinger. The 21-year old commander, one of the Regiment's greatest soldiers, worked in the icy stream helping to construct a footbridge. Once across and in the town his men knocked out or repulsed the counter-attacking tanks and half-tracks by firing bazookas and throwing gasoline-filled bottles.*

*Another example of the gallantry and daring of the small boyish officer occurred earlier on Sept. 24th when he was still a platoon leader. Misdirected fire from our own artillery began falling on hastily prepared positions of Co. A. Bell left his dugout and sprinted for the nearest radio 500 yards away across the area being shelled. Ten 240mm shells burst around him as he ran, and a fragment from one of them wounded him knocking him down. He was able to get up and dash on to the radio, where he succeeded in stopping the shelling.*

\* \* \*

## MY PROMOTION FROM GEN. PATTON

### RESTRICTED

### HEADQUARTERS
### THIRD UNITED STATES ARMY
APO 403

SPECIAL ORDERS
NUMBER 277                              1 December 1944

### —EXTRACT—

2. Following O this comd are temporarily promoted to gr indicated in AUS w/rank fr date of this order. (Auth: Par 3 Cir 90 Hq ETO US Army 17 Aug 1944):

### 1ST LT TO CAPT

Orval E. Faubus, Inf
John S. Foster, Inf
Milton Ginsburg, Inf
John M. Safley, FA (TD)
Clyde S. Smith, FA
Burr Sutter, Inf

### 2D LT TO 1ST LT

James L Corlett, FA
Charles V Litherland, Inf
Donald B Parish, Inf

By command of Lieutenant General PATTON:

HUGH J. GAFFEY,
Major General, U.S. Army,
Chief of Staff

OFFICIAL:

R. E. CUMMINGS,
Colonel, Adjutant General's Department
Adjutant General.

A TRUE EXTRACT COPY:

CHARLES L. FELDMAN
Captain, A.G.D.,
Asst. Adjutant General.

Uberkinger, France
Dec. 4, 1944

The S-1, Lt Ginsberg, placed in my hands today enough cases of courts martial to make a lawyer rich in the private practice of law. So I guess I'll not be doing much in the lulls of fighting except to work on them. Very unfortunate that we have to deal with such things in combat. But so long as there are human beings there will be human errors [and failures] and someone will be engaged in straightening them out.

Today Lt Ginsberg and myself received our promotions to Captains, and Lt Parish his promotion from 2nd to 1st Lt. The latter fellow was mighty pleased. When I think back, it was more gratifying to get that promotion than this one. I have never been too concerned about rank, but when Hitler and the Japs say "quits," then I'm going to be as happy as if I were young again.

The most gratifying aspect of my advance in grade was the fact that others seemed pleased at my good fortune, especially the enlisted men.

First to congratulate me; Maj McElroy, 2nd, Col Byrne. My first (and as yet only) set of captains bars [given to me by] a big strapping officer of the engineers, Capt Louis H. Johnson, Lueders, Texas.

* * *

Today, the 3rd Bn advanced quite successfully and took a number of towns. The 2nd was held up and pinned down all day, just after crossing a stream in its push toward a town. We are fighting SS troops today, Hitler's bad boys. Co K had ten PWs. They asked them about Hitler and if they were still for him. Four said, "yes" and "Heil Hitler." So only six ever got back to regtl PW point. I have not confirmed the story but it has been generally accepted.

Lt Cooper of TDs is back with us. He has had a twin brother killed in action in Africa, and another [brother] has been wounded in the war. [Cooper was also wounded] That makes three "purple hearts" in his family. "And that's enough," says Lt Cooper, "for one family."

[A casualty[48] not mentioned in the Journal].


Heckenransback, France
Dec. 6, 1944

Time: 1220:

We spent the night in this little battered, manure-smeared town. It is like all the others through this section, the grey, colorless peasants clumping about in their mud-covered wooden "sabots."

Some gather their household and personal belongings, as much as possible, and move to the cellar or to a neighbor's house to make room for our CP establishment. The manure piles from the barns, mixed with straw, are always piled in front of the combination barns and houses and always steaming in the ever-present dampness and rain. Still no outside clothes lines because garments would never dry hanging outside.

We are moving up again now. Our troops, with the 134th on our left, are looking across the Saar into Germany.

So we're moving again.

---

48  1st Lt. Corbitt B. Rushing, Co F, Baltimore, Md., a replacement, listed LWA Dec. 4, did not return.

[Hamback, France]
December 7, 1944

Time: 0045

We are now set up in the town of Hamback. The building we found for a CP is a very fine one; must have been rather prosperous occupants. We set up a "liaison room" in the bath. We installed a telephone as is our custom, so that visiting officers and junior officers have a place to stay without cluttering up the operations room.

From the upstairs window there is a view of the green rolling country that is actually beautiful in spite of the war scars. Most of the country is open, carpeted with meadow or fresh winter-resistant small grain. From a high eminence can be seen a number of towns connected by the net work of roads. Just to the east is the Saar River Valley, which we will soon cross.

I know this section will be (and has been) truly beautiful, when all the dead horses, cows, etc. have been removed; the craters filled, the bridges rebuilt, the roadway again lined with grass, and the shrapnel scars on the trees have healed. One certainly gets tired of looking at the muck and the mire, the death and destruction.

*  *  *

All evening and tonight, the big guns in the low draw near by have been speaking in thunderous tones as they hurl their shells across the Saar into the enemy positions.

Yesterday as we drove along the muddy road we could see, off to the north, a town or city burning, with high columns of smoke and great, leaping flames.

*  *  *

Tonight, after the darkness gathered, we had about three hours of leisure and for a time subdued our troubles in a card game. Participating were myself, Lt Sperl, Lt Parish, Lt Quillen, Lt Silverman, Capt Bonham and Capt Hare. Lt Cooper, the TD officer, was on a mission. The movement of TDs and the work of engineers is very often done at night while the darkness prevents enemy observation. Tonight was Lt Silverman's first game and he certainly did not have beginner's luck.

*  *  *

We are encountering a great deal of mines now. Today, while "sweeping" a road, Lt Botton[49] lost three of his men, one killed instantly and two injured. We heard one of the injured died but this not confirmed. The soldier killed, a big husky fine-looking fellow, picked up a mine that was booby-trapped. The tired grey eyes of the slight young Botton have looked upon many such tragedies. He has had as many close calls as most officers who lead rifle troops.

*　*　*

Pvt Bock[50] is on duty with me tonight. Our Kraut radio has the front broken, but still operates. We are getting some good German music now. Pity all their [German] talents could not have been directed into useful and worthwhile channels. I think I'd better get a little rest as I have some work that must be done tomorrow.

*　*　*

Heard that Capt Brochu[51] returned to duty today. Lt Sperl is here to get the list of 20 men and one officer who can go to the states on 30 day furlough [rehabilitation.] My God! What a hope! What a change for the men in the lines. To be eligible, a soldier must have been wounded twice and have been decorated for bravery.

Wiesviller, France
Dec. 15, 1944

From our CP at Hamback the group moved to Siltzheim, leaving me behind with Sv Co to investigate 27 courts martial charges. First time I had ever been behind the regtl CP during an action. That work certainly wore me down. I was interviewing the 27 accused men, many stories of hardship, heartbreak and suffering. I have just about concluded the investigation now, and have recommended as much leniency as I can safely justify.

There at Hamback I spent two nights with Charley Glatzer, "Red Cross Charlie," of Cleveland, Ohio. He is cer-

---

49　1st Lt. Kenneth I. Botton, AT Co, New Brunswick, N. J., an original with the outfit all the way.

50　Pvt. Bach had relatives in Germany, understood the language, and sometimes translated portions of the radio programs for me.

51　Capt. Brochu had returned when he could have remained away longer.

tainly a wonderful guy. While at Siltzheim at Capt Heil's CP, I stayed one night with Lt Brown[52] (hit at Mortain), Lt Charley [G.] Bell[53] of G Co (hit first day at St. Lo) and others returning to the unit. There were Lt Kohler,[54] Lt Rowe[55] and Lt Woods[56] also. I was glad to see them again but sorry to see them here. One of them said Lt Trask had gone to the States which I hope is true. I heard that he might return to duty soon.

The young Lt Charles [W.] Bell[57] of Co A has finally been evacuated. A shell hit too close and the concussion was too much.

Capt Brochu is not doing so well. He has been transferred to Sv Co as assistant to Maj Hughes.

Sgt Wilber Curry,[58] my old friend of Co F, was killed. He was one of the few who fell the day before we crossed the Saar River. Two of our Bns are in Germany tonight. The first troops crossed the border day before yesterday, Dec. 13, 1944.

In the Saar River crossing, one of our Bns, the 2nd, caught the Krauts asleep and really slaughtered a bunch of them. Our troops crossed in the darkness of early morning and caught them before they had awakened. [They were not attacked in their sleep. They were caught unawares before they had time to awaken and organize.]

\* \* \*

I saw our contingent of 20 EM, among whom are Sgt Koch, and one officer, Lt Jeff Wright,[59] off on their way to

---

52 1st Lt. Kenneth H. Brown, Co B then to Co A, Puente, Calif., an original, out with wounds for four months, returning to duty.

53 1st Lt. Charles G. Bell, Co G, Binghamton, N. Y., original, out for five months with wounds received the first day at St. Lo, returning to duty.

54 Richard H. Koeller, Co I, La Crosse, Wisc., a replacement, Ft. Benning classmate, returning to duty after wounds.

55 2nd Lt. Travis R. Rowe, Co M, address unknown, an original, returning to duty after wounds.

56 1st Lt. James R. F. Woods, Co M, Palo Alto, Calif., an original, returning to duty after wounds.

57 1st Lt. Charles W. Bell, Co A, Valentine, Texas, an original, evacuated as sick, shell concussion, Dec. 7, did not return.

58 Sgt. Wilbur Curry, Co F, Troy, Ohio, friend since Camp Rucker, listed KIA about Dec. 10. He had been wounded previously on Nov. 9.

59 1st Lt. Jeff D. Wright, Co B, address unknown, a replacement.

the States on 30-day furloughs. I was so glad of some one's good fortune. But the thought of it . . . home . . . with comfort and tenderness and loving kindness, far away from the harshness, death and filth of the battle field. The phrase, "From death unto life," kept going over and over in my mind, and that is just what it meant for some of them. Even by now some of them would likely have been casualties.

\* \* \*

There are many tales of heroism of the last few days. Lt Shamhart, plat ldr of the engrs, was killed. One of his men was badly wounded by an S-mine while seeking shelter from arty and mortar fire. He was bleeding badly and the lieut dashed out to get him, tripped another mine and was killed.

\* \* \*

Unusual: The Germans laid a big mortar shell into the muzzle of one of our 60s and blew it to pieces.

Back at Gremercy Forest, when the little youthful Arthur Liagre[60] and his asst gunner were fighting off a Kraut assault after their MG had jammed, Liagre with his pistol and the asst gunner with his carbine, a bullet fired by the Germans entered the muzzle of the carbine.

\* \* \*

Most amusing incident of the past two days, listening to Lt Cooper, the TD officer, tell stories of the colored folks in the South (Lt Scott Cooper, Henderson, NC). Perhaps the busiest man around the CP and elsewhere has been the engineer captain, Fred Waters, son of a regular army officer "from everywhere" as he says. Capt Zurman [tank commander] of Stanford, Conn. is also with us again.

\* \* \*

Had a card from Margaret Cull with the return address "Margaret and Gary Brent Cull." The card was beautiful with a touching sentiment and there were also two pictures of a very cute little boy who will never see his daddy.

\* \* \*

I am so tired, I had to force myself to write this. Lt Quillen and myself are just about "under the weather." I

---

60  Sgt. Arthur Liagre, Co F, Detroit, Mich., a friend since activation of the 320th.

must stop and get some rest, for tomorrow (great, good fortune) I go to Div Rear CP for a trip to Paris and a week's school there as Information and Education officer. Glatzer says it will be a wonderful trip and has given me the address of a French friend of his who will act as guide for me should I have time to "sight see."

Lt Clark is back with us again. He assumed his former duties of liaison officer and is doing fine. He is unrolling bed roll now on the dirty floor where we sleep.

The Krauts have shelled our town each night but no hits on us.

Two days now have been generally clear and free from rain, most unusual weather. I don't think the weather could have possibly been worse for an offensive.

\* \* \*

Outside the winter lightning [flashes of the big guns] flickers along the horizon, the near flashes gleaming on objects nearby. The winter thunder [the sound of their explosions] booms and crashes, and goes echoing through the streets of the towns, out over the fields and down the valleys of this German borderland. We are pushing into Germany, into the outposts of the Seigfried line.

Now I must stop for I have grown very tired (as Lt Cooper says) "of this tuable (terrible) wah (war) in this fah away land."

\* \* \*

## IN THIS FARAWAY LAND

*Lt Scott Cooper, of Henderson, N.C., the brave, co-operative commander of the TDs attached to our unit, became a warm friend. As liaison and general trouble shooter for the 320th, ofttimes on duty when others slept, I dealt more often than my fellow officers with the commanders of attached forces and liaison officers from other units. I learned to like and admire the pleasant, affable Cooper. We often visited at odd moments when opportunity afforded. He had a pronounced southern accent and could imitate to perfection, President Roosevelt. His imitation of the president went, "Ah hates wa-ah! Eleanah hates wa-ah! We all hate wa-ah!"*

*He often said to me, many times late at night as he came in from some difficult, dangerous mission, "Judge, Ahm*

*awfully tiad, of this tuable wah, in this fah away land."*
*(I'm awfully tired of this terrible war in this faraway land)*
The memory of Cooper's statement suggested the title
for this book.

* * *

## CASUALTIES

During the period of Dec 8th to 15th the following officer casualties occurred which, except for one, terminated their
services with the Regiment.

Capt Carl H. Beasley, CO of Co C, Hellarm, Pa., a replacement, with the company as far back as Aug. 14, evacuated as sick Dec. 7, did not return; 1st Lt Aleck F. C. Greene,
Co C, Laramie, Wyo., a replacement, probably took command
for a time as the company had now lost five officers since
the push began on Nov. 8th, later returned to duty; 2nd Lt
Douglas H. Nichols, Co A, Newark, N.J. a replacement, listed KIA Dec. 8th; 1st Lt Samuel Pascal, Hq Co of 1st Bn,
Pittsburgh, Pa., a replacement, listed LWA Dec. 9, did not
return; 1st Lt William Dickterenko, Co C, Roderfield, W. Va.,
a replacement, listed LIA Dec. 9, did not return; 1st Lt
Wybras S. Delune (or Delaune), Co F, Morgan City, La., a
replacement, listed LWA Dec. 9, did not return; 1st Lt Warren E. Wilke, Co I, Batavia, Ill., a replacement, listed DOW
Dec. 14th.

* * *

## CROSSING OF THE SAAR

In crossing the Saar River and Canal, where all bridges
had been blown, Sgt Clyde V. Manning of Oceania, Calif.,
protected the engineers as they put in a treadway in the 2nd
Bn sector, from the fire of Germans entrenched on the opposite hillside. He was reported to have fired for an hour
and a half, mowing down the enemy troops as they tried to
climb out of the upper ends of the trenches. When it was
all over only about 40 Germans remained who could surrender and some of them were wounded.

Capt. Charles F. Guilford of Dearborn, Mich., Co. B
Commander, then led his troops forward to expand their
narrow bridgehead. The Nazis launched a counterattack led
by two tanks and 10 half-tracks, and Guilford was forced to
withdraw his men to the protection of the river bank. He

then went forward 300 yards to establish an OP accompanied by his communications sergeant, Edward H. Doster of the Bronx, N.Y. From the OP they directed artillery fire on the German armor, breaking up the attack.

* * *

## LT JOHN DAVIS AT SAAREGUEMINES

The city of Saareguemines is split by the Saar River. The 134th drove through a maze of trenches and pillboxes to the outskirts of the western half. Lt Davis led a night patrol of Co G, 134th, into the city, captured an 88 intact, killed eight enemy troops and made such a commotion that the Germans withdrew across the river. Other elements of the regiment entered the city as the 320th was pushing seven miles through the Saareguemines Forest. By Dec. 7th Patton's forces held the entire west bank of the Saar River.

* * *

John Davis, combat veteran of the 35th Division, after returning home, served two terms as governor of North Dakota, and was narrowly defeated in a race for the U.S. Senate. Later he served as National Commander of the American Legion.

## CAPTURED MATERIAL IN SAAREGUEMINES

A G-2 report compiled by Lieutenant Colonel John T. Hoyne showed that the 35th had captured the following equipment in Sarreguemines:

| | | | |
|---|---|---|---|
| Machine guns | 234 | 75mm SP assault guns | 2 |
| Rifles | 1,132 | 88mm SP assault guns | 6 |
| Mortars | 29 | 40mm guns | 2 |
| Radios | 5 | Nebelwerfers | 2 |
| Bazookas | 112 | Grenades | 2,150 |
| Pistols | 208 | 88mm AT guns | 3 |
| Tank Mk VI | 1 | Command car | 1 |
| Vehicles | 4 | Mines (Misc.) | 18 |
| Motorcycles | 6 | Vehicles (Misc.) | 11 |
| Trailer (small) | 1 | Ordnance Shop (complete) | 1 |
| 20mm guns | 10 | Power Shovel | 1 |
| AT guns | 2 | Volkswagons | 3 |
| Burp guns | 134 | Half-tracks | 6 |

| AMMUNITION | Rounds | Artillery _____ | 6,530 |
| Small arms _____ | 50,500 | Bazooka _____ | 1,500 |

*—From 35th Division History*

\* \* \*

## ENGINEERS PERFORM AT SAAR CROSSING

*Lt Col Botchin's 60th Engineers performed gallantly at the crossing of the Saar. First Lt John S. Parker's Co A, repaired a railroad bridge for crossing of 134th foot troops. Other engineers supplied assault boats for the crossing of 1st and 2nd Bns. of the 320th. With a bridgehead of infantry for protection and a smokescreen laid by the 81st Chemical Smoke Generating Co., the combat engineers worked without stopping for 48 hours, first putting a treadway bridge over the canal and then two artillery bridges over the waterways.*

*Tanks, TDs and vehicles loaded with supplies rushed across to the footsoldiers. Then in attacks against fierce resistance, the 35th pushed to the swift Blies River, the last barrier to German soil. In the advance, nearly a thousand Russian, Polish and Anti-Facist Italian PWs were freed and an airfield captured.*

*Banner headlines in the States and Allied countries announced that Patton's Third Army had breached the line of the Saar and was ready to push into the Fatherland.*

\* \* \*

## INVESTIGATION OF THE DEFECTION

*From Dec. 7 to Dec. 15, a period of 10 days, only two entries were made in the Journal. Most of that time I was busily engaged in the investigation of 27 courts martial cases of alleged defections in the ranks of one company. (See Dec. 15 entry) It was necessary to interview each of the accused as well as numerous witnesses. All statements had then to be typed for signatures and the signatures obtained. To the completed statements in each case were added my review of the testimony and recommendation as to possible courses of action. The file was then placed in the hands of the Colonel for his review and afterward forwarded to higher headquarters for the final decision on action to be taken. The task required several days with hours and hours of steady work from early morning to late at night until it was finished.*

The alleged defections occurred, or began, in the dark night of Nov 7-8 in the initial jump-off of the Alsace-Lorraine campaign. According to much of the testimony the men of this particular company, or a large number of them, were left standing for some time, leaderless, in the darkness in an open area between two woods. They had advanced from one woods and were awaiting H-hour to attack the enemy in the next. The rain was pelting down and the temperature wavered just above and below the freezing point. There was no place to sit down and little opportunity to take cover as the whole earth was a sea of mud and water. The solders were becoming wet and miserable. To the front the enemy guns were flashing from the Stygian blackness, shells were passing overhead and the troops were within range of enemy small arms fire. However no casualties from enemy action were reported in the group at the time.

Finally in the absence of any direction or encouragement, except from some non-commissioned officers who were equally confused, some of the soldiers, seeking shelter, began to fall back to the woods from which they had advanced. Others followed. If all had remained there, as some did, they might later have been found by their first sergeant and company officers, who reportedly searched in the woods for those absent when the hour of attack came. By that time the accused soldiers had left the forest and withdrawn still farther, finding refuge in the buildings of the towns in the rear.

Once having reached a place of comfort and safety with no one to urge them back to duty, the defectors remained away from their company until the hard fighting of the 5-day battle was over. Later on in the campaign some of the same soldiers, having skulked away from the dangers and hardships of the front during this attack, "bugged-out" again during the next fierce battle in which their unit participated beginning on Nov. 18th.

Such a situation is comparable to a frightened boy traveling along a dim road at night past dark woods and cemeteries, beset by fear of dangers on every hand. The faster the scared boy walks, the faster he wants to go. Finally, unless the fear is controlled, the boy, in panic, will break into headlong flight which does not end until he reaches a place of safety. Having once run from danger, real or imagined, the frightened youth will flee again when next faced with the same conditions. The best and almost the only solution to such a situation, is to control the fear when it is first faced. This the alleged defectors had failed to do.

A few of the defectors, early replacements, had been good soldiers. Two of the accused had been members of a squad which, except for them and one other soldier, was wiped out at Mortain. However most of them were more recent replacements not yet inured to the hardships and dangers of battle.

The temporary lack of direction during a critical period when faced with the fearsome flashes and explosions of the enemy guns in the lonely blackness, coupled with the extreme discomfort of the terrible weather conditions, were the mitigating circumstances to be weighed against the severe transgressions the defectors had committed. Still, it had to be remembered, approximately 85% of their comrades in the same company faced the same or comparable circumstances, went forward into the battle, and remained at their posts of duty. The same was true of the men of the other companies, who endured the same or similar hardships and dangers without defection.

At the time of the investigation, some of the accused were back in the lines doing their duty with their company. These were permitted to continue with only light punishment inflicted by a special court. Others willing to return were permitted to do so and suffered only slightly greater punishment. Some of the greatest offenders faced a general court with power to impose the most severe penalties. However, even the worst of the defectors, I learned later, because of the mitigating circumstances in this particular incident, got off with comparatively light punishment as compared to the extreme penalties that could have been inflicted.

It was with a feeling of relief that I finished the investigation, although later I was a witness in some of the trials. To me the inquiry was more difficult than duty with the advancing troops. Coupled with my illness the interrogations brought on a depression which was difficult to overcome.

Even before the inquiry began I had taken on a ghostlike apperance, and had lost appetite and weight. I had seen the same sickly condition develop in others, both men and officers. Sometimes those so afflicted would recover and go on. Often they could not, in which case they were evacuated.

*After hospitalization some recovered and came back to the front lines, while others never returned.*

\* \* \*

## LESSON OF THE DEFECTION

*There is a theory that two different lights, set in the lamps of justice and properly tended, will guide any orzanization to success and greatness. One light is the bright, white beacon of reward before; the other is the dull red warning of stress behind. The reward must be carefully evaluated and justly bestowed, the stress carefully controlled and properly administered. The first light is to beckon men to the proper achievement of deserved aspirations and just ambitions; the second is to restrain men in the improper acquisition of undeserved comforts and ill-gotten gains.*

*To attain success, reward is used to encourage men in the application of strength and diligence; to avoid failure, stress is used to restrain men in the indulgence of weakness and idleness. The bright gleam says this is the right road, and lights the way forward; the dull glow says this is the wrong way, and darkens the road backward. One beckons eternally, the other forbids always.*

*Without rewards in war, as honor for self, victory over the enemy, the respect of comrades, a clear conscience, and praise and reward by authority for duty properly performed, there would be no incentive to face great danger and remain bravely true to comrades and country. Without penalties, as disgrace for self, defeat by the enemy, the scorn of comrades, a clouded conscience, and condemnation and punishment by authority for duty failed, there would be no restraint on flight from danger and the cowardly betrayal of both comrades and country. Without praise and reward for those who go forward, and condemnation and punishment for those who withdraw, the infection of weakness spreads, corrupting the whole.*

*No matter how justified the actions of the defectors might appear under the circumstances in this particular case, punishment was absolutely necessary. They had shown weakness and cowardice and hidden in places of safety away from their posts of duty, while their comrades with strength and courage had borne the brunt of the battle at their appointed places of danger. Had those who yielded to weakness, even*

*under extremely adverse circumstances, escaped punishment,
the word of such escape would have spread through the
ranks. Other troops, all with varying degrees of weakness,
would have concluded that deserved credit and earned reward for the performance of duty, had been replaced with
undeserved benefits and unearned gains for dereliction of
duty. Discipline and pride, the basis and spirit of any military unit, would have been corrupted and destroyed. No military organization worthy of the name would have remained.
Never again would the company have advanced in the face
of great danger, and never again by its men would a victory
have been won.*

## PATTON USED REWARD AND PENALTY

*Gen Patton must have understood and used the two-light
theory. Constantly he searched among his troops for the virtues of strength, merit and ability. Whenever he found those
qualities, he was quick to promote and otherwise reward the
men who possessed them. At the same time, if, in his search
for virtues, he discovered cowardice, selfishness and maling-
ering, he was equally quick to condemn and punish those who
showed such defects. The same could be said, with varying
degrees of emphasis, of other commanders, but Patton somehow got his points over better with the troops. His flair for
the dramatic, which got him publicity, gained for his troops
the credit which they deserved.*

*Under Patton's command, when we were given a task
and performed well, we had full confidence our performance
would be noted and the deserved credit would be received.
If our performance was unusual and spectacular success attained, there would be, we felt, recognition and any appropriate reward he could grant. At the same time if, through
fault of our own, we failed, or success was less than it should
have been, we knew we would catch hell. Equally important,
knowing we deserved punishment, we would attribute no in-
justice to him who inflicted it.*

*As a commander Patton wanted to be a winner. As sold-
iers we wanted to win the war. So, we had a mutual purpose.
To win the war, - "get it over with and go home" - we
knew we had to do battle and win victories over the enemy.
We couldn't do battle and overcome the foe if there were too
many who skulked away to places of safety just when they*

*were needed most. Therefore we liked Patton's glorification
of the courageous men of combat, and his condemnation of
those who showed the white feather.*

*Patton knew the great value of reward for merit and
achievement, and the unavoidable necessity of punishment
for weakness and failure. Through the calculated use of personal drama and the deliberate promulgation of certain
policies, he kept constantly ahead of his troops the bright
gleam of hope for the rewards of success, and behind them
always the dull glow of fear of the consequences of failure.*

*If Patton had no profound understanding of what moves
men to greatness, or of what keeps them from low failure;
if his personal dramatics were not intentional nor his policies deliberate, then, it must be admitted, his natural personal traits and instinctive actions achieved the same results.
If he knew and understood, he was a warrior trained; if he
knew not, a leader born. Perhaps he was both.*

*Whether Patton's personal traits and military methods
were deliberate or instinctive, it matters not. In any event,
his traits and methods instilled into the men under his command a higher spirit and a greater drive, which made the
Third Army the greatest offensive force on the Western
Front. His army may have been the best in the world. Certainly it was superior to any force it faced in battle. And
that degree of greatness by which the Third Army possibly
excelled all others, came from one source alone, - the personality, the spirit, the figure of Gen George S. Patton.*

## A BRIDGEHEAD IN THE FATHERLAND

*In the blackness of night, Dec. 12, 1944, at 0100 hours,
four GIs of Co K, 137th, paddled softly in a small boat across
the Blies River toward the German shore. When the prow
touched the soft bank, the first 35th man to set foot on Nazi
homeland jumped ashore. He was 1st Lt. Clarence Sprague,
Catskill, N.Y., accompanied by Pfc. Richard Iles, Pittsburgh,
Pa., Pfc. Charles Golumbek, Newark, N.J., and Pvt. John
Friday, Madison, Wisc. They reconnoitered for several hours
and quietly returned.*

*On the afternoon of Dec. 12, following the seizure of
Bliesbruck, two B Company men of the 320th, S/Sgt Elvin
C. Hammonds of Clinton, Mo. and James W. Johnson of
Clifton, W. Va., forded the Blies River and walked on to*

cross the German border, thus becoming the first 320th infantrymen to step on the "sacred soil" of the Fatherland.

Co C of the 134th led by S/Sgt Thomas Wese, Beverly, W. Va., and seven men from the 60th Engineers were the first to stay and fight, capturing 65 Nazis. A picked Nazi guard battalion opposed the crossing under orders to die before allowing Americans to remain on German soil. More elements of the 134th re-enforced the bridgehead and, under Capt. William Denny, held on. Casualties were high. All officers of Co. B were lost except one.

Meanwhile 3rd Bn of 320th raced to Bliesbruck, while 1st Bn, 320th, spanned the Blies in a surprise attack and took Hill 512. A solid wall of German resistance was then met which was broken by the charge of the 654th TD Bn and the 737th Tank Bn. Germans were annihilated in cellar strongholds of farms and cities as town after town fell in the enlarging bridgehead on German soil. Then the Division was ordered to hold and consolidate. Its relief began one day later by the 87th and 44th Inf. Divs, and was effected on Dec. 20-21.

There was more important work for the battle-wise 35th. Runstedt's winter offensive in the Ardennes had made alarming progress. Gen Patton, with approval of the High Command, was marshalling his best divisions to throw against the southern flank of the last great Nazi drive.

\* \* \*

## TO I & E SCHOOL AT PARIS

With a jeep and driver I left the 320th Headquarters in the forenoon of Dec. 16, reaching Nancy that day where I spent the night with troops of the Regimental Personnel Section. It took most of the next day, driving in the open jeep in the bitter cold, to reach Paris. We found the facilities where the 6-day Information and Education (I&E) School was being conducted and checked into our quarters about 1600 (4 p.m.).

\* \* \*

Paris, France
Dec. 19, 1944

Tonight I am here in my quarters in the Belgian Building of "Cite Unniversitaire." Two days of school are finished. Very interesting, much of it group discussion during which one hears some good comments and always gets some off color stuff from any crack pots who may be in the crowd. The main purpose is to get us oriented and properly prepared to get the education program working when the war ends. Many of the units can use the program to a certain extent now. But there is very little, if anything, that can be done for the Infantry until the war ends. You cannot teach, lecture, or instruct in the battle lines. Besides that, a man engaged in a life and death struggle has no thought for anything but his own immediate problems.

\* \* \*

I stayed all night in Nancy on 16th with my good friend, Capt Arstrong. Lt Sperl and myself sought a bath, my first since Nov 7. The bath house was closed when we arrived, and Lt Sperl, who parleyvoos the language within limits, at first got a "no." But some compassionate woman took one look at me and indicated they would accomodate us.

After we were in the bath, each in a separate tub in the same room, Sperl, more as a jest, called for one of them to wash my back and give me a shampoo. He was having quite a joke out of the affair, giving directions and carrying on a conversation which I knew little or nothing about. I was so tired I didn't care what was going on except that the warm water felt heavenly and I was really quite grateful that he did get someone to shampoo my hair and scrub my back. The lady who came in was a kind, motherly woman and well old enough to be my mother. Sperl was having a lot of fun but it would not have made any difference to me if it had been Heddy Lamar. Then another nice one came by and he got her to work on him, and finally, as they were ready to close, another came and stood in the open door and watched the proceedings. It amuses now to think of the incident (I was too tired then). I know this would sound very strange to most Americans but it is a not unusual French custom in which they see nothing strange whatever, and is no more immoral [to them] than putting the children to bed at home.

\* \* \*

We arrived in Paris in afternoon of 17th and found our way without difficulty to the City University, driving the whole distance in open jeep with Pvt White (of Kansas). Major Lloyd L. Paynter, [Omaha, Nebr.,] also of the 35th

Div, had arrived earlier and had already been assigned quarters for the two of us. After registration, I lay down on my bunk, the softest in many weary days. I fell asleep, missed supper, and so undressed and continued my rest sleeping from four (1600) in the afternoon until 0730 next morning. Other arrivals hurried out to see what attractions the "City Beautiful" had to offer.

After such a night's rest and a day of comfort in the class room, I consented to accompany Major Paynter to the town. We are some 10 or 12 miles from the heart of the metropolis. Well, riding the "Metro," the train or trolley transportation system of the city, was certainly some experience. Until you catch on to the way the system works, it is very confusing, and I must confess I didn't know most of the time which way I was going. I was still too tired to react to most things intelligently. I just followed the major. He speaks French, but, either not too well or his accent is bad. Most of the Frenchmen seemed to have difficulty understanding.

We didn't see much. We spent most of the time battling the "metro" system and the crowds. I thought the buses and trains of America were crowded before I left the States, but never like the "metro." Many times they packed in like sardines and that isn't a shade exaggerated. After they had crowded as closely as possible, other passengers shoved and pushed them tighter and closer to make room for more. When certain ones wanted to dismount, whole segments or sections moved until they untangled at the door. A frail person would actually be in danger of injury. The trains run swiftly and halt only briefly. All stations are underground and most of the track. I think it is classed as a subway. The major and I had difficulty finding our way out of some of them.

Another interesting feature of the city, we could not help note, were the prostitutes, who accosted us everywhere we went. Some were quite attractive, others not so good. They worked singly and in pairs and once there were three together. Usually the major talked to them as a matter of curiosity and would then tell me what they said. However they can all speak enough English [to indicate quite clearly their wishes] (the Americans have been here long enough for that). Prices ranged from 200 to 1,000 francs.

Once we were hurrying along the sidewalk through the crowds and someone brushed into me and a voice said, "Hullo,

Baby." I discovered a very nice looking, plump brunette walking beside me. "Oh, you can speak English," I said. She could she indicated and said something else I didn't catch. "How much English can you speak?" I asked. "Three hundred francs," was the reply.

Charley Glatzer and the others at the CP will get a great kick out of that one.

\* \* \*

I haven't yet seen the city during day-light. That I must do if I have to cut a class or stay even a day longer.

There are many beautiful women in Paris, but at night it is difficult for a stranger to tell the ordinary people from the ones mentioned before. Perhaps in day-light the prostitutes won't appear quite so numerous. They are interesting as a part of humanity and always present factor of war conditions, and are a part of the tragedy of war and bad economic conditions. Like war, I think prostitution can be prevented by sane and sensible planning.

\* \* \*

The German counterattack is somewhat alarming. [the Ardennes offensive] Perhaps it is a harbinger of the end, as was the last German thrust in World War I: perhaps not.

I know the comfort here, the touch of civilization, the recalling of ideas and learning, is in such great contrast with what I left at the front, that the difference is incomprehensible. The return to combat will be hard indeed.

Paris, France
Dec. 21, 1944

Suffering from a severe cold. Last night Major Paynter urged me off to the city to see a show with him as he had already secured tickets and had transportation in his command car. We saw the "Folies Bergeres," a variety show, some numbers of great beauty and others of hilarious comedy. The dialogue was in French but, as the numbers had a great deal of pantomine, they were easy to understand. Some of the scenes had such beauty as I have never seen on the American stage, and I do not refer to those of the lovely women almost in the nude.

However my brief glimpse of Paris (so far) has certainly confirmed its reputation for beautiful women.

Today, during our one half-holiday from studies, I spent the entire time going to hospital for an X-ray of my chest, ordered by the doctor this morning.

After my return just at nightfall, I got some dough-nuts and coffee at the Red Cross room (missed all my meals today) and then to try to forget my misery, I sat through the movie in the class-room building. There were scenes of home life, a darling baby, and the soft voices of women that could be understood. Made me very lonely at times . . . it has been, so long out there in the slimy mud, with the stinking manure piles in the damp, wrecked villages, and the smell of dead cows and horses . . . and dead men, . . . and with the road ahead looking just as long and difficult as the one behind.

And so to keep from thinking, in my loneliness now, of the boys out there, . . . those who are forever gone, . . . and those who are to go; and to keep from thinking of the tender, little, gentle hands of my little boy, and others waiting for me far across the cold dark waters, I will take my sleeping medicine and seek oblivion and rest.

\* \* \*

The German Wermacht pushes on tonight, as yet unchecked. From their bloody tracks in the sticky mud will spring many tears and heartaches for loved ones of those who died as they sought to stop them. In spite of the blanket of security silence, we know casualties are running heavy.

\* \* \*

This would not be considered by many as a very happy night in Paris. And it is not, but illness cloys all pleasures.

Paris, France
Dec. 22, 1944

Even more ill today than before, so only a few brief sentences.

The German counterattack must be of alarming proportions, as all military personnel of this area have been ordered to remain in billets from 2000 to 0600. So, no one is out tonight which wouldn't have made any difference to me anyway. Everywhere the MPs and French authorities are checking everyone. The Major and I went down to the clinic and had to show our identification cards upon re-entering the grounds. A great deal of military traffic is pouring by outside . . . re-enforcements I presume, streaming north to check, to counterdrive.

* * *

Wonder which of my comrades have fallen or been hit in the last few days since I left. One of my class mates saw Lt Kuh in town but I did not get to go see him.

* * *

*When I returned to the 320th on Christmas Day, the following officers had been finally lost. Others had been evvacuated for illness or wounds who would return.*

*1st Lt. Edward J. Collins, Co K, Gaffney, S.C., a replacement, listed SWA Dec. 16, did not return; 2nd Lt. Robert J. Kuehn, Co K, Sturgeon Bay, Wisc., a replacement, listed KIA Dec. 16; 2nd Lt. Eugene M. Zeilanski (or Zielanski), Co B, Rochester, Minn., a replacement, listed LWA Dec. 17, did not return; 2nd Lt. William L. Mosely or (Moseley) Jr., Co G, address unknown, a replacement, evacuated as sick Dec. 21, did not return; 2nd Lt. Travis R. Rowe, Co M, address unknown, an original recently returned from hospital, evacuated as sick Dec. 23, did not return.*

* * *

From The<br>
MADISON COUNTY RECORD<br>
Jan. 4, 1945

CAPT. ORVAL E. FAUBUS'<br>
CHRISTMAS LETTER

With the Third Army,<br>
Dec. 25, 1944

This Christmas in embattled Europe will not be remembered long by some, for their memories will die with them. But for us who survive it can never be forgotten. The weather is clear, very unusual as compared to that of the past several weeks, and when I look at the far distant stars through the pale moonlight, it brings to mind the line from the Christmas carol, "It came upon a midnight clear."

It is very cold now in this war-scarred land. Today as I drove down the Moselle Valley to rejoin the unit after a brief absence, the children were skating on the frozen ponds and canals. The bleak and frozen landscape is covered with a light blanket of snow, which somewhat softened the battle scars on the buildings, the trees, and the countryside. The bridges were tumbled into the cold running river, every span blasted into crumbling ruins. The sun was shining as I traversed the winding road into the great fortress city of Metz, but it seemed only to accentuate the chill which gripped the whole region into seeming immobility. It was cold, cold as I drove along in the open jeep, and I could not help thinking that those who fall in the fighting now cannot go long unattended if they are to live.

My regiment (and division) was in Germany across the Saar River after fighting all the way across the disputed provinces of Alsace-Lorraine from near Nancy. That was the toughest campaign yet for us. The enemy was no more numerous, nor did they fight better, but the weather was so bad (as you have probably learned from the news). The enemy used extensive demolitions; every bridge was blown; the roads were cratered; there were road blocks and ditches, and many, many areas sown with mines and booby traps. There were some new mines made of glass and plastics which our detectors would not pick up, and we lost men because of them. And there were the ever-present, all-prevailing rain and mist; there were flooded areas; and mixed with the endless vistas of mud, mud, sticky, clinging, sloppy mud, were the dead, stinking cows and horses, village manure piles, the wrecked vehicles, until my soul has become sick of the sight, the smell and the memory.

Finally at long, long last, we were pulled from the line for a rest. Then the big show springs up to the north of us, and - we move tomorrow. So perhaps soon you shall hear of us in a new country.

It was on the banks of the Saar that I received the letter from W. H. Fritts of Thorney telling me of the death of his son, Pfc. Hugh Fritts. I have written of him several times before as we had been in the 35th Infantry Division since we both joined it in California in February, 1943. Before hearing from Mr. Fritts I had two letters returned to me, which I had written to Hugh, marked "deceased," so I knew that he was gone. He fell in the battle for the Moselle bridgehead when Patton's troops were the first to cross that stream in early September. He was one of the finest boys I have ever known and a brave and good soldier.

I have written but very little for some time. I have been about half-sick, half-well, caused by the miserable climate. Today I received several letters and two Christmas packages which were the best gifts I could have wished for under the circumstances. Will you who have so kindly written please accept this line, and my apologies for not answering soon.

Several have asked me, so I will tell you, Alta's middle name is Moselle. It was that region south of Nancy that I mentioned as being the most beautiful of any through which we had fought. But that was in the autumn when the leaves were just coloring, when the plums were ripe and the grapes hung in purple clusters on the vine.

It was just at the close of September that we ran out of gasoline and artillery ammunition. I am convinced, as is every soldier and officer with whom I have discussed the matter, that had this not occurred, the war would have been over before the winter set in. At that time the enemy was disorganized and demoralized. The infantry was working with the armor and the fighter-bombers. Together we were killing and capturing thousands [of the enemy] every day. They had not been able to set up a defense line anywhere, but we had to stop and dig in, and for a time we fought the old type trench warfare of World War I. By the time we were to jump off again, on Nov. 8, they were ready for us. And now the Germans are on the offensive in Belgium and Luxembourg.

I know this letter is not well written and I fear may not make sense at times. Occasionally I have thoughts I would like to convey to you but when I come to write I do not then think of them. Many, many things have happened. I think my record of them, kept as faithfully as conditions would permit, will already fill a book.

A few unusual occurrences: The little baby-faced Arthur Liagre, a machine gunner in the platoon I used to command, was fighting off a German attack back in the Gremercy Forest. The MG jammed but he kept working on it and firing as much as he could until the enemy was quite close. Then he pulled his pistol and with his assistant gunner who was armed with a carbine (small rifle) fought them off with those weapons. In the course of the fight a bullet fired by the Germans entered the barrel of the carbine.

Just recently the enemy dropped a heavy mortar shell into the muzzle of one of our smaller ones and blew it to bits. The mortar crew had taken to their holes and miraculously no one was even injured.

Once an artillery shell creased the side of a liaison plane. One-half inch more contact and it would have been blown to bits in flight.

My friend 1/Sgt Harold Rinert, [Dodge City, Kans.] of E Co., after many days in combat was given a battle field promotion to 2nd lieutenant. In his first day as an officer he was wounded and while being evacuated the Huns shelled the medical jeep with mortars. One shell went between his legs and through the floor of the vehicle. It was a dud or he would have been blown to pieces.

Tales like this are numberless and almost everyone has had his narrow escapes.

And there is the letter written by one of the men of this regiment to another soldier. When it arrived at its destination the other soldier had been killed so it was returned. When it came back the writer had been killed in action. Therefore there was no one to claim it, as both the writer and the one to whom it was written are dead.

As I said, we have been briefly out of the line but I do not think for [it will be] long. It seems a bit strange not hearing the thunder of the artillery after listening to it for so long. Right now we are amidst the dark grey stone walls of the fortress of Metz. Occasionally a raiding member of the Luftwaffe roars low over the stone buildings and the ack-ack and machine guns cut loose with terrific bang and clatter. The shells and flares light up the sky and the tracers cut thousands of gleaming paths across the Christmas heavens. When the hubbub subsides the pale, cold Christmas moon is still shining, and I hope that somewhere its light falls on someone who has had a happy Yuletide, like a little boy I'm thinking of far, far to the westward.

Best wishes,

Capt. Orval E. Faubus
Hqs. 320th Inf.,
APO No. 35, c/o P.M.
New York City, N.Y.

## CHRISTMAS DINNER IN METZ BY PATTON'S ORDER

*As is noted from the Journal entries I remained ill while in Paris. I would have thought my illness the main reason I was sent, had not my orders come from Division headquarters. I was a good selection to attend the school, but perhaps the Colonel recommended me because of my condition.*

*I left Paris to return to the unit on Dec. 24 and reached the regimental rear CP at Nancy late that same day, driving all the way in an open jeep in the bitter cold. At Nancy I learned the Division had been pulled out of Germany, back along the bloody trail we had made across Alsace-Lorraine, and all the units were now in Metz. The withdrawal of the 35th Division had begun as soon as the seriousness of Runstedt's offensive was known. In fact Gen Patton had given instructions to his division commanders to make plans for the move before the order was received.*

*Not having time to reach my unit on the 24th I spent the night at Nancy, again with members of the 320th personnel section, although some of them had gone to Metz to join the main headquarters. On Christmas day my jeep driver companion and I drove down the valley along the winding river into which all the bridges had been tumbled, either by our bombers or Hitler's withdrawing troops as we drove them from the area. We passed through the battered villages and towns and other war wreckage, traveling over the frozen landscape in the bitter cold, rejoining our unit in the afternoon.*

*The 320th's depleted ranks following the terrible Alsace-Lorraine campaign had been filled with replacements. Consequently we had regained some of our wounded, both men and officers, who had recovered and returned, but by far most of our replacements were new troops. Some companies were slightly over strength in assignments.*

*That evening we had a fine Christmas dinner in comfortable quarters. Because of the hardships the troops had known for so long, it was by Gen Patton's personal order that the 35th Division remained a day longer in Metz that we might have our dinner there. This was another of the many instances we discovered of Patton's concern for the combat troops he commanded.*

*That night we were bombed by German planes and saw a wonderful display of our own ack-ack and anti-aircraft machine guns. The Christmas fireworks were unlike any we had seen before or since. (See Dec. 25th letter to hometown newspaper).*

*By daybreak the next morning the entire Regiment had entrucked and was on the way to the Battle of the Bulge in the Ardennes. The 320th in one 24-hour period traveled from Metz across three countries, France, Belgium and Luxembourg, a distance of 93 miles, detrucked, went forward and deployed. Within another six hours the troops of our regiment were in combat against Runstedt's forces. The Journal for the Ardennes campaign began shortly before daybreak on the morning of Dec. 27, our first day of combat in the great Battle of the Bulge.*

CHAPTER VI

## THE ARDENNES
### and
## THE VOSGES MOUNTAINS

Berg, Luxembourg
Dec. 27, 1944

It is now 0512 after a night of duty. We have our CP
in this little village while other parts of the company are
quartered in nearby town of Ell. We set up here shortly before nightfall after coming in truck convoy from Metz. So
in one day we were in three countries as we crossed parts
of Belgium enroute. The frontiers were unnoticed; they mean
little or nothing in this war.

Just to the north the lightning is flashing along the
horizon and the thunder rolls down to us. In a short time we
will be pushing into the left flank of the raging German drive.
Right now  Sgt Bridgewater is awakening the Colonel and
other members of the staff to move up as the drive begins.

Lt Cooper rejoined us. He came in about 0200, looking
very worn and weary. He's been fighting with his TDs with
the 5th Div. He is his same cheerful self.

Activity buzzes now, so more later.

\* \* \*

*As the first encounter with the enemy began in this
fierce battle, our troops after wading or swimming the icy
Sure River, advanced four miles, siezed three towns - Boulaide, Baschleiden and Flebour - and captured 35 Germans.
Lt Henry O. Tietjens of Carrolton, Missouri and Lt Byerly,
both old originals, got four jeeploads of hot chow to the men*

*across the river by using jerricans, rocks and planks to fill*
*gaps in a poorly demolished bridge above the water.*

\* \* \*

Boulaide, Luxembourg
Dec. 28, 1944

No writing last night. It is very cold, and our quarters, where we had the CP, were so crowded that there was no room for other than necessary personnel. There was no heat at all in the small room where I slept, so I rolled in my sleeping bag early and did not arise until late. I still continue, half-well, half-sick, and am hardly any use to anyone or to myself.

Our troops got across the SURE River yesterday and today. One platoon of I Co waded the freezing water, waist deep, and set up a defensive perimeter while the engineers built a foot bridge for the rest of the battalion. I don't see how they could stand the cold. Although it was clear and the sun giving a dim hazy light, it was far below freezing and the snow and ice melted not at all. The only smudges on the white earth were where shells had landed, making a crater and scattered the dark earth in a circular smudge over the snow.

We moved to this place at noon. All during the remainder of the day the sounds of battle have rolled over the countryside just in front of us. We can hear the coughing of the mortars. The Germans have thrown a few shells into town, but most have landed to the front of us. The MGs carried on a spirited engagement most of the afternoon. Our TDs laid into some German MG positions and blew the hell out of them. Now 2220, I can hear the mortars and artillery still trying for each other.

We have a warm room tonight on the 2nd floor, not a safe place at all, but much better than being out in the snow on the frozen ground. The troops will be dug in of course, those who do not occupy buildings, and keep from freezing in the holes.

How different it is now to the war of the summer when we could set up a CP or sleep almost anywhere. If we hit the concentrated artillery of the "Nebelwerfers," of which the Germans are using a lot on this front, we will probably be digging in our CPs again.

\* \* \*

I wish I could feel like working once more. It takes the greatest effort to write even this much. I have written to no one except Alta for days, and very briefly and not very often to her.

\* \* \*

Lt Quillen got "shot at" tonight by one of the guards. He was riding in a jeep with his driver when they were challenged. They stopped and then, through a misunderstanding, started up again, and the guard put a shot through their gas tank. That put them to an abrupt halt and Lt Quillen walked over to the guard who asked him the sign. Quillen replied "I did know it but you've scared me so bad that I've forgotten it now." They got the matter straightened out all right. It was highly amusing to the rest of us, in fact, about the funniest incident in some time.

\* \* \*

The hilly rolling country of this section of Luxembourg looks much better than the mud of Alsace-Lorraine. I think it would be very beautiful in peace to one who was not ill or half ill at least.

\* \* \*

We had about a three-hour bull session tonight. Lts Quillen, Parish, Cooper, Silverman, Capt Scherer and myself, with Col Northam getting in on a part of it. That was my principal activity for the day. I hope that I can feel better during coming days. I am just no good at all in my condition. And now, if the Krauts don't zero in on us, I'll try to get some rest.

[Casualties[1] not mentioned in the Journal].

Boulaide, Luxembourg
Dec. 29, 1944

No move today, as we were unable to advance, except slowly, against the positions ahead. There are many [enemy] MG positions. The word from the 2nd Bn is that every time

---

1 1st Lt. Kenneth H. Brown, Co A, Puente, Calif., an original, formerly of Co B, evacuated as sick Dec. 26; WOJG Edwin K. Stearnes, Sv Co, Tucker, Ga., an original, evacuated as sick Dec. 26; Capt. Conrad P. (or B) Pitcher, CO of Co L, address unknown, a replacement, evacuated as sick Dec. 26; none returned. (Pitcher was in the attack on Nov. 8, then was out as of Dec. 9, evidently returned to duty and again evacuated.)

a man sticks his head up he is fired upon. Second Lt Sweeney,[2] one of my old section leaders in the wps plat, was hit today. He was evacuated and the word was that he was not too badly wounded. He just recently received his battlefield promotion to 2nd Lt from Plat Sgt. I have learned that Sgt Wilbur Curry, had he lived, would have gotten his promotion (battlefield) to 2nd Lt.

\* \* \*

One of Lt Cooper's officers came in tonight and reported the loss of two TDs to tank fire, with 8 men killed and others wounded. Lt Cooper's old plat Sgt had an arm blown off in the melee while pulling a wounded man from one of the stricken TDs.

\* \* \*

Planes strafed our position today. Two men were killed and two wounded at the crest of the hill about 100 yards from this building. Lt Silverman was caught on the road in a jeep but managed to escape. He picked up one of the wounded men, who was shot through the neck, and brought him to the aid station but he died shortly after arriving. The killed and wounded were members of Capt Rennes engineer company.

The planes that did the strafing were P-47s, our fighter bombers, but we suspect were flown by Krauts. They have been pulling that stunt quite frequently in this offensive. Lt Cooper saw one shot down while with the Fifth Div and the German pilot was captured. He had just knocked out a jeep, a 2½ T trk and an ambulance, killing five wounded men. Some doughboys shot the pilot but some officer came along and sent him to the hospital in the next ambulance.

However it is possible these planes today were our own, as some P-47s did some strafing for the 137th on our left. Still this is to the rear of their positions and one of Lt Cooper's TD units was strafed which had our identifying panels plainly displayed.

(I hear a plane strafing now, 2320, and it must be Kraut for it is too close for ours)

Now that it is over, the funniest sight of the day was Lt Clark after he had dived into the corner when we heard the roar of the plane's MGs. The others broke pell mell for

---

2  2nd Lt. Joseph B. Sweeney, Co F, Chicago, Ill., an old original NCO, a friend since Camp Rucker, recently awarded a battlefield commission, listed LWA Dec. 29, did not return.

the door and headed down stairs. Lt Clark rose and followed. That is, except for Lt Cooper who was looking out the window to see the planes. His identification confirmed other reports.

Shortly he and I went down into the street to see if anyone was hit, but luckily no one was touched. There was momentary hubbub and excitement downstairs, of course, with many heading for the cellar or preparing to go if the planes returned.

\* \* \*

*In the CP at Boulaide, as was usual and proper, the Colonel and senior staff had the safer rooms on the ground floor and in the cellar of the stone building which we occupied. The junior staff and liaison personnel had a second floor room with one window which faced the battle lines to the north.*

*When the P-47 strafed the town and the building in which we were situated, it came from the north. The bullets could have entered the window and killed or wounded most if not all those in the room. The ricochets would have done the most damage.*

*At the time the room was full, containing 12 to 18 men and officers. I was seated on the left of a long table near the center of the room barely out of direct fire through the window. Lt Cooper was in the right hand corner beside the window. When the plane roared through, its MGs chattering, and the bullets rattling through the streets and smacking into the walls, everyone broke for cover. Some fell flat, then got up and ran. That is, everyone broke for cover except Cooper and myself. I did not move at all but sat observing the whole thing. Cooper leaned over slightly and peered out the window. In the quietness which followed the passage of the plane and the exodus of personnel from the room, he said quietly, "Judge, that was a P-40." (one of our own planes)*

*It was then I noticed Lt Clark lying in the right rear corner of the room. He was on his back, his hands and feet in the air in the same manner that a pup or a cat will fall on its back and throw up all four feet for protection. He looked so comical that I burst out laughing. Angered by my laugh, he scrambled to his feet and ran after those who were already gone, leaving Cooper and I alone.*

*The plane was already gone. There was no use to run then unless it returned or another came along.*

\* \* \*

I said the sight of Lt Clark piled into the corner was funny, yet that was the perfectly natural reaction and might have saved his life, while I could have lost mine sitting at the table where I was writing. On the other hand he could have been killed while I remained unscathed. One never knows.

That incident was funny because we have little or nothing else at which to laugh. Just like it was uproariously funny to see Lt Quillen after he was fired upon by the guard. Perhaps some things about the incident were funny, but out there on the sun-lit crest today two men lost their lives. They were working along unaware of any immediate danger or that the end was near, when the plane roared in and the heavy 50 Cal MGs blasted their bodies and their lives and blood flowed out of their beings as rapidly and irrevocably as the air from a punctured balloon. And with them died many hopes of things that were to be, now never to be fulfilled, plans never to be performed and joys never to be tasted. Their own and those of loved ones waiting for their return, who will now receive the fateful messages. I did not know either of them but the tragedy of the incident is as real to me as if they had been my brothers.

For if such can happen to them it can, and may well, happen to me and my own. I do not know how many of our Infantrymen died today or how many are in agony out there tonight, but certainly some are.

\* \* \*

At our CP in Arsdorf the other night, I talked awhile with Pfc Bush the runner for my old F Co. He told me little Art Liagre was the MG section ldr and was now a sergeant; said he appeared to be proud to make good; that there were three of them (he and two brothers) in the Army and now all of them were sergeants. Bush said there were only 15 left of the original 185 in the Co which came overseas. Now there are less for I hear that Sweeny was hit today. Lt Shupe,[3] another who got a battlefield promotion, was also hit today.

\* \* \*

---

3  2nd Lt. James R. Shupe, Co G, Freeman, W. Va., an old original as a sgt., was wounded but later returned to duty.

Now past midnight. I have felt much better today and hope I can improve still more with the coming days.

[A casualty[4] mentioned earlier in the Journal].

Boulaide, Luxembourg
Dec. 30, 1944

Now 1345:

We were shelled today at 1130 and twice since then. A flock of shells just now came into Cn Co area.

This is a critical battle. We know we are in an area that is vital to the Germans if their big counteroffensive is to be successful. So we are getting what we expected, hell and more hell all along the front. If we can hold and crush Von Runstedt's bulge, perhaps the war will be shortened. I don't know enough of the big picture to guess. We are too interested, as we must be, in our own local situation.

\* \* \*

When the shelling started at 1130, everyone started for the basement. As I came out of the liaison room Col Northam, who was shaving in another upstairs room, was going down, lather still on his face and holding his hands in front of his head as if to shield it. Lt Cooper came back to get his helmet and was the last to get out. There was no room in the basement, so I sat down with Capt Ginsberg beside the wall in his department. Lucikly only one (that I know of) was hit in the town. There were some shrapnel marks on our building.

I wish I could remember all the remarks that are made in this liaison room. I know I can't remember them and the situation is not conducive to recording them at present.

\* \* \*

They just brought in a PW. Not many of them get back to the IPW men in this engagement.

\* \* \*

We are sweating it out in our liaison room with its window on the side from which the shells come. Lt Cooper sits

4  2nd Lt. Ernest J. Jones, AT Co, address unknown, an original listed in unofficial record as DOW Dec. 28. This must be in error for I wrote in the Journal entry of Sept 21 that we had received word that Lt. Jones' wounds had proved fatal. I could find no record of any other officer by the name of Jones in the 320th.

down and says, "These thick walls will stop shrapnel or an ordinary shell, and if one comes in that window, it's fate. So I'm not going to worry about it."

We knocked off a lot of Krauts yesterday, last night and today. There were wounded Germans in front of G Co last night, crying and complaining, who could not be aided by either side.

\* \* \*

The battle is terrific. There is constantly the sound of artillery, mortars, MGs and small arms, and often the roar of strafing planes, rocket mortars [nebelwerfers], and the heavy firing of tanks and TDs. I think when one gets down to the basic issue . . . he must ask God to take care of his soul, for there is nothing any power can do for the body and mind. Collectively our fate is in our hands and that of the high command. Our personal fortune is in the hands of fate.

\* \* \*

The earth is still in the grip of winter. The snow remains the same, in the bitter cold, except where the vehicles and marks of shells and gunfire disturb its whiteness. And here and there of course are the bloodstains.

\* \* \*

Now a MG duel sounds out above the general clamor of the battle. That German MG has the most hateful, deadly, menacing sound in all the world. It is not so terrifying or nerve-shaking as the artillery and mortars, but it still seems more hateful.

The duel continues.

## THE SANTA FE COMBATS THE ADOLPH HITLER DIVISION

*After the 4th Armored Division, with the 35th Infantry Division on its immediate right, had driven into Bastogne and relieved the garrison, the Germans launched a hard driving counter attack on Dec. 30. The attack, principally through the sectors held by the 134th and 137th, was led by the 1st SS Panzer "Adolph Hitler" Division, aided by 167 Volksgrenadier Division. The objective was to cut, at all costs, the Arlon-Bastogne Highway and re-surround the city and the troops there.*

In the initial drive of the Nazi counter-thrust, Villers-la-Bonne-Eau was surrounded and elements of K and L Companies of the 137th Regiment were cut off. Our 654th Tank Destroyer Battalion and the 701st Tank Destroyer Battalion of the Fourth Armored Division helped to stand off the charging Panzers destroying 11 tanks during the attack.

Gen Futch's artillery did the usual superior job in support. In the words of the 35th Division History, "All day and night the battle raged, finally with the assistance of the Air Corps and close proximity fused artillery, it [the attack] was broken, and the elite 1st SS Panzer (Adolph Hitler) Division lay lifeless, broken and destroyed upon the field of battle."

Attempts on Dec. 31 to relieve the cut-off units of the 137th, were in vain. They were given up for lost when it was learned from German prisoners that they had been either killed or captured. The Nazis blasted holes in the walls of the houses from which the men fought and then turned flame throwers on the men inside.

Of the 235 men missing from the 137th that day, a majority were from the lost elements of K and L companies.

It took 13 days of fierce fighting for the 137th again to take Villers-la-Bonne-Eau, five days of assault for the 134th to capture Lutrebois, and several days of fierce attack for the 320th to take Harlange.

When the counter-attack by Hitler's finest division failed and the Americans again advanced, it signaled the final failure of the Fuhrer's great Ardennes offensive. From then on for the German forces it was fight, hold and withdraw. And again the veteran Santa Fe Division had performed well at a crucial point at a critical time.

* * *

From The
MADISON COUNTY RECORD

WITH THE THIRD ARMY

Somewhere in Luxembourg
December 31, 1944

Dear Home Folks:

As I write this the old year is coming to a close, and the new one is being born. I guess the greatest wish of most of us is somewhat of a double hope - that the New Year will see the end of the war and the safe return of loved ones.

Tonight is mostly clear with a pale moon riding high with broken clouds flying across its face. The evening, or western star, seems to shine with especial brightness. To our north in the shelled towns, fires are burning with a red glow, the flames and smoke leaning with the winter wind as it sweeps across the frozen, snow-blanketed earth. Bright flashes, some white, some deep orange, light up the horizon and the snowy hills as the big guns continue to thunder. Occasionally there can be seen balls of orange flame from air-bursting shells, and flashes of orange as others plow with deafening, earthshaking thunder into the frozen ground. Planes drone through the starry heavens, plowing in and out of the broken clouds, their bombs crashing into dimly outlined targets below. Or with deep-throated, terrifying roar the air-craft sweep with flaming guns over villages, roads and troop positions.

As you know I am with General Patton's famous Third Army. And from the news you already know that we have been moved north to help take care of the German push. We are now in the snowy Ardennes where Runstedt mounted his offensive. My unit is in a strategic spot so you know the going is tough.

This is winter war with a vengeance. It is quite different from the tough little corners of hell we had in the hedgerows of Normandy, or the push across the Vire River south of St. Lo, or the terrific battle of Mortain where the 320th Infantry rescued the now famous isolated battalion of another division. Then we were fighting with the American First Army. After that we joined Patton's forces and drove across central France, across the Loir, the Seine, and the Marne Rivers, taking town after town and sending back PWs by the hundreds. Then we established the Moselle bridge head and held it against the biggest counterattacks up to that time. Then the Army swung northward and our regiment was the first to reach and cut the main highway and railroad running from the city of Nancy to the German border, which helped greatly in the fall of that Nazi bastion. Then our supply of gasoline and artillery shells gave out and the whole army had to hold up, dig in and defend until new supplies were brought up. A little over a month later we began the drive across

Alsace-Lorraine which took us across the Saar River into Germany, and the awful mud and rain and stench of that campaign I can never forget. Yet from all that this campaign is different in many ways. But in one respect they have all been the same, and that is that in any campaign anywhere, war is just what General Sherman said it was.

A short time ago I received from home an article, "How A Nazi Quits," from the December 2, 1944 issue of Collier's magazine. It mentioned several times Major Woodrow Anderson of Crosses, Arkansas. That was the time I met Major Anderson which I mentioned to you in a previous letter. Everything dealt with in that article happened in my unit. The colonel mentioned, is my commander (and a prince if I ever knew one). The Lieut. Frank Gardner mentioned was a fellow officer and good friend of mine, and one of the bravest men I have ever known. Later he was promoted to captain and a short time thereafter was killed in action when the 320th Infantry Regiment cleared the Chateau-Salins Forest. I could add a great deal to what the correspondent wrote but there is not time or space here. I have not seen Major Anderson since that time which was in July before St. Lo fell.

Oh yes, you asked about my bets that the war would end on November 11th. Well I paid off of course (the money is no earthly good here anyway). There were some with whom I had made wagers that were killed and others were wounded and evacuated, and those I could not pay and neither could I have collected. But I still think I would have won had we not run out of supplies at a critical time. (Will profiteers, strikers, and loafers please note.)

I don't think I need mention to you folks at home that the war is not yet won. If you get any truth from the papers (which I think you do) you know that the going is tough and the slaughter on both sides terrible. We know the Germans still have twice as many troops on the Russian front as we are fighting on the whole Western Front. Hitler spoke tonight and he has chosen death rather than surrender and is trying to get all the people of Germany to do likewise. His greatest and perhaps his only hope is to divide us from Russia and thereby gain a peace that will save him. I hope no one is foolish enough to listen to the arch-fiend for a single minute, for the Russians are the greatest allies we have.

It is now past midnight and the New Year has been born, but there is no joy here because of the arrival. There are only breathless longing hopes amid the despair of this snowy battlefield. This next thought is sad indeed, but I know that in this frozen, flamelit, thunderous vortex of hell, there are many who welcomed this New Year who will not see its first dawn, and many more who will not survive its first day. My prayer is that God will grant all the fallen the peace in the next world that was to them here denied, and give to those who live the peace and good will upon earth that all deserve who work or fight for freedom.

Capt. Orval E. Faubus,<br>
Hqs., 320th Inf. Regt.,<br>
APO No. 35, N. Y., N. Y.

* * *

Boulaide, Luxembourg
Jan. 2, 1945

Still no progress against the Germans in our sector. They hold firmly the town of Harlange which we have been attacking. If we had tanks we could go in and take it. But Infantry, no matter how brave, cannot advance across open ground and dislodge a well fortified enemy. Capt Zurman and his tankers have not returned to us.

I have been to medics today for treatment of my sinuses, which are very sore and badly infected. It is the most unpleasant and difficult thing, for me to endure a sinus treatment.

Right now I'm ill, I don't know from the sinuses or the medicine Maj Smith gave. So this must be brief. I must lie down before I fall down.

* * *

Last night we lost two of our old originals who have been with us constantly, Capt Vignes[5] and Capt Kuhlmar, S-1 and executive of First Bn respectively. A driver, whose name I did not learn, was also wounded. It is not thought either was fatally injured. They were all injured when a truck, carrying blankets for their Bn, ran over mines which

---

5 Both Vignes and Kullmar recovered and returned to duty. Vignes also listed as serving in 2nd Bn Hq; Kullmar was originally CO of Co A.

were exploded. The mines were laid by the 137th Inf Regt, and should have been guarded or marked. What a travesty that those two fine officers should go through almost six months of combat uninjured by German fire, only to be wounded, perhaps killed, by our own mines.

\* \* \*

Bright spots of yesterday and today, quite a bunch of letters from my friends and loved ones.

Lots to write about now - but as the British say, I just don't feel up to it.

\* \* \*

News tonight of a German drive in the Saar Valley. Hope they don't get any of that region back as it cost us too damned much to get it from the Krauts in the drive which just recently ended.

[A casualty[6] not mentioned in the Journal].

Boulaide, Luxembourg
Jan. 4, 1945

We have made the acquaintance of a very interesting character connected with the 42nd Chemical Mortars which are supporting us in this action. He has a handle bar mustache which is really a beaut. Red in color, it, and his actions, remind me of an old friend I used to have back home known as "Babe" Deaton. He has been dubbed "Colona" by some of the other officers, principally Clark, and now the greeting is "Where's Hope?" and his reply, "No Hope, No Hope!" He is Lt Charles E. Slater of Buffalo, N. Y. Of course Clark and Parish have immediately taken him to their bosoms, he being an "Up-stater" and a Republican. Lt Slater has seen a lot of action, having landed with the first troops in Africa. He has been through Tunisia, Sicily, Palermo and Cassino, and then came up with the Seventh Army through southern France. It is really a fine bunch I have to work with here.

\* \* \*

The snow is heavier today and the fighting. The 2nd and 3rd Bns took over 100 PWs today. They gained the outskirts

6 1st Lt. Charles Lower, Co L, address unknown, a replacement with us at least since early Sept., evacuated as sick Jan. 3, did not return.

of Harlange but were thrown out by tanks just at nightfall. Some compare the fighting with that of St Lo as there is almost ceaseless and constant pounding of artillery. I don't know the extent of our casualties, but Lt Sunderland[7] of E Co was killed. Two more of our old originals were wounded, Lieuts Lakeness[8] and Cammack[9] of Cn Co.

\* \* \*

Day before yesterday I went to medics for treatment of my sinuses. Yesterday I was so ill that I arose from my bed roll only once during the day. Today I have felt little better. My fellow officers urge me to go back to the hospital for treatment. I've been trying to hang on, but I can't hold up much longer if I don't get better. I can do very little work. I have to force myself to do this little writing, and that with the greatest difficulty. I must have lost 25 or 30 lbs in weight in past two months.

Today I received the fruit cake from Mr. and Mrs. Allen Presley of Huntsville which they wrote they had mailed in October. My fellow officers, Clark, Parish, Slater, Silverman, Cooper, Quillen and Ginsberg, and Charlie Glatzer, shared it with me. It was very good. Right now the packages and letters from home are the only bright spots in the gloom and discomfort of combat.

It is a weird sight now, to step outside and see the great gun flashes on the white, newly-fallen snow. They [the guns] have thundered all day, and several enemy shells have whistled past here. Once when we were upstairs one whistled so close that Lt Quillen dived for a corner sending a chair clattering. Another time Slater, who was sitting near the window, involuntarily held his paper before his face as he crouched. As if a paper would be any protection against the flying steel fragments if they had come our way. But such are men's actions although they laugh at them the next moment. Lt Slater seems to be a pretty cool fellow.

\* \* \*

7  1st Lt. Starr S. Southerland (or Sutherland) Jr., Co E, address unknown, a replacement, listed KIA Jan. 4.

8  1st Lt. Leslie A. Lakeness, Cn Co, address unknown, an original, listed LWA Jan. 4, did not return.

9  1st Lt. Elbert Cammack, Cn Co, Geneva, Fla., with us a long time but his name is not in the original list of officers at Camp Butner. Possibly an early replacement, he recovered from his wounds and returned to duty.

Have learned that Capt Brown[10] and Lt Wilson[11] were evacuated for wounds received today, and Lt Lower for illness. I did not learn the names of any enlisted men who fell today, but there were several. Lt Col Hannum [CO of 2nd Bn] had his britches torn by shrapnel when Lakeness and Cammack were wounded.

* * *

I wonder when this slaughter is going to cease. The Germans will have no man power left at all. Those who are being drafted at home will be given infantry training now and will find themselves in combat as replacements with a minimum of delay.

Had a letter from my friend, Woodrow Ledford, who is now in a replacement depot training as an infantryman. I await with dread the day when I shall learn he is either wounded or killed. (So far as chances go, I think one has a better opportunity of evading a death sentence after it has been imposed by the courts in the States, than he does of escaping death or injury as a front line infantry soldier in this conflict.)

The mortars continue to give out their death dealing chant, aided by the heavier pounding of the artillery. Occasionally the terrifying noise of the nebelwerfers (minniewerfers, or screaming meanies), as if grinding something from a rusty barrell, sounds out through the night. The shells from this weapon arch through the air and come down in a cluster of "whumps." Of course you're just unlucky if you're caught where they fall. [We first faced this weapon at Mortain and again in the Ardennes.]

* * *

And now the big clock, with the pleasantly toned musical chimes, strikes the hour of midnight. As my damned head is so sore that I can hardly think at all, I'll stop writing and see if I can sleep another night upstairs in my bed roll without being scared out of it.

Two things which I have seen everywhere in Europe are religious symbols, and large beautiful clocks with musical tones.

---

10  Capt. Eugene G. (or C) Brown, CO of Co I, Harsay, Mich., a replacement, listed LWA Jan. 4, did not return.

11  1st Lt. Raymond C. Wilson, Co L, Wheatland, Ind., a replacement, wounded, recovered and returned to duty.

I shall never forget the beautiful church at Pontpierre. The glass, which had been shattered from the stained windows, crunched under my feet as I walked up the aisle. The beauty of the colored, stained glass windows, the intricate construction, the rich cloth and curtains by the altar and pulpit, the figures of the saints, all were most impressive. And I shall never forget the haggard-faced, unknown officer who knelt, praying, his muddy boots sticking back underneath one of the seats.

\* \* \*

## GERMANS STILL FIGHT FIERCELY

*In the fight for the woods approaching Harlange our troops were supported by the 216th, 219th and 179th FA Bns., the 3rd Chemical Bn., and our own Cannon Company. Col Reed's 216th alone fired 2,358 rounds and Capt Ekstrum's Cannon Co more than 1,000 rounds on Jan. 3 in helping repel two counterattacks.*

*On Jan 4 the 3rd Bn overran 10 MG emplacements and one mortar emplacement, taking 88 PWs and killing about 100 enemy troops.*

*Earlier the 2nd Bn wiped out a counterattack of 80 Germans, killing all except four who were captured. The dead enemy soldiers could not be removed and froze in the snow in the grotesque positions in which they had fallen. Such attacks showed the fanatical zeal with which the enemy sometimes fought in the last great Nazi offensive of the war.*

\* \* \*

## SLUGGISH REACTIONS IN THE "WHITE JUNGLE"

*During this terrible period in the "white hell," foxholes were lined with ice, water froze in canteens, and medics carried blood plasma under their armpits. The deeply snow-clad area would have been beautiful had it not been for the tenacious, deadly conflict. Overhead in the sometimes blue sky the high flying planes left vapor trails in their wake, outward bound or homeward bound to and from Germany. Some of those which flew closer did not look so good for there were some enemy planes on strafing missions.*

*In this "white jungle" close-quarter fighting in the icy fir forests, soldiers on both sides sometimes reacted sluggish-*

*ly. T/Sgt Arthur E. McLaughlin of Black Rock, Arkansas, an E Company platoon sergeant, set off at dark to contact Co G. He encountered some soldiers digging in the frozen ground.*

*"G Company"? he asked, although by the time he spoke he had realized they were Krauts.*

*"Nix"! one of the Germans replied, and continued chipping at the ground.*

*McLaughlin turned slowly, and just as slowly walked off through the snow. He was well back to his own positions before the Germans opened fire on him.*

*1st Lt William W. Dodge, Co G, Perry, Missouri, returned with a patrol and reported to Capt Head that there were a number of Germans asleep in their foxholes but clicking their boots together because of the cold.*

*"Good"! it is reported the CO exclaimed. "Let's go throw in some hand grenades and warm 'em up."*

*The mission was a success and a number of Germans were eliminated. Their exhausted state is demonstrated by the report that one grenade tossed in a hole rolled on top of a Nazi without exploding and the German went on sleeping and clicking his heels. The second grenade, no dud, warmed him up for a time and then left him cold forever.*

\* \* \*

From The
MADISON COUNTY RECORD
Feb. 8, 1945

## CAPT. ORVAL FAUBUS WRITES FROM HOSPITAL
### Somewhere in France, Jan. 8, 1945

Only a short time now until the lights go out for rest, but perhaps I can put together a few lines to you beforehand. I am now in a hospital in an "old world" city of northern France. No, I have not been wounded, but the cold, damp climate and the rigors of winter war, coupled with my sinus trouble, have almost proved my undoing. However, I shall be back to the front in about three days, and my stay here when concluded will have been about a week.

I have seen another phase of the war here, which Paul Corlett described in his letter of Aug. 20, (I just recently read it, which shows the length of time it often takes for news to reach us), "The care of the wounded." I have seen the dead and wounded in many and varied ways on the battlefield, but this is my first time to see how they are cared for farther back than the aid stations.

I can say that the attention is the best possible and there is nothing but admiration among us for the Medical Corps, and to us the members of the Army Nurse Corps are the "Angels of Mercy." I guess we members of the Infantry love them more because we need them more than anyone else.

There is every conceivable kind of wound to be seen and it would only horrify you if I could describe them. Sometimes I feel a bit of shock myself and I should be quite used to such scenes by now. Some of those with lesser wounds and illness not very severe are, in a way, quite happy. It means to them a respite from the uncomfortable and uneasy hell of the front lines.

A lot of Americans have died in this battle with the Germans in their big offensive. They struck in the American sector of the front, but now the British are in it also, and they are wonderfully good soldiers. A lot of our prisoners have been murdered by SS troops of the German Army. A hatred such as I have never seen has sprung up among us against Hitler's armies and all of Germany.

There are two chaplains in the ward with me, and one, Chaplain Vermillion of Portland, Oregon, says it is the judgment of God on the Germans for their evil. Well, they certainly are going to reap what they have sown, but at what a great cost to us. However, there is no alternative but to push it through to a conclusion and give the aggressors all the hell possiblle.

The other chaplain, John T. Stratton, formerly a Baptist minister of Oklahoma (he knows the young Baptist minister at Fayetteville quite well) remarked: "It was quite a shock to me when I first realized that I could hear planes and shells going overhead and knew they were going to kill people, and feel glad, but now I do, and I can't help it."

That is the way everyone of us feels, and I mean everyone. It gladdens our hearts to see dead Krauts, and if you don't understand that just remember that the faster they are killed the more of your boys will come back to you. They have sown the storm and I pray to God that they will reap the destruction that should be theirs.

Yesterday was my birthday, and I have had many thoughts of the good cakes that my mother, and then Mrs. Alonzo Ledford, and then Alta, use to bake for me each time that anniversary came around. Perhaps there'll be another cake, another time.

Today the snow fell steadily, the fluffy, white flakes floating gently down. They made deeper the cold covering which already blankets the frozen earth. I wondered how anything so soft and gentle as snow could contribute so much to the harshness of the situation, yet, that is just what it does for it makes it easy for the now defending enemy to spot us as we attack. (The weather has seldom, if ever, been in our favor since the invasion started). Too, the wounded must be attended soon after they fall or they will perish, and for those not hit the snow greatly increases the hardships.

I hope to write again soon from the battle of Rundstett's Bulge.

> Capt. Orval E. Faubus
> Hqs. 320th Inf. APO No. 35
> c/o P.M., New York City, N. Y.

*   *   *

## COMMENDATION FROM XII CORPS

The following letter is another attestation to the fine achievements of the Santa Fe:

Major General Paul W. Baade
Commanding, 35th Infantry Division
APO 35, U. S. Army

My dear General Baade:

I want you to know that the 35th Infantry Division, when it transferred from the XII Corps, took with it the respect and admiration of our entire Corps.

Your record in combat has been a distinguished one on the Western Front. Beginning with your unforgettable drive from Le Mans through Chateaudun and Orleans, the 35th Division conducted itself with the greatest distinction through one brilliant success after another. Your spectacular operation against the city of Nancy, and your part in the securing and exploiting of our bridgehead across the Moselle, were forerunners of an even more difficult advance over 45 miles against most stubborn resistance by some of Germany's finest fighting forces. The manner in which you battled across Lorraine to cross the Saar and Blies Rivers in the face of bitter opposition, and finally to smash across the border into Germany, was even more remarkablle when we consider the frightful conditions of weather you were forced to endure. Your gallant and determined fight against record rainfalls, floods, bitter cold and the pillboxes of the Maginot Line is in the highest traditions of the military service.

Every officer and every soldier of your Division will share your pride in the enviable standards of courage and professional skill you have set during these past bloody months. Please accept for yourself, and for all members of your command, my sincere appreciation of the heroic achievements of the 35th Infantry Division.

Very sincerely,

/s/ M. S. Eddy
/t/ M. S. EDDY
    Major General, U. S. Army
    Commanding


1st Ind.

HQ. 35th INF. DIV., APO 35, U. S. Army, 9 Jan. 1945

TO: Officers and men 35th Infantry Division.

The glory of the historic achievements of this Division during the past six months now belongs to the ages. It is a brilliant page in the history of the military forces of the United States. To each of you, and to your fallen comrades, I can add nothing but to express my deepest appreciation and humble pride in being your commander. Proud of our past, confident in our future, let us go forward to even greater heights as we drive on in this our greatest test.

/s/ Paul W. Baade
/t/ PAUL W. BAADE
    Major General, U. S. Army
    Commanding

# FIRST HOSPITALIZATION

On Jan. 5th I reported to Maj Smith for sinus treatment and he decided to send me out for hospitalization. Col Northam came to the aid station to discuss the matter as the headquarters did not wish to lose my services. However, after discussion I was evacuated, and given a letter requesting that I be kept at a forward hospital in order that I might return sooner to my unit. I might as well not have had the message for all the consideration it received upon reaching the first medical stations.

Upon reaching the hospital at Thionville, France, I was placed on the first cot nearest the quarters used by the staff. According to my observation, my physician felt I was about to crack up and wanted me watched carefully.

My doctor, one of the kindest who ever cared for me, treated my sinus condition each day and the hospital personnel kept me under close observation.

While there I lost my wrist watch with the luminous dial. It was taken from the wash room by some hospital orderlies moments after I left it there. I made an effort to recover the watch but to no avail. I had looked at the glowing numerals to note the time on many dark and lonely nights, syncronized it many times for H-hour, and had timed the German artillery on numerous occasions. Its disappearance was like the loss of an old friend.

After a stay of only six days I checked out of the hospital to return directly to my unit. Reaching the 35th Evacuation Hospital at Luxembourg by evening of the first day, I found it crowded with casualties from the still raging Ardennes battle. A cot was found for me in the attic of the large building so close to the roof that there was insufficient room to stand. I had almost to crawl beneath the roof and around the cots of wounded to get to my bed.

I visited briefly with a nurse as she came by on her duty rounds, crouching and crawling in the narrow passageways. She was the busiest I have ever seen, giving shots, pills and other medication. Working hurriedly she barely had time to get to her last patient before returning to the first to begin her rounds all over again.

When I got back to the 320th on Jan 13 it had moved from Boulaide, Luxembourg into the battered bastion of Bastogne in Belgium. The 35th Division which had held the

— 478 —

*right flank for the 4th Armd Division as it drove through the German lines to reach the beleaguered garrison, had now joined elements of the 101st Airbourne and other units in the city. The battle was still raging. Some of the 320th had a slight respite from the fighting during the move.*

*On arriving at the CP I was received by my fellow officers with open arms and unusual pleasure and enthusiasm. However, before I had opportunity to become 'lightheaded," each officer went to his gear and bedroll and returned with a handful of courts martial cases and administrative work which they handed to me with evident relief. After my departure the work regularly given to me had been divided up and assigned to a number of officers. The opportunity to get rid of the extra work by returning it to me was the basis of my enthusiastic welcome.*

Bastogne, Belgium
January 14, 1945

Someone said today is Sunday. I am now back with my unit, rejoining them late yesterday afternoon here in battered Bastogne.

I was evacuated for hospitalization on Jan 5, and late in the evening of that day reached a hospital, the 106 Evac, in Thionville, France. I remained there until Jan. 11, at which time I got an ambulance driver to sign me out so I could return. He took me to the city of Luxembourg where I contacted the 35th Evacuation Hospital and spent the night. Next day I caught an ambulance to Arlon, Belgium, spending the night at the Div Rear CP with Capt Armstrong, Lt Sperl and W/O Frazier. Next morning (yesterday) I rode the mail truck to Sv Co and came on up here with Charley Glatzer.

\* \* \*

Right now two of our Bns are attached to the 6th Arm Div and the other is tied in on the right of 502nd Regt of the 101st Airbourne. We are fighting with Gen McAuliffe's "Battered Bastards of Bastogne." They seem to have assumed a part of the name we have applied to ourselves for some time, "Baade's Battered Bastards." There are a lot of "Battered Bastards" in Europe now. [In the 320th Inf we often referred to ourselves as "Ben Byrne's Battered Bastards."]

— 479 —

We had an air strike this morning on a patch of woods in which enemy positions are holding up the advance of 1st and 3rd Bns. It has been shelled since, but when the infantrymen attacked, a few minutes ago, they were still facing heavy automatic fire.

The snow still covers the landscape and is very deep in many places. The truck which I rode from Arlon had difficulty getting through many drifts. The engineers are sweeping the roads but yesterday a brisk, icy cold wind kept sifting the dry white snow back into the road way.

I found the old CP group about the same, - Clark, Parish, Silverman, Quillen, Capts Bonham, Ginsberg and Haley. Lt Botton is here now; also Capt Scherer of the 216th FA; Lt Cooper of "Highroad Charlie" is not with us now. The staff is the same.

\* \* \*

Have learned that Lt Walsh,[12] one of the old originals, was wounded and evacuated. Capt Abbot[13] was killed in action. Glatzer told me that Sgt Cain[14] of G Co was killed the day before he was to go back to Div Rear to receive his commission as a 2nd Lt.

\* \* \*

There was some heavy shelling yesterday soon after I returned. Soon after word came in that one of the 216th FA batteries was hit and Lt Allen[15] was killed. Eight EM were wounded. I regretted very much to hear the news as I became good friends with Lt Allen when we attended Military Intelligence School together at Camp Ritchie, Md., shortly before we came overseas.

He was a Mississippi boy and, as Capt Scherer said of him, "One of the finest officers I have ever known." Previously he had been wounded at St Lo on the day we first jumped off on July 11, and was evacuated to England. He rejoined

---

12  1st Lt. Edward G. Walsh, Co E, formerly Co H, Detroit, Mich., an original, listed LWA Jan. 11, did not return.

13  Capt. John E. Abbott, Jr., CO of Co K, address unknown, listed KIA Jan. 5. Capt. Abbott's men respected him highly. It was related to me that they were so affected by his death that they "advanced as one" in marching fire and overcame the enemy opposition.

14  Sgt. Cain of Co G, KIA, an old friend since Camp Rucker. At St. Lo I had reports that he kept his company and another from panic in that battle.

15  1st Lt. Ernest B. Allen, 216th FA Bn, Miss.

us at Brin just before the jump off on Nov 8 through Alsace-Lorraine.

\* \* \*

I was quite pleased to learn that Capt Head[16] got to return to the States in our last quota of one officer and 13 EM. He was one of the closest friends I had left as he and his wife had an apartment in the same building with Alta and me in Newton, Ala., along with Lt Silverman and Lt Trask. I am happy to know that his wife and twin boys are waiting for him at Little Rock, Arkansas, and then he plans to see his relatives in Kansas. I did not get to see him when he started home as he left while I was in the hospital.

Armstrong and Sperl said he came back to Div Rear with no equipment and no extra clothing wearing only a field jacket for an outer garment, and announced, "I'm ready to go! Where's that boat that's going to the States?"

[Casualties[17] not mentioned in the Journal].

Bastogne, Belgium
January 15, 1945

Now 1540. Still here in Bastogne which is still being shelled. Most of the CP group has now gone forward, Col Byrne and Lt Silverman at dawn this morning, and more of the staff about an hour ago. Most of Hqs Co and the S-1 and S-4 sections must remain here, because the forward CP is set up in a lone house on a snow covered hill, and there is not sufficient room.

Col Solomon, Chief-of-Staff, and Lt Col Renfro, G-3, came by a moment ago. I gave them what I knew of the situa-

---

16   Capt. Clifford M. Head, Co I, Topeka, Kans., an original. He returned to duty from the States before the war ended.

17   2nd Lt. George T. Ramsden, Co G, Oceanside, N. Y., an original, evacuated as sick Jan. 5; 1st Lt. Daniel C. Lawler, Co H, Glendale, Calif., a replacement, listed LWA Jan. 5; Capt. James F. McDermont, Med Det, address unknown, a replacement, listed LWA Jan. 9; Capt. Carl (or Karl) M. Rague, Med Det, address unknown, a replacement, listed DOW Jan. 10; 1st Lt. Edgar A. Wade, Co L, address unknown, a replacement, who had previously returned to duty after recovery from wounds, listed KIA Jan. 14; 1st Lt. Charles G. Bell, Co F, formerly Co G, Binghamton, N. Y., an original, evacuated as sick Jan. 14; 1st Lt. Jay S. Levey, Co A, Cressen, Pa., a replacement, listed LIA Jan. 14; none returned. When Ramsden and Bell went out in this battle, no original officer of Co G remained. All had gone for good, some having been wounded as many as three times.

tion and directions to the Fwd CP. I have always found both of these officers very agreeable to work with.

I was on duty last night and the artillery thunder was continuous throughout the night as it has been since my return. It has slackened somewhat today as our lines have moved forward. Just at dusk last night I watched some shells come into the center of Bastogne, some of which set a fire which was still glowing red long after darkness. Several shells came in yesterday, one of which damaged Milt's jeep and wounded two men of the 101st Airbourne unit nearby. Luckily none of our men were hit. There haven't been many enemy shells today but some landed rather close while I was talking with Col Solomon.

I intended to write last night but a combination of work and drowsiness prevented. The weather is very cold. The night was clear, the many stars shining much brighter than usual over the cold snow-covered earth. Many of the men cannot endure the cold and we have a considerable number of casualties from frost bite. How any of them endure the rigors of the winter war is difficult to understand.

Our 1st Bn is fighting today in the town of Oubourcy. They got into the town this morning by attacking in the darkness before dawn. They crossed the open ground and closed with the enemy before he was alerted and have been fighting it out all day. A number of PWs have been taken and sent back, including some German officers.

(A very big shell just came into the town with a terrific explosion. 1630 - as I write this line another followed. Milt arises saying, "Where's my helmet just in case I need it?" I don't think a helmet would help much against those shells. A helmet is mostly for morale purposes anyway. A hard-flying shell fragment or bullet can slice through one as if it were paper).

Now 2330 - I counted 21 of the big shells which came in during the shelling, the last three quite close. Have been writing some letters and now to bed.

\* \* \*

While I was away to the hospital Lieuts Gangemi,[18] John Kelley,[19] Wade[20] and others returned to duty. I want to see Kelly and Gangemi as soon as possible.

\* \* \*

The total PWs today amounted to 215 including a Bn commander.

Bright picture now, the rapid advance of the Red Armies on the Eastern Front.

\* \* \*

Last night the liaison group had some very heated (or interesting) discussions on various subjects. We had two new officers in our group from the 6th Armd Div, one representing tanks and one artillery. Subjects ranged from "what to do with Germany," world peace, lynching, social problems and racial relations. Remark of Col Byrne, "Judge, has merely changed from his ordinary court room voice to his supreme court voice."

[The Col sent Capt Bonham to quiet us down - He made the remark later when we continued the discussion in subdued voices, and sent Bonham in again with new orders. The discussion then ceased.]

[Casualties[21] not mentioned in the Journal].

Bastogne, Belgium
January 16, 1945

Today our unit took Mechamps. PWs are still being sent back tonight.

The day has been clear; very good for air activity and I hope they made the most of it. Tonight great fleets of bombers were roaring over high in the starry heavens. This is the

18    1st Lt. Felix M. Gangemi, Co F, Freeport, L. I., N. Y., the only original officer of Co F who remained, and he had been out for a long time with wounds.

19    1st Lt. John P. Kelly, Co K, Broken Bow, Nebr., was the last original officer of his company to be evacuated. He went out with wounds early in Sept.

20    1st Lt. Edgar A. Wade, (See No. 17) He was killed in action before I wrote in the Journal of his return to duty.

21    1st Lt. Cecil McClister, Jr., Co B, address unknown, a replacement, listed LWA Jan. 15, did not return; 2nd Lt. Albert J. Gibeau, Co D, Carthage, N. Y., an EM awarded a battlefield commission, listed KIA Jan. 15.

first night Bastogne has not been shelled (could happen yet; plenty of time left as it is only 2330.)

The way Co A of the 1st Bn took Oubourcy yesterday was really an achievement. I think I can get Pvt Whitey Hanson's story of the happening.

Still no mail today, so I guess transportation problems have really held it up.

\* \* \*

Replacements are now coming in to the infantry regiments who are only 18 days out of the States. That is a rapid change; a very short time for a change from America to the world of combat; from heaven to hell. It troubles my heart when I think of them, but one must not think of such things. But perhaps it is better for them than for those who have been here so long.

\* \* \*

Lt Reynolds[22] was killed yesterday. We lost some more officers whose names I can't now recall.

\* \* \*

Just before dark I watched an artillery battery firing from about a half mile out back. A great red ball of flame would blossom out from the gun position, and a black smoke ring would float upward. Then the shell would produce that ear-battering bang as it passed over head, followed immediately by the concussion from the explosion which would slap against the tin shed nearby as if struck a hard-blow by a plank.

\* \* \*

[An officer[23] lost not mentioned in the Journal].

\* \* \*

## CAPTURE OF OBOURCY

*From Pvt Whitney Hanson and others I obtained some of the details of the remarkable achievement of Co A in capturing the town of Obourcy, four miles NE of Bastogne on*

---

22  1st Lt. Max T. Reynolds, Co H, address unknown, a replacement, was in the fighting as far back as Nov. 18, became Ex O of Co B, listed KIA Jan. 15.

23  2nd Lt. Erwin G. Buzzell, Co M, address unknown, a replacement, sent back to another unit for unknown reasons on Jan. 16.

January 15. (Listed on map as Bourcy; known to us as Obourcy, why I do not know.)

In the darkness before daybreak the company advanced across a mile of open terrain. As the lead troops neared the town an enemy outpost fired on T/Sgt William A. Fried of Lexington, Illinois, a platoon guide. As the outpost continued to fire on Fried, a squad under S/Sgt Samuel S. Graham of Newark, N. J., rushed the post and killed the three Germans manning it. Pfc Charles P. Briner of Henry, Illinois, crawled around a haystack and captured a MG and two gunners. Pfc Joseph J. Calea of Detroit, Michigan, took a 75mm anti-tank gun by killing one German and taking two prisoners. In the meantime other GIs had siezed the first four houses capturing the enemy in them.

Now the Co C men observed communication wires running from the fifth house. Pfc John O. Beal of Gates Center, Kansas, dashed through fire now laid down by the arousing Germans, killed the guard in front of the building and cut the wires.

The German Bn Commander had his CP in the cellar of the building. When the wires were severed, there was no longer any central direction by the commander over the German troops.

When the supporting tanks arrived, Capt Norman C. Carey of Springfield, Ohio, the Co A Commander, ran out under fire to direct them, coordinating their attack with that of his men. The German defenders had orders to resist to the last man and the Co A riflemen had to throw more than 150 grenades into the tank-shelled houses.

By mid-afternoon Obourcy had been cleared of the enemy and the town was firmly in our hands. The entire German battalion staff of eight officers had been killed or captured. In all, 123 of the enemy were captured and 38 killed. Co A, which was at one-third strength, lost one man killed and five wounded.

\* \* \*

## TRAGIC DEATH OF SGT JARVIS OF CO H

After fighting into Bastogne and helping effect the relief of the 101st Airborne Division and other units there, the 320th Infantry with elements of the 101st jumped off to the east astride a railroad track with the mission of pushing *the enemy back and linking up with the 84th Infantry Division. The attack in the foot-deep snow went well for about a mile until stiff resistance was encountered in two patches of woods about 300 yards apart. Our troops were bogged down until late afternoon when tanks and tank destroyers reinforced G Company on the left and E Company on the right.*

*With the help of the armored vehicles G Company cleared the patch of woods to its front, taking about 75 prisoners. Then the Germans began running from the woods on the right as E Company advanced with its supporting armor. Lt Travis E. Hendren of Cleveland, N. C., and Sgt Jarvis, full name and address unknown, both forward observers for the 81mm mortar sections of Co H, began taking pot shots at the fleeing Germans. Hendren was using a German rifle taken from a fallen enemy soldier and Jarvis was using his GI .45 caliber automatic pistol. The Germans were running short distances and then falling in the snow in an effort to evade the small arms fire. Sgt Jarvis became quite excited, according to Lt Hendren, claiming he was felling the Germans at 300 yards range with his pistol.*

*An outstanding soldier from Tennessee, Sgt Jarvis had fought all the way from St Lo without receiving a scratch. A few days after the engagement with the enemy east of Bastogne, the sergeant was on his way to Paris by truck to spend a 3-day leave, when the vehicle was wrecked and Sgt Jarvis was killed.*

\* \* \*

CONFIDENTIAL

HEADQUARTERS 35TH INFANTRY DIVISION

APO 35 US ARMY

SPECIAL ORDERS)
NO        13)                    15 Jan 1945

EXTRACT

1. A general court-martial is aptd to meet at the Rear Echelon, 35th Inf Div, at 0930 17 Jan 45, and thereafter at such time and place as mil necessity may require and the President of the court may direct, for the trial of such persons as may properly be brought before it:

## DETAIL FOR THE COURT

COL DOUGLAS G DWYRE FA Hq 35th Div Arty

LT COL THOMAS E COONY FD Hq 35th Inf Div
*Law Member*

MAJ CHARLES L MCGEE CAC 448th AAA Bn

MAJ ROY M MATSON MC Hq Sp Trp 35th Inf Div

CAPT JOHN W CARSON INF 654th TD Bn

CAPT ELBERT B O'KEEFE INF 134th Inf

CAPT LOUIS W BROWN JR INF Hq Sp Trp 35th
Inf Div

CAPT NATHANIEL M SAGE JR IGD Hq 35th Inf Div

CAPT JOHN O SHOEMAKER INF 137th Inf

CAPT ORVAL E FAUBUS INF 320th Inf

1ST LT BEN A SMITH JR JAGD Hq 35th Inf Div
Trial Judge Advocate

1ST LT JAMES E JUDSON FA Hq 35 Div Arty now
on SD with Hq 35th Inf Div
Asst Trial Judge Advocate

CAPT WALTER W WAGNER AGD Hq 35th Inf Div
Defense Counsel

1ST LT THULE B KNIGHT INF 134th Inf
Asst Defense Counsel

Unarraigned cases in the hands of the Trial Judge Advocate
aptd by par 1 SO 178 Hq 35th Inf Div 20 Oct 44 are trfd to
the Trial Judge Advocate herein aptd.

The employment of an enl reporter, if available, is auth,
otherwise, the employment of a civilian reporter is auth.

By command of Major General BAADE:

MADDREY A SOLOMON
Colonel, G S C
Chief of Staff

OFFICIAL:

RICHARD G CHADWICK
Lt Colonel, A G D
Adjutant General

\* \* \*

Bastogne, Belgium
January 17, 1945

Our units are being relieved tonight . . . tomorrow all move back a short distance . . . later there is a long move coming up. Quartering parties are going out tomorrow headed by Capt Ginsberg. Shoulder insignia must be covered and vehicle markings obliterated. That doesn't look like the rest we had hoped to get, but seems to indicate commitment in a vital sector some where else on the front.

Today, as per orders, I went back to Div Rear at Arlon, and sat as a member of a General Courts Martial. It is a very distasteful and unpleasant task to me and always leaves me in a state of depression from which I sometimes have difficulty in recovering. I especially disliked the General Court because some of the members seemed so self-righteous and so harsh in their judgements. Some of the charges were for "misbehavior before the enemy" and I seriously doubt if anyone is qualified or competent to sit in judgment on a case of that nature who has not seen or experienced combat at the front. The combat soldier has lived in another world which others know nothing about.

* * *

I rode into Arlon with Milt and his driver "Buff" in an open jeep. The snow hangs on here and does not melt and each succeeding storm, as the one today, deepens the drifts and adds to the weight borne by the evergreens (firs I think) and the roof-tops. I hitch-hiked back, riding as far as the Sv Train area in a truck with a load of replacements just coming up to join the unit. All of these, a considerable number, were fresh from the States. They had sailed from America on Jan 1, crossing on the Queen Mary in six days, landed in Scotland, rushed across the island, across the Channel and through France, right up to the front. I talked with one officer, Lt Roberts, who had spent Christmas with his family. It is quite a different situation to reach in so short a time. Two boys from Springfield, Mo. had entered the army last July 17, which was after we had entered combat. I had not the heart to tell any of them what they might see here of what might happen to them, or how soon some of them would cease to exist. Because of their rapid transit to the front, some of them will be killed and their families will receive death notices by telegram from the War Department before they even get one letter from them [the soldiers] mailed from overseas.

Old Gen Sherman spoke a tragic truth in his brief remark "War is hell."

And so it was that we rode in almost total silence, the several miles along the icy, winding roads of the snowy Ardennes through Belgium and Luxembourg, past the dark snow-laden forests of fir, through the quaint villages, and then the battered towns of the late battlefields from which we had driven the enemy, past the fire-blackened, gutted frames of stone farm houses. For being so late from the States they did not want to talk of home, and there was nothing of the battlefield I wanted to tell them. They will learn of its horrors and hardships too soon as it is.

\* \* \*

Lt Silverman just called me from the Fwd CP to tell me the late news (gotten from the radio) of the Russian drive. Warsaw has fallen before a tremendous one day assault of the Red Army. The southern drive is almost on the German Silesian border, and they are driving on other fronts. It is the best and most heartening news in many days. Perhaps this is the beginning of the end.

\* \* \*

This Capt Fitzpatrick, who was special counsel for some of the defendants in today's trials, is really quite an intelligent and personable fellow.

Lt Col Williamson, the Judge Advocate, [35th Div Staff] is a former prosecuting attorney of the Southern Missouri Ozarks. He seems to be a very reasonable fellow, friendly and pleasant to work with.

\* \* \*

Lt Morgan[24] and Lt McLister were seriously wounded on the 15th. Lt Gibeau was killed. [See footnote No. 21] Morgan is one of our oldtimers, now evacuated for 2nd or third time. The others had joined us after we entered combat.

\* \* \*

---

24  1st Lt. Henry G. Morgan, Jr., Co C and Hq 1st Bn, Birmingham, Ala., an original, wounded first day at St. Lo, returned in late Oct., listed LWA Jan. 16.

Our troops reached their objective today without too much difficulty. If we are relieved as planned our part in the Battle of the Bulge in and around Bastogne will have ended. We held the right flank and the shoulder of the corridor when the 4th Armd Div drove in to make connection with the Bastogne garrison. The 35th Div then defeated the desperate efforts of the enemy to cut the corridor, and so contributed much to the success of the campaign to eliminate the "Bulge." We joined the 6th Armd Div in turning back the last attacks on Bastogne, and then drove back the Germans to a safe distance [from Bastogne] for the first time.

[From Metz we went into the Ardennes with over-strength companies, - more than 186 men and officers. Some companies came out with only 31.]

[A casualty[25] not mentioned in the Journal].

* * *

## CAPTURED EQUIPMENT IN BASTOGNE

*Enemy equipment captured in the Bastogne engagement included:*

| | | | |
|---|---|---|---|
| Rifles | 1,321 | AT gun (puppchen) | 1 |
| Pistols | 116 | Panzerfaust | 40 |
| Machine pistols | 312 | Teller mines | 48 |
| Machine guns | 263 | Rifle grenades | 75 |
| Bazookas | 267 | Bayonets | 12 |
| Mortars (80mm) | 27 | Vehicles (Misc.) | 17 |
| Mortars (50mm) | 5 | Arty. carriages (horse | |
| Mortars (120mm) | 14 | drawn) | 2 |
| Grenades | 1,053 | Bicycles | 3 |
| AT guns (75mm) | 8 | Personnel carrier | 1 |
| Guns (88mm) | 10 | Motorcycle | 1 |
| Wagons | 18 | Volkswagons | 10 |
| Howitzer (105mm) | 1 | Com. and Rcn. cars | 4 |
| Howitzers (75mm) | 2 | Trucks (1 1/2 ton) | 11 |
| AT mines | 12 | Trailers (1 ton) | 4 |
| Guns (40mm) | 2 | Half-tracks | 3 |
| Guns (20mm) | 2 | Tanks (all types) | 16 |
| Nebelwerfers | 7 | Horses | 180 |

25  1st Lt. Robert McDonald, (or McDonnell), Co H, address unknown, a replacement, listed LWA Jan. 17, did not return.

| | | |
|---|---|---|
| Radios _____ 24 | Machine pistol _____ 32,000 | |
| Telephones _____ 35 | Mortar (50mm) _____ 4,940 | |
| Binoculars _____ 12 | Arty. (88mm) _____ 1,077 | |
| | Mortar (80mm) _____ 4,200 | |
| Ammunition: Rds. | Puppchen _____ 20 | |
| Rifle and MG _____ 220,800 | Arty _____ 1,027 | |
| Rocket _____ 80 | Mortar (120mm) _____ 60 | |

*Enemy prisoners taken numbered 1,034, and there were killed and wounded in greater numbers.—From 35th Division History.*

## 320TH REGT AND PVT HANSON HIGHLY COMMENDED

Out of thousands of military units in the ETO the 320th Infantry and Pvt Whitney K. Hanson, N. Y., N. Y. were singled out by the highest echelon of Command, for special commendation for news stories written at the front and sent out through channels.

The commendation originated at The Communications Zone, ETO, and came through Hq 12th Army Group, Lt Col John M. Rudding; Hq Third U. S. Army, Maj James T. Quirk; Hq 35th Inf Div, Capt Leo B. White; to the 320th Public Relations Officer.

The commendation follows:

FROM: COMMUNICATIONS ZONE, ETO.

PUBLIC RELATIONS SECTION EAM/vc

APO 887

18 January 1945

SUBJECT: News Stories from the 35th Infantry Division.

TO: Public Relations Officer, 12th Army Group, APO 655.

1. The Public Relations Officer of the 35th Infantry Division and the members of his staff, are to be praised for their untiring efforts to publicize the achievements of the 35th Infantry Division and for the superior caliber of the material submitted.

2. Stories have been neat, accurate and well written to a high degree. The attached story by Private Whitney Hanson is cited as being specially meritorious. It is hoped that more work by this soldier will be forthcoming.

3. Frequently submissions from the 35th Division have been used as models for other divisions.

4. Such excellent work will aid tremendously in bringing home to Americans the brilliant job soldiers are doing in this theater.

For the Public Relations Officer:

EDGAR A. McLAUGHLIN,
Lt Col, G. S. C.
Deputy PRO and Executive

INCL.

\* \* \*

## COMMENDATION FROM 6TH ARMD DIV

### HEADQUARTERS 6TH ARMORED DIVISION

Office of the Commanding General

APO 256, US Army
20 January 1945

SUBJECT: Commendation.

TO: Commanding General, 35th Infantry Division, APO 35, U S Army

1. The 6th Armored Division was reinforced on 6 January 1945 by the 3rd Battalion, 320th Infantry, and on 12 January 1945 by the balance of CT 320, which remained with the Division until relieved on 18 January. During this period, these forces were engaged in holding a considerable portion of the Division front and took part in attacks on 13 January to 17 January inclusive. These operations were well carried out and were successful. The combat team acquitted itself in a highly creditable manner throughout, and by its reinforcement, the Division was able to accomplish its mission.

2. I wish to particularly commend the regimental and battalion commanders: Col Bernard A Byrne, Lt Col Joseph D Alexander, Lt Col Warren T Hannum, Jr, Lt Col William Walton and Lt Col Kenneth H Read for the skill and determination with which they carried out their missions and particularly for the splendid attitude and cooperation that they exhibited at all times. The combat efficiency of their units, reduced in strength as they were and subjected to se-

vere weather conditions, as well as fatigue, was of the highest standard. The 6th Armored Division personnel have acquired a feeling of confidence in their association with this combat team and will welcome an opportunity to join efforts with it in the accomplishment of our common objective whenever the occasion offers.

s/ R. W. Grow
R. W. GROW
Major General, USA
Commanding

1st Ind

PWB/w

HQ 35TH INF DIV, APO 35, U. S. Army, 23 January 1945.

TO: Commanding Officer, 320th Infantry, APO 35, U. S. Army.

It is with pleasure and congratulations for this accomplishment that I forward this commendation.

s/ Paul W. Baade
PAUL W. BAADE
Major General, USA
Commanding

Reproduced at
HQ 320th INF
27 January 45

\* \* \*

Sainlez, Belgium
January 23, 1945

Time: 0400

The relief was as planned and we moved out of the line to some villages a short distance back of the front and spent the night of the 18th.

On Jan 19th we moved in convoy to city of Metz and took up quarters in some dirty stone buildings on the southern outskirts. The 20th, 21st and 22nd have been spent here. [Evidently Sainlez, France, but written in the original as Belgium.] Have been so busy that I did not write a letter until today. Have been on night duty: busy with work of the CP, and some paper work of my own. It is now 0420, Jan 23.

Milt has arisen and is moving about. He is now taking off for some point to the south and east. We have received orders to join the Seventh Army, so the rumors of 10 days or two weeks rest were apparently unfounded. I guess we're on our way to another battle for the Germans have been gaining in the Seventh's sector around Strasbourg. It seems this veteran division is rushed from one critical point to another.

The weather is still very cold and the earth snow covered.

Quite a number of old veterans of our unit returned to us today and yesterday. They included Capt Alloway,[26] Lt Goodchild[27] and Pvt Blackmoore.[28] The latter used to drive for members of the staff and occasionally for me.

Now I think I shall try to get one hour's rest. Milt has "parte" for our next location.

\* \* \*

Bilderstruff, France
January 23, 1945

After some difficulty and confusion, we arrived at our present location. No one seemed to know where we were supposed to go. The Colonel had to halt the convoy on the road for some time while he found "what the score was" from our new headquarters. We are now with the Seventh Army, and tomorrow we move up to the front in the Vosges [Mountains] and must relieve a regiment by midnight tomorrow night.

It seems we are the "trouble shooters" for all the American Armies in France. We have now served with three of them.

Maj Jamieson, the Bn Comdrs and others are not yet back from Paris. I expect they will be surprised on their return to find us here instead of Metz.

The weather today was very cold; snowy with grey skies. This afternoon and night the snow has been sifting steadily

---

26  Capt. Curtis Alloway, originally Co L, became CO of Co K, Kansas City, Mo., an original, returning to duty from wounds the second time.

27  1st Lt. James C. Goodchild, Co C, Saco, Maine, an early replacement, wounded Nov. 8 and continued in the line, wounded and evacuated Nov. 18, now returning to duty. Later became CO of Co C and promoted to captain.

28  Pvt. Jack "Blackie" Blackmore, an original member of I & R Platoon, Liberal, Kans., returning to duty.

down. There is no wind and the white flakes settle gently on the scarred buildings and ruins, and the already white earth. Again it is reminiscent of snow fall in the Ozarks, if I look only at the flakes and the forest trees.

Again I have a cold and feel worse than at any time since I returned from the hospital. I have neglected almost all my correspondence. It is an effort to pen these few brief words.

Chief pastime of spare moments is listening to the wonderfully good news from the Russian front, and the programs of music from the USA. Very nostalgic, the latter. And there is always the bitching, mostly for pastime, the arguments and repartee among those whom we call the "junior officer" group, myself, Capts Bonham and Scherer, Lts Quillen, Parish, Clark and Silverman. Capt Ginsberg is included part of the time.

As we move early tomorrow, the others have spread their bed rolls on the dirty floor and have already crawled into them. My mind refuses to function so I shall lie down also. I wonder how long it will take to get accustomed to sleeping on a good bed when we can again have access to some of the comforts of civilization. I have had none of my clothes off, except coat and boots, since night of Jan 11, when I slept one night in the 35th Evac Hospital near Luxembourg. Some nights I have almost frozen with all my clothing on and wrapped in all the bedding I have.

And there are many others whose hardships are greater than mine.

\* \* \*

Wingen, France
January 27, 1945

Time: (0330)

We moved up to the front on the 24th and relieved another unit as planned. We have now been holding this sector since then making the third night in this place. We have a very nice set up for a CP and this sector is not yet very active. The personal feelings of most of us are that we'd like to spend the rest of the war here if the Russians can end it before too long. There are some artillery shells exploding about the town. Don't know if they're premature bursts of our own, on the way out, or enemy "packages" coming in.

The snowy Vosges Mts. in which we now fight resemble very much some portions of the Ozarks. I think of home every time I glance at any part of the landscape.

Maj Jamieson, Lt Mody[29] and others, returned today from their trip to Paris.

Most amusing incident of past two days, Capt Scherer, with the captured German SS cap on his head and a monocle in his eye, giving a good imitation of a German officer summing up the news from the war zones with special attention to the "Situation on the Eastern Front."

Now too sleepy to write - so must stop - and as I stop the eerie whine of a [enemy] shell helps me to punctuate these lines.

[A casualty[30] not mentioned in the Journal].

\* \* \*

## PRAISE FROM GEN. PATTON

Once again the officers and enlisted men of the Santa Fe received the gratitude and commendation of their Army, Corps and Division Commanders:

## HEADQUARTERS III CORPS
## OFFICE OF THE COMMANDING GENERAL
### APO 303, U. S. Army

200.6 GNNCG            25 January 1945

SUBJECT: Commendation.

TO: Commanding General, 35th Infantry Division, APO 35, U. S. Army.

1. The following letter from the Army Commander is quoted to all III Corps units which participated in the relief of Bastogne:

---

29   1st Lt. Raymond W. Mody, Sv Co, S-4 for 1st Bn, Detroit, Mich., an original. Mody, Byerly, S-4 for 2nd Bn, and Keith, S-4 for 3rd Bn, all originals, had grown most proficient in their supply duties during the long period of combat.

30   1st Lt. Daniel W. Tedder, Co C, address unknown, a replacement, evacuated as sick Jan. 27. He had returned to duty from wounds received Nov. 8. This time he did not return.

HEADQUARTERS

THIRD UNITED STATES ARMY

Office of the Commanding General

APO 403

20 January 1945

SUBJECT: Commendation.

TO: Commanding General, Officers and Men of the III Corps, APO 303, U. S. Army

"1. The speed with which the III Corps assembled, and the energy, skill and persistency with which it pressed its attack for the relief of BASTOGNE, constitute a very noteworthy feat of arms.

"2. You and the Officers and men of your Command are hereby highly commended for a superior performance.

"3. You will apprize all units concerned for the contents of this letter.

/s/ G. S. Patton, Jr.
/t/ G. S. PATTON, JR.
Lieutenant General, U. S. Army
Commanding."

1. The Corps Commander is gratified to transmit the Army Commander's commendation to the units of Corps troops and divisions participating in the relief of BASTOGNE. The uncertainty of the enemy situation, the stubborn enemy resistance, the disregard for losses and the team work which all units displayed in gaining the goal of relieving BASTOGNE were the contributing factors that made the operation such an outstanding victory, and will be highly valued in the history of each unit.

2. The Corps Commander adds his commendation for the performance of this task well done.

3. The contents of this letter will be made known to all officers and enlisted men of your organization at the earliest practicable time.

/s/ John Millikin
/t/ JOHN MILLIKIN
Major General, U. S. Army
Commanding

330.13                    1st Ind.                    PWB/mla

HQ. 35th INF. DIV., APO 35, U. S. ARMY, 9 Feb 45

TO: Unit Commanders, 35th Infantry Division.

 1. From St. Lo to BASTOGNE the path of this Division is well marked by monuments to Victory. Your performance has been magnificent.

 2. I desire that the above commendation be read to all of your officers and enlisted men. To it I add my congratulations for this splendid achievement.

/s/ Paul W. Baade
/t/ PAUL W. BAADE
  Major General, U. S. Army
  Commanding

\*   \*   \*

### PRINT THE DAMNED STUFF IN ENGLISH

*Artillery shells with the new "posite" fuse (proximity fuse) were being used in the Vosges. This was a shell with a new type fuse which had been developed causing the shell to explode when it came close to an object. Thus air bursts could be had any time such a shell was fired, making our artillery fire much more effective. To "hit the dirt" or get in a hole, good protection against the contact fuse shells, was little or no protection against the shells with a proximity fuse. To obtain an air burst with the old type fuse a timing device had to be set. With the new fuse this was unnecessary. Our supporting artillery may have had a limited supply of the new shells in the Alsace-Lorraine Campaign. Now the new, more effective ammunition was plentiful.*

*Our positions in the Vosges were in a region of hills and valleys. Consequently we had some shell bursts in our own positions. When the elevation for a shell was insufficient in passing over a hill top in our own area, it exploded within our lines before reaching the enemy positions.*

*Lt John Kelly had a most unusual and humorous experience in this region with another type of artillery fire. Because our lines were lightly held and an enemy offensive similar to the Ardennes was feared, a constant check was kept on enemy activity by means of patrols.*

*John and his platoon sergeant were making one of the nightly patrols in a dark forest region between the lines when some of our own artillery shells exploded in the area. John and the sergeant called back on their radio to make sure the artillerymen knew to keep the area clear. All arrangements were clearly understood and those directing the artillery could not understand how the misdirected explosions occurred.*

*After being reassured John and his sergeant resumed the patrol. Shortly another shell came into the trees over their heads and they flattened out on the earth. Following the explosion they heard, as they lay on the ground, a strange rustling. Then paper objects began dropping about them. They retrieved one of the papers, got down under their raincoats for concealment in order to use a flashlight for examination, and found the paper object was a pamphlet printed in German.*

*"Dammit, Lieutenant," the sergeant said to John in angry disgust, "Call them up and tell them if they're going to keep shootin' that damned stuff in here to print it in English."*

*John always got a hearty chuckle from the recollection of the sergeant's reaction when relating the incident to me.*

*Our own artillery was firing propaganda shells on the enemy positions, some of which were falling short and landing in the patrol area between the battle lines.*

*It was our experience that for some reason artillery rounds other than high explosive, as propaganda shells, white phosphorous and others, did not have the same accuracy as to range. This probably accounted for the short rounds on Lt Kelly's patrol which the artillerymen were carefully seeking to avoid.*

\* \* \*

Wingen, France
January 29, 1945

Considerable confusion reigns in the considerable hustle and bustle as we prepare to move again. The 179th [Inf Regt] of the 45th Inf Div is moving in to relieve us, and there is not room for both our units in the shelter available. So our unit is trying to get out as theirs comes in. Lt Quillen, as usual, is the busiest man about. It is rather uncomfortable, to say the least, to bustle out into the winter night in the deep snow. I hope we find a place to thaw out at the end of our move tonight.

— 499 —

As I write this, seated in the CO's room, a very comfortable place right now, (I've already given up my quarters to the incoming troops) Capt Scherer, always proud of the 216th FA, says not to forget the 160th FA which is relieving them.

Seems we're in for a long move this time, into our fifth country on the continent, and to fight with another American Army (the fourth one for us.)

Lt Silverman went away yesterday to spend a week with the Air Corps but this move will bring him back immediately I guess.

Lt Byerly [2nd Bn S-4] was to go to Paris for a week's schooling on the AEP but this move may prevent that.

We're all sorry to leave here; we had a good set up. One Bn was in reserve while the other two held the line. The troops were getting some rest. I was busy every day, and part of almost every night, with administrative work, but we had good quarters and were comfortable. We all thought this was too good to last, and so it was.

Snow has fallen every day since we've been here except today. It is a beautiful country here now - the snow, white and deep, clings in heavy coats to the evergreens which are spread over the steep forested hills. The streams flow dark and cold between their high, white banks, and wind crookedly along the deep narrow valleys.

Which reminds me. I would have been glad to stay here until the Russians finished the war, and I heard others express a similar hope.

Remark of Lt Col Alexander when informed we were to move again, "Where have the Germans broken through this time?"

It is a fact that we have been out of the lines only 15 days since we entered combat on July 8, 1944, north of St Lo. A large part of that time [the 15 days] has been spent in moving us from the Saar to Metz - to Luxembourg - back to Metz - and to the Vosges.

Said some member of our unit one day, tired and disgusted with the constant battle and pushing, "Well, it's the same old story. The Russians and the 320th push ahead." We're going to another sector to push now, I'm sure. Perhaps if we do well, we'll soon meet the Russians as they're certainly pushing fast enough at this time. [As fate would have it, the 320th was atchd to the 83rd Inf Div, which was the first American outfit to meet the Russians at the Elbe River in what is now a part of East Germany.]

Today was a very pretty one for winter. Much of the time there was sunshine on the snow-white hills. Several times we could see, through the light, broken clouds, deep throated bombers roaring high through the pale blue sky, homeward bound from bombing missions in Hitler's Germany. The third Reich is constricting now, and the bombers' targets are growing fewer and easier to find. At long last, the war is coming home with a vengeance to German cities and towns and to the German people, and may they get their fill of the hell and destruction which the German nation let loose on the world.

\* \* \*

While we wait tonight, for the relief to be completed, our talk turns to past experiences, the friendliness of the people of Luxembourg, the piles of dead Germans around Bastogne; the liberated cities of Central France with the FFI parades and the shorn heads of the women collaborators, and I recall Col Northam's haircut at Courtenay. Maj McElroy has the most accurate memory for dates and places. We listen for awhile as Col Byrne describes, in his inimitable way, some of the scenes to the CO of the regiment that is relieving us.

Red Cross Charlie has come in. When he learns we are bound for Mastrich, Holland he pulls out his tiny French pistol and [in jest - he is a non-combatant] says, "I'd better load up my shootin' iron." It is easy to guess we will go from there into the big push into the German Rhineland plain.

\* \* \*

Our radios pick up almost constantly now, German propaganda broadcasts in English - seeking desperately, almost hysterically, to foster distrust and fear of the Bolsheviks (Russians). It is their last trick and they are playing it to the fullest extent, for all it is worth, in an attempt to create disunity among the Allies, and gain a peace that will save their criminal necks. I'm sure our leaders will not fall for any of their lying propaganda. It would be a betrayal of those who have died and will die before the conflict is finally ended. Germany must be completely crushed and must accept our terms without negotiation. We must not listen for a moment to any pleas for special consideration. Force is the only thing which the German people, in their present state of mind, can understand and respect.

Petersbach, France
January 30, 1945

Our CP now is a big hall in the town of Petersbach. We arrived okeh traversing the snow covered roads last night without incident. Sammy O'Brien [liaison from Div Hqs] reached us some time after midnight with our orders for the move, and Maj McElroy, with his customary speed and dispatch, soon had the orders ready for the various units of our regiment. Representatives from some of the units were called in to get their copies and instructions. Lt Parish carried them to others. I think his work was done by 0430 this morning. I took over his duties in the CP while he was out. Traveling last night was not too difficult as the snowbound country was bathed in bright mellow moonlight.

Our move is to be by train and motor. About 800 men will go by our organic motors and the remainder in the charge of Col Northam, assisted by Maj Jamieson, will go by train, the old 40 and 8, so well known to the veterans of World War I. The cars are open, built of slats like our cattle cars of the U. S. No doubt it will be very cold riding in them, but it is cold in the motor vehicles also. There is no comfortable side to war in winter, except when we occasionally get situated in buildings during a fairly static situation, which has occured so seldom to us.

Lt Clark is sour and without smiles because he has to go on the train. Sid has not yet returned, hope he doesn't get lost. Milt went on ahead yesterday with 3 or 4 days rations. He is to select our bivouac area in Holland before we arrive. Maj Hughes, Capt Shamla[31] and assistants are the busiest people now, as service and supply are the biggest problems in a situation of this kind.

* * *

Many among us are growing optimistically hopeful now because of the wonderful progress of the Russians. I grow

---

31  Capt. Richard J. Shamla, Sv Co, Regtl TO, Glenco, Minn., an original, with us all the way.

a bit breathless sometimes myself, but I try to hold my hopes in check. When peace and home seems too near it becomes too painful, and often brings one close to the breaking point.

\* \* \*

Lt Adams[32] just came in and I told him of our classmate, Lt Don C. Craig, [North Platte, Nebr.] who recently joined the Division. Lt Craig is now acting as aid to Gen Sebree. I went through basic training with him at Camp Wolters, Texas. We were assigned to the same platoon while in OCS at Ft. Benning, and were together two weeks at Camp Robinson after graduation. Now our paths have crossed again in the battle lines of the snowy Vosges. Lt Craig came over during the fall with the 99th Div and saw combat with it before joining the 35th.

Don has a brother, Lt Col Craig, who has been with the 35th Div for some time.

Col Byrne is enthusiastically telling the world news to all visitors to the CP this morning. I think the Colonel, like myself, is longing very much to get back to a warm sunny clime. I know he is very much in love with his pleasant Hawaiian home, and dislikes the cold almost as much as I. And the news he relates this morning is good. Russian armies sweeping into the province of Brandenburg toward Berlin. German armies trapped in East Prussia, another pocket forming around Danzig, mop-up of industrial areas in Silesia, even substantial gains in the West, and the German people and the radio broadcasters growing more alarmed and hysterical by the hour. And there are successes in the Philippines and other sectors of the Pacific War. Also we suspect the building up of large forces, of which we are being made a part, for the big assault on the Rhineland in the West. Things could break rapidly for us, but we are prepared if the struggle is much longer.

---

32 1st Lt. Robert W. Adams, A/T Co, Canton, Ohio, an original, a Ft. Benning classmate, wounded Aug. 11, 1944, recovered and returned to duty.

Somewhere in Holland (MHEER)
February 1, 1945

Time: 0445

I would not attempt to write this, but for a combination of circumstances. I have been assigned as duty officer and so must remain 'downstairs'; my bed roll is somewhat wet and very cold; there is a little stove in this beautiful Dutch room, and electric lights that work. So I made a fire in the stove, and while my bed roll dries, I can write by the light of this civilian electric light, seated in a chair at a very nice table, all of which is very wonderful.

It has been a very uncomfortable move, all the way from the Vosges to SE Holland from the Seventh Army to the Ninth, [the 292-mile trip was one of the longest infantry moves of the war] all the way over roads banked high with snow and, most of the distance, caked with slippery ice. Tonight as we crossed a part of the former Runstedt Bulge the vehicles rolled over glassy roads, which were narrow lanes between minefields not yet removed from the shoulders. There is as yet no report of anyone being so unfortunate as to slide off the road in one of those areas, and most of the vehicles have now arrived. [The 320th had moved 450 miles in January.]

Some time or at some point between here and the deeply snow-covered Vosges, the weather moderated. Now the snow is becoming slush and the hard earth a soft quagmire. As I write I can hear the water gurgling in rivulets from the roof and down the drain pipes, and I know it is beginning to run in muddy streams through the gulleys and along the ditches beside the roadway. The heavy overcast has also given way, for while outside a moment ago I could catch faint glimpses of the moon through the light, rapidly flying clouds, and could see for quite some distance over the Dutch countryside.

* * *

Impressions on arrival: Scarcely anyone was in a pleasant mood after the long, arduous journey. Milt was as uneasy as an old hen with ducklings in a rainstorm, in his attempts to keep things quiet in this building. Col Bryne and Maj McElroy had already gone to bed and he did not want them awakened, and, it being in the early hours of morning, he did not want to disturb the Dutch villagers too much either. But new arrivals kept coming in with much banging of equipment and loud talking. He would grab his flashlight and with a ferocious bulldog look on his face, make a rush for the doorway as if he were going to tackle an unfriendly intruder.

During one interval, when things were fairly quiet, Milt had gotten seated. Then in bursts Capt Haley demanding, in a loud, high-pitched, almost hysterical voice, if he is "going to hang my extra 25 men from the rafters."

"Lets keep our voices down," barks Milt in an intense subdued tone, and after a further exchange of words, rushes out with him to solve the quartering problem for the communications section. He returns presently with a smiling, satisfied look on his face. Captain Haley had simply failed to find all the rooms assigned to him. "Why Christ! He could billet them if he had twice as many," concludes Milt.

Capt English, S-1 for the 3rd Bn, comes in looking very worn and tired. "No problems," he replies to Milt's query, "Just wanted to know when the rest of the troops will be in." But none of us know when those on the trains will arrive. He and Milt discussed the billeting problems, and English, who at first seemed to have the easiest one, now has the most difficult. He was assigned an old castle which was to be all his own for his Bn. "I thought I could billet a thousand troops in that," he said, "But it seems we miscalculated. Now I know of one room we entered from four different directions and counted four times." So he is short of space because, in addition to the miscalculation mentioned above, many of the rooms leak and are hardly usable. These old world castles are confusing.

However English is still very cheerful, in a tired way, about the whole thing. When Lt Quillen brings in his bottle of whiskey, still two-thirds filled, English picks it up, shakes it and asks, "How is this?" "I tell you," replies Quillen, who does not like that particular brand, "It's strictly piss, but it's all I've got." Then almost everyone, especially Lt Quillen, drinks it like a long lost desert wanderer quenching his thirst at a fresh mountain spring.

Things finally grow quiet. Lt Parish finishes his checking of the units and goes to bed at 0515. Now 0610 and the only noise is the gurgle of the water from the melting snow, the occasional passing of a truck, and the early morning crowing of the cocks in the Netherland farm yards.

The good news from the Russian front fills me with a pent-up hope that the war may soon end, and this awful bloodshed will cease. I hope the brave Russians are not losing too many of their heroic fighters. So many of all nations have died. I think of those I know, Braffit and Cull, Fritts and McCormic, and their faces pass through my memory followed by many others. At quiet times like these, when there is no one astir and there is only me, slowly and laboriously penning these lines, I often feel their presence. The big smiling Porta is showing me the pictures of his family; Zintas is arguing politics and making wagers; Gardner exclaiming that you must not let it get the best of you; the imperturbable Gillis about the business of war as calmly as if it were maneuvers; Braffit, never pausing in his activity, exclaiming, "Damn, Faubus, this is rough. When's it going to end?"; the fair young Cull with tenderness in his eyes and voice telling me the latest news from pretty Margaret and showing me pictures of his baby boy whom he will never see; Underwood describing to me his part of the Ozarks. That recalls the letter so filled with pathos from his wife; and I realize once more that I shall never see them again, except as I see them now.

Mheer, Holland
February 2, 1945

It is now the afternoon, (1715). I have been busy throughout the day compiling the "after action" report for the month of January. It is a story of bitter battle amidst deep snow in Luxembourg and Belgium, and then of travel, Bastogne to Metz to the Vosges, then back to Belgium and to

Holland, via Nancy, Void, Commercy, St. Mihiel, Verdun, Sedan, Boullion and Liege. I don't know what route the trains took but they have not all arrived yet. The first train, on which Col Northam and Maj Jamieson rode, came yesterday and I find they had a very comfortable trip. Pvt Whitey Hanson[1] says the journey was much more comfortable than if they had come by motor in the usual manner.

While more comfortable than [for] some, the trip was still very uncomfortable to me. My knees ached and were slightly swollen by the time we arrived. Sightseeing was practically nil, our view being confined chiefly to the roadway and the dirty snow heaped along its shoulders, and of course we saw nothing at night. My ration of liquor was all that kept me from suffering the first day, and whether it helped Sgt Kearns and Sgt _____ or not, they still seemed to get a lot of pleasure from helping me drink it. On the second day the weather had moderated and the cold was not so severe.

\* \* \*

Lt Silverman returned today. He had been assigned to an "Air Arm" near Dijon, where he could have had a nice week, but he was ordered back to us as soon as he arrived and finally caught up with us.

\* \* \*

To clear my mind for work, and at the same time get some exercise, I took a walk at noon up on the rise of ground to the east of the village. A moderately warm west wind has cleared away the snow, except for a few remaining drifts, laying open to the view a country side covered with a carpet of green. It looked so refreshing after the days of snow. Where the grass grew the ground was quite firm in spite of the thaw. The wind, though continuous and strong, was not severe and had lost its chill. As it came in from the sea and over the country-side in great long sweeps, it felt to my face and hands like a caress.

When I had reached the top of the green hill, I could look down on a large part of the picturesque village, made up of the stone houses and divided into parts by the winding

1  Pvt. Whitney K. "Whitey" Hanson, Sv Co, N. Y., N. Y., wrote news stories on the 320th's activities for the Public Relations Section of Division. Occasionally I worked with him.

muddy roads. On the slope to the north was the church, indispensable to any European village, its tall, intricately-graven spire rising above the imposing building and dominating, as always, the settlement which clusters about it, just as its influence controls, to a great extent, the lives of those who live in the dwellings. From the village itself, in every direction, the slightly uneven country rolled in green swells, interspersed by small woodlands, crisscrossed by the hedges and roads and dotted occasionally by buildings. To the east across a knoll, an orchard marched in even rows.

I returned by a winding muddy road, splashing along in my big overshoes in the lowest places on the firm ground washed bare by the water from the melting snow. Passing close to a Dutch house I saw two childish faces with rosy cheeks and round eyes pressed close against the window as they peered at me. They answered my greeting with shy grins. The householder waved from his seat near the window and a woman stepped from behind the curtains with the friendliest of smiles.

These kind Dutch people have been as good to us here as anyone could possibly be. Many of us are billeted or sheltered in their homes. I have heard only words of praise for them from all the troops. Their homes are beautiful and wonderously clean, neat and well kept. Almost all Americans could take lessons from them in that respect.

*　*　*

The remainder of the troops (3rd Bn) arrived today.

This is much nicer even than the Vosges. The snow is now gone - the sun shone brightly for awhile today and all the troops are out of the battle lines getting some rest. As before I fear this is too good to last.

We now have information that we are to relieve a British division on the extreme left of the Ninth Army along the Roer River line in Germany. The going will likely be tough for there the Germans will have their artillery massed more heavily than perhaps any other part of the Western Front.

*　*　*

The people with whom I am sheltered have the village Post Office. The establishment is about the size and style of the village post office in America. I bought a set of Neitherland stamps from them. They are very kind and serve us delicious tea at every opportunity. Capt Scherer and I had a cup with them a few moments ago. He can understand a little bit but I can grasp very little of what they try to say.

[Two "Old Originals"[2] pass from the scene].

Mheer, Holland
February 3, 1945

With the help of Sgt "Smokey" Dodd and Sgt Mosher, I have been showing an orientation film to the troops today. It is a very good one, designed to guide us in our attitude toward the Germans and our conduct while occupying the country. We've been all over the countryside to the various villages where the different units are located. Our first projector went bad and, with the help of Lt Quillen, I got another by going almost to Maasterich to Div Rear. That disrupted the whole schedule which was not going too smoothly anyway because of the lack of a suitable place to show a movie.

\* \* \*

Well, I thought I could write some, but find I'm too tired. Tomorrow we relieve the British Division[3] on the plains by the Roer.

\* \* \*

Yesterday the ground hog got a good look at his shadow even though a brief one. Today was mild for February. Last night a British plane roared over our CP and crashed nearby, and all that could be found of the unfortunate pilot was some intestines and some bits of flesh. I observed the scattered wreckage today. Last night a buzz-bomb exploded not far away. Tonight one passed over while we were showing for the 2nd Bn.

Today I got to see my old friends, Lts Kelly and Gangemi. There are now only about eight EM of the old originals [180] left in Co F. [Among them Archie L. Jones, Haynes, Ark. and Sgt. Coy E. Johnson, Johnson City, Tenn.] I saw them tonight and got to talk briefly with them. Pfc

---

2  Capt. Victor H. English, Hq 3rd Bn, Portland, Oregon, evacuated as sick Feb. 2; Capt. Curtis H. Alloway, Co K, Kansas City, Mo., listed Tdy Feb. 2, probably returned to the States as a member of the Rehabilitation Furlough group. Two "old originals," they did not return.

3  We relieved the 52nd British Infantry Division.

Bush is now evacuated as well as Lindsey. Lane[4] got to return to the States and Arkansas in the last quota, - I was so glad to learn that. Good news of one's friends is so seldom heard here. My good friends Capt Hare and the Chaplains, Capts Tarpley and Stone, are still fine. Other old acquaintances I was glad to see, Cpl Estell,[5] Sgts Quested and Lockhart of 2nd Bn Hqs, and that ardent CIO advocate and skillful gin rummy player, the rough-looking, good-hearted Lt Peterson, Com O of the 3rd Bn. I won't soon forget the time he and his wire crew laid a line in to the town of Torigny ahead of the rifle troops way back in Normandy in July.

Tonight is as clear as June skies in the Ozarks and the stars twinkle throughout the immeasurable heavens almost as brightly as they once did in peaceful America. During my brief glances at their gleaming brightness I was forcefully reminded by the criss-crossing searchlights, the drone of planes, and the occasional blossoming of the orange ack-ack, thrt there is as yet no peace here.


Mheer, Holland
February 4, 1945

Now 1330:

The day is gray, forbidding and rainy. The roads are streaks of mud as we move to relieve the British Division. This morning as we ate breakfast, Dominees indicated the streaming window panes through which could be seen the raindrops and said, "Right on schedule!" Seems we do have inclement weather for almost every move.

The chill has returned to the air. Last night, before the rain, the ground froze.

Very shortly we must be off. The Colonel and staff and most of the troops have already departed.

---

4 Sgt. Lensy P. Lane, Co F, Garfield, Ark., returned to duty before the war ended, and was one of the four men still remaining with Co F at war's end - who crossed the channel with the 320th.

5 1st Sgt. Jack T. Estoll, Hq Co, 2nd Bn, San Francisco, Calif., came home with the unit after the war. I cannot be sure he is the same person mentioned in the Journal. I can find no further information on Sgts. Quested and Lockhart of 2nd Bn Hq.

Birgden, Germany
February 4, 1945

Now 2000 hours. We moved up to the new area along muddy roads through the misty rain of the gray day. At first there were the comparatively clean and orderly Dutch villages, but when we crossed the German border there was a decided change. If there had been no marker of the international boundary, we could have been able to determine where the line ran by noting the destruction which existed after Holland ended and Germany began. From then on we drove through a country pock-marked and scarred with shell craters, trenches and fox holes. The houses often had been reduced to piles of rubble, and the forests and orchards to areas of scarred stubs. The ground in forest areas was littered with the shattered tree tops and branches.

The British, whom we relieved, told us there was a hard battle for the area, and neither they nor the Americans were stingy with the artillery when it came to blasting the Germans from their positions. I had the thought that if the Germans could see this desolated section of their "Fatherland" they would surrender now in order to spare other sections of their country from like destruction.

\* \* \*

Tonight we operate a joint CP with the British as the relief of their units by ours goes on. Some positions are under enemy observation and the relief must be effected under cover of darkness. These British officers and Tommies are regular guys, but to most of our men their accent or brogue sounds very funny. It certainly has to be a desperate situation when they pass up their tea, usually at 1000 and 1600, or at any time they can brew it. Some who have observed them say the situation is never that critical. One of our Bn Cmdrs reporting to their Bn CP during the process of the relief was greeted, "Oh, I'm frightfully sorry, old chap, you are just too late for a spot of tea." Those arriving anywhere near the proper time were welcomed with "I say, old man, won't you have a spot of tea?"

I guess "having tea" is a very bright diversion in the heavy gloom of war. I think the tea itself is very delicious. Unlike most Americans, I much prefer it, and think it much better than our coffee. But perhaps that is because I never had the coffee habit before entering the army.

Overheard as one British officer talked over the telephone, "Oh, I don't mind. Not a bit." - and again, "Yes, I'm quite happy about the whole thing."

Birgden, Germany
February 5, 1945

Today, we are getting settled into the old routine of the front, after the pleasant though brief stay in Holland, and again familiarize ourselves with yet another area. Within a few hours it seems as though we had lived here a long time. Perhaps it is because the activity is so much the same. Certainly the shell holes, the ruined buildings and piles of rubble, the now worn vehicles plowing through the sloppy mud, the sound of the artillery ringing in our ears again, and the misty rain sweeping at intervals over the soaking German plains are all very familiar to us.

The whole area over which our regiment has now assumed control has many mines and booby traps; "Lousy with them," the British said. The Tommies have all gone today but a constant reminder of their recent presence are the signs posted along the highways, "Roads cleared of mines to verges." Our regtl staff has voiced a unanimous opinion they were the most courteous and cooperative unit we have ever relieved. Comment by Lt Quillen on a different angle, "God Damn! They had more transportation in their hqs co than we have in the whole regiment. They know how to live." They certainly did have some wonderful "establishments" fixed on their big highwheeled lorries. They looked as comfortable as a good American house trailer and much more substantial.

We do not go poking around the ruins here, nor do we walk on the inviting green sod in the yards and fields. We stick to the roads or beaten paths no matter how filthy or deep the mud. To do otherwise is inviting death from the hellish machines the Huns left behind.

The whole regimental area is fairly quiet with only desultory artillery fire. Occasionally there is mortar and machine gun fire on the forward outposts. The busiest people are the engineers who work constantly to keep the roads in passable condition, and who keep clearing out minefields with deafening explosions. Lt Donovan[6] and his I & R Platoon are kept busy with their OPs and RCN details.

---

6 Formerly Sgt. Richard C. Donovan, I & R Plat, Baltimore, Md., mentioned often previously. He was awarded a battlefield commission.

Birgden, Germany
February 6, 1945

This morning I slept late having been on duty the previous night. Upon arising I staggered sleepily from my "quarters" in a stone building into the nearby roadway and was almost run down by Lt Quillen who was guiding a clubmobile into the area. My God! those doughnuts and coffee certainly did go good for my morning meal, and those American Red Cross girls looked fine. It was a nostalgic reminder of the times when I used to order the same food from some pretty waitress for my morning meal while traveling in the States.

During their noon rest the ladies came over to our liaison room and chatted with the officers for a few moments. Two of them had dinner at the Officer's Mess. There seemed to be a constrained air among us and no one felt fully at ease. The fact is we had to be very careful of what we said. To have spoken in our usual manner might have been very embarrassing to all present. For it must be said that the language and conversation of men at war would not be suitable for mixed company, nor the homes or public places of the world we left behind. Some one remarked later that the incident was a reminder of how far we had come in many ways from what we are wont to call culture and civilization.

Perhaps the Red Cross workers did not know that they were as alone in a man's world as they have ever been or perhaps ever will be. For miles in either direction from here, the civilians have left or been evacuated. All these settlements are strictly GI towns. The inhabitants may use their rough language freely with assurance that it will not fall on tender, womanly ears, and free to answer the calls of nature whenever and wherever they choose without danger of offending soft, feminine eyes. Except, of course, in case of an "invasion" such as we had today. Then the GI inhabitants are as alert as if the enemy had infiltrated our lines and were roaming among our positions.

It is true, however, that as a rule the front line troops have to concern themselves only with the enemy. Except in the case of refugees, the sight of a lovely figure or the sound of a soft voice is not for them. Had this not been a quiet sector we would not have had the clubmobile here. Most of the girls would go to the front positions if permitted (I think because they do not realize the danger) but officers have orders not to take them into dangerous areas.

Birgden, Germany
February 8, 1945

It is now 0540 on morning of the 9th. I have been on duty during the night. Throughout the hours of darkness planes have droned overhead at more or less regular intervals. Artillery booms occasionally. All night the searchlights have played across the sky, sometimes reflecting their "artificial moonlight" back to the earth from the clouds above.

\* \* \*

Today Capt Wilson [of AT Co] showed me one of the "shu" (pronounced "shoe" but spelled differently) mines which his mine platoon[7] had secured while clearing the area. It consisted of a one-pound charge placed in an all-plastic or wooden case with a simple firing devise which could be tripped by pressure from above, as a person stepping on it. The only metal about the contraption was the firing pin, which makes it next to impossible to locate with a mine detector.

An artilleryman of Capt Scherer's unit was killed since we came here. He stepped on one, which smashed his leg between the knee and hip, and fell on another which practically blew him in two at the waist.

\* \* \*

Tragedy still further stalks on this quiet front. Two 3-man patrols have been lost without a trace. With one of them was an old veteran of the unit, who had been selected to return to the States with our next quota. He was to return to the rear tomorrow. Thus it is often by such a narrow margin of chance, or whim of fate, that joy or grief is brought to a soldier or his loved ones.

\* \* \*

Lt Byerly is to go to Paris tomorrow for a week's training in preparation for setting up the AEP when the war is over.

\* \* \*

---

7 Lt. Kenneth I. Botton, A/T Co, New Brunswick, N. J., was in charge of the mine platoon.

Interesting items in the mail today: a letter (forwarded by Alta) from my old friend, Stephen W. Bowker of Jonesboro, Ark, with whom I did basic training at Camp Wolters, Texas. He is now a warrant officer, junior grade, and stationed on New Caledonia.

A letter from my friend, Ruby V. Hughes of Whitener, Ark, who says my letters from the war fronts are the finest he has seen, and urges me to write a book of my war experiences when the conflict is over. My due appreciation to him, of course, but right now I'm thinking of doing my job and, at the same time, getting through safely to the end. Everything else must be, and is, subordinated until that goal is reached. It is only then that one in the combat infantry can think of plans for life, love, and happiness, and the possible satisfaction of one's ambitions. I know Mr. Hughes understands as he was a doughboy in World War I.

*  *  *

A letter from Sgt Koch[8] who reached his home in America after a journey of 40 days.

Birgden, Germany
February 11, 1945

Still busy today with administrative work. With my assistants, Pvt Winters[9] and Backhoven,[10] we have turned out enough typewritten work to fill a large volume.

Last night, for a time, was clear with the stars twinkling brightly. Then there was rain and mist. This morning there was ice on the puddles. As I drove past a German cabbage field the green leaves were crisp with frost. About two miles to the west was a snow line and in that direction the fields were white and the forests fringed with lace. By noon the snow was all gone and at intervals the almost daily mist and rain was sweeping over the flat German plains. During one

---

8 Sgt. Don A. Koch, Lima, Ohio, one of the originals with Co F, who was in the first quota of EM and officers to obtain a rehabilitation furlough to the States. They left the lines on Dec. 15 in Alsace-Lorraine.

9 Pvt. Winters, no other information, a stenographer and typist, who assisted me in administrative and legal work.

10 Pfc. Charles F. Bachofen, Hq Co, Elizabeth, N. J., a highly skilled stenographer and typist, my most regular assistant in the great amount of administrative and legal work done.

clear period, two enemy planes came from the east, flying fast. The AA guns, stationed throughout the area, opened up with a terrific clatter. Some distance to the west both planes were seen to burst apart in the air and fall in smoke and flames, bringing joy to the heart of every watcher.

Tonight rain fell quite heavily for some time with a drumming patter and a drip, drip, drip through the shell holes in the wrecked buildings, and splashed steadily into the puddles under the eaves.

Now 0100 - It is quiet again, and Milt, Clark and I, after late discussion, are going to our bed rolls in the damp stone buildings. Sid is on duty tonight.

Col Northam, lucky man, left today for a seven day leave in London.


Birgden, Germany
February 13, 1945

Now early morning after all night duty (0700) and work yesterday. Spent the day at Capt Heil's CP investigating courts martial charges. In the afternoon, while Pvt Winters finished typing some statements, I went with Capt Heil to the Dutch town of _____ where I had a shower. Things are getting almost luxurious as that is the second bath in a week. The other bath in a large tub with plenty of hot water was positively a pleasure, and was the first (on Feb 9) since leaving the hospital on Jan 11.

Aside from the pleasure of the bath I was quiet amused at Clark and Ginsberg who were oh-ing and ah-ing in the next compartments. "Ah-h-h, what a sensation; Oh-h-h-h, this is really marvelous; I tell you this is positively luxurious!" exclaimed Milt.

The baths, hundreds of them, are in a wonderful stone building. They must be owned cooperatively by the miners for a sign at the entrance reads "All Allied Service men are welcome to have a bath on the coal miners of _____."
[At time of writing I could not recall the name of the town] They are certainly wonderful and I know of nothing that would be more appreciated.

\* \* \*

Picture that stuck in my mind.

The rear echelon soldier walking down the street of a Dutch town with a gorgeous woman on each arm, as our battle stained doughboys moved up to the front.

Battered town of Gilenkerchen.

The blasted forest, filled with fox holes, with the foliage cut from the pines. The fragments of boughs carpeted the ground. About one tree in five, badly battered, was yet standing. The rest were splintered stubs.

[An "Old Original"[11] goes home].

\* \* \*

From The
MADISON COUNTY RECORD
March 15, 1945

## NEWS AND COMMENT

(By Ruby V. Hughes)

LETTER—

Here is one from Captain Orval Faubus, written upon the soil of the country which "has fed the people who have authored most of the hell of the past several years." He enclosed some French and German currency of the series of 1944. The letter speaks for itself and no comment could add to the glory of the beloved Captain so loved and honored by all of us at home:

Somewhere in Germany,
Feb. 13, 1945

Mr. Ruby V. Hughes,
Whitener, Arkansas

Dear Mr. Hughes,

Just recently I received your very welcome letter. I am going to save it as one of the finest compliments I have ever

11  1st Lt. James R. F. Woods, Co M, Palo Alto, Calif., listed as Tdy Feb. 13. He probably was returned to the States on a rehabilitation furlough. Lt Woods, an original, previously wounded and returned to duty, did not return from this assignment.

received. Thank you very much although I know I can never write as well as your words implied. Just the same it is nice to receive a rose sometimes even though it is not fully deserved.

There is no way for me to express to you the depth and the sincerity of my desire to make others see the horror and the cost of war. I have never really tried to do that in my letters, for censorship rules would not permit, even though I felt I had the ability, which I do not. My reason: I think if everyone fully understood what war is like, there would be no more conflicts of this kind. The heartbreak and hardships, the loneliness and frustrated longing caused by war are so much more than the glory and small benefits (if any) which it brings, that the comparison of difference is not comprehensible.

Of course I don't need to talk about this to you. For you, Mr. Hughes, were a "Doughboy" of World War I, and realize as well as I that there is no harder, more dangerous job in all the world.

Tonight my unit holds positions on German soil; the soil has fed the people who have authored most of the hell of the past several years. Of course I know it isn't the fault of the land itself. It was and is the perverted and wrong ideas the people had in their heads. I once heard a minister preach a sermon entitled "It Makes a World of Difference What You Believe," and since that time I have come to realize that he hit the head of the nail the squarest blow of any I have ever seen struck. If these German people, along with many others throughout the world, had had right ideas instead of wrong ones, the world could have been at peace, they could have been much better off and I could have been at home getting the greatest pleasure from listening to my little boy read his primer, which he has learned to do since I went away. Yes, when you come to think of it, millions of dead would have yet lived, millions more of the maimed would still be whole, and the slaves in Germany would yet be free. "Know the truth, and the truth will make you free." (Scripture once quoted by Robert Reed of Combs).

I have always enjoyed your column in the Record. So just keep it going. I wrote that to you in a letter some time ago, which you may not have received. Lives are lost in crossing the ocean so we must expect the loss of letters and supplies as well. Thank you for your letter and the copy of the Record.

Your friend,

Capt. Orval E. Faubus
Hqs. 320th Inf., APO 35,
New York City, N. Y.

* * *

Hulhoven, Germany
February 24, 1945

I'm so tired that I just couldn't force myself to write long hand, so I'll try the typewriter as it seems to require a bit less effort.

Our troops have moved to the River Roer all along our front. Most of the movement was accomplished before day-break yesterday (starting at 0330, 23 Feb.) [The 320th crossed the Wurm River on Feb. 23.] The First Bn was fighting most of the day. The Second ran into so many mine-fields and booby traps that its mission was not accomplished until nightfall. Sometime after dark Lt Parish had to go get some engineers to go up to the battalion to help get some wounded men from the mine fields. There were two aid men which the Bns own men got out, but they had to have engineers with special equipment to get one man who was far out into the mined area. He was still lying there in the cold and rain far into the night while they worked their way out to him. The aid men were wounded trying to go to him when he was first hit. There were "shu" mines and "S" mines mixed together.

We had some more Air Corps officers and enlisted men with us again last night. I don't think they were impressed by any favorable conditions which they found us enjoying.

* * *

On night of 22 Feb we could see our Air Force striking the German city of Duisburg. The sky was lit up by flares and bomb flashes for almost an hour as the bombers pounded it. The thunder was almost continuous. The multi-motored planes were leaving vapor trails high in the clear, moon-lit sky on their way home.

A great bombing raid must be about the most terrifying thing in the world. The great artillery barrage yesterday

— 519 —

morning reached along the whole front. It recalled to my mind the morning of Nov 8, 1944, when we jumped off across Alsace-Lorraine from the Gremercy Forest. To me there was another similarity. On Nov. 7, I had gone to town of Nancy for a bath and had stayed a short time afterward. I sat in a hotel lobby for a short time and talked to some other officers, one of them being Lt Botton. On Feb. 22 I went with a bunch of enlisted men in a truck with Pvt Chabina[12] to Maastrich, Holland. There I saw a show and then sat around the Red Cross Club and chatted with some officers, one of them being Lt Botton. Again when we got back to the unit, big things began to happen. Lt Botton recalled the incident of our pass to Nancy during the course of our conversation and remarked that things would probably start rolling again. We had no idea that the big push was impending at that very moment.

I hope this one is more successful in bringing the war to a conclusion, and I pray that it is less costly and does not entail so great hardships for the men. [as Alsace-Lorraine]

* * *

Before the push was well under way we had lost one of our old original officers, who is one of the best. Lt Ermelbauer[13] was wounded on the 22nd while doing some demolition work. A part of his injuries was a broken leg.

Surely, surely the war will be over before he is ready to return to duty with us. He is a very personable fellow, well liked by everyone, as well as being a very efficient officer. I remember that he performed services during the crossing of the Marne-Rhine Canal at Somerviller which won for him quite some distinction.

* * *

The thought which has stuck in my mind today and keeps lingering is "smoke of battle." As I came up toward the new CP this morning in a jeep with driver Lanier[14] and Pvt Whitney Hanson, there was smoke rising in a number of places from within our own lines, as from the white smoke

---

12  Pfc. Joseph F. Chabina, Regtl Hq Co, Crabtree, Pa.

13  1st Lt. Carl Ermelbauer, Hq Co, 3rd Bn, New York, N. Y., cited for his work at Rhine-Marne Canal the night I had charge of the crossing, an original, listed LWA Feb. 22, did not return.

14  Pfc. Henry L. Lanier, Hq Co, Ferreston, Texas.

shells the enemy was laying in pairs into the town of Drem-mond. I counted [smoke shells] six in a short space of time. And there was the truck burning fiercely at the "hot" cross-road after being hit by enemy artillery.

Farther out there were the black puffs from our shells landing on the enemy, and everywhere there were fires, big ones and little ones. There was one tall pillar of very black smoke which reached up to the clouds and then spread out and blended with the grey overcast. The intermingling of the whole lent a sort of hazy atmosphere to all the sounds and activity of battle.

\* \* \*

As we approached the crossroads the enemy were laying in a few. The soldiers we met had scared looks on their faces and were casting apprenhensive glances. A Negro truck driv-er leaned out of his cab, attempting to wave us down and shouting, "Don't go up theah! (there) Don't go up theah." We drove on and another landed with a "Wham" right on the target. About 75 to 100 yards from the crossroads center a lineman was repairing a broken telephone wire. "Give 'er hell!" he said as we drove by, waving us on. Then at my urg-ing Lanier took us through in a hurry. We had to make a sharp turn to go to the right, and I never knew a vehicle had to slow down so much to make a turn. We drove over a fresh scar in the road about 15 yards past the RJ center. We passed the vehicle, still burning and sending up its column of black smoke, a good marker for the enemy artillery and a sure sign of his success.

Before I can finish this page the day will end and an-other of war, filled with death and destruction, will begin. The midnight hours are resonant with the thunder of our artillery and the terrible "whuump, whuump" of landing enemy shells. Occasionally machine guns send out their chat-ter of death, and there are rifle shots which sound isolated and miniature among the heavier instruments in the terrible symphony,—the symphony of death played by the legions of the damned.

\* \* \*

Lt John Kelly has joined our immediate group, having been assigned as executive officer of the Regtl Hqs Co. Lt Quillen is assigned to Service Co as Special Service Officer. A very happy change for both, as Quillen likes the work he is now doing, and any change is a happy one from that of rifle platoon leader which Lt Kelly was in K Co.

Lt Cooper, "High Road Chawlie," was around again tonight. He is now Co Cmdr of his unit. They were getting their TDs up to the front now that we are pushing again. Because he always comes around when things are hot, I have come to associate him with war at its worst. Wish I could see the humorous and likeable fellow under pleasant circumstances some time.

Lt Col Northam, Capt Bonham, Lt Silverman and Sgt Kearns have not yet returned.

Guess they're all having a wonderful time. I thought Kearns would rather have gone to Paris than London but I guess not. As for me I'm ready for my rehabilitation pass to the States but I would settle for the London trip since I don't see any possibility of the other.

\* \* \*

A Kraut plane is droning overhead. Just a little while ago the fiery ack-ack and gleaming tracers followed one across the sky.

\* \* \*

I am again having trouble keeping going, and doing my work, because my sinus is becoming bad again. I get so pentup and irritable that I wonder anyone can get along with me. I have even neglected my correspondence which is bad as it causes my mail to fall off, and that is the one little ray of light that shines through the gloom of the war. Well, there is another ray beginning to show now. The winter is passing and soon the weather will be more bearable. Perhaps we shall soon see roses blooming in Germany, if they have them there and I suppose they do. I shall never forget the beautiful roses of North Carolina, nor those of England which I saw blooming along the quaint hedges and grey stone walls of Devon. There were also roses among the stinking bodies and destruction of Normandy, and there were thousands of fragrant wreaths and bouquets [of other flowers] for us from the liberated people of Central France.

\* \* \*

Lt Donovan is now a First Lieutenant, glad to see good fortune for some one - Lt Peterson has become S-1 for 3rd Bn, - Sgt Manning is acting as S-2. Everytime I see him I think of the night at Somerviller when the shell went in the next room and he was slightly wounded as he stood just outside the door. Big Sgt Porta was there then, giving out more help and moral encouragement than anyone I have ever seen - God rest his brave soul.

* * *

Lt Parish is DO tonight. Seems the more I know him the better I like him. Good fortune has enabled me to again build up a circle of friends. I'm terribly scared when I allow myself to think, that something will happen to some of them in this push.

* * *

### SIGNATURES

S/Lt B. J. CRADDOCK                 370 Ftr Grp
Robert Lee, Texas               401 Sqd. (Ftr)
    (Out spoken, talk of "clobberin' up the Huns)     APO 151

S/GLEN CALDWELL, 1st Lt.            370th FG
2076 N. Raymond Ave.             401st FS
Pasadena, California             APO 151
    (Curly hair, quiet)

S/E. K. BARRETT, 1st Lt, A. C.
1820 Keith Drive
Whittier, California, 43-724
    (Handsome - with the girl in Belgium)

S/L. C. BOWER Jr.             370th Ftr. GP
60 Allison Street             401st Ftr Sqd
Newton, Massachusetts            APO 151
    (Does not drink, very quiet)

S/BILLY BROWN
Truscott, Texas
    (With the accent that reminds me of home, soft-spoken)

These Air Corps "boys" listed above spent two days and nights with us at Birdgen, Germany. They were pleasant fellows and well liked by all of us. It was a "quiet" period for us and we swapped experiences and information and had quite an enjoyable visit with each other.

* * *

UNFORGETTABLE MEMORIES:

While the Air Corps officers were with us we were going to bed late one night in our damp, battered stone quarters. There was one Air Force EM with the group as their driver. Going to bed with us in our room he looked around and inquired, "Where are you going to sleep?"

"Where we always do." I replied as I crawled into my bed roll on the floor.

The Air Force man was astounded that we had no better sleeping facilities. He set up his folding cot with other equipment and lay down without any further words.

---

As we moved up in attack to the Roer River along the muddy roads in the misty rain, I noticed a three-man patrol of Tommies who had fallen to enemy fire. They had advanced across an open field, the point man almost reaching the fence before all were cut down. They lay face downward in perfect formation where they had fallen, their weapons and bodies pointed toward the enemy, their helmets and uniforms bathed in the rain. Someone, perhaps the Dutch, had planted the beautiful black and gold flag of The Netherlands above the body of the point man. The gorgeous colors of its wet, silken folds waved gently above the brave dead Tommy [in the draft] as the vehicles drove by.

---

When the Negro soldier shouted to us as we approached the "hot" crossroads, Lanier the driver, as if afraid to ask, inquired, "What did he say?"

"He said not to go up there," I answered.

His face tightening, Lanier replied, "That's what I thought he said!"

---

[A casualty[15] not mentioned in the Journal].

## COMBAT ENGINEERS

*On the night of Feb 24-25, two enlisted men of Co A, 60th Engineers, performed a heroic act. A stone bridge across the Roer River had for several days been denied to the enemy by the 161st Field Artillery's skillful use of artillery inter-*

---

15 2nd Lt. Isadore Warshaw, Co A, Detroit, Mich., a replacement, listed LWA Feb. 24, did not return.

*diction fire. Hundreds of shells, fired on the bridge position at the rate of no less than one per minute, had kept the enemy away from the approaches. When the 134th Regiment took Hilfarth and pushed through the town, foot troops raced across the bridge.*

*Then the two engineers, T/5 James Stanislav of Lynbrook, N. Y., and Pvt Harold Wright of Jersey City, N. J., slipped through enemy automatic fire, cut demolition wires on the bridge, removed the charges and dropped them harmlessly in the river.*

*Capture of the bridge intact made possible a rapid crossing of the Roer River in that sector. The Germans had counted on the stream to hold up the 35th advance.*

\* \* \*

Hulhoven, Germany
February 26, 1945

Time: 0618

A night of duty. The wind has whistled and howled through the streets of the battered town and went through the branches of the trees in front of the CP with a sort of sighing. The big guns whoom, whoomed in single rapidity, or rolled in great volleys all night, the concussion shaking and rocking the walls of the buildings as if it were sometimes in an earthquake.

Not much activity in our lines as we still hold the line along the river without crossing. Joplin on our right is to make an assault crossing this morning, and we have already given them supporting fire. Had two of the few remaining "oldtimers" on the line during the night's activities, Capt Trossen[16] of 3rd Bn and Capt Tobin[17] of 2nd Bn. Capt English, evacuated for illness some days ago, has not yet returned to duty.

\* \* \*

A shell just burst in the town, 0629, very near.

\* \* \*

---

16 Capt. Kenneth F. Trossen, formerly CO of Co K, now 3rd Bn Hq, Chicago, Ill., an original.

17 Capt. Robert B. Tobin, formerly CO of Hq Co, 3rd Bn, now in Hq 2nd Bn, Pistol Point, Texas, an original.

Lt Parish obtained from Capt Watkins of F Co the outcome of the effort to rescue the wounded man in the mine field. He was there in the field where he had fallen, from about 1500 until 2130. One foot and part of his leg was blown completely away and the other was so badly shattered that it hung crazily, the foot pointing in the wrong direction. The wounded soldier remained conscious all the time, and appeared quite happy when his rescuers reached him. He had managed to apply a tourniquet to the stump to stop the bleeding and had bandaged his wounds, although very crudely of course. With his shovel he then "dug in" in the field. Another of his buddies had fallen near him, [dead] and he had made his fox hole behind him so that the body offered some protection from enemy fire. He had not taken his wound tablets, but with all the wonderful drugs we have now to prevent infection, he will probably live. It is likely he will lose the injured foot and leg also, but not certain.

Another soldier in the mine field hit one of the "Shu'" mines and his leg and foot was blown from his body and landed in a roadway 30 yards away. When he fell his back hit another and he was killed instantly. Of the several casualties suffered by F Co, all were from mines except one.

\* \* \*

Seems we're in for trouble. Another shell just came in with a terrific wham.

\* \* \*

Our light plant has gone bad, and my lonely candle has just burned out. So will have to work in darkness and with flashlight until daybreak.

[Another "Old Original"[18] is lost].

Hulhoven, Germany
February 27, 1945

A busy day of administrative work until I'm in no mood for writing.

Sid and Bonham have returned from Paris and Col Northam is back from London. After "batting the breeze" with Sid and Kelly and at the same time working, I find it

---

18  1st Lt. Charles V. Litherland, Hq 2nd Bn, St. Francisville, Ill., an original, evacuated as sick Feb. 28, did not return. He was promoted to 1st Lt. at the time I became a captain.

is now getting late. Clark is sleeping after a day in Mastrich during which he visited his "interesting acquaintance" there. Parish is on duty, Bonham is moving about as usual seeing about the affairs of the Co. Ginsberg is sweating out some work I've turned over to him which goes to Division. He and I argue to beat hell sometimes and he is damned near as stubborn as I.

The 134th is across the river on our right and has made good progress. Other forces push on toward Cologne farther south. Looks like it might be a wild day for us tomorrow and the following days. Seems we are to work with the 8th Armd Div. We are to cross the Roer River and cut north - work behind the Siegfried defenses in a move to entrap German forces there and still farther open the line.

The artillery around us continues to thunder loudly as it hurls shells across the river into positions still held by the Germans. Sounds like some coming in to the NE, but none landing here. German planes have struck both to our north and south, but none have hit our positions.

If our luck can only hold a few weeks longer!!!

March 1, 1945

Now, at 1126 we are in a temporary CP in this German town. Our troops began moving shortly after dawn this morning, and pushing on rapidly to the north. We spent the night farther south after crossing the Roer.

Col Alexander with his Third Bn is leading the drive with our attached tanks, the doughboys riding the iron behemoths as they drive steadily on with earth shaking roar. Just now word has come that he has been well received and is sending back some "cellar doors" (code name for PWs).

Our CP at present in an old feudal lodge. All over the place is evidence of the Nazi party and its influence. Books, maps, banners, insignia, and pictures of Hitler and the Nazi leaders. Looking around I can see evidences of their waning power. I write hunched over a window ledge in an attached room inclosed by windows on three sides. The battle was not so fierce here and most of the glass is still intact, very unusual so far in Germany. Just outside is a German rifle, freshly broken, and an empty mess kit. We have passed their barbed wire entanglements, their abandoned fox holes and emplacements. The road blocks have been shoved aside or bypassed.

— 527 —

In this house itself, most everything has been removed. They left the grand piano and the pile of music sheets stacked on it. And now as we work for the Nazis' destruction, some one gets enough leisure from the work to pick out a tune on the white keys.

The sun was bright this morning when we started, but now the day has grown grey and overcast. It is beginning to rain. Some of the drivers spread shelter halves over their equipment. Most are now busy eating their cold K ration. A few make hot coffee with the miniature gas stoves. There is no noon hour, and each man eats his own ration when he feels so inclined or when he has time.

Communication is by radio, and the messengers go back and forth from the radio vehicles to the CP.

Those who ride and fight with the tanks today won't have as much leisure to eat as we. Our mission is to reach Venlo and contact the British. We are half way there already, and if completely successful, will have outflanked and cut off a large segment of the Siegfried defenses. I wish the rain would hold off, for the ground is now comparatively dry, and it helps us to utilize our armor and it lessens the discomfort no end.

* * *

I saw a few civilians peering from the windows in this town. Someone said there were some Dutch who had been brought here from Holland by the Germans. I have not had time to check the story.

Those who are gone, if and when they return, will find their places completely destroyed in many cases and damaged houses and furniture in the others. The home in which we stayed last night was a very nice one with very expensive furniture and glass ware. Our soldiers do not inflict much needless damage but they certainly do not take any pains to protect the stuff. Why should they? "If the Germans had not started the war we would not be here" expressed their attitude.

* * *

Our troops just brought in two Russians who came into our hands in some way as we advanced. Wisecracked someone (Sgt Kozeil[19] I think), "They by-passed Berlin." We will

19 Sgt. Koziel, Regtl Hq, with the unit a long time in training and combat, - no other information.

probably find they are Russian PWs impressed into the German Army.

* * *

Outside some of the trees are scarred and clipped by the arty fire. I can see through the window a perfect cross [church] in the woods made of white wood laid bare by the flying [shell] fragments. It shines out white and clear from the dark brown of the tree trunks and the dark green of the foliage of the evergreens. Its outline has grown clearer still since the lowering clouds and flying mist has made deeper the glooming shadow of the forest.

* * *

Moving up again 1315. We are halted momentarily on a soggy, rutted road leading through a German forest of evergreens, now heavy and dripping with the rain. So far no artillery to bother us.

I'm riding as I usually do with the 193 radio car and crew, Sgt Tom Gaughan (in charge), Sgt Harold Noll, T/5 Joe Hussey, and T/5 Arnold Rossi. Fieldsteel is with us today instead of Sgt Kearns, as he has not yet returned from London.

* * *

We soon moved out of the woods and proceeded through open country, the roads encompassed on either side by green fields.

* * *

What a day this has been. It is now 0120 (March 2) and things have just now quietened down. We continued to roll all day, and just at nightfall we began setting up this CP. Tonight there are about 24 miles of the Seigfried Line Defenses which are no more, so far as offering protection to Germany is concerned. They still hold a number of defenders who are hopelessly cut off from the rear.

Leaving Dalheim we drove on through the towns of Arsbeck, Neider, Kruchten, Ober-Krutchen, Bruggen, Bracht, Bruch, Kaldenkirchen and into the town of Venlo. The attack was led by Col Alexander's 3rd Bn, which was spearheaded by Capt Kurtz's K Co and two companies of Negro tankers. The Co[mpany] of light tanks led most of the way, and those black boys proved to be good fighters. Today's action was more or less in the nature of an adventure after some of the hellish battles we've been through. So we don't know how the colored boys would be if there was only unrelenting hell as we have seen it several times, but they did all right today.

There are about 250 PWs in the pens, sent in by us today (TF Byrne), and more being rounded up tonight.

\* \* \*

As the command group came into Venlo, the battle here was going sharply. MGs were talking, interspersed with rifle fire. The tanks were blasting holes through houses in which Nazis were resisting or hiding. There was arty and mortar fire. The Huns laid a barrage on the road just after we started moving, following a pause, and the first shell hit squarely in the middle of the road about 5 seconds behind our 193 radio car. We kept going and drew away from the barrage.

It forced Parish and Lt Cooper to take shelter in a house. Cooper turned back to his TDs and Parish came on to the CP location on foot. The mortar shell which missed us got two boys from M Co. The mortar fire and some heavy artillery fire continued in the town around us until a short time ago.

\* \* \*

Among the many, many scenes of the day, a few of the unforgettable ones are —

The group of PWs in one of the towns where we paused briefly. They were unmistakably happy as a whole that they had been captured. They complied willingly with all directions, smiled often, talked and smoked.

The German civilians hurrying to the appointed place, as directed, to hear the military government officer give them instructions and the new rules and regulations under which they will now live. I watched them closely. Some appeared at a loss as to how to receive us. A few appeared disdainful and with a "so what" attitude. Others seemed to have a sort of frightened friendliness. I think most were thankful that they would not be shot, as many thought when our troops first entered the town.

I talked briefly with Sgt Koontz[20] of 2nd Bn (who had just gotten himself a fine P-38 pistol) and he said the civilians

20 Sgt. Koontz, 2nd Bn, with the 320th since Camp Rucker, one of the few originals still with the 320th (Sgt. Alfred C. Koontz, Auburn, Nebr., was listed with 1st Bn Hq; might be the same.)

were waving white flags, crying and begging to surrender when they first entered the town. Those Negro tankmen fired at anything that did not suit them.

There was one very shapely, medium sized lass of about 18, the only pretty one I saw in that town, who seemed very displeased about it all.

There was a very beautiful raven-haired lass who smiled in very friendly fashion from a doorway in another little German town. I think her pleasure at seeing us was unmistakable but she is probably an imported Pole or Yugo-Slav laborer.

\* \* \*

The hundreds of abandoned fox holes, trenches, emplacements, barbed-wire entanglements etc. which were a part of the Seigfried defenses.

The bridges over the AT ditches and small streams were not blown because the speed of our advance caught the enemy away from their prepared demolitions. Our engineers removed the charges and the bridges remain intact.

\* \* \*

We began to meet people who smiled and waved and gave the V-sign. At first it puzzled us for I could see their pleasure was genuine and then we figured out that we were again approaching Holland. At Kalden-Kirchen the crowds, led by their priests, wearing orange robes, almost overwhelmed us. It was reminiscent of Central France. Many of the Dutch speak English, and they told us they had been hungry for five years under the Germans. One lady wept with joy and said we would never know how happy we had made them.

Some GIs, cheered on by the Dutch, began wrecking the local Nazi Hqs until their officer, in hot anger, called them from the building and put a stop to the activities. I looked the place over and found it to be a very elaborate place. Nothing but the best for the "supermen."

\* \* \*

I started to write these last few pages at 0120 and it is now 0545. The morning hours have been very busy. A volley of six artillery rounds came in about 0230 landing close enough to send fragments rattling against the building. Three more followed in about five minutes. It woke several of those who were sleeping and some of them, among whom were Bowman,[21] Magallanes and Bockhoven, came from their beds and stood around awhile. Magallanes moved his bed downstairs before again retiring.

At intervals all through the night, just at this moment, rifle shots, MG and Burrp gun fire have sounded out through the moon-lit stillness. The entrapped Krauts are trying to slip through our lines and get back toward their own forces in the Fatherland. A force of 200 succeeded at one point, getting across the main road, from the west to the east. They captured an officer and an EM from the "Jumbo" unit and took them along. The officer escaped and gave us the information.

* * *

The Dutch resistance movement has been very helpful here. The 3rd Bn says the resistance movement now has 60 PWs which they are to turn over to us tomorrow (about 3 hours from now, today). Already we have 43 from 3rd Bn besides those turned over to Div yesterday. There is a young girl Dutch resistance leader who reads and writes English very well.

Which reminds me that Quillen asked a Dutch youngster, "Parlai Francais?" - and the reply, "No, No, Parlai Englais."

* * *

It is very chilly these morning hours. There is not enough fuel and I am cold. My eyes are closing on me.

## TASK FORCE BYRNE

*The drive of Task Force Byrne was spearheaded by Col Alexander's 3rd Bn. Col Alexander chose Co K headed by Capt Kurtz, who in turn designated a platoon to lead commanded by 2nd Lt Royal A. Offer of Adams, Nebraska, a former enlisted man who had won a battlefield commission.*

*After crossing the Roer River on the afternoon of February 28, the column advanced nine miles. The next day the task force made 23 miles behind the Siegfried Line defenses, seized 16 German towns, turned back into Holland and liberated Venlo. The next day the blitz invaded Germany again,*

---

21  Probably Pfc. Russell M. Bowman, Regtl Hq, Hanover, Pa.

*the third time in the war for the 320th, plunged 15 miles and captured Sevelen at the end of the day.*

*Lt Offer related that one of his men had a bullet hole in his left leg and his right leg was almost blown off by an anti-tank shell while riding one of the lead tanks. Yet he kept shooting, killed three German soldiers manning an anti-tank gun and forced the German officer to surrender. A staff sergeant with four bullet wounds, three in his chest and one in his stomach, kept his squad together, helped two of his men who were hit, and refused to dismount from his tank until the battle was won in the town of Straelen. Three hours later the wounded were evacuated.*

*Sevelen was secured against heavy German mortar and artillery fire. Here in this town were found the stacks of German propaganda leaflets, especially prepared for the 35th Division with a beautiful reproduction of the division patch. Undistributed, with the ink still moist, the leaflets welcomed the division troops to their positions in Holland and warned that the Roer River defenses were impregnable.*

*In this, the fastest and most successful drive by the Ninth Army, it is perhaps significant that the push was spearheaded by a division with long experience in Gen. Patton's Third Army.*

Venlo, Holland
March 2, 1945

All night without a wink of sleep and now I am just about past going. Col Alexander jumped off in the lead again this morning, heading back into Germany again. This makes the third time for this regiment to invade the Fatherland. The General has been here and raised hell and gone stamping away in that imperious way of his.

Not until 0620 this morning did I receive the message, containing instructions and orders for today's action. That leaves mighty little time for planning and execution of a military operation as important as this. The Colonel arose immediately had the staff aroused and began work.

As we worked there came the damndest screaming roar I have ever heard, which grew louder like the scream of a shell, and then exploded with a terrific bang. It was too large for a shell, we knew, and too fast for anything but a rocket. The guards at the door saw the missile burst just before striking the ground after passing over the CP. I knew it was not a flying bomb and it could not be V-2, so I was dead sure, for a moment, that the Krauts had sprung a new V-weapon.

A little later another went by with express train roar, and my belief was just about confirmed. Then someone reported that the strange things were jet-propelled planes. The first one had exploded in the air while in flight. They travel so fast, it is said, that an AA gun cannot track them. I can well believe that after this morning's experience.

\* \* \*

As I write the Huns are throwing some more shells into Venlo.

Germany
March 4, 1945

I moved from Venlo late in the evening with the Hqs Co group. As we moved out the fires built by the GIs, to keep from freezing while waiting for the column to move, were glowing brightly in the gathering darkness. The day had been cold, with alternating sunshine and squalls of snow. One moment the sun would be bright over the chilly landscape, and in the next the snow-flakes would be flying from low grey clouds, clothing in temporary whiteness the streets and buildings and kissing the face with moist softness. The American doughboys, talking to the Dutch people and their newly-made Neitherland girl friends, said a hasty good bye and climbed into the vehicles when the order for movement was given.

\* \* \*

Our tank-riding doughboys and the Negro tank crews continued to do a wonderful job. They pushed on to the German town of S_____, took it in quick sharp fighting and then pushed on. When we caught up the Regtl CP was in ____ miles beyond. The Krauts were shelling the hell out of _____ and they caught it as we passed through. As we turned a corner in the streets, I could hear stuff falling which was knocked down by the [shell] fragments. I was riding with Capt Bonham, Lt Kelly and the driver, Lanier. We got on through the town, but a shell hit an ammunition truck of the 1st Bn behind us, burning it and another truck. One man from 1st Bn was killed.

\* \* \*

The Germans attacked our troops in the town just after we had gone through. There was a very noisy battle in the houses and streets for a time. [The battle had begun before we cleared the town.]

Capt Ginsberg, Capt McCormic and Sgt Gwizdala[22] captured 19 Krauts at one point while looking for a CP location. Gwizdala was still guarding them beside the road as we drove by.

Sgt Novak[23] came into the CP with some PWs from the 1st Bn. He reported that a C Co road block had shot up a white German ambulance filled with German soldiers, as it careened down the road towards S_____ from _____ where we now are. We had gotten off the road just soon enough to miss it. [The ambulance did not contain wounded. It was used offensively by German soldiers.]

\* \* \*

During the night an American was shot through the stomach when he challenged some unidentified person.

\* \* \*

During the 3rd we remained at _____. The doughboys and tankmen were held up by road blocks and demolitions, and stronger resistance. One tank was lost when the enemy threw open a barn door revealing an SP gun which opened up on it.

Progress today was limited. It can be understood when it is seen that two of the four remaining Rhine bridges are in our Div sector. The 137th was committed on our right but also failed to reach the river. The Nazis are using almost everything they have left on this side of the river to hold the bridges so they can withdraw their remaining troops which I understand includes the First Paratroop Army.

Information from a PW discloses that there is an assembly area for a German Div just to front of 1st Bn posi-

---

22  Sgt. Victor H. Gwizdala, Sv Co, Bay City, Mich.
23  Sgt. Novak, with us a long time, no other information.

tion. Col Walton[24] called in about 2230 that they were getting a counterattack from the Germans. Now 2345 I can hear sporadic rifle and MG fire, some of it German. For the past two hours there has been as great if not the greatest pounding of artillery that I have heard in this war. Gen Futch has released all restriction on the amount of artillery ammunition that can be used during the night. All the guns in the Division, plus some from Corps and Army, are pounding the assembly area of the German division and the road leading to the bridge across the Rhine.

\* \* \*

I have been ill last night and today, caused by severe sinus pressure in left side of my head. I find my ability to endure very much lessened, and sometimes feel very lonely and weary of the warfare.

\* \* \*

Never to be forgotten. The night ride through the German countryside, lit up by the light of burning hay stacks, houses and barns, and the flashes of guns and shells. The slanting flames alternately glowed red and white as the freezing wind waxed and waned. In the fluid situation one could not always be sure if he was meeting friend or foe.

\* \* \*

On the drive up from Venlo in the darkness we missed by minutes and sometimes seconds, arty barrages, one pitched battle in the streets of a town, and groups of Germans on foot or in vehicles as they crossed or used the same road.

Once we came to a fork in the road with no idea which road to take. As Lanier halted the jeep I looked at a line of fires glowing brightly across the countryside and indicated the road that led in the same direction. It was the right way. Those Negro tankers fired on everything - horses, cows, men, vehicles, haystacks, barns, houses and other buildings. The line of fires marked the path of their advance.

\* \* \*

24 Formerly Capt. William Walton, S-3 of 1st Bn, now Lt. Col. Walton, CO of 1st Bn, Newton, Kans., with 35th Div since its activation in Dec. 1940; with 320th since it was organized. While still a captain he was CO of 1st Bn briefly after Maj. Gillis was killed. Soon promoted to Major, he again became CO when Col. Walker was wounded on Nov. 18; promoted to Lt. Col. in late Dec.

Lt Silverman is on duty tonight. My turn comes tomorrow (already the morrow comes). So I guess I'd better give my tired and irritated eyes a rest. That is, if I can take enough aspirin to deaden the pain in my jaw and ear, and if the counterattack does not develop too much. But I know it would take a strong force to get through our men. There is always possibility of infiltration.

I can hear the mortars coughing now, followed by the explosions of the shells.

## T F BYRNE CONTINUES TOWARD THE RHINE

*As the drive continued the 2nd Bn took the lead with Co F as the spearhead. The fighting was hard with heavy casualties at times. Co F lost another commander when Capt Watkins was killed on March 5.*

*Sometimes there were swift clean strokes with few or no casualties. 2nd Lt Vivian G. Palmore of Mattoax, Virginia, another former EM with a battlefield commission, directed such a platoon action at Hillmanshoff. The German positions were in two big houses surrounded by a thick hedge. The artillery poured in a 10-minute barrage. Then tanks smashed up to 100 yards of the positions. Then the platoon from farther back dashed in with marching fire. Palmore said the Germans just couldn't get going.*

*A truck load tried to escape and were riddled by fire from four BARs wielded by Sgt Joseph C. Anzalone of Independence, Louisiana, and Pfcs Joseph J. Madanski of Painseville, Ohio, Howard E. Kroeger of Blackduck, Minnesota, and William T. Brewer of Rockmart, Georgia.*

*The assault started at dusk and S/Sgt Glenn E. Metcalf of Huntington, Indiana said they were still killing or capturing Germans at nine o'clock. They were last-ditch Nazis and didn't like being taken, but the platoon finally got about forty prisoners. Palmore's platoon did not have a casualty.*

Vicinity of Hogenhof
Germany
March 7, 1945

We spent the night of the 6th in town of Kamp, moving up to this point about noon. The fight with the Germans in the pocket still rages. Our regiment, with the 137th Regt and one command of 8th Armd Div, is pressing this last

German pocket west of the Rhine. We are pressing the southern flank from just north of Cologne, and the Br and Canadians are pressing on the west and north. The fighting is still fierce.

So many things have happened, but I have been too ill to write. If it were not for the medicine which I have gotten from Maj Smith to numb the pain, I would not be able to endure. I have remained up tonight until midnight purposely so that I could sleep when I lie down.

We have a new British officer as liaison from another Division which is relieving the one to our left. W/O Frazier is with us tonight, and the liaison officer from Corps, and the one from the tank unit which is fighting with us. Lt O'Brien and Capt Ginsberg have gone to Paris on pass.

I have so many pictures in my mind of the past few days. The factories still smoking on the flat plain as we advanced and occupied the towns. The fresh holes made by the big shells through the thick walls; the fragments of vehicles and patches of tarp and uniform high in the trees beside the road where a direct hit had blasted them into the air; the German civilians, submissive and obedient but not downcast; the smoke of the big guns creeping over the damp green sod after it puffs out with terrific concussion and then drifts away over the country side, over the Rhine and on into Germany; the white-speckled ack-ack in the sky as the Kraut gunners try for our planes as they zoom and roar over their positions; the black spotted farmlands, where the shells have landed in the green sod.

While I stood briefly in a church, now being used as a shelter by our troops, a GI was playing the chapel organ and a Negro soldier was singing with deep feeling an old familiar religious hymn. Strange assemblage and a strange scene for such a place. Other battle-stained GIs listened with weary, strained faces turned toward the singer and the player. Another Negro trooper slept the sleep of exhaustion upon a soiled, silken pallet.

*   *   *

On the 5th Capt Watkins[25] of F Co was killed while his Co was leading the advance with the colored tankers. The

---

25  Capt. James M. Watkins, CO of Co F, listed KIA March 5. Watkins, a replacement, was a fine officer. The only address I could find was 309 Jefferson Street, (town and state missing).

tank Co Comdr had a leg blown off and a tank plat ldr was wounded. By yesterday afternoon one Co of our tanks had lost all its officers except the maintenance plat ldr, whose duties were more or less somewhat to the rear of the front elements. The Co also lost 8 tks, 5 yesterday, 3 day before.

Lt Ellis of the TDs was mortally wounded yesterday. Lt Cooper, who is now the TD Co Cmdr, got to him with a jeep and brought him out. Both legs were torn through with shell fragments and he was wounded in both hands and arms and in the face. His mouth was bandaged so that he could not speak. Cooper said when he looked at him on the ground that Ellis winked at him and there were signs of a grin on his face. Later we had word from the medics that a part of his jaw and mouth was torn away by the shell fragment that struck his face.

Eulogies are no good to a man out here, but everyone who knew Ellis came as near to loving him as one can love out here. As an officer and combat man not many equaled him and few if any excelled him. And now unless medical and surgical skill can work another of its many wonders, the voice to which one instinctively loved to listen, may not speak anymore. He had an irrepressive, sunny, kindly personality, the like of which I have seldom if ever seen.

It is ironic to recall that Cooper had said to us just the day before that if he had three more plat ldrs like Ellis he could sleep 24 hours per day, and that he certainly hoped he did not lose him.

*I had learned to like Lt Ellis because he was always calm, efficient, pleasant and most cooperative. I never once heard him raise his voice in anger or impatience. Quiet in manner, his comments were never hasty, always completely free of malice or criticism but sometimes filled with wit.*

*Once we were hearing of a great administrative difficulty into which one of the arty officers had fallen. After listening for some time Ellis remarked, "Well, he's up that well known tributary without the proper means of locomotion."*

*It was the first time I had heard such an intellectual phrasing of the old Ozark Mountain saying, "Up salt creek without a paddle."*

A great part of one platoon of the Negro tankers were either killed or captured when they spearheaded into a town and were cut off. The bodies of some were found, badly beaten about the face, and one shot through the forehead. One was recovered alive after other troops fought into the town. He was badly bruised from beating. He said the Nazis beat them after they were made prisoners. He was in too bad a condition to question further and was rushed on back to the hospital.

* * *

After Lt Koehler with Co I had captured and occupied one of the towns here, two German civilians (men) approached him, and said they had forty volunteers (women) to service his troops. Col Alexander told me of the incident. I must get the details from Lt Kohler.

Capt McCormic,[26] after visiting the burgomeister of one recently occupied town, and giving him the new orders and laws of the military government, was then faced by the burgomeister's daughter, a lucious thing they say, who spread her arms invitingly and said "I am now yours. You may do with me as you wish." Whereupon the captain had to explain that he could not do that as the Americans did not do things in that manner, etc. Sprained his tongue I guess in doing that.

I have to laugh at Capt Scherer who, every time the incident is mentioned, pulls his hair and with an expression of acute suffering exclaims, "Oh, my dying ass." The expression has no particular significance. It just happens to be one commonly used by him.

(Both the above occurences on March 5.)

* * *

In the morning eleven battalions of arty will lay on selected targets in the German pocket, following which we attack, followed shortly by 137th on right.

We are getting quite a bit of artillery tonight most of which we suspect is coming from across the Rhine. We'll be paying them back as soon as we get the pocket mopped up.

* * *

I'm groggy from the medicine. One more incident: When the 3rd Bn with the tankers captured the town of Sevelen, a

---

26 Capt. William N. McCormic, East Orange, N. J., CAC or Military Government affairs officer attached to our regiment.

print shop was found which contained a number of leaflets printed specifically for the 35th Div. They were to be distributed to us in the defensive positions down on the Roer River.

Strange that we should advance so far and capture the particular town in which the propaganda designed for us was being turned out.

\* \* \*

Lt Parish is now our liaison officer from Division while Sam[27] is gone. Tonight he got bracketed by fire from a German plane while on his way down here.

Now, as I write those last words above, a shell whistled eerily overhead and crashed beyond. I may need a larger sleeping portion than I have after all. And being ill certainly does not add to ones ability to "take it" in this business.

[A loss[28] not mentioned in the Journal].

[Camp Pittsburgh, France
Nov. 27, 1945

The following is a copy of a propaganda sheet which I first saw during our push up to the Rhine in early March 1945. It had a beautiful reproduction of the division patch. I could not secure a copy for my files at that time, but today I am copying this from a copy in the possession of Pfc Gordon S. Jones of _____. He sent the original home, but showed me the copy today and gave me permission to copy same.

---

27  1st Lt. Samuel G. O'Brien, originally Co L, then Regtl Hq as liaison to Division, on leave at that time.

28  2nd Lt. Russell W. McAnally, Co F, Huntsville, Ala., a replacement, listed MIA March 6. Later listed KIA.

## WELCOME

## MEN OF THE 35TH DIVISION

*Considering the fact that you are newcomers, we would like to do everything to make you feel at home. We extend to you a cordial greeting and a hearty welcome to the Rur Valley! (Roer Valley)*

*We regret that you must come to this unpleasant district, but, as usual, you have to take over this section where the air is heavy with lead. The British have been withdrawn from here, because this same atmosphere didn't suit them very much. As always, under these conditions, the British prefer to let you do the work.*

*You have tried to veil your arrival here by doing such things as removing your divisional insignias. Nevertheless, a little bird told us all about it.*

*Before you arrived, there were other divisions here who didn't fare so well, namely: the 84th, the 102nd, the 229th, and, not to be forgotten, the British. They all got knocked about a bit. You can see that you won't have an easy time of it against the Rur defense lines.*

*As we said before, we shall try to make you feel at home. We hope to make every day here seem like "the glorious Fourth" - there'll be plenty of fireworks.*


## WE KNOW WHAT YOU ARE MEANT TO DO.

## WE KNOW, ALSO, WHAT YOU WANT TO DO

### YOU WANT TO RETURN HOME
### AS SOON AS POSSIBLE ! ! !

#### (BETTER ACROSS
#### THAN A CROSS)

The Germans meant too distribute the above to us while we were in the Roer River lines just across the border from Holland. They didn't get them out in time. We started the drive to the Rhine on March 1, and captured stacks of the propaganda sheets in the printing shop in a town up near the Rhine River, after we had advanced about 60 miles in three days. There is a note in my "journal" of the incident, made at the time it occurred.]

Venlo, Holland
March 9, 1945

Yesterday, Buff drove me back from the forward area to Div Rear where I have been a witness before a general courts martial. I am also a member of the court, but have been excused from sitting because of illness. Yesterday and today I have been treated by the medical officer here, and just this moment have returned to the personnel section of 320th from the latest treatment. I am staying with Capt Armstrong and Lt Sperl at this place.

Have had no word from the regiment as to its activities today, so don't know if it is still in the line or not.

The good news of course is the bridgehead across the Rhine established by the First Army. If it can be held it may measurably shorten the war. [The First Army's foothold across the Rhine was gained by capture of the Remagen railroad bridge by infantry before it could be blown up]

I was one of the last to go through the mess line at the evening meal yesterday. In the short time the unit has been here, the people have already learned that the kitchens will give away the leftovers after all the troops are fed. There was already a group waiting anxiously at the door when I went in, men, women, girls, boys, and little tots with their pans or bowls in their hands. There was one little tot [I noticed] in particular of about four or five years, round head with brown hair, very fair skin, and big brown eyes. He had gained a place at the head of the crowded mass and was sort of ducking underneath the others to avoid the crowding as he clutched in his tender, stubby hands his metal container in which he hoped to get some food. He cast a glance from his brown eyes at me as I entered. I stopped, smiled at him, and ran my fingers through his closely cropped hair. But it was no smiling matter with him. He was deadly serious, and watching anxiously about the food. And it was the same with the others. This was no pleasure-seeking, merry line of commuters waiting for a bus, or anything like that. I felt a bit remorseful to enter ahead of them especially when I looked back at the little brown-eyed boy in the red sweater, brown knee pants and clubby wooden shoes, whose air of seriousness never for a moment left his face. But it is the rule that all military personnel must be fed before any leftovers can be given away, so I went ahead. I do not think I could have eaten at the moment had it not been for the thought that there would be considerable food left, and the little boy, so like my own when I saw him last, would get something for himself.

I finished eating shortly and went out by a side door. The cooks had taken what they had left and placed it on the side walk by the street. Instead of ladeling it out, as I fully expected, they just set the containers down and turned the people to it.

Just as I came out, they made a rush for the food. There was no effort to form a line or maintain any semblance of order. They just rushed it and dived in for all the world like I used to see the hogs run for the garbage when I was back on the farm. The first ones of course secured the dippers or spoons, others dipped their bowls into the food; some of it was wasted; one man finally picked up one of the big pans and poured the remainder into his vessel. In such a melee of course the weaker and less hoggish were crowded aside. The little tots got not a dribble; some of the girls and women smiled shame-facedly and stood aside, their vessels empty; others tried half-heartedly to get a portion of the food which was gone almost immediately.

And where was the little brown-eyed boy in the red sweater and wooden shoes? I spied him running around the fringe of the struggling mass, his pan gripped in one chubby hand, the wide-eyed serious look still on his face, eagerly seeking a way into the food. But the surging mass was too much for his light and tender form. After the others cleared away, he got to the pans, and taking a big, longhandled spoon which he used in a very unskillful manner, he, oblivious to all else, was securing a few tiny driblets which he was putting into his empty pan.

Then one of the cooks brought out another pan, almost filled with stew. He held on to this one and dipped out the stew to the hungry civilians who immediately rushed up and surrounded him. I ran over and grasped the little Dutchman around the waist and carried him over. The Sgt filled his small pan. I removed from his hand the spoon which he still held and placing both of them on the pan so he could hold it, set him down to one side. Hardly taking his eyes from the vessel he turned and set out, as straight as a homing bee, to where ever he was going. I don't think he ever noticed me or the sergeant, or anyone in particular around him. He was too engrossed in the food.

He was very light when I lifted him, and again for the umpty-ninth time I cursed the Germans with deep and bitter feeling. What untold suffering those dumb, non-thinking, egotistical, goose-stepping klouts have inflicted needlessly on untold innocent thousands. Greek children dead of starvation in the ditches, little hungry Dutch urchins, Poles and Russians raped and enslaved, the smoke of cremation for the executed of all nations rising without a break for month after month, the pillage, the death and the ruin, and added to all that the many, many aching hearts in the countries untouched by battle, and Brent Cull's little boy fatherless forever.

I am sometimes made to wonder if any judgment or penalty can be too severe for them.

*[Following the entry of March 9, because of illness and a heavy load of administrative work I wrote nothing in the journal until I had reached the hospital in Kempen, Germany.*

*Upon reaching the Rhine River the armies paused for replacements, supplies and administrative work. The pain had grown so severe in my face that Maj Smith's medics said I must be hospitalized. I stayed another day to help with courts martial. All day long we labored, from early morning until nightfall, completing case after case. Then without eating, I was evacuated reaching the hospital before midnight.*

*In one of the hospitals, I was so wakeful that I slept none at all the entire night, yet lay perfectly quiet. The sheet was pulled up over my face as if I were dead. Two nurses came around and pulled back the sheet. I looked up, had the thought and then said to them, "Well, two angels of mercy instead of one."*

*All through the night the duty nurse made the rounds each hour. She found me each time completely wakeful. Finally she said, "Why don't you go to sleep?"*

*"Well, it's like this," I told her. "If I go to sleep I won't get to see you when you come around."*

*After that she quietly avoided my cot on her rounds thinking perhaps that she had awakened me before.*

*Examination revealed infected sinuses and "neuralgia of the face" which I could tell was puzzling to the doctors.]*

\* \* \*

## END OF RHINELAND CAMPAIGN

*On the night of 9 March, after 3 days of advancing against stiff resistance from Kamp through Millingen and Huck, Task Force Byrne took the town of Drupt in a swift attack preceded by a heavy artillery bombardment. Drupt protected the center of the road net of the Nazi bridgehead at Wesel.*

*The 134th then passed through Task Force Byrne and stabbed swiftly forward toward the two remaining bridges over the Rhine in the Ninth Army sector. The 35th plan was to capture intact the Wesel Bridge. But on 10 March, the Nazis pulled their shattered remnants back to the east bank and blew the two magnificent bridges just before the 134th reached them. Farther south, the 137th captured the town of Wallach.*

*The Santa Fe was on the Rhine! The last Nazi troops facing the division had been driven across the river in the Ninth Army zone by the attacking Santa Fe, leaving 4,775 prisoners.—From 35th Division History.*

\* \* \*

The following letters were received and transmitted by General Baade to the men of the Santa Fe:

HEADQUARTERS XVI CORPS

OFFICE OF THE CORPS COMMANDER

APO 197, U. S. Army

12 March 1945

TO: Commanders of all units participating in Operation "Grenade."

On March 10, 1945, the XVI Corps successfully completed its mission in Ninth Army's Operation "Grenade." From 23 February until the completion of this operation, this Corps has undergone many types of combat, including a river crossing, rapid pursuit of the fleeing enemy and tough, slow fighting against a determined enemy who, by every form of defensive fighting, was attempting to protect his last escape routes across the Rhine in the Wesel Area.

In these operations both battle seasoned units and units with no previous battle experience have participated. All have demonstrated the highest degree of courage, energy, aggressiveness and determination. The successful results that have been achieved are a credit to every participating unit. New and bright pages have been added to the histories of your organizations—pages filled with heroic acts of individuals and outstanding accomplishments by units.

I desire to thank every officer and man who participated in these operations for his contribution and assistance in driving the enemy from his positions along the Roer River with the ensuing pursuit for a distance of approximately fifty miles, and, finally, in forcing his withdrawal across the Rhine. I know the same high order of accomplishment will be demonstrated in the future operations necessary to crush our enemies and bring peace to the world.

> /s/ John B. Anderson
> /t/ JOHN B. ANDERSON
> Major General, U. S. Army
> Commanding

The 35th Division Commander added the following message to Santa Fe troops:

In every campaign in which you have fought you have defeated the Germans handily and elicited the praise of the Corps Commander. To the above glowing tribute I add my congratulations and admiration for the fighting qualities you continue so consistently and so magnificently to display.

> /s/ Paul W. Baade
> /t/ PAUL W. BAADE
> Major General, U. S. Army
> Commanding

* * *

In Hospital at Kempen - Germany
March 15, 1945

Pfc Dale A. Heller, Co L, 320th Inf, who is also a patient here, gives me the following information which came as a surprise to me.

Pfc David Carl Stroud, Co L, 320th Inf, of Aurora, Arkansas, was killed in action by a German sniper's bullet in the Battle of the Bulge in Luxembourg. He is the son of Clarence Stroud of Aurora [Ark.] with whom I am well acquainted.

Stroud joined the unit just before battle of Mortain about Aug 6th to 8th and participated in that battle from Aug 9 to 12.

He was made a member of the MG Section of the Wpns plat of L Co from the beginning, at first an ammo bearer, and later asst gunner. He served with Pfc Heller all the time after that.

"We always shared fox-holes together," said Heller.

Heller remembers that Stroud had a birthday while we were in the holding positions in Gremercy Forest during October or previous to Nov 8, when we jumped off from there into Chateau Salins Forest. It was his 20th or 21st birthday. In the attack on Fresnes on Nov 8, Stroud's canteen was shot off his belt and a piece of shrapnel went through his trousers but not his underwear. He and Heller slept in the cold wet woods that night. Heller says they dug about three or four fox holes in the Gremercy woods. Each hole would flood and they would dig another.

Just before the crossing of the Saar River, a rifle was discharged accidentally while a group of the men were in a cellar, and five men were wounded slightly by the flying fragments, including Heller and Stroud.

Stroud was hit just below the eye and was evacuated for hospitalization rejoining the unit for duty 10 days later while it was in Gersheim, Germany.

Heller was hit in right cheek by a sniper's bullet which ricocheted when it struck the edge of a fox hole they were digging. The wound was not serious enough for evacuation. The sniper had been pinging away at them for some time. This was just before the capture of the town of Gersheim and before Stroud had returned to duty.

The two were together Xmas Day in Metz. They had a six-hour pass together in Metz, and had a good Xmas dinner. All the Regiment was there and moved next day to Belgium and Luxembourg.

During the fighting in the woods near the town of Harlange, Luxembourg in the first days of January (1st to 4th estimated) the wound in Heller's cheek became infected and he went back to the Bn aid station. It was while he was back there that Stroud was hit by the sniper's bullet. Heller was told of the incident when he went back to the Co two or three days later. The best Heller can remember Stroud was standing outside of his fox hole in the deep snow which covered all the country at that time. The bullet struck him over the left eye and came out at the temple. He lived a short time but was not conscious. His body was brought out perhaps part way before he died. Heller does not know. Perhaps I can learn more of the details if I can see Sgt [Gerald R.] Lauer of L Co when I return to the unit.

Pfc Heller joined the Regiment as a replacement during our second engagement just after the fall of St Lo. It was before the big air strike on July 25. He has been with the unit all the way. He came to this hospital yesterday with some kind of ear trouble. He does not know yet what will be done with him here. He has been almost deaf for 6 weeks. Home address: 500 East 9th St., Berwick, Penna.

Of course, I did not know Stroud was with the Regiment, and he probably had no knowledge of my being with it. The GI clothes and the strain and dirt of combat changes one's appearance so much, so that if we ever saw each other, as we may well have on more than one occasion, we did not recognize each other.

\* \* \*

In Hospital at Kempen
March 16, 1945
APO No. 35

Pfc Orval E. Larsen, Hqs Btry, 127th FA
The above man came into the hospital yesterday suffering from an eye ailment. The doctor removed something from his eye and he says he is now ready to go back.

The strange coincidence is - on the night we spent in Venlo, Holland while I was on duty in the CP, it was reported to me, while I was on duty that night, that an O and EM had been captured by a party of about 200 Jerries who were making their way through our lines in an attempt to escape. It was also reported that the O escaped but the EM was still held.

Upon getting acquainted I find that this soldier is the one. He was freed about 25 hrs later when a spearhead of the 8th Armd Div cut them [his German captors] off. About 125 Jerries were captured and the EM freed.

Notes: German civilians laughed at him, when he marched along as a PW with the Jerries. A little later he marched back with the Jerries as PWs. Larsen says he marched about 25 miles with the Germans.

The O, Maj Moore of Salt Lake City, Utah, escaped when our own Inf opened up on the German column near Venlo.

The Germans [who captured Larsen] ate with the civilians. They split up into small groups and got food from the homes. Larsen was returned to his unit thru 8th Armd. [Div] Home address, Box 95, Steuben, Wisc.

Interesting coincidence: when I went to take the soldiers full name I find his first name and middle initial are the same as mine.

In 32nd General Hospital
Aachen, Germany
March 17, 1945

I left the 108th evacuation hospital yesterday morning arriving here about noon. This unit, just recently arrived here, is not yet operating as a general hospital. So I will be sent still farther back before my ailment is treated. My throat is slightly improved but the pain in my left jaw and left side of my head is very severe. I notice part of the diagnosis is neuralgia of the face. The X-rays show three impacted wisdom teeth which have never come through, which the doctors think are causing most of the pain. There is also definite sinus infection in both cheeks and forehead. The two ailments make a bad combination. I do not feel so badly as long as I can keep down the pain with drugs, but now I'm getting mighty sick of the drugs.

* * *

This building which houses the hospital is one of the few in the city that is not ruined. Most of the main city is a chaotic, jumbled mass of crumbled stone and dirt, mixed with crushed household furnishings and furniture. The bulldozers have scraped the debris from the streets to make way for traffic, leaving it piled high on the sidewalks. In only a few places did I note cleared places on the sidewalks where a few remaining civilians were living in crushed rooms amid the wreckage, for all the world like an animal living in his burrow in a rock pile.

\* \* \*

Someone said this was formerly one of Herman Goering's baby factories where they turned out supermen.

In 298th Gen. Hospital
Liege, Belgium
March 20, 1945

I developed acute appendicitis during the night after arriving here. That must have been night of March 17. The doctors were undecided for a time between the diagnosis of appendicitis and kidney stone, but I think have decided on the former.

I was well enough to arise this morning and take a shower in the shower room. First bath in over a month incidentally. My jaw and head bother me considerably but the doctor says we'll get to that when this other is cleared up.

Spring has been blowing in at the tent door with the March winds. I'm so glad the weather is becoming mild again. Without, the countryside has a coating of green sod. There are other promises of the new season, which the calendar says will be here tomorrow.

There is an almost incessant roar of planes overhead. Some are transports taking patients to Paris and the UK, where some (blessed thought) will fly on to the States. There are the fighter-bombers, the infantry-man's friends. Also the pursuits, the mediums, and the big four-motored jobs which are now giving the German cities such a pounding. The hell and the pounding seems to increase for the Germans but still the dumb klouts hold out.

News comes of the collapse of the Remagen Bridge but the bridgehead is now secure. There are several here who

— 551 —

crossed it. One can keep up with all the combat units by talking to the patients in the hospital.

Must rest . . .

*  *  *

Now evening. All day the winds have fought with the tent and forced their way in at the door. When I step outside to go to the latrine they whip at my robe, and I can feel the spring in their touch as they push or caress my body. They are not good for my sinus affliction and my whole head is sore. Many times today I have had to bake my head by the fire to drive the pain from my teeth and jaws. The pain in my side seems to be fading away.

The winds make me think of home. They sweep in from the west. Coupled with the coming spring they create in my heart a nostalgic longing. At home this was the time of year which had such promise, new life, carrying out of new plans. It was the time when life began in earnest on the farm. But that is too far away to think about.

*  *  *

Life here is different, vastly different from the front. There is much suffering of course, but the strain of battle is missing. There are soft voices and occasional lilting laughter in feminine tones, something we have not heard in many weary months.

I pray that all is well with my comrades and find myself longing at times to be back with them. But I know I can't make it until I get some relief for my sore head.

298th Gen. Hospital
Liege, Belgium
March 21, 1945

I went to breakfast in the mess hall for patients this morning for the first time. Whom should I see but Lt Perkowski, the Brooklyn boy who was ambushed and wounded by the Jerries at Gremercy Forest in late September. Of course he wanted to know of many of his acquaintances. I did not realize so many of them had gone until I began to try to recall what had happened to those about whom he asked.

I find that he had been discharged from the hospital as cured of his foot wound. Some where along the line in the Repo Depot system he had developed sleeplessness and an inability to rest and had been returned here for treatment. Perkowski always was somewhat of an odd fellow but he doesn't seem himself anymore. I doubt if he can take it or be much use even if he is sent back to the front. I noticed he asked me twice about some of our acquaintances and had difficulty remembering some things I thought he should know.

He made a few remarks about the night he was wounded and captured. After their jeep had been hit by MG fire and overturned in the ditch, about 20 Krauts closed in on them from both sides. Perkowski was already knocked out, so on his advice the sergeant with him, who was the only one who had his hands on a weapon, gave up. He said, "One of them took two shots at me with a pistol as they withdrew. I rolled over into the ditch." He then lay there in the cold, wounded, in our arty and mortar fire throughout the night. "It was terrible," he remarked in pained memory.

I know it is such that breaks a man, the discomfort coupled with the pounding of artillery, the terrible shriek of the speeding shell and the earth shaking explosion which spreads the death dealing, jagged splinters: the never knowing when or where.

\* \* \*

The calendar was not wrong in its promise today. This was good enough for the first day of spring, hazy sunshine from faintly cloudy skies through which the planes continued to fly with almost never ending roar. In the air was a faint touch of warmth, which was like a promise of more balmy days to come.

\* \* \*

More X-rays and examinations. Perhaps tomorrow will come a decision on what action to take in my case.

Not much of interest here, except the nurses and few Red Cross girls, who are reminders of the world we knew before we sailed from home to combat. And there are so many for them to look after that they scarcely have a word for each and everyone. Therefore they can make few (if any) happy, but many lonesome. It is the personal touch that gives the zest and fullness to life.

\* \* \*

Amusing incident today: Two members of the GI camp personnel in the barber shop to get haircuts. They argued and then scuffled over who should be first, until one gave way and said "All right! I'll get you fixed up." He spoke fluent French and the one in the chair not a word except perhaps "oui" and "cushay a'vec." So the French speaking soldier began telling the French barber how to cut the other's hair. He was telling him all wrong of course. The barber would begin and the GI in the chair, as uneasy as a hen on a hot rock, would start waving his hands and protesting. He must have been a plow boy once for he kept saying "Whoa! whoa!" when he thought the clippers were going too far. He would then turn to his buddy and with intermingled curses, pleading and threats, urge him to desist, and then turn back to the barber and talk to him in English which he could not understand. The barber would look at the other [GI] and he, with suave, urbane and self-confident manner, would again tell him how to trim the hair. All the while he kept up a running conversation with his uneasy buddy, "Hell, it'll grow out in a week. You'll be restricted for that long and then it'll be all right. You don't want to get married here any how, Joe." He smoked his pipe, spat out the door and greeted acquaintances going by, while his buddy pled, and cursed. Oh, he was a smooth one. The barber finally caught on to what was happening and stood back and laughed until he had to hold his sides. These irrepressible GIs!

But that could never happen at the front. In the first place no two GIs there would argue about who was first, and no one would have the heart to try to pull such a joke. If he did the other wouldn't give a damn, because he wouldn't care how or whether his hair was cut. There is humor in the front lines of a strange, indefinable type. It seems to be of things which have already happened. No one would pull a practical joke on another if there was any possibility of it hurting him, because he might be killed the next minute and therefore give cause for regret. There is a consideration for each other among combat troops which is touching.

* * *

Life here in the hospital sometimes brings me close to the breaking point. During the long night hours some men curse and groan and call for relief from their suffering. Occasionally one prays with a deep and anguishing earnestness. . .

298th Gen. Hospital
Liege, Belgium
March 22, 1945

A day of spring with warm sunshine. I could even get enough warmth standing by the door to help my sore head and shoulders. The clear sky made an open pathway for our planes which continued to fill the air with their deep throated roar.

\* \* \*

Today another dental examination which disclosed an ulcerated tooth. Maybe the seat of part of my trouble has been discovered. I dread that drilling on my teeth like I dread artillery fire. Honest-to-God, I'd shoot a dentist for drilling my teeth if he weren't doing it for my own good. I feel much better today, but there is not much of interest here. Now nearly time for "lights out." (at 2200)

\* \* \*

[While I was away these commendations came to the Division].

## HEADQUARTERS NINTH U. S. ARMY
## OFFICE OF THE COMMANDING GENERAL
### APO 339, U. S. Army

330.13 (GNMCS)                                    15 March 1945

SUBJECT: Commendation.

THRU: Commanding General, XVI Corps, APO 197, U. S. Army.

TO: Commanding General, 35th Infantry Division, APO 35, U. S. Army

1. Assignment of the 35th Infantry Division to Ninth Army a few weeks ago afforded me a feeling of particular gratification. I am frank to confess that this feeling is prompted in part by the fact of my previous association as one-time Commander of the organization. Aside from this warm personal interest in the division, I am also mindful of the splendid achievements of the division since the early days of the invasion.

2. With reference to the participation of the division in Operation "Grenade" just concluded, I feel that the performance of your organization was one of the outstanding features of the entire operation and undoubtedly contributed greatly to the speedy reduction of the northern portion of the Army zone of advance. The skill with which the division made its crossing of the Roer River and the speed and power with which it raced up the Army left flank, progressing up to twelve miles a day, was most impressive. Significant also was the staying power evidenced by the division when, after extended operations in the advance, it smashed German resistance in the critical area west of Wesel. It is one of the few of the participating divisions which fought in the operation from H-hour of D-day to the completion of the action on 12 March.

3. It is unnecessary for me to point out that the performance of the 35th Infantry Division in Operation "Grenade" constitutes another glowing chapter in the splendid record achieved by the unit in this theater of operations. Please express to every officer and man of your organization my most sincere appreciation for their individual contribution toward the accomplishment of a difficult mission in a superb manner.

/s/ W. H. Simpson
/t/ W. H. SIMPSON
Lieutenant General, U. S. Army
Commanding

\* \* \*

AG 330.13 GNMTA      1st Ind.
(15 March 45)

HEADQUARTERS XVI CORPS, APO 197, U. S. Army, 21 March 45

TO: Commanding General, 35th Infantry Division, APO 35, U. S. Army.

1. The outstanding performance of your Division in the "Grenade" operation has been thoroughly covered in the Army Commander's letter of commendation.

2. May I add my sincere and heartfelt thanks for the contribution of your splendid Division to the successful accomplishment of the mission of this Corps in the operations that have recently been successfully completed.

3. I am greatly pleased to forward the Army Commander's commendation, in which I concur wholeheartedly.

/s/ John B. Anderson
/t/ JOHN B. ANDERSON
Major General, U. S. Army
Commanding

\* \* \*

AG 330.13            2nd Ind.            PWB/emn
(15 March 45)

HEADQUARTERS 35th INFANTRY DIVISION, APO 35, U. S. Army, 24 March 45

TO: The officers and Enlisted Men of the 35th Infantry Division.

It is with distinct pride that I again transmit a letter of commendation to you. Your glorious achievements, challenging as they are, have been surpassed each time you enter a new phase of combat. With the praise of the Army and Corps Commanders ringing in our ears, let us cross the Rhine and enter the heart of Germany with even more determined dash and vigor to FINAL VICTORY.

Godspeed to each of you!

/s/ Paul W. Baade
/t/ PAUL W. BAADE
Major General, U. S. Army
Commanding

\* \* \*

THE MADISON COUNTY RECORD
April 12, 1945

From
CAPT. ORVAL E. FAUBUS

Somewhere in Belgium,
March 23, 1945

Dear Home Folks:

It has been a long time since I have written. My last letter was sent some time in mid-winter from a hospital in France. A lot has happened since then. I was there six days. Then I rejoined the regiment while it was fighting in and around Bastogne, Belgium.

It can now be revealed that we were on the right of the Fourth Armored Division when it drove the corridor into that city and relieved the tired survivors of the garrison. Because the best route for counter-attack lay through the sector held by our division (35th Inf. or Santa Fe Div.), it was busy for days standing off savage enemy thrusts while other forces halted the German drive farther west and began slowly to press it back. Then we moved into Bastogne and, joining up with another armored division and the airborne troops, fought the Germans back from the town. It has not been my unhappy lot to be closer to any bigger artillery than the Germans used on us there. The shells came screaming into the battered place with a terrific wham, and every evening and night during the same hours.

I cannot tell you all about our part in the Battle of the Bulge. You have already read that it was the most costly battle in American history. I shall never again see a dark shade on a field of white without remembering the dark shell craters in the snow. Later we again saw the city of Metz. "A week or ten days rest," we were told and on the third day we were on our way to the Vosges mountains where the new German offensive was threatening to retake the city of Strasbourg. We fought with the Seventh Army in those snowy mountains (more like the Ozarks than any I've seen in Europe) until that Nazi threat receded.

Then back across France and Belgium to billets in Holland. No one could treat us better than those Dutch people while we were there, but two days after all arrived we moved to positions in the front lines along the Roer River. There we held, shelling and being shelled, watching the flying bombs come over, until time to make our way through the minefields and start driving for the Rhine.

After we broke through the German lines, my regiment, with attachments which included two companies of Negro tankers, drove north behind the Seigfried line. We were known as Task Force Bryne after our regimental cammander. The first day we rolled up 26 miles of the line and entered Venlo, Holland, from the German side and contacted the British who were across the Maas river. I guess we are the only force which has come out of Germany itself to liberate a part of a conquered country. Next morning we drove northeast back into Germany to contact the Canadians and then on to the Rhine. You could tell our trail across the Rhineland by the trail of smoke and fire. Those Negro tankers set on fire every hay stack, barn or other object that would burn that came within range of their guns. Their fingers never strayed far from the triggers of their weapons, and they certainly were not stingy with the ammunition. We moved so fast that sometimes there were Krauts behind as well as before and to the right and left. Before we got to the Rhine our task force had 1200 prisoners and almost everyone could claim credit for the capture of some German soldiers. White flags of surrender were waving by every farm house and from the windows of the towns.

I have now been in combat with my regiment in all four of the American armies, and in five countries on the Western Front. We have had more than eight months of combat with only 15 days out of the line in all that time, and most of those days were spent in moving from one hot sector to another. I never thought any infantryman would last that long but a few have. We have killed or captured members of more than twenty German divisions which we fought at one time or another during that period. They ranged from SS divisions, the best in Hitler's army, on down to Volksgrenadiers. The greatest number faced were parachute units which rank next to the SS as fighting troops.

A few days ago I left my unit and am now in a hospital here in Belgium. I hope soon to be well enough to return. I'd hate to miss the final wind-up after being in so much of the war. Of course I don't want to go back. No one ever wants to go back to the front after learning what it is like, and no one will ever know what it is like unless he has been there.

The weather is growing better now. The new season which the calendar promised on the 21st is really here. There have been several days of good spring weather, and through the happy sunlight of the clear skies the planes have roared almost incessantly. And all of them ours, most of which are bound for Germany to pour on the Nazis the hell which they deserve.

I want to express my deepest sympathy to the relatives of those who have gone on the "long journey." I know your loss is irreplaceable, but theirs was a journey we all must take some time. The great tragedy and pathos lies in the fact that their going was so untimely, and all because of the brutality and unjust ambitions of those we fight. To those who have been wounded, I wish a happy recovery.

I have learned that Congressman [James W., Berryville, Ark.] Trimble's youngest brother was in the fighting around Bastogne at the same time we were there.

May I acknowledge letters from the following men in the service which I know I have not answered:

S/Sgt. John Vanlandingham (Pinnacle community), who when he wrote had had 35 missions with the Air Force. From what he said I think he was in the big air strike which I saw from near St. Lo before we broke the German lines. He is now back in the States (blessed thought) stationed at Chanute Field, Illinois.

Pfc. Ernest H. Walden (Marble) a combat engineer somewhere in the Philippines. Seems those boys over there are doing a very good job. He mentioned Cecil Harper and we both regret deeply the news he gave (which all of you now know, and which I, too, learned from other sources). [Harper was KIA]

Cpl. James D. Reed (Huntsville) who is somewhere in the ETO. He mentioned meeting Leland T. Lewis (Hartwell) in the city of Reims, France.

Pvt. Roy B. Bowman, [Huntsville] a tanker, writes that he has already had three of the big iron monsters shot from under him. Hope he is still okeh.

Cpl. Millard C. Sisemore [Japton] has also written, and says Paige Thomas [Japton] is somewhere near him, but I have been unable to hear from either of them since.

Also good luck and a "write again please" to Cpl. Joe F. Baker, Pfc. Denver Samples, Cpl. Everett Samples, Pfc. Arthur Tice, Sgt. Elbert R. McMurray, Pfc. Everett C. Hill, Erlis Lawson and Pvt. Julian (Woodrow) Ledford, all here somewhere in the ETO. And the same to you in the Pacific Theater which includes Pfc. Robert M. Ward, Pvt. James D. Watson, Pfc. Paul W. Harriman, Pfc. Oscar Dunaway and others out there.

Sincerely,

Capt. Orval E. Faubus
Hqs. 320th Inf.,
APO No. 35, c/o P. M.,
New York, N. Y.

## CHAPTER VIII

## CENTRAL GERMANY CAMPAIGN

298th Gen Hospital
Liege, Belgium
March 25, 1945

The stirring news yesterday was word of the crossing of the Lower Rhine by the British, Canadians, and the Ninth [American] Army. Since the Ninth Army crossing is just up the river from Weisel, I'm sure my unit is in it. I had written to Sid telling him where I am, and thought he might drive back to see me and bring me my mail. Now I know he cannot come.

Wonder who will be gone when I get back. At the time I left I can think of Capt Trossen, Lt Col Walton in 1st Bn, Lt "Curly" Williams,[1] A Co, who was going to the States in about two days, and Lt Goodchild of C Co.

In 2nd Bn were Capt Tobin, Lt Gangemi (of F Co), Capt Hare and Maj Smith.[2]

In 3rd Bn were Lts Carpenter and Peterson, and a Lt known as "Fighting" Leo Thomas[3] of L Co.

The Hqs group, Hqs Co and Sv Co as they have been for some time, Capt Wilson, Lt Adams and Lt Wright in AT Co and Capt Eckstrum of Cn Co. I can't remember right

---

1  1st Lt. Leo K. "Curly" Williams, Co A, Atoka, Okla., an original, listed Tdy March 13, rehabilitation furlough to the States, did not return.

2  Originally Capt. Harvey A. Smith, CO of Co H, now 2nd Bn staff, Denton (or Forsan) Texas, an original.

3  1st Lt. Leo E. "Fighting Leo" Thomas, Co L, Lima, Ohio, an original, listed as Tdy March 16, rehabilitation furlough to the States, did not return.

now whether Lt Larson[4] is still there or not. There are others I can't think of now, but not many of the old originals. Only a few of those still there have been there all the time. For example Gangemi, Hare, Eckstrum and Thomas were out for long periods with wounds. The supply officers for the Bns, Lts Mody, Byerly and Keith were still there. They have been very lucky.

Up until today the weather has been clear and sunny. Yesterday great fleets of bombers continued to go out to batter industrial Germany or to support the Rhine crossing. In the evening they were going home, their flights looking slightly thinned and with a few stragglers, the westering sun glistening with silvery sheen on their sides.

Today is cloudy but as yet the ceiling is high, leaving room for the planes to continue their operations. There have been a few drops of rain. Now at noon the sky is somewhat lighter.

The radio music on this Sabbath seems to fill me with melancholy and a brooding longing. I did not get to attend church services because I was being treated at the clinic. This is the first time I have been conscious of the day-of-the-week in many, many weeks. Soon will come Easter and there will be Sunday services and dinner and egg hunts in the homeland. The Sweet Williams will bloom and the bush honey suckles (azaleas) will give out their wonderfully sweet, over-powering fragrance, and I will not be there. I think of the time Farrell found his first Easter egg. He was yet so small that both tiny pink hands were scarcely enough to hold the colored oval-shaped object, and he was, oh, so thrilled.

My Sunday prayer? Just keep him safe and well, Oh Lord, and I will not ask more of Thee.

The end of the war and our own home coming, we must, collectively and individually, shape and determine by our own efforts.

* * *

0410. As we sat about the ward this afternoon, there came in a USO musician. I recognized him immediately as the hand organ player that was with Don Rice's show at Brin-sur-Seille last fall, when they played for our battle weary doughboys before we jumped off toward the Saar. He

---

4 1st Lt. Melvin L. Larson, Cn Co, address unknown, previously evacuated with injuries in Oct., did not return.

still had his accordion and played tunes which the patients called for. Many men looked up and smiled who had evinced little interest in anything before.

There was quite a bit of gay repartee between the organ player and the rough and ready officer from S. C. (with a broken knee). This fellow of course called for the tune "A little bit south of North Carolina." One of the first things he said to the nurse and ward boys when he came in was "Gee, I sho am glad to see y'all go to work." He is the lively, irrepressible type, who with ready wit and humor, is the life of the crowd wherever he may be.

This USO player also recognized me, as I had given some orientation lectures at the shows they held for our GIs. He is Chester Sholls of Westchester County, New York. He expressed a wish to have a picture of me because I looked like Will Rogers.

Made me recall that my good and kindly friend "Red Cross Charlie" said the same thing when he looked at the picture I had made in Nancy.

298th Gen Hospital
Liege, Belgium
March 26, 1945

There was sunshine this morning, but this afternoon dark, lowering clouds brought rain from the west.

The fresh grass shone a bright green after being bathed by the scurrying showers.

News from the fighting fronts is exceptionally good.

I used to notice the weather because its changes offered variety and a change in work. Usually on the farm it meant rest. [It also determined whether we would have a good crop or a failure.] Here I am sensitive to every change because it means good fighting conditions advantageous to us, or bad conditions favorable to the defending enemy.

\* \* \*

There is a terrible taste in my mouth from the rotten hole where the dentist removed the abscessed tooth. [A deactivated (dead) tooth which had become abscessed and was poisoning my whole system.]

\* \* \*

I read a book today "The Turning Wheels," first in many months.

* * *

[An acquaintance made in the hospital was Capt. Walter W. Brewster of Bearden, Ark., serving with Headquarters, 28th Infantry Division.]

298th Gen. Hospital
March 29, 1945

Still in hospital here, not much improved. Don't know yet what they are going to do with me. I told the "Doc" yesterday I was ready to go back, but I guess they will remove the impacted teeth first.

Cloudy weather today with some rain. The showers galloped across the green swells of the Belgium landscape in sudden dashes. The sound of the drops on the ward tents was like the beating of running feet.

I grow tired of the waiting here. I am more nervous and restless than when at the front. I find myself listening for the big guns and missing their thunder, the sight of the drifting smoke and the smell of the powder. So long have I been a part of the activity, the hurrying, the confusion, the anxiety and sometimes the stark fear and grief, the hate and the anger, that even here, this close to the war, I feel a let down. Well, guess I'll be back soon, and then I'll find myself wishing to be away from the slaughter.

PWs do a lot of the work here. They sweep the wards, carry wounded about on stretchers, in fact most of the work of that type. Others are painting tents and sodding the area. The nurses, doctors and other medical personnel go about their work, apparently pretty busy all the day.

More wounded came in today, including airborne and paratroops who landed beyond the Rhine. They have many stories, which indicate that, although it was war with plenty of shooting and killing, it was not the hell we have endured several times. Reports from the front bear out the indication. There is continued rapid progress against light and disorganized resistance. Only in spots is there fierce resistance and hard fighting. It seems from today's "Stars and Stripes" that the beaten and rugged old Santa Fe Div has hit one of those spots. They have encountered a suicidal group of paratroopers near the town of Gladbecken just north of Essen.

One story from an airborne patient. They had landed, cleared out the enemy and consolidated. One of the men was striding along with his carbine on his shoulder when a German popped out of a doorway, his hand drawn back to throw a grenade. The soldier forgetting his carbine, whips out his 45 and it leaps three times with a bang! bang! bang!.

The German wilts to the ground the grenade falling in front near his feet. "Huh," says the American, holstering his smoking pistol, "Just like in the movies," and goes on his way.

Another: A German tank, armed with the long barrelled lethal 88, was temporarily abandoned in confused fighting. A GI, a new recruit not long from the States, slipped up and put two thermite grenades in the muzzle of the gun. Next morning they kept watch and shortly after dawn a German approached and entered the tank. After a bit the observer using a sound-powered telephone line which they had rigged up during the night, called up some others who were working with him and directed them "I think the Jerries are ready now. Move out across that open space where they can see you." The other GI's moved out where they could be observed by the Germans and they took the bait. They threw a shell into the gun and fired. There was a terrific explosion within the tank and parts of the gun went flying through the air. There were three Germans in the tank, but when the turret was opened no body could be found. There was only a mixture of bodies, uniforms, equipment, and pieces of the tank.

The thermite grenades had almost completely sealed the muzzle of the gun, and when the Krauts fired they got a bigger dose of the medicine than they had intended for the GIs.

298th Gen. Hospital
Liege, Belgium
March 31, 1945

Yesterday the "Doc" cut out and pulled out one of my impacted molars. So last night and today I have been pretty much under the weather. Was able to read again this afternoon and feel much better tonight.

These drugs can almost make one forget he is ill at times.

More wounded came in today from over the Rhine. Some are in pretty bad shape, and of course we don't get the worst cases back here. They are kept in the field hospitals and treated there because they cannot stand the strain of the journey to the rear until their condition has improved.

The airborne officer with the lung wound is better now. Yesterday and today he was able to get out of bed briefly. He suffered a lot for several days and I could hardly sleep for listening to his complaints. [moaning] To keep up his body heat and appetite, a part of his prescription was two shots of liquor daily. One day he was sitting propped up in bed and suddenly said "Say, what about my shot of liquor." We all laughed (that were able) for we knew he was improving. [The doctors took a needle as large as a finger and inserting it through his back, drew a half gallon or more of fluid from his lungs a number of times. For a time we doubted he would survive.]

Almost invariably the talk in the wards, among those who are able to talk, turns to the Germans, their dumbness, their cruelty, their vast and stupid egotism, and what will be done with Germany. There is unanimity on one point. Germany must be controlled, no matter the length of time, whatever is necessary to prevent her making another war.

* * *

*After arrival at this hospital I developed a case of appendicitis. Just when it seemed surgery would be necessary, I got better and three or four days later the pain was almost gone.*

*On the day after the appendicitis attack began, I had a case of the giant hives. Great white welks, which looked like blisters, broke out on my arms and body. They stung and itched but I paid them little heed.*

*The next day I picked up a Readers Digest and there was an article about the disease. The article said the ailment could be serious and related how a tracheoctomy had to be performed on a patient in the elevator of a hospital in order to save the patient's life. There was insufficient time to get him to the operating room.*

*I thought how ironic it would have been, after what I had been through, to die from the hives on a hospital cot because no one knew what was wrong. Three days later a doctor, having heard of my case, came to interview me about it. He was doing research on the ailment. It seemed very little is known about the disease.*

298th Gen. Hosp., Liege
April 1, 1945

I have learned from those around me and from the radio that today is Easter Sunday. The air-ways this morning were quite filled with music and services appropriate to the occasion, which was all the difference it meant to me. Of course there was no pause for the combat troops. Some of them may not have known; - some of them died today.

News from the war fronts indicates the progress of all Allied armies is good. Still it is discouraging to think about, even though we are moving rapidly. For behind the headlines and the newspaper stories I can see the tired GIs, and in their drawn and weary faces the look which is seen in no others. For every town taken I know the price is paid in killed and desperately wounded. Behind the sound and fury of the battle about which the correspondents write, following up the advances which sound so good to us all, are the GRO boys (grave registration) who gather up the dirty, bloody bodies and haul them away in trucks like loads of wood to some American cemetery in Europe. Just as I, or any of my friends, will be hauled away whenever anyone of us meets his end. For no one can waste time with the dead, except to bury them in the hastiest and most simple way possible, as long as there is a war to win and the living to care for.

All of which reminds me of some of the incidents related about the GRO squad headed by "Smokey" Dodd, who is quite a character and has become quite legend in the 320th. He was headed back toward the rear one day with a trailer load, the vehicle filled to capacity. Someone, Maj Hughes I think, hailed him and asked if he could take another body. Bringing the truck and trailer to a stop Smokey looked at him in that expressionless way of his and answered, "Well, I guess so, Major, if he doesn't mind riding in the front seat in my lap."

Red Cross Charlie told me of another member of the group, also quite a character, but whose name I cannot now remember. Charlie was watching him gather up bodies one day, some of which were Krauts and, having lain out for some time, were overly ripe. I do recall it was in that period of awful mud and rain in Alsace-Lorraine. Charlie, not inured to such proceedings, was having a rather unpleasant time just watching. This particular individual, grinning at

Charlie's discomfiture, waded out into a pool of mud and water and seized a long dead soldier by the leg and started dragging him out to where he could be loaded on a stretcher. [He was "getting the best" of Charlie by showing how the work was done] Reaching the edge of the pool he looked around and was much surprised to find he had only a leg. Both flesh and clothing had parted where the thigh joined the body, leaving the remainder still lying in the pool. It was Charlie's turn to laugh at the soldier.

\* \* \*

This first day of April has been reminiscent of the gale-laden spring days in the States. All day, and even now as the darkness settles, the strong gusts of wind have shaken the tents with popping and flapping so that it was difficult at times to hear the radio or to carry on a conversation. The electric light bulbs swung to and fro casting wavering shadows. The westerly wind has borne in from the sea light rain and mist. The bright green of the new grass and the dark upturned sod stood out prominently against the grey of the horizon with the dark clouds overhead.

\* \* \*

I think I shall be well enough to return to my unit without having the other impacted teeth removed. So as soon as this one heals I think I shall be off. I am more pent up here than when I was at the front, and here I am doing nothing useful. I hope to avoid the replacement depot system but may not be able to do so. My unit is so far away that I cannot reach them by telephone.

\* \* \*

While I have written, Jack Benny's program ("Sad Sack Benny," he says), has been on the air. No matter how low my spirits I have to laugh at some of the gags, which is good. As old "Honest Abe" said, "laughter is medicine," and certainly many in Europe need that medicine.

[*"The Sad Sack" was the most famous cartoon strip of the war in Europe. Drawn by Sgt George Baker and appearing in the weekly magazine, YANK, the strip took its name from the central and almost only character, a nondescript, lowly GI, who was always unlucky and unfortunate, and most of the time wound up with the raw deals of which most sol-*

*diers imagined themselves the recipients. The creator took the name of the character from the universally known GI phrase, "a sad sack of s - - t," widely used to describe any unpleasant, disgusting or deplorable situation or character. In adopting the title, "Sad Sack Benny," in his broadcasts to the troops, the great comedian was establishing instant raport and understanding with his listeners.]*

298th Gen Hospital
April 4, 1945

I was to return to my unit today but this morning my jaw was much worse, so I'm here for another day at least. I walked out to the tram line yesterday and rode the trolley to Liege. After some inquiry I think I have found a fast way to get back to the unit. A truck comes each day from Corps Hqs to pick up its quota of "Stars and Stripes" at the Liege office. I can catch a ride on that truck to Corps Hqs and from there to my division.

*     *     *

Yesterday was a day of sunshine and showers. It was like an ordinary life - a succession of smiles and tears and an occasional storm. Life in combat is not ordinary. It is like a long and dreary winter which will not end until the peace and the home coming.

Tomorrow is Farrell's birthday. In a way it is an anniversary for me too, for I never really began to live life at its fullest until he came along.

Evacuation has been slow in this hospital recently and there has grown up a circle of acquaintances among the sick and the wounded. The joker of the crowd now is the fellow who was for a time so ill. When he was so ill, with a tube sticking through a hole in his back to drain matter from his shrapnel punctured lung, one would never dreamed he was such a humorous personality.

The fellow across from me, with a bullet hole through his abdomen which punctured his guts, has quite an odor. He seems a wonderfully nice fellow. He is a very sick man but is slowly improving.

298th Gen. Hospital
Liege, Belgium
April 6, 1945

It is now 1035. Soon after lunch today I will "take off" for my unit. The hospital authorities are permitting me to sign out on my own to return to the regiment. I have made arrangements to catch a ride on the vehicle which hauls the "Stars and Stripes" to the Corps Hqs. From there I can get a ride or else call the regiment for transportation.

\* \* \*

This 104th Div artilleryman is going strong. He is kidding a couple of Air Force officers. Calls them members of the Ninth Luftwaffe, and wants to know how many points a member gets for the Iron Cross. He says they kill more Americans than Germans so they should get Iron Cross decorations and he called them Lutwaffe. He adds, "You bombed me so often I got nervous."

He and the Rebel from S. C. have their ups and downs. The Rebel says he hopes the arty joker will get a cluster to his purple heart the day he gets back to duty, and the artyman replies that he hopes the wings will drop off the plane which flies him [the Rebel] across the ocean toward America.

Usually the talk is not so rough but they seem to enjoy their word play.

\* \* \*

I guess I'm foolish for not going through the repo system for it would probably take three or four weeks. By that time the war might be over. But here I go and should be there in 3 or 4 days.

\* \* \*

*I left the hospital on the afternoon of the 6th, riding the tram into Liege where I rented a room in a hotel to spend the night. I was up the next morning at 0300 and over to the publishing house by 0400, some time before the carrier arrived for the papers. I took off with him in the darkness before dawn on April 7. (I could have stayed in Liege a few days and no one would have known the difference). We traveled across Belgium and Holland into Germany, up to the Rhine and across the stream on a pontoon bridge. I reported to 320th regtl CP, rejoining my old buddies, and was under enemy arty fire before the sun went down in the Battle of the Ruhr Pocket.*

*One thing is worth remembering about the 298th Gen Hosp at Liege. It had been under fire when the Germans were directing the buzz bombs (rhobombs) on Liege. When a bombardment was under way, the hospital staff had to get the patients out of bed and down on the floor under the cots. Those who could, both patients and hospital personnel, went to bomb shelters. The hospital was hit a number of times and there were casualties. There was a story of a doctor and nurse who got married and spent their honeymoon at the hospital under the bombardment of the rhobombs. One night the apartment in which they were sleeping was struck by one of the missiles.*

*Because they had been under fire, the personnel of the 298th were more understanding, sympathetic and considerate to the wounded than those of any other hospital in which I was a patient.*

Germany
April 11, 1945

I have rejoined the Regiment, which I find attached to the 75th Div and fighting on the north edge of the Ruhr Pocket. Tomorrow, if plans are fulfilled, the Regiment will take the city of Dortmund.

Fortunately the Regiment has not been engaged heavily during my absence, and the circle of acquaintances is about the same. Pvt John Dudley, who was one of the most colorful characters in the 320th, fell into a mine shaft while looking for a store of cognac, [and other supplies] and was killed. A soldier from L Co, riding a motorcycle without lights along a dark road, ran headlong into a jeep and was killed. Deaths in battle grow common place so it is the ones that occur otherwise that are noticeable.

This conquered section of the Ruhr is teeming with people. Women predominate. War has taken the men. Almost all Germans appear well dressed. The slave labor, French, Poles, Russian and others, are shabby, lean, often in pitiable condition, but are happy. [because of the coming of the Allied armies.]

Many, many are along the roads attempting to walk home, perhaps hundreds of miles. As I drove along the road in the late afternoon of this warm sunshiny spring day, I observed many who had grown so tired and weary that they had dropped on the grass, exhausted. Others plodded wearily ahead. Many of the Russians and Poles are remaining in their barbed-wire stockades or with the farmers for whom they worked, until we join up with the Russians, and then they can go home.

Capt McCormic, the CAC or Mil Govt officer, is a much worked and worried man. One German came and complained to him that since we came his Russian slaves had not worked so hard and he wanted something done about it. The captain informed him that the Russians and Poles were to work only if they wanted to, and that if he or anyone else came to him (the Capt) with such a complaint, that he would have the slaves hitch him to a plow like a horse and work him as long as they liked.

For the most part the slaves have been kept in barbed wire inclosed stockades, living far too many to the room in rough barracks, with only the most meagre furnishings. They were beaten, tortured, seduced, raped or killed at the whim of the overseers and guards or the farmers or factory owners for whom they worked. They were paid a little, sometimes amounting to perhaps a dollar per week or per month. They had no protector, or law, or higher authority to which to appeal for justice or for mercy.

Yesterday, Red Cross Charlie, Sid, Brochu and I visited such a camp, set off in an out-of-way place near our CP. Things I saw there I can never forget. Capt McCormic estimated it would hold about 600 when filled to capacity. I did not make an estimate. McCormic told me that during the three years it had been in operation, 1300 babies had been born there. They had been delivered by a former Russian doctor, a woman, assisted by two midwives. The inmates were Russians and Poles. There was the plump young woman (almost all were plump, especially the Russians, and you could hardly notice their starvation unless you looked at their sunken almost lusterless eyes) whose face was splotched, blood-shot and blue from a beating administered shortly before the camp was liberated. I noticed signs of beatings in the faces of three or four others.

The big, cruel looking strands of barbed wire, which made the fence, had signs hanging on them printed in two languages, "Anyone touching this wire will be immediately shot."

They could not tell us much for Charlie and Sid could not speak their language. Some of them could speak only a little German. When Charlie would speak his few words of Russian or Polish, their faces would light up with smiles like the sun coming from behind a cloud.

They related that the guards used to stand at the stockade gate and hit them with their rawhide whips or clubs when they were ordered in or out of the stockade.

Most of the inmates were women (or girls) of about 18 to 30. Many were very pretty. Some had been brought to the camp at age of 14 or 15. There were a few older women. I noticed 3 or 4 old or middleaged men. There were several youthful men or boys. One followed us around wanting to join the American Army. There were small children ranging from infants to age two or three, most if not all born in the slave camp. Many of the women were pregnant, perhaps 1/3 or 1/2 or more. Some were sired by the German masters for there was no such thing as refusal. With every effort to please they were still beaten too often, and some killed.

I did not find out if the Germans permitted marriage but we do know it was not encouraged.

There was the mad girl, crazy as a loon, a sickening and heart rending sight to see. When she first saw us she came immediately to a salute. She was doing all manner of the aimless, senseless things which one in her condition does, picking up buttons and then spilling them, adjusting her ragged, dirty clothes, heaping up the straw pile in which she worked and then scattering it. Once she grabbed up an object, which I first took for a rotten skull, and gnawed on it ravenously. She got a great mouth full and I observed it was a rotten beet. One of the Russian women stormed at her and she spit it out. I had to turn away to keep from retching.

She had become insane four months ago when a child was born. The doctor in the camp could not help her and the Germans would not. If they had done anything it would have been to take the poor creature and kill her.

Most of the camp inmates laughed at her antics, much as we have come to laugh at the hardships and danger of the front lines. They, like us, have come to laugh at misery, thus accepting unconsciously nature's insurance against the misery itself.

Before we left two Russian girls sang, in very sweet voices, some Russian folk song to the accompaniment of an instrument like our guitar or mandolin. I could not understand the words but there was haunting melody and pathos in the music.

\* \* \*

*When I rejoined the 320th, the following officers in addition to Thomas and Williams, were gone.*

*Capt Ancrum Waring, Jr., Med Det, Charleston, S. C., a replacement, evacuated as sick March 9, did not return; Capt Peter A. Miceli, Med Det, address unknown, a replacement, trfd to Ninth Army, March 17.*

*Three officers, all replacements, were trfd to 102nd Inf on March 20; 2nd Lt Howard L. Angell, Co A, Tulsa, Oklahoma; 2nd Lt Stanley A. Revzin, Co A, address unknown; 1st Lt James W. Leisner, Co L, address unknown.*

*Three officers, all replacements, were trfd to 84th Div on March 20; 2nd Lt George S. Schonewald, Co L, address unknown; 2nd Lt George W. Walsh, Co M, address unknown; 2nd Lt Howard F. Wiseman, Regtl Hq Co, address unknown.*

*2nd Lt Paul E. Roberts, Co L, Esperance, N. Y., a replacement, listed LWA March 28, did not return.*

*2nd Lt Joseph J. Donovan, Co G, Baltimore, Md., an EM awarded a battlefield commission, listed LWA March 30, did not return. (The address may be incorrect as it may have been confused with that of Lt Richard A. Donovan).*

*S/Sgt. Archie L. Jones, Haynes, Arkansas, an old friend of Co F, had been evacuated the second time. Later he returned to duty.*

\* \* \*

## PVT DUDLEY AND MARLENE DIETRICH

*While I was away in the hospital and before the 35th jumped off in the Central Germany Campaign, the famed movie actress, Marlene Dietrich, visited the Division area on a tour of entertainment for the troops. After one of her shows a group of GIs, including Pvt John Dudley of Mortain fame, watched nearby as the actress prepared to leave.*

*Dudley's companions challenged him to get Miss Dietrich's autograph. As her vehicle started away Dudley dashed out into the street and flagged it to a stop. Not only did the actress give him her autograph but visited with him for a time and then threw her arms around his neck and kissed him goodbye.*

*Needless to say, Pvt Dudley was the envy of the watching soldiers.*

*Much was written and said during the war about the entertainment of the troops by stars of screen and radio. Many of the stars made many appearances for the men of the armed forces, but the combat troops had few, if any, opportunities to see them. I recall that Bob Hope entertained the 35th troops at Camp Rucker while we were still in the States, and Bing Crosby and Miss Dietrich appeared at different times at Division Headquarters in September 1944 during combat in France.*

*Miss Dietrich came to the continent soon after the invasion armies broke out of the beachhead in Normandy, and became the most faithful entertainer of the troops in Europe.*

*From what I could read and hear about the famous actress, it seems she remained on the continent, devoting full time to appearances before audiences of GIs until the war ended. Once the allied armies had liberated large sections of The Fatherland, I read about her making a return visit to her former home in Germany.*

*One of her shows gave rise to an oft quoted line among the American troops in Europe. As related to me by one of my friends, perhaps Lt Sam O'Brien or Lt Ernest Zielasko, who saw the show at Division Headquarters, Miss Dietrich came on the stage and waited for the catcalls and whistles of the GIs to subside. Then turning to the master of ceremonies she inquired, "What shall I do?"*

*"Give them what they want, Marlene," he answered.*

*Again after waiting for quiet she asked, "What is it they want?"*

*The instant reply of the MC was, "It ain't spam!"*

*The reply, in show parlance, brought down the house, for spam was the most universally disliked of all the GI rations served to the troops in Europe. Afterwards any time any question arose as to the object of an individual's thoughts, the instant rejoinder was, "It ain't spam!"*

\* \* \*

# FIGHTING IN THE RUHR POCKET

*On March 31 in the Battle of the Ruhr Pocket, Company F, led by Capt John M. Roberts of New Haven, Conn. after the death of Capt Watkins, engaged in a fierce fight for the Prosper Coal Mine as the 2nd Bn was forcing a crossing of the Emscher Canal. An estimated 100 Germans were emplaced in a huge slag pile, in mine shafts and buildings, while a reported eight to ten thousand civilians - Germans and foreign workers - were kept below in the tunnels by armed guards.*

*Capt Roberts related that everything was thrown at the enemy force, but after each barrage the Nazis would still be there firing. Cannon Company fired 950 rounds and Sgt William Chambers said the mortars fired 500 shells. Sgt Loren McKinney and Sgt Thomas Bendig manned two .30 calibre machine guns which fired 12,500 rounds.*

*A 9-man patrol led by S/Sgt Glen Metcalf crossed the Emscher on a railroad bridge under cover of a smoke screen and machine gun fire. Then Lt Vivian Palmore of Mattoax, Va. led a platoon which cleared the mine buildings of enemy and freed the thousands of civilians.*

## UNUSUAL PATROL

*An unusual experience in the fighting of the Ruhr Pocket was that of 2nd Lt Omer D. Whitwell of McKinney, Texas. He led a patrol of Co K, guided by two Russians, into the town of Schalke, where, in the darkness, they mingled with the soldiers and civilians in the streets of the town, and watched the socializing, including dancing and drinking in the cafes and bars. With the aid of the Russians the patrol talked its way past a half dozen or more sentries except one who was killed with a knife by one of the Russian guides, and another, the last one encountered, who was captured and brought back as a PW. The EM on the patrol were Sgt Walter Hrbacek of Chicago, Pfc Wesley Bryan of Philadelphia and Pfc Erwin A. Lord of Berkeley, Calif.*

\* \* \*

## WITH 75TH DIVISION

On April 11th and 12th the 320th was attached to and fought with the 75th Division in the clearing of Holthausen and the attack on Dortmund. Then the Regiment, after a link-up with the 95th Division in the attack, was pulled back to the 35th for the plunge far into Germany.

* * *

Brambauer, Germany
N. of Dortmund
April 11, 1945

Near the slave camp were the remains of a British bomber which had been shot down some time ago. It had burned after falling, and pinioned in the charred wreckage were the roasted remains of the pilot. His white teeth were glaring in the dull light of the evening and his skull had crumbled away. A piece of his uniform which had not burned showed the blue of the Royal Air Force. Charlie picked up a piece of it and there fell from the pocket the scorched half of his identification card, which I noted and picked up. The number was legible and from it he may be identified. Other words showed him to be one of the Dominions, a youth from far across the sea, "fallen in the cause of the free" here in Naziland. I thought of him and the enslaved Russians, the connection and their common cause. He was the forerunner of the power which drove back the German Army and opened the gate of freedom, we hope forever, to their barbed wire prison.

* * *

April 13, 1945

In the grey hours of dawn of the 13th I was lying in my sleeping bag when I heard some one say, "Roosevelt is dead." I knew that it was true for no one would jest about that. It came as a stunning, cruel blow in the face to me. Then when the shock of the news began to wear off, I knew the blow was a mortal one. For like the crown laid down by Alexander the Great which no one else could wear, the place in world affairs left vacant by his death cannot by any other be filled.

But for me and the millions of others, who loved him as a leader for the right, and the lowly and oppressed, the time of mourning must necessarily be brief. For now without his leadership we must work all the harder for the victory for which he planned, and with even greater zeal for a world free from want, fear and war, in accordance with his ideals.

On the road from Brambauer
April 13, 1945

We are rolling in convoy through the heart of Germany. Leaving the pocket to be finally liquidated by other forces we are on our way to the moving front near Berlin.

The spring is here in its fullness, the fruit trees and flowers in bloom and, after last night's heavy showers, the pale green foliage shining in all its new spring freshness. The sun is just breaking out. We're rolling.

\* \* \*

1400. - - Now halted about 20 Km short of Hamm. The country is a vast expanse of green, well developed and with many farms and villages. We are now out of the great industrial section of the Ruhr. (Many moving - [Unfinished]

\* \* \*

1500. - Now on a German superhighway rolling toward Bielefield.

\* \* \*

1600. - We have detoured from the superway and are now N of Paderborn. Here are signs of battle when the first troops drove through. A burned out American armored car, a German tank with the long barrelled 88, an overturned German armored car, the fox-holes, the defenses and road blocks now over run.

The death of President Roosevelt dominates the news, as it does the thoughts of all of us who are not actually fighting at the moment.

We are moving again . . .

\* \* \*

Now another halt for some unknown reason. Perhaps it was to allow the big truckloads of gasoline, accompanied by a roaring tank, to go by.

Here the road is lined with evergreens, their darker hue contrasting with the pale amber of the new foliage on the other trees. There is a radio silence [for military messages] imposed during our movement so the operator in our command car keeps almost constantly turned to a good radio program. The music is touchingly beautiful in spite of our speed and the new scenes never seen before. We have covered 82 miles already. Very good for a military convoy. The country is very open now, compared to the industrial Ruhr. It has been level and smooth; the land appears very rich; everywhere are the farmers working in the fields and gardens. Many are spading up the ground - a very slow process. I guess it is the only means for many of them because the German military took their horses for the army.

Those along the roads are on foot or riding bikes. Others push carts of every kind and description. I have seen a few horse drawn wagons.

All along the roads are the refugees, the slave laborers, now freed by our advancing armies. Most are heading, by any means available, toward the west, to get out of Germany and away from their former masters. The natives of France and the Low Countries are of course going home.

We move again . . .

* * *

Now 1645. - We pause again on the green German plain. Now very near the town of Hamelin on the Weser River, the storied location of the exploits of the Pied Piper who freed the German town of rats and piped all the children away into a mountain because the town council failed to pay the promised amount of money.

We have observed about 50 truck loads of German PWs on the way to the rear. They are a dirty, bedraggled, beaten lot. One truck had some women in it. One full truck load were dressed in grey tan uniforms, perhaps Hungarians or Italian Facists.

There are more and more slaves on the roads. One commandeered German vehicle had in big letters on the side, "Paris, France, we go to France." Another had, "France and Belgium" and "Vive la America." Just now 3 refugees passed on foot, two of them men and the other a dark-haired, young woman. Many, many are walking, just now a column of middle-aged men, weighted down with their packs and bundles, plodding very slowly with the fatigue of a day's journey upon them.

Now exactly 1700. The sun's rays are slanting and the shadows are long over the new green, or the dark broken earth of the fields. Even now it is dropping behind a hill, one of the few on the northern plains, and into a mass of dark clouds. "Cloudy in the West," but I hope it does not rain too much.

— 579 —

Just heard a transmission from Ankara, Turkey, in English, expressing the deep grief and regret of the Turkish nation at the death of our beloved president.

* * *

Friendly children, talking to us in German and waving as we move very slowly through a town. A bunch of girls with flowers, chatting happily. Some as beautiful as the tulips they were holding.

*I noticed that the comely young women all wore a badge sewn on the upper part of a blouse. All appeared near the same age and similarly dressed.*

*I asked one of the German-speaking GIs about the badge. It read Deutches Mutter (German Mother) he told me. The town was the location of one of Hitler's baby factories. The women were unwed German mothers. The emblem worn on the blouse was the badge of honor for each, signifying that she, as an unwed girl, had given birth to one or more children for the replenishment and glory of The Fatherland.*

*The GI, during our brief stop, obtained for me one of the cloth badges which I kept for a souvenir of the war and Hitler's Germany.*

1720. - Now in the storied town of Hamelin beside the Weser River. Two girls are carrying water from the stream and up the high bank across the pavement where we are parked. On the far bank a couple sits in close embrace and our GIs are bringing out their field glasses. We move before they can get a close look. The river has a number of big boats anchored in its placid waters. One has a French tricolor hanging from its mast and the others have flying the white flags of surrender. Shots can be heard from the town on the other side.

We move up a little farther and there is bomb damage. The bridges are blown. We are moving very slowly, traffic difficulties. They are here at the pontoon bridge which we have now reached.

There are many signs of recent combat. Burned out buildings, broken lamp posts, shattered trees, and the debris in which I can see a number of German caps. None of the premises orderly or clean, so we know we are near the front again.

We cross the Weser on a pontoon bridge.

Ribbensdorf, Germany
April 14, 1945

We are west of Magdeburg where fighting is reported to be still in progress. It got dark shortly after the last entry above and I could write no more. Our destination had been changed while enroute; the convoy became broken up and we wandered about most of the night. Many of us never reached the assembly area until this morning. Sid, Scherer and O'Brien did not arrive until about noon. At one time last night there were only two other vehicles with our command car. I think we visited several German towns which had not yet been "conquered."

At one time about 0200 we stopped in a town, at the time with Cn Co and a few other vehicles, and aroused a civilian, and Sid found out from him where we were.

But that didn't help much as we still didn't know where we were supposed to go. It was quite a mixed up affair. I would have really been uneasy if the Germans had been in a fighting mood. [In the confused fighting brought on by the rapid advance into Germany, two American generals were killed and a number of German generals were captured far behind us.]

But now at 1900, we have received a situation and an order which indicates that there are forces organized to our front and to the south who are really putting up a fight. We have been ordered to join the 83rd Div which has a bridgehead over the Elbe south of Magdeburg. They are fighting to hold it and to go to the assistance of 2 armored bns over the Elbe north of the city. The Germans still hold Magdeburg in force on this side of the river. There are seven German divisions to our south and rear which really puts us out on a limb farther than we have ever been before. In this closing battle a lot of lives will probably be lost.

\* \* \*

I visited a PW [Allied] group today which our forces have recently liberated. There were about 400 Britishers and Dominion troops and 500 to 600 Americans. Their conditions were deplorable and the stories of hardship and suffering were overwhelming. I cannot even try to set them down now for they were too many and I am too tired. They had been marched about over Germany losing many of their number from exhaustion and starvation. Some were shot by their German guards. Their condition could hardly have been worse. Some of the British had been prisoners since Dunkirk. Others at Tobruk, etc. More details later.

## THE AMERICAN AND BRITISH PRISONERS

*Capt Sid Silverman and I with some enlisted personnel were among the first, if not the first, to reach the British and American PWs. Upon the approach of the Americans the German officers and men had surrendered to the PWs. In overall charge of the some 1100 PWs and the dozen or so Germans, their roles now reversed, was an American sergeant from Texas.*

*Many of the men were in deplorable condition, unable to rise lying in their own filth. Within two minutes after our arrival Sid and I had dispatched a message to the medics and to Red Cross Charlie for all the aid that could be sent.*

*The PWs had been halted at their present location for only 3 or 4 days. Information from them revealed that they had been in a prison camp in East Germany. When the Russians approached, their captors marched them toward the west. When the Americans approached from that direction, their march was turned back toward the east. One soldier had kept a daily record which indicated they had marched back and forth across Germany for about 1400 miles.*

*There were some Anzacs in the group still wearing their big black western-type hats. Some of them and the British had been captured in Africa at Tobruk and other places before America entered the war.*

*Many PWs had been lost on the long march. They became ill or exhausted and died along the way. Sometimes one or more would be shot by one of the more ruthless guards because they could not keep up, or for taking a raw cabbage or beet from a field.*

*We learned that the Germans allowed at least some of the Red Cross parcels to reach the PWs. Some of the Anzacs and Americans said they would never have survived without the food parcels.*

*The Texas sergeant and others vouched for their former German captors at the camp. The German officers and soldiers who surrendered to them had not been with them long* but, according to the sergeant, had done everything possible for their welfare while there.

The reader might well surmise that an attitude of great joy would be found in such a situation. Such is not the case. These PWs, like combat veterans, had been drained of almost all emotion by the harrowing hardships they had endured.

Discipline and compassion were apparently the predominant attitudes remaining. There may have been in some a quiet joy, but it was not apparent. Their pale, flacid faces showed little if any emotion. Many were, of course, too ill to feel anything.

\* \* \*

## REACTION TO TRUMAN'S INAUGURAL ADDRESS

By chance and circumstance, which always determined any activity other than combat, a number of us had an opportunity to listen by radio to the speech of Harry S. Truman when he assumed the duties of the presidency following the death of President Roosevelt. It may have been when we were gathered to receive the order which sent us plunging approximately 180 miles into the heart of Germany to the Elbe River.

We received the address by way of the Armed Forces Radio network on Maj McElroy's little radio, which he had kept with him since our stay in England, or perhaps even longer. Among those present in addition to McElroy, were Col Byrne, Col Northam, Maj Jamieson, Capts Silverman and Ginsburg, several other officers and a number of enlisted men. It was a rather large group for combat conditions, almost as many as could crowd into the room.

Compared to the mellifluous tones of Roosevelt, the midwest twang of Truman's voice was less appealing to many listeners. However, we were not concerned with the sectional dialect. In a regiment which boasted men from every state in the union, we had long ago learned that dialect, or fluency of speech, did not make the man. Nor did it matter from what part of the country a man came. There were good men from all sections. The important attributes to us were integrity, courage, fortitude and dependability, qualities which made a man, - in the language of the front - "fit to take along," one who could "deliver the goods" at a time when "the chips were down."

— 583 —

*With the great confidence of the men of combat in Roosevelt as a war leader, there was naturally great interest in the quality of the leadership to be provided by his successor. We were concerned about President Truman's understanding and knowledge of what we were doing, of the great sacrifices being made, and of the obligations of world leadership which he had now assumed. To us the attitude of the speaker and the content of the speech were all important.*

*The men listened with a quiet, sober intentness. Not a sound was made nor a voice heard, except the one coming over the radio, and fortunately there were no interruptions, as we heard the speech of our new leader.*

*When the message had ended - a message received on a dinky little radio at a battle command post thousands of miles from the place of delivery - there were audible sighs and exclamations of relief and satisfaction. We had a new leader, we were convinced, not only of knowledge and understanding but of courage and decision as well. Whether or not all of us survived, we could now push on with confidence to the approaching end of the great conflict.*

*As we hastily broke up the impromptu gathering to return to our various tasks, one of those present appropriately summed up the situation for those who had listened. Quoting the statement attributed to George Washington when he heard of the courage displayed by the Continental soldiers at Bunker Hill, someone remarked, "The liberty of the country is secure."*

*President Harry S. Truman, we concluded, would "do to take along."*

\* \* \*

Calbe, Germany
April 15, 1945

We have just arrived at this place (about 1400) and have set up our CP in some houses on the edge of the town. I arrived while Bock was clearing the civilians from the house. One lady was hastily packing some things, meanwhile shedding tears and talking in tones of self-pity. Bock remains unperturbed and ushers them on their way. He, like me, cannot recall any instances wherein the Germans had compassion on the Jews, the Poles, Russians or others.

\* \* \*

Our move last night was without incident except that we were halted for some time while waiting for our advance parties to return to show what areas had been selected for bivouac. While we waited some ack-ack blossomed in the sky and a few planes droned overhead; to the east were many red flashes and flares as Allied planes made their nightly, bombing run over Berlin. It was too far to hear the sound. We are yet some 60 or 70 miles from the German capital.

We spent the night, or that portion after midnight, in the town of Brundy. This morning the work was going on in the farm-yard around the CP. The Polish laborers, wearing on their right chest the letter "P," emblem of their servitude, doing the housework and driving the big cream and reddish colored draft horses hitched to the big lumbering farm wagons or huge carts. The Russian slaves wear the emblem "OST" on their clothing. As we were moving out a very pretty girl passed by with that insignia on her sweater. I asked "Russke?" She smiled and replied [nodded] in the affirmative.

* * *

I think the Russian and Polish governments will have to send delegations throughout Germany after the war to round up some of the slave laborers. Many of them were brought here when very young. Some, having no home or family to whom they can return, will just lack the initiative to go back to their country. In some cases, we have learned, their former masters treated some of them very well. But the great numbers who have slaved in the factories and lived in the slave camps are ready and anxious to go home.

Tornitz, Germany
April 15, 1945

Just arrived here after another displacement of the CP (now 1920). The CG of the 83rd Div, Maj Gen [Robert C.] Macon, just visited us to get the latest situation. We were just setting up the CP and there was a great deal of confusion. He was in the room before Maj Hughes happened to catch sight of him and call, "Attention." He was nice, very business like and not at all austere.

* * *

The CP at Calbe was close beside the Saale River over which the 2nd and 3rd Bns were making assault crossings.

The upstairs window offered an excellent view of the operation. First the artillery laid down a barrage on the targets across the river. The landing shells threw great plumes of dirt into the air and clouds of dust and black smoke billowed upward. The guns shifted from target to target. A few white phosphorous shells made great, bright red flashes followed by clouds of white smoke. All this could be seen before the sound of the explosions reached us, whamming into our building across the flat, green, German plain.

Shortly the mortars began coughing and we waited while the shells arched their high angle path over the troops and began exploding in clouds of dust on their targets. A few moments later we could see the dark forms of the infantrymen advancing in spread out formation over the green field and across the brown roads. There were the two lead scouts and a third one following closely, and a 100 yards or so back the thin lines of the squads and platoons. It was a picture of war seldom seen so plainly and safely. Luckily the enemy did not have any artillery or SP guns in position or the troops could not have advanced so easily. He could also have knocked out the window from which we watched and put us into the cellars. Rifle fire was mingling with the coughing and exploding mortars, now both friendly and enemy, as we moved out from that CP to our new location. A few moments later a wounded GI and five PWs were ferried back across the river. Fighting has grown more brisk as our troops advance farther and the darkness falls on the plains by the Elbe River.

\* \* \*

And now my good friend, Lt John Kelly, says to take a drink of his Scotch, that it will give me inspiration to do what ever I am now doing so diligently. One very often is in need of inspiration amidst the fatigue, the strain and the danger. Now there is an added strain, the thought that one can yet lose his life, and some will lose their lives, with the great conflict so near its culmination. So many, many things are happening too, that it is impossible to write of them, and still more impossible to remember. They are seen and noted as they occur, and then fade from the mind and memory as completely as the ripples created by a falling pebble disappear from the surface of a pool.

\* \* \*

2240. After the evening meal most have gone to bed. We have had very little sleep for the past few nights. Parts of the attacking battalions are still active but most of their units have now posted security and settled down for the night.

Lt Silverman has set his wife's picture before him and is writing to her. He pauses often, his mind far away. Only other remaining person is Sgt Howard of the Engineers who is also writing.

\* \* \*

Impressions of the day. As we were loading up this morning, Dominees singing, as if to himself, to the tune of "Don't Sweetheart Me" the words, "Don't Fraternize, if you don't mean it." This non-fraternization is a much discussed subject up here.

The "OST" and the "P" emblems on the breasts of the slaves.

The wild ride last night through village towns and countryside not knowing what we would meet.

Every MP guide along the way [during daylight] surrounded by a gathering of the liberated laborers, happy at the coming of their liberators and their regained freedom. Many stood by the road and saluted every passing vehicle. The Germans themselves, goggle-eyed at the motorized military might overrunning their country.

In the courtyard of the farm center, where we spent last night, a notice and instructions in eight different languages, including English, which forbade smoking in certain areas about the premises. The notice in German also made nine languages. This indicates that the Nazis intended to have English slaves also in addition to their many others.

\* \* \*

Capt Scherer, in a loquacious mood today, telling us of his romance with his wife. Says he never told anyone, "I love you" except her. I have often heard him say that for a long time after we entered combat he had a great fear that he would get a letter from his wife and would get "knocked off" before he could read it.

\* \* \*

"The Star Spangled Banner" played at the close of a radio program, brings to my mind the thought that this is

Sunday and today they buried our departed chief. [Franklin D. Roosevelt] The cause of freedom and right, and the poor and the oppressed, has lost one of its greatest champions.

\* \* \*

Last night after darkness fell, four of our MP road guides were fired upon by German snipers. The liaison officer from the CAV group now with us, Lt Obreter, said one of his sections had one man killed last night by a German burrp gun. The killing occurred in a rear area. This is undoubtedly the work of SS men. We get information from the slave laborers that there are a number of them in civilian clothes in certain areas.

\* \* \*

The Krauts just laid in a heavy round not far away. Enemy arty fire so far has been sparse in our sector. Today the 2nd Armored bridge-head over the Elbe north of Madgeburg was lost. The one to the south has been enlarged slightly by hard fighting. It is now just to our left and we may be thrown into it at any time. Another round just came in. The night may not be too peaceful.

[Casualties[5] not mentioned in the Journal.]

### Extract from G-2 Report of 83rd Inf (Thunderbolt) Div of 16 April, 1945

CALBE (D7774) had been occupied by 83rd Div Hqs three days. An officer of the Div Judge Advocate Section, armed with a carbine, was walking alone on the street early afternoon 15 April. When rounding a small bend in the street, the Officer was fired upon by a civilian who had stepped from a doorway. The shots went astray, but the shots of four American soldiers, who were but a short distance away, found their mark as this Nazi youth fell dead.

**Empty foxholes?** A concussion grenade was hurled from a foxhole at a ¾ ton truck of Div Mil Gov detachment when traveling along the road in vic D262658. Two men in German uniforms had been observed in the foxhole by the occupants of the truck and by prudently speeding up, the grenade fell to the rear of the truck.

---

5 2nd Lt. Omer D. Whitwell, Co K, McKinney, Texas, a replacement, listed LWA April 15, did not return; 2nd Lt. Clifford C. Rock, Co G, Antigo, Wisc., a replacement, listed MIA April 16, later listed KIA; 2nd Lt. Frank Von Borstel, Co H, Grass Valley, Oregon, a replacement, listed MIA April 16, later listed KIA; 2nd Lt. Burton K. (or S.) Wheeler, Co I, address unknown, listed LWA April 16, did not return.

**Climax in OHRDRUT:** Albert Schneider was the Mayor of Ohrdrut, a small town 17 km from GOTHA. A concentration camp is situated on the top of the hill nearby, in which three thousand Russians, Poles, Jews and others were systematically beaten to death, starved and shot. The day before the arrival of the American troops 33 sick inmates were shot by SS Men. Their bodies were still on the grounds of the camp when the Germans left. Among the murdered was an American flyer.

Schneider joined the Nazi Party in 1933 and became a troop leader (Ober Truppfuhrer) in the SA. He was made mayor of Ohrdrup six years ago. The mayor had a good reputation for honesty and was considered a fair administrator. Though harsh toward local people, Schneider was never guilty of actual cruelties, according to statements of his fellow citizens. Town people describe him as a conscientious man. Nevertheless because of his Nazi background MG intended to remove him from office as soon as a suitable non-party member could be found.

When the Americans occupied Ohrdrup the mayor as well as the citizenry denied knowledge of the autrocities committed in the camp. The MG officer decided to take Schneider to the camp to show him the bodies of the murdered inmates. The mayor was profoundly moved by the sight. He said, "I did not believe that Germans are able to commit murder in a brutal manner. There were rumors in town but we did not believe it." The MG Officer ordered him to take representatives of the population to the camp the next day. Considering it an excellent idea Schneider promised to prepare a list of prominent members of the community. The mayor and the representatives were supposed to appear at the MG office at 0800 hrs next morning. When the mayor failed to appear at the fixed hour, the MG officer sent a soldier to his home. (The mayor and his wife lived at the house of Mr. and Mrs. Arthur Singer, his brother-in-law and sister). On the back porch on the second floor the sergeant found the mayor and his wife, their wrists slashed, held upright by cords around their necks. They had committed suicide the night before. In town, people believe that the mayor felt responsible for the atrocities committed in the camp area. They assume this to be the only reason for the suicide. A hand-written note was left by the mayor reading: "Forgive us for this in your house, but it cannot be helped." (See: VIII Corps)

* * *

## UNUSUAL RESCUE

*In the fighting near the Elbe while attached to the 83rd Div., a platoon of Co I led by 1st Lt Harold E. Ganzel of Menasha, Wisc., was captured at dawn April 16th while holding an outpost in a large barn. Their position was assaulted by superior numbers of Germans using Panzerfausts, hand grenades and a flame thrower which set the barn's hay on fire. The platoon was forced to surrender.*

*The Germans were sighted by 2nd Lt Kleber Trigg, Jr., Bastrop, Texas, from Cannon Company's observation post 500 yards back. Trigg called for battery fire and ten direct hits were scored on the barn. Men were seen to run out, hands overhead, and it was thought the Krauts wanted to surrender. A German civilian was sent to the barn under a white flag to instruct the enemy to come in or be blasted by more shell fire.*

*The civilian returned with the information that the men with upraised hands were American prisoners, who were being forced to stand there to prevent further firing by Cannon Company.*

*Lt Trigg then observed the Germans starting to march the Americans across a field to the rear. Thinking quickly, he ordered his gunners to lay fire just over their heads. Then, lowering the range step by step, the shells dropped in closer and closer to the Germans and their prisoners. The Germans were driven back to the barn. An agreement was then made and the Co I men were freed. —from 320th History.*

\* \* \*

### 320TH LAST TO ATTACK

*On April 15 the Division Command Post moved to Burgstall and, on the 16th, a total of 1,759 prisoners were taken for the day, a new record for a 24-hour haul. On the 15th at 1300 Combat Team 320th, on orders from the 83rd Division, made the last coordinated attack, by a unit of the 35th, to cross the Saale River. —from 35th Division History.*

Gross Rosenburg, Germany
April 17, 1945

Time: 2158:

I am writing in S-1, S-4, CP room, Sgt Koziel, Sgt Harding[6] and T/5 Gwizdala present. We are using candle light. We have just been bombed by German planes.

---

6 Sgt. Harding was a part of Regtl Hq personnel; no other information.

Reports so far indicate one killed, Frizone[7] of I & R. Holloway[8] of I & R wounded and also Sgt Barnes[9] of CP plat. The bombers may have been aiming at the pontoon bridge near by across the Saale River. We just crossed it at noon to move here from Tornitz.

Holloway has not been found yet so we don't know his status.

This is the town in which K Co, Commanded by Capt Kurtz, had such a battle with the Krauts in the early morning of the 15th. The Germans counter attacked our bridge-head in considerable force. They reached the bridge site, killing three engineers and wounding others.

Co I, situated nearby, drove them from the bridge and they went into the town where K Co was located. There was close in fighting as dawn came with the Germans firing bazooka shells (or Panzerfausts) into the buildings. When day light came the K Co men drove them from the town after killing more than 20, capturing about 40 and wounding others who were also captured.

Co G was not so fortunate. It had advanced toward Panztez and was cut off. One platoon, except two men, was lost along with one HMG Section and an arty FO. Some of them may have been captured. At dawn and on up into the morning every line Co, except L, was engaged. The enemy was beaten back by noon and the bridge-head was saved. Fortunately the enemy had no artillery, but it was one of the hardest small arms battles for the Regiment for some time.

Capt Bonham has just come in and reports that Holloway has been found. He suffered a broken arm and a flesh wound. The vehicle in which he and Frizone were riding is burning. It cannot be reached yet because the 50 caliber ammunition is exploding. The body [Frizone] will be picked up when the fire subsides. Three civilians were killed by the same bomb. No report of casualties from other bombs yet. Sgt Seilling just came in to ask Maj Hughes for trucks to haul back 80 PWs taken today. He has gained information

7  Domenic Frisone, I & R Platoon, an early replacement, N. Y., N. Y., KIA April 17.

8  John Holloway, I & R Platoon, address unknown, an original who had been with the 320th all the way, wounded, did not return. Sgt William Dickson, another I & R original, was hospitalized during the fighting in the Ruhr Pocket, later returned.

9  Sgt. Barnes was with us all the way. No other information.

from them that they took 31 American prisoners in the fighting with our regiment on the 14th and 15th. The enemy probably has them across the Elbe by now, so they are lost to us until further advances are made.

* * *

All three men hit tonight were old originals with the Regiment.

* * *

Another of our old original officers went home today on the rotation plan, Capt Tobin[10] of the 2nd Bn Hqs. While I was in the hospital Lt Thomas and Lt Unland[11] were fortunate enough to experience the joy of a visit to the States under the rotation system.

On the day I rejoined the regiment, the first group to go to the States returned for duty. Sgt Koch and myself and the others rode from Div Rear back up to the Regiment together. I had hoped when I bade them good-bye in the mud and rain of Alsace-Lorraine last December that I would not see them back in the war. But now they are back sweating out the closing days of the conflict like the rest of us.

Just got Milt to present me with one of his pictures. It is a striking likeness. He has that dour, harried look which he wears after long hours of work, or during unpleasant situations like when he has to rise early on cold and dismal mornings or when there isn't much bodily comfort to be had. Some of us have grown mighty close during these long months of combat and during the months of training which preceded our active entry into the war.

* * *

Prize remark in the cellar during the bombing made by Lt Clark, "Capt Scherer is mad because the others didn't stand at attention and let the regular army go first."

New addition to the headquarters group while I was away, Lt Preston,[12] a very amiable and likeable young fellow. He is Hqs Co executive officer. Lt Kelly is attached, unas-

---

10 Capt. Robert B. Tobin, 2nd Bn Hq, Pistol Point, Texas, an original, listed Tdy April 17, a rehabilitation furlough to the States, did not return.

11 2nd Lt. James M. Unland, Pekin, Ill., first with Co A, then Co B during Alsace-Lorraine Campaign, a replacement, rehabilitation furlough to the States; did not return.

12 1st Lt. Roy W. Preston, originally Co H, now Regtl Hq, Seneca, Mo., an original.

signed, and taking care of courts martial investigations, which relieves me of that burden, "Thank God!"

There are some slave laborers at this place, French, Russian and Polish. A French laborer had married a Russian girl here and they have a baby. They got ready to leave after we arrived. They piled their few belongings on a cart, put the baby on top, and were fixing to set out for France pulling the vehicle. They were afraid to take one of the horses left by their former master. Some GIs caught one of the horses, hitched it to the cart, set the woman up on top and placed the reins in her hands. They departed tearful but happy. Sometime later they returned the horse after stopping at another house in the town. Perhaps they intend to wait for transportation by some other method.

There are hundreds and thousands of those slave laborers. I keep thinking of the sign, in eight languages including English, posted in the courtyard. Many times when I see these people in servitude I think, "There, but for the Grace of God and the strength and unity of the Russian, British, and American armies and others, goes one of my relatives or friends."

Now 0040, the 18th. And so to bed with many thoughts, and many acts of heroism unrecorded.

Capt Kurtz's Co K freed 23 of our men in the battle here, that had been taken [prisoners] from other companies.

In a town nearby the burgomeister and his wife had, upon the approach of the Americans, locked themselves in their house and slashed their wrists. Our troops broke into the house, then called for a doctor. Capt Shumate and Capt _____ went to the place. The two Germans had to be forcibly evacuated to the hospital for treatment. Seems a pity to waste time on such people.

There are two heavy, leather horse whips hanging with the coats and hats in one of the closets of this house. The slave laborers said they were often used to beat them when they displeased their masters. Once the Russians refused to work because they had been given no food. The mayor summoned the police, rounded up the Russians and publicly administered the whippings himself.

I think the truth of the matter is that many of those [Germans] with respect for the decencies of mankind, met

\* \* \*

one of three fates, the concentration camp, death, or exile, and all those remaining acquiesced or supported the inhuman policies of the Nazis.

\* \* \*

## SGT. WASSON DIDN'T MISS THE FURLOUGH

Sgt. James Wasson of Miami, Oklahoma (another address listed as Dennis, Kansas), a forward observer for H Company's 81mm mortar platoon, and 2nd Lt Winfred Young of Joplin, Missouri, also Co H, were attached to a rifle company in an attack in the Elbe River area. Although unknown to them, less than a week's fighting remained for the 320th and the war itself would end in three weeks. They did know the 320th was attached to the 83rd Division which had the only Allied bridgehead over the Elbe River only about 40 miles from Berlin, a point nearer the German capital than any Allied force, and Sgt Wasson was on his last day of combat duty, having been notified the previous day that he had been selected for a 30-day rotation furlough to the States.

Moving up with the rifle company Sgt Wasson and Lt Young took a short cut, got temporarily lost, were surprised by three Germans manning a machine gun nest, and captured. Two of the enemy soldiers started with them to the German PW collecting point. On the way they passed through a forest single file, one German leading and the other in the rear. Anticipating that their captors could not understand English, the lieutenant and the sergeant discussed the possibility of escape. Said Wasson, "I'm just not going to miss that furlough so let's jump them."

At a propitious moment Sgt Wasson swung the SCR 300 radio he was still carrying while Young used his steel helmet. They bashed their captors in the head knocking them senseless and made their escape.

Next day before leaving for the States while relating the incident to Lt Travis E. Hendren of Cleveland, N. C., Sgt Wasson said, "The way I figure, it will take a lot more than two Krauts to make me miss this hard earned furlough."

\* \* \*

Gr Rosenburg, Germany
April 18, 1945

Attached is a proclamation posted by the mayor of the town of Breitenhagen after its occupation by Col Alexander's

Third Bn, but before he [the mayor] was interviewed and instructed by Capt McCormic, our mil gov officer. Could it be that some feel a guilty conscience? Perhaps some did not know of the atrocities as reported by the mayor in the intelligence report here attached, but certainly all knew of the work of the slaves and of their miserable conditions and the punishment inflicted on them.

## PROCLAMATION

To the population of Breitenhagen:

I hereby decree that everyone who is still in possession of a weapon surrender same immediately at the town hall.

1. Starting immediately every citizen has to obey and to follow all orders of the American military authorities.

2. You must execute all orders which I receive and pass on to the population.

3. Citizens who do not obey these orders will be punished according to American law.

4. Every citizen has to cooperate with the American troops of occupation.

5. Men of the Volkssturm are ordered to surrender all weapons of all kinds in their possession including Panzerfausts to the town hall. Those who do not comply with these orders will be considered hostile and will be punished according to American law.

6. All applications and requests will be accepted in the town hall as heretofore.

7. I request the population to cooperate with me to wipe out the system of a guilty government.

Breitenhagen, April 16th 1945
The Mayor
in behalf of; signed Schnitzendoebel

This proclamation posted in town of Breitenhagen after occupation by Lt Col Alexander's 3rd Bn on April 17th 1945.

* * *

Incident of last night. I had gone out back to have a better view of the ack-ack and MG fire on the German bombers. After the first two sticks of bombs had fallen scattering some debris about, I had gone into a cellar with some enlisted men. One GI, pretty well inebriated was climbing up the stairs, proclaiming, "They couldn't hit shit! They couldn't hit shit!" When another stick of bombs began exploding, he turned and dived clear to the bottom of the stairway, knocking to the straw-covered floor another man and myself. I thought he showed a decided lack of faith in his assertions, or perhaps he was not including himself in the class with the article he was naming.

We have again captured large stores of liquors, cognac, rum, wine, etc. There is an eggnog mix, already bottled, which is really delicious. There have been a lot of people who had all they wanted to drink. There was perhaps $5,000,000 worth in one underground warehouse.

Yesterday the civilians were looting a warehouse filled with shoes, stockings, thread and such articles. Lt Silverman discovered what was going on. He herded them out and placed a guard over the storehouse of goods. I hesitate to make an estimation but there was a vast amount of the goods.

The civilians had also begun to loot the liquor caches but that was soon stopped and this valuable war commodity taken into custody.

I am, even yet, sometimes appalled at the terrible waste and destruction of war, aside from the still worse killing and maiming.

* * *

It is now late at night. I have written until a late hour, and no one is up except Lt Kelly and myself and the sentries.

We were bombed again tonight. Some of the missiles fell very near sending us to the cellars. There are no reports of casualties in our immediate area this time.

Seems we are all going into the bridge head area tomorrow unless plans change. Two Bns are already across the river over [President Harry S.] Truman Bridge. It has grown customary, so everyone says, for the 320th to be in the hottest spots.

I regretted very deeply, as did all those about me, to hear tonight of the death in action of correspondent Ernie Pyle. Every doughboy felt that the famed writer was his true friend. [He more accurately described the conditions of war than any other writer.]

Capt Brochu has come to regiment as captain of the MP detachment, and Capt Cleves[13] has gone on detached service to train replacements somewhere in a repo depot.

Funniest incident of the day; Brochu describing how he is going to run his "88 Club" when he gets home.

[A casualty[14] not mentioned in the Journal.]

Walternienburg, Germany
April 19, 1945

We are now across the Elbe River in the bridgehead established by the 83rd Div. We are attached to the 83rd, have been since moving down to this area.

This is now the hot spot of the front, this being the only bridgehead over the Elbe River.

I think everyone is a bit uneasy, especially Capt Scherer. Capt Ginsberg just came in and asked if we all had swimming trunks. Capt Scherer immediately thought the bridge was out.

The Elbe here is almost as big as the Rhine where we crossed at Weisel. The Germans bombed us again tonight. If they could hit our bridge with a bomb, artillery or a floating mine, it would put us in a precarious position.

*   *   *

Clark is waiting to take an overlay to Div Hqs. He has imbibed freely of egg-nog mix and cognac as Milt is now doing; Capt Scherer is feeling pretty good too; so the comedy goes on, as we wait for Clark to go on his mission, sweat out the artillery and the return of the German planes. When a shell comes in, someone says, "Pass me the armor plate."

---

13 Capt. Mark B. Cleaves, originally Sv Co. then CO of Co K, address unknown, a replacement, did not return.

14 2nd Lt. Robert L. Williams, Co K, address unknown, a replacement, evacuated as sick April 18, did not return.

## FROM CAPT. ORVAL FAUBUS

Somewhere in Germany,
April 16, 1945

Dear Home Folks,

I have now been back with my regiment for some days and we are far into Germany. I signed myself out of the hospital and returned directly to my unit by the hitch-hike method. Another officer from the same regiment left the hospital two weeks before I did going through the regular channels and has not yet returned. The way things are going I might have "made" the war by going through the replacement depot system. But here I am with the sound of artillery in my ears as I write, and about as close to Berlin as any American unit. In fact we were close enough last night to see bombing of the German capital by American planes but still too far away to hear the sound.

I joined my unit in the Battle of the Ruhr when I returned. After the resistance there weakened we were rushed mile after mile across Germany to our present positions. Without even waiting for us to catch up on our sleep we were again committed. Today we made another river crossing and there is another ahead of us tomorrow. Or I should say yesterday we made a crossing and there is another ahead of us today, for it was on the 15th and it is now the early dark hours of the 16th. * * * *

I have seen much in the past few days. Everywhere we have gone we have found the slave laborers by the hundreds and the thousands. I never dreamed there were so many in Germany. I visited one of the camps which we have liberated and looked at it closely. There were rough frame buildings erected in the form of a hollow square around a pool of dirty water, in the style of the early day American stockades. The furnishings were meagre in the extreme. The camp was surrounded by a fence of heavy, cruel-looking barbed wire on big high posts. Posted on the fence were signs in two languages, "Anyone approaching this fence will be shot immediately." And needless to say the German guards carried out the threat without the slightest hesitation.

Of course the place stank because there were no facilities for sanitation. Fourteen people lived in each room which we would consider small for five or six persons. The place held from 300 to 600, depending on how many slaves the German masters needed in that area, and was about 100 yards long and 50 yards wide.

There was only one entrance and exit from the camp. The officers with me [Silverman, Glatzer and Brochu] could speak some German, Czech and Russian, so they talked to the inmates. * * * * The slaves were taken out in whatever numbers needed by the Germans and for whatever purpose their masters desired. * * * * The Germans furnished no medical aid, for they didn't care if the inmates died or not. Hitler would conquer more territory and get more slaves if the present captives did not survive.

* * * * The great majority of the slaves are Russians, Poles and French. The first are forced to wear the emblem "OST," the Poles the letter "P", and the French the letter "F". There are many other nationalities - Dutch, Belgium, Danish, Norwegian, Hungarian, Czech, Slovak, Italian, etc. All are agreed on one thing - the Germans are all alike and no good.

The next day I visited a group of about 1,000 PW's freed by our forces, 600 Americans and 400 British. Their condition was much worse physically than that of the slaves. The Americans had been prisoners since the Battle of the Bulge. The British had been taken at different times, some at Dunkirk. All the British agreed wholeheartedly that they would long ago have died had it not been for the Red Cross parcels they received. The Americans had received only two packages each since their capture and seemed to be in worse condition than the British. The Nazis did everything possible to cause bad feeling between the two groups. All the captives were dirty, filthy and covered with lice. Some could not rise from where they lay and had to be evacuated to the hospital. I saw officers and men, who have known long months of the hell and misery of combat, turn away in tears when they saw the pitiful condition of those emaciated prisoners-of-war.

* * * *

This letter is being finished on the morning of April 19, now a little past midnight. I guess you folks at home think the war is just about over. True, it is reaching its closing stages, but that is small comfort to those who are killed or maimed in the final battles. As I have said before the last battles can be just as fierce and hellish as the first. To the combat soldiers, war is still war. In a recent 48-hour period my regiment made three moves totaling 274.7 miles and established a bridgehead over a river. During the next 24 hours the bridgehead was held against strong counterattacks in which there was much close-in fighting.

We have been bombed two nights in succession. Our anti-aircraft couldn't seem to hit the enemy bombers and they laid their deadly loads among us. The bombing interrupted the writing of this letter tonight.

All men of the fighting fronts have been saddened by the news of two recent deaths. The first, that of our great commander-in-chief, President Roosevelt, and the second—the news came tonight—that of Ernie Pyle, the foot-slogging doughboy's friend, killed in action in the Pacific. I never had the pleasure of meeting the famed correspondent but was very near him several times, and I saw a number of the things about which he wrote.

If you see any pictures of "Truman Bridge" you can now know that a part of President Truman's old outfit, the 35th Infantry (Santa Fe) Division has crossed the Elbe River on it.

When I returned to the regiment my three-weeks collection of mail had just been sent out to me in the hospital. It has not returned. I don't know when I will get it and I was very disappointed.

Spring is in its fullness here now. The fruit trees and the wild flowers are in full bloom. The grass on the flat German fields is a bright, velvety green. The ground is dry and firm, good to plow, and also good for tanks and trucks. The shells make dust clouds for the first time since last summer. The streams smell of fish, and I think of a line and pole and the banks of White River. Sometimes when the smell of the cordite is not too strong I can catch the fragrance of the blossoms, and the balmy breeze carries the aroma of the new season.

It would be such a good time for the war to end; such a good time to bring peace to the world and joy to our hearts and to yours. But it seems the hard-headed, egotistical Krauts will not surrender, will not give up the ill-gotten gains nor free from bondage their slaves, until we occupy every foot of their country. That we will do, and when it is finished, I hope that no one asks for mercy for the Nazi or German war criminals.

My best wishes,

Capt. Orval E. Faubus
Hqs. 320th Inf.

\* \* \*

Walternienburg, Germany
April 20, 1945

Still in the Elbe bridgehead sweating out the durability of the pontoon bridge behind us.

Contrary to our expectations the bombers did not return tonight. There has been very little artillery on the battalions and still less on the Regtl CP area. So far this has not been a very tough experience on this side of the Elbe.

Word has come that unless plans change, we will be relieved and go to rejoin the Division tomorrow.

\* \* \*

It is likely that the great Russian drive now in progress has saved us from fighting here. According to the G-2 intelligence the Germans have enough forces available and in reach to eliminate our bridgehead if they should choose to commit them.

\* \* \*

## COMMENDATION FROM EISENHOWER

### HEADQUARTERS 35TH INFANTRY DIVISION
### APO 35, U. S. Army
### DAILY INFORMATION SHEET
### NUMBER 59

#### OFFICIAL

1. ORDER OF THE DAY. The following Order of the Day issued by the Supreme Commander will be brought to the attention of all troops of this command:

To Every Member of the AEF.

The Battle of the Ruhr has ended with complete success. Following hard upon the final destruction of the German forces west of the Rhine, the Twenty First Army Group thrust powerfully across that river with the U. S. Ninth Army under its command.

Simultaneously, rapid drives across the Rhine and from the Remagen bridgehead by Twelfth and Sixth Army Groups provided the southern arm of a great double envelopment which completely encircled the entire German Army Group "B" and two Corps of Army Group "H," whose mobility was rendered almost zero by our magnificent and tireless air forces. Thereafter, in the pocket thus created the Twelfth Army Group eliminated twenty-one enemy divisions, including three Panzer, one Panzer Grenadier and three Parachute divisions. Over three hundred seventeen thousand prisoners of war were captured including twenty-four Generals and one Admiral. Many tanks and more than seven hundred fifty guns were destroyed or taken. Booty is immense and still being counted. The enemy's total losses in killed and wounded will never be accurately known.

The rapidity and determination with which this brilliant action was executed tore asunder the divisions of Field Marshal Model, and enabled all army groups without pause to continue their drive eastward into the heart of Germany.

This victory of allied arms is a fitting prelude to the final battles to crush the ragged remnants of Hitler's armies of the west, now tottering on the threshold of defeat.

(Signed) DWIGHT D. EISENHOWER, 20 April 1945

\* \* \*

## COMMENDATION FROM MARSHALL

### HEADQUARTERS 35TH INFANTRY DIVISION

### APO 35, U. S. ARMY

DAILY INFORMATION SHEET    21 April 1945

### NUMBER 55

#### OFFICIAL

1. COMMENDATION. The following congratulatory message from the Commanding General, Ninth United States Army, 12 April 1945, is published for the information of all troops:

1. The following Message has been received from the Chief of Staff, United States Army:

MY CONGRATULATIONS AND ADMIRATION TO YOU, YOUR CORPS AND DIVISION COMMANDERS AND TO ALL YOUR MEN FOR THE MAGNIFICENT JOB DONE IN THE ADVANCE TO THE RHINE AND THE CROSSING INTO THE RUHR.

Signed: MARSHALL
Chief of Staff

2. It gives me great pleasure to pass to you and the personnel of your command this congratulatory message from General Marshall.

I wish to add my own congratulations and commendations to you, your officers and men for superb manner in which you have accomplished these great tasks. The advance to the Rhine and the crossing into the Ruhr will undoubtedly rank high in the annals of history as an outstanding military achievement.

I desire that this communication be read to all troops as early as practicable.

W. S. SIMPSON
Lieutenant General, U. S. Army
Commanding

## HITLER'S FROGMEN

*During the Regiment's attachment to the 83rd Division the unit was in the Elbe River bridgehead from April 19 to 21 inclusive. While there we captured two German frogmen from whom came the 320th's strangest and most unbelievable story of the war.*

*The span on which we had crossed the wide, swift river was named the President Truman Bridge. It was the only link with friendly forces for the troops across the stream. If the bridge were destroyed German forces could then attack and kill or capture the American troops on the east bank and eliminate the bridgehead. The bridge was a pontoon span - pontoons being hollow boat-like structures filled with air. They are lashed together from bank to bank and a roadway laid on top. Anything which breaks the ties, permitting the pontoons to float away, or which punctures the pontoons*

*allowing them to sink, will destroy such a crossing. There-*
*fore wrecking of the bridge was easy if it could be hit.*

*The Germans continually tried to destroy the bridge by*
*shelling with artillery, bombing from planes, and by float-*
*ing mines down the stream from above to explode on con-*
*tact with the structure.*

*To protect the bridge from the floating mines, the en-*
*gineers constructed a boom of logs across the stream above*
*the bridge. However, the current was so swift the boom could*
*not be continuous and gaps had to be left in the chain of*
*logs. Consequently, a few of the floating charges of explosive*
*would slip through the spaces in the boom. Likewise when*
*a charge exploded upon contact with the logs, blowing holes*
*in the barricade, mines could slip through before repairs*
*could be made.*

*To still further guard the bridge from the floating mines,*
*GIs armed with rifles and carbines were posted a few feet*
*apart on the span, lying on the upper edge with weapons*
*cocked, their eyes constantly on the swirling blue-green wat-*
*er. When a floating mine was noted the soldiers fired into*
*the approaching object to cause it to explode before touch-*
*ing the bridge. Some floating explosives which got by the*
*log boom, were detonated by small arms fire and one GI was*
*knocked unconscious by the concussion when the mine got*
*too close before exploding.*

*All efforts to knock out the bridge failed, and evidently*
*Hitler tried a last desperate measure.*

*The two captured frogmen were apprehended in the*
*bridgehead in the vicinity of the pontoon span after they had*
*crawled from the stream. One was taken by personnel of the*
*60th Engineers, and the other by two C Company soldiers,*
*Pfc Oswald D'Amadio of Belleville, N. J., and Pfc Erwin J.*
*Danielack of Milwaukee, Wisc. The Company C riflemen saw*
*a figure emerge from the water and flit from tree to tree.*
*They opened fire and the frogman surrendered.*

*The Nazis wore tight-fitting rubber suits and helmets*
*with wool camouflage hoods, and looked a lot like Buck Rog-*
*ers cartoon strip characters. Their faces were blackened and*
*both were equipped with pistols, knives and waterproof*
*watches. D'Amadio and Danielack said they thought their*
*captive was Batman come to life or a man from Mars.*

*The two strange looking figures were escorted to 320th Headquarters where they were questioned by our IPW team. Their appearance was no more strange than the story they told.*

*The two frogmen said they were members of a seven-man team of Naval Swimmers, and had just come from a personal audience with Hitler in Berlin. The order for their mission, they stated, was given directly by the Fuhrer himself. They were instructed, they said, to proceed to the Elbe River above the President Truman Bridge, and there, properly equipped with underwater suits and gear, and carrying large charges of explosives, the frogmen were to enter the stream and be carried by the current to the bridge which they would then destroy.*

*The frogmen had proceeded according to orders, but after entering the stream they found the water swift and cold, and they could not hang on to their heavy loads of explosive. After losing the charges and becoming unable to accomplish their mission, they climbed from the stream and were captured. They disclaimed any knowledge of the whereabouts of the other members of Hitler's team of Naval Swimmers.*

*A strange story indeed. But it is no more strange than many of the now documented occurrences in the underground bunker in Berlin which was Hitler's refuge and command post during his last days.*

*For the German commanders and for Hitler the conflict was long since a lost cause. The Third Reich, its armies shattered and supplies depleted, was crumbling to complete ruin. Many German cities were already demolished and now German territory was being overrun daily from both east and west by overwhelming military force. German people by the millions were now being subjected to the same indignities and hardships of conquest which the once invincible Nazi conquerors had previously carried to the peoples of other nations.*

*Yet, in the face of all these dire realities, the Fuhrer continued to give unrealistic orders to commanders of mythical armies for grand offensives impossible of accomplishment. His subordinates, all of whom must have recognized the actions as a grand pretense, still continued to pay complete deference and homage to this strange madman by accepting the orders and moving to carry them out. Thus was continued* to the very last the blood-letting and fiery destruction of a war, which, in its final stages, had become for Hitler and his close henchmen the most fantastic drama of make-believe in the history of the world.

There was that next to last strange act in the underground bunker - the wedding of Hitler to Miss Eva Braun, his mistress and companion for several years. It was as if the German leader, after a dishonorable public career of complete disregard for the most elementary rights of nations and peoples, and after a regime of bloody, illegitimate war for rapacious, illicit gains, had, at the last by the marriage, sought to clothe his private life with some semblance of personal honor and legitimacy.

Then finally, in a weird and dramatic finish to a career unparalled for scientific butchery, the man who had brought about the execution and burning of more human beings than any other in the history of mankind, now, by his final act and last directive brought about the extinction of two more lives - himself and his wife - and the burning of one more body - his own. The woman who had become Mrs. Adolph Hitler only for the purpose of death, was either killed or took her own life. Hitler died by his own hand, and a few followers, in accordance with his last order, placed his corpse on a funeral pyre.

I am inclined to accept as truth the story of the captured frogmen as told to our prisoner-of-war interrogation team, not alone for the reason that it parallels to a remarkable degree the fantastic directives and activities of the Nazi leader in his last days, although the similarity lends credence to the story, but for another reason as well.

During our ten consecutive months of almost unbroken combat with the enemy we had taken thousands of captives of the Nazi Army, and questioned hundreds and hundreds of them for military intelligence and other information. During all this time in all our experiences with the many prisoners-of-war, we had never discovered any tendency of the German soldiers to use their imagination for such tales. Either they lacked the capacity, or had not the inclination for the contrivance with words, necessary to match the frogmen's story.

Mahlpfrehl, Germany
April 23, 1945

We moved out of the bridgehead on 21st. We came north
across the wonderfully green flat plains which stretch away
from the west bank of the Elbe. There were flurries of rain
which left the country fresh and clean. The air was cool. The
apple trees, which were in glorious bloom in the south around
Magdeburg, are just putting forth pink buds in this region.
The nearby forests, evergreen mixed with beech with shining white bark and pale amber foliage, have soft, grassy
floors over which the deer bound soundlessly. Both today
and yesterday flurries of hail and snow have briefly but furiously assailed the advancing summer on the North German
plains.

Artillery thunders heavily over by the Elbe. German
stragglers are rounded up from the by-passed pockets in
town and forest.

Wonderful rumors about peace, about Army of Occupation, float about.

There is good news of the progress of the Russians and
our forces.

* * *

## AMERICANS MEET RUSSIANS FROM 320TH GROUND

The first formal link-up of the American Ninth Army
with the Russian forces occurred on Tuesday, May 1, 1945.
Major General Robert C. Macon, commander of the 83rd Infantry Division, with officers and men of his command, met
the Russians of the elite Sixth Guards Division under the
command of Colonel Alexis Ivanov in the small town of
Cobbelsdorf.

Thus the 320th Infantry had helped to take and hold the
ground, the Elbe River bridgehead, from which occurred the
long sought link-up with the Russians, heralding the complete
overrunning of Nazi Germany and the end of the war. —
Source, 83rd Thunderbolt of May 5, 1945.

* * *

From
## 83RD THUNDERBOLT
May 5, 1945
(83rd Division Newspaper)

## VETERAN 320TH
## INFANTRY OVER
## ELBE WITH 83rd

Veteran infantrymen of the 320th Regiment, 35th (Santa Fe) Division, President Truman's World War I outfit, contributed greatly to the success of the Thunderbolt Division's drive across the Elbe.

The Regiment, under the command of Col. B. A. Byrne of Bradenton, Fla., made two river crossings during the short time it was attached to the 83rd. 320th doughs first made an assault crossing of the Saale River and cleared its south bank for a distance of six miles to where it joins the Elbe. During the operation seven towns fell to them.

Following the fighting across the Saale, the Regiment crossed the Truman Bridge into the Elbe bridgehead to join Thunderbolt infantrymen fighting on the east side of the river. Lt Thomas M. Leirer of Bernie, Mo. was the first 320th soldier from the President's home state to cross the bridge named in his honor.

Being attached to another division was not a new experience for Byrne's doughboys. Since entering combat in Normandy, they have been assigned to four divisions outside their own. They have participated in most of the important campaigns and battles on the Western Front, including St. Lo, the Vire River, Mortain, the Moselle River, the drive across Alsace-Lorraine, the Saar River, the Battle of the Bulge at Bastogne, the Vosge Mountains, the Roer River, the push to the Rhine, the Battle of the Ruhr and this latest lightning thrust with the Thunderbolt.

An interesting sidelight on this present attachment was the capture of three Nazi demolition men garbed in underwater swim suits by doughs of Co A. [The 320th History says the men were from Co C.] The suicide swimmers were caught as they were trying to reach the Truman Bridge with their dynamite charges. Thus it fell to men from the President's own division to stop one of the attempts to destroy the bridge named after him.

FROM
83RD THUNDERBOLT
May 5, 1945
(83rd Division Newspaper)

---

## CONVOY GETS FOOD
## TO ALLIED PWs

A convoy of mercy consisting of ten trucks and a jeep, specially painted all white with huge red crosses and the words "Canti Internationale de la Croix Rouge" conspicuously lettered on each, went through Thunderbolt lines recently in the area held by the 3rd Bn of the 330th Infantry.

With the exception of Lt Joseph A. W. St Onge of Holyoke, Mass. and his driver, Pfc Larry Key of Neptune, Tenn., both from the 3rd Bn, 330th, [83rd Div] the rest of the men were white-clad Swiss. The trucks were loaded with more than 55 tons of medical supplies, food and clothing for Allied PWs held by the Germans.

After arriving at the take-off point, it was only a matter of minutes before the convoy was on its way across No Man's Land. The American officer led the way through a specially charted lane in a protective mine field.

"It felt funny to be passing all those civilians beyond our outposts," said Key, "and they looked as if they couldn't figure it out, either."

At a pre-arranged point near the town of Flatz, the American part of the mission was completed and St Onge and Key turned back toward 83rd lines as the trucks disappeared into a thick woods held by the Jerries.

"We felt pretty helpless out there all alone," smiled St Onge, "but we got back safely - - didn't even see a Kraut."

## *ENEMY BOOTY TAKEN AT THE ELBE*

*The 35th Division captured and destroyed immense stores of enemy equipment in the Elbe operation. The list was so long that it reads like an inventory of the Nazi defeat. A few of the major items included:*

| | | | |
|---|---|---|---|
| *Tanks, all types* | *29* | *RR locomotives* | *50* |
| *Half-tracks* | *9* | *Airplanes (fighter and* | |
| *Trucks (1/2 ton or more)* | *145* | *recon)* | *100* |
| *Ambulances* | *9* | *Barges* | *3* |

MGs, 20mm _____ 239
MGs, smaller caliber __ 1,675
Machine pistols _____ 171
Rifles _____ 9,476
Bazookas _____ 370
Mortars (50mm, 80mm,
   120mm) _____ 60
Arty. pieces _____ 167
SP guns _____ 16
Rocket guns _____ 20
Railroad guns _____ 2
V-2 bombs _____ 65
V-1 bombs _____ 126
TNT, tons _____ 101 1/4

### Ammunition:

Arty. (rounds) _____ 1,275
Bazooka (rounds) ____ 2,000
Small arms (rounds) 575,000
Grenades _____ 21,775
Mortar (rounds) _____ 1,500

Mines (all types, includ-
   ing glass) _____ 2,001,150
Machine gun (rounds) 10,000
Searchlights _____ 120
Range finders _____ 6
Electric generators _____ 56
Field radios _____ 80
Radio receivers and trans-
   mitters _____ 100
Ordnance warehouses, con-
   taining 20mm, 30mm,
   50mm guns, approxi-
   mately _____ 600
Stocks of spare parts,
   clips, drums _____ 2
Oil, all grades
   (gals) _____ 100,000
Canned goods (carloads) __ 8
Civilian clothing
   (carloads) _____ 2
Airplane motors _____ 20

The Elbe operation, (mostly by the 320th) netted 5,976 prisoners. In the Hanover area, where all the Division had moved by April 27, 3,000 more were taken. After the first week in May, the 35th Division's total of prisoners taken during the war, ran well over 31,000. —From 35th Division History.

### UNUSUAL CAPTIVES AND DISCOVERIES

In one day, 24 April, Santa Fe troops captured SS Major General Heinz Jost and the Clauswitz Task Force Command-er, Lt. Gen. Unrein. Jost, listed in Shaef's "Who's Who in Nazi Germany," head of the Gestapo in foreign countries, was captured by 2nd Lt. Darrel Droslem and S/Sgt. A. Roh-leder of Counter-Intelligence Corps, who found him in a house at Magdeburg. Unrein, in civilian clothes and riding a bicycle, was captured by a 35th Reconnaissance Troop patrol under Cpl. Mike Waseline.

A party of seven MP's headed by Major Hal Briggs took an entire Hungarian airfield near the Elbe. The garrison was carrying on with all the routine of an American army camp *and included families of the Hungarian officers and a detachment of "WACS."*

\* \* \* \*

*The Anti-Tank Company of the 137th discovered three hundred railroad cars filled with V-1 and V-2 bombs, ammunition, arms and medical supplies.*

\* \* \* \*

*In the Grasleben Salt Mine, Goebel's "morgue" was unearthed 1600 feet underground by 35th intelligence officers, Capt. John S. Foster and Capt. Barnaby Keeney. The files contained information on all Nazi officials together with their photos. Also cached in the mine were the vital financial, realty and historical records of Germany's biggest cities as well as looted rare books and museum treasures. Found buried in four feet of salt were record transcriptions of Hitler's speeches. —From 35th Division History.*

At the 100th Evac Hospital
May 3, 1945

Entered hospital on April 25 from Weferlingen, location of Div Rear. Underwent an operation for appendicitis that day. Have now sufficiently recovered to be placed on list for evacuation to Gen Hospital. Probably won't go today. There is a wind and cold rain is peppering on the tents from slate gray clouds. My Doctor is Capt Grant, N. Y.

Very efficient nurse.

[Met Pvt Marion Hester, 65 Sig Co, from Newport, Ark.]

May 8, 1945
195th Gen Hospital
Near Rheims, France

The announcement has come over the radio that a general surrender has been arranged and the war will soon end. Resting last night on a nice soft bed with white sheets, the first time in my two weeks illness, I fell asleep with shots, explosions and the shouts of the celebrating French ringing in my ears.

The four days spent at the "stop over" station run by the 50th Field Hospital were miserable indeed. Yesterday I was flown in a C-47 from a point just west of Magdeburg in Germany to this hospital. There were 24 litter cases to a plane plus some walking patients. The flight was 2 hrs 20 minutes.

Now on my soft bed in the balmy spring air of France, much warmer here than Germany, and a new day beginning filled with glorious sunshine. The war is near its end. The foliage of the green trees casts dark, flickering shadows on the grassy lawn. The pretty nurses, neat and shining in their pin-stripe uniforms (first I've seen), are bustling about their duties of the hospital.

Seems like it might be the dawn of a new era.

I know this won't mean much at present to the men fighting the Japs. When one is engaged in a life-and-death struggle—and so every battle is to the men who fight it— nothing else matters much. But it will mean a lot to them as soon as our might can be shifted to the Pacific Theater.

## LAST HOSPITALIZATION

*On April 24 I was sent to Div Rear Hqs to participate in a general courts martial. On the morning of the 25th I was to sit as a member of the court with other officers on a capital offense case. A Negro GI was to be tried on a charge of rape of a German girl. I had developed a case of appendicitis, which I reported to the president of the court. Another officer of the court, a veterinarian with some medical experience, examined me and confirmed my illness. The President of the court released me, because if my condition worsened, forcing me to leave during the course of the hearing, a mistrial might result.*

*Leaving the court, I reported to Lt Sperl and Capt Armstrong, our 320th personnel with Div rear, returned to my quarters and lay down. My fever continued to rise and before long things were hazy and I was unsteady on my feet. An ambulance was summoned and the GI medics loaded me inside. We bounced, it seemed for hours, over the pot-holed German roads, finally reaching a field hospital (100 Evacuation).*

*Minutes after arriving I had been examined, divested of my clothing and placed in the operating room. I barely had time to glance at the physician and the nurse and exclaim, "Only one angel of mercy?" before I was put out by the ether.*

*I woke up the next day on a folding cot with only GI blankets, my abdomen very painful, and feeling somewhat nauseated from the anesthetic. All around me were wounded.*

*The hospital was a huge tent set up with stakes on the German plain, with the cots setting on the grassy, cold ground. There were no compartments. All the sick and wounded were on rows of cots in one huge room. There were no sheets and no pillows. GI blankets, folded or otherwise, served all needs. The folding, canvas cots sometimes set unevenly on the ground. Toilet facilities were provided by an old-fashioned one-holer set outside. It seemed to be a quarter of a mile away as I was forced to walk to it on the second day after my operation.*

*I soon became aware of other patients, some in serious condition. Beside me on the right was a strong young soldier who had been wounded by shell fragments. The doctors had cut him three quarters in two, in order to remove the shrapnel from his innards and the walls which housed them. Fortunately no fragments had entered his lungs. During the two or three days he was still "out" - unconscious under the influence of drugs - his lurid, frontline language would turn the air blue. Neither the nurses or the patients showed any sign of heed. Later when he was conscious and we were all happy that he was recovering, we jokingly told him of his unconscious expressions. He blushed like a bashful country boy, which he evidently was, and was terribly embarrassed.*

*At my feet two rows away over by the flapping tent wall lay a soldier who had been shot through the head with a bullet. His head was encased in a bloody bandage which was not changed during the two or three days he was kept under sedation. At intervals he begged for "somebody" to help him. "Won't somebody help me?" he pleaded over and over again, "won't somebody help me!" Ropes had been tied aroung him and around the cot, loosely binding him to his crude bed. In his struggles and pleading he was often on the point of tumbling from the cot in spite of the bonds. At such times the wounded near him would reach out from their beds as best they could and keep him from falling to the cold ground. Later medical personnel would come, push him down, adjust his covering and tighten the ropes. At other times he was pleading, "I've gotta shit, I tell you, I've gotta shit."*

*The extent of his brain damage could not be determined, we were told, and it would not be known until the sedation wore off, whether or not he would ever again be lucid. Near the end of the three-day sedation period he had given up on "somebody" and pleaded for his "Mommy." "Mommy, please won't you help me? Please, Mommy, won't you help me?" he called over and over. As I listened with worried heart, I had concluded from his expressions and dialect that he was a country boy from the South.*

*Finally the sedation was stopped and we waited breathlessly as the hours passed. Then he awoke. After a time he looked around, and then spoke, as calmly and sanely as anyone in the big room. Man! What a relief to us who had listened to his unconscious pleadings through the long hours of the days and nights. He was a country boy from Georgia. He would recover.*

*To my back and to the far right by the front wall of the tent was apparently the most seriously wounded man. A nurse worked with him for some time one night, saving his life by running her finger down his throat to help remove the phlegm from which he was smothering. However, the "save" was only temporary. The next night we heard him die there, apparently at the time unattended. Wakeful in the early hours I observed the medical personnel, hurriedly and as quietly as possible, remove his body as the dawn was breaking over the huge tent on the German plains.*

*While I was there it rained often, not the slow, steady patter, the clinging mist or the wind-blown storms of the past winter, but frequent gusts of spring showers, the large drops assailing the canvas roof and walls with sudden drumming like the sound of horses galloping across the flatlands. The rain squalls alternated with brief periods of sunshine. The sunlight had little warmth, and could not remove the chill from the western wind blowing through the loose tent flaps at the front and underneath the sidewalls.*

*As is often found, most of the hospital personnel were fine, but some were not. Each morning one GI entered the tent, made a pretence of helping one patient near the back entrance, and spent his entire time there gabbing and complaining. Apparently he was never reprimanded or ordered to do more. Most of us thought he needed some combat duty, or a courts martial for dereliction of duty.*

*At one time a nurse, who always had an imperious manner, made me literally furious by ordering me to eat some food left on my tray. However, I returned no words and almost gagged as I poked some of it down my throat. Of course she did not know that for days before entering the hospital, I had been nauseated by the sight of GI food.*

*During my last days of combat, almost since my return to the 320th from the hospital at Liege, there was only one item of GI food that I could eat consistently. It was fruit cocktail - chopped mixed fruits from the C-ration cans. Upon our move to the vicinity of the Elbe River on April 14, a huge underground storehouse of liquor was captured by our forces. Among the many different beverages was some of the finest bottled egg nog I have ever tasted. A favorite drink of many was a mixture - poured from the bottles into a glass - of about one-third cognac and two-thirds egg nog. Almost all the time some one in our group - officer or enlisted man - had received a fruit cake from home which was always shared with buddies. As a result of these circumstances I had subsisted the last days before entering the hospital on fruit cocktail, fruit cake, cognac and eggnog.*

*On May 3 or 4 I was transferred from the 100th Evacuation Hospital to a "stop over" station run by the 50th Field Hospital. The first facility was an evacuation hospital, so called because patients were received, given emergency treatment and then, as soon as their condition permitted, evacuated to more adequate and comfortable accommodations in the rear areas.*

*The "stopover" station, located by an air strip for evacuation of patients by air, was even more uncomfortable than the 100th Evac. The planes landed and took off from a grassy field. The first four days no one left as rain drummed on the tents, muddied the field and prevented flights. Finally a break in the rainy weather permitted planes to land on the slick grassy strip on May 7.*

*The one distinct memory I have of the stay at the "stopover," other than the discomfort, is of the soldier who had lost both arms and both legs. He was of course depressed and disconsolate, and we were at a loss as to how to approach him and of the best method to deal with him. Once a nurse, explaining the delay in transportation, and trying to be helpful and considerate, said, by way of encouragement, "We're going to get you out of here!" The soldier began to weep and said, "Nobody wants me around anymore."*

*While on the flight on May 7 over the checker-board fields of Germany, personnel from the cockpit of the plane came back and reported to us that news had come on the radio that a general armistice had been arranged and that the war was over. We had little reason to doubt the report.*

*History has since recorded that the report, although true, came from a premature and unauthorized announcement. The official announcement was made the following day, May 8, and I heard it in the 195th General Hospital near Rheims, France, as recorded in my brief entry in the Journal on that date. The next day I slipped out into a hospital corridor to listen to Churchill's victory statement.*

*After our flight had ended, we learned that a locked wheel in take-off caused a crash of one of the hospital planes flying wounded from the "stopover." The crash occurred after our plane was safely in the air. I did not learn the fate of crew or patients involved. I have often wondered if the mishap proved fatal to anyone and if the soldier, who had already been so unfortunate as to lose both arms and legs, were aboard.*

✳   ✳   ✳

[While I was away in the hospital the 320th received the following commendation, one of many during the combat period.]

HEADQUARTERS 320TH INF

APO 35 U. S. ARMY

10 May 1945

TO: ALL OFFICERS AND MEN OF THE 320th INF.

I transmit with pride the following commendation for your characteristically outstanding performance in our last attack upon the enemy before his final and total capitulation.

HEADQUARTERS 83RD INFANTRY DIVISION

OFFICE OF THE COMMANDING GENERAL,<br>APO 83 U. S. ARMY

SUBJECT: Commendation.

TO: Commanding Officer, 320th Infantry Regiment, APO 35, U. S. Army

1. The 320th Infantry Regiment with supporting artillery was attached to the 83rd Inf Div from 15th of April to 21st of April 1945. During that period many demands were made of you. Initially you cleared the enemy from the area between the Saale and the Elbe Rivers in the Division zone.

This operation was essential if the bridgehead were to be expanded to the south and southeast. By performing it with speed, your troops contributed materially to the successful conclusion of our mission. The 83rd Division is aware that as a direct result of your excellent cooperation it became possible to establish a second bridge over the Elbe, thereby insuring the security of the bridgehead itself. [The second span across the Elbe was named the Franklin D. Roosevelt Bridge.]

2. On the 19th of April you relieved CCR, 2nd Armored Division, east of the Elbe River and took up defensive positions along the north flank of the Division bridgehead.

3. The spirit of cooperation with which you and your troops worked with us was an important factor in the successful holding of the bridgehead. Please extend to every officer and man of your command, and attached units my sincere appreciation and thanks for their courageous and untiring efforts.

(Signed) ROBERT C. MACON
Major General, U. S. Army, Commanding

1st Ind

Hq, 35th Inf Div, APO 35, U. S. Army

TO: Commanding Officer, CT 320, same station.

3 May 1945

It is with pleasure that I transmit this commendation and add my personal congratulations for the continued splendid performance of your combat team while attached to another division.

(signed) PAUL W. BAADE
Major General, U. S. A., Commanding

2nd Ind

Hq 320th Inf, APO 35, U. S. Army

TO: All Officers and Men, CT 320.

9 May 1945

1. Ten months ago you struck at the well-equipped and highly organized enemy who was stubbornly attempting to destroy our newly won beachhead in Normandy. With cour-

age and skill, and in spite of every obstacle offered by terrain, weather, and always by the enemy himself, you drove him from the hedgerows at St Lo, thru Torigni Sur Vire and across the Vire River. At Mortain you broke the back of Hitler's finest troops and marched in victorious liberation across France, thru Chateaudun, Montargis and Joinville; across the Meurthe, the Moselle, the Rhine Marne Canal, to drive thru Buisonncourt to Mazerulles. You drove our enemy from the Foret De Gremecy and after hard defensive fighting advanced doggedly to clear him from the Foret de Chateau Salins and the Morhange area; and by assault across the Saar and Blies Rivers into Germany and the finger of the Siegfried line. Thence in bitter weather you continued your victorious progress at Boulaide in Luxembourg and Bastogne in Belgium; defended in mid-winter high in the Vosges mountains; then took in your stride the crossing of the Roer River and your sensational dash thru Venlo, Holland to the last defenses of the Rhine. Your part in the clean-up of the Ruhr and final culmination of this long campaign in expansion of the Elbe bridgehead have brought to a victorious conclusion a period in which you have taken every objective and destroyed the enemy wherever you met him. You are now in the heart of a once powerful enemy's homeland, who has surrendered unconditionally to our Armies as the result of the superb achievement of you and your comrades.

2. Time and again your achievements have been of such high calibre as to receive commendations from your superiors. Not only while fighting as part of your parent division, but also when attached on occasions to the 4th Armored Division, 6th Armored Division, 75th Infantry Division and the 83rd Infantry Division.

3. I deeply appreciate that our goal could not have been reached so rapidly, effectively, and with such low casualties, but for the fine spirit of cooperation evidenced by your ever willingness to tackle new tasks and your high espirit de corps. Individually and as members of this proven regiment you may well be proud of your glorious record.

(signed) B. A. BYRNE
Colonel, 320th Infantry, Commanding

21st General Hospital
Mirecourt, France
May 18, 1945

I was transferred to this hospital by train some days ago. I am to leave tomorrow for replacement depot. Hope to get back to my unit soon.

I have had no word from the unit since I entered the hospital on April 25, and of course no mail either.

I'm glad to get out, although I'm not fully recovered at all. The time drags interminably here. I was never so listless in my life. I have absolutely no energy or ambition. It must be the let down after the long period of strain and the high pitch of living at the front.

### [END OF THE JOURNAL]

\* \* \*

The above brief entry of May 18 was the last made in the Journal. I was too listless at the time to write, and remained so throughout the following year I remained in Europe. I had to force myself to perform the most basic tasks necessary to go on living. When functions were assigned to me as duty, I could do them, but not without difficulty. Otherwise, I did nothing except brief correspondence with an occasional letter to the home town paper.

\* \* \*

## THE AIR FORCE OFFICER'S MIRACULOUS ESCAPE

The main item of interest I recall from the last hospital, was the story of an Air Force officer who was shot down while on a strafing mission over Germany in the closing days of the war. A leg was injured when he parachuted from his stricken plane, and he was soon a captive.

His captors took him into the nearby city where he was paraded between lines of angry civilians who heaped invective upon him. They spat upon him as he passed and threw garbage, manure, and other objects. Upon reaching the steps of city hall in charge of the Home Guard troops, he was set upon by angry bystanders and flogged unmercifully. His captors did not interfere.

Finally he was put in a car and driven into the country by two fat Nazis with Swastika arm bands. They stood him out in the roadway and he realized they had brought him there to kill him. He begged for his life with word and gesture. (He must have been very eloquent, for he was most effective in describing the situation to us. His undoubted truthfulness, the intensity of his manner, yet good humor and lack of bitterness as he related his story, created riots of laughter among his hearers. His narrative was highly humorous to everyone).

Standing alone in the open road before his would be executioners, the airman saw his pleas were to no avail. He broke and ran, although not very well with his injured leg. They fired on him with pistols and he was wounded twice although not seriously. The Nazis (I've forgotten the number, perhaps two) pursued him firing as they ran. His pursers were fat and in not too good physical condition, so he managed to remain out of reach for sometime. They finally ran him to earth beside a farm house on the bank of a stream, where he sought refuge with the farm family residing there.

By word and gesture he again plead for his life with the farmer and his family. They could not understand his language but could understand the situation from the circumstances - a bleeding, exhausted, fleeing American pursued by two fat Nazis armed with pistols. In what must have been a rare act of courage as well as compassion, the farmer and his wife, joined by a member of the Wehrmacht (a regular German soldier) who came along, refused to yield him to the Nazis. The farmer's wife and daughters dressed his wounds and the farmer gave him water to drink. In the meantime he observed that a message was sent, as various individuals continued to come and go. After what seemed an interminable wait to the Air Force man, a squad of regular German soldiers appeared and took him in charge. He was transported to a regular prison where, as I recall his story, he was treated properly by the Wehrmacht until the invading Allied Armies effected his release.

At the hospital it appeared his injured leg would probably make him a handicapped person the rest of his life. He could walk but only with great difficulty, and there apparently was no improvement.

The killing of prisoners, especially airmen, by the German populace was not at all unusual. We found many unmarked graves of Allied personnel. In fact special teams of investigators were sent into Germany immediately behind the invading armies, to search out and determine the fate of airmen shot down behind the lines during the conflict and to locate the graves and identify as many as possible.

The manner of this airman's escape was most unusual, including the courage of the farmer and his family and the intervention of the Wehrmacht with the intentions of the Nazis. However it was no more unusual than the flyer's telling of the story - apparently without rancor or bitterness, yet with deep-felt thankfulness and continual amazement at his escape. The relating of the experience was actually hilarious to his listeners. I soon discovered an unspoken conspiracy among his fellow patients to get the story retold at every opportunity. Any new arrival at the hospital was prompted to engage the airman in conversation and elicit the story of his experience. We lay on our bunks or gathered about his, at times holding our sides in laughter (somewhat painful to me because of the yet unhealed appendectomy) as he retold the story.

I made the last entries of the Journal in a German notebook which I picked up somewhere sometime before this last hospitalization. In this notebook I find the name - Capt Everett Lindley, Air Corps, 24 King Oak Terrace, Weymouth Heights, Weymouth, Mass. I believe this is the Air Force officer who told the story of his remarkable escape.

Other officers with whom I became acquainted in that hospital were: Lt Walter Phillips, Route 30, Box 37, Lynchburg, Va; Lt Lester Kurtz, Odd, Va; Capt Stanley Stromm, 1053 N. Huey St., South Bend, Ind.; and Lt Edward Williamson.

I do not remember when I left the hospital although I'm sure soon after the 18th. I do not recall whether I went through a repo depo. I do remember that I was in charge of a troop train of soldiers from the hospital to somewhere. There were no coaches. We rode in empty box cars with no equipment whatsoever except our meager gear.

A soldier became very ill and developed a high fever. Somehow or other, I summoned an ambulance to meet the train at a stop. The soldier was removed to be taken to another hospital.

Once when our train was stopped on a siding, the troops in the car just ahead of mine, discovered crates of beverage in a car on another track immediately beside ours. Soon an enterprising GI hopped from the car ahead, squeezed through a narrow opening into the car containing the beverage, and shortly emerged his shirt bulging with hidden objects. Another followed, and then another and another, entering and leaving the beverage laden car one at a time through the narrow passageway.

A number of French gendarmes were on the station platform and one of them turned and discovered what was going on. He stopped the last GI, took some liquor from him, but allowed him to re-enter the troop car. Other gendarmes gathered and they gestured and expostulated excitedly to each other and then with the GIs. The troops were mostly combat men who had been inactive for some time in hospitals. Soon a lively controversy developed between them and the gendarmes.

I then piled out of my side-door pullman and walked up to face the GIs. "Men," I said, "I may have seen what happened. If you don't stop the discourtesy and controversy, get back and keep quiet, we'll have to search your car. You know what we will find."

Everything was quiet as I returned to my car, except the gendarmes gesturing and stomping about uncertainly. Presently the train moved out, ending the episode.

The box cars weaved, rattled and jolted as we sped along. Sometime later, as the train made a brief halt, a GI jumped from the car ahead and dashed back to where I sat by the door looking over the countryside. "Here, Captain," he said as he set two bottles of beverage beside me, "We wanted you to have this." Turning, he dashed back before I could utter a word, and climbed back on the already moving train.

I don't even remember what the beverage was. But it was good! And I felt good. If it hadn't been for such GIs, I thought, the Nazis would have all the beverage, and nearly everything else also.

(A search of my 201 file reveals I left the 21st General Hospital on May 19. Capt Edward L. Callahan and I were placed in charge of the contingent of about 200 troops leaving the hospital for a replacement pool. Orders of May 24 sent me from the 18th Reinforcement Depot back to the 35th Division, and orders of May 28 reassigned me to a place of duty in the 320th Infantry.)

* * *

RETURN TO 320TH; CHANGES IN PERSONNEL

On May 30th I rejoined the 320th on the German plains near Hanover, where the entire 35th Division was engaged in occupation duty.

From personal contacts then, and the checking of records later, I found the following changes in personnel.

Capt Homer W. Kurtz, Collinsville, Illinois, had gone on Tdy April 25 - a rehabilitation furlough to the States. I feel sure he did not rejoin the Regiment in Europe. Kurtz, one of the finest combat officers of the 320th, had started out as a first lieutenant in the role of S-2 for the Third Battalion, later was given command of Co K and promoted to captain. Calm and collected always, soft-voiced and slow to speech, his hazy appearing eyes seemed to take in all about him in a time of crisis and battle. He led Co K in one of the last pitched battles by a 35th Division unit with a German force in the town of Gross Rosenburg, Germany at the Saale River bridgehead.

Well known to the Regimental staff, as well as the headquarters group and the entire Third Battalion, he had performed notably on many occasions, being among the first to reach the Lost Battalion at Mortain, and commanded the infantry company which, with the supporting armor, spearheaded Task Force Byrne, rolling up 26 miles of the Seigfried Line and liberating Venlo, Holland. He was one of the few original line officers who made it all the way, experiencing many, many narrow escapes, as the smashing of the CP over his head by a mortar shell near St Lo and the crashing of the tree between him and Porta as we moved across central France. Among his many close friends and companions who were lost were Braffit, Frederickson, Porta, Ermebauer, Perkowsky, Hermanspan, Orr, Brimhall, Alloway, Woods and Leo Thomas.

Three veteran medical officers, original members of the 320th who had gone all the way, had been transferred. Capt. Forrest A. Rowell, Jr., Hastings-on-the-Hudson, N. Y., who had rendered yeoman's service in charge of the First Battalion Aid Station where he had treated thousands of the wounded, injured and ill, was transferred to 35th Division Headquarters. Capt John E. McKeigue, Cambridge, Mass., and Capt Morris Himmelstein, address unknown, both of whom had likewise treated thousands of 320th men, had been transferred, the first to 110th Medical Battalion and the second to the 60th Engineer Battalion.

Another old original who had weathered the storm, but not without being wounded and a considerable time in the hospital, was gone. Capt Henry H. Hare, Los Angeles, Calif.

was sent on Tdy, a rehabilitation furlough to the States, on May 12, four days after peace was declared.

Another old original, who must have been out a considerable time with wounds, had gone to the States. Capt Lester L. Remley, commander of Company L, who had entered combat as a first lieutenant and platoon leader in the same company, went on Tdy April 26, the day after the 320th withdrew to an area beyond the sound of the German artillery.

Others who had gone, all replacements, most of whom had had considerable combat experience, were: 1st Lt James Alfieri, Co D, Buffalo, N. Y., one of the great combat leaders of the 320th, Tdy to the States on May 3; 1st Lt Lewis W. Thorne, Co D, Fairmount, W. Va., transferred to 35th Div Hq on May 2; 1st Lt Baxter A. Baltz, Sv Co, address unknown, transferred to 6th TD Group on May 6; Capt William P. Breeden, Hq 2nd Bn, Baltimore, Md., transferred to 9th Army; 1st Lt Raymond P. Street, Co H, Baltimore, Md., transferred to 84th Division; and Lt Col Fielder P. Greer, Hq 3rd Bn, address unknown, transferred to 8th Division.

All this was good news, because it meant these officers, some my close friends, had survived the war and returned home, or after a period of duty elsewhere would return home.

There was, to me, one very sad ending. On May 17 1st Lt William H. (Bill) Quillin, of Regtl Hq and Sv Co, Texarkana, Texas, with whom I had developed a very close friendship, was evacuated as sick. I had the highest regard for his qualities as a man, his compassion for others, and his efficiency and devotion to duty as a soldier. His evacuation caused no concern among his friends as it was anticipated that in the hospital he would recover, and after recovery be sent directly to the States, or would return to the outfit before going home.

Then we received the sad news of his tragic death. He was killed in the crash of a hospital plane while being flown out of Germany to a hospital in France. How sad indeed that he had survived the storm of shot and shell through ten months of warfare over 1600 combat miles with four armies on the soil of five countries, only to lose his life when the conflict had ended. I was deeply saddened by the news of his death, and the sadness was accentuated by the untimely and tragic circumstances. His loss constituted for me another of a number of life long regrets.

Charles Glatzer, alias "Red Cross Charlie", alias "Croix Rouge Sharlee," Cleveland, Ohio, Red Cross field representative with the 320th Infantry.

Capt. Milton Ginsburg, St. Paul, Minn. The picture was presented to me just after the German bombers hit us in Gros Rosenburg, Germany the night of April 17, 1945.

Capt. Homer W. Kurtz, center, Troy, Ill., K Company Commander and one of his platoon leaders, Lt. Royal A. Offer, right, Adams, Nebr., a sergeant awarded a battlefield commission, somewhere in Germany. (photo from Capt. Kurtz)

Capt. Charles Brochu, Cleveland, Ohio, somewhere in Europe after the war.

Faubus, left, and 1st Lt. Richard Donovan, Baltimore, Md., I&R Platoon leader, shortly after my return from the hospital. The picture was snapped by Ralph E. Rawson during a lull in April, 1945 when we had pulled out of the Ruhr Pocket battle and were preparing for the plunge deep into Germany.

Capt. Faubus pauses in his travels on a German autobahn after the war. A modern highway built by Hitler's Germany, a "have not" nation, before the war, and long before we had such a highway in the States.

Lt. Travis E. Hendren, left, Cleveland, N. C., and Lt. Winifred Young, Joplin, Mo., Co. H, 320th, during convoy break near Hanover, Germany. The war was evidently over as the trees appear to be in full foliage. (photo from Lt. Hendren)

President Harry S. Truman in white suit leads the columns of 35th Veterans in a reunion parade on Main Street in Little Rock. He is flanked by Secretary of War Louis Johnson in white shirt with cane, and a battery mate of WWI carrying the 129th Field Artillery banner. On the other side in the dark suit wearing white hat is Arkansas Governor Sid McMath, Gen. Harry Vaughn in uniform and another 129th FA battery mate. Behind Johnson the tall man in dark suit and white hat is Gen. Joe Nickell, then Adjutant General of Kansas.

Five generals, all 35th Division Veterans, at a Little Rock reunion. Left to right, Joe Nickell of Topeka, Kans.; Ralph E. Truman of Springfield, Mo.; Warren Wood of Gering, Nebr.; Butler M. Miltonberger of North Platte, Nebr.; and Charles H. Browne, Sr., of Horton, Kans.

Some 320th men get together at the Little Rock reunion. Left to right, Faubus, Sid Silverman, Col. Northam, John Miller (216th FO with 320th), Maj. Leach and Red Cross Charlie. Last man on the right unidentified.

Months later, I learned from members of the 320th, Lt Quillin's wife came to Camp Breckenridge, Ky., where she tried without success to obtain from members of the outfit, something of the details of her husband's death. No one could be helpful to her because his death occurred after he left the outfit. Just as I found my own situation during my periods of hospitalization, Quillin was probably alone so far as having near him a close friend or acquaintance. There were probably no individuals who knew him personally at the scene of his death, and even if there were, they probably died with him in the crash.

\* \* \*

On May 31 Gen. Baade announced that he had received official notification from SHAEF officials, that the First Battalion of the 320th Infantry, and the 737th Tank Batalion, had been cited by President Truman for the rescue of the Lost Battalion at Mortain on Aug. 11-12th. The Lost Battalion was a part of the 120th Infantry Regiment of the 30th Division. Everyone was proud of the rare Presidential Citation. Capt. Davis, Lt. Prescott, Lt. Orr and others who lost their lives there, as well as Maj. Gillis, Capt. Gardner, Sgt. Porta and other heroes of the battle who died later in other engagements, would have been pleased to know their heroism had been recognized.

\* \* \*

## CHAPTER IX

## THE 320TH AND THE 35TH AFTER WAR'S END

### OLD ORIGINALS REMAINING

With the war over and the 320th now on occupation duty, of the original 78 officers in the 12 line companies when the Regiment entered combat, only 14 remained. Only two of those were with their original companies, and both of these officers had been out for considerable time with wounds. However a few, as Thomas, Remley, Williams and Alloway, had been sent home on rehabilitation furloughs in the closing days of the war and did not return.

Those remaining were:

Company A - Capt Kullmar, now a major in 1st Bn Hq.

Company B - Capt Ekstrum, now commander of Cannon Company.

Company C - Lt Dalton, with his company, and Lt Morgan, with 1st Bn Hq.

Company D - 1st Lt Roman W. Knopke, Crookston, Minn. with 1st Bn Hq; 2nd Lt Kirksey O. Looney, Crane, Texas, with Sv Co; and 2nd Lt Jack Sabata with Sv Co.

Company E - none.

Company F - Lt Gangemi, with his company.

Company G - none.

Company H - Capt Smith, now a major in 2nd Bn Hq; and Lt Preston in Regtl Hq.

Company I - Lt Brochu, now a captain in Regtl Hq; Lt Head, now a captain, returned from furlough to the States and took command of Co G.

Company K - Capt Trossen, now in 3rd Bn Hq; Lt Zimmerman, a capt in Sv Co; Lt Kelly, with Regtl Hq.

Company L - none.

Company M - Capt Bonham, now commander of Regtl Hq Co.

In the supporting units the following original officers remained:

Cannon Company - none

Anti-Tank Company - Capt Wilson with Lts Wright, Botton and Adams, with their company; Lt Zielasko, now with Division Headquarters.

Medical Detachment - Maj Smith and Capts Shumate and Cacioppo, with their company; (Capts Rowell, Himmelstein and McKeigue were transferred, perhaps after the war ended.)

Service Company - Maj Hughes, still S-4 and Captain Heil commander; Capt Armstrong with Lt Sperl and WO Frazier, still running the personnel section; Capt Shamla with Lts Keith, Mody and Byerly and WOs Ball and Patterson with their company; Capt Leach, now a major with 3rd Bn Hq.

In the command units the following original officers remained:

Hq & Hq Co 1st Bn - Capt Vignes and Capt Walton, the latter now a Lt Col and CO of the Bn; Lt Carpenter and 1st Lt Eugene A. Duffy of Batavia, Illinois.

Hq & Hq Co 2nd Bn - Lt Henry O. Tietjens of Carrolton, Mo.

Hq & Hq Co 3rd Bn - Lt Harold E. Peterson, the communications officer. (Capt Hare of 2nd Bn, and Capts Tobin and Kurtz of 3rd Bn, had been sent to the States on rehabilitation furloughs in the closing days of the war)

Regtl Hq - Col Byrne, Lt Col Northam; Majors Jamieson and McElroy; Capts Hailey, Tarpley and Stone; Lts Ginsburg, Silverman and Faubus, the last three now captains.

Of the approximately 160 officers of the Regiment who had shipped from the States, about 50 remained with the 320th at the end of the war. Of those who remained almost 50% had been casualties at one time or another. Some of the originals who wound up with the unit at war's end, had spent almost as much time in hospitals as in the battle lines. I recall that at least one, Lt Henry G. Morgan, had been wounded three times.

\* \* \*

# WE HEAR OF FORSYTH AND ROBERTS

In the closing days of the war and shortly after the General Armistice on May 8, we heard of the release of some of our men from the German Prisoner-of-War Camps, who had been captured during the conflict. We heard of the release of Capt Forsyth who was captured at Mortain when Capt Davis was killed. We did not hear of T/5 McCartney, who was lost at the same time.

1st Lt Grover C. Roberts of Company C, Pine Bluff, Ark., wounded by gunshot and captured July 12, the second day of our attack on St Lo (my unofficial record listed him as MIA July 22) was released from the German Prisoner-of-War Cages by the advancing American Armies on May 3.

\* \* \*

# ADDITIONS TO OUR CIRCLE; OCCUPATION DUTY

During the occupation duty in Germany and the 320th's stay in France before returning to the States, there remained eight of the close circle of the original officers of regimental headquarters - Col Byrne, Lt Col Northam, Maj McElroy, Maj. Jamieson, and Capts Ginsburg, Silverman, Haley and me. Of these Silverman had been wounded, and I had been hospitalized twice briefly during combat, and a longer period, the last time, at the war's end. The others had been present all the way except for short periods of leave. Lts Parish and Clark, early replacements, were still around, although Clark had been hospitalized briefly. Capt. Bonham had joined the group about Nov 10th after four months hospitalization for wounds, and Lt Kelly was added in early April after a lengthy hospital stay to recover from wounds. Both were still present. Glatzer, "Red Cross Charlie," was happily, still with us, and Capt Brochu was in command of the MP Platoon. We missed Capt Scherer and Lt Cooper, who had returned to their respective units.

2nd Lt Martin I. Sellings, Newark, N. J., with us all along as a sergeant with the IPW team, was made a commissioned officer, and remained with the group. Another original officer of the Regiment, 1st Lt Roy W. Preston, Seneca, Mo, was brought to headquarters from Company H during the last month of the war. Lt. Donovan, an EM who had earned a commission, continued as commander of the I & R platoon.

Among the new members of our close circle was 1st Lt Travis E. Hendren of Cleveland, N. C., who joined the 320th on Sept. 19 as a platoon leader in Company G. He was wounded on Nov. 8, the first day of the Alsace-Lorraine Campaign, but recovered, returned and was assigned to Company H as the 60mm mortar platoon commander in time for the Ardennes Campaign. Wounded the second time on March 8 in the Rhineland drive, he again recovered and returned and was assigned to Regimental Headquarters in May. Other new members of our circle, all replacements, were 1st Lt Donald C. Villemaire, Burlington, Vt; 1st Lt Thomas M. Leirer, Bernie, Mo; 1st Lt Robert Shapiro, Bronx, N. Y.; and Capt Elwyn A. Bierie, Catholic chaplain from St. Louis, Mo.

The two Protestant chaplains, Capts Tarpley and Stone, both originals, had survived the conflict and were still present. We did not see them often as they spent most of their time with the battalions.

We saw a great deal of Majs Hughes and Smith, supply and medics respectively, of Capts Shamla, Heil and Armstrong, Lt Sperl and WO Frazier, all of Service Company, as well as the battalion commanders, Lt Cols Walton, Hannum and Alexander, and members of their staffs. However, each command group, whose members daily worked closely together, became a small circle of associates, while contact with others was less frequent. So each unit became a close circle of friends - the companies, the battalion staffs, the medical and supply groups, as well as our own.

The period of less than three months was a pleasant time. The combat veterans were so glad to be alive that almost all else was secondary. There was much to do, especially in the administrative field, but our duties were not burdensome and we performed them with dispatch and pleasure. Our unit continued superbly efficient and with high morale.

Lt Clark obtained instruments and formed a 320th band which became quite good, although under his leadership the emphasis was on jazz and a type of music called "boogie-woogie." These tunes were not especially to the liking of Col Northam and myself but that didn't bother Clark who directed them with gusto.

Chaplain Bierie, we learned, had been a student for two years in Germany before the war and could speak the language like a native. In traveling about the Coblenz area he contacted a number of acquaintances he had made as a student years before. The chaplain became quite useful in helping to locate needed supplies and items which we wanted to acquire, as additional food and souvenirs. He could also easily locate the best beer and wine and, by acting as interpreter, expedite the purchase of the same.

* * *

## CHARLES BROCHU AND "CLUB 88"

Lt Charles Brochu had joined hqs Co as comdr of the MP platoon. The MPs always had duty which Brochu directed with dispatch and efficiency. He had a well drilled and disciplined unit, and it was always interesting to see him fall them in for duty or fall them out afterward.

Brochu was that rare combination of excellent parade ground soldier and combat leader without superior. He had a machine gun like laugh which was seldom missing in combat and never in the pleasant days after the war had ended. He smoked a cigarette in an interesting, unusual manner, holding it delicately between his finger and thumb, taking short puffs, and delicately flicking off the ash with his little finger.

Like any platoon leader of a company of the line in combat, Brochu had had a rough time. His experiences were probably worse than most. He had faced small arms fire and artillery shelling innumerable times, and had been knocked unconscious by the concussion of exploding shells. He had experienced so many narrow escapes that long before war's end he no longer noted nor tried to remember the number. Once when he thought he and his men had killed two of their own comrades, he almost cracked up. The incident occurred in the dismal cold blackness of night on Nov. 8 when Charlie and his platoon members were first to fight their way into the fiercely defended town of Fresnes at the beginning of the terrible Alsace-Lorraine campaign.

During the bull sessions after the war he would sometimes describe his experiences. The thin line of riflemen is deployed as Charlie's platoon leads the advance with him near the center for best control. They don't know how far the leading riflemen will get, or just when the Germans will open up, but they know the fire is coming. Then, at some point, there comes the deadly, hateful purr of the German machine guns accompanied by small arms fire. Every man goes down. Some are hit, some are not. Some will rise, others won't. At times there was German shelling once the men got into the open.

— 630 —

When such a situation had developed, Charlie would quickly seek shelter behind tree, boulder, bank or building. Propping his back against something, he would quickly light a cigarette, and, as he puffed, would evaluate the situation and then give directions. If he could utilize friendly mortars and artillery, or perhaps an attached tank or tank destroyer, fine. But most of the time the advance had to be continued by the riflemen covered only by friendly automatic and MG fire.

In this activity, Charlie was engaged in the greatest game of all, with the highest stakes known to individual men - pitting his life and the lives of his men against the German lives, with the great advantage with the enemy. It was a game in which no man could survive indefinitely, and in which few lasted very long. In fact, a brief span of such activity was the rule rather than the exception.

There were more pleasant subjects and happier occasions with Charlie Brochu. The most hilarious times were when he described the nightclub he was going to establish in Cleveland, Ohio when he returned home. Known as Club 88 in recollection of the dreaded German artillery gun, the facility would have several sections. There would be a Purple Heart Room, a Combat Infantry Badge Room, and among others, a place which could be entered only by the presentation of an Army K-ration box top. Charlie could imitate almost to perfection the incoming sound and explosion of a shell from the powerful German field piece. Puffing his cigarette and flicking the ash with his little finger, he would begin his presentation, imitating a radio announcer.

"Good evening, friends! Welcome to Club 88 in downtown Cleveland. This music is coming to you courtesy of Club 88 by way of station KNGY." Then, with a rising crescendo, the terrifying sound of an incoming 88, "W-h-a-a-a-a-ah, BAM!" Then in the loud silence immediately following the deafening explosion, waving gently his cigarette arm and cigarette like a baton, Charlie would softly intone, "Time on my hands, and you in my arms."

It was hilarious!

I wish he could have established the Club. It would have been great to visit, especially if Charlie were there, puffing his cigarette, flicking the ash with his little finger, smiling and giving out his staccato laugh while chatting with the customers.

At some disremembered place in Europe, the time now also forgotten, Charlie and I saw each other for the last time. We corresponded briefly after I returned home. In fact, he was one of the first of the very few to read my war diary and urge its publication. Then we lost touch and it has now been perhaps 20 years since I have heard of the combat soldier "par excellence," Charles Brochu. In all the years since the war I have never been in a club or heard a club radio program without remembering his planned introduction of Club 88.

\* \* \*

## 1ST LT ROBERT SHAPIRO, BRONX, N. Y.

Lt Shapiro was a big, strong fellow, short and handsome in appearance, and quiet and courteous in manner. He was always friendly but seemed to have lost interest in living. He was silent and somber. We tried to include him in on everything but with little or no success. He just didn't participate and remained quietly withdrawn.

Then one night we were having a comradeship party in my second floor quarters. There were John Kelly, Red Cross Charlie, Sid Silverman and others. We ran out of wine or anything else to drink except the beer stored in the basement of John's quarters across the street, and the only beer available there was in a good sized barrel. The beer could be obtained by removing the bung (stopper) from the side of the container and replacing it with a spigot. The problem was to get the barrel to my quarters.

Shapiro, the strong man of our group, happened to be around and offered to help. Alone, he carried the barrel from the basement, across the street and up the stairs to my room. As he came through the door of the room the bung struck the door jam and was knocked out. Within a moment beer had spewed on us and all over the room. I'll never forget Shapiro's chagrin and consternation, nor the unrestrained hilarity of Red Cross Charlie and the others.

The German girl in the house, hearing the commotion, came to see what was wrong. She took one look, and with an expression she had picked up from the GIs, "Oh, my aching back," ran for the mop.

First, we stopped the loss of beer by replacing the stopper, then with the help of the German girl cleaned up the room, after which she withdrew, and the party continued.

We persuaded Shapiro to remain. Already the center of attention he became the life of the party, and seemed to have a wonderful time. After that he was not the same. Following the incident it appeared to us that to him life again seemed good, and he enjoyed it with the rest of us.

Charlie Glatzer and I often laughed together afterwards, about how the knocking of the bung from the beer barrel and the spewing of the beer over the room proved to be the salvation of Lt Shapiro.

* * *

## RELIGIOUS FREEDOM RESTORED

During the period with the 320th near Hanover, Germany shortly after my return, the people of the occupied area held a day-long religious ceremony. It was a beautiful spring day with flowers in bloom in great profusion. The occasion included a parade with the church leaders in colorful religious regalia with equally colorful religious symbols and banners, and many wreaths and bouquets of flowers carried by the marchers. Many of our troops watched the picturesque parade in which almost all the people participated. Religious service and ceremonies followed at the churches.

Late in the afternoon the religious chiefs, still in their colorful garb, accompanied by the mayor in formal dress including a silk top hat, came to the 320th Headquarters to thank us for permitting them the privilege of engaging in the spiritual activity. Only myself and one EM (I think it was Cpl Ostapczuk) were in the headquarters and were caught by surprise at the unexpected visit. There was much bowing and formality on the part of our visitors as they made known the purpose of their call. We received them courteously but without much formality. They said the religious affair was the first of its kind in many years as Hitler had not permitted such ceremonies. We stated that as Americans we were glad to see religious freedom restored to them and to their country.

A few days later the Regiment moved to the southwest to its new zone of occupation. The Division's area with Coblenz as the center, was part of the same area administered by the American Army of Occupation after World War One.

The base ball stadium at Coblenz, built by the first Army of Occupation many years before, was restored by the 35th Division and renamed the Santa Fe Stadium. Dedication

— 633 —

ceremonies included a military parade with the belated awarding of decorations earned during combat, and a baseball game between teams of the 106th Division and the Santa Fe in which a number of former big league stars participated. The Santa Fe Division team was the winner.

I stood on the sidelines while the military parade was in progress. I noted German civilians watching from the second story of a nearby house. They laughed gleefully and critically at the sometimes awkardness of the American soldiers and the lack of precision in the movement of the units. They didn't know that almost all these men were civilian soldiers, hurriedly trained for combat, some of whom may never before have participated in such a formation. And, I thought, they failed to remember that the American Army, of which this outfit was a part, had participated in the defeat of their precision-drilled and parade-conscious army, and had conquered their entire country.

While in the new area I did administrative work and went on missions for the regiment, making two or three trips to Idar-Oberstein farther up the Rhine, a center for the manufacture of jewelry, precious stones, trinkets and metal emblems. Our regiment had placed a large order for regimental crests and cigarette cases, the latter engraved with the battle route of the unit. We could never get delivery of the full order while the unit remained in Europe, nor could I obtain delivery in the months after the Division returned home.

On a return journey from one of these trips, my driver and I picked up a German soldier hiking wearily along the road going home. As it happened we took him all the way to his home in a town on the lower Mozel River (Moselle in France), arriving there after nightfall. When he knocked on the door and made his presence known, there followed as joyous a reunion as I have ever heard. (We couldn't see in the darkness).

As we started to drive away the soldier came dashing out. He wanted us to wait while he secured some wine to present to us in appreciation for the ride we had given him. He obtained and gave us, as I recall, four bottles. I then had the thought that the German soldier's family might have wine for sale and made the inquiry. It seemed they did, and I bought as many cases as the already loaded jeep would hold. The price was very low.

Arriving back at our headquarters we were storing the wine in the cellar of the house in which we were billeted. The man of the house, a former German officer in the Wehrmacht who had returned home, was helping us. We remarked that we would have a wine party right away.

"Oh, you can't," said the German, We wanted to know why. "Because wine is not good until it sets quiet and still for at least two weeks," he replied.

"Well this won't have a chance to get good," we laughed.

And it didn't. Still, the white Mozel wine of the Rhineland area in Germany is by far the best beverage of its kind that I have ever tasted, even after transportation in a jeep and no chance to "set quiet" for at least two weeks.

* * *

## LT JOHN P. KELLY

During this period one of my companions was Lt John Kelly of Broken Bow, Nebr (or was it Broken Arrow? Even yet I can't ever be sure without checking). John was the quiet gentleman, a poet at heart, so un-warlike in his appearance even in battle dress, the gentle combat soldier who had survived.

We spent a number of quiet evenings together in his quarters just across the street from mine. On some occasions when there were just the two of us, we read poetry and drank wine. I had a book "Pack up Your Troubles," an excellent collection of poems, which I had taken from storage in my foot locker after the war had ended.

John would quote some poetry, and we would have a glass of wine; then I would quote and we would have another glass. When our memory of quotes was exhausted, I would get the book, read a passage of poetry, after which we would have another glass. We repeated this, the two of us in the quiet room, until the hour grew late and John would go to bed. Then, alone, I would read another poem while having another glass of wine, and myself retire.

Years later, after returning home, I learned that John was working for the Justice Department in Denver, Colo. On a trip through the area I stopped in Denver to visit my aunt and her husband, Mr. and Mrs. J. S. (Jess) Johnson. I called John by telephone at the Justice Department and when he came on the line, without identifying myself I inquired, "John, how would you like to read some poetry and drink some wine?"

Without hesitation he exclaimed, "Gees, Judge, where are you?" He had remembered as clearly as I. Since my relatives would be bored with our reminiscing, John and I went to a cafe somewhere in Denver. We had a meal, so unlike the GI food we had eaten together so many times, and had another drink "for old times sake." We toasted our comrades, both living and dead, now sleeping in many graves in the military cemeteries of Europe, or scattered to the four winds of the earth after the war had ended.

* * *

## OTHER OFFICERS OF THE 320TH INFANTRY

After the War some of the veterans of the conflict were sent on temporary duty to the States, and a few others were given assignments with various units in Europe. When the decision was made to send the Division to the Pacific Theater, many high point veterans were transferred from the organization.

New officers and men joined the Santa Fe Division to bring its units again to full strength. Consequently, some officers and men came home with the Division who had not fought with it in Europe.

The following officers, not heretofore mentioned, served with the 320th in Europe, and most of them came home with the unit. Many of them saw combat with us in the later campaigns of the war and some even earlier, while others were transferred to our regiment after the conflict ended. Some came from other combat divisions, while others may have arrived in Europe too late to engage in the actual fighting.

In the list, those enlisted men awarded commissions, were veterans of combat with the 320th, some of them "old originals" who came overseas with us.

Without access to officials records it is impossible for me to determine which of the following officers, all replacements except the enlisted men who were commissioned, saw combat with the 320th, or joined the regiment after the war ended.

## REGIMENTAL HEADQUARTERS

Capt Walter S. Nelson Jr., Atlantic City, N. J.
CWO Albert E. Surmont, Morristown, N. J.

# FIRST BATTALION HEADQUARTERS

Capt Fred C. Miller, S-3, Ogdensburg, N. Y.
1st Lt Henry G. Peterson, S-2, Des Moines, Iowa
1st Lt H. C. Thompson, Camp McCoy, Wisc.

## HEADQUARTERS COMPANY, FIRST BATTALION

1st Lt Ralph C. Evert, Jr., Com O, Philadelphia, Pa.
2nd Lt Russell W. McBride, A&PO, Carbondale (or Joliet), Ill.
    (EM awarded a battlefield commission)
2nd Lt Elmer L. Appelhans, MTO, Holcomb, Kansas.
    (EM awarded a battlefield commission)
2nd Lt Daniel P. Dineen, Springfield, Mass.

## COMPANY A

1st Lt Daniel C. Stewart, St. Daniels, Pa.
1st Lt Rodney P. Scoville, Schenectady, N. Y.
    (Commanded a platoon in Co A as far back as Nov. 8)
1st Lt John E. Sherman, Compton, Calif.
2nd Lt John R. Westphal, Chicago, Ill.
2nd Lt Lamoine E. Heiman, Eau Claire, Wisc.
    (EM awarded a battlefield commission, one of the great
    combat soldiers of the 320th)
2nd Lt Leo C. Lyon, Ventura, Calif.
    (EM awarded a battlefield commission)
2nd Lt John F. Cottrell, Oak Ridge, Tenn.
2nd Lt Paul S. Tramel, Hatfield, Pa.
2nd Lt Robert M. Rehor, Hermon, N. Y.

## COMPANY B

Capt Frank V. Rosson, Jr., CO, Palmyra, Va.
    (Joined Co B as platoon leader on Aug 1)
1st Lt Robert E. Seitz, Joliet, Ill.
1st Lt Gus Miller, New Orleans, La.
1st Lt Martin S. Turner, Arkansas City, Kansas
1st Lt Bernard J. Grachek, Fremont, Ohio
    (EM awarded a battlefield commission)
2nd Lt Harry A. Thompson, Columbus, Pa.
2nd Lt Alan G. McIlvaine, Jenkintown, Pa.

## COMPANY C

2nd Lt Stanley King, Pe Ell, Wash.
    (EM awarded a battlefield commission)

2nd Lt Arthur J. Raymond, Norfolk, Nebr.
2nd Lt Harold C. Heimann, Monroe, La.
2nd Lt William E. Murphy, address unknown
2nd Lt Wayne C. Stacey, Kexar Falls, Maine

## COMPANY D

Capt Earl Lynch, CO, Cincinnatti, Ohio
1st Lt Robert E. Phillips, Macon, Georgia
1st Lt John V. O'Brien, Brooklyn, N. Y.
1st Lt Jack L. Bush, Salem, Ind.
1st Lt Ford L. Thompson, Minneapolis, Minn.
1st Lt Charles E. Radcliffe, Mertztown, Pa.
2nd Lt McRae Werth, Lexington, Ky.
2nd Lt Robert H. Shannon, Hatfield, N. J.

## SECOND BATTALION HEADQUARTERS

Maj. Robert F. Wilson, Charlotte, N. C.
1st Lt Robert G. Venema, S-2, Gladewater, Texas
2nd Lt William F. (or M) Martone, address unknown
(Joined Company E not later than March)

## HEADQUARTERS COMPANY, SECOND BATTALION

Capt John W. Walleigh, Jr., Ardmore, Pa.
1st Lt Edwin H. Ward, A/T O, Artesia, N. Mex.
2nd Lt William M. Mack, Com O, Dickinson, N. D.
(Em awarded a battlefield commission)
1st Lt Arthur E. Thomas, MTO, Pawleys Island, S. C. or
Fayetteville, N. C.
1st Lt Mack G. Reed, New York, N. Y.

## COMPANY E

1st Lt Ben W. Crume, Jr., New York City, N. Y.
(With Co E as far back as the Ardennes Campaign)
1st Lt Gilbert L. Gaumer, Houston, Texas
1st Lt Ralph B. Shwartz, Struthers, Ohio
1st Lt James E. Moore, Jr., address unknown
1st Lt Nicholas T. Zackeo, Brooklyn, N. Y.
2nd Lt Williamson T. Hough, Lawrence, Kansas
2nd Lt Edmund S. Watkins, Houston, Texas

# COMPANY F

1st Lt Charles S. Sancic, Washington, D. C.
1st Lt John F. Scully, Yonkers, N. Y.
1st Lt Clair R. Snyder, Elmira Heights, N. Y.
(Also served in Co G)
2nd Lt Ross M. Miller, Montezuma, Kansas
1st Lt Frank B. Edwards, Oakland, Calif.

# COMPANY G

1st Lt Edgar T. Snipes, address unknown
1st Lt Jerry P. Richardson, Little Rock, Ark.
1st Lt Robert A. Sanders, Corning, N. Y.
1st Lt Donald S. Severence, Syracuse, N. Y.
(Saw combat with the unit)
2nd Lt Robert D. Foley, Rochester, N. Y.
1st Lt John R. Patrick, Central City, Pa.

# COMPANY H

1st Lt Russell B. Winger, Dayton, Ohio
(With Co H as far back as Nov 18)
1st Lt Arnold Hallenger, Goodhue, Minn.
(EM awarded a battlefield commission)
1st Lt Joseph R. Shafnacker, Sayresville, N. J.
2nd Lt James K. Humphrey, Washington, D. C.
1st Lt Michael Prosak, North Coplay, Pa.
2nd Lt John D. Gettinger, Sullivan, Ind.
2nd Lt Ernest R. Schmidt, Chicago, Ill.

# THIRD BATTALION HEADQUARTERS

Lt Col Kurt G. Ratke, Fond du Lac, Wisc.
Maj Frank W. Marshall, Jr., Concord, N. H.

# HEADQUARTERS COMPANY, THIRD BATTALION

1st Lt Lloyd H. Baker, A/TO, Lake Crystal, Wisc.
2nd Lt Earl R. White, A&PO, Manhattan Beach, Calif.
2nd Lt Robert L. Cates, Com O, Asbury Park, N. J.

# COMPANY I

1st Lt Ronald A. Taylor, Jr., Bethel, Conn.
(Joined Company I not later than April)
2nd Lt Theodore J. Dulchinos, Chicopee Falls, Mass.
2nd Lt Arthur J. Herald, Pontiac, Mich.

## COMPANY K

1st Lt Arthur E. Stringer, Jr., Metcalf, Ga.
1st Lt Frank Mekachonis, address unknown
1st Lt Arthur A. O'Leary, Jr., Belmont, Mass.
2nd Lt Kenneth M. Stewart, address unknown
2nd Lt James C. Robertson, Holly Ridge, Miss.
    (With Co K as far back as Nov. 8, evacuated, recovered
    and returned to duty after that date)
2nd Lt George E. Moore, Silver Springs, Md.
2nd Lt Charles C. Slater, Chicago, Ill.

## COMPANY L

Capt Julius G. Resnick, CO, East Liverpool, Ohio
    (Joined Co L as platoon leader Nov. 14, later executive
    officer, became commander Dec. 27)
1st Lt Franklin E. Chaffey (or Chaffee) address unknown
1st Lt Ted R. Savage, Hammon, Okla.
1st Lt Richard O. Kiser, Springfield, Ohio
2nd Lt Richard E. Rutledge, Haleyville, Ala.

## COMPANY M

1st Lt Albert C. Henderson, CO, Seattle, Wash.
1st Lt Glenn L. Stonecipher, Patterson, Calif.
1st Lt Robert J. Hourigan, Kingston, Pa.
    (A platoon leader in Co E as far back as January, '45)
1st Lt Harold E. Becker, address unknown
1st Lt Alvin F. Woolslayer, South Bountiful, Utah
1st Lt Larry E. Wells, New York, N. Y.
2nd Lt Harold M. Shepher (or Shepherd), Chandler, Okla.
2nd Lt Robert L. Huey, Erie, Pa.
2nd Lt Oliver K. Colson, address unknown
2nd Lt John F. Kneeland, Lewistown, Maine
1st Lt David E. McGeorge, Pittsburgh, Pa.

## SERVICE COMPANY

1st Lt Charles A. Little, Chicago, Ill.
2nd Lt Charles T. McCreary, Pittsburgh, Pa.
CWO Harry R. Shildt, San Antonio, Texas
Capt Bruce F. Glenn, Morrisville, Pa.

## CANNON COMPANY

1st Lt Glenn O. Nowels, address unknown
    (With Cn Co as far back as December, 1944)
1st Lt Stanford L. Clem, address unknown
    (FO for Cn Co as far back as Ardennes Campaign)
1st Lt Harold A. Ames, Greenville, Texas
1st Lt John T. Randall, Chicago, Ill.
2nd Lt Darrol L. Dunham, Nickerson, Kansas
2nd Lt John J. Humphrey, Washington, D. C.
1st Lt Kenneth R. Arney, Woodburn, Oregon

## ANTI-TANK COMPANY

1st Lt Lee R. DeRouen, Cheneyville, La.
1st Lt Robert C. Green, Fort Worth, Texas
1st Lt John M. Van Antwerp, Tacoma, Wash.
2nd Lt Robert D. Figgs, Valley Falls, Kansas, or Chicago, Ill.

## MEDICAL DETACHMENT

Capt Thomas T. Upshur, DC, Sumter, S. C.
Capt Paul C. Jenks, MC, Burlington, Vt.
Capt Vernon A. Ingle, MC, Montebello, Calif.
Capt Philip J. Atrim, Attica, Kansas
Capt Milton Berman, New York, N. Y.
1st Lt Irwin C. Cole, MC, Chicago, Ill.
1st Lt Arthur Horwitz, MAC, Beverly Hills, Calif. or Chicago, Ill.
    (EM awarded battlefield commission)
1st Lt Herbert Freedman, MAC, Portsmouth, N. H. or New York, N. Y.
    (EM awarded a battlefield commission)
1st Lt James C. Keener, MAC, Detroit, Mich.
    (EM awarded a battlefield commission)
1st Lt Robert L. Deuel, Detroit, Mich.
Capt H. M. Scherer, New Philadelphia, Ohio

From
## THE MADISON COUNTY RECORD
## NEWS OF OUR BOYS

— V —

## FROM CAPT. ORVAL E. FAUBUS

Hq 320th Regt.,
July 6, 1945

What the Mail Brings—

Rejoining my regiment about May 30 near Munster, Germany, I found quite a collection of mail, due principally to my two hospitalization periods within 3 months, but also to delay in transit. It seemed a bit strange to be reading some of the letters in June, as one dated Dec. 8, 1944 from my sister, Cressye, Fullerton, Calif., which said, "Bonnie has gone to town to do some Christmas shopping." Also the Christmas card from my cousin, Mrs. Ruby Bookout of Springdale whose husband, Hank Bookout, has been in the European Theater longer than I. Another Yuletide greeting from Mr. and Mrs. Leonard Elvington was mailed from Omak, Wash., and an Easter greeting in March.

Almost every letter brought news of service men or showed a touch of the war. My sisters, Connie, Cressye, Bonnie and June, write that for more than a year they, with Dad, were helping to build C-47 Transport planes like the one which flew me out of Germany as a patient. Bonnie's husband, Pvt Raul Salcido, has sailed as an infantryman to the Pacific war. June's husband, Pfc. Verle Hall of the Marines, has returned home after many missions on the big bombers in the Pacific.

Uncle Will Joslin of Combs says Virgil Judy and Lorin Combs are home on furlough; Clyde Ritchie has been discharged; Arlin Judy is in the Pacific and Henry Thornsberry, after three years in that theater, is on his way home. Aunt Ada McChristian of Foreman, Ark., sends news that my cousin, Tom Oril McChristian, is supervisor of a Navy plant in Oklahoma. Aunt Minnie Johnson of Denver, Colo., sends news of her son-in-law, Dale Reich, in the service.

My most faithful correspondents among the relatives are Mr. and Mrs. L. A. Nelson of Huntsville who write the doings of the old home town. Another is sister-in-law, Ruby

Faubus, who writes the news of the many Arkansawyers in Washington State where Elvin (my brother) is employed.

Mr. and Mrs. Everett Ball write from Derby, Kans., and friends of courthouse days in Huntsville, Pauline Hillard, Mary Roberts, Gayle Johnson, Adry Gaskill and the Elmer Olivers, send welcome letters.

Cousin Dave Thornsberry and wife, Ruby, of Combs send news that Ruby's brother, Earl Rogers of the 29th Inf. Div., has been wounded twice and is now in Germany. It was his division which mine first relieved when we entered the battle lines in Normandy. It moved a bit over to the left and then the 29th and the 35th attacked side by side to take St. Lo. They also tell that Herbert Thornsberry has been home on furlough, and Shelby Thornsberry is in the European Theater.

The most laughs from any letter were derived from one written by Cousin Fred Thornsberry who is now cross tie inspector at Rogers.

A letter from Uncle Hiram and Aunt Carrie Thornsberry of Combs makes me long for strawberry shortcake and fried chicken. Word comes from old friends like Wm. Simmons of Huntsville and the Alonzo Ledfords of Pinnacle. The John Millers of Combs are now in Washington. Clay McBroom of Huntsville tells of changes in the county seat.

A former student, Mrs. Opal (Davenport) Glenn of Asher, sends the address of her husband, Pfc Everett Glenn in the European Theater. Her brother, Pfc Truman Davenport of Pinnacle, is at a convalescent hospital at Camp Carson, Colo., recovering from wounds. Another ex-pupil, James Caler of Thorney, writes that his brother, Roy Caler, also a former pupil, was also in the forces which engaged the Germans at St. Lo. Mrs. Lee Yarbrough of Huntsville sent the address of her husband who is serving in the Field Artillery in this theater.

Letters from servicemen - Ex-teacher Paul Corlett now doing his bit with the Navy; Pfc. Jimmie Rogers of the Engineers in Europe, whom I saw at Fayetteville when we were both privates; Pvt Paul W. Harriman in the Pacific; Cpl Millard Sisemore of the engineers and Paige Thomas, both still in Europe; Cpl Arvil R. Shipp on the Marianna Islands in the Pacific; Pfc Asie Easterling of the Combat Engineers who has seen Alsace-Lorraine; Pfc Dave Jones serving in an Ordnance unit in Nancy, France; Pfc Earl L. Sams of the 324th Inf Regt in Germany; and Pvt Denver Samples of the

Signal Corps, Rhiems, France. Warrant Officer S. W. Bowker of Jonesboro, Ark., an acquaintance of basic training days, sends some strange money from New Caledonia in the South Pacific; Pfc Julian Woodrow Ledford of the Medical Corps writes that he served a month with the infantry in Europe, got initiated to the artillery and bullets and had his quota of close calls; and my cousin, Pvt Leslie Jones of Tahlequah, Okla., has been wounded the third time while fighting with the 80th Inf. Div.

W. M. Eubanks of Huntsville tells of his three sons in the service - William Roy, with the Fifth Army in Italy; Gifford Paul and Jesse Fred, both with the First Army in Germany. Clyde Clark of Springdale tells of his boy in service in Italy, then in the hospital, but I hope by now fully recovered.

Weighted with sorrow was the letter from Mrs. Jesse Ledford of Fayetteville which relates the death of her son-in-law, Pfc Donald Riggs, killed in action with the 26th Inf. Regt in Germany, and buried at Henri Chapelle Military Cemetery in Belgium. His wife, Letha Lee, was a pupil of mine at Pinnacle. Equally sorrowful was the news from Marion Bayles of St Paul of the death of his son, Pfc Marion E. Bayles Jr., who once worked with me in the forests of Washington, killed in action with the veteran 78th Inf Div in the First Army's push to the Rhine.

A veteran of World War I, W. B. Dixon of St. Paul, told where he was stationed during the first occupation of Germany; Ruby V. Hughes of Hindsville inquired if we are paid in German marks, we are - of American issue; and from Sherman Clark, the Sage of Hock's Creek, came an eloquent commentary on the death of President Roosevelt. Another doughboy of World War I, Elmer Oliver of Huntsville, sent a German post card which he picked up on the battlefield during the first great conflict. It followed me to Belgium and back to the "Fatherland" before I received it. I have sent it back, so the card has now crossed the Rhine four times and the ocean three during the two great wars.

Congressman J. W. Trimble, whom I still think of as the "Judge," sent an invitation to visit as soon as possible.

There were letters from Alta, and last but not least, a greeting card "To My Father" and scrawled in large irregular letters across the bottom, by a childish, unskilled hand, the signature "FARRELL."

And there were the copies of the Record which are always gladly received.

Capt. Orval E. Faubus

\* \* \*

## THE REGIMENT DEPARTS GERMANY

After moving to the Coblenz area it was generally accepted that the veteran Santa Fe Division would remain on occupation duty until it could be returned home. Then we heard that pleas had been made from officers in the upper echelon of command for duty in the Pacific. Soon we received word that the 35th would be hurried home where all personnel would be granted leave, after which the Division would be sent to the Pacific War.

In accordance with the new plans, on July 10 the Santa Fe Division was relieved of duty in the Coblenz area by elements of the 10th French Infantry Division.

On July 11th and 12th the 320th with other elements of the 35th moved by motor and rail to Camp Norfolk assembly area near Sommesous, France. Here we were billeted in tents set up in open fields. Preparations were under way to transport the Division via England to the States and thence to the Pacific. High point men, who did not volunteer for the Pacific War, were transferred out, and low point men were brought in to fill the ranks to the authorized strength.

\* \* \*

## HONOR GUARD FOR PRESIDENT TRUMAN

On July 11 the Santa Fe Division was signally honored. Of all the combat units in Europe the 137th Infantry Regiment of the 35th Division was selected as the guard of honor for President Harry S. Truman. At Camp White Tie near Brussels, Belgium, the regiment received the President, who was en route to the Potsdam Conference. The 137th was originally a National Guard unit from President Truman's home state of Missouri, and was federalized for active duty when the Division was activated in December, 1940. Also, the President had served as a captain in the 129th Field Artillery of the 35th Division in France during the first World War.

\* \* \*

# WE ALMOST LOSE SILVERMAN

Soon after arriving at Camp Norfolk some one discovered a short distance away a stream in which was a large pool. During my short stay with the unit there we sometimes went to the pool in the afternoon for swimming and a means of getting a bath.

On one of these occasions the group included, besides myself, "Red Cross Charlie," Capt. Silverman and Lts. Hendren, Leirer and Preston. The stream flowed into the pool along the edge of a gravel bar toward the opposite bank which caused a sharp turn to the right. The sharp turn caused the current to circle, creating a sort of whirlpool in the center in which the water swirled round and round. Consequently a floating object thrown into the pool, about 60 by 80 feet in size, would float in circles for some time before being caught by the exiting part of the current and carried down stream. A diving board projected from the bank facing the current as it flowed into the swimming area. Downstream perhaps a 100 yards distance were the remnants of a dam which had been destroyed.

On this occasion Sid, Hendren, myself and perhaps a few others were in the pool or around the edges while Leirer and Preston, fully dressed, were exploring the dam. There wasn't a real good swimmer in the crowd. I could barely stay afloat for brief periods while Sid could not swim at all, so we had our station on the gravel bar where the bank sloped into the round, deep hole of water.

Sid was trying to learn how to swim and I had showed him what I considered a safe way. Following my instructions he would wade out until the water came up to his shoulders, and then paddle back to the bank. Using this method, if he tired, or for any reason had to stop, he could always touch bottom and wade back to the gravel bar. Sid had been doing this for some time while I occasionally made an excursion into the water.

Returning to the bank from one of his practice trips, Sid got too close to the stream which entered the pool. When he let down, his feet touched bottom but the swift current swept him backward carrying him to depths over his head. Standing on the bank I saw him go under, and plunged for him immediately. I reached him, but because of my lack of skill, I could do nothing toward getting him to the bank. Then

I felt Sid release me and push me away. I struggled to the bank and gave the alarm.

Hendren was the first to hear and immediately plunged from the diving board into the center of the pool where the struggling Silverman was rising and sinking. Hendren could get hold of Sid, but he had not the skill to get him to shore. Time after time he brought him to the surface, sometimes kicking Silverman's body into the air. Fearing the death grip of the now drowning man, he avoided holding on to him. Finally completely exhausted, Hendren caught hold of the diving board and pulled himself from the water to recover his breath.

Observing early that Hendren couldn't properly handle the situation, we kept up our importuning shouts for help. We could see Leirer on the dam, who could hear our cries but in the roar of the stream couldn't understand what we were saying. Finally we made him understand something was wrong and he shouted for Preston who was downstream beyond the sound of our voices. They both came rushing back and arrived just after the exhausted Hendren had crawled from the water. At that moment, the already unconscious, limp body of Silverman, caught in the circling pool, swirled near the surface, his dark hair showing through the dark green water near the diving board. Preston dashed out on the board, bent down and grasped the inert form by the hair, and quickly dragged the body to the shore. He stretched Silverman out on the sloping bank, his head downward, to drain the water from his lungs. In a few moments Sid had regained consciousness, and a short time later appeared to be all right.

What a relief! What a relief! when Silverman had recovered. In the minds of all was the unspoken thought - what a ludicrous distortion of fate it would have been for this intrepid man of combat to have drowned in this small hole of water no larger than an indoor swimming pool, with comrades around him, after his life had been preserved through all the perils of combat. He had been wounded by an S-mine near St. Lo which took the lives of two of his close friends, and, in a rare act of loyalty and devotion, had returned the following day to the lines, his hand encased in bandages and his arm in a sling, forsaking the safety of a hospital where he could have remained for two weeks. He had escaped the deadly strafing of the plane that day on the crest of a hill near Boulaide in the terrible Ardennes battle, - strafing which killed three soldiers and wounded others nearby. He had been bounced by exploding 88s, avoided the flying shrapnel of the enemy artillery, narrowly missed the thousands of zipping bullets which had come his way, and come safely through many missions in the blackness of night during ten long months of combat.

After the avoidance of the near tragedy at the pool, we all felt sudued in a strange sort of way. We continued for some time to shake our heads in seeming disbelief, that the life of such a veteran of combat could be lost in an activity which offered no apparent risk, in a place where, with the caution we were exercising, there was so little danger.

After awhile we gathered our belongings and together went to a small cafe in a little village nearby. We ordered some food and then some beer. Soon Glatzer, always the one to bring cheer whenever possible, began leading us in some silly French songs, one of which is used to teach the French language to children in school. Sid, although not yet feeling completely well, joined the singing. Then we parodied, "Oh, Once There Were Three Fishermen," substituting the names of our comrades. By the time we returned to camp we had, in a sense, by the custom long before made necessary by combat losses, put the near tragedy behind us.

The event, because it had turned out well, had now become one of those experiences which we could recall with jest and laughter. Many other occurrences had not turned out well, resulting in the loss of the lives of our comrades. Of those who had been lost, we always spoke soberly, with an attitude of respect, and reverent memory for friends we would never see again.

I cannot recall now the whereabouts of "Red Cross" Charlie while Sid was in the pool. It seems he was on the gravel bar with me. However that doesn't seem right because Charlie was a trained wrestler and quite athletic. Surely, if he had been present, he would have been able to help in the rescue. He might have been downstream with Preston, or it is possible he joined us later at the cafe and was not at the scene of the near tragedy. I made no notes at the time and can now write of the event only from memory.

Some time later I mentioned to Sid that while we had hold of each other underneath the water, he had released his grasp and pushed me away.

"Yes," he explained, "I remembered that you could bare-ly swim, and I thought if I were going to drown, there was no reason to take you with me."

His cool, clear thinking and voluntary release of a would-be-rescuer under such circumstances, showed the unexcelled self-discipline and self-control developed by many of the veterans of long experience in combat.

\* \* \*

## I JOIN THE 75TH, THE 35TH GOES HOME

Along with many other highpoint men, I was transferred from the Regiment not long after we arrived at Camp Norfolk. I was assigned to the First Battalion, 289th Regiment of the 75th Infantry Division at Camp Oklahoma City. The 75th had entered combat during the Ardennes Campaign, fighting on the northern flank of the Bulge. Later the 320th was attached to the Division and fought with it in the Ruhr Pocket, although I did not recall that experience at the time I joined the unit. The men of the 75th had learned much of war, but even so, had been in combat only about four months compared to our ten. I did not observe many tired, strained, faces among its officers and men such as the "Old Originals" in the 35th Division.

Then came news of the victory in the Pacific. Shortly afterwards I visited the old outfit for the last time. I recall that my old buddy, Milt Ginsberg, was one of those who had volunteered to stay with the 320th for duty in the Pacific War, a decision he seemed to regret at times afterward. When I arrived at the regimental area I found great rejoicing and much celebration of the end of the War with Japan. That was the happiest I have ever seen Milt. I rejoiced with him, and all the others.

When I left that evening to return to my post of duty, I had, without knowing it at the time, said farewell forever to the 320th Infantry Regiment as a military organization. Likewise it was the last time I ever saw Col Byrne and many more of my fellow officers and men of the unit. When I took my leave of them I was saying good bye to even more. For in the days to come there would not again be found the unpar-alled comradeship, the selfless devotion to duty, the high meas-ure of discipline and good order, the absence of pettiness and envy, or the unmatched standards of honor, all of which we had known as we struggled together in a great conflict for the principles of justice and freedom.

Plans for the movement of the Division to the States were so far advanced that no change was made in the schedule. As a result all the troops with the 35th, including the low point men, got home ahead of high point men who had been transferred to other units.

The 137th Regiment sailed on the SS Cristobel on Aug. 23, arriving on Aug. 31 at Boston Harbor and Camp Miles Standish. From there the troops went on leave to assemble later with other units at Camp Breckenridge, Kentucky.

Beginning on Aug. 15 the Division, including the 320th, and less the 137th, moved, in a four-day period, to the Port of Le Havre for transportation to England. The 35th departed from Southhampton, England on Sept. 5 aboard the Queen Mary - the world's third largest liner afloat, and holder of the trans-Atlantic crossing record. The Santa Fe arrived at New York Harbor in five days, Sept. 10. From there the troops entrained for Camp Kilmer, New Jersey - where the "Old Originals" had staged prior to sailing to combat - and then scattered throughout the country on 30 and 45 day furloughs.

When the men of the 35th reassembled at Camp Breckenridge, the Division's strength was quickly cut. High point men were discharged back to civilian life. Their job in the war was finished. The low point men, and those who wanted to remain in the Army, were transferred to other active units.

On Dec. 7, 1945, four years after Pearl Harbor, the 35th Infantry ceased to exist as a unit of the Army of the United States.

The tracks of the Santa Fe had come to an end, but some old veterans of the Division, proudly wearing the blue and white wagon wheel shoulder patch, were still leaving individual trails about the continent of Europe and other places.

Other high point men of the 320th joined the 75th, among them Capt Ekstrum, formerly of Co B and Cannon Company. Whenever any of them came to the unit, we always had a joyous reunion.

## CHAPTER X

## EUROPE AFTER THE WAR

### VISIT TO GREAT BRITAIN

With the 289th Infantry of the 75th Division, there was little to do except the ordinary military housekeeping chores. About one-third of the men and officers were on leave most of the time, with trips to the United Kingdom, Denmark, Belgium, Switzerland and various parts of France. Shortly after joining the Division I made a seven-day tour of England and Scotland, but took no other leave.

On the trip across the channel to London, I observed on the ship a considerable number of Polish troops, both men and women. As we moved slowly in port, either at the beginning or ending of the brief voyage, we discovered a warship flying the Polish national colors. As if drawn by a magnet the Poles, aroused by the sight of their flag, gathered by the rail nearest the war vessel and spontaneously burst into song, singing the national anthem of their country. It was quite a moving experience to observe the incident. Their intense longing for their homeland, from which they had been exiled by the war, was keenly apparent.

At that time with the Allied banners crowned with victory, the Poles were expected to return to their country and set up a free government of their own choosing. Sadly such was not to be their happy fate. Poland fell under the Communist yoke, and those brave Poles who did return have lived under a form of repression only slightly less severe than that from which they had escaped by the defeat of the Nazi conquerors.

The tour of Scotland was especially interesting. I visited Edinburgh, a great educational center, and walked up and down Prince's Street, claimed by many to be the most attractive in the world. In the beautiful park beside the street were two objects of particular note. Growing flowers formed the Roman numerals of a clock, all the works underground except for the moving hands, which told the time of day as accurately as any other time piece. Nearby, growing flowers formed pictures of Roosevelt, Churchill and Stalin, the features so well shaped that they were as easily recognized as would be any photograph of the three famous personages. What detailed planning and meticulous care was required on the part of the gardner, to shape the perfectly formed numerals and outline of the clock, and the striking likenesses of the three world figures.

I spent one day sailing on Loch Lommond, taking passage up and down the lake on a regular passenger boat of considerable size. It was one of those rarely beautiful days on the British Island. The sun shone from cloudless heavens of flawless blue, and the azure hue of the sky was reflected by the clear water of the lake. Flocks of white sea gulls followed the craft throughout the voyage, often catching in mid-air particles of food thrown from the moving vessel.

The passengers were about 50 percent tourists - armed forces personnel - and the other half residents of the region. Among the latter were a Scottish grandmother and her two charges, - twin grandchildren about four years of age, a boy and a girl, dressed in the colorful Highland Kilts. The little girl was quite tractible, but the little boy was up and down and constantly chattering. Once the grandmother rushed over to him and exclaimed, "David! How aboot resting your tongue for a moment?"

After a time another tourist and myself offered the twins - they were the object of much attention partly because of their colorful dress - some chewing gum. They regarded the proffered objects with rapt attention, and it was readily apparent the gum was strange to them. We soon found it was the first they had ever seen. The children did not know how to unwrap the sticks of gum, and still less what to do with them afterward. The grandmother with an attitude of great concern rushed over to us and, in the dialect made familiar by the writings of Robert Burns, exclaimed in rapid speech, "Dinae waste it on them! They dinae what tis! Dinae waste it on them! They dinae what tis!"

What a refreshing experience for a change. On the continent (except for our initial contact with the rural French residents) and in urban England, the people had come to regard all American soldiers as capitalists. They not only took without hesitation everything that was offered but often unashamedly asked for whatever we had. Groups of English urchins followed GIs asking, "Gum, Chum?" French youngsters requested "Choc-co-lat," and sometimes asked for "cigarette pour Papa?" (a cigarette for Papa?) Once we noted an amusing switch. A middle aged Frenchman asked, "Cigarette pour babee?" (a cigarette for baby) meaning, we supposed, his wife or daughter.

The emphasis of the word, waste, by the Scottish grandmother reminded me of my father. When we children were growing up he often urged us either to consume or to save the already prepared food and "not let it go to waste." Dad had probably never read any back issues of Poor Richard's Almanac (he would have if they had been available) but constantly urged thrift for all the family and never himself wasted anything. He saved empty buckets, cans and jars for possible future use, scraps of leather, extra bolts and nuts, pieces of metal and planks, unused boards (shingles), even used nails, bent or straight. Once he paid me five cents per hundred for extracting and saving the used nails from the decayed roof of an old barn. Almost always Dad found a use for everything that was saved, either in the repair of our tools, harness and vehicles, or in making something new.

I recall also that Mother always saved the buttons from worn out clothing. The buttons were reused to replace those lost from clothes in use, or to place on new, homemade garments.

As I grew older I had thought that my father's urge to save came from the difficult conditions under which he had been reared and in which we still lived while he was bringing up his family. After hearing the emphasis on waste by the Scottish grandmother and observing more of the traits of the residents of Scotland, I concluded that his thrift came from our Highland ancestors, and the inherited trait was merely encouraged by the less than modest circumstances in which we lived.

Later I found a monument or marker on which were inscribed the names of the great Scottish clans, and the particular plaid or tartan for each. I bought a few items of my clan, Forbes - Faubus is a derivation or offshoot of the name. (The first immigrant of my Scottish ancestry landed in America in 1750.) No true Scotsman, I was informed, ever wears any tartan except that of his own clan.

## WITH THE 289TH INFANTRY

While with the 289th at Camp Oklahoma City I was in charge of a formation of troops almost every day. At one of the assemblies, I had the pleasure of decorating a member of the Nisei, a Japanese American. Like myself, a high point man transferred to the 75th, his award earned during combat, had finally caught up with him. During the war two combat battalions made up of these troops were recognized as being among the finest combat units of the war.

The commanding officer of the First Battalion, 289th Infantry was Lt. Col. Henry K. Fluck of Somerset, Pa. Others among my fellow officers there were Arnold Rawitz of Newark, N. J.; H. P. Jacobs of Brooklyn, N. Y.; Alfred C. Boorman of Muskegon, Mich.; William H. Mayhall of Coolville, Ohio; Lowell M. Brooks of Vermillion, S. D.; Walter A. Miller of Schenewes, (near Cooperstown), N. Y.; A. V. Hummel of Clearfield, Pa.; Charles L. Lory of Los Angeles, Calif.; Irving Smorask of Long Beach, Calif.; John L. Green of Bowling Green, Ky.; U. S. Alexander of Minneapolis, Minn.; Jno. G. Manners of Pryor, Okla.; and Kenneth A. Hale of Watrous, Pa.

## DETERIORATION OF THE ARMY

Some time in the autumn, the date and circumstances now forgotten, I was transferred from the 75th Division to Camp Pittsburg, near Rheims, France. Duty here included military house keeping and servicing transient troops being deployed home.

By now the high discipline and good order for which the American Army up to then had been noted, had disappeared. Gone was the unit loyalty and the excellent "espret de corps." Everyone was bitching, including doctors and Red Cross personnel, even the chaplains, except a few of us old combat men who were glad just to be alive.

The Red Cross man at Camp Pittsburgh was just the opposite of "Red Cross" Charlie. He spent most of his time in Paris and took care of the needs of the men not at all. A

Catholic chaplain declined to write the parents of a Catholic soldier who was accidently killed or had committed suicide. I shouldered the task in his stead, and assisted another chaplain in the funeral service. Men took off without authorization for various places, mostly Paris, returning when they were ready or not at all. A guard detail list would be posted and only a few of the men would appear. These, and other infractions of rules and regulations, were transgressions for which disciplinary action would formerly have been swift and certain.

The camp was a sea of mud most of the time, but billets and tents were comfortable compared to maneuver or combat conditions. Food was adequate, there were USO and Red Cross personnel on duty all the time, and leave was easy to obtain. Yet no one was happy. Everyone, it seemed, wanted to go home at once, or else to run about Europe or engage in black market activity. Those who had been most responsible soldiers during combat in the finest American Army ever put together, now declined and often refused, to accept any responsibility or to perform properly any assigned duty.

Agitation and complaints, fanned by editorials and news in the official publication, "Stars and Stripes," became rife. Open and defiant demonstrations broke out. Officers were uneasy and often uncertain how to handle them. Some were frightened at the possible consequences. One demonstration and protest meeting, which I ignored, occurred in Camp Pittsburgh, but drew only a small number of protestors.

The camp commander, Col. Frank R. Williams, was a very fine commander, and his executive officer, Lt. Col. Russell O. Harris, was very helpful. Col. Williams did the best he could under the difficult conditions. He finally designated me as commander of the headquarters company and camp personnel. The number of men under my command fluctuated from 50 to 600 creating a most difficult administrative problem.

The personnel files were in the worst possible shape. There were 135 men assigned to the company on paper who could not be found. I enlisted the help of some experienced personnel non-coms and some combat sergeants in an attempt to set the records in order. We found many individuals listed on more than one order, some on as many as three different directives. Therefore if these soldiers reported for duty to their new stations on one set of orders, as undoubtedly most of them had, they were missing and presumed to be AWOL at other places. Finally, by diligent research of the files, we accounted for all except 25 of the missing men.

Gradually, by fairness, kindness, understanding, pleading, cajolry and threats of disciplinary action, some of which were carried out, I was able to bring some semblance of order out of the confusion and mass chaos. I had no commissioned officer to assist me most of the time - only non-commissioned officers and a few willing privates.

I wrote the following at Camp Pittsburgh, France, Nov. 30, 1945.

"Life here in the Assembly Area Command is the dullest yet to Americans in the ETO. Dissatisfaction, discontent and morale are the worst I have ever seen. A few want to be discharged to work in Europe, or to wait and come home with their European wives. The great majority of the men have one all consuming desire - to go home as soon as possible.

The personal problems of the men are almost innumerable. Being in command of the largest group of men in this camp, a battery of about 400, a host of those problems are dumped into my lap. A commander is responsible for so much - morale, behavior, information, cleanliness, sanitation, property, etc. The past month has been the busiest in my army career (excluding combat). I have worked every day including Sundays and holidays, and part of the time at night."

Toward the end of my tour of duty at Camp Pittsburgh I was placed in command of the large area designated for the use of deploying troops. Assigned to assist me were one officer (possibly 1st Lt. Homer K. Presson), one enlisted man and 70 German prisoners-of-war.

The lieutenant was very good at handling the German prisoners and kept the area well policed (cleaned up) and ready for the transient troops. He had learned a few German phrases and used them effectively. The PWs worked under leadership from their own ranks without any American supervision. Sometimes, especially on rainy or cold days, the lieutenant, on an inspection trip, would find them idling in the tents they were cleaning.

"Ferstein ze arbiten?" (Do you understand work) the lieutenat would inquire.

"Yah, yah, yavold," (Yes, Yes) the Germans would reply.

"Mock schnell!" (Damned quick) was the lieutenant's rejoinder, and the work would proceed expeditiously.

My general assistant was the enlisted man, who was fresh over from the States without having heard a gun fired in anger. My company clerk and other office personnel were German prisoners-of-war, as well as my jeep driver.

In the area in my charge were thousands of dollars worth of GI material, - tents, blankets, stoves and cots, and mess halls complete with equipment. Technically and legally I was responsible for the equipment and could be charged with its loss. The PWs were basically honest, as most Germans were found to be, making the property quite secure during the day. However at night when the PWs were confined, most of the camp could have been hauled away by GIs or French civilians without discovery during the time of the theft.

I asked Col. Williams about security for my area, and he gave me the name of a Regular Army unit nearby which could supply troops for guard duty. I called the unit and the commander said a contingent of troops would be sent. Since guard duty is always considered a most responsible assignment, I had the PWs fix up a comfortable billet for the men of the guard detail, with everything arranged to meet their needs.

In due time the sergeant of the guard, a Negro, reported to me. His detail was made up entirely of Negro soldiers, which was perfectly all right with me. I took him first to the quarters which had been prepared for the guard detail, then showed him the area to be secured, and described the various posts which I had worked out ahead of time. I explained that each member of the detail would have only one day's duty of not more than four hours walking post, which could be broken up as the sergeant directed, to be followed by two days without any duty at all.

Two days later I checked the area to see how the detail was functioning. I could find no guard anywhere but had no time to check further then. The next night I checked and again found no men on guard anywhere.

I decided to go to their quarters to determine why no guard was posted as had been directed.

Taking my enlisted assistant in the jeep with the German driver, I went to the large Bronson hut which served as quarters for the guardsmen. Upon approaching the building we could hear commotion and the sounds of revelry. It took only a glance to reveal what was going on and why no guards were at their posts. The big hut was filled with drunken GIs and French prostitutes.

At considerable risk from the drunken Negroes, being at the time unarmed except for a flashlight, I apprehended as many of the prostitutes as possible. At one time I had to rescue my enlisted assistant, who reported that some of the women and GIs had escaped into the dark woods to the rear of the building. The German driver remained seated in the jeep watching the proceedings by the headlights of the vehicle. I have never seen a man laugh harder that the driver, as he watched the prostitutes being herded, disheveled and barefoot, through the cold, deep mud to the vehicle. The dozen or more females we were able to apprehend were transported to military police headquarters, a few blocks distant, and turned over to the American police. From there they were handed over to the French gendarmes. I'm sure that was the end of the incident so far as the prostitutes were concerned. The American authorities had no jurisdiction over French civilians.

As for security of the property in my area, I concluded it was useless to rely further on the guard detail for any assistance. All should have been courtmartialed for dereliction of duty, but from past experience I knew it would be difficult to obtain convictions since, because of the darkness, I could have personally identified, in a trial, no more than two or three of the drunken soldiers. By threatening courtmartial proceedings I got the entire detail withdrawn from my area by 10:00 A. M. the next morning. With the one officer, one enlisted man and the prisoners-of-war, we maintained the security of the area as best we could. With no guard at all the area was far more secure, than with the soldiers who had been provided, who had failed to post a guard at any time.

## LT MORRIS BART

Not long after the unpleasant episode with the guard detail, I had a stroke of good fortune. I discovered one evening a newcomer sauntering forlornly about the billeting area for the regular personnel. He had just arrived and was awaiting the assignment of quarters, which was difficult because of limited space. I invited him to share my quarters, a rather spacious room where I was alone at the time, and helped him to move in. He was Lt. Morris Bart of Knoxville, Tenn., who had been a liaison pilot in a flap flap with an artillery unit during combat.

A more quiet, friendly, helpful fellow I have never met. I got Bart assigned to duty with me and asked him to search out and list all the equipment in my jurisdiction. I didn't want to be charged with so much lost property that it would require the rest of my life to pay for it, and there was no way to account for the military equipment without an inventory. We didn't know then that all this mattered little. All the property was soon given away to foreign countries, mostly to France. We were still trying to act and work in a responsible manner and according to the proper regulations we had learned.

Bart and I visited much in our room at night, never going out for any function, and declining the opportunities for pass to the nearby towns. We naturally related to each other some of our war experiences.

One of Bart's venture's which I considered quite amusing, occurred shortly before the war ended. He was making a trip in his little plane, flying across enemy territory, when he felt the call of nature. There being no provision to answer such an urge in one of those little aircraft, he picked out a likely field and set the plane down behind the enemy lines. Leaving the motor running he got out, but before he could finish the homeguard German forces were coming from the woods across the field toward him. He finished, jumped in the cockpit, gunned the engine and took off, a few shots whistling by as the plane lifted.

I always thought it most unusual and very funny, that a man would land a plane behind the enemy lines, and risk being killed or captured, just to "take a leak."

Bart could have departed for the States two months or more before he left, but voluntarily stayed with me longer to help get the property list in order. He remained out of pure friendship for me, as well as a sense of duty, although not much patriotism was being shown by the American forces in Europe at that time. Then, with misty eyes, we reluctantly said goodbye at Camp Herbert Tareytown near Le Havre after leaving Camp Pittsburgh. Before leaving, Morris visited a town on the coast to see, standing in the town square, a statue of Jean Bart, one of his ancestors.

He had a Swiss fiancee who preceded him to the States where they were married after he arrived home.

## LT LLOYD BORCHERDING

Another happy development for me at Camp Pittsburgh was the arrival of Lt. Lloyd Borcherding. A pleasant, affable officer from Hooks, Texas, near Texarkana, he replaced Lt. Presson who had been transferred. With all the discomfort and problems of the camp, Borcherding was as happy as could be with me because his previous duty had been even more unpleasant. Not only had discipline failed in his former unit, but dissension had broken out with sometimes attacks on officers. Grenades were thrown into their beds at night and casualties had resulted. Our service together was most pleasant. A dutiful officer who was of great help, Borcherding's cheerful, willing attitude was quite remarkable amidst the heedlessness and complaints of so many others.

## CAMP HERBERT TAREYTON

The unpleasant winter duty with the discontented forces at Camp Pittsburgh ended in the early spring of 1946. Transferred to Camp Herbert Tareyton near the port of Le Havre, I soon found myself in charge of the huge sprawling camp and, as headquarters commandant, in command of all American forces there.

The principal difficulty at Tareyton was to hold in check the black market selling of everything in camp. Items being stolen and marketed included not only clothing but cots, blankets, weapons and kitchen equipment. Again, as I later learned, it didn't matter much so far as the property was concerned. It was the breakdown of discipline, law and order, and the encouragement of dishonesty which proved so damaging.

The principal black marketeers were soldiers, both black and white, who jumped ship to avoid returning to the States. They would return, hide out in the camp, steal and market army goods. With the income they were leading the "Life of Riley" in the bordellos and hotspots of Paris and other French towns. Some were finally stopped by being captured and turned over to the MPs where they were held until placed, still in custody, aboard ships returning home.

RESTRICTED

HEADQUARTERS
CAMP PITTSBURGH
REIMS GARRISON AREA

SPECIAL ORDER)                    APO 806
NUMBER        26)                 28 Jan 46

E X T R A C T

21. A Special Court-Martial is appointed to meet at Camp
Pittsburgh, France at 1000 hours on 28 January 1946, or as
soon thereafter as practicable for the trial of such persons
as may properly be brought before it.

### DETAIL FOR THE COURT

CAPT ORVAL FAUBUS (INF)
CAPT JOSEPH P HOLENHAM (MC)
CAPT ROBERT J KUHLMANN (FA)
1ST LT EARL K BUCHAN (INF)
1ST LT CHARLES H GILL (INF)
2ND LT CHARLES E BLAKE (INF)

1st LT MILES B SHOOKMAN (QMC) Trial Judge Avocate
1ST LT MYRON H EBERLE (INF) Ass't Trial Judge Adv
1ST LT MORRIS BART JR (FA) Defense Counsel
2ND LT LEONARD F WLODAZEWSKI (INF) Ass't Defense Counsel

All unarraigned cases in the hands of the Trial Judge
Advocate of the Special Court appointed per Par 9, SO No.
23, this Hq, dtd 25 Jan 46, will be brought to trial before the
court hereby appointed.

### BY ORDER OF COLONEL WILLIAMS:

CECIL E. SULLIVAN
2nd Lt., Infantry
Adjutant

### COMMUNISTS MOVE TO TAKE OVER

Once Chaplain Beirie, before leaving for the States, attended a conclave of high Catholic Church officials some-

where in Germany where he met and conversed with the top church officer in the country. Upon his return he related to me the confidential warning which the Catholic leader had sent personally to President Truman. The gist of the secret message was that the President had better move with dispatch to assume firm control in the American zone or the Communists would take over all of Germany and move into other countries further west.

The chaplain and I agreed the warning was timely. Most American soldiers at the time had no interest in political events but those of us who were politically aware could see the trend of the times. Having Russia as a much needed ally, without whose help we could well have lost the war, had brought about a warm feeling for the Soviets. The ravages of their country and the persecution and imprisonment of the Russian people by Hitler's military forces and his Gestapo political machine, had created a sympathy among Americans and many others for almost everything Russian. In our gratitude for the help of the Red Army in defeating Hitler's awesome war machine, there was a tendency to forget the tyranny of the Communist system with its merciless purges and executions, and the supression of many of the freedoms in which we believed. Also, it was the policy of the Allied forces, which occupied all of Germany, to remove from all political offices those who served during Hitler's regime, as well as all workers in key positions in communication, transportation, education, news media and other fields, who were adjudged sympathetic to the Nazi Party.

Taking full advantage of this situation, the Russian Communists attempted to get their Red German agents into political offices and key positions in industry even in the zones controlled by the Americans, British and French. The Communists also became super active in the Low Countries and in France. Throughout these countries in every village and town, Communist speakers could be seen almost daily, haranguing crowds from their soap boxes in open meetings in the public squares or from forums in public buildings.

At one time the Communist Party of France, feeding on the conditions created by the ravages of war and the uncertainties and disruptions which followed, almost took over that country by political means. It elected large numbers of officials including the governing bodies of many towns and provinces. I recall that the city of Rheims had a Communist mayor and other city officials while I was stationed near there in the latter part of 1945 and early 1946.

Failing in this legitimate effort the Communists later on planned a takeover by their favorite means - demonstrations, disorder and barricades in the streets. Without the determiniation and courage of Charles De Gaulle, who mustered the French armed forces to maintain order, I am convinced the French Reds would have carried out their plan, and might have succeeded.

## WINSTON CHURCHILL DEFEATED

There were Leftist trends in other areas favorable to the Communists. During my furlough in England and Scotland, I spent much time listening closely to the talk of the people. I was alone among my American comrades in correctly forecasting the results of the British elections. A Labor government was elected and installed, as the people turned out of office Winston Churchill, Britain's greatest leader during its time of direst peril and most urgent need.

The greatest spokesman of freedom during the century and perhaps for all time, Churchill had by his unmatched eloquence and inspiring courage, saved England from defeat in its time of greatest danger. By his perseverance through military misfortune after misfortune, and his unwavering determination in the face of almost insurmountable odds, he kept England in the war, while he prayerfully waited for the help he hoped would come from America, without which he knew he could not win. His words kept hope alive in the hearts of the free as well as the already enslaved. His actions held at bay the fearful German war machine, behind which had developed a repression seldom equaled in human history, a system of slavery of vast proportions which included millions of nationals from the conquered countries, and a new, scientific barbarism with the most systematic and appalling torture and butchery of human beings in the history of the world.

At that time my sentiments were pro-Labor Party rather than Conservative. It appeared that those who had compromised with Hitler and signed the Munich pact, thus consigning the great Czech people to Hitler's enslavement, were among those in the Conservative ranks. Such cowardly, selfish acts of appeasement as Munich, had contributed to the

— 663 —

rise of the German leader until his war machine threatened the whole world, and brought us into the conflict. And there were still then in England within the Conservative Party, those who believed in the existence of a class of the high born who never worked. Realizing that without work no one would ever have anything, and having struggled for all I had ever obtained, I could not in anywise accept such a theory.

Still Churchill, though a Conservative by label, had opposed the appeasement of the "Little Corporal," as he termed Hitler, and, by his attitude during the war, had rejected the idea of a privileged class whose members performed no useful labor. In the face of these facts, I, like the great majority of Americans at that time, found it difficult to understand his rejection by a people whose very lives and freedom he had been instrumental in saving. To turn the great leader out of office before there could be returned home from victory, the men he had so greatly inspired, and the armies he had so ably directed, appeared completely unjustified.

## THE YALTA AGREEMENT

Churchill was not so naive as to believe that we could easily do business with the Soviets, which was contrary to the hopeful view of the Americans. Years after the great conflict, the thought was expressed that Churchill wanted the Western Allied Armies to drive farther to the east when opportunity afforded in the closing days of the war. However, according to the terms of an agreement worked out at Yalta and Teheran by Roosevelt, Stalin and Churchill, a line of demarcation had already been established which precluded a deeper penetration by the British and Americans without breaching the contract. Gen. Patton had probably advanced too far when he liberated Prague, the capital of the freedom-loving Czechs, and the 320th Regiment and the 83rd Division had crossed the agreed line in the Elbe River bridgehead. That was the reason our advance stopped, approximately two weeks before the Armistice, when our armies could easily have driven to Berlin and beyond. The American Armies having reached the agreed line of demarcation, and in some cases advanced beyond the boundary, were ordered to stop and wait until the Russians reached our lines.

The agreement reached by the Big Three at Yalta and Teheran, to which Churchill may have been a reluctant partner, contained a number of items affecting Europe other than the establishment of a line between the Red Army and the forces of the Western Allies.

It is generally understood that the agreement (1) made no mention of the Baltic states of Latvia, Esthonia and Lithuania, forcibly occupied by the Red Army even before the war began. (2) The Red Army would occupy eastern Austria and northern Iran while the British and American armies would take over the other portions of those countries. (3) The Russians were granted full sway over Poland, Czecho-Slovakia, Hungary, Rumania and Bulgaria, while the British and Americans would be in control in France, Luxembourg, Belgium, Holland and Denmark. (4) Germany would be divided, the Russians taking the eastern part, with the British in the north, the Americans in the south, and the French occupying certain sections in the west along the Rhine. (5) The Big Three powers would share in that strange three-way division and control of Berlin, deep within the Russian Zone. (6) When the issues of the war had been finally settled, the agreement called for the withdrawal of military forces from all occupied countries except Germany, permitting these formerly independent states to establish freely organized governments of their own choice. (7) The ultimate fate of Germany would be determined eventually by conference of the Big Three with France participating in the consultation.

## THE AGREEMENT BROKEN

How has Soviet Russia on the one hand and the Western Alliance on the other, lived up to the terms of the agreement? Before very long all the nations under the hegemony of the two Western powers were completely free, and British and American troops were withdrawn from western Austria and southern Iran.

On the other hand, Latvia, Esthonia and Lithuania have disappeared as free nations, having been incorporated by armed might as integral parts of Red Russia. In addition huge chunks of Poland and Rumania, and sections of Germany, Czecho-Slovakia and Bulgaria were annexed to the Soviet Union. The Red Army has not been withdrawn from a single country it fully occupied. Puppet Communist governments were set up in Poland, Czecho-Slovakia, Hungary, Bulgaria and Rumania, and the peoples of those countries remain in complete subjugation to Russian Communism. The subjugation is enforced by the tanks and guns of the Red Army, and the political and economic decisions are made by Russian Commissars. Red Army troops continued to occupy the parts of Austria and Iran under Soviet control, and only the courage and determination of President Harry S. Truman finally impelled their withdrawal from those countries. Likewise the daring and audacious use of the Berlin Airlift by President Truman was necessary to thwart the Russian effort to take complete possession of the former German capital city.

It is tragic to recall that the Poles and Czechs who escaped their countries to fight heroically with our armies, and some with the Russian Armies, did not gain that for which they fought - freedom in their homelands. Among the thousands upon thousands of slave laborers we found and liberated within the borders of the Fatherland, some of whom I personally conducted out of Germany, the Poles, Czechs, Slovaks, Rumanians and Bulgarians were not permitted to return to freedom in their own countries. Those who went home still live, 25 years later, under a form of Communist tyranny.

Because of Russia's part in the war, the heroic defense of the Red Army against the attack of the Nazi juggernaut and the suffering of the Russian people from Hitler's invasion, the Soviet government was entitled to every consideration in shaping the terms of the war settlement. However, after receiving due consideration it is now plain that the Soviets have not lived up to the terms of the agreements reached by the three heads of state. It should be equally plain to all fairminded people, after the Hungarian freedom fighters were drowned in blood spilled by Soviet guns, and the slight movement to freedom in Czecho-Slovakia was chilled by Russian tanks, that a Communist system of tyranny prevails over all these countries. It should likewise be clear that the system of government in those formerly free nations is imposed by an outside force and maintained by terror and military might. It is also apparent that the peoples of these subjugated countries, given the freedom of choice which we Americans still exercise, would overwhelmingly reject the Communist tyranny imposed upon them by a foreign power - Soviet Russia.

The unfolding events since the war often lead to speculation. Was it wise to trust the Communists to keep an agreement with those they had professed to fear, and had consistently condemned for a quarter of a century prior to the outbreak of World War Two? Was it good judgment to accept the terms of an agreement which placed the Western Allies in a position from which it was impossible to intervene if the pact were violated?

I feel certain that President Roosevelt believed that by the terms of the agreement, he had reasonably assured the freedom of the Czechs and the Poles in their own countries, - the very areas in which the war began. Tragically, this has not been the case.

Would it not have been better to rely on the fairness and good judgment of the leaders of Britain and America, dealing from a position of strength, rather than risk the freedom of so many brave people to the terms of an agreement of the kind so seldom kept? Was it wise to place too much faith in a nation whose leaders had never espoused the principles of freedom for which we fought, and which might never have been our ally in the conflict except for Hitler's invasion?

If there had been no agreed demarcation line, and our commanders, such as Gen. Patton, had been permitted to drive deep into Czecho-Slovakia, Austria and Germany, a position of strength would have been established from which to negotiate for the freedom of those we fought to save. If this, or some other course, had been chosen, rather than blind faith in a pact to which the Soviets never in the least adherred, millions of people might now be free who are today inextricably trapped behind the Iron Curtain.

## GEN CHARLES DE GAULLE

Some time in the late spring of 1946, in preparation for the abandonment of Camp Herbert Tareyton, I was sent with a jeep and driver to Frankfort, Germany, to deliver the camp records to the American Army Headquarters. I found the offices of the headquarters in a large, modern, multi-storied building. Everything was polished and shining. There were dozens of civilian typists and clerks, and still more enlisted men and officers clothed in clean, pressed, dress uniforms and highly polished boots and shoes. I couldn't help but marvel at the great contrast with the battle conditions we had known during combat, and afterward the crude, meagre furnishings of the redeployment camps set in the mud of France.

On the return journey our route crossed and followed, for a distance, the main highway leading from Paris to Coblenz. On this road we met a large French convoy composed mostly of civilian cars, and pulled over to let the speeding vehicles pass. I noted insignia of rank on a number of vehicles, and banners flying from others. Then in one car I caught a good look at the tall, angular figure and the prominent nose of the ruler of France, Gen Charles De Gaulle. The French leader with quite a retinue, was on his way to Coblenz for a public ceremony about which I read the next day.

The public ceremony was held in the stadium, built by the American Army of Occupation during its stay in the area following World War One, and which the 35th Division had repaired, refurbished and renamed the Santa Fe Stadium during our brief tour of duty there. The facility, toward which the Frenchmen were speeding as I saw them pass, now bore the name of Stad De Gaulle.

Two of the cars, not yet equipped with new rubber, fell out of the convoy with flat tires. Still carrying out the spirit of aid to an ally, my driver and I stopped and helped some rather fat, well dressed French civilians repair the tires. I was impressed that they didn't appear very appreciative.

## RETURN TO NORMANDY

My duty in Europe nearing an end and Camp Herbert Tareyton in the closing stages of American control, I made my final journey in France before returning home. I returned to Normandy for two purposes - to view again the scene of our initial baptism of fire and see how the area looked in peace, and to visit the graves of some of my comrades who fell early in the struggle.

## GENERAL BERNARD LAW MONTGOMERY

Taking a jeep and a GI driver I journeyed the short distance down the coast and approached the Omaha Beach area on the road network leading through Caen. As we drove into the city I was forcefully struck with the battered and ruined condition of the buildings and the complete absence of the inhabitants. The outlying sections through which we drove were as vacant as No-Man's Land.

Very little repair had been made of the destruction of war wrought in the battle almost two years before, when Gen. Montgomery's force of British and Canadians sought to capture and hold the city on the left flank of the Normandy Invasion. The invasion successful, the Caen sector then became the hinge of the breakout effort from the beachhead area. Consequently the city had been pounded by artillery and bombs of both sides as the lines of combat swayed back and forth, before the Germans were finally driven to the east.

As we approached the heart of the city we discovered the reason for the absence of people in the outskirts. The inhabitants had gathered at a central location for a public ceremony. Crowds lined the streets and sidewalks for a parade, which was then in progress. The driver, at my direction, pulled our jeep to one side at the edge of the crowd to let the parade pass.

To my astonishment, having had no advance information of the ceremony, Bernard Law Montgomery, the famed British general who had led the Allied forces in the great battle there in June and July of 1944, was leading the parade. Standing erect on the side of a British military vehicle, turning his beret-clad head from side to side, the famous war leader, referred to as Monty in the press, and as "I-am-God" Montgomery in the unrecorded comments of our circles, was acknowledging the cheers of the crowds by slight, restrained, upward waves of his right hand. As I noted his austere manner and, to me, appearance of extreme confidence, in the only personal view I ever had of one of Britain's greatest heroes, the thought occurred to me then, as it has many times since as I have read of him in the news, that the title by which he was unofficially known in our circles was completely appropriate.

## MILITARY CEMETERIES

The ceremony and parade over, we drove along the streets of Caen through the dispersing crowds on our way to the Omaha Beach area.

In response to a sign of invitation to visitors, we stopped briefly at the mayor's office in the small village of St. Mere Eglise, the first French hamlet to be liberated in the Great Invasion. In signing the visitor's register I noted that Cardinal Spellman had affixed his name in the book only the day before.

In a military cemetery a short distance inland, I found the grave of Sgt. Horace Barnes of Huntsville, killed while fighting with another division in the Normandy Invasion. A few feet away in the same cemetery was the grave of Gen. Roosevelt, son of President Theodore Roosevelt, who had died of a heart attack while commanding one of the divisions in the beachhead fighting. Also buried there was Lt. Rufus Garrett of El Dorado, Ark. the husband of the former Agnes Soule, a classmate of high school days in Huntsville.

Situated on a slight plateau overlooking the beach and the sea to the north was a larger cemetery with the entrance toward the hedgerowed country to the south. Here I found the grave of Sgt Wallace Brent Cull. In this cemetery the uniform white crosses and Stars of David emblems were standing over the resting places of many other former comrades. Most of them had fallen in the hellish hedgerow fighting in the struggle for St Lo which preceded the great break through with Gen. Patton's armor. In response to requests previously received, I took a number of pictures which were mailed to relatives of the fallen heroes.

In one cemetery was a lone, unknown soldier kneeling by a white cross. He was visiting the grave of a brother. Finding he had no transportation, my driver and I took him with us for the balance of our tour.

## THE STONE HOUSE CP, NORMAN HOSTILITY

Finishing the tour of the cemeteries, I searched and found the stone house in the Norman orchard, where Maj Jamieson and I had spent our first hours under enemy fire, as we learned what we could of the situation and combat conditions before our comrades of the 320th joined us in the battle lines. The gaping holes in the walls of the house, and in the walls of other nearby buildings, had been repaired.

Some 200 feet to the south I looked on the side of a hill for the deep dugout which had served as part of our command post, and which housed Col. Byrne, Col. Northam, Maj. McElroy, Sgt. Kearns and others. Here in this area each had borne his particular burden and performed his assigned task in the fierce engagement which was the "baptism of fire" for the men of the regiment. The dugout had been filled, and the growing grass was obliterating the scar over the spot where the excavation and embanked earth once sheltered my comrades from enemy bullets, shells and bombs.

I recall that my visit to the area was on a Sunday, perhaps in early May, and a number of civilians, perhaps 15 to 20, were gathered at the site of the stone house. The attitude of those present, mostly young people - I did not observe an elderly person in the group - was rude and unfriendly. Only one showed enough courtesy to respond to a few questions and an explanation of my visit. How unlike the attitude of the French people we had encountered in other sections in earlier times. I had heard that considerable pro-German sentiment existed among some of the residents of Normandy. I never had an opportunity to determine the truth or falsity of the information, but I do know that I found among those gathered at that particular spot on that specific day, a more hostile posture than we had encountered even among the residents of conquered Germany.

Proceeding farther south to the location of other former battle lines, I was able to find, still remaining, two foxholes which I had dug. One was on a hillside close beside a hedge at the site of our command post from about July 21 to 27th. It was the hole into which I had crawled while watching our ack-ack try for bombing and strafing German planes, and where I heard Magallanes agree with Col. Byrne that the fireworks looked like a Fourth-of-July display, "only more serious, sir." From this place I had gone for my first bath after entering the lines; we were located there when Lt Underwood was killed; and we were there during the great bombing raid.

## CHANGES IN NORMANDY

However, it was difficult to identify our former areas of battle. The trees, shrubs and vines, which the Germans had forced the Norman farmers to allow to grow in order to provide better concealment and defense, were now neatly trimmed; the fields and orchards were cleared of weeds, briars and brush, and some in cultivation, thus wiping out the tracks of many war vehicles; the foxholes and dugouts were filled and the scars rapidly being obscured by grass and flowers; the buildings were mostly repaired and the fences rebuilt. Even the breaks in the hedgerows, which served as partitions between the fields and plots of Norman ground, had been closed. The many poles, placed upright in the ground of fields and level areas as hazards for our invading planes, gliders and paratroopers, had been removed. The war wounds of the countryside were quick to heal. Normandy after a year of peace, and almost two years after the conflict raged on its soil, looked a great deal unlike the Normandy of war which we had known.

The least change was to be found in the battered town of St. Lo. Very few repairs had been made, in fact some structures were beyond repair but none of these had been removed. The most notable difference, from the time we first occupied and passed through the city, was the aging of the ruins. The crumbling walls and columns, now weatherbeaten and flecked with cobwebs, towered over the piles of rubble like ghostly guardians of the battle scene. To those who participated in the campaign - the many unknown and obscure who struggled there and the few renowned who directed the strategy - the decaying columns were grim reminders of the hell which reigned over the men of both armies, as they valiantly fought for the vital crossroads, the possession of which was the key to success in a battle that will live in history so long as this civilization shall last.

As I trudged reflectively through the ruins of St Lo, I noted scattered on the ground and on the floors of wrecked buildings, the rusting shrapnel and shell fragments. Two years after the battle had raged, the pieces of metal from the exploding shells were still piled, in some places, as thickly as pebbles on a gravel bar. Taking a glass jar I filled it two-thirds full of various sizes of the hellish, cruel objects to keep as a souvenir of the great battle. Some where along the way the jar of fragments was misplaced and lost.

## OMAHA BEACH

Returning to the coast at Omaha Beach I stopped to view once more the scene of the historic landings. I walked from the cemetery across a level, cleared border to the crest of a hill overlooking the landing area. Reaching the crest, I was startled by sudden, terrific detonations on the slope below me. I involuntarily ducked and had a flashing thought of hitting the dirt. Some slight debris fell in my area but most of the fragments from the explosions fell down the slope to my front.

I soon discovered that a crew of German prisoners-of-war was clearing minefields laid by the Nazi forces before the invasion. I had approached the area as the crew was exploding some of the mines. As I walked to a safer place, I thought how ironic it would have been for a combat veteran, who had gone unscathed through all the campaigns in Europe, to meet death from a German mine on Omaha Beach two years after the battle there. I recalled our casualties at the Elbe in the final battles, the deaths of Pvt. Dudley and Lt. Quillin, and the near drowning of Capt. Silverman.

The landing area was easily recognizable but there were great changes. The surface of the ocean which had been filled with a myriad of ships during those eventful days almost two years earlier, was now empty. Not a single live vessel could be seen afloat on the wide expanse of the sea. The sky above the water near the shore, filled then with countless barrage balloons surging at the ends of steel cables, was likewise vacant. The trail up the slope, once well-worn and filled with an endless line of plodding troops in battle gear, was windblown, fading, and void of any passing soldier.

The main remaining signs of the hectic, intense activity which once prevailed over both land and sea, were the masts and hulls of sunken ships in the shallow water, and a few wrecked tanks and amphibious vehicles scattered on the sandy beaches and adjacent slopes. Clearly visible also in the rising and falling ocean, was the breakwater of sunken vessels, placed there to create a more placid area in the water near the shore for the unloading of troops and supplies.

Another evidence, of course, was the perfectly ordered rows of hundreds and hundreds of white crosses interspersed with the Stars of David in the manicured cemetery, located at the top of the slope above the beachhead area, over which floated in the bright sunlight, waving gently in the breeze, the Red, White and Blue of the American flag.

Gone was the continuous thunder of the big guns from the front a short distance inland, and gone the man-made lightning of the explosions. Absent was the roar of war vehicles climbing the slope. The shouts of working, fighting men had faded into silence. The planes no longer droned through the skies above. The barrage balloons had fallen or been hauled down. The ships had sailed into the distance. The marching men had trudged away, to a rendezvous with battle, and some with death.

Now the inexorable forces of nature - the beaming sun, the driving wind and the pelting rain, together with the growing grass, the unrelenting, timeless movement of the ocean, the persistent gnawing of insects and animals of land and sea, and the inflexible processes of decay - were fast obliterating all the physical evidence of man's greatest beachhead military effort and achievement. In time, all visible signs will disappear. The gray hulks of the sunken ships will rot away or sink into the mire of the ocean's depth; the abandoned wrecks on shore will be claimed by rust and decay; the faint trails will fade into windblown spots of drifting sand as unmarked as any other area of endless beach; the discernable excavations and shellholes, gradually filling with earth and rotting leaves, will be blotted out by the covering grass. Far and near, throughout many lands, death, which comes to all men, shall overtake the surviving participants of the landings, and remove all recollection of the great event from the minds of the living.

When the persistent, irreversible ravages of time which cannot be stayed, have worked their unrelenting will, until the last trace and the final memory is forever gone, then shall the Great Invasion live only in the tablets of history, and in a few erected monuments inscribed with fading words on markers of stone.

As I turned from my last look at the now tranquil scene of former action by many men of great uneasiness, the waves lapped at the hulks of the rotting ships. The flag flapped idly and the grass waved gently as a breeze swept through the silent crosses. The birds, their music silenced or unnoticed during the landings, twittered in the shrubery and sang in the trees. Nearby was the sound of a few voices in conversation and, farther away, the noise of a single motor vehicle as it moved inland along the quiet road.

## DEPARTURE FROM EUROPE

Back at Camp Herbert Tareyton, the camp with all its equipment was, pursuant to orders, turned over to the French Army. Orders were written transferring all American personnel, some to other units and camps in France, the others to return home. In making the transfers, I forgot to include myself on orders abandoning the army facility, and technically, perhaps, I should still be at the camp. However my orders to return home, issued from a higher headquarters, suffviced to get me on the ship. I carried my luggage to the dock and was helped aboard.

As the troop transport pulled away from its berth, the many tugs at the docks accompanied it outside the harbor. On signal the small vessels pulled up, blowing, in unison, their hoarse whistles in farewell.

As the ship gained speed my gaze turned shoreward. The tugs were returning to the harbor. Through the haze and smoke shown the outline of the war battered docks and buildings of the Port of Le Havre. On the slopes beyond the battle-scarred city, the greenery of spring was visible in the fading fields and woods.

As sight of the shore became dimmer with the growing distance, I thought of the many experiences since first landing on the soil of France - the booming guns, the charging tanks, the rattle of small arms, the diving planes, the night watches, the dangerous missions, and lastly, the deterioration of the great American Army. I recalled the many wonderful comrades I had known, and realized that I was bidding farewell to a period of life that would never come again. And finally, my recollection prayerfully turned to those in eternal sleep in the alien soil of the countries they had died to make free.

## Chapter XI

## HOME AND CIVILIAN LIFE

I came home on a new troop transport, the good ship "Ernie Pyle" and thought of the beloved correspondent every foot of the voyage. It was a pleasant trip in the month of May. Two years earlier during the same month, we had crossed the other way, destined for battle.

A thrill of pride came into every heart as there came into view that great symbol of freedom, "The Statue of Liberty." We debarked at New York and troop trains disbursed across the country carrying the returning troops to stations nearest their homes. On the long ride to St. Louis a white major slept in a bunk on one side of me and a Negro non-com on the other.

From St. Louis I secured my own transportation by rail. I got off the train at Fayetteville, Ark. in the early daylight of a spring morning. Unloading my baggage I placed it in the depot and alone walked to the main business section along the streets of the awakening town. I went to a cafe for breakfast and then to a barber shop and got a hair cut. Later I came across an acquaintance, Roy Bowman, a returned veteran wounded in France, and hitchhiked the remaining 30 miles to Huntsville with him.

After a period of leave I reported for duty at Ft. Sheridan, Ill. There I helped supervise the discharge of returning soldiers. Regulations permitted the soldiers to keep many items of clothing. However most of the soldiers dumped all their possessions into the bins except one outfit to wear home. They were anxious to get out of the army and to be rid of the symbols and trappings of army life. I'm sure many of them had need of many items of the clothing later on.

While at Ft. Sheridan I spent two days in Chicago as the guest of Col. Alexander. He had returned to civilian life and gone back into the real estate trade. He couldn't regain the business which he had enjoyed before going to war. Later he went back to the Army and served until retirement. Once he came through Little Rock while I was governor and was my guest at the executive mansion. It was a genuine pleasure to award him an Arkansas Traveler certificate. We have since lost touch (contact we would have said in the war) but wherever he is I wish him well. He is a gentleman of the highest degree and was one of the finest combat commanders of the war.

After a brief stay at Ft. Sheridan I was transferred to the Fifth Infantry Division at Fort Campbell, Ky. I reported for duty there to Capt Armstrong, our 320th personnel officer throughout the war, then serving as adjutant of the Fifth Division. Other 320th men at Camp Campbell included Lt. Preston and Lt. Col. Hannum.

Here I had perhaps the most pleasant assignment during my entire period of Army service so far as working conditions were concerned. I was made Assistant Judge Advocate for the camp with ample office space and civilian employees as secretaries. The duties were mostly paper work with regular office hours. Occasionally there was a trip to a nearby town to check with civilian authorities on difficulties experienced by personnel of the camp.

Soon I was ordered to Ft. Sam Houston, Texas for separation from the service. After a period of leave my termination was final on Nov. 15, 1946.

* * *

When I arrived home from Europe I found that the Democratic Party had made me the nominee for the office of county judge. I did not feel like making the race and wished to withdraw. I contacted the party officials, informed them of my wishes, and asked them to meet, accept my withdrawal and select another nominee. Three young veterans had been selected as Democratic nominees to seek three other county offices at the same time. When they learned that I was to withdraw, they informed the party leaders, I was told, that they would not continue.

The party leaders then insisted that I stay in the race, arguing that the Democrats would have great difficulty in fielding a slate of candidates if I should quit, and that I owed an obligation to the party. They reminded me that I had asked for and received the support of the party and of the people for county office before going to the war.

Reluctantly, I agreed to continue, and campaigned as best I could. I was the most experienced campaigner on the Democratic ticket, while the Republicans had a number of experienced men. Our young Democratic veterans were completely inexperienced in seeking votes.

I had a few civilian clothes and at times wore army garments. One day a friend approached and said to me in intense, subdued tones, "For God's sake! Get out of those army clothes! It's costing you votes everyday."

I thought, "How ironic, indeed! That the clothing I had worn while defending every liberty and privilege we enjoyed, including the right to vote and the right to campaign, would be offensive to the civilians at home." I continued to wear army garments as I had the need.

I lost the race to my Republican opponent, (by 105 votes - 2340 to 2235), a man who had remained at home serving in county office throughout the war. (My opponent was a fine man, an excellent politician, and made a good public official. He and I have remained personal friends.)

All the veterans running as Democratic nominees went down to defeat. The Democrats elected only one candidate in the races for seven major county offices. Not a veteran himself, ironically, the successful Democrat defeated one of the only two veterans running as Republican nominees. Six non-veterans were elected. Of the six war veteran candidates of both political parties, only one was victorious, a Republican, and he opposed a veteran running on the Democratic ticket. It was a case where the choice had to be a veteran.

The urgency of the war was gone. The high appreciation that once was felt for the men who left home to defend the country, had faded away. Except for a few civil service positions, veterans no longer had any preference in any way and were shown no consideration whatever which was not given to everyone. We were back in the battle of civilian life, in politics, business and otherwise. To use an old Ozark Mountain expression, "It is dog eat dog, and the Devil take the hindmost."

In fact veterans were at a disadvantage. Many were worn and weary, others shell shocked and wounded. Ofttimes they were broke. Their former jobs were held by others, and their former business had been swallowed up by the competition, as was the case with Col. Alexander. In my case the office I held when I went to war, and the office I sought when I returned, had been taken over by the political opposition which had become entrenched while I was away. Too, many veterans had lost, or failed to develop a civilian skill. We had grown proficient and skillful in war, and this proficiency and skill we found worse than useless in the life to which we had returned.

The situation was a forceful reminder to many veterans of the poem, said to be carved in the face of stone at the great fortress of Gilbralter.

> "In time of trouble, and not before,
> God and the soldier we implore;
> The trouble o'er, and all things righted,
> God is forgotten, and the soldier slighted."

There was a vacancy in the position of postmaster at the Huntsville post office at the time of my political defeat. An applicant had already been selected for appointment, but decided to remain in another position which he already held in the teaching profession. This left the postmastership open for other applicants, and Congressman J. W. (Jim) Trimble, himself a veteran of World War One, called me and inquired if I wanted the appointment. I thought about the matter for 24 hours, and informed the congressman I would accept.

In the matter of employment, I was much more fortunate than most returning veterans. For that area, the postmaster's position at Huntsville was a good job. I was fortunate also in that chance and circumstance had made the position available at that particular time.

My first appointment was as acting postmaster. Later I gave up the position to serve in the state administration of Gov. Sid McMath. In the meantime I took the Civil Service examination for appointment as permanent postmaster, and won the top spot on the list of applicants. At the recommendation of Congressman Trimble I was appointed to the position by President Harry S. Truman. With the approval of the two U. S. Senators from Arkansas, my appointment was confirmed by the U. S. Senate and I was formally installed as postmaster at Huntsville on Jan. 1, 1952.

By fulfilling my duties properly, I had job security, perhaps until retirement. However, in slightly more than a year I gave up the position to become a candidate in the Democratic primaries for the Democratic nomination for Governor of Arkansas. But that is another story.

It will suffice to say here that my efforts in the campaign were successful, and that later, as chief executive of my state, I was to see again the 101st Airborne Division which the 35th helped to relieve at Bastogne. Surviving 35th veterans of the Ardennes Campaign will recall the terrible losses suffered when the Division plunged into the snow-covered hills on the right flank of the Fourth Armored Division, which drove through the Nazi forces to reach the troops in the encircled city. The 35th then defeated the crack combat unit of the German Army, the Adolph Hitler SS Division, and thwarted the Nazi effort to again encircle Bastogne. Then the Santa Fe Division moved into the city, linked up with the 101st Airborne troops and fought with the paratroopers to drive the enemy forces back toward Germany.

In 1957 the 101st Airborne Division was ordered to Arkansas by President Eisenhower with directions to occupy Little Rock and all of Arkansas if necessary, during the so-called Little Rock Crisis. The unit was flown in huge transport planes from Fort Campbell, Ky., to the Little Rock Air Force Base. From there the heavily armed paratroopers, with unsheathed bayonets affixed and shining, spread out to occupy the capital city.

As had been the case when he backed Montgomery instead of Patton in the effort to end the war against Hitler in 1944, Eisenhower, a great American and a well intentioned man, in this instance, again yielded to heavy pressure and made a decision against his better judgment. But that, too, is another story.

## MADISON COUNTY'S WAR EFFORT

In Madison County no one kept up the "Roll of Honor" - the names of those in the Armed Forces - when I had to discontinue the list after entering the Service. Men enlisted or were called to the colors in increasing numbers, induction calls from the county sometimes numbering more than 100. Not as many passed the physical examination as in the early calls. In my group on May 17, 1942, 21 of 23 were accepted. In a group much later only 5 of 22 passed the examination; in another 14 of 44 and another 23 of 41 called. In a group of

64, called on Dec. 9, 1943, 23 were accepted among whom were Clay True Garrison, postmaster of Marble, for the Army, and my youngest brother, Darrow Doyle Faubus of Combs, for the Navy.

The superintendent of schools at Huntsville, Frank W. Cannaday, joined the Army; the principal, Prof. Henry Burke volunteered for the Air Corps; and the English teacher, Paul E. Corlett, entered Naval service.

Jack and Felix Brashears, sons of the county's only undertaker, entered the service, and J. Clark Hawkins, Jr., one of the county's two druggists, went into the Navy. Rudolph Setzler, the county agent, and Paul Inzer, assistant administrator of the Farm Security Administration, resigned their positions for Naval service, and Miss Frances Bruehl, the county nurse, resigned to join the Army Nurse Corps.

Miss Gayle Johnson, band director and teacher in the high school, was named the Women's Army Corps recruiter for Madison County and among those who enlisted were Misses Bessie R. McChristian, Mary E. Fields, Elsie Benson and twin sisters, Bessie and Dessie Caler. Miss Eleanor Ann Gaskill volunteered for service in the women's division of the Marines.

Judge John K. Butt, Chancellor of the district of which Madison County was a part, volunteered for Naval service and resigned his position, and in Washington the district's former Congressman, Clyde T. Ellis, joined the Navy. Entering the same branch of service, was the county's best known native of Germany, Bill Basecke, leaving his position as manager of Huntsville's best industry, the Pet Milk Company plant.

Elmer Jesse Haskins, Steve Montgomery, Earle Hargis, Dan R. Smith, George Rankin, the latter with two brothers as Jap prisoners, and hundreds more entered the various branches of the Armed Forces until more than 1,400 people from Madison County were serving or had served their country in the great war. The number was approximately one-sixth of the entire population of the county.

Madison Countians supported the war effort and backed up their sons and daughters in the armed forces in many other ways.

In the first war bond drive, the State Farm Bureau organization offered a decorated flag to be awarded to the county with the highest percentage of sales based on quotas established by the state officials directing the drive. To begin the county drive the local American Legion Post (WWI members) held a small party and in one hour sold enough bonds to exceed the quota. By the end of the campaign Madison County had exceeded its quota by more than 400%, leading all 75 counties of Arkansas, and the flag was proudly flown from the county courthouse in Huntsville.

In the same month, Madison County raised 250% of its quota of donations for the Red Cross. The total amount contributed amounted to $5,708.84 of which $1,058.30 came from private donations and $4,650.54 from the proceeds of the old-fashioned pie suppers described in the introduction to this book.

The second war bond sale quota was exceeded, and the Red Cross quota was oversubscribed by more than 200 per cent.

The third war bond sale quota of $184,000.00 was exceeded. The sum invested in this one drive amounted to $22.00 for each man, woman and child in the listed population of the county. When it is considered that the contributions of those in the Armed Forces were not included, their purchases being credited elsewhere, and not a single war industry or military facility existed in the county or adjacent areas, the effort of the hill farmers and workers of the region must be rated as nothing less than remarkable.

In the sixth war bond drive, McConnell Chapel, a small community just south of Huntsville, was the first to exceed its quota. Bond purchases were obtained by conducting a public auction at the community school house. Frank Murphy, an aging, rugged mountaineer who would have been rated by grammarians as less than proficient in use of the King's English, but who knew well the mountain people and their language, sold a white rooster over and over until he had raised $4,500.00. Roberta Harris, a young, part time postal clerk, finally took temporary possession of the bird by investing $1,000.00. The county exceeded its quota of $105,000 in sales by 210%, while the state average was 123%.

In November 1944 a war fund drive was initiated to raise funds for some war purpose, perhaps for the United Service Organizations (USO). The county was given a quota of $1,291.00 by the state directors. The people donated $4,387.76, exceeding the quota by 339.9%, breaking all state records and winning national recognition - perhaps setting a national record. Again almost the entire amount was raised in dozens and dozens of old-fashioned pie suppers held in nearly every community in the county.

At the urging of committees appointed by the government, the people gave tons of scrap metal for the making of munitions for the war effort. The heaps of donated scrap iron piled by every farm house were collected by Army trucks operated by Army personnel sent from Fort Chaffee near Ft. Smith more than 100 miles away. (There would have been more but junk dealers had bought up much of the scrap metal and resold it to Japan in years before the war began. The mountain people recalled that we got some of it back at Pearl Harbor, and wondered why the sale of the metal to Japan was permitted in the first place.)

A move was also initiated to close all businesses in Huntsville one-half day of each work-week. The purpose was not for rest, not for recreation, but to permit owners, operators and workers in the stores and shops to work in their Victory Gardens.

The American Legion post of Huntsville raised funds with which to buy supplies, and the Legion members prepared and served breakfast free to all men called for induction before they left the county seat bound for Camp Robinson at Little Rock. It was a service much appreciated by those going away. Local businessmen contributed still further by paying for advertisements promoting the war bond drives. The local newspaper published free of charge the notices of the various fund drives and other efforts, announcements of pie suppers and auctions and the lists of donors whenever available. At the same time its columns were filled with news of the comings and goings, and the deeds of the servicemen, and with many of their letters, written first from the training camps and finally from the far flung battlefronts of the earth.

In the few church buildings in the county, and in the many school houses which served also as places of worship, there resounded often the voices of the ministers and the people praying for the safety and wellbeing of their sons who had gone away to war, and for the restoration of peace to the world. Perhaps no member of my group will ever forget the voice of the countrywoman unashamedly lifted in prayer as we boarded the buses for our departure. The memory followed me all the days afterward and lingers with me still.

They were, for the most part, a praying people, - these relatives and friends who said goodbye to us. But they were also a people who backed up their prayers with work and deeds, which after all is said and done, constitutes the only true faith. For is it not written that "faith without works is dead."

To say that one could be proud of his heritage among such a people of such a region, seems too weak a statement. Perhaps never have a people, so happily situated at such a safe distance from the carnage of the battlefronts, and with so little detailed knowledge of the cruel repression and inhuman autrocities of the foe, so wholeheartedly and so nobly supported their country in such a great effort against an enemy so far away.

## WHAT NOW

Remembering the spirit and deeds of those times, not so far agone, in contrast with the attitude and happenings in our country in today's world - the lawless mobs of demonstrators, disorderly conduct at public meetings, open flaunting of smut and immorality, organized attacks on law enforcement officers, disruption of the courts of justice, the selfish demands for unearned contributions, the discordant cries for support without work, and the unredressed indignities to the men of our armed forces and their families who suffer because of service to their country, - leads to dismay and wonder.

Can we restore sufficient faith in our system of government, our country and its leaders, to halt the trend to destruction of that which was once so nobly and unselfishly defended and, for a time, preserved? Can we restore the attitude and spirit which created the unity of purpose and the high devotion among the people, which in turn made possible the orderly defense of our nation against the most terrible tyranny that ever threatened to engulf the earth in the greatest conflict of all mankind?

We have still a great people. But do we have the sense of patriotism, the reverence for the Deity, the respect for the rights of others, the due regard for orderliness, and the willingness to labor, which are necessary for our survival as a society, a form of government, and as a nation of freedom?

Or have the unruly, immoral, rude, shiftless, cynical dissidents in our midst, gone too long undisciplined?

These are great questions for the now young generation, to whom have been handed the freedom and privileges which we fought to preserve.

## THE RETURNING

Taking up the pursuits of civilian life, I joined with other veterans in a group organized to participate in the last rites for those who lost their lives in the war, and whose bodies were returned home for reburial. Among those returned (whose funeral service I directed) was a 35th veteran, my former friend, Pfc Hugh Fritts, Company I, 137th Infantry.

My former schoolmates, Charles Rankin, Henry Rankin and Sidney Marcum, were freed from the Japanese prison camps, and returned home. Returning also from those prisons were Blake Vanlandingham, Loren Brandenburg, George S. Wylie and others.

Percy G. Bolinger and a greater number of prisoners-of-war returned from the German prison camps.

Numbers of wounded came home, including Calvin Watkins of the Army, who lost an arm and a leg in the battles in France, and J. B. Hathorne who lost a leg.

Then came the Korean War and a number of veterans who were members of Reserve and National Guard units were called to colors again for that conflict. Among them was my brother-in-law, Raul (Ralph) Salcido, then living in Huntsville, who saw combat in Korea and got back safely.

With that war finally ended, the nation became embroiled in another struggle in Indo-China. My nephew, Raul's son, Reginald (Reggie) Salcido, Buena Park, Calif., was called to that conflict. Wounded twice in battle in South Viet Nam, he was returned to hospitals in the States after suffering severe injuries when hit the second time. He has now recovered and back in civilian life.

J. D. Hill, already making a career in the Navy, survived the war in the Pacific. He retired after 30 years service, and then headed the Office of Economic Opportunity in my administration. A heart attack in 1966 proved fatal.

Lt. Van Albertson, one of the first called into service from the county, remained in the Army after the war, rising to the rank of general. He retired about 1967, built a home on the banks of War Eagle River, and now is an attorney at Huntsville.

Oral E. Evans, his feet frozen in the snows of the Ardennes, barely escaped the slaughter of American troops by Hitler's SS men, known as the Malmedy Massacre. He returned home to later find employment as a law enforcement officer in my administration, a position he still holds.

My brother, Doyle, returned safely from Naval Service to his home at Combs. He worked for a time in my administration and is now serving his third term as Circuit Clerk and Recorder of Madison County, the same, elected, political office I held when I entered the service.

And what of the little boy I had left, with whom I had such a rare and deep understanding, and whose mere presence and company had brought me the greatest joy I had ever known?

At his grandfather's (J. S. Faubus) house on Greasy Creek in early April, 1944, I had held him up while he blew out the candles on his fifth birthday cake. I left the next day to return to Camp Butner to go overseas.

While I was at war he had become six, entered school, began to have new experiences and make new acquaintances. Some time while I was away, my influence removed, the memory of me growing dim, the little boy I had known had taken his books in hand, gone out the doorway, looked both ways before crossing the street, fixed his eyes and his interest on his fellow pupils and teachers, all new acquaintances, stepped shyly through a strange school house door, and was gone forever.

All little boys with complete faith in Dad, always disappear. They grow into larger boys, then into young men, and finally mature adults.

After a time following my return, we again developed a closeness. Farrell had the rare experience of being with me on the road, as an unknown worker when we had to campaign, in thirteen successive elections. He grew to be an astute analyist of political sentiment.

Always anonymous, he sat on curbstones on the streets, or on boxes at the crossroads groceries and took in the conversations of businessmen, merchants, clerks or rugged mountaineers as they discussed the current political campaigns. He ordered sodas at the small town drug stores and, while consuming them, listened to the remarks of young people and housewives. Sometimes he entered the pool parlors, often wearing a campaign button of an opposing candidate, and at an advertent moment raised a political issue. Then, when others entered the discussion, he evaluated the sentiment. He watched the crowds during my speeches, noted the strong points from expressions, applause and comments afterward. Because of his objectivity - seeking the facts whatever they were - and his ability to evaluate, he became one of my most trusted advisers. This was especially true of the reaction to the effectiveness of our campaign efforts. He could also give valuable information as to our strength or weakness in almost any section of the state, and was sometimes helpful in determining the effectiveness of the opposition's efforts.

Farrell graduated from the Huntsville High School, attended Arkansas Tech at Russellville for one year, one of the finest colleges in the state, Little Rock University, then a private institution, one year, after which he entered the University of Arkansas at Fayetteville and graduated in the school of law. He made the second highest grade in his group while taking the Arkansas Bar examinations, and became a licensed attorney.

Later he served as an assistant in the Attorney General's office in Little Rock, and for a time was deputy prosecuting attorney in Madison County. He served most of a two-year term in the Arkansas General Assembly as a member of the House of Representatives from Madison County, a position he won at a special election.

Turning to the field of education, he was a teacher in the Huntsville schools for two terms. He now resides at Huntsville where he has established an office for the practice of law.

## 35TH DIVISION REUNIONS

Shortly after the war the 35th Division Association, an organization of veterans of the Santa Fe Division of World War One, was re-activated and the veterans of the Division of World War Two were invited to join. The practice of holding an annual reunion, discontinued during the global conflict, was resumed.

The first post-war gathering was held in Kansas City, Mo., June 5, 6 and 7, 1947. Thousands of veterans with members of their families came from all over the Union, the heaviest attendance being from the four-state area of Kansas, Nebraska, Missouri and Arkansas.

The stellar attraction was the President of the United States, Harry S. Truman, himself a member, and a former president of the association. He attended the reunion proudly wearing the arm band of the 129th Field Artillery, in which he served as a captain in France in WWI. His address to an audience which packed the huge municipal auditorium, was the highlight of the event.

As President Truman with his party marched down the aisle of the auditorium to the stage, he was trailed by our former Supreme Commander in Europe, Gen. Dwight D. Eisenhower, then the President's Chief of Staff. As the former GIs, their families and friends cheered the President, many also called out to the famous general, "Hello, Ike! How are you, Ike?"

The greetings to Eisenhower were friendly, and the seeming familiarity of the calls was not meant to be discourteous in any way. The General responded, - not too openly because it might appear disrespectful to the President - with that typically boyish grin and shy nods of his head. Unconsciously by his seemingly bashful friendliness he was still making points and keeping open that personal pipeline to the people which later aided so much in his election to the presidency.

All radio networks broadcast the president's speech, and two networks carried Gen. Eisenhower's address. Television had not yet come on the scene for such events.

Jack Benny, not yet 39, headed a cast of 25 movie and radio stars. Benny served as master of ceremonies for two shows, one each on separate days.

Distinguished foreign guests included the French Ambassador, Henri Bonnet, who came from Washington, D. C., and a famed French Maquis (FFI) leader, Georges Pierre Lavally, also a flying ace of France in WWI, then Mayor of St. Lo, and a comrade-in-arms of the 35th in the battles which liberated his city. Lavally flew to the Reunion from France "to greet his friends of the American Army who helped liberate his city and his country from the hated Nazis."

Three governors were listed on the program to speak to the veterans - Phil M. Donnelly of Missouri, Frank Carlson of Kansas and Val O. Peterson of Nebraska.

The Reunion was organized and directed by Maj. Gen. Ralph E. Truman (Ret), a cousin of the president, and commander of the 35th when it was activated and during its training days at Camp Robinson. He was assisted by Kansas City Mayor, William E. Kemp, and a host of officials and private citizens. Mayor Kemp gave the official welcome. Coordination for the Division veterans with the some two dozen committees appointed by the mayor, was handled by Gen. Truman, then president of the Association, aided by Mahlon S. Weed, Albert Thomson, Don Ashlock and Joe Nickell.

Among the many distinguished guests and committee members were Judge Bennett Champ Clark of the U. S. Court of Appeals in Washington, Justice William A. Smith of the Kansas Supreme Court, Congressman Wint Smith and Errett P. Scrivener of Nebraska, and former Congressman Randolph Carpenter of Kansas.

In Gen. Eisenhower's party was his brother, Milton Eisenhower, then president of Kansas State College, Manhattan, Kansas.

In the president's party were Admiral William D. Leahy and Maj. Gen. Harry Vaughn.

Generals included L. T. Gerow (of the night attack order in Normandy), Paul W. Baade, our 35th Division commander throughout the war, and more than a dozen others.

Also among the guests were Junior Spurrier, Bluefield, W. Va., our Congressional Medal of Honor winner in Alsace-Lorraine; the oldest veteran, the Rt. Rev. Father William Hart, 140th Inf., then 82, of Anoka, Minn.; and Pat Kilroy, Co F, 134th Inf., of Philadelphia, Pa. Then there were dozens more well known officers and officials, and hundreds and hundreds of the unknown, obscure rank and file, who were more interested in visiting with former buddies than seeing the dignitaries or attending the various functions.

In the years immediately following the great homecoming reunion at Kansas City, other large and successful gatherings were held at St. Louis, Topeka, Little Rock, Springfield, Mo., and Kansas City, Kansas. At an early Topeka reunion, Airman Joe Foss, flying ace of WWII and the first jet ace of the Korean War, was our special guest. Later we were governors of our respective states at the same time. At a later Topeka gathering I occupied a place on the platform during the parade beside Alf Landon, the Republican nominee for president so overwhelmingly defeated by Franklin D. Roosevelt in 1936. Mr. Landon and I had a very nice visit.

One of the larger reunions was at Little Rock during the administration of Gov. Sid McMath. At that affair Gen. Truman led the parade as Grand Marshall. The row of dignitaries heading the procession and flanked by the President's 129th Field Artillery batterymates, included President Truman, Gov. McMath, Secretary of the Army Louis Johnson and Gen. Harry Vaughn.

During my attendance at these early reunions I was nominated and elected to the position of fifth vice-president of the Association. Year by year I was elevated in office until elected president in 1954. Consequently, in 1955 I was privileged to preside as president at the Reunion in Little Rock during my first year as Governor of Arkansas. President Truman, no longer in office but still a faithful attendant at the reunions, was there and was our guest at the Executive Mansion.

I have many impressions of Harry S. Truman: his winning battle as an underdog for the U. S. Senate in Missouri; his chairmanship of a Senate committee to weed out inefficiency and waste in the war effort; his speech on assuming the presidency, heard at a battle command post in Germany; his upset victory over Thomas E. Dewey in the campaign for election to the presidency in 1948; his courage in forcing the withdrawal of Russian troops from Iran and Austria and his audacious initiation of the Berlin airlift; his order for American troops to oppose the invasion of South Korea by Communist troops of North Korea. All these were impressions held by an unknown, obscure, private citizen as he observed a public figure.

I have other impressions from personal contact. His stance on the platform as he charmed an audience, especially effective with small gatherings; his gracious attitude in the president's office; as a guest at Little Rock; as a host at the Truman Library at Independence, Mo., and as a combat comrade at the reunions.

I recall another impression, formed only as a distant, unknown observer. That was Truman's portrayal of courage, appreciation and loyalty to an old friend when, as president, with no further need of help, he flew from Washington to Kansas City to attend the funeral of Tom Pendergast.

We of his old 35th Infantry Division, and all other men of combat, who knew so well the true meaning of loyalty, had our high regard for him confirmed. Among others, even his critics, the respect for him increased at this act of loyalty toward a man, who had helped him in a time of need as he struggled upward. Certainly with the reputation the press had created for "Boss" Pendergast, the gesture could not be labeled as a move to improve his political image.

I got to know Harry S. Truman rather well. I met him when I was a completely obscure private citizen, and while I was governor of my state. I met him when he was president and highly popular, and afterward when he was again a private citizen, his prestige and influence waning, his critics many. He was always the same - alert, friendly, charming, frank and outspoken.

It is my opinion that it will be a long time before our country again has a leader and world figure the equal of President Truman for ability, decision and humility, - a man for whom the expression is quite appropriate when it is said, he could "walk with kings, nor lose the common touch."

Of all the men I have met, both high and low, there were none more gracious and charming than Harry S. Truman.

After President Truman left office and the Division Association could no longer claim as a member the President of the United States, and when the advance of years brought inactivity to the group's most illustrious member, interest and appeal in the reunions declined. Gradually the attendance dwindled until now, much smaller numbers are found in attendance, and the outside interest and publicity are mere shadows of the former attention and notoriety.

For years the faithful workers who continued to organize and promote successful gatherings were Gen. Ralph E. Truman, Springfield, Mo., Gen. Charles H. Browne, Sr., Horton, Kansas, Gen. Joe Nickell, Topeka, Kansas, Warren Osgood, Little Rock, Ark., "Gunboat" Smith, Wichita, Kansas, Gen. Mahlon S. Weed, Kansas City, Kansas, John Cobb, St. Louis, Mo., and a few others, most of them veterans of both wars. I always worked with them in making the preparations for the Little Rock reunions, of which there were at least three.

Easily the most outstanding individual in these working groups was the former commander of the Division and former president of the Association, Gen. Truman. Gracious in manner, the general was outspoken and direct as a gunshot in a discussion, and sometimes as blunt as a sledgehammer in his methods. A cherished and unswerving ally in a debate or parliamentary struggle, he was likewise a dreaded foe when in opposition. He upheld what he thought was right, condemned what he thought was wrong, and spoke what he considered to be the truth in the bluntest, plainest, strongest language I have ever heard used in meetings of public discussion. Sometimes it seemed he sought not merely to win, but to bludgeon and crush completely his opposition at the same time.

Yet, when a word battle was over, he would forgive, forget and be gracious. I have heard him say at the close of a meeting to an opponent over whom he had just triumphed, "All right, Goddam you, now that I've whipped you, come on and I'll buy you a drink." Or if he had lost, he would say, "All right, Goddam you, now that you've beaten me, I think you ought to buy me a drink." And he might add, "I still think you're wrong, but I hope it works."

He was always open minded in a meeting. If some one presented facts, or brought forth new information, he listened attentively. I have seen him give way with a gracious wave of his hands and the words, "I'm wrong. Let's do it your way."

But if he were not convinced, any opponent had better be prepared for a brutal, bruising battle on any issue about which he felt strongly. Gen. Patton would have treasured Gen. Truman as a division commander in his army.

Gen. Truman remained active in civic and public functions. He accepted an assignment from the Governor of Missouri for an examination of the state prison system and recommendations for improvement. He did a thorough job for which he was highly commended.

With the approval of the government in Washington, he worked for some time on an assignment to secure the establishment and erection in Cuba, of a monument to the Americans who fought there in the Spanish-American War. After much study, several trips to the island, and negotiations with the Cuban government, considerable progress had been made toward fulfillment of the project.

Then the Castro-led revolution took over in the southern republic. Gen. Truman did not give up, but continued his efforts. With the press-sponsored idea that Castro was the George Washington of Cuba - an idea with which most officials in Washington seem to agree - the general hoped that the government would become stablized and friendly, and the project on which he had worked so hard could be completed.

Then I saw the general at an executive committee meeting of the 35th Division Association in Little Rock. He had just returned from another trip to Cuba. He related to me personally, and later in a speech to the committee members, what he had discovered in that country.

Whether or not Fidel Castro was a Communist was beside the point, Truman said. (It was already known that his brother was a Communist and had received training in Russia). The Communists, he reported, had taken over every post of power in Cuba and were rapidly Communizing the entire country. Many non-Communist Cubans, - businessmen, professional people, members of the press and members of the government - had become aware of the direction Castro's government was taking, and were begging for understanding and assistance. Already some Cubans were fleeing the country, and others were preparing for flight if they could escape.

Efforts for the establishment of the monument were hopeless, Truman concluded, although Castro's agents kept up a facade of negotiations, (as Communists always do for the purpose of deception). The general related that the government was anti-American, pro-Russian and undoubtedly Communist, and that all freedom in Cuba was systematically and relentlessly being crushed. He had also learned that many Cubans, including some of his personal friends, were already confined under shocking conditions in political prisons.

Gen. Truman's report to us was at a time when the government in Washington and the entire American news media, were still assuming the stance, that Castro was a freedom-loving revolutionary with a belief in the democratic processes similiar to the views held by the leaders of the American Revolution. I recall that shortly before Truman's report I had spoken to the Illinois Press Association at Peoria at its annual convention. Preceding me on the program was a prominent American lawyer who portrayed Castro and the Cuban Revolution in a favorable light. The mere mention of the thought that Castro was a Communist and that Communism was being installed in power at our very doorstep, would elicit a shake of the head in disbelief.

A few days after Gen. Truman's report to us, the first nationwide story broke in the press of the true developments in Cuba. Soon thereafter the truthful story, confirming completely the general's private report, of Communism's seizure of the first country in the Western Hemisphere, was being made known. When Castro had kept up the deceptive facade of a believer in freedom for a sufficient time to enable his Communists agents to seize all posts of power and to crush all liberty in the island, he suddenly dropped the deception. In a speech to Cubans and to the world, he proclaimed himself a Marxist and stated that he would be "until the day I die."

Later Gen. Truman personally helped to obtain the release from prison of some of his Cuban friends, including members or former members of the Cuban Diplomatic Corps. In these efforts he called on me for assistance as the Governor of Arkansas - aid which I was glad to give, although it was weak and ineffectual compared to the assistance that could have been given by the federal government.

The Cuban developments raise many serious questions. The way the government, or at least the Congress, was deceived by the Cuban Communist leaders; the promulgation by the press and some political leaders, of Castro as "the George Washington of Cuba"; and other misinformation about the Cuban situation to which the American people were subjected, all can be viewed with dismay. The manner in which the developments were handled in Washington casts serious doubts on the effectiveness and accuracy of the great Committees of Congress, especially the Senate Foreign Relations Committee, in keeping the Congress or the people properly informed. Even more serious doubts are cast upon agencies of the federal government, as the State Department and the CIA, as to their effectiveness in keeping properly informed the highest officials of the Nation.

Can it be that the leaders of our great country and the proper agencies of our all-powerful federal government, were so ill-informed as to be ignorant of the Communist nature of the Castro take over in Cuba? Or is it, as some say, that too many of our leaders harbor the concealed belief that Communism is merely another form of democracy, and are sympathetic to its spread?

Truman and Gen. Browne were old comrades and buddies. His favorite form of address for his old friend was "Hard Nose" Browne. Also a good friend of Smith, he never addressed him other than "Gunboat."

There was a very close relationship between Gen. Truman and Warren Osgood of Little Rock. I was told that during their early days in Missouri, Osgood was a captain in a

National Guard unit in which the general and his more illustrious cousin, the president, were sergeants. I never thought to inquire if it were true.

Osgood was a quiet, unobtrusive, steady workman, a gracious companion and a true friend. In the years of our association when we had the pleasure of working together, I never once heard him raise his voice above a well modulated, friendly tone, or ever once used a word of profanity. An employee of the Veterans Administration at the beginning of our acquaintance, he later retired. He was a long time, close, personal friend of both Gen. Truman and President Truman, yet never once did he use that relationship for ostentation or advantage.

A foursome that could always be seen at any of the reunions was made up of Gen. and Mrs. Truman, and Mr. and Mrs. Osgood. They were very close and quietly enjoyed their time together in the manner of old and trusted friends.

Then Mrs. Osgood died, and Warren, missing her companionship, became almost a recluse. He seldom left the house and attended no public functions except one or two reunions which occurred while he yet lived. Then Gen. Truman answered the last call to report for duty to a new assignment in the unknown land, and Warren was summoned not many months later. Only Mrs. Truman, the last survivor of the constant foursome, remains.

Among this group of leaders of my close acquaintance, who did the planning for the Little Rock reunions, the first to die was Gen. Browne. A short time later, "Gunboat" Smith departed, and Harry Johnson, another oldtimer, died the year after he had sponsored the Reunion in his home town of Wichita, Kansas. With the deaths of Truman and Osgood, only Joe Nickell remains. He has been adjutant general of the National Guard of Kansas through a series of administrations since the end of WWII.

Gen. Charles Browne, Jr. of Horton, Kansas, succeeded his father, Gen. Browne, Sr., as a leader in the Association's affairs. Now retired, he was the last commander of the 35th Infantry Division, a National Guard unit in the same states of the unit's origin for WWII. The Division was deactivated in one of the many reorganizations of the National Guard by the Department of the Army in recent years.

Among the new leaders in the activity of the Association and the annual reunions, are Sid Silverman of Detroit,

Charles "Red Cross Charlie" Glatzer of Cleveland, Col. J. D. Alexander of Chicago, Ray H. Rawlings of Topeka and L. D. Kerr of San Antonio, Texas. They provide able assistance to the old veterans who still carry on - Gen. Weed, Gen. Nickell, John Cobb and Howard Faulkner of Leavenworth, Kansas.

William "Bill" Dixon of Kingsville, Ohio, a sergeant of the I & R platoon, 320th Infantry, WWII, is the president of the Association for the term 1970-71. Dixon, an original member of the 320th, survived the entire conflict with one period of hospitalization, and returned home with the Division.

## 35TH VETERANS

Since the war I have been able to renew acquaintance with some former comrades through the Reunions of the 35th Division Association, and to hear of others through the 35th Divisionaire, the publication of the Association. But, as is well realized, the contacts and associations, except in cases where former comrades live in the same areas, are brief. Each is busy with his own problems of earning a living, making a career and other difficulties. Some have done well, while to others fate has been unkind, just as in combat when some were wounded, captured or lost their lives while others survived.

It would be a difficult, if not impossible, task for any veteran of a combat unit such as ours, to reestablish contact and account for all the close friends with whom he trained and fought, and who touched his life in a number of ways. I have made no effort to do this, but I feel constrained to mention a few and some things that happened to them.

Col. Byrne was able to achieve his oft mentioned dream of building a home on a beautiful beach in Hawaii after his retirement from the Army. Then tragedy struck in another way. Those closely associated with the Colonel will recall the many times he referred to his children, Sandy and Tippy, a boy and a girl. In the one letter I received from him he wrote that his son was killed in Korea while serving as liaison officer, "the same function you performed for me so often" during the war. His daughter married a captain in the paratroop forces. While making a jump his parachute only partially opened and he was badly injured, perhaps permanently.

1st Lt. Thoms M. Miller, the little man who was a mighty warrior as forward observer for the 216th Field Artillery

with the Third Battalion, 320th Infantry, was a member
of a prominent law firm in Oklahoma City. After a time he
heard of our 35th Reunions and attended one at Little Rock
with his wife and children. Some months afterward I got
a call from his friends. He was killed in a car accident while
driving home alone. I flew to Oklahoma City and was a pall-
bearer at the funeral service.

John E. "Old Chief" Snyder, the medic who braved the
bullets and shells so many times to give aid to the fallen,
even enemy soldiers, returned home whole and well. After
becoming a civilian he was driving one day along the road
near his home at Silver Creek, N. Y., when he came upon a
car wreck in which there were a number of badly hurt people.
"Old Chief" stopped and while aiding the injured, as had
long been his habit, another car plowed into the wreckage
and struck him. Badly hurt, he survived but his broken back
will keep him in his wheel chair the rest of his life. A familiar
scene at the reunions is that of "Chief" Snyder being wheeled
about by his buddies. They call him "savage" and say he
knows little of the finer things of life, and he replies by
threatening to raise a war party and "lift your scalps." Often
"Red Cross" Charlie arranges to travel with "Old Chief"
when attending the reunions, to help him as he enters and
leaves cars or planes.

1st Lt. Grover C. Roberts, wounded and captured by the
Germans on July 12 in Normandy, and released by the
American Armies on May 2, 1945 east of Munich, was called
to military duty again in the Korean War and served in that
conflict. He now lives at Pine Bluff, Ark., his home at the
time of WWII.

Another 320th officer who saw service in the Korean
conflict is 1st Lt. Kenneth H. Brown. He then lived at Puente,
Calif.

Sgt. Fred Smead of the I & R Platoon, Yakima, Wash.,
suffered a severed spine in wounds received in Normandy
after the breakout. Paralyzed from the shoulders down, he
finished law school after returning home, and now is an attorney at Chatsworth, Calif.

Col. Northam, a West Point graduate, remained in the
Army, and attended a few of the early reunions. Maj. Jamieson and Maj. Hughes were last heard from in California. Maj.
McElroy is a prominent attorney at Grand Forks, N. D., as
is Capt. Ginsburg at St. Paul, Minn. Capt. Silverman, a

special guest at my first inauguration, is a member of a large contracting firm in Detroit, and Lt. Keith is a prominent attorney in the same city.

Lt. Knopke is now in Kansas City, Mo. and the last I heard Lt. Sperl was an attorney in New York City. Capt. Hare has retired as a college professor in Los Angeles, Calif. Lt. Trask has reared his family in Iowa, and I have lost touch with Capt. Head.

Capt. Bonham moved from Nebraska to Wyoming where he is now state bank commissioner. His home is in Cheyenne.

Capt. Heil is at Dennison, Ohio, and Maj. Leach at Davenport, Iowa. Lt. Byerly and Sgt. Koch are still at Lima, Ohio.

Col. Alexander is back in Chicago, and Maj. Smith is somewhere in Minnesota. "Red Cross" Charlie is still knocking around Cleveland, Ohio, and Capt. Brochu has dropped into the vast ranks of the unknown.

In 1954 I had come to the closing day of one of the hottest political campaigns, weather wise and otherwise, in the history of Arkansas (for ten straight days the thermometer ranged above 100 degrees, going as high as 111.) On Monday afternoon before the voters went to the polls the next day, I was making my next to last speech in the Democratic runoff primary campaign. I spoke to a large audience in the beautiful park square in the center of Marianna, county seat of Lee County. When I had finished I walked through the crowd shaking hands. Presently I was faced by a man with weatherbeaten appearance dressed as a laborer. He stuck out his hand and said, "Do ye know me?"

I looked closely and replied, "I can't call your name but you're from the old 35th Division."

"I'm Archie Jones," he answered, "Company F, 320th Infantry."

He was one of the four surviving "Old originals" who had crossed the English Channel for Normandy with Company F, who were still present for duty with the same company when the war ended. As best we can remember the other three besides Archie were Sgt. Coy E. Johnson, Johnson City, Tenn., T/5 Henry C. Calhoun, Atlanta, Ga., and Sgt. Lensy P. Lane, Garfield, Ark., all of whom I had helped to train as a former officer of the company.

After I became governor Sgt. Jones and I re-established contact, but the life of a chief executive is so busy that there was seldom any opportunity to visit.

Then, one day many months later, I was, by special arrangements, visiting West Helena on a tour of public facilities and industrial plants of the city. I had learned that Archie was a work foreman and the union labor steward at an industrial plant which was on the schedule for my visit. When we came to this industry, I said to the committee of well dressed public officials, Chamber of Commerce leaders and business executives, "I want Archie Jones to take me through this plant." Archie met me in his work clothes, and we had a nice visit as we toured the facility followed by the committee members.

During my administration we constructed a fine, new bridge, a toll facility, over the Mississippi River at Helena. I recommended Archie to the Highway Department for employment there and he was accepted. Before I left office he had worked up to the position of foreman of the toll collecting crew, a position he still holds.

Lt. Gangemi of New York, although hospitalized for long periods of time, was the only original officer of Company F to return home with the 320th. While governor I received a letter from my old comrade. He was present, he wrote, standing nearby my seating area at the Gator Bowl football game at Jacksonville, Fla. He did not come over to greet me, he related, because I was with a group of dignitaries and he feared he would be intruding. (I was with Mayor Hayden Burns of Jacksonville, later governor of Florida, the then governors of Florida and Georgia, and perhaps other dignitaries.) I replied to Gangemi that I would rather have met and visited with him than to have seen the game (if it had been necessary to make a choice), although the Arkansas Razorbacks won the Gator Bowl contest by defeating Georgia Tech. What a wonderful opportunity to have visited with a fellow officer of my old company F, at the game or afterwards. I felt a sense of loss that Gangemi had not let me know of his presence. Such opportunities are rare and seldom come again. Gangemi and I have not met since the war.

At the National Governors Conference I visited often with Lt. John Davis, then governor of North Dakota. He missed the last conference of his four-year administration while engaged in a campaign for the U. S. Senate which he lost by a narrow margin. Later I renewed acquaintance with him when he visited Arkansas in 1967 as National Commander of the American Legion. I joined Gov. Winthrop Rockefeller (infantry) and former Attorney General Bruce Bennett (air corps) in welcoming Davis who spoke to the Arkansas Legion Convention at El Dorado.

While Chief Executive of Arkansas I had the pleasure of knowing two other 35th veterans who served as governors of their respective states. Bill Avery, a U. S. Congressman from Kansas, was elected governor of his state, and Warren E. Hearnes was elected governor of Missouri. We attended the meetings of the National Conference of Governors in 1965-66 while I was serving my last term in office.

From the ranks of the 35th veterans have come a president, at least four governors, several congressmen and many other public officials.

At a Southern Governor's Conference in North Carolina Lt. Hendren and family were my guests. Hendren now has a high position with the Vocational Agriculture Division of the Education Department of that state.

At a National Governor's Conference in Cleveland, Ohio I visited with "Red Cross" Charlie, Capt. Heil, Capt. Silverman and others. Silverman flew over from Detroit for a small 320th get-together after the Conference ended. At a National Conference in Minneapolis I had an extended visit with Capt. Ginsburg. Several times while attending football games at the Cotton Bowl at Dallas, Texas, I had opportunities to visit with Col. Jack Tingle, formerly of the 35th Division Judge Advocate Section.

Sgt. Ted Woods of the personnel section of the 320th throughout the war, was a resident of Helena, Ark. We renewed acquaintance after returning home, and when I became governor I appointed him to the Publicity and Parks Commission. Later he served as director of the agency as my administration continued to improve and expand the Arkansas State Park System, increasing from seven to 34 the number of state operated parks and recreation areas.

Any chief executive has an unlisted telephone number in his residence, which is answered by himself or a close confidant. Then there is a listed number which is answered by other members of the family or employed personnel. If the governor answered the listed number calls, he would soon be spending too much of his time talking to crackpots, inebriated callers and hecklers, some of the latter using vile and abusive language.

On one occasion while governor I returned home one evening at about the hour of eleven (2300 in the military). There was no one in the executive residence at the time, - the members of my family were away and the employees had gone home. As I unlocked the back door and stood alone in the empty house, the listed number telephone began ringing. Something prompted me to take the call although I had not personally answered that telephone in perhaps four or five years. I put aside the urge to answer as a superstitious thought, but the prompting returned. When I was strongly prompted the third time I lifted the receiver and replied. The caller was Lt. Donald Villemaire of Burlington, Vt. whom I had not seen or heard from since we parted in Europe a dozen or more years before. We had a nice visit via long distance telephone, and that is the last time I have heard from him.

On one occasion while attending a Southern Governors Conference at Lexington, Ky., we visited with the former wife of Sgt. Cull, then remarried, and his son. Some years later while still governor, I received a letter from a Masonic official in Florida. The son, Gary Brent Cull, then grown, married and living in Florida, had applied for acceptance as a member of a Masonic lodge in that state. I was glad to sign his petition for membership and write a letter of recommendation for the son of Sgt. Cull, the first man in Company F to die in the 320th Infantry's first assault on the hellish hedgerows in Normandy. I have had no further news of the family since that time.

Once on the way home from a Southern Governor's Conference in the East, I stopped at Knoxville, Tenn., for a brief visit with Lt. Morris Bart, my friend and helper at Camp Pittsburgh, France. Later we were in attendance at the same time at a football contest at the Cotton Bowl in Dallas, Texas. The movie, "Battle of the Bulge" was showing at a theatre in the city, and we slipped away together to see it. The scenery in the film was quite unrealistic, the earth being only partially covered with snow. We recalled that all during that fierce engagement the soft substance lay white and deep over the entire mountainous region of the Ardennes.

I have been able to renew acquaintance a number of times with Lt. Lloyd Borcherding, my happy helper at Camp Pittsburgh. He still resides at Hooks, Texas.

Capt. Arthur D. Wilson, AT Co., now at North Andover, Mass., writes that Lt. Kenneth I. Botton died early in 1971 at his home in New Jersey. Sgt. Koch writes that Pfc. Charles Bachofen of New Jersey died in 1970. He was one of the best stenographers with whom I ever worked. Somewhere in the musty, aging files of the 320th's records, are reams and reams of typewritten material which came from Bachofen's skillful hands, and which have outlasted his dutiful body and his understanding heart.

Shortly after I returned home, Capt. Scherer, the Regular Army officer who was the 216th Field Artillery forward observer with the 320th, visited one night with me at Huntsville. He was on his way with his family to a new post on a change of stations. I have never heard from him since that time.

Edward H. Miller, Jr., of New York State, joined the 320th while it was on maneuvers in Tennessee. He went all the way as a member of Headquarters Company of the Third Battalion. He now lives on Lakeshore Road, Fort Erie, Ontario, Canada.

Through political channels while still governor, I heard of Capt. Tobin, one of the old originals who survived all the way with the 320th. At that time he had been elected and was serving as sheriff of his home county in Texas.

Well known to most of the soldiers of Company F during training days was big, red-haired Clarence "Red" Montgomery of Forest City, Ark. He suffered a leg injury while in training at Camp Butner which kept him from going overseas with the 320th.

While serving in the McMath administration after the war I was aiding in the arrangements for the visit of Vice-president Alben Barkley to Arkansas to attend the Poultry Festival at Springdale. At that time a minor minion in the government, I was not included among those who met and accompanied the vice-president.

While Barkley was speaking at the main event in the football stadium at Fayetteville, I was seated to one side in the audience near the post of some members of the State Police. Presently one of the troopers approached, engaged me in conversation and then inquired if I were not once a lieutenant in Company F of the 320th Infantry.

As soon as he made the inquiry I recognized the trooper as "Red" Montgomery, one of my trainees at Camp San Luis Obispo, Camp Rucker, Tennessee maneuvers and Camp Butner.

After that first post war meeting, we saw each other quite often. Once when accompanying me and my group by car on the way to a Southern Governors Conference at Greenbrier, W. Va., we were passing through the war time Tennessee maneuver area. A drunken driver forced my car off the road and struck the vehicle being driven by Montgomery. He was injured and spent some time in a hospital in Lebanon, Tenn. before returning home.

After a fine career as a member of the Arkansas State Police, in which he advanced to command of a district, Montgomery suddenly resigned to become a candidate for sheriff of St. Francis County. Against odds he won the race, has since been re-elected three times, and is still in office at Forrest City.

After our visit in Denver I saw John Kelly on one other occasion. We were both attending a 35th Division Reunion in St. Louis. We had a long visit, and he told me of a book he had read entitled, "Nostalgia for War." We knew how the writer felt. We too remembered the orders and the marching, the booming of the big guns belching smoke and flame, the terrifying screech of incoming "freight," the rattle of small arms, the deadly purr of machine guns, the coughing of mortars, the zooming of planes, the awe-inspiring sound and sight of tanks in full charge, the roar of trucks in the dark as armies moved, the watches in the lonely night, and that indefinable, vast uneasiness as H-hour approached in the dawn.

We weren't homesick for the hardships of training or the dangers of battle, we concluded, but there were some things we missed in civilian life which we had known with our fellow soldiers. We were lonesome for the unequaled fellowship we had found in the ranks of our comrades. We missed the pleasure of the deep and abiding friendships. We longed for the manner in which the men of battle dealt with each other - in complete frankness and genuine honesty with all pretense and sham removed. We wanted again the opportunity to openly disagree with a buddy, and then be able to go on a dangerous mission with him in complete trust and faith. We yearned for the association with men of great differences, yet so devoid of prejudice and so imbued with loyalty that we could go out together to fight and die, for each other and for the common cause of freedom. We longed for the spirit of the men of combat - a spirit motivated by bravery, honor, compassion and sacrifice, with the absence of pettiness, envy, jealousy and falsehood. We wished again to see the recognition of worth, the pardon of honest error, the quick condemnation of malicious wrong and deliberate failure (as the only way to remove the bad and preserve the good), and the unswerving loyalty of men to each other based upon the true and noble.

We figured that the writer of the book was not homesick for war, but like us, he yearned again to see the unexcelled standards of duty and honor, and to feel once more the incomparable comradeship brought forth by hardship and danger as free men bravely struggle for a great cause.

There are few false or weak men in the battle lines of a great combat unit such as ours had been. They are weeded out in many ways - by deferments, rejections at the induction centers, the seeking and finding of soft berths in the army itself, the failures in training, the crackups as we approached the sailing date and the battle lines. Then there were those willing enough to stay in the lines but who were not constitutionally fitted to stand the strain of combat. Finally there were a few who ran out on their buddies on the field battle.

So, John and I thought, perhaps by chance and circumstance, together with endowed ability properly used, and through the process of elimination, with luck never to be left out, we had become members of a select group. Perhaps there would never be again, for us, a time and place where we would be members of a large group of men so devoted to duty and to each other. Neither would we enjoy again the comradeship and the high standards of honor we had known, nor the respect for rules and law and the strict discipline without which the combat units could not have survived.

I can hear John as he would say, "Well, Judge, it'll take a greater philosopher than I to come up with the answer. I don't know." And with that short laugh I had learned to love so well he would add, "And if some one comes up with an answer, he might be wrong."

John continued to work for the Justice Department until there was a change of national administration. It was ironic that he was terminated from his job after the election to the presidency of Gen. Eisenhower, our commander in Europe, whom we had so much admired.

Moving back to Broken Bow, he engaged in the practice of law. Some time after our last meeting John got married.

Later from our correspondence I learned of the birth of his child. He seemed supremely happy.

Then one day I received a letter from his sister. She wrote, "You must have been a very good friend of John's. I know he thought a lot of you. I thought you would want to know that he died suddenly of a heart attack."

I remember having the sadly lonesome thought, "Well, it's a wonder his tired, combat heart held out this long."

For me, some of the pleasure and interest in life went out upon the receipt of that message. Our friendship was something special. The death of such a friend is a loss seldom made up in the years afterward.

Of course I did not know all about John Kelly. But I knew him when all pretenses were removed, when defects were quickly noted, and virtues were treasured above all else. And I can say that he is one person in my life whom I never knew to commit a wrong, or to influence another to do wrong. Yet he never pointed a finger at his erring brethern.

## LAST FORMAL CEREMONY FOR THE ORIGINALS

At the last formal parade of the more than 3,000 men and officers of the 320th held at Camp Butner, N. C. before going overseas, Col Byrne permitted the junior officers of his staff to replace the senior members in reviewing the formation. It was an interesting experience to view a parade of my comrades from such a strategic position.

It was inspiring to see the companies and platoons of trained men take their places, and then the officers respond to the front and center orders for reports. Then all the units of the regiment wheeled, turned and marched to the music of the band past the reviewing stand. The guidons with attached banners streaming in the wind, identified each company. The colors of the flag, flanked by the honor guards, flowed in the breeze. Three thousand marching feet struck the earth in unison with the beat of the drum, as the troops did eyes right for the reviewing officers.

Later we were to recall that this was the last such ceremony for the men and officers - the "old originals" - who made up the 320th at that time. Soon after this final ceremonial formation we entrained for the port of embarkation and together crossed the ocean and entered combat on the continent of Europe.

It was the last parade of the unbroken ranks of men who had become comrades and friends through long months of training with each other. They would never be together again for such a ceremony, and, for such a formation, it was the last time the officers and noncoms could give, for these men, the report, "All present or accounted for!"

## 25 YEARS AFTER WAR'S END

Now 25 years after the global conflict ended, what of the great in many fields whose names were household words and known to all the GIs of the far flung battlefronts.

Gone are Roosevelt, Jack Garner and Henry Wallace; gone Churchill, Attlee and Edens; gone are Stalin and many of his marshalls; gone DeGaulle and Petain, and gone Mussolini, Hitler, Goering, Goebels, Tojo and Yamamoto. Following their fallen comrades of battle were Eisenhower, MacArthur, Patton, Marshall, Stillwell and McNair, as well as Rommell, Runstedt and Model. Gone also are Willkie and Herbert Hoover, and now Dewey.

Of all the great war time leaders in their countries there remain only Harry S. Truman, Hailee Selassie, Chiang Kaishek, Marshall Tito and Rudolph Hess, the latter now an aging prisoner, the most noted, remaining defendant of the War Crimes Trials.

Of the American military leaders the two most famous remaining are Gen. Omar Bradley and Gen. Walter LeMay, the latter praised highly during the war as the great fleets of bombers of his command ceaselessly pounded Nazi Germany both before and after D-Day.

Among the Britons, Gen. Montgomery still survives.

Preceding the outbreak of the war, Max Schmeling, the German prize fighter, once touted by Hitler (perhaps through no fault of Schmeling) as a representative of the "Master Race," was beaten in less than one round by our great U. S. champion, Joe Louis. The news media carried stories of how lights were burning brightly throughout Naziland as the populace prepared to celebrate following an anticipated victory by the German. The lights of the potential celebrants quickly went out on news of the Louis victory.

During the war Schmeling entertained German troops while Louis entertained Allied soldiers. Both still survive.

Among the great names of the entertainment world who helped boost the morale of Allied troops, Clark Gable, Carole

Lombard, Tyrone Power, Joe E. Brown and Gary Cooper are gone. Remaining are Bob Hope, Bing Crosby, Marlene Dietrich and Jack Benny, the latter now having reached the age of 39 and still going strong.

The combat veteran, knowing already of the great number of buddies who have preceded him, and noting the numbers of the great and the near great who have gone on, can face the approaching H-hour of the Last Crossing and the Final Jump-off, with the realization that the numbers there to greet and welcome him into the Grand Encampment across the Great Divide, will soon greatly exceed the count of those awaiting the last Line of Departure.

## THE HOPES AND ACCOMPLISHMENTS OF THE GI JOES

Who were these GI Joes, and what were their hopes, as they valiantly struggled in faraway lands in the greatest war of history? As a result of their sacrifice, what were the worthwhile accomplishments of the Great Endeavor?

These men and women of the Armies of Freedom were from homes, families, churches, communities and countries which they cherished. For the most part they were obscure, law abiding, working people, looking not for gain or glory, but seeking merely to do an unpleasant, dangerous job, so they could return to that which they had left.

The ranks of the armies were not drawn from gangs of idlers, or from disorderly crowds shouting down speakers attempting to exercise the right of free speech. Nor did they come from lawless mobs of demonstrators engaged in smashing windows, burning and looting while shouting obscenities at firemen, law enforcement officers and decent citizens doing their duty. Neither did they come from groups living in "communes" as devoid of morality as any house of prostitution.

The soldiers viewed with dismay, and almost disbelief, the suppression of freedom of speech, freedom of the press, and all religious liberty in the countries of our main antagonists. It was difficult for them to comprehend that all labor unions had been abolished; that all fraternal organizations, as Masons and Elks, had been suppressed; that all civic groups were disbanded.

Equally alien to these troops from the free countries, was the practice of forced labor in Germany and Italy for their own nationals. And then there was the most extensive, inhuman system of slavery of modern history, imposed by the Nazis on the millions of people, forcibly imported to Germany from the lands overrun by the Nazi legions.

The soldiers of the Western Alliance viewed with complete disgust and the strongest condemnation the reprehensible Nazi breeding pens wherein were confined selected, unwed girls, who were persuaded or coerced to mate with carefully selected Aryan men in order to give birth to pure Aryan, illegitimate children for the building of a super race "for the glory and replenishment of the Fatherland." To Americans, and all other decent people, this cold, heartless system was a denial of the deeply cherished right of love and marriage, and the brightest of all hopes - the establishment of a home where children could be reared with loving kindness by parents in a decent, Godly atmosphere.

Lastly there were the most horrible facilities of all - the concentration camps - institutions for the mass extermination of millions of helpless, innocent people.

After capture of the camps by British and American forces, it took some time for our troops and officials to fully realize the awful purpose of the facilities, and to recover from the shock and revulsion. The institutions, and the systems of operation, were then carefully examined, and the facts documented.

The inmates of the camps were gathered from throughout Germany itself, and from the far corners of the countries overrun by the Nazi military machine. Those apprehended in town, city or countryside, were herded on to trucks and railroad cars. Whole convoys of motor vehicles and special trains, all loaded to fullest capacity with the hapless captives, with no thought of convenience or sanitation for the human cargo, converged on the already prepared centers of concentration. Once arrived at their destinations, the unfortunates were disgorged into the massive prisons, there to be kept only for the time required for their disposal.

Executions were carried out by means of mass slaughter - gas chambers, lethal injections or wholesale murder with machine guns. Many inmates were starved to death, others killed by cruel labor, some shot, still others had the life brutally beaten from their bodies, and some were destroyed by inhuman experiments.

After the victims were slain, or died from any cause, the bodies were divested of everything of value - clothing, shoes, trinkets, rings, and even gold and silver fillings in the teeth. The bodies were then tumbled indiscriminately into mass graves, or burned in huge crematoriums constructed for that sole purpose.

In the huge camps with crematoriums, the number of executions each day was not determined by guilt or innocence of the victims. There was never a thought of a trial. Of those confined none were ever accused of any crime. They just happened to be Jews, Poles, Russians or members of other unwanted groups. Or they were handicapped people - cripples, mentally retarded, consumptives and mentally ill - who were likewise removed to make way for the super race.

Neither was the number executed determined by the number of victims available - the truck convoys and the special trains continued to run and the camps were always full. The number executed was not determined by sex, age or former standing in life. All alike were slain and the bodies fed through the doors of the fiery furnaces. This was confirmed by mountainous piles of shoes taken from the bodies - shoes of children, shoes of women and men, shoes of young and old, shoes of office workers, farmers, fishermen and professional people, shoes of the poor and shoes of the rich, all kinds, of every size and description.

The number of lives snuffed out each day was determined by one thing - the capacity of the crematoriums - the number of bodies the flames could reduce to ashes each day. That is why the smoke from burning bodies, continuously arose into the heavens, 24 hours each day for month after month as the huge furnaces operated to maximum capacity.

Yet, so systematic were the Nazi monsters who operated these facilities, that no body was ever fed into the furnaces until the teeth had been checked and an imprint stamped across the chest, "Inspected for fillings."

Some of my comrades will recall, as I do, the stories related to us by the people of Holland, of how the Nazis apprehended inhabitants of that country. When the conquerors had established firm control and all freedom was crushed, the only diversion in the restricted activity of the Dutch people was to attend the cinema (movies).

Then one day in the midst of the show when the theater was filled with viewers, the lights were suddenly flashed on, and the iron-heeled, booted, uniformed Nazis entered and strode to the front. Ordering the people to remain in their seats, the Nazi officers came back down the aisles designating individuals. As an individual was pointed out, the person was seized by other German soldiers, hustled outside and unceremoniously loaded on to waiting trucks. No person so taken was permitted to say goodbye to loved ones, to send a message, or to gather any item of clothing or other personal belongings. When the trucks were loaded they roared away, and no word was ever again heard from the captives.

In their methods of selection, the Nazis took husbands from wives and wives from husbands, parents from children and children from parents, brothers from sisters and sisters from brothers, neighbors from neighbors and sweethearts from sweethearts. Those taken were transported to unknown destinations in Germany, where many wound up on the farms and in the barbed wire enclosed slave pens as slave laborers, while others were sent to the concentration camps where they were liquidated.

After this occurrence was repeated a few times, the Dutch no longer went to the cinema or any other similar place of congregation. The people went only to their places of work and to the church for worship, hoping they would be safe from apprehension in the house of God.

Then suddenly and without warning, the Nazis repeated the same act in the churches. They violated the sancity of the places of worship by interrupting religious services, using the same methods to make captives of those who were to be enslaved or exterminated in the Fatherland.

To all these appalling, infernal indignities to the universal mind, the eternal spirit and the physical body of man, these soldiers of freedom were unalterably opposed. The depth of their devotion and committment to the principles of freedom and the defense of their country was proven in many ways. In my own unit it was Silverman returning to the battle lines his wounds unhealed; Pillow and Gardner going AWOL from a replacement depot to return to combat; Dezinnick declining the safety of a training camp to return to the danger of the front with his comrades; the selfless work of Braffit and Porta, always above and beyond the call of duty; the return of Brochu before it was necessary; and thousands and thousands of other unrecorded acts of heroism and sacrifice of countless men, whose deeds are now, and will forever remain, unknown and unsung.

Amidst the hardships and cruelty of the conflict, these men of battle did not lose their belief in the democratic processes nor forsake the ideals of equality and freedom which they held as private citizens. Both on and off the battlefield, these beliefs and ideals, together with their daily, multitudinous, individual acts of fairness, kindness and compassion, made Americans the objects of the highest admiration by all with whom they came in contact. The greatest dream of millions of people was to some how become an emigrant to this great land which maintained such freedom, provided such affluence, produced such men, and which had created overall such a glorious way of life. This impression of America existed not only among the peoples of the allied countries, but among the residents of the nations we opposed on the field of battle.

These Americans fought to preserve for themselves and their posterity, their families, homes, schools, churches, jobs, businesses and all the other privileges, freedoms and opportunities which they cherished. They fought to bar from the shores of their homeland the disastrious and repulsive results of the tyranny which had overcome so many. They fought to save the nation itself. In all this they were successful.

The sacrifice of those who struggled and the blood of those who fought and died in the Great Endeavor - the successful invasions and the battles which followed - purchased freedom for millions of slaves behind the enemy lines, relieved from military rule the millions of inhabitants of the conquered countries, and preserved freedom for millions of freemen who had not yet been overcome by the Nazi tyranny. The advancing forces of the great Allied Armies finally reached and opened the cruel barbed wire gates to the slave pens, and smashed the iron doors to the appalling liquidation centers. They tore away the doors to the crematoriums where the bodies of the hapless victims were consumed by the fire which burned continuously, and which was never extinguished during Hitler's rule. Not until the capture of the camps by Allied soldiers was there removed from German skies the smoke from the most inhuman, diabolical facilities ever established by human hands.

Even in Germany, which authored the hell of combat which we had endured to oppose the tyranny to which the country likewise gave birth, religious freedom was restored. This was clearly denoted by the religious ceremony at Hanover. Also the armies of freedom, although ruling Germany as conquerers, lifted from the minds of the Germans themselves the grim fear of brutal, rapid reprisal by the Nazi rulers for any act or word that displeased them.

To rid the world of a system of tyranny which violated every precept of decency, every just law of man and all the sanctified laws of God, was reason enough to work, fight, struggle, bleed and die. But there were greater hopes in the hearts and minds of those who fought under the banners of freedom.

The success of Allied armies in the global conflict resulted in more than the removal from the earth of the evil consequences of Nazi tyranny. The principles of human justice, published forth to the world by the spokesmen of America and Great Britain, were heard and heeded everywhere. The words kindled the fires of liberty, and lighted the candles of hope for a better way of life, in the minds and hearts of untold millions of every race and creed, of every walk of life, in every clime and country of the world.

Millions of people are now free to decide their own form of government and determine their own destiny, who were then under rule of countries foreign to their own. In many free countries the democratic processes, without which true liberty cannot be permanent, have been improved.

In those countries where the most extensive, efficient systems of repression continue, the rulers have found it necessary to construct and maintain barriers to prevent the flight of their own people. Yet every day there are those behind those walls who risk their lives to escape through the Iron Curtain or the Bamboo Curtain. They seek to flee from their homes and native lands in order to share the liberty and privileges which we enjoy. Could there be any greater proof of the superiority of our system of government over any other now in use? Yet there are those, even in our own country, who "have eyes but will not see."

As these GI Americans bore their burdens, endured the hardships, shed their blood and gave their lives on the sea, in the air and upon the land in World War Two, they had the hope that their accomplishments would be of lasting benefit. They hoped that never again would it be necessary to invade the shores of any land to drive out repression; that others would not be enslaved as were those they liberated; that the barbed wire camps they destroyed would not again confine the victims of slavery. They hoped that those appalling places of butchery - the concentration camps - which they captured and which were later destroyed - save for a few preserved as proof of Nazi guilt and man's inhumanity to man - would never again deface the soil of any land. They hoped the fires which they extinguished in the furnaces of the crematoriums would never be rekindled, and that the vile stench from the burning bodies of innocent victims would never again pollute the purity of the air, nor the smoke blot the face of heaven.

These battle-stained soldiers shared in the higher hopes and ideals proclaimed by their leaders. They believed in Roosevelt's Four Freedoms - freedom of expression, freedom of worship, freedom from want, and freedom from fear - and they were uplifted and inspired by the unexcelled eloquence of Churchill's phraseology of freedom. They felt that the success of Allied arms would result in the eventual removal of tyranny from the earth, and that somehow their sacrifice would make it possible for all people everywhere by their own efforts, to establish freedom in their own countries, provide for their own material wellbeing, and create for themselves a way of life equal to that which they so much admired in America.

These men of combat hoped that the world would continue to improve until all men lived in freedom in their own lands, governed by the rule of reason and law, under governmental systems and officials of their own free, peaceable choosing. Then would be realized the dream for which man has struggled through the ages, the good life under freedom for all mankind.

An impossible dream, this hope of freedom, peace and plenty for all men, everywhere?

Perhaps so. Certainly, without the qualities of honor, loyalty, labor, discipline and patriotism, the dream will vanish.

When I was a barefoot boy in ragged overalls, my teachers and my parents said to me, "Hitch your wagon to a star and climb toward it and you will succeed."

We know one never reaches the star, and seldom is the complete fulfillment of a dream ever realized. But the struggle upward toward a goal lifts an individual from the gutters of failure and disgrace, and places him on firm ground above the infested swamps of weakness and corruption.

Perhaps a larger dream, even if not completely attainable, can do the same for mankind.

Anyway, what ever the dreams for human progress, it can be truly said that the hopes of mankind for their fulfillment, were, for a time, preserved, and measurably advanced, by the struggle and sacrifice of my combat comrades - those devoted, loyal, kind, generous, good-humored GI Joes - those idealistic, heroic, magnificent Americans of World War Two.

# TABLE I

## TOTAL CASUALTIES, INFANTRY DIVISIONS
Battle and Non-battle
(Based on 14,089 TO Strength in Each Division)

| Inf. Divs. | Casualties | Percentage of Orig. Strength | Inf. Divs. | Casualties | Percentage of Orig. Strength |
|---|---|---|---|---|---|
| 4th | 35,545 | 252.3 | 84th | 9,811 | 69.6 |
| 9th | 33,864 | 240.4 | 103rd | 9,369 | 66.5 |
| 1st | 29,005 | 205.9 | 102nd | 8,825 | 62.6 |
| 29th | 28,776 | 204.2 | 70th | 8,201 | 58.2 |
| 3rd | 28,400 | 201.6 | 63rd | 8,019 | 56.9 |
| 90th | 27,617 | 196.0 | 75th | 8,016 | 56.9 |
| 45th | 26,449 | 187.7 | 42nd | 5,949 | 42.2 |
| 36th | 26,157 | 185.7 | 76th | 5,556 | 39.4 |
| 30th | 26,038 | 184.8 | 69th | 3,347 | 23.8 |
| 2nd | 25,884 | 183.7 | 65th | 2,302 | 16.3 |
| 35th | 25,488 | 180.9 | 17th | 3,020 | |
| 80th | 25,472 | 180.8 | (no number for wounded) | | |
| 28th | 24,840 | 176.3 | 89th | 2,080 | 14.6 |
| 83rd | 23,980 | 170.2 | 66th | 1,947 | 13.8 |
| 5th | 23,487 | 166.7 | 71st | 1,869 | 13.3 |
| 79th | 23,457 | 166.5 | 97th | 1,318 | 9.4 |
| 8th | 21,056 | 149.4 | 86th | 1,282 | 8.8 |
| 26th | 16,851 | 119.6 | 82nd | 456 | |
| 44th | 13,748 | 97.6 | (no number for captured or | | |
| 104th | 13,407 | 95.1 | non-battle casualties) | | |
| 78th | 12,257 | 87.0 | 13th | No Combat | |
| 100th | 12,215 | 86.7 | 101st | (listed 11,468 bat- | |
| 99th | 11,987 | 85.1 | | tle casualties, no | |
| 87th | 11,587 | 82.2 | | number given for | |
| 94th | 10,810 | 76.7 | | non-battle casual- | |
| 106th | 10,671 | 75.7 | | ties) | |
| 95th | 10,204 | 72.4 | | | |

## TOTAL CASUALTIES, ARMORED DIVISIONS
(Based on 10,870 TO Strength)

| Armd. Divs. | Casualties | Percentage of Orig. Strength | Armd. Divs. | Casualties | Strength Percentage of Orig. |
|---|---|---|---|---|---|
| 6th | 12,816 | 120.1 | 11th | 5,137 | 48.2 |
| 7th | 10,502 | 98.4 | 14th | 4,296 | 40.3 |
| 4th | 10,496 | 98.4 | 8th | 2,454 | 23.0 |
| 10th | 8,381 | 75.5 | 13th | 739 | 6.9 |
| 5th | 7,146 | 67.0 | 20th | 395 | 3.7 |
| 12th | 5,976 | 56.0 | 16th | 243 | 2.3 |
| 9th | 5,411 | 50.7 | | | |

(Based on 14,454 TO Strength)

| | | | | | |
|---|---|---|---|---|---|
| 3rd | 16,122 | 111.5 | 2nd | 13,867 | 95.9 |

## TABLE II

### BATTLE CASUALTIES ONLY, ALL DIVISIONS

| | | | |
|---|---|---|---|
| 4th Infantry | 22,454 | 94th Infantry | 5,607 |
| 29th Infantry | 20,111 | 87th Infantry | 5,555 |
| 9th Infantry | 18,631 | 6th Armored | 5,526 |
| 90th Infantry | 18,460 | 102nd Infantry | 4,867 |
| 30th Infantry | 17,691 | 100th Infantry | 4,790 |
| 28th Infantry | 15,904 | 10th Armored | 4,697 |
| 35th Infantry | 15,406 | 63rd Infantry | 4,547 |
| 83rd Infantry | 15,248 | 103rd Infantry | 4,543 |
| 2nd Infantry | 15,066 | 70th Infantry | 3,966 |
| 1st Infantry | 15,003 | 75th Infantry | 3,954 |
| 79th Infantry | 14,875 | 9th Armored | 3,952 |
| 80th Infantry | 14,480 | 42nd Infantry | 3,598 |
| 8th Infantry | 13,458 | 5th Armored | 3,554 |
| 3rd Infantry | 13,101 | 12th Armored | 3,436 |
| 5th Infantry | 12,475 | 11th Armored | 3,216 |
| 101st Infantry | 11,468 | 17th Infantry | 3,166 |
| 36th Infantry | 11,258 | 76th Infantry | 3,126 |
| 45th Infantry | 10,458 | 14th Armored | 2,896 |
| 3rd Armored | 10,105 | 69th Infantry | 1,556 |
| 26th Infantry | 9,956 | 8th Armored | 1,313 |
| 106th Infantry | 8,163 | 66th Infantry | 1,098 |
| 78th Infantry | 7,890 | 65th Infantry | 1,052 |
| 104th Infantry | 7,011 | 89th Infantry | 1,006 |
| 2nd Armored | 6,751 | 97th Infantry | 934 |
| 84th Infantry | 6,561 | 71st Infantry | 783 |
| 95th Infantry | 6,370 | 86th Infantry | 760 |
| 7th Armored | 6,150 | 13th Armored | 493 |
| 44th Infantry | 6,111 | 82nd Infantry | 456 |
| 99th Infantry | 6,103 | 20th Armored | 76 |
| 4th Armored | 5,988 | 16th Armored | 12 |

## TABLE III

### CASUALTIES WORLD WAR TWO

328,000—Americans lost their lives.

3,814—from Arkansas lost their lives.

241,000—bodies buried in 356 cemeteries.

18,558—bodies buried in isolated places.

19,000—missing.

After the war many bodies were brought home for reburial in cemeteries of their home communities. There were 250,000 identical caskets provided for this purpose. The total cost was $195,000,000 to $215,000,000. The average cost for returning a body was $700.00.

TABLE IV

ARKANSAWYERS IN THE 35TH DIVISION

| 134th Infantry Regiment |
| --- |

Adair, James V., Wilson
Allen, Jewel T., Star Route, Delight
Alman, Sol, Little Rock
Andrews, Bert, Rt. 1, Clarksville
Armstrong, Eugene, Ash Flat
Alexander, Jesse M., Leachville
Braden, Troy E., Rt. 2, Leachville
Balls, Jack W., Rt. 1, Ft. Smith
Bowden, Alfred L., Rt. 3, Dardanelle
Burns, Hunter D., Augusta
Branch, Roy F., Nashville
Banks, Louie V., Rt. 2, Dardanelle
Barlow, Vernon O., Huntington
Black, Wilbert J., Armstrong Springs
Barnett, Thado C., Rt. 1, Trumann
Bates, Herbert G., Rt. 4, El Dorado
Brady, Melton T., Rt. 2, Blytheville
Cable, Thomas R., Rt. 3, Rector
Cunningham, Bruce A., 742 Highland, Helena
Colvin, Steele H., Rt. 2, Lamar
Chesshir, Walker F., Rt. 5, Nashville
Crowell, Howard L., Tuckerman
Chalk, Melford E., Higden
Drain, William Durf, Star Rt., Asher
Durham, Robert C., 921 W. 11th Ave., Pine Bluff
Dozier, Hugh E., 225 Union, Osceola
DeWoody, John S., Rt. 2, Prescott
Drury, John T., Colt
Duncan, Odis E., Rt. 1, Wesley
Ernest, Lester L., McRae
Ellis, Kenneth W., 316½ W. 18th, N. Little Rock
Frasher, Paul, Midland
Finnegan, Charlie H., 800 S. 12th, Fort Smith
Fine, John W., Star Rt., Rogers
Flatt, Tolly I., Rt. 3, Dover
Fields, J. R., Dixie
Goble, Ed L., Rt. 1, Mena
Griffin, William H., Jr., Rt. 2, Little Rock
Griggs, Ralph Y., Rt. 3, Malvern
Green, Archie S., 411 Wills, Morrilton
Hale, Edgar C., 1923 Cumberland Ave., Little Rock
Harrington, Edward K., 301 S. East, Morrilton
Hale, Aubrey J., Rt. 1, Perry
Harvey, Cecil R., 814 Rock, Little Rock
Hannibal, Russell G., 1415 S. Martin, Little Rock
Harbin, Robert L., Rt. 1, Hot Springs
Hauswirth, Everett M., 1700 Park, Little Rock

TABLE IV (Continued)

Jones, James M., Palestine
James, Dewey L., Jacksonville
Lahodney, Darrell, Leawood Circle, Little Rock
Lingle, John E., Rt. 1, Pollard
Linke, John K., 4615 Edgemere Drive, North Little Rock
Lewins, Thomas M., 123 Federal, Hot Springs
Landers, Lonnie H., 731 S. Main, Rector
Langley, Joe L., Rt. 1, Conway
Lake, Leonidas, Booneville
Mullen, Jack F., Cave City
Meller, Julius R., Cherry Valley
Matock, Henry M., 216 S. B, Rogers
McDanield, James M., Rt. 1, Tyronza
Mathis, Estel, Rt. 1, Bentonville
Nelson, William M., Crawfordsville
Neal, James C., 303 Archer, Hot Springs
Nations, William A., Rt. 1, Hope
Pigeon, Antone E., Rt. 2, Westfield
Passmore, Buell A., Bauxite
Peter, Leonard R., Mountain View
Partain, Leonard D., Rt. 2, Siloam Springs
Phillips, Harry, Dumas
Preston, John W., 2001 Chester, Little Rock
Price, Joe B., Dyer
Passmore, Built, Leachville
Rutledge, Doyle L., Rt. 1, Belleville
Robinson, Carl C., Rt. 1, Malvern
Reinheimer, Dan W., 225 East A St., North Little Rock
Riley, James H., El Paso
Rice, Earl M., 312 Haywood, Rose City, N. Little Rock
Smith, Oscar A., Parks
Stockton, Wm. H., 1614 Woodrow, Little Rock
Seagraves, Wm. C., Dalton Rt., Pocahontas
Smoot, Ben M., Jr., Beebe
Schmidt, John J., Floral
Smith, Elmer E., DeWitt
Shinn, Cletis W., Rt. 3, Russellville
Sheets, Howard R., 18 N. Border, Hot Springs
Spence, Ralph R., Rt. 1, Scranton
Sinyard, Kingery E., Rt. 1, Hope
Stanley, Ernest K., 5304 B. St., Little Rock
Self, Elbert E., 1213 Sycamore, N. Little Rock
Tate, Samuel L., Bonnerdale Rt., Hot Springs
Turner, Arnold E., Rt. 1, Lamar
Taylor, Raymond B., 202 Cross, Little Rock
Taylor, James P., Donaldson
Vickers, William H., Ward
Vincent, Clifford L., 1511 S. Cedar, Little Rock
Womack, Garland W., Box 32, Cabot
Whelchel, Clifford F., Rt. 1, Corning

TABLE IV (Continued)

Webber, Eugene R., Box 101, Mountain Home
Wood, Thomas J., Rt. 5, Pine Bluff
Weston, Everett H., 315 E. 19th St., Little Rock
Wright, Wesley M., 1519 W. 7th St., Little Rock
Whittenburg, William W., Rt. 3, Atkins
Webb, Jewell W., Walnut Ridge
Wilson, Luther C. Jr., Rt. 4, Sheridan
Youngblood, Dallas H., Selma

### 137TH INFANTRY REGIMENT

Acree, William H., Ft. Smith
Adkins, William W., 1824 Allis, Little Rock
Asay, Wallace M., 819 Cypress, N. Little Rock
Asbell, Don C., Box 525, Rogers
Avery, Loyd L., Nimmons
Arnold, Rufus K., Bald Knob
Abott, Roy K., Terry & Ida Sts., Hot Springs
Burnett, Malcolm D., 1305 Rock, Little Rock
Ballard, James A., Oil Trough
Briney, James P., Box 17A, Pine Bluff
Berner, Leonard R., 1101 W. 23rd, North Little Rock
Bryan, Clarence L., Big Flat Rt., Marshall
Carmical, Dudley L., Collins
Clapper, Clair L., Rt 3, N. Little Rock
Clemens, William F., Box 623, Fordyce
Coffman, Lawnie B., Hector
Casey, Stanley H., 676 Main, Batesville
Cossey, Claud, Bee Branch
Cowling, Jesse R., Mineral Springs
Cunningham, James H., Harrisburg
Dodson, Foy L., Rt. 1, Lewisville
Dugger, George W., Box 159-K, Faulkner Rd., Little Rock
Donnell, Bernard B., Enright
Frizzelle, Reginald E., 4309 W. 25th, Little Rock
Forsgren, Eugene W., 701 N. 18th, Fort Smith
Fulmer, Charles T., 208 Georgia St., Pine Bluff
Funderburg, Fred L., Box 51, Monticello
*Fritts, Hugh, Star Rt., Thorney
Greenwilt, Harold V., Rt. 1, Hazen
Gambill, Elmer E., Rt. 2, Jonesboro
Geddis, Roy W., Norfolk
Gentry, Earl A., 809 W. 22nd, Little Rock
Godfrey, L. W., Rt. 1, Booneville
Gore, Joy T., Hatfield
Gilreath, Rueben H., Enright
Grover, Carl H., Mallard Pt., Mt. Home
Hovarter, Edgar M., Rt. 2, Rosston
Heedick, Wayne, Rt. 1, Heber Springs
Hemphill, Elbert, Star City
Herrin, Tilman L., Rt. 1, Bismarck

TABLE IV (Continued)

Hill, Delbert R., Cushman
Howanietz, Albert F., Garner
Huckabee, Theodore,, Black Rock
Jones, Riley C., Russellville
Jones, Charles W., Rt. 2, Booneville
Kelley, Horace E., 1607 W. 9th, Pine Bluff
Little, Opio R. Jr., Rt. 1, Lavaca
Lincomfelt, Clyde W., Rt. 1, Clarendon
Mitchell, William R., Rt. 3, Russellville
Manes, David L., Camp
Martin, Willie F., Rt. 1, Trumann
McCallister, Elvan J., Rt. 6, Little Rock
McGuyre, James T., Rt. 3, Van Buren
McLean, Charles S., Cedar Drive, West Helena
Moffett, Grady G., Bassett
McKelvey, Paul C., Rt. 5, Paragould
May, William B., Blytheville
McGuire, Gerald W., Rt. 2, Beebe
Metsgar, Doyle C., Foreman
Niehaus, Theodore E., 606 Wolfe, Little Rock
Nichols, Howard G., Rt. 3, Ozark
Owens, Olen, 106 S. 9th, Van Buren
Owens, Joe, Vimy Ridge
Patrick, Robert L., 107 N. 18th, Ft. Smith
Petty, George W., Rt. 1, Amity
Pickens, David D., Glendale Rt., Star City
Pool, Johnie H., Searcy
Richmond, Budd W., 701 S. Martin, Little Rock
Riley, Romie C., Antoine
Rinehart, Orvel O., Rt. 1, Adona
Robinson, Loren D., Rt. 3, Box 167-B, Rogers
Ruddick, Wayne, Rt. 1, Garfield
Stallcup, Odie T., 124 Virginia, Fayetteville
Sholty, Edward R., Calico Rock
Sullivan, Byron M., Malvern
Swain, James L., Rt. 1, Branch
Schrable, Lewis N., Little Rock
Sinnett, Richard E., 2423 Cedar, Little Rock
Smith, John L., 719 Orange, North Little Rock
Springer, Paul, Siloam Springs
Scholes, Harold D., Ashdown
Thach, Leland, 723 N. 6th, Ft. Smith
Thevenet, Allen J., 1800 Battery, Little Rock
Ussery, Vitol, 1124 W. Barraque, Pine Bluff
Wallace, George M., Rt. 4, Little Rock
Walter, Harrold F., 412 E. 1st St., Stuttgart
Watkins, Ernest E., Rt. 1, Bald Knob
Wells, Leonard G., Cash
Wells, Vernie M., Rt. 1, Mt. Home
Worthen, Orbit L., Rt. 6, Pine Bluff

TABLE IV (Continued)

Wygal, Harold D., 5301 "A" St., Little Rock
Wallace, J. C., Heber Springs
York, Isaac H., Rt. 5, Nashville

## 320TH INFANTRY REGIMENT

Adams, Olive N., Camden
Aleshire, Jacob H., Mena
Allen, Aubrey D., Rt. 2, Morrilton, (also in 134th)
Alston, Phillip, Rt. 3, Ozark, (also in 134th)
Anderson, Raymond J., 1014 N. 2nd, McGehee
Arthur, Earl C., Buford
Ashley, Cary E. Jr., 1801 Maryland, Little Rock
Babitt, Homer C., Rt. 1, Donaldson
*Barber, Harry L., Rt. 5, Searcy
Barnett, Leo C., (Jonesboro), Nettleton
*Barrow, David B., Rt. 3, DeQueen
Baty, Robert S., Rt. 2, Widener
*Beeler, Raymond, Rt. 1, Black Rock
Belue, Meldon D., Ft. Smith
Benefield, Hampton R., Rt. 3, Emerson
Berman, Fred, 900 Barber, Little Rock
Biggerstaff, Robert W., 616 St. Mary, Van Buren
Blackwell, Lloyd, Mena
Bobo, Troy F., Rt. 1, Hope
Brown, Joseph O., 110 S. College, Fayetteville, (also in 134th)
Brown, Lloyd E., (Carlisle) Rt. 1, Lonoke, (also in 137th)
Brownlow, Frederick R., Rt. 2, Parkdale
Brummitt, Frank S., 742 South Porter St., Stuttgart
Bunn, James B. Jr., 108 Lee, Osceola
Burdine, Roy L., W. Main, Magnolia
Burnett, Willie C., Rt. 2, Crossett
Burns, Joe F., Mansfield
Busby, Hershel D., Piggot
Busick, Porter M., Patterson
Carpenter, Louis E., Rt. 1, Lonoke
Carter, Robert D. Jr., Bald Knob
Cary, Elbert, 612 Abeles, Little Rock
Cato, Doil I., Rt. 1, Boydsville
Chin, Ting G., Little Rock
Churchill, James E., Hector
Coley, Floyd F., Rogers
Copeland, Albert R., Elkins
Cowan, Henry S., Fayetteville
Crawford, James M., Rt. 3, Rogers
Crawford, Joe M., Ellis
Currington, Desmond A., Rt. 3, Malvern
Daniel, Henry, St. Joe
Davis, Dan L., Calion
Dime, Edward J., Bonanza
Downum, Lewis B., Rt. 1, Lowell (also in 137th)

## TABLE IV (Continued)

Dryer, Charles W., 1510 S. Church, Jonesboro
Dunigan, Leonard, Blockton
Edwards, John H., Rt. 5, Searcy
*Elrod, Ralph, Jr., Rt. 2, Malvern
Epps, Clifton M., 1415 Bishop, Little Rock
Farmer, James D., Rt. 1, Mansfield
Gann, Nolan E., Rt. 3, Mena
Gilliam, Albert R., Rt 1, Beebe
Goodwin, Glen E., Kensett
Grabowski, Conrad W., 516½ S. 16th, Ft. Smith
Harris, Meade A. Jr., 223 E. 21st, N. Little Rock (also in 137th)
Harrison, Byron R., Rt. 1, Roland
Harmon, Glen W., Piggott
Harp, Arthur L., Winslow
Heard, Porter A., Palestine
Heath, James A., Box 344, Trumann
Heim, James E., 1515 W. 25th, Little Rock
Henderson, Arvle J., Rt. 4, Rosston
Henson, James E., Caldwell
Horn, Raymond E., Rt. 3, Malvern (also in 137th)
Huett, Gene R., Rt. 1, Springfield
Jackson, James H., 906 Branch, Morrilton (also in 137th)
James, Hoyt R., Ozark
James, Nolan, Rt. 2, Rosebud
James, Tildon M., Rt. 2, Benton
Johnson, Alonzo C., Star Rt. 1, Lake Village
Johnson, Robert H., Rt. 1, Adona
Jones, Archie L., Box 44, Haynes
Jones, Donald F. Jr., 21 Longfellow Lane, Little Rock
Jones, Hencle L., Rt. 1, Shirley
Kesterson, Fred, Dierks (also in 134th)
King, James A., Rt. 1, Bono
King, Reece B., Rt. 2, Clarksville
Kirkpatrick, Bobby M., 1117 Ringo, Little Rock
Kratzmeyer, John J., Rt. 1, Malvern
Lackey, Richard E., Norfork
Lamkin, Berl D., (Jonesboro), Nettleton
Lane, James F., 812 W. 4th, Little Rock (also in 137th)
Lane, Lensy P., Rt. 2, Garfield
Langley, Albert C., 507 W. 3rd, Prescott
Langley, James D., Rt. 1, Morrilton
Lawrence, Kenneth C., Rt. 1, Pine Bluff
Lassiter, Pat H., Jr., Rt. 2, Belleville (also in 219th FA Bn)
Lee, Robert E., Arkadelphia
Linneman, Lauren E., 2216 Main, Little Rock
Lyles, David J., Hamburg
Madlock, Calvin E., Patmos
Mashburn, Charles D., Williford
Mason, Reynard E., 331 Cook, Little Rock
Matthews, William J., Faber

TABLE IV (Continued)

May, Joe L., Rt. 2, Rosston (or Hope)
McCauley, George E., Mineral Springs
McGathy, Clifton, Boydelle
McKinney, Artice D., Huttig
McLaughlin, Arthur E., Black Oak
Medlock, Mariel G., Poughkeepsie
Montgomery, Clarence E., 1733 N. Division, Forrest City
Moore, Charles R., Rt. 1, Blytheville
Moreton, Wayne W., Rt. 2, Ft. Smith
Nabours, Benjamin F., 607 W. Bennette, Morrilton
Nutter, Johnie H., Hensley
*Orr, Elbert T., 319 W. 8th., N. Little Rock
Orton, James R., Rt. 2, Pine Bluff (also in 134th)
Palcne, Fountain, Rt. 1, Westville, Okla.
Paul, Hallion, Higginson
Perdue, Emon E., Rt. 2, El Dorado
*Perser, Albert B., Leola
Peters, J. D., Rt. 1, Atkins (also in 134th)
Pettigrew, Luther E., Rt. 1, Horatio
Phillips, Clarence, Rt. 4, Greenwood
Pokornik, John, Rt. 1, Mineral Springs
Poppy, Alfred B., Ola
Price, Will H., (Beere) Beirne
Priest, Miles Jr., Ward
Pullen, John D., Rt. 3, Lamar
Rauls, Greely A. Jr., 721 2nd, Pine Bluff
Ritter, Charles F., Winthrop (also in 137th)
Roberts, Frank, Rt. 1, Prattsville (also in 134th)
Robinson, James O., Kensett
Rosser, Ollie W., Rt. 2, Cotton Plant (also in 134th)
Rosson, Wm. S., Rt. 1, Crossett (also in 137th)
*Rowe, Carl E., Rt. 2, Emmett
Rowe, James G., Rt. 1, Van Buren
Russell, Rex A., Jr., Marianna
Sample, Charles, Floral
Sasser, James M., Mulberry (also in 134th)
Scott, Loyde, Bono
Sharp, Johnnie M., Tyronza
Sherman, Robert T., 1886 Izard, Little Rock
Shoptaw, Nathan L., Redfield, (also in 137th)
Shoup, William O., Rt. 1, Jonesboro
Simmons, Louis M., 902 Warner Ave., Jonesboro
Simpson, Paul E., Rt. 1, Clarendon
Skender, John J., Rt. 4, Hamburg
Slankard, James H., Hartford
Sloan, Jack A., Cotton Plant
Smith, Jay D., Little Rock
Sommey, (or Summey) Wayne M., Rt. 1, Garfield (also in 134th)
Spears, Wilburn S., Coy
Spencer, Edward D., Chidester

TABLE IV (Continued)

Stalnaker, Zane T., Rt. 1, Smithville (also in 134th)
Standley, Glen C., Woolsey, (also in 134th)
Stanley, Roy L., Rt. 1, Prairie Grove, (also in 137th)
Stephens, Herman W., Rt. 1, El Dorado
Stone, Henry B., 48 Aggie Rd., Jonesboro
*Stroud, James C., Aurora
Stumbaugh, Don I, Rt. 2, Dover, (or Atkins)
Swafford, Vilas A., Moran
Sweeden, John H., 204 S. Cherokee, Morrilton (also in 137th)
Talkington, Rupert C., Rt. 3, Dover
Teague, Marion N., 702 Front, Nashville
Thomas, Odis, Cherry Valley
Tomlinson, Webb H., 521 W. Main, El Dorado
Townes, Charles E., 127 S. Hill, Fayetteville (also in 134th)
Trafford, R. B., 310 E. 5th, North Little Rock
Traylor, Benjamin F., 1705 W. 8th, Little Rock
Tucker, Clarence R., Rt. 1, Hartford
Veteto, Richard Q., 116 Carlton Terrace, Hot Springs
Watson, Herman B., Rt. 1, Tinsman
Watt, Wm. R., 410 E. 1st, Fordyce
Wells, Thomas L., 212 S. 3rd, Van Buren
Whilchel, Clinton A., Rt. 1, Corning
White, Charlie M., Rt. 1, Bonnerdale (also in 134th)
White, Paul S., Rt. 1, Cabot
Willis, William H., Rt. 1, Poughkeepsie
Wilson, Carl L., 510 S. Commerce, Russellville
Wilson, Glen D. Jr., Dyer, (also in 134th)
Wilson, Grover E., Dierks
Wilson, Meredith E., 1102 N. Izard, Forrest City
Wolfe, Robert R., Rt. 1, Hamburg
Woods, Robert E. "Ted", 1018 Perry, Helena
Yates, Wayne, 603 Northwest, Morrilton

## 60TH ENGINEERS COMBAT BATTALION

Brown, J. D., Box 144, Stuttgart
Conzel, Earl T., Route 5, Malvern
Hill, Charles A., 1726 West, Texarkana
Jewell, Ben, Amagon
Julian, Joseph A., 302 Walnut, Corning
Mashburn, Amon A., Rt. 1, Little Rock
Massey, Irving H., Bonnerdale
Nowell, Thomas E., 402 E. Highland, Malvern
Rhine, Rolland H., Fox

* * *

## 127TH FIELD ARTILLERY BATTALION

Cather, William N., Rt. 1, North Little Rock
Farmer, James C., 1607 Maple, N. Little Rock
Sarras, Louis P., Jacksonville
*Wright, Dallas M., 123 4th, Benton

TABLE IV (Continued)

## 216TH FIELD ARTILLERY BATTALION

Brisco, Clyde O., Rt. 1, Berryville
Chambliss, Norman T., Rt. 2, Newport
Coffman, Lawrence B., Hector
Gimblet, N. A. (Bus) Jr., Box 35, Levi Station, North Little Rock
Hand, Henry A., Box 484, Mt. Home
Johnson, Nolan, Hagarville
Lee, Thurman, Aly
Meriweather, Wilburn C., 204 Scott, Little Rock
Nichols, Paul W., Rt. 2, Paragould
Rice, Lawrence E., Rt. 2, Warren
Tice, Herman C., 728 Appianway, Little Rock
Webb, Thomas J., England

* * *

## 219TH FIELD ARTILLERY BATTALION

Bennett, Otis W., Rt. 4, Nashville
Branscum, Joseph E., Ash Flat
Chissoe, William Jr., 1804 S. Pierce, Little Rock
Dickens, Vernon E., Trumann
Dollar, Jim L., Prim
Dyke, Cecil O., Rt. 2, c/o D. R. Kennemer, Benton
Finley, Arthur T., Grapevine
Fonck, Howard L., 239 East A St., North Little Rock
Hall, Donald E., 1900 Cumberland, Little Rock
Jones, Pawnee E., 126 Victory Courts, Conway
Kemper, Arthur R., Houston
Kolb, Myron D., 2500 State, Little Rock
Lane, Carl W., 1810 W. 6th Ave., Pine Bluff
Liles, Johnnie L., Heber Springs
Madden, Howard H., Rt. 1, Ashdown
Mills, Ben F., (KIA), Jonesboro
Pickens, O. C. Jr., 920 Warner Ave., Jonesboro
Shaver, Claude N., Cherokee Village

* * *

## 35TH HEADQUARTERS COMPANY

Campbell, Ray, Everett
Cutler, Kenneth M., Rt. 1, Gurdon
Davis, Oscar L. Jr., Foreman
Fowler, William K., 915 W. 6th, Hope
Miller, Sterling E., 2623 Wolfe, Little Rock
Mitchell, William Y., Dyess
Pinkley, Cecil P., 802 W. Allen, Springdale
Poole, Ray B., Piggott
Seaman, Jack F., Box 751, Little Rock

* * *

## 35TH RECONNAISSANCE TROOPS

Walker, Carl V., 1005 N. Fourth, Fort Smith

TABLE IV (Continued)

## 35TH QUARTERMASTER COMPANY

Hays, Harry G., Little Rock
Houston, Clayton, J. L., Rt. 1, Trumann
Wheatley, Calvin E., 424 E. Second, Little Rock

\* \* \*

## 161ST FIELD ARTILLERY

Howell, Henry E., 5205 Woodlawn, Little Rock
Meyers, John S., S. Ninth St., West Helena
Trudell, Lawrence L., 9 Bryn Mawr Drive, Little Rock

\* \* \*

## 129TH FIELD ARTILLERY

Howard, F. L., Rt. 5, Hot Springs

\* \* \*

## 142ND FIELD ARTILLERY

Markley, A. D., Huntsville
Peek, Robert M., 2400 N. Pierce, Little Rock
Rogers, William R., 500 Vinson, Fayetteville
Scott, Brad, 135 Fairview Rd., Little Rock
Thompson, Jerome F., 28 Shannon Drive, Little Rock

\* \* \*

## 138TH INFANTRY

Major, John T., Rt. 4, Mt. Home

\* \* \*

## 139TH INFANTRY

Douglas, William J., 234 Hillcrest, Mt. Home
Whiteley, Frank J., Kingston

\* \* \*

## 140TH INFANTRY

Scheibner, Carl F., 221 Rosetta, Little Rock

# MADISON COUNTAINS
## WHO GAVE THEIR LIVES
## FOR THEIR COUNTRY

In order that their names will not soon be lost in the incomplete and scattered records of the war and the fading memory of man, the names of those men from my native county who made the supreme sacrifice for their country, are included in this book.

For each breath drawn in freedom, each meal eaten in peace and each day of work or play in security, all who have lived since they perished should give constant thanks to them and their fallen comrades. To them who gave their lives, and to those who risked the same, we are indebted, always.

This list includes residents and natives of Madison County, Arkansas, or those with close connections with Madison County relatives, who lost their lives in World War Two.

### KILLED IN ACTION

Carroll A. Smith, Navy, Pacific
Claude Lafon, Army, Corregidor, Philippines
J. D. Nelson, Navy, Pacific
Marion Yeargin, died in Japanese prison camp
Pfc Thomas V. "Louie" Long, died in Japanese prison camp
Billie Hughes, Navy, Pacific
Samuel Franklin Pullen, Navy, Pacific
T/Sgt Conley A. Neal, Army, England
Pvt Donald L. Stewart, Marines, Pacific
Sgt Kermitt E. Phipps, Army, Corsica
Sgt Carl Swift, Air Corps, Pacific
Lt Rufus N. Garrett, Army, France
Cpl Curtis D. McElhaney, Army, France
    (One of five brothers in the Armed Forces)
Lt Ray McFerrin, Italy
Pvt Verlin D. Johnson, Army, France
Pvt Paulie J. Lewis, Army, Belgium
Pfc Henry N. Moppin, Army, France
Pfc Carl Dean Counts, Army, France
Harold J. Brisco, Army, Belgium
Pfc Hugh Fritts, Army, France (35th Div)
Dell Shrum, Army, Luxembourg
Pvt Cloys Burnett, Italy
Pfc Olen L. Ball, France
Sgt Hugh H. Barnes, Army, France
Pfc James Thomas Garrett, Army, France
Sgt Clifford Clark, Army, Italy
Pvt Jack S. Combs, Army, Luxembourg
Pfc John R. Litterell, Army, Luxembourg

T/Sgt Everett Dutton, Germany
Charlie W. Edmondson, Luxembourg
Pfc Thomas Jefferson Barber, Army, Germany
Pvt James Washington Barber, Army, Philippines
Pfc James C. Stroud, Army, Luxembourg (35th Div)
Lt Robert E. Frost, Air Corps, Germany
Pvt Marion E. Bayles, Jr., Army, Germany
Pvt Sherman Lee Baker, Army, France
Orval E. Gilliam, Army, Italy
Pvt Olaf Haught, Army, Germany
Ensign Paul K. Spradling, Navy, Pacific
Pfc Clay L. Burns, Army, Germany
Pvt Elbie Lee Eaton, Army, Luzon, Philippines
Pfc Cecil Harper, Army, Leyte
Pfc Donald Riggs, Army, Germany
Sgt Roy Ivan Brown, Marines, Okinawa
Pfc Ernest Paul King, Marines, Iwo Jima
Pvt Claude W. Todd, Army, Luzon, Philippines
Pfc Carl Samuels, Okinawa
Pvt Nolen Eugene Jackson, New Guinea
Pvt Jim Whiteley, Leyte
Alva Hoskins, New Guinea
Sfc Wyatt Patton Moore, Navy, Pacific
Pvt Dorlan McCown, Okinawa
Pfc Virgil McCoy, Army, Germany
Pfc Watson Whittemore, Army, Germany
Lt Arthur D. Erwin
T/5 Raymond D. Hallam, Germany
Pvt Orlan David Howard, Army, English Channel
T/5 Norman B. Misunstad
Pvt Aubra Shrode, Germany
Pfc William J. B. Walls, Luzon, Philippines
Capt Terrill E. "Smokey" Stover, Navy Air Corps, - lost on a
    flight in the Pacific. Stover had appeared on a national radio
    program, "The Fighting Five," and was the star of the popular
    movie about an aircraft carrier, "The Fighting Lady," He
    visited his parents, Mr. and Mrs. J. S. Stover of Rockhouse
    shortly before he was lost in action.

Died in the Service of illness or non-battle injuries as explosions,
plane crashes, auto accidents or other causes.

Pvt Floyd Walker, Army, Japan
Cpl Ray Hobbs, the States
Phm2/C Conley Skaggs, the States
Pvt Boyd Edens, Army, the States
Pvt Gordon O. Harriman, the States
Pvt Winifred R. Smith, the States
Dwight Armes, Navy, the States
Pvt Earl K. Williams, Army, the States
Maj Seth W. Duncan, Air Corps, the States

## LOST THEIR LIVES IN VIET NAM

Pfc Charles Phillip Glenn, Army
Lt. Col. Roy Everett Couch, Army
Pfc Bobby McElhaney
Terry Gilliam
Carey Siler

\* \* \*

(The most popular song of WWII. We heard it many times on the German radio while in combat and German PW bands played it often after the war at the request of American troops.)

## LILE MARLENE

### I

Underneath the lamp post by the barrack gate,
Standing all alone, every night you'll see her wait.
She waits for a boy who marched away,
And though he's gone, she hears him say,
"Oh promise you'll be true, Fare thee well Lile Marlene,
Till I return to you, Fare thee well Lile Marlene."

### II

Underneath the lamp post by the barrack gate,
Standing all alone, every night you'll see her wait.
For this is the place a vow was made,
And breezes sing her seranade,
"Oh promise you'll be true, Fare thee well Lile Marlene,
Till I return to you, Fare thee well Lile Marlene."

### III

Underneath the lamp post by the barrack gate,
Standing all alone, every night you'll see her wait.
And there in the lamplight, it is said,
A halo shines above her head.
"Oh promise you'll be true, Fare thee well Lile Marlene,
Till I return to you, Fare thee well Lile Marlene."

### IV

Underneath the lamp post by the barrack gate,
Standing all alone, every night you'll see her wait.
And as they go marching to the fray,
The soldiers all salute and say,
"Oh promise you'll be true, Fare thee well Lile Marlene,
Till I return to you, Fare thee well Lile Marlene."

\* \* \*

# WHY CAN'T WE GO HOME

(This song was improvised by the GI Joes and officers in Europe after the War, and sung to the tune of Lile Marlene. The words were obtained from Col. J. D. Alexander, 1628 S. Prospect Ave., Park Ridge, Illinois, who served in both the 137th and 320th Infantry)

Oh Mr. Truman, why can't we go home?
We have taken Berlin, and we have conquered Rome.
We liberated the master race,
And still you say no shipping space,
Oh, Mr. Truman, why can't we go home?

We have met the Russians, we have crossed the Rhine,
We're tired of drinking vodka, and tired of Mozel wine,
We're not permitted to fraternize,
Cause General Ike says that's not wise.
Oh, Mr. Truman, why can't we go home?

Oh, Mr. Truman, we have all the points,
We're tired of living in all these foreign joints.
We don't want to go to the C.B.I.,
We'll leave that for some other guy,
Oh, Mr. Truman, why can't we go home?

| | |
|---|---|
| ack-ack | — anti-aircraft shells exploding in the air |
| AEF | — American Expeditionary Force |
| AEP | — Army Education Program |
| aid man | — enlisted medical personnel who give first aid to wounded |
| air burst | — a shell which had a time fuse and was set to burst in the air. They were more effective because the fragments ranged downward, as well as outward from burst, and could kill and wound men in fox holes |
| aptd | — appointed |
| armd | — armored |
| arty | — artillery |
| asst | — assistant |
| AT | — anti-tank |
| atchd | — attached |
| auth | — authorized |
| BAR | — Browning automatic rifle |
| barrage | — a concentration of artillery shells fired into an area by a number of guns |
| bazooka | — a weapon with a barrell similar to a metal gas or water pipe which propelled an explosive charge. Used at close range as an anti-tank weapon or to blast holes through walls of buildings. A two-man weapon. One soldier held the barrell on his shoulder while his team mate inserted the charge from behind. The weapon got its name from the large, pipe-like musical instrument made famous in his radio shows by the great comedian, Bob Burns of Van Buren, Ark. A similar German weapon was called a panzerfaust. |
| big stuff | — slang for heavy artillery |
| bitching | — soldier slang for complaining, many times just to relieve pent-up feelings and thus only half serious. |
| Blue Unit | — code name for third battalion (three battalions in a regiment) |
| Bn | — battalion |
| Bosche | — term for the German enemy, a carryover from WWI. |
| Burp (bur-r-r-p) | — gun, - a hand carried automatic weapon, machine pistol, used mostly by the Germans. |
| CAC | — Civil Affairs Corps whose personnel established military government for the conquered areas. |
| Capt | — captain |
| cav | — cavalry |

| | |
|---|---|
| CG | — commanding general |
| cn | — cannon |
| co | — company |
| CO | — commanding officer |
| Col | — Colonel |
| coll | — collecting |
| combat time | — ran on a 24-hour basis. It began after midnight. One minute after midnight was written 00:01; one o'clock A.M. was 01:00; six o'clock a.m. was 06:00; noon was 12:00; one p.m. was 13:00; six o'clock in the evening was 18:00; 11:45 was 23:45 and twelve midnight was 24:00 |
| comdr | — commander |
| Com O | — communications officer |
| Corps | — a high eschelon command, above division and below army command |
| contact fuse | — the fuse used on a shell which explodes as soon as it strikes, or comes in contact |
| CP | — command post |
| cpl | — corporal |
| C & R | — command and reconisance |
| CR | — crossroads |
| C-ration | — last indefinitely until opened, as canned goods; would spoil after opening - could be eaten without cooking or could be heated |
| ctr | — center |
| CWO | — Chief Warrant Officer |
| DE | — destroyer escort |
| delayed fuse | — explodes a short time after conact, which enables a shell to penetrate a breastwork or wall of a building before exploding |
| DC | — Dental Corps, a department of the Medical Corps Division. |
| Div | — Division |
| DO | — duty officer |
| D-ration | — a ration prepared to last, could be carried for several days; would not spoil |
| DOW | — died of wounds |
| dud | — a shell that fails to explode when it hits |
| Eighty-eight 88 | — German direct fire gun, artillery, long range, hard hitting; for a time the best gun in the war. Late in the conflict our forces developed some guns for tanks and TDs which may have been as good. |
| Eighty-one 81 | — 81mm mortar - a larger longer barrelled, longer range weapon; heavy mortar |
| EM | — enlisted men, a term to distinguish from officers |
| engr | — engineer |
| enl | — enlisted |

| | |
|---|---|
| FFI | — The Free French underground resistance forces (pronounced FFE) |
| flap-flap | — a small plane used by artillery forward observers to spot enemy targets and to direct artillery fire on the targets |
| FO | — forward observer |
| fwd | — forward |
| Gen | — general |
| G-1 | — division personnel section - keeps rosters, records |
| G-2 | — division intelligence section, information of enemy |
| G-3 | — division operations section, as plans, training, logistics |
| G-4 | — division supply section, food, clothing, ammunition, weapons, equipment |
| H-hour | — time set for jump off in the attack |
| HMG | — heavy machine gun |
| H-minus-12 | — 12 minutes before the designated time for attack |
| H-plus-12 | — 12 minutes after designated time for attack |
| hqs or hq | — headquarters |
| Huns | — term for the German enemy, a carryover from WWI |
| Inf | — infantry |
| IPW | — interrogation of prisoner of war |
| I&E | — information and education as the information and education program |
| IEP | — information and education program |
| I&R | — intelligence and reconisance |
| JA | — Judge Advocate, a military legal officer |
| Jerry - Jerrys | — a slang name for Germans |
| Joplin | — a code name for the 134th Inf. Regt. |
| Juniper | — a code name for the 320th Inf. Regt. |
| Jury | — a code name for the 137th Inf. Regt. |
| Justice | — a code name for the 35th Inf. Div. |
| KIA | — killed in action |
| km | — killometers |
| K-ration | — one flat, easy-to-carry package containing a meal and cigarettes; most often carried in combat; last indefinitely without spoiling |
| LIA | — light injury in action, battle |
| LMG | — light machine gun |
| LO | — liaison officer |
| Long Toms | — long barrelled, long range artillery |
| Lt | — lieutenant |
| Lt Col | — lieutenant colonel |
| Luftwaffe | — German Air Force |
| LWA | — light wound in action, battle |

| | |
|---|---|
| MAC | — Medical Administrative Corps, kept records but were not physicians |
| machine pistol | — a small automatic weapon used by the Germans; it amounted to a hand carried machine gun |
| MC | — Medical Corps |
| Maj | — major |
| medics | — medical personnel |
| med | — medical |
| Med Det | — medical detachment |
| MG | — machine gun |
| MIA | — missing in action |
| MII | — military intelligence and information |
| mil govt | — military government |
| moaning minnie or meme— | GI term for a certain artillery shell used by the Germans. It made an eerie, moaning noise in its flight and was nearly always used at night. We concluded it was used for psychological purposes, - to induce fright in the quiet loneliness of the night |
| mortar | — a hollow tube weapon - it is set up on a metal base plate and adjusted for range at an angle on a tripod. The shell is dropped into the mouth of the tube. When it hits the bottom a charge detonates, propelling it back out of the tube and through the air. The shells go high, dropping on the target. It could not be heard on its flight, thus the only warning was the distant cough of its firing. It was a dreaded and dangerous weapon, and was used to drop shells into houses, holes and valleys where artillery shells could not strike. |
| MP | — military policeman |
| MR | — morning report |
| msg | — message |
| msgr | — messenger |
| NBI | — non battle injury, an injury from other than enemy action |
| NCO | — non-commissioned officer |
| nebelwerfer | — a sixteen or 24-barrelled mortar used by the Germans. The weapon fired its load of shells in rapid succession. The nearest anyone could come to describing the sound of its firing, "like grinding something out of a rusty barrell." |
| No-man's-land | — area between battle lines of opposing forces which is controlled by neither and which no man can use |

| | |
|---|---|
| non-com | — non commissioned officer (corporals and sergeants) |
| non-combatant | — medical, chaplain and other personnel who do not bear arms and who do no fighting |
| Normandy hedgerows | — these were fences between, or enclosing the fields of Normandy built of sod two feet or more in thickness and often six feet or more in height, interspersed and overgrown with briars, weeds and bushes, including a very tough growth such as bois d'arc or hawthorne. Nothing could get through them and they were difficult to overrun even by tanks. An enterprising GI finally designed a device, a huge blade attached to the front of a tank, which could slice through a hedge row. By that time much of the hedge row fighting had ended, and there was not sufficient time to equip tanks with the device. TDs could overrun some hedges. These hedgerows were excellent fortifications for a defending force. The Germans had dug holes in the hedgerows for MG emplacements and riflemen. MGs properly emplaced firing through these holes could sweep entire fields with deadly fire and cut down the American attackers as they came over the tops into the open fields. Also it was most difficult to locate and knock out such defense installations. |
| OP | — observation post |
| Panzerfaust | — German anti-tank weapon, the counterpart of the American bazooka |
| Panzer units | — German armored or tank units |
| par | — paragraph |
| pers | — personnel |
| Pfc | — private first class |
| plt | — platoon |
| POW | — prisoner of war |
| pt | — point |
| Pvt | — private |
| PW | — prisoner of war |
| RCN - recon | — reconissance, scouting |
| Red Unit | — code name for first battalion |
| repo depot | — replacement depot where troops were assembled for return to their units, or to send up as replacements for casualties |
| rhobomb | — a German rocket bomb, often called a buzz bomb |
| RJ | — road junction |
| S-1 | — regimental personnel section |
| S-2 | — regimental intelligence section |

| | |
|---|---|
| S-3 | — regimental operations section |
| S-4 | — regimental supply section |
| sabot | — wooden shoes worn by Europeans |
| SCM | — Special Courts Martial |
| Sec | — section |
| Sgt | — sergeant |
| shrapnel | — fragments from exploding shells, bombs, or mines, jagged pieces of metal from which wounds were much worse than from bullets. |
| SIA | — serious injury in action, battle |
| sixty mm mortar | — 60mm, a small, short barrelled short range weapon, light mortar |
| smoked or smoke screen | — an area is covered with smoke to mark targets, or the location of friendly or enemy troops, or to obscure visibility |
| SO | — special order |
| SOP | — standard operating procedure |
| SP | — self-propelled |
| SS | — Hitler's finest troops with fanatical Nazi ideology |
| strafing | — a plane sweeps over an area firing on targets with MGs. |
| SWA | — serious wound in action, battle |
| TD | — tank destroyer - a tank like vehicle with a powerful gun, designed to destroy tanks |
| tdy | — temporary duty |
| TF | — task force |
| The Stars and Stripes | — newspaper published by Armed Forces personnel for the Armed Forces and delivered to them without charge. |
| tks | — tanks |
| Tommy | — English soldiers, slang |
| trfd | — transferred |
| tracer | — a bullet coated with substance that makes it glow in its flight |
| T/Sgt | — technical sergeant |
| Volks-sturn | — German home guard troops, of inferior quality to regular German troops, used for combat in closing stages of the war. |
| Wehrmacht | — Regular German Army |
| White Unit | — code name for second battalion |
| wps or wpns | — weapons |
| WO | — warrant officer |
| WOJG | — warrant officer, junior grade |
| zeroing | — getting the correct range to lay shells directly on a target |